Bilingual Schooling in the United States

A Sourcebook for Educational Personnel

Bilingual Schooling in the United States

A Sourcebook for Educational Personnel

By

Francesco Cordasco

Professor of Education, Montclair State College

Former Educational Consultant, Migration Division
Commonwealth of Puerto Rico

With a Foreword by
A. Bruce Gaarder
United States Office of Education

WEBSTER DIVISION, McGRAW-HILL BOOK COMPANY
New York St. Louis San Francisco Auckland Bogotá Dusseldorf
Johannesburg London Madrid Mexico Montreal New Delhi
Panama Paris São Paulo Singapore Sydney Tokyo Toronto

Editorial Development: Winifred M. Davis
Editing and Styling: Linda Richmond
Design Supervision: Pedro A. Noa
Production: Karen Romano

Text Design and Cover: Libra Design

Library of Congress Cataloging in Publication Data
Cordasco, Francesco, 1920–
    Bilingual schooling in the United States.
    Bibliography: p.
    Includes index.
    1. Education, Bilingual—United States. I. Title.
LC3731.C668   371.9'7   76-29056
ISBN 0-07-013127-9

For
Carmela Cordasco and Filomena Tiesi
For Whom Language Was Everything

A significant step was taken by the New York Board of Education in 1922. The introduction of the teaching of the Italian language in school and the establishment of parity with French, German, Latin, and Spanish was the result of a long campaign.... In the campaign to have the Italian language added to the curriculum, one of the most important among the many reasons put forth was that it would aid in the adjustment problems and in the Americanization of the Italo-American group.... While there is no way of determining the extent of the benefit derived from the addition of Italian to the curriculum, Italian language teaching has probably been a medium of cultural rehabilitation and acted as a preventive for social disorganization. It made provision of a medium of communication in the home, strengthening home ties. It helped mitigate the Italo-American sense of inferiority by gaining for the Italian student and the Italian groups social and ethnic status and probably a decrease in discrimination through the concept of the cultural worth and prestige of Italian civilization.

Leonard Covello, *The Social Background of the Italo-American School Child* (1944)

TABLE OF CONTENTS

Foreword

Bilingual education is a relatively simple matter if it is concerned solely with children and other learners who have chosen voluntarily to study through a language other than their own native tongue or whose parents have so chosen for them. This is individual, academic, or elitist bilingualism. It occurs happily all over the world. Bilingual education becomes exceedingly complex, however, when it is based on involuntary, obligatory, collective bilingualism, the kind that occurs when two peoples, with two languages, are found within a single nation, one subordinated to the other. In that case children and adults of the subordinate group have little choice but to become bilingual. The dynamics of these two kinds of bilingualism and bilingual education are quite different each from the other.

It is, of course, true that the pedagogy of bilingual education—what happens in the classrooms—is always important, but in the case of such education based on collective bilingualism, even more important are the political considerations and the political decisions that must be made. For example, is it the intention of the financial supporting sponsors to strengthen and maintain that other language or is the program designed to hasten its disappearance? Likewise, despite the great importance of pedagogy (including, of course, the teachers, their competence, and their attitudes), it is probable that children take most of their signals from the adult world outside the schools and the school yards.

Stated otherwise, the success of a program of bilingual schooling based on collective bilingualism depends largely on two factors, power and prestige: the political and economic power of the subordinate people and the prestige, i.e., the extent of prestigious use, of the subordinate language.

Professor Francesco Cordasco's compendious sourcebook is timely in two senses. First, it is needed to enlarge our understanding of an important subject. Second, there is need for action now, without delay, if the subordinate languages—particularly Spanish and the indigenous Indian tongues—are to maintain the positions of relative strength which they now hold. This is true because of another characteristic of collective bilingualism: its instability. This kind of bilingualism is essentially a way of mediating between two monolingual peoples. The bilingual individuals are needed because they alone can establish communication between two groups with different languages. But if the day comes when all or almost all of the subordinate group is bilingual (members of the dominant group very seldom learn the subordinate tongue) there is no longer need for the weaker language, no longer need for intergroup mediators. No people needs two languages for the same set of purposes. Massive language shift can then be expected, and the next generation will speak only one tongue, the dominant one.

Bilingual Schooling in the United States is indeed timely and pertinent to those who do not want to see a massive shift away from their own native tongue.

A. Bruce Gaarder
U.S. Office of Education **xi**

Preface

According to the 1970 census, some 5 million youngsters in the United States come from homes in which the generally spoken language is other than English. Estimates based on a sampling in several states suggest that between 1.8 and 2.5 million American schoolchildren need bilingual education. (Bilingual education uses two languages—English and the one the child uses at home—to develop listening, speaking, reading, writing, and other academic skills; concomitantly, the student learns about the history and culture associated with both languages.)

Widespread efforts in the early 1960s to incorporate bilingual education components into the American school curricula resulted in the enactment by Congress in 1967 of the Bilingual Education Act (as Title VII of the Elementary and Secondary Education Act). The Educational Amendments Act of 1974 revised and strengthened the 1967 statute: in federal fiscal year (FY) 1975, congressional appropriations for bilingual education were $85 million (authorizations call for $140 million in FY 1976; $150 million in FY 1977; and $160 million in FY 1978). At least four states (Illinois, Massachusetts, California, New Jersey) have laws providing for special instruction for children who do not speak English; and the 1974 U.S. Supreme Court ruling in *Lau v. Nichols,* which required San Francisco schools to provide bilingual education to non-English-speaking pupils (largely Chinese), will undoubtedly accelerate this trend. [1]

A multiplicity of needs will have to be met if the efforts in bilingual education are to be successful. A major need (critically felt) is a text that will introduce thousands of pre- and in-service teachers to bilingual educational practices, techniques, programs, and historical backgrounds. As yet, no such text exists. A variety of materials in teaching English as a second language (TESOL) exist. [2] Abstruse linguistic monographs, largely, have little use in classrooms. Where competent texts have been published, a regional frame of reference has precluded their national use. [3]

Bilingual Schooling in the United States is intended as a basic sourcebook for training the educational personnel needed in bilingual education. Comprehensive in its coverage, it is the first clearly designed text addressed to the training required in this critical area. *Bilingual Schooling in the United States* is a compendium of documents, program constructs, theoretical-practical statements, and related

---

[1] See, generally, F. Cordasco, "The Challenge of the Non-English Speaking Child in American Schools," *School & Society,* vol. 96 (March 30, 1968), pp. 198–201, which is an adaptation of testimony before the Committee on Education and Labor of the U.S. House of Representatives in support of the proposed Title VII (June 29, 1967); and for recent developments, see F. Cordasco, "Spanish Speaking Children in American Schools," *International Migration Review,* vol. 9 (Fall 1975), pp. 379–382.

[2] See, as representative of TESOL texts, Harold B. Allen and Russell N. Campbell, *Teaching English as a Second Language,* 2d ed. (New York: McGraw-Hill, 1972).

[3] Cf., for example, Paul R. Turner (ed.), *Bilingualism in the Southwest* (Tucson: University of Arizona Press, 1973); and Frank Pialorsi (ed.), *Teaching the Bilingual* (Tucson: University of Arizona Press, 1974).

materials. It provides a dimensionally coordinated instructional-learning tool for the pre- and in-service teacher. It is intended as a classroom text for undergraduate-graduate classroom adoption but will equally serve as a main reference in bilingual education for library acquisition (academic, municipal, state, and federal) and, in a very broad sense, will prove useful to general readers. For the specialist in bilingual education, it provides a convenient repository of basic documents to which continuing reference is made.

The framework for the text has been flexibly defined. Part I (*Historical Backgrounds*) provides materials on nineteenth- and early twentieth-century efforts in bilingual education, the experience of immigrant children in American schools, de-ethnization-Americanization and enforced assimilation, and the history of immigrant language maintenance. Part II (*Typology and Definitions*) furnishes a wide range of definitions of bilingualism and a schema for a fully fashioned typology of bilingual education and articulates the central questions and concerns in bilingual education. Part III (*Linguistic Perspectives*) brings together representative documents in which the contributions of linguists and language teachers to bilingual education are clearly perceived and out of which the insights of sociolinguistics derive. Part IV (*Programs, Practices, and Staff Development*) surveys programs and practices in bilingual education (including the problems that are inevitable in administration, supervision, and implementation) and sketches the parameters of staff training, with a fully developed conspectus for graduate study. The appendixes provide an overview of court decisions and legislation affecting bilingual education in the United States and a corpus of abstracts that describe representative projects (federally funded) currently under way; and the bibliography is an introduction to the vast resources that are available. I am not unaware of the tendentious ideologies that impinge on any discussions of an area as nationally sensitive as bilingual-bicultural education, and I have purposely eschewed controversial encounters. These prolegomena (and they entertain legitimacy) correctly belong elsewhere.[4]

I have incurred many obligations in the preparation of *Bilingual Schooling in the United States*. My first indebtedness is to those individuals whose materials appear in this *Sourcebook*. In the area of linguistics (keenly aware of my limitations as a sociologist) I found the resources of the Center for Applied Linguistics and the Georgetown

---

4 See, in this connection, Alfredo Lopez, *The Puerto Rican Community: Notes on the Re-Emergence of a Nation* (Indianapolis: Bobbs-Merrill, 1973); and the vast repository on Mexican-Americans, Carlos E. Cortes (advisory ed.), *The Mexican-American*, 21 vols. (New York: Arno Press/New York Times, 1974). On the ideology of the new ethnic studies, see Andrew M. Greeley, *Ethnicity in the United States: A Preliminary Reconnaissance* (New York: John Wiley, 1974); Nathan Glazer and Daniel P. Moynihan (eds.), *Ethnicity: Theory and Practice* (Cambridge: Harvard University Press, 1975); and F. Cordasco, "The Risorgimento of Italian-American Studies," *Journal of Ethnic Studies*, vol. 2 (February 1975), pp. 104–112. ("The ethnics want to be respected. To be Polish, Italian, Slovak, Slovene, Lithuanian, or even Irish is to be the object of greater or lesser amounts of disrespect and contempt among America's intellectual and cultural elites. As the man from Yale remarked, 'If there is an inferior race, it has to be the Italians.' Just as blacks, women, and Spanish-speaking are climbing into the upper middle-class professional and intellectual world, so are the Catholic ethnics. And they are becoming more and more conscious that they have been cast in the role of scapegoat for certain social ills. There is no evidence that the ethnics are any more angry at black militancy than anyone else in the society, but there is substantial evidence that they are angry at being typecast as society's worst racists, of being stereotyped as having stereotypes, of being treated with contempt on the grounds that they are more likely to have contempt for others. As Professor Joseph Schwab once remarked, 'Students who are told that they should try to sympathize with Polish people as well as with black people turn up their noses in contempt. "How could anyone sympathize with them?" ' ") (Greeley, op. cit., p. 286).

University School of Languages and Linguistics truly invaluable. Dr. John H. Hammer, of the former, was particularly helpful. A special obligation is owed to Joanna F. Chambers, research librarian of the Dissemination Center for Bilingual Bicultural Education and to Dr. A. Bruce Gaarder of the U.S. Office of Education, who generously furnished sage counsel. Professor Joshua A. Fishman was particularly helpful, and the major contributions he has made to bilingual scholarship have placed all academicians in his continuing debt. It is not inappropriate to observe that my views (vis-à-vis linguistics and bilingualism and the tensions of these last years) are congruent with those of Professor Fishman. I can only inadequately acknowledge the debt owed to Dr. Leonard Covello, who initiated community-centered school practice in the East Harlem barrio of New York City and from whom I learned the magnitude of obligation due children by American society and its schools. Of course, any faults discerned in the present work must be attributed solely to me. In a true sense, the volume's wellsprings and motivations lie in the ethnic community of my youth and in the dynamically multifarious ethnic communities in which I have sojourned and worked: contexts in which language and culture are the animating forces of existence.

Francesco Cordasco
Montclair State College
January 1976

Introduction

The concepts that make up both the theory and practice of bilingual education are not without controversy. In a nation as diversified in its origins and makeup as the United States, controversy (and, inevitably, the ideologies that infuse both languages and cultural differences) intrude into any history of bilingual education in the United States and assume a formidable part of contemporary bilingual practice. It could not have been otherwise, for the issues inherent in a policy of bilingual education (and its concomitant practices) in any society present great problems which must be understood and resolved.

In the historic hearings before the United States Senate Special Subcommittee on Bilingual Education in mid-1967 (hearings which culminated in the enactment by the Congress of Bilingual Education Act), the doyen of Mexican-American educators, Dr. Herschel T. Manual, approached the issue of bilingual education, with great care, in these terms:

> But first, let us examine our objectives. Is the school right in its emphasis on English?
>
> The answer depends, in part, on the kind of community we wish to build and the relation of the individual to the community. One possibility is a community, a State, and a nation in which the identity and power of subgroups, based on ancestry, language, or other origin, are emphasized.
>
> In such a community, the individual identifies himself strongly with the subgroup and looks to it as his agent in the community at large. The community is thus a combination of predetermined and relatively fixed subgroups, which both cooperate and compete with each other.
>
> It would be possible to consider the Spanish-speaking people of the Southwest as such a group, and to make effective membership in that group the goal of education for its children. The bearing of such an objective on language policy is clear. If a child is to be prepared primarily for effective action within a subgroup, major attention may properly be given to his native language and relatively little to the second language.
>
> In sharp contrast is the concept of a united community composed, not of fixed subgroups, but of individuals who work together in the community at large regardless of ancestry or native language.
>
> My vision is that of a city, a state, a region, a nation, in which divisions are on issues, not on ancestry or native language. I want the Spanish-speaking children—as indeed every child—to be, to feel and to act as a full member of the larger community working for the common good. And I want to avoid like the plague the conditions that divide us and tend toward the isolation of members of a subgroup from the larger community.

Now, obviously, if people work together, they must have a common language. If persons of different language are to participate effectively in common activities, one or both must learn the language of the other.

In the Southwest, and in the nation at large, English, as all know, is the native language of the great majority of our people, and it is the primary language of commerce, industry, government, education, and news media. Conditions inherited from the past, not some arbitrary ruling and not some attempt to Anglicize children, make it necessary for every child to become proficient in the use of language if it is to participate fully in the affairs of the larger community.

Now, on the side, and dimly, I should remark that since Spanish is the first language of many of our people, it would be helpful, very helpful, in communication and personal relations, if English-speaking children would learn Spanish. They should have that opportunity in the early school years.

The school has been right in its emphasis on English and this emphasis on English must continue, but it has not been right in its neglect of the child's home language. Although English is a basic necessity for the non-English-speaking child, as every child, his native language should not be lightly cast aside. The home language of a child is an individual and community asset which the school should help develop from the child's first enrollment. To leave the development of his native tongue to the later school years is too little and too late. A developed native language can assist the child's learning in other fields than language.[1]

Professor Manuel's reasoned commentary (with its acknowledged primacy for English in the United States) butts against a constellation of dissident views: some ideological, others abstrusely linguistic, and still others psychosocial. If clear agreement and congruence of views exist on the need for bilingual education for American children (there is no unanimity of view for the need), there are, still, seemingly intractable questions that envelop the definitions of bilingual education, its typologies, its programs (and their evaluation), and the psychosocial components that accompany it.

For Mexican-Americans and Puerto Ricans, programs in bilingual education directly intrude into the new unity and militancy that characterize vigorous postures which defy acculturation and assimilation: e.g., the *La Raza* movement (and the pursuit of *Aztlán*, the ancient home of Mexican Indians) in the Southwest; and, for Puerto Ricans, the proliferating discussions that center on the island and its relationships to the mainland and on the very issue of Puerto Rican independence itself.[2] This new consciousness is clearly evident in the observations of a Puerto Rican political scientist:

The problems faced by a Puerto Rican in his society are magnified and multiplied when he migrates to the United States. Regardless of what Glazer and Moynihan argue in *Beyond the Melting Pot*, the American ethic is a messianic one, and all ethnic groups are required to assimilate culturally as a

---

[1] U.S. Congress, Senate, Committee on Labor and Public Welfare, *Hearings before the Special Subcommittee on Bilingual Education,* part 1, 90th Cong., 1st Sess., May 18, 19, 26, 29, 31, 1967, pp. 215–216.

[2] The issue is explored in David Vidal, "All Sides Agree That U.S. Tie Is a Key Problem," *New York Times,* October 16, 1975. See, also, news dispatch by Vidal, "Puerto Rico Seeks Way Out as Economic Woes Mount," *New York Times,* October 15, 1975.

condition for achieving a share in the material and spiritual goods of American society. This is particularly true for Puerto Ricans, whose process of assimilation to what Glazer and Moynihan call the "Anglo-Saxon Center" starts in the Island of Puerto Rico itself. The intellectual and moral colonization of Puerto Ricans is merely continued and intensified on the mainland, but what I have called elsewhere "the colonialist syndrome" is the result of a deliberate policy on the part of the American and the colonial government geared towards the destruction of the trend in Puerto Rican society that has historically been the main obstacle to the complete cultural assimilation of our country: namely, the trend towards independence. Frantz Fanon's insights into this problem are extremely useful for the understanding of Puerto Rican society, not from the point of view of the colonizers like Tugwell, but from that of the colonized themselves.[3]

The contemporary contexts of bilingual schooling in the United States directly impinge on the ideologies that herald the energetic emergence of peoples who find in their cultures and languages the instrumentalities of an evolving enfranchisement; and it would be hazardous to suggest otherwise. In many ways, the ideologies of race, culture, and language (if not new phenomena in American history) have a special importance at this point in time. For bilingual education, they have a crucial significance. How successful bilingual education proves in the United States will depend on how congruent its programs become with the aspirations of the ethnic communities to which the programs are addressed; on the awareness by American educators of the new American ethnicity; on the very participation of ethnic communities in program formulation and evaluation; and on the cogency of those bilingual typologies that (in carefully constructed bicultural frames) can best achieve desired objectives. Although there is a long history associated with bilingual educational effort in the United States, the contemporary effort in bilingual education has little relationship (certainly, no causal connection) with the earlier effort. The contemporary effort in bilingual education comes directly out of the restive social contexts of the American 1960s. It is part of that decisive challenge, formulated out of the civil rights struggle and the quest for educational opportunity, to the pervasive policies of American schools that discriminated against the children of the poor: a challenge that combated both cultural assault (which deprived children of their ancestral languages) and enforced assimilation. And so bilingual education became still another weapon in the capacious armamentarium of the social reformer against an intransigent establishment.[4]

---

[3] Manuel Maldonado-Denis, *Puerto Rico: A Socio-Historic Interpretation* (New York: Random House, 1972), pp. 319–320. A Puerto Rican independentist addresses the issue in more abrasive terms: "Committed as they were to the most reactionary tendencies in the political arena, in the economic structure, and in the class struggle, the assimilationists wanted Puerto Rican culture integrated into what U.S. sociologists call the 'melting pot.' Hence their irrational advocacy of English teaching in public schools, their reveries of the Puerto Rican as a North American, their concept of education to develop 'good and loyal American Citizens.' " Juan Angel Silén, *We the Puerto Rican People: A Story of Oppression and Resistance* (New York: Monthly Review Press, 1971), pp. 96–97.

[4] See, generally, F. Cordasco, "America and the Quest for Equal Educational Opportunity: A Prolegomenon and Overview," *British Journal of Educational Studies*, vol. 21 (February 1973), pp. 50–63; and F. Cordasco (ed.), "Poverty in America: Economic Inequality, New Ideologies, and the Search for Educational Opportunity," *Journal of Human Relations*, vol. 20 (3rd Quarter 1972, [special issue]), pp. 235–396.

HISTORICAL BACKGROUNDS OF BILINGUAL EDUCATION

The schema introduced by Theodore Andersson and Mildred Boyer in their *Bilingual Schooling in the United States* best illustrates nineteenth- and twentieth-century practice in bilingual education:

First Segment: Public Elementary Schools
Phase I: 1839–1880
German was the only non-English tongue admitted as a medium of teaching except for French in Louisiana and, from 1848, Spanish in New Mexico. The heyday of the public bilingual school was before the Civil War.
Phase II: 1880–1917
There were German-English bilingual schools in Cincinnati; Indianapolis; Baltimore; New Ulm, Minnesota; and in an unknown number of rural places. In other schools German was taught as a subject, but not used as a medium of instruction. Norwegian, Czech, Italian, Polish, and Dutch were also occasionally taught but not used as teaching mediums.
Second Segment: Non-Public (Chiefly Parochial) Elementary Schools
Phase I: (Before 1800)
German schools flourished throughout the country. Also this period saw the beginning of many French schools in New England and many Scandinavian and some Dutch schools in the Midwest. Many of these schools were not actually bilingual in their curricula; they were non-English schools where English was taught as a subject.
Phase II: (After 1880)
This period saw the multiplication of French and Scandinavian schools as well as the founding of numerous parochial schools especially for Catholic newcomers from Eastern and Southern Europe: e.g., Poles, Lithuanians, Slovaks.[5]

The efforts suggest a very limited range in the rapidly developing American public schools of the period; an overwhelming identity with the powerful German community; and, almost inevitably, a continuing identity with the religious schools of late-nineteenth-century immigrants from eastern and southern Europe.

One fact, however, is preeminently clear: the American public school movement (what Lawrence A. Cremin in his *The American Common School* called "an historic conception")[6] did not encourage the preservation of languages other than English. The multiplicity of state statutes that expressly forbid instruction in any language other than English is a grim attestation of the fact.

---

[5] Theodore Andersson and Mildred Boyer, *Bilingual Schooling in the United States*, vol. 1 (Austin, Texas: Southwest Educational Development Laboratory, 1970), p. 17. This impressively large work (2 volumes, 620 pages) was compiled pursuant to an amendment to the laboratory's Title IV contract with the U.S. Office of Education and published by the U.S. Government Printing Office. The greater part of volume 1 is an annotated bibliography. Volume 2 is a series of appendixes incorporating a wide range of materials relating to bilingual education in the United States. Out of print for some years, the work has recently been reissued with an introductory essay by F. Cordasco in a single-volume format by Blaine Ethridge (Detroit, 1976).

[6] Lawrence A. Cremin, *The American Common School: An Historic Conception* (New York: Bureau of Publications, Teachers College, Columbia University, 1951).

In the period of the great migrations to the United States (circa 1880 to 1920), the children of immigrants found American schools inhospitable and largely alien. As I have noted elsewhere: "In the effort to respond to the immigrant child, it is important to note at the outset that no overall programs were developed to aid any particular immigrant group. Although there was little agreement as to what Americanization was, the schools were committed to Americanize (and to Anglicize) their charges. Ellwood P. Cubberley's *Changing Conceptions of Education* (1909), which Lawrence A. Cremin characterizes as a 'typical progressive tract of the era,' saw the new immigrants as 'illiterate, docile, lacking in self-reliance and initiative, and not possessing the Anglo-Teutonic conceptions of law, order, and government...' and the school's role was (in Cubberley's view) 'to assimilate and amalgamate.'"[7] Assimilation, as a national policy, ostensibly meant the repudiation of the native languages that the children of immigrants brought to American schools. It is this theme that I have explored in "The Children of Immigrants in the Schools," in "The Challenge of the Non-English-Speaking Child in American Schools," and in "Educational Enlightenment Out of Texas: Towards Bilingualism."

It is appropriate that any compendium of materials on bilingualism in the United States draw from Joshua A. Fishman's classic *Language Loyalty in the United States*. In a very real sense, Professor Fishman sought to redress grievous wrongs against immigrants and their progeny in America. In a poignant introduction to the volume, Einar Haugen observed:

> Joshua Fishman has done us all a great service in building up a more positive image of the immigrant in this book. He has brought to light a facet of the immigrant's life in this country which has remained unknown and unheralded even by most historians of immigration, let alone historians of America. He has demonstrated the importance of seeing the immigrant as one who brought with him in his native language a pearl of great price. He has portrayed the efforts of immigrants to maintain their linguistic identity against overwhelming odds. He has documented the cost to each immigrant group of the loss which they endured when their children or their children's children refused to speak the old language. Many capitulated without a struggle, but some trait of stubborn self-assertion, some streak of pride, made many others rally to their language and wage a fight which would have been called heroic had others been there to witness it. Against indifference and contempt even the gods fight in vain, but these fighters for a doomed ethnic medium have at least been given belated recognition through the vast and patient research effort of Professor Fishman and his associates.[8]

---

[7] F. Cordasco, "The Children of Immigrants in the Schools: Historical Analogues of Educational Deprivation," *The Journal of Negro Education,* vol. 42 (Winter 1973), pp. 48–49. These themes can be further pursued in some of the new revisionist American educational historiography, e.g., Colin Greer, *The Great School Legend: A Revisionist Interpretation of American Public Education* (New York: Basic Books, 1972); and, generally, in F. Cordasco, "The Historiography of American Education," in F. Cordasco and William W. Brickman (eds.), *A Bibliography of American Educational History* (New York: AMS Press, 1975), pp. 26–34. For Cubberley, see Lawrence A. Cremin, *The Wonderful World of Ellwood Patterson Cubberley: An Essay on the Historiography of American Education* (New York: Bureau of Publications, Teachers College, Columbia University, 1965).

[8] Einar Haugen, "Introduction," in Joshua A. Fishman, *Language Loyalty in the United States: The Maintenance and Perpetuation of Non-English Mother Tongues by American Ethnic and Religious Groups* (The Hague: Mouton & Co., 1966), p. 9.

Professor Fishman defined the framework of his investigations in very broad terms: the study of language loyalty in the United States encompasses American ethnic historiography; the twin processes of de-ethnization–Americanization and the concomitant conflicts in the enforced acculturation that accompanies assimilation; and the history of immigrant language maintenance. Professor Fishman's concern with the last of these is set in the dimensional contexts of American sociocultural history and pragmatically related to contemporary needs:

This is a study of the self-maintenance efforts, rationales, and accomplishments of non-English speaking immigrants on American shores. It is not a study of the assimilation of American immigrants and of the resultant formation of the supra-ethnic American nation. The two processes— de-ethnization and Americanization, on the one hand, and cultural-linguistic self-maintenance, on the other—are equally ubiquitous throughout all of American history. They are neither necessarily opposite sides of the same coin nor conflicting processes. Frequently the same individuals and groups have been simultaneously devoted to both in different domains of behavior. However, as a nation we have paid infinitely more attention to the Americanization process than to the self-maintenance process. As a result, we have tended to be insulated from some of the most stirring cognitive and emotional processes within ourselves and throughout the rest of the world. This study represents an all too preliminary attempt to redress this imbalance in attention. Such redress would seem to be particularly appropriate at the present time when non-English language skills have been recognized as scarce and vital commodities in the conduct of our nation's international relations. Is it possible that we have appreciable but as yet unrecognized resources of these scarce commodities? Is it possible that these resources are being wasted as a result of apathy and ignorance? It is unfortunate that these questions were not asked and answered years ago.

What do we—citizens and social scientists—know about culture and language maintenance efforts in the United States? Very little indeed. How many of us, even among professional historians or students of religion in America, know that a Polish National Catholic Church grew up on *our* shores, rather than in Poland proper, because so many Polish-Americans were distressed by the policy of American Catholic leaders toward language and culture maintenance? Or that a similar state of affairs almost came into being among Franco-Americans in New England? How many of us know about the language problems that convulsed several German and Norwegian Lutheran denominations for well over half a century, or of the language issues that have influenced Jewish ethnic, religious, and intellectual life in America? Certainly, few serious students of American mass media know that the nearly defunct German press of today is a vestigial remnant of hundreds of periodic publications that appeared as recently as sixty years ago and that once represented a major force in American journalism. Few serious students of American education are aware of the bilingual *public* elementary schools that existed in several states until quite recent years. One purpose of this study is to introduce such information into the mainstream of American awareness. [9]

---

[9] Fishman, op. cit., pp. 15–16.

Language Loyalty in the United States is an invaluable repository of formal language-maintenance resources and institutions in American society. Its epilogue, "Language Maintenance in a Supra-Ethnic Age: Summary and Conclusions," sets into a meaningful historical perspective the contemporary realities of bilingual practice.

TYPOLOGY AND DEFINITIONS OF BILINGUAL EDUCATION

A typology of bilingual education derives from a set of definitions on which there is some agreement. Any attempt at definitions of bilingual education encounters difficulties because of the complex psychological, linguistic, and social interrelationships that are inherent in bilingualism itself. Although its components are essentially undefined, bilingualism is instruction in *two* languages, the use of both English and the child's native tongue as media of instruction in the school's curriculum; but this definition (which I have found most useful) is, at best, very limited. It carries with it the limited perspectives of contemporary American needs and relates largely to the unmet educational needs of language minorities in the United States.

An adequate definition, necessarily, would be much more complex. The range of definitions of bilingualism is suggested in the selection from Theodore Andersson's and Mildred Boyer's *Bilingual Schooling in the United States* entitled "Definitions." In it, Einar Haugen provides succinct definitions of "language," "dialect," "correctness," and "bilingualism." These definitions make intelligible the admirable perspective provided by William F. Mackey, who observes:

> Bilingualism cannot be described within the science of linguistics; we must go beyond. Linguistics has been interested in bilingualism only in so far as it could be used as an explanation for changes in a language, since language, not the individual, is the proper concern of this science. Psychology has regarded bilingualism as an influence on mental processes. Sociology has treated bilingualism as an element in culture conflict. Pedagogy has been concerned with bilingualism in connection with school organization and media of instruction. For each of these disciplines bilingualism is incidental; it is treated as a special case or as an exception to the norm. Each discipline, pursuing its own particular interests in its own special way, will add from time to time to the growing literature on bilingualism. But it seems to add little to our understanding of bilingualism as such, with its complex psychological, linguistic, and social interrelationships.
>
> What is needed, to begin with, is a perspective in which these interrelationships may be considered. [10]

Any definition of bilingual education must deal with the misconception that ESL (English as a Second Language) is a form of bilingual education. This is a sensitive issue and not easily resolved, but the cautions expressed are well worth heeding:

> ESL *is* an important component of bilingual education; but unless the home language is used as a medium for teaching a part or the whole of the curriculum, we believe education cannot properly be called bilingual. To call ESL programs bilingual only causes confusion. Thus, for example, in a U.S. Office of Education report of Projects to Advance Creativity in Education

---

[10] William F. Mackey, in Theodore Andersson and Mildred Boyer, op. cit., vol. 1, pp. 11.

(PACE) entitled 'Bilingual Education Projects—SR-68-25 Projects Funded in FY 1966, FY 1967, and FY 1968,' there are reported descriptions of selected planning and operational programs funded under Title III of the Elementary and Secondary Education Act. The foreword, dated August 12, 1968, defines bilingual education as 'the use of two different languages, such as English and German, in the regular classroom educational process.' In spite of the title of the document and in spite of the definition of bilingual education given, the list includes projects which are definitely *not* covered by the definition. Thus, 'bilingual education' is used as an official label to designate not only ESL projects, but also a project for the transfer of student records by data processing equipment and general cultural awareness programs. Such indiscriminate use of the term renders it meaningless.[11]

An impartial examination of contemporary bilingual education programs reveals continuing confusion on the role of ESL methodologies.[12]

A fully fashioned typology of bilingual education is in the schema provided by William F. Mackey. In it, Professor Mackey seeks an objective typology "based on criteria that are observable and quantifiable"—criteria "found in the pattern of distribution of languages in (1) the behavior of the bilingual at home, (2) the curriculum in the school, (3) the community of the immediate area within the nation, and (4) the status of the languages themselves: in other words, bilingual education is a phenomenon in four dimensions."[13] Professor Mackey's typology is more fully dimensionally sketched in the contexts of urgency that Jeffrey W. Kobrick explores in "The Compelling Case for Bilingual Education," and in the experiences of Puerto Rican children that I have delineated in "Puerto Ricans on the Mainland: The Educational Experience," and in "Spanish Speaking Children in American Schools" which (in a broad frame of reference) examines the consent decree signed in federal court in 1974

---

[11] Ibid., p. 12.

[12] How abstruse some of these methodologies are can be discerned in the animadversions of a leading theoretician of ESL: "Closely related to this is the subject of 'bilingual education.' Four current trends are noteworthy [in bilingual education] and warrant attentive consideration by educators everywhere: (1) The effort to make non-English speakers literate in their native tongue through school *language* programs; (2) The desire to teach pupils to read in their native tongue *before* teaching them to read in English; (3) The teaching of curriculum areas such as science, social studies and mathematics in the native tongue so that non-English-speaking pupils—upon entering the mainstream of the school—will not lag behind their age peers; (4) The increasing attention to the teaching of foreign languages to English speakers (with emphasis on the language spoken by the non-English speakers in the community) so that early communication between the groups will be possible. Controlled experimentation is needed, however, particularly with reference to the first three trends noted above. Recurring questions throughout this text which are applicable here and which need to be answered include: (1) How old are the learners we are talking about? (2) What proportion of students in the school and in the community are non-English-speaking? (3) How many native languages are involved? (4) Does the native language have a written language? (5) What proportion of time will be spent on the development of the native language and on the development of English? (6) Should the same curriculum areas be taught *concurrently* in the native language and in English (adapted, naturally, to the level of the learners' ability) or should there be a time lapse between the knowledge given in the native language and similar knowledge given in English? If so, how long should the English component be deferred?" Mary Finocchiaro, *Teaching English as a Second Language* (New York: Harper & Row, 1969), pp. 6-7.

[13] William F. Mackey, in Theodore Andersson and Mildred Boyer, op. cit., vol. 2, p. 65.

by the New York City Board of Education "to establish a major new program to improve the education of all Spanish-speaking pupils." The New York City federal consent decree is a small part of the greater political effort that Professor Joshua A. Fishman recommends in "The Politics of Bilingual Education," and which heralds, in his words, a day "when more and more genuine bilingual education, for all those who want it, regardless of income, mother tongue or language dominance, will be part of the variegated picture of American education."

A typology of bilingual education, inevitably, must intrude into those areas in which the difficult issues of assimilation and pluralism are encountered. These are the twin concerns of Professor Rolf Kjolseth in his "Bilingual Education Programs in the United States: For Assimilation or Pluralism?" in which he maintains that the vast majority of programs in bilingual education aim at assimilation in the dominant culture rather than preservation of ethnic differences. It is a harsh assessment, brilliantly conceptualized, and furnishes the background against which the assessments of contemporary bilingual practice are to be understood. It is in Dr. A. Bruce Gaarder's "Bilingual Education: Central Questions and Concerns" that Professor Kjolseth's piercing enquiries are enjoined:

> For our purpose here, the most fundamental distinction is between voluntary bilingualism, developed in individuals, and obligatory bilingualism, which is a collective or group phenomenon. In the former case, the individual becomes bilingual of his own free will or that of his parents. The new skill is acquired from members of the family, tutors, or servants, from sojourns abroad, in special schools, or from simple foreign language study. Obligatory, collective bilingualism takes two main forms, but the principal one is the result of contact and conflict between two peoples in a single state or under a single government: a dominant people and a dominated people. The latter group becomes bilingual by necessity, from their need to eat, to survive.
>
> Thus, the bilingualism of Americans or Frenchmen or Argentinians who learn Russian or German is voluntary, elitist, academic. The bilingualism of Puerto Ricans or Mexican-Americans (Chicanos) who have to learn English, of Catalans in Spain who must learn Spanish too, of Indians in South or North America who must learn Portuguese or Spanish or English—this is obligatory and collective. They dynamics—social, political, pedagogical—of the two kinds of dual-language acquisition are different and incompatible. [14]

And if one is constrained to agree with Dr. Gaarder ("compulsory bilingualism is an unstable, self-destructive linguistic phenomenon, for no people needs two languages for the same set of purposes"), it must readily be agreed that he has sharply defined continuing, pressing concerns in the goals to which bilingual education would aspire: "Clearly there are three major ones [goals of bilingual education], each in basic opposition to the others: (1) development of a more effective, more 'humane' one-way bridge to English; (2) more effective education for children whose mother tongue is not English, plus the long-term development and maintenance of that mother tongue; and (3) provision of a source of jobs in education and of preferential treatment for members of the ethnic groups involved." [15] Any typology of bilingual education in the

---

[14] A. Bruce Gaarder, "Bilingual Education: Central Questions and Concerns," *New York University Education Quarterly,* vol. 6, (Summer 1975), p. 2.

[15] Ibid., p. 4.

United States (in its contemporary programs and practices) can ill afford to neglect these conflicting goals.

LINGUISTIC PERSPECTIVES

There is little doubt that linguists and language teachers have an important role to exercise in bilingual education programs. That questions exist as to the nature of the role can hardly be denied. Some of the questions are asked in the remonstrances expressed by Professor Bernard Spolsky:

> When a scholar finds his field becoming relevant to the society in which he lives, he is easily tempted to assume he can cure all the ills he sees. Applied linguists are no exception; many have jumped from seeing how language education might help those who do not speak the standard language, to a belief that language problems are basic. Thus, in a recent article Garland Cannon (1971) speaks of the "original linguistic causes" of discrimination and seems to argue that the solution of "bilingual problems" will lead to a new millenium. Reading an article like this, one is reminded of the enthusiasm with which the new methods of language teaching were propounded in the fifties and early sixties; give us the money and the machines, we said, and the linguists will show you how to teach everyone a foreign language.
>
> This belief in the existence of linguistic solutions explains linguists' disappointments when they find programs in English as a second language, or as a second dialect, or in bilingual education, being greeted with suspicion by the community for which they are intended. Serious-minded, honest, and well-intentioned applied linguists are discouraged when the NAACP condemns programs using Black English as part of an "insidious conspiracy" to cripple Black children ("Black Nonsense": editorial in *The Crisis* [1971]) or when ESL programs are characterized as arrogant linguistic imperialism (editorial in *El Grito* [1968]). How can we be wrong, we ask, both when we try to recognize and preserve the child's language (as in bilingual or "bidialectal" programs) and when we try to teach the standard one (as in ESL or ESOD programs)?
>
> The difficulty has arisen, I suspect, because linguists and language teachers have seen their task as teaching language: they have not realized that it is teaching students to use language. Thus, they have often ignored the place of language in the wider curriculum of school and in society as a whole. Take the example of literacy. We argue for adult literacy in English as a means of getting jobs, ignoring (or probably not knowing) that unemployment patterns are not controlled by linguistic but by economic and racial factors. A Mexican American is out of work not because he can't read, but because there is no work, or because the employers don't hire Mexicans. [16]

Professor Einar Haugen has posed the question in these terms: "One of the problems that has concerned some of us for a number of years is to ask what contribution linguists could make to the study of bilingualism. In the rapid growth of linguistics that we see taking place before our eyes, there is a danger that the kinds of problems which bilinguals face may be neglected. The topic of bilingualism has interested psychologists and educators more than it has linguists, and much of the

---

[16] Bernard Spolsky, "The Limits of Language Education," in Bernard Spolsky (ed.), *The Language Education of Minority Children* (Rowley, Mass.: Newbury House, 1972), pp. 193–194.

literature on the subject is written by non-linguists. This is surprising in view of the fact that linguists are (or ought to be) bilingual by definition, and one would expect them to take an interest in their own problems."[17] Professor Haugen is addressing himself to the efforts, for some time under way, to establish a new interdisciplinary field under the name of *sociolinguistics* and specifically to Professor Joshua A. Fishman's charges that linguists were methodologically and theoretically rigid in their conception of language as "a pure, monolithic structure" and of language contact as resulting in "harmful" interference.

These issues are best pursued in Joshua A. Fishman's and John Lovas's "Bilingual Education in a Sociolinguistic Perspective." The conclusions that Professors Fishman and Lovas articulate in this paper are a necessary framework for a correct and dimensionally adequate appraisal of the problem:

> After a hiatus of more than half a century we are just now reentering the first stages of genuine bilingual education at public expense. We are just overcoming the deceptive and self-deluding view that teaching English as a second language is, in itself, all there is to bilingual education. We are just beginning to seriously ponder different curricular models of real bilingual education. This paper stresses that such models have societal implications, make societal assumptions, and require societal data for their implementation and evaluation.
>
> We are just beginning to realize that public schools should belong to parents, to pupils, to communities. We are just beginning to suspect that these may be legitimately interested in more than learning English and affording better and bigger TV sets. We may soon arrive at the disturbing conclusion that it is not necessarily treasonous for pupils, teachers, parents, and principals to speak to each other in languages other than English, even when they *are* in school, even when they *know* English too, and even when the languages involved are their *own mother tongues*!
>
> However, we still have a very long way to go. We still do not realize that the need for bilingual education must be viewed as merely a disease of the poor and disadvantaged. We still do not realize that alternative curricular approaches to bilingual education make tacit assumptions and reach tacit decisions concerning the social roles of the languages (or language varieties) to be taught. We still do not realize that these assumptions and decisions can be empirically confirmed or disconfirmed by sociolinguistic data pertaining to the communities that our programs claim to serve. By and large, we still do not know how to collect the societal data we need for enlightened decision making in the field of bilingual education.
>
> We are learning all of these things the hard way—which may be the only way important lessons are learned in the world of public education—but we are learning! Thank God for poor Mexican-American parents and their increasingly short tempers. Because of their number and their growing organization our grandchildren have a chance of getting a bilingual public education in the United States without necessarily being either poor or even Hispanic.[18]

---

[17] Einar Haugen, "Linguistics and Dialinguistics," in James E. Alatis (ed.), *Bilingualism and Language Contact* (Washington: Georgetown University Press, 1970), p. 1.

[18] Joshua A. Fishman and John Lovas, "Bilingual Education in a Sociolinguistic Perspective," *TESOL Quarterly*, vol. 4 (1970), pp. 221–222.

fessor Fishman has reexamined these issues in "Bilingual Education and the ture of Language Teaching and Language Learning in the United States," and it is with this important statement that I have introduced Part III.

In "Bilingual Children: A Resource Document," Professor Muriel Saville-Troike perceptively develops the concepts of child language acquisition (i.e., how language is learned, how mothers talk to children, the sequence of language development, language and physical maturity, language and concept development, boys versus girls, the effects of socioeconomic status, and finding out what children know) and she explores the phenomenon of becoming bilingual (i.e., learning a second language, interference phenomena, optimum age for second-language learning, and psychological factors). These discussions make poignantly more meaningful the profiles of bilingual children (Mexican-American, Puerto Rican, Indian) that are appended.

The issues raised by Professor Fishman are enjoined again in the presentations of professors Dell Hymes and Susan U. Philips. In "Bilingual Education: Linguistic vs. Sociolinguistic Bases," Professor Hymes examines what he considers a fundamental mistake in bilingual educational program practice (itself deriving from linguistic theory): the equation of competence in a language with competence in ways of speaking. In her paper, in turn, Professor Philips presents data (largely corroborating Professor Hymes's thesis) from an American-Indian case. The issue is neither abstruse nor esoteric. Professor Philips's conclusion (i.e., that Indian children fail to participate verbally in classroom interaction because the social conditions for participation to which they have become accustomed in the Indian community are lacking) is a reaffirmation of the need for sociolinguistic perspectives. Both Professor Hymes's and Professor Philips's papers were presented at a Georgetown University round table on languages and linguistics, and the discussion appended to each of the papers sharpens the criticality of the issues.

PROGRAMS, PRACTICES, AND STAFF DEVELOPMENT IN BILINGUAL EDUCATION

Most programs in bilingual education are federally funded. Almost without exception fiscal support derives from the national Bilingual Education Act (1968/1974) which is Title VII of the Elementary and Secondary Education Act. For the most part, programs and practice in bilingual education are a reflection of Title VII guidelines, both constraining and ambiguously left undefined. It would be invidious to characterize as somewhat exaggerated the sentiments of educators who convened in 1974 to identify criteria that would serve as guidelines for the design and content of academic programs to train bilingual-bicultural teachers. Their unrestrained praise of the Bilingual Education Act is unquestionably deserved: "Bilingual-bicultural education has become one of the most significant and widespread movements in American education in the twentieth century. Not since the Renaissance has there been such a general acceptance of the idea that the goals of education might best be served by offering instruction in the native language of the learner. The passage of the Bilingual Education Act in 1968 helped bring about a major change in our educational philosphy, from a rejection or disparagement of other languages to a respect for their validity and their value as mediums for learning. The cultures of their speakers have come to be recognized as forming a valuable part of our national heritage, and as occupying an important place in our pluralistic society."[19] The materials in this section

---

[19] *The Linguistic Reporter* (October 1974), p. 4.

are supplemented and enhanced by Appendixes A and B, which gather legislative and program exhibits. These should be noted first.

An overview of court decisions and legislation affecting bilingual education in the United States is articulated from a diversity of materials in Appendix A. These include major federal court decisions; a notice of federal statutes; basic trends in state statutes; excerpts from court decisions, constitutions, and statutes affecting bilingual education; the text of the Bilingual Education Act as amended in 1974; and related statutes. A wide range of programs in bilingual-bicultural education funded under Title VII of the Elementary and Secondary Education Act is representatively collected in Appendix B. Each program is described in the form of an abstract which includes statistical data, narrative statements regarding staff development, management activities, instructional materials used (purchased or developed), instructional content areas, classroom organization, parental and community involvement activities, and a description of the evaluation component of the project.

In "The First Seventy-Six Bilingual Education Projects," Dr. A. Bruce Gaarder provides an analytical schema and a set of criteria for judging the probable effectiveness of bilingual schooling projects. He also perceptively applies the schema and criteria to the first seventy-six such projects funded by the U.S. Office of Education under the Bilingual Education Act and offers cogent comments on and critical appraisals of the entire program. Professors Curtis Harvey, Carmen Elena Rivera, and Gloria Zamora deal with a variety of concerns in bilingual education, i.e., programs which meet students' needs; the administration, supervision, and implementation of bilingual-bicultural programs; and the philosophical basis for staff development in bilingual-bicultural programs. This last concern—staff development—is a critical issue since "teacher training institutions are under increasing presure to meet the rapidly growing demand for bilingual teachers, and states are moving swiftly toward bilingual teacher certification. Yet, there has been little agreed-upon direction for teacher training."[20]

The Center for Applied Linguistics (CAL) has issued teacher competency guidelines which derive from the discussions of a conference convened by CAL in August 1974. These guidelines are relatively comprehensive: *teachers*

> Seven major areas in which bilingual teachers should have competence were defined: language proficiency, linguistics, culture, instructional methods, curriculum utilization and adaptation, assessment, and school-community relations. The competencies specified within each of these areas are considered essential for effective performance in the bilingual classroom. The manner in which teacher training institutions formulate programs to develop these competencies will vary, thus the focus of the guidelines is on the skills and abilities which should be required for certification, rather than on specific courses or number of credit hours.
>
> Two points were stressed throughout the discussions: First, an extensive amount of the teacher's training should be conducted in the mother tongue. This is important for many obvious reasons, the major one being to provide the future teacher with specialized terminology required to present course content in the child's first language. Second, the teacher training curriculum must provide for on-site training in the community very early in the program, and continuing throughout the training period. Student teaching should extend

---

[20] Ibid.

beyond the classroom to extracurricular activities, the playground, and school programs involving the parents and community. There is not other way the teacher can develop the communicative competence required, nor perception of roles, functions, styles of socialization, and learning within the community nor can sensitivity to culture be developed adequately on campus.[21]

I have sketched (with Professor Eugene Bucchioni) some of the parameters of staff training in "An Institute for Preparing Teachers of Puerto Rican Students"; and I have provided a fuller conspectus, together with Professor Robert Miller, in "A Conspectus for the M.A. in Bilingual Education and M.A. in Teaching English as a Second Language: A Program Proposal." Although these M.A. proposals respond to critical needs for staff training in bilingual education in New Jersey and the northeastern United States, their rationale, matriculation requirements, program structure, and courses would be essentially congruent with those recommended by professionals working in bilingual education elsewhere. The realities of program visitation and evaluation are sketched in my memorandum on "The New Bedford Project for Non-English Speaking Children," which describes educational efforts under way in the largest Portuguese community in North America.

---

[21] Ibid. The guidelines are presented in considerable detail under the following rubrics: (I) Language Proficiency; (II) Linguistics; (III) Culture; (IV) Instructional Materials; (V) Curriculum Utilization and Adaptation; (VI) Assessment; (VII) School-Community Relations.

1

Historical
Backgrounds

The supra-ethnicity of the American Dream could not have found a better instrument for the enfeeblement of primordial ethnic particularities (including the displacement of ethnic languages) than the frenetic and polyglot American metropolis and the American "ways of life" which developed in it. In these inauspicious surroundings the maintenance of ethnic languages became more conscious than it had ever been before, but without either a great tradition or a little tradition to maintain it.

Joshua A. Fishman

Bilingual Schooling: An Historical Sampling

There is probably not a nation in the world without some bilingual population, and bilingual schooling has also been widespread. But the origin and status of bilingualism in different countries, as well as the national policies underlying bilingual education, have varied so widely that care must be taken in interpreting the results. Clearly, we cannot assume that practices which have succeeded abroad under entirely different circumstances will necessarily succeed in the United States. They may, or they may not. On the other hand, we would be foolish indeed to ignore the experience of others in other settings. Without any attempt at complete coverage, we have therefore selected a few examples to lend perspective and to give us an orientation. Let us, however, begin with a review of the situation in the United States.[1]

BILINGUAL SCHOOLING IN THE UNITED STATES

The history of public bilingual schooling in our country divides itself into two main parts: pre-World War I and post-1963. Kloss (1942 and 1963), who has studied this subject in great detail, distinguishes in the first part two segments and two phases:[2]

First Segment: Public Elementary Schools
  Phase I: 1839–1880
    German was the only non-English tongue admitted as a medium of teaching except for French in Louisiana and, from 1848, Spanish in New Mexico. The heyday of the public bilingual school was before the Civil War.

---

[1] The reader will find it useful to refer to the varied matter contained in the appendices. [The reader is referred to the bibliography in the original source: Theodore Andersson and Mildred Boyer, *Bilingual Schooling in the United States*, vol. 1 (1970).] Especially relevant to this chapter are Appendix C, Demographic Data; Appendix J, From Egypt to America: A Multilingual's Story; and Appendices K through U, which contain basic information on a dozen different American ethnic groups.

We also call attention at the very outset to a basic book, Joshua A. Fishman's *Language Loyalty in the United States*, which should be within reach of every educator interested in bilingual schooling.

[2] In a personal communication to us, from which we quote and paraphrase.

From Theodore Andersson and Mildred Boyer, *Bilingual Schooling in the United States*, vol. 1 (1970), pp. 17–40.

Phase II: 1880–1917
There were German-English bilingual schools in Cincinnati; Indianapolis;[3] Baltimore; New Ulm, Minnesota; and in an unknown number of rural places. In other schools German was taught as a subject, but not used as a medium of instruction. Norwegian, Czech, Italian, Polish, and Dutch were also occasionally taught but not used as teaching mediums.[4]

Second Segment: Non-Public (Chiefly Parochial) Elementary Schools
Phase I: (Before 1800)
German schools flourished throughout the country.[5] Also this period saw the beginning of many French schools in New England and many Scandinavian and some Dutch schools in the Midwest. Many of these schools were not actually bilingual in their curricula; they were non-English schools where English was taught as a subject.

Phase II: (After 1880)
This period saw the multiplication of French and Scandinavian schools as well as the founding of numerous parochial schools especially for Catholic newcomers from Eastern and Southern Europe: e.g., Poles, Lithuanians, Slovaks.

[3] See Frances H. Ellis (1954) for a detailed account of the Indianapolis program between 1869 and 1919.

[4] Kloss (1942), pp. 615–682; Kloss (1963), pp. 95–109.

[5] Dr. Kloss has communicated to us a one-page tabulation, published under the title "Die Deutschamerikanische Schule" in *Jahrbuch für Amerikastudien*. Vol. VII (1962), pp. 159–160, and which we reproduce herewith. Kloss writes:

In 1962, I published the following tabulation, giving data from 1900 (the figures were taken from Viereck, but the capital letters A, B, C have been added by me):

I. Enrollments in Programs with Highly Developed German Studies in Elementary Schools

Place	Private	Public[1]	Total	% of All Pupils
New Braunfels, Tex.	120	240A	360	100
Tell City, Ind.	120	500C	620	96
Belleville, Ill.	960	2,026A	2,986	71
New Ulm, Minn.	330	575A	905	90
Carlstadt, N.J.	122	486C	608	95
Erie, Pa.	1,985	4,830B	6,815	66
Milwaukee, Wis.	10,525	21,190B	31,715	62
Cincinnati, Ohio	10,700	17,287A	27,987	50
Cleveland, Ohio	8,041	17,643A	25,684	40
Evansville, Ind.	1,365	2,480C	3,845	36
Hamilton, Ohio	450	1,017C	1,467	32
Columbus, Ohio	1,580	3,980A	5,560	22
Dayton, Ohio	1,320	2,203A	3,523	25
Saginaw, Mich.	250	1,130A	1,380	33
Baltimore, Md.	7,250	8,450A	15,700	16
Indianapolis, Ind.	1,861	4,537A	6,398	18

[1]*A=dual medium schools*
B=German mere branch of study
C=precise status of German unknown

(continued)

(footnote 5, continued)

II. Enrollment in Programs with Less Highly Developed
German Studies in Elementary Schools

Place	Private	Public [1]	Total	% of All Pupils
New York, N.Y.	18,240	60,000B	78,240	25
Buffalo, N.Y.	5,030	7,030B	12,060	17
Hoboken, N.J.	870	980C	1,850	20
Sheboygan, Wis.	1,870	744C	2,614	55
Davenport, Iowa	430	3,400C	3,830	56
Chicago, Ill.	25,340	31,768B	57,108	19
Denver, Colo.	530	2,861C	3,391	15
Lancaster, Pa.	980	580A	1,560	25
Akron, Ohio	750	75C	825	11
Toledo, Ohio	1,868	1,932C	3,800	18
La Crosse, Wis.	893	560C	1,453	25
Houston, Tex.	350	816C	1,166	20

[1]*A=dual medium schools*
B=German mere branch of study
C=precise status of German unknown

III. Secondary School Enrollment in Cities Where Public
Elementary Schools Teach No German

Place	Private	Public [1]	Total	% of All Pupils
St. Louis, Mo.	16,850	148B	16,998	17
Detroit, Mich.	7,180	250B	7,430	15
Newark, N.J.	5,180	500B	5,680	14
Louisville, Ky.	4,530	150B	4,680	14
St. Paul, Minn.	2,180	443B	2,623	9
Brooklyn, N.Y.	7,150	960B	8,110	5
Allegheny, Pa.	2,560	150B	2,710	11
Peoria, Ill.	1,020	150B	1,170	12
Dubuque, Iowa	1,850	175B	2,025	30
Rochester, N.Y.	2,180	448B	2,628	9
Pittsburgh, Pa.	7,128	160B	7,288	13

[1]*A=dual medium schools*
B=German mere branch of study
C=precise status of German unknown

Kloss has reminded us of the considerable number of non-public Franco-American schools in New England between the two World Wars. These included both elementary and secondary schools as well as colleges. Kloss also mentions the Chinese, and a considerably larger number of Japanese, afternoon schools in Hawaii and on the West Coast. For an account of other afternoon or all-day parochial schools of newer immigrant groups, the reader is referred to Fishman's chapter on education in his *Language Loyalty in the United States.*

Rebirth of Bilingual Schooling, Miami, 1963

In an effort to meet the educational needs of the children of the Cubans who pour into Miami at the rate of some 3,000 a month the Dade County, Florida, Schools undertook in 1963 a completely bilingual program in grades one, two, and three of the Coral Way School, Miami, with plans to move up one grade each year. The first director of this program was Dr. Pauline Rojas, who had had long experience in Puerto Rico. At first, participation was made voluntary and a few parents chose to have their children follow the all-English program. By the end of the first year, however, the bilingual program had won almost unanimous approval and it was no longer necessary to offer the unilingual option. Approximately half of the instruction is given in Spanish by competent Cuban teachers and half in English by American teachers. The American and Cuban teachers working in the same grade form a cooperative team and confer frequently in order to coordinate their teaching.[6] In addition to this notable bilingual program, which has now been extended to two other elementary schools, Dade County offers Spanish as a subject in every grade from one through twelve in all other Miami schools. To start with, there were equal numbers of English- and Spanish-speaking children in the Coral Way School, but now the balance is steadily shifting in the direction of the Cuban children. The socioeconomic level is also declining; for, as the Castro regime continues, more lower-income Cubans are seeking escape.

An evaluation of the achievement in the Coral Way School in language arts and arithmetic shows that the bilingual program is as effective as the regular program in English. Dr. Mabel Wilson Richardson, the evaluator, writes: "It must be noted here that, in addition to performing as well as the control group in the regular curriculum, the English-speaking pupils were learning a second language and the Spanish-speaking pupils were learning to read and write their native language."[7] The Dade County bilingual program has the distinction of being the first public elementary school program in this second period of bilingual schooling in the United States, and it is also widely considered as one of the best.

One year later, in 1964, two noteworthy programs were launched in Texas, one in the Nye School of the United Consolidated Independent School District in Webb County, outside of Laredo, and the other in the San Antonio Independent School District.

---

[6] For a description of this and one other Spanish program in the Dade County Schools see Gaarder and Richardson (1968) and Bell (1969).

[7] Richardson (1968).

United Consolidated Program

An interested school board and an enthusiastic superintendent were responsible for the launching of this program in the first grades of Nye School, in which half the children are English speakers and half Spanish speakers. In 1965 the program was expanded into the second grades and in 1966 into the third grades. In 1966 too the other two elementary schools in this sparsely populated school district—with an area slightly greater than that of Delaware—began their bilingual programs in grade one and planned to move up one grade at a time. The teaching, in English and Spanish in all elementary school subjects, is done by bilingual teachers who are native speakers of Spanish and fluent also in English. They move without effort back and forth in Spanish and English, using each language about half of the time. In the fourth grade, where the self-contained classroom changes to the departmental organization, Spanish is continued as a subject one class period a day. An evaluation of learning in mathematics reveals that bilingual learning—for both Anglo and Mexican American children—gives better results than does learning in English alone. The enthusiasm of school board, administration, and teachers has enabled this program to prosper, to attract numerous visitors, and even to entice families to move into the district.[8]

San Antonio Independent School District Program

There are by now (1969) at least two other school districts in San Antonio that have bilingual programs, but the one in the San Antonio ISD is the oldest and best known in the city. It was begun in 1964, under the direction of Dr. Thomas D. Horn of the University of Texas at Austin, and has been carried forward chiefly by Dr. Elizabeth Ott of the Southwest Educational Development Laboratory. Orignally it was a reading-readiness program in English for Spanish-speaking children in selected schools in neighborhoods which are all Mexican American. New materials were prepared and new teaching techniques were developed. These were used for thirty minutes in the morning and thirty in the afternoon, in English in one experimental stream and in Spanish in another. By 1967 the success of the program was sufficiently recognized to permit a somewhat greater emphasis on the use of Spanish, starting in grades one and two, and to designate it as a bilingual program. The teaching in Spanish is all done by native speakers, either the regular classroom teacher or another who exchanges with the regular teacher. The subject matter stresses the self-concept and includes language arts, science, and—recently—social studies. The relatively limited emphasis on the use of Spanish—some eighty minutes a day—suggests that, in contrast with Dade County and United Consolidated, this program is more concerned with transfer than it is with maintenance of Spanish as such. Spanish is used essentially to build the self-concept of children and to facilitate their learning of English as the eventually exclusive medium of learning.[9]

---

[8] See Texas Education Agency (1967).

[9] Ibid.

Other Bilingual Programs in the United States[10]

Bilingual programs began in Pecos, New Mexico, and in Edinburg, Texas, in 1965. In 1966, similar programs started in the Harlandale Independent School District of San Antonio; in Del Rio, Texas; in Zapata, Texas; in Calexico, California; Marysville, California; and Rough Rock, Arizona. The following programs began in 1967: Las Cruces, New Mexico; Hoboken, New Jersey; Corpus Christi, Texas; Del Valle, Texas (Creedmoor School); and St. Croix, Virgin Islands.

This list, consisting almost exclusively of public elementary schools, is merely suggestive. With the exception of Navajo, taught along with English at the Rough Rock Demonstration School, the two languages concerned are Spanish and English. Approximately ninety percent of the BEA [Bilingual Education Act] proposals submitted in 1968–1969, and of the projects funded, involved these two languages.

For further information on current bilingual programs we refer the reader to Appendix V, Bilingual Programs in the United States. [The reader is referred to Appendix V in the original source: Theodore Andersson and Mildred Boyer, *Bilingual Schooling in the United States*, vol. 2 (1970).] Part I consists of programs known to have existed in May 1969, fifty-six in number, of which forty-nine were in preprimary or elementary grades, four in secondary schools, and three in colleges. A second list consists of the seventy-six projects which have been funded under Title VII, BEA, for 1969–1970. We have indicated with an asterisk fifteen projects which are continuations or transformations of programs in the first list.

Summary

Twelve years ago there was nowhere in the country any perceptible interest in organizing bilingual programs in public schools. And yet a potential must have existed, for soon after a successful program was launched in Miami, it was followed, as we have seen, by increasing numbers each year. We do not know exactly how to account for this rapid change in public temper. Did the relative success of FLES (foreign languages in the elementary school) suggest the bilingual pattern? Or was the example of such non-English medium schools as the Lycée Français in New York a cue? Or the bilingual schools in Latin America? Or should one instead seek the explanation in the tremendous changes taking place in our society, such as the Supreme Court Desegregation Decision of 1954 and the increasing search for identity and self-assertion on the part of ethnic groups and low-income classes? Whatever the explanation, opinion has evolved rapidly and the American public now seems to be of a mind to give this experiment a new try.

BILINGUALISM AND BILINGUAL SCHOOLING IN OTHER PARTS OF THE WORLD

In sampling bilingualism in other parts of the world we shall first consider Switzerland, the only officially plurilingual country we know of, then take up four officially bilingual nations: Belgium, Canada, Finland, and the Union of South Africa. Thereafter we shall see what can be learned from a selection of officially monolingual countries that have nevertheless to deal with minority languages.

---

[10] Ibid.

Official Bilingualism and Multilingualism

Most countries in the world, however many languages may be spoken within their borders, have only one official language. A few are officially bilingual. And Switzerland occupies a unique position with three official languages—French, German, and Italian—and one additional nationally recognized language, Romansch.

Switzerland

Of Switzerland's three official languages, German is spoken by seventy-four percent of the population, French by twenty percent, and Italian by four percent. Romansch, which also enjoys national recognition, is spoken by one percent of the population. In addition, German-speaking Swiss have a language or dialect for intimate use in the home or among close friends, known as Swiss German or Schwyzertütsch. The contact of these various languages does not cause any notable friction. Switzerland's language policy is based on the "territorial principle": that is, in a given canton the language of the majority is official and speakers of other languages are expected to learn and use it. But a "personality principle" is used at the federal level, according to which any individual may be attended to in his own language, no matter where he lives. Individual Swiss citizens are not notably more bilingual or more plurilingual than other Europeans. Their elementary schooling takes place in their respective mother tongues, and a second language is learned at the beginning of the secondary school. Cases of teaching in and through more than one language in the Swiss elementary school have not been reported.[11]

Belgium

Popularly considered a bilingual country, Belgium is more accurately described as a combination of two officially unilingual areas separated by a fixed linguistic boundary, which crosses the middle of the country from east to west. The present language legislation dates back to 1963, at which time the government legally separated the country into the two areas (the territorial principle). In the northern area, only Dutch is available for administrative services and Dutch is the medium of instruction in all publicly supported elementary and secondary schools. To the South, only French is used, in the same fashion. Matters of national concern are announced bilingually. Brussels and the immediately surrounding area have both Dutch and French schools and are the only parts of the country to enjoy a special bilingual status. The hostility between the two language groups appears to be beyond immediate alleviation. The French-speaking Walloons of the South feel that since theirs is a language of international prestige they have little need to learn the other official language, Dutch. The Flemings, on the other hand, feel incensed by the attitude of the Walloons and do not see why the Flemings should carry the entire burden of communication, particularly since they are in the ascendency, both numerically (about sixty percent) and economically. Neither group seems to be motivated to learn two languages in order to build one unified bilingual nation. By resorting to the territorial principle the government hopes to maintain a degree of tranquillity in this sharply divided nation.[12]

---

[11] For a brief report on Switzerland as a plurilingual state see Canada (1967), pp. 79–80. See also Welsh (1966).

[12] Canada (1967), pp. 77–79.

Canada

Canada's two official tongues, English and French, are both international languages of prestige, but English speakers outnumber French speakers about two to one and have a great economic advantage. Canada's commonwealth status and proximity to the United States in addition tend to favor the English Canadians. For this reason, the pressure is greater on the French speakers to learn English than on the English speakers to learn French. Until five years ago, French-speaking Canadians were treated legally as a minority. At that time, the government created the Royal Commission on Bilingualism and Biculturalism, to study the thorny language question. This Commission, created on a temporary basis, produced or elicited 400 briefs by representatives of the two official languages as well as by different linguistic minorities, including Ukrainians, Poles, and Italians. One hundred research reports were also produced, which will be used by the Commission in preparing its official report of twelve volumes. At this writing, three volumes have been published: *A Preliminary Report of the Royal Commission on Bilingualism and Biculturalism*; Book I, *A General Introduction: The Official Languages*; and Book II, *Education*. Minorities other than the French-speaking are waiting for more adequate treatment of their problems in a later volume. These initial volumes, though they cannot be expected to satisfy all factions equally, represent an admirable effort at objectivity and scholarliness. They stand as a kind of model of what needs in the first instance to be done in countries where language and culture differences constitute serious problems.

A multilingual country like Canada[13] should be fertile ground for bilingual education, and indeed there are extensive efforts by language groups to maintain their languages and culture in private schools. The two official languages are of course taught extensively in public schools, where the common pattern is to use the majority language of the particular province as the medium of instruction and to teach the other official language as a subject. Bilingual schooling in the sense defined by the Draft Guidelines to the Bilingual Education Program (Appendix B) [Andersson and Boyer, vol. 2 (1970).], that is, using two languages as mediums of instruction for part or all of the curriculum, is rare in Canada, as it is in most nations.

---

[13] See Canada (1965), p. 95. This table names the following languages or language groups, with numbers and percentages:

Language (groups)	Number of Speakers	Percentage of Population
German	563,713	3.09
Ukrainian	361,496	1.98
Italian	339,626	1.86
Dutch	170,177	0.93
Indian and Eskimo	166,531	0.91
Polish	161,720	0.88
Scandinavian	116,714	0.63
Jewish (Yiddish and Hebrew?)	82,442	0.45
Others, not stated	492,137	2.69
TOTAL	2,454,562	13.45

Worthy of note is the unusual case of Welland, a city of 40,000 located in southern Ontario, a few miles west of Niagara Falls. The 8,000 Franco-Ontarians living in Welland are completely isolated from the French-speaking communities living in the northern and eastern parts of the province. Nevertheless, thanks to the fact that the Welland public schools provide education for the French-Canadian children in their mother tongue, both French and English speakers of this small city have been able to preserve their own language and culture in educated form.

"Some of the French Canadian children in Welland are accommodated in French-language classes in English-language schools, but the majority of them attend schools in which all the pupils have French as their mother tongue."[14] In two such schools French is used as the exclusive medium of instruction in K through 6 as well as the medium of communication in the classroom and gymnasium and on the playground. In grade 3 English is introduced as a subject and continued through grade 6. Upon completion of grade 6 the children move to a "senior public school" (grades 7 and 8), where French continues to be the language of instruction for most subjects. "With the opening of Confederation Secondary School last September [1968], it became possible for the French Canadian children of Welland to continue their bilingual education throughout the secondary grades within the publicly supported school system."[15]

In thus emphasizing teaching French speakers in and through French the Welland schools do not neglect English but rather take advantage of the local circumstances.

Although English as a school subject is new to the Grade 3 French-speaking pupil of Welland, English as both a spoken and written language is familiar. Except for the hours he spends in school, he is immersed in a predominantly English environment. Although French is the language of his family, he also hears English at home—whenever the radio or television set is turned on. In all probability there are English-language newspapers, magazines and books in his own home. In the streets of Welland, on buses, in restaurants and stores the French-Canadian child hears English spoken and he sees that street signs, public notices, and advertisements are in English. There are English-language movies, comics, and children's magazines readily available. Although he has had no formal instruction in how to read or speak English, he does have some notion of the usefulness of English and it may be assumed that he has a greater motivation to become functionally bilingual than has his English-speaking counterpart living in some other Ontario town or city where French is rarely, if ever, seen or heard. The very factors which facilitate the acquisition of English as a second language by French-speaking children in Welland at the same time increase the difficulty of preserving and cultivating their mother tongue; English language and culture are ever-present and all-pervasive.[16]

In an effort to determine how successful this bilingual education for French-speaking children is, Giroux and Ellis, with the assistance of the Ontario Institute for

---

[14] Giroux and Ellis (1968), p. 2. Our description is based on this study, supplemented by a personal visit.

[15] Ibid.

[16] Ibid., p. 3.

Studies in Education, have measured reading achievement of grade 6 pupils in both French and English.[17]

> In both speed and comprehension the reading achievement [in French] of the average grade 6 pupil in Welland is similar to that of the average grade 6 pupil in an urban area of the [French-speaking] province of Quebec. . . . It was found that the average French-Canadian grade 6 pupil in Welland reads English with the speed and comprehension of an English-speaking Ontario child who is about eighteen months younger. After only three years of studying English as a school subject, the Welland pupils obtained a median score of 19, which is equivalent to a grade level of 4.7.[18]

In commenting on the possible relationship between French and English reading achievement, Giroux and Ellis conclude

> that there is a tendency for pupils who earn high scores in the reading of French to also earn high scores in the reading of English and for pupils who earn low scores in the reading of French to also earn low scores in the reading of English. There is certainly no evidence that competence in reading one of the languages interferes with reading the other language.[19]

Another significant experiment is taking place in the middle-class English-speaking community of St. Lambert, located just across the St. Lawrence River from Montreal, in the Province of Quebec. The parents of the English-speaking children of a Protestant elementary school, having read about the results of recent research in early elementary school learning, contacted several staff members of McGill University, including Dr. Wilder Penfield, former Director of the Montreal Neurological Institute, and Professor of Psychology Wallace E. Lambert, head of a group of productive researchers in bilingualism. They discussed the possibility of an experiment in their school. In 1966–1967 one first-grade class was taught exclusively in French with the attendant testing and research supervised by Lambert.[20] The results were so satisfactory that it was decided to continue the experimentation for three years. In 1967–1968 the pilot experimental class was followed through grade 2, which remained all-French except for fifty minutes of instruction each day by a teacher of English. At the same time different experimental and control classes were started in the first grade.[21] And in 1968–1969 the project was expanded into the third grade and replicated in grades 1 and 2.[22]

---

[17] The procedure is described on pp. 5 ff.

[18] Ibid., p. 6.

[19] Ibid., p. 7.

[20] For a detailed report see Lambert and Macnamara (1969).

[21] Gratifying results are reported by Lambert, Just, and Segalowitz (1969).

[22] The authors had an opportunity to visit this school in April 1969 and were most favorably impressed by the interest expressed by several parents and the principal, by the skill and dedication of the teachers, by the performance of the children, and by the effective research collaboration of Lambert and his team.

For a summary conclusion we shall let the researchers speak for themselves:

The results of this experiment to date indicate that the type of bilingual training offered these children is extremely effective, even more so than was originally expected. The similarity of the findings for two different sets of first-grade classes, involving changes in teachers, methods of instruction and modes of testing and analysis, speaks well for the stability and generality of the effects produced by the experimental program. These effects demonstrate a very high level of skill in both the receptive and productive aspects of French, the language of instruction; a generally excellent command of all aspects of English, the home language of the children; and a high level of skill in a non-language subject matter, mathematics, taught through the foreign language only. The results for the second year of the French program, during which a minimum of training was given in English, show a general improvement in French and English language achievement and in mathematics so that the second year experimental class performs as well as, and in some cases better than, either English or French control classes in most abilities examined. Impressive as the grade 2 results are, however, they should be considered as tentative until they are replicated with new sets of classes in 1969. Their significance will become clearer, too, as the scope of the research is broadened to include an examination of the impact of the experimental program on the ethnic attitudes of the children and their parents, relative to the control children and their parents. It would be surprising if a program of the sort offered the children did not affect their self-conceptions, since they have become progressively more bicultural, perhaps much more so than their parents.

Finally, it is felt that plans should be made to study the effects of the same type of experimental program on English-speaking children from somewhat lower social-class backgrounds and on children with an even broader range of intelligence scores. To be of general value to a region or nation that is serious about developing a bilingual and bicultural citizenry, the children from working class backgrounds and those of limited intellectual endowment should be given every opportunity to capitalize on a program as promising as this one now appears to be. In other words, it should not be a program for the privileged classes only. Similarly, it is hoped that certain French Canadian schools will see the obvious advantages of such a program for their children.

Finland

For a capsule description of the harmonious bilingual situation in Finland we resort to the *Report* of the Royal Commission on Bilingualism and Biculturalism in Canada: [23]

In Finland, there are two main languages: Finnish and Swedish. The two languages have had many years' experience of association—for 600 years present-day Finland was part of the Kingdom of Sweden. Only in modern times, however, have they existed in a state of legal equality. Earlier, Swedish, as the language of learning, administration, the church, and commerce, had characterized the educated classes, and more particularly the civil service, the clergy, and the economic elite. From about 1840, the forces of Finnish nationalism began to gain momentum. The movement culminated in the 1919

---

[23] Canada (1967), pp. 75 ff.

Constitution. Both Finnish and Swedish were declared national languages of Finland, and citizens were guaranteed the right to use either language in their relations with the administrative authorities. Article 14 of the Constitution also provided that "care shall be taken that the rights [of both populations] shall be promoted by the state upon an identical basis."

This sweeping promise of equality is at first sight surprising, since the minority group who spoke Swedish accounted for only 11 percent of the population in 1919. Admittedly, they had formed 14 percent in 1880, but by 1960 this population had declined to 7 percent of 331,000 persons in a total population of 4,100,000. Yet, while the numerical strength of the Finnish-speaking citizens explains the comparative rapidity with which they established parity with those speaking Swedish, the past pre-eminence of the latter largely accounts for the present position of formal equality between the languages. Another factor is the usefulness of Swedish in increasing contacts between the Nordic countries: the status of Swedish is an affirmation of Finland's position as one of these countries.

Though it was not always so, language rarely seems to be a subject of serious discord in Finland nowadays. Given the smallness of the Swedish minority and the lack of widespread individual bilingualism (some 11 percent had a knowledge of the two languages in 1969), it is accepted on both sides that the equality spoken of by the Constitution should be implemented principally by regions. Such a territorial principle restricts an individual's right to receive services in his own language to certain defined districts. As the Swedish-speaking community is for the most part concentrated in the coastal areas and in certain cities and towns rather than scattered across the country, this is not as great a restriction as it might first appear.

The commune is the unit of local government in Finland. It will be officially bilingual if it includes in its territory a linguistic minority of at least 10 percent of the population or at least 5,000 persons. If the proportion of the minority is smaller, the commune will be unilingual in the language of the majority, whether Finnish or Swedish. For administrative purposes, one or more communes may form a district; this will be unilingual if all the communes making it up are of the same language. But if there are bilingual communes or communes of different languages, the administrative district will be considered bilingual. School districts, whose boundaries do not necessarily coincide with those of administrative districts, are similarly organized; for more than a given number of students who speak Finnish or Swedish, an education in their own language must be assured.

This, in a very broad outline, is how the people of Finland have established linguistic equal partnership. By impartially subjecting minorities of both language groups to the territorial principle, on the basis of the most recently available census figures, they have met their constitutional requirement of official equality. Yet at the same time they have never lost sight of the practical limits imposed by the country's demography and history on the provision of equal service.[24]

---

[24] For a much more detailed treatment of the Finnish situation the reader is referred to T. Miljan, *Bilingualism in Finland*, a research report submitted to the Royal Commission on Bilingualism and Biculturalism. See p. 211 of Book I, *General Introduction: The Official Languages*. Miljan reports, for example, that the normal pattern for a Finnish school child is to receive his education through his mother tongue and to study the second official language as a subject starting in grade 5. See also Wuorinen (1931).

Union of South Africa

In his Inaugural Address at the International Seminar on Bilingualism in Education, held in Aberystwyth, Wales, in 1960, Dr. E. G. Malherbe, Principal and Vice-Chancellor of the University of Natal, refers to his country as "the most bilingual country in the world today." He adds that "it has administratively applied bilingualism in schools in a more universal and thoroughgoing way than any other country I know of."[25] We shall use Malherbe as our main source of information on the Union of South Africa.[26]

> When the four Provinces were united into the Union of South Africa in 1910, one of the main principles laid down in the Act of Union was that: "Both the English and Afrikaans languages shall be official languages of the Union and shall be treated on a footing of equality and possess and enjoy equal freedom and rights and privileges."
>
> Every child in every school throughout the Union is taught both English and Afrikaans as languages, with the second language being started not later than one to two years after beginning school. The results of this official policy are reflected in the census figures, which show a steady rise in bilingualism amongst the white population of 7 years and over, during the last 40 years.
>
> Afrikaans is a highly streamlined form of the 17th century Dutch brought to South Africa by its first permanent settlers. It is a very flexible medium of expression in all fields, technical as well as literary. It is able to draw on modern Dutch when necessary for technical terms, and uses it as supporting literature in the higher classes. In its short span of life as a language it has developed a literature in poetry and prose, the best of which compares favourably with that of older literatures. It has proved a very successful medium of instruction over the whole educational range from the kindergarten to the university. Its spelling is phonetic and can for that reason alone be learnt far more easily at school than English.
>
> At present roughly 60 percent of the three million white population speak mostly Afrikaans *at home*, and 40 percent English.
>
> In 1918 (i.e., 42 years ago) the percentage who could speak both English and Afrikaans was 42 percent. In 1921 it had risen to 51 percent; in 1926 to 58 percent; in 1936 to 64 percent; in 1946 to 69 percent; in 1951 to 73 percent. If one takes the age group of 10–64 years, the percentage is 78 percent bilingual. This was in 1951. (Today I am sure it must be over 80 percent.) The number who spoke Afrikaans only was 8 percent and English only was 14 percent. . . .

Commenting on the organization of schools, Malherbe distinguishes between language as a subject and language as a medium:

(A) *Language as a subject:*

> Though the regulations differ somewhat in the four Provinces, it can be assumed that all white and coloured children in South African schools are taught both official languages, English and Afrikaans, *as subjects*. All indigenous African pupils are taught their vernacular language as well as at

---

[25] United Kingdom (1965), pp. 8 ff.

[26] For another succinct description see Canada (1967), pp. 80–82. See also Aucamp (1926), and Malherbe (1946).

least one of the official European languages. For the moment I shall limit my observations to schools for white pupils.

This is the general position in a nutshell as far as the legislative requirements are concerned.

Obviously the child begins to learn his first language as a subject right from the start. But as to *when and how* a beginning should be made with the study of the second language as a subject, this becomes a question of *educational method.*

According to the best educational theory in South Africa today, both official languages should be taught to all pupils *as subjects* right from the beginning. *But with the following important provisos:*

(i)   The child must hear the second language first, then learn to speak it, then to read and write it.

(ii) The young child must under no circumstances learn to *read* or *write* the second language until it can do so in the first language. This is a necessary proviso, particularly where the one language is phonetic (e.g., Afrikaans) and the other (English) is not phonetic in its spelling.

(iii) It does not matter much how early in school life the child starts with the second language, provided that it follows the mode of acquisition of the first language in learning it. This is best achieved in free association with other children who speak the second language. And, failing the presence of such children, the second language should be introduced *conversationally* through games and other interesting experiences of intrinsically educational value to the child, e.g., simple stories from the fields of history, geography, nature study, etc.

Used in this way, the language lesson (whether in the first or the second language) becomes ancillary to the other subjects, instead of being something sterile by itself. . . .

(B) *Language as a medium:*

In South Africa the child must be taught at least up to the end of the primary school through the medium of the home language, i.e., the language which the child understands best. This is determined by the school inspector. Only in the Province of Natal does the parent have a choice in the matter.

The second language may be introduced as an additional medium beyond the primary stage. In Natal this may be done earlier.

The home (or family) language medium principle is more strongly entrenched in the educational enactments in South Africa than in any other bilingual country.

As an educational principle, the use of the child's home language as a medium of instruction, especially in the early stages, is sound. Education, to be effective, must utilise the child's own environment and experience as a foundation on which to build.

Malherbe then describes the various types of schools:

(1) *The unilingual or single-medium school:*

Here children with Afrikaans and English home languages respectively are segregated into separate schools, even though they live in the same community or town. Thus only one medium of instruction is used throughout the school, except when teaching the second language as a subject. The majority of schools in the larger towns and cities are of this type. This type of school organization has led to the artificial "kraaling off" [separation] of children into two distinct and sometimes socially hostile groups, even where they come from homes and communities where both English and Afrikaans are currently spoken. This not only deprives children while at school of the benefit of associating on the playground with children of the other language group—thus diminishing the opportunities of hearing and using the second language—but has also had important social and political consequences. By accentuating language differences it has caused a set-back to the process of developing a corporate national feeling of South Africanism amongst the younger generation.

In general there are four different principles according to which the media of instruction are determined in bilingual (or trilingual) countries:

(a) the home;
(b) the religious allegiance;
(c) local geographical area;
(d) the political unit (the State).

A logical consequence of the separate-medium type of school organisation has been in fact that we have now four English-medium universities and four Afrikaans-medium universities. . . .

(2) *Parallel classes:*

Here Afrikaans and English home language children go to the same school, but are taught in separate classes. The only time they will hear the second language spoken is in the language lesson and on the playground.

(3) *Dual medium:*

This takes several forms in practice (a) where some subjects are taught through Afrikaans and others through English medium to the same classes: (b) where both media are used alternatively: (i) in the same lesson, by repeating completely or partially in the one language what has been said in the other language, (ii) on successive days of the week. The situation in (b) is feasible only when the teacher is fully bilingual. . . .

(4) *A combination of the parallel class and dual-medium systems*, the former being more common in the lower classes and the latter more common in the upper classes.

Types (2), (3) and (4) are usually grouped together under the generic term *Bilingual School* to distinguish them from the single-medium school.

In 1938 I made a study of over 18,000 pupils in over 200 representative primary and secondary schools in South Africa to ascertain *inter alia* the effect which these various types of school organisation had on (a) their progress in their first and second languages respectively, and (b) their content subjects by using either or both first and second languages as a medium of instruction. (The results have been published in "The Bilingual School"—Longmans, 1946.)

In short it may be stated that where English and Afrikaans children attended the same school, either with the method of parallel classes or of dual medium, (a) they gained in proficiency in their second language over those in separate single-medium schools, while their first language was unimpaired; (b) by the time they reached Standard VI (i.e. the end of the primary school), they were in no way behind in their content subjects as a result of their second language being used as medium of instruction.

Bilingual or Plurilingual Countries Having One Official Language

We have selected about a dozen countries in this category with the thought that they will suggest something of the diverse conditions—linguistic, cultural, political, etc.—which affect education. Not discovering any better procedure, we shall take them up in alphabetical order.

Ceylon

Ceylon, an independent nation within the British Commonwealth since 1948, has unresolved language and educational problems. The majority of the population are Sinhalese (about 6,000,000) and the largest of the minority groups are the Tamils (about 2,000,000). All others—Moors, Burghers, Malays, etc.—comprise less than 1,000,000. In 1961, after much discussion, Sinhalese was made the single official language of the country. As a result, the minority groups, especially the Tamils, feel that their best interests are not adequately protected, and there are frequent language disputes.[27]

China

In China, despite the presence of sometimes mutually incomprehensible languages, or dialects, what may comprehensively be called Chinese is spoken by ninety-five percent of the population and ninety-five percent of all speakers of Chinese—some of whom are to be found in almost any part of the world, from Singapore to New York—live in China. The national language of China is Mandarin (or Kuo-yu), which is also one of the five official languages of the UN.[28]

There are eight subgroups of non-Chinese languages spoken by the ethnic minorities in China including Taiwan. Many of these languages never had any fully developed scripts until, interestingly, the advent of the People's Republic of China, whose policy approximated that of the USSR with regard to minority languages. The general thrust generated by Peking was to help the minority people either to perfect or to create written forms for their languages. The theory was that these people must first be helped to become literate in their own way to facilitate their education, and then along with improved education would come the incentive to join in the main-stream of Chinese society, to the extent of wanting to learn the national Chinese language in addition to their own. For example, in 1955, a script was developed for the Chuang Minority Nationals in Kwangsi Province, Southeast China, using the Latin alphabet as the basis.[29]

Within the subgroup of minority languages in Taiwan, nine different forms of speech have been identified, with a total of about 160,000 speakers.[30] The government of the Republic of China in Taiwan so far has encouraged only academic interest in studying these languages; there has been little activity to promote their use. (Kai-yu Hsu)

---

[27] See Macrae (1939).

[28] See also Appendix R, Chinese, by Kai-yu Hsu. [Andersson and Boyer, vol. 2 (1970).]

[29] American Consulate General in Hong Kong, "Survey of Mainland Press," No. 1068 (June 14, 1955), p. 1.

[30] Chung Lu-Sheng, *The Phonology of the National Language*, Taipei: 1966, pp. 10–12.

Faroe Islands

These Islands in the North Atlantic comprise a county of Denmark. The local language, Faroese, is one of six distinct written languages of Scandinavia. The written form of Faroese was developed about 1846 by V. U. Hammershaimb, and in 1912 the use of Faroese in schools and churches was to some extent authorized. Since 1938, teachers are free to use Faroese as the single language of instruction, reversing the trend of the preceding period.

Greenland

Greenland, which until 1953 was a Danish colony and which since that time has become an integral part of the realm, has a Danish-Greenlandish bilingual program in its elementary schools. Instruction in Greenlandish, the mother tongue of the Eskimos, is emphasized at the beginning and then Danish is added to the curriculum. It is generally considered that the Eskimos of Greenland receive a more suitable education than they do in Alaska or Northern Canada. However, the Danes are not satisfied and continue to study the problem.

India

India represents what is perhaps the most complex multilingual situation in the world. In the Census of 1961 "every individual was asked to give his mother tongue. A total of 1,652 different names of mother tongues were returned, of which 1,022 could firmly be classed as Indian languages."[31] Even though this multiplicity of tongues may be reduced to "twelve major languages of Indo-European or Dravidian origin,"[32] the problem of education is complicated. Addressing a Conference of Provincial Ministers of Education in 1949, Minister of Education Manlana Azad stated: "India is a vast country with many languages. We must accept unreservedly that all these languages are Indian languages and deserve equal treatment. . . . What objection can there be if a minority in a particular province speak or learn in a language other than that of the majority. . . . Even if our aim is unity, it cannot be achieved by compulsion or imposition. . . .We should approach this problem with large-hearted generosity and try to meet the wishes of the minorities in a manner which will leave no ground for dissatisfaction or complaint."[33] This expresses an irreproachable sentiment, and to this day nearly all minority languages are used as mediums of instruction, at least in the lower forms of the schools. The trouble comes when national unity is sought, for Hindi, the national language, is spoken by only one-third of the population. As a medium for higher education it competes poorly with English, which also serves as the best medium of communication among well-educated Indians and as a link language with the world outside. After more than a decade of controversy a tolerable formula has been worked out. Recognizing the tendency of regional languages to become the mediums of university education, the Central Advisory Board proposed in 1962 "that

---

[31] Julian Dakin et al. (1968), pp. 12–13. Our brief account is based on this chapter.

[32] Ibid., p. 16. Kloss states that there are fourteen (not twelve) official languages (including Sanskrit). See his "Problèmes linguistiques des Indes et de leurs minorités," in *Revue de Psychologie des Peuples*. Vol. XXL (1966), pp. 310–348.

[33] Julian Dakin et al. (1968), p. 36.

any university adopting a regional language should continue to provide facilities for instruction in English and Hindi. . . .The National Integration Council, while conceding that regional languages should become the media of university education, warmed to the theme of Hindi as the eventual, and English as the transitional, link between universities. . . . The link language formula satisfied everyone because it left open the question of timing."[34] This is the language policy today, reflected in a speech by Mrs. Gandhi on August 15 (the Indian national holiday), 1967, in which she said, "In the present-day world, we cannot afford to live in isolation. Therefore there should be three languages, regional, national, and international."[35]

Mexico, Guatemala, Peru,[36] and Ecuador

Monolingual Indian populations in these countries have been for many years a serious problem for any educational program. Increasingly in the past two decades, the governments of these countries have sponsored programs in which the Indian languages are used as mediums of instruction in the early grades of special schools, while at the same time the children are introduced to Spanish as their second and national language. The Summer Institute of Linguistics, whose teams of linguists are engaged in research in these languages, has assisted in such programs by cooperating in the development of writing systems, in the preparation of basic primers and readers, and in the vernacular side of teacher training. (Sarah Gudschinsky)

Paraguay

"In Paraguay, two languages, Spanish and Guaraní, have co-existed for the past three hundred years in relative equilibrium. A high percentage (52%) of the community is said to be bilingual and almost the entire community (92%) can speak the aboriginal language, Guaraní."[37] Rubin points out that "Paraguayans are unique in Latin America in the importance they give their aboriginal language, Guaraní. In all other . . . countries the Indian language is relegated to a secondary position—it is the language of the lower class or of the still extant aboriginal groups."[38] In Paraguay Guaraní is the language of intimacy, of love, of poetry, and of jokes.[39] The explanation for this unique situation is to be found in the close interaction between the Spanish conquerors and the Guaraníes from the very beginning. The latter were willing to collaborate with the Spaniards for their mutual protection, and a high percentage of Spanish-Guaraní households were established.[40] The children learned Guaraní from their mothers and from the servants, and Guaraní became quickly the language of the home. There is a high degree of loyalty to Guaraní, which is considered to be the

---

[34] Ibid., p. 53.

[35] Ibid., p. 61.

[36] Burns (1968).

[37] Joan Rubin (1968), p. 14.

[38] Ibid., p. 21.

[39] Ibid., p. 16.

[40] Ibid., p. 23.

national language *par excellence*, though Spanish is the official language and is also highly respected.[41] The fact that the two languages are used for different roles makes for the great stability of both.

Philippines

One of the earliest pieces of serious research on the effects of beginning education in the child's mother tongue was done in the Philippines in the late forties. The Iloilo experiment demonstrated the superiority of this form of instruction.[42] Current experimentation in the use of two languages in the primary grades is being carried out under the sponsorship of the Language Study Center of the Philippine Normal College, Bonifacio P. Sibayan, Director.[43] In general the first two years of schooling are conducted in the child's home language, and the rest of the elementary school in Tagalog (Filipino, Pilipino), the official language, with English studied as a subject.

The Union of Soviet Socialist Republics (USSR)

The European nation with the greatest variety of experiences in bilingual schooling is presumably the USSR. The Soviets were from the beginning committed to allow the ethnic minority groups considerable freedom in their educational planning. With some 200 distinct languages, spoken by about forty-five percent of the population, the USSR became the scene of extensive language-development. The principal languages were standardized, writing systems were developed for unwritten languages, and well over sixty languages began to be used in primary schools and in some instances past this level.[44]

In the 1930's a new policy was initiated, which emphasized the role of Russian in the Soviet communication network and limited the use of the minority tongues. The more important minority languages, however, continued to be used as mediums of instruction in primary and to a lesser extent in secondary schools.[45] It is reported that some 700 schools make some use of foreign languages like English, French, German, and Chinese as languages of instruction in various subjects.[46] Mackey adds that there

---

[41] Ibid., p. 21.

[42] Pedro T. Orata, "The Iloilo Experiment in Education through the Vernacular," *The Use of Vernacular Languages in Education*, monograph 8 on fundamental education, Paris: UNESCO, 1953, pp. 123–131.

[43] Prator (1956). See also: Bonifacio P. Sibayan, "Some Problems of Bilingual Education in the Philippines," *Philippine Journal of Education*, Vol. XLV (1966); ____"Language Planning in the Philippines," paper read at the Thomas Jefferson Cultural Center, mimeographed, 10 p. See also Sibayan (1968); ____ "Pilipino, English and the Vernaculars in Philippine Life," *The Catholic Teacher*, Vol. XIV (January 1969), p. 1–12; ____"Planned Multilingualism in the Philippines," in Thomas A. Sebeck, ed., *Current Trends in Linguistics*, Vol. VIII, *Linguistics in Oceania*, The Hague: Mouton & Co. (in press); and G. Richard Tucker, "An Assessment of Bilingual Education in Philippine Context." See interim report attached to correspondence with Work Page No. 1, Philippine Normal College Bilingual Experiment, 1968-1969.

[44] Eric Goldhagen (1968). See especially Jacob Ornstein's chapter entitled "Soviet Language Policy: Continuity and Change." See also Kreusler (1961).

[45] Eric Goldhagen (1968).

[46] H. H. Stern (1969), p. 82.

are more than twenty Pedagogical Institutes for Foreign Language Teaching and at least four times this number of Special Language Schools in which, from the first grade, a foreign language is used almost exclusively as modern history and economic geography of the foreign country are taught in the foreign language.[47]

United Kingdom

As E. Glyn Lewis remarks in his chapter on "Bilingualism—Some Aspects of Its History," there has been in Britain "a long, almost unbroken, tradition of bilingualism of one form or another over large areas of the country. Latin, of course, was a living language in these islands as it was on the continent. . . . Latin was spoken by members of all classes of the Celtic population. . . . It was probable that the Romanised Britons were bilingual exactly as the well-to-do-classes in Norman England a thousand years later."[48] Lewis continues: "In the 13th century French was spoken practically everywhere, certainly everywhere that mattered. It was the language of the court, and of society; it was the language of administration, of parliament, of the law courts, the church and monasteries. It was the language of schools, which forbade the speaking of English, much as Welsh was forbidden in Wales in the 19th century."[49]

In our day, the Celtic minority languages, having long since retreated to the edges of Great Britain, are struggling manfully to maintain themselves. Welsh-English bilingualism is still active in parts of Wales.[50]

The Constitution of Ireland lays down in the famous Article 8 that "(1) the Irish language as the national language is the first official language. (2) The English language is recognised as a second official language. (3) Provision may, however, be made by law for the exclusive use of either of the said languages for any one or more official purposes, either thoughout the State or in any part thereof."[51] Proponents of Irish-English bilingualism see it as the only way of maintaining the Irish language and culture. Others, while sympathetic to the desirability of maintaining the ancestral heritage, point out that Irish speakers account for only three percent of the population, according to the 1961 Census. Recent surveys show that "about 83 percent of the population did not believe that Irish could be restored as the most widely spoken language. . . ."[52] Apparently the motivational factor is lacking. Even those who are sympathetic to the maintenance of Irish have little reason for optimism.

In Scotland Gaelic plays a feeble role in the schools.[53]

---

[47] Xronika, *Inostrannije Jazyki v Skole*, 1960-1968.

[48] United Kingdom National Commission for UNESCO, *Bilingualism in Education*, London: Her Majesty's Stationery Office, 1965, p. 71.

[49] Ibid., pp. 72-73.

[50] Ministry of Education, "The Place of Welsh and English in the Schools of Wales." London: Her Majesty's Stationery Office, 1953. See also Jones (1966).

[51] See the chapter by Colmán L. O'Huallacháin, O. F. M., "Some Development in the Irish Republic: Language Teaching in Ireland," in Peter Strevens, ed., *Modern Languages in Great Britain and Ireland*, Strasbourg: AIDELA, 1967.

[52] Macnamara (1969), p. 17. See also Macnamara (1966).

[53] Scottish Council for Educational Research, *Gaelic-Speaking Children in Highland Schools*, London: 1961.

Summary

This cursory sampling of a dozen bilingual or plurilingual communities is intended to be no more than suggestive. An American educator will perhaps detect among these foreign settings an occasional feature that matches the situation in his own bilingual community. He will probably have more questions than answers. Is bilingualism a good thing for a community or a nation? Should it be confined to the home and to use among intimate friends? Or should it be supported through instruction in the schools? How do languages relate to social roles? What are appropriate roles for the home language, for a second language, and for foreign languages? Are there essential differences between local languages and languages of wider communication? What makes some languages prestigious and others not? What determines community attitude toward a given language, toward bilingualism, toward bilingual schooling? How should majority and minority language groups interact? Does the power advantage of the majority or dominant group imply special responsibility toward the minority groups? How much do language problems and intergroup tensions result from ignorance—of the nature of language; the process of language learning; the inter-relationship of language, culture, and society, etc.? In the chapters that follow we cannot presume to give definitive answers to all of these questions, but we hope that the information we have gathered will be suggestive of some lines of thought.

Some Facts about Bilingualism in the United States: a Socio-Historical Overview

Non-English languages of the continental U.S. are commonly classified into three groups: (1) indigenous languages, (2) colonial languages, and (3) immigrant languages.

1. The indigenous population is estimated to be as great as or greater than when European colonization began in earnest. Nevertheless, many of the original tribes have disappeared entirely. The Federal Government has vacillated between policies oriented toward forced de-tribalization and tribal autonomy. This on-again, off-again treatment has greatly weakened the ability of Indians to retain their languages and their interest in doing so.

Of the nearly 300 separate American Indian languages and dialects extant, only roughly 40 percent have more than 100 speakers. In the case of about 55 percent of these languages, the remaining speakers are of advanced age. These facts imply that many of the languages are destined to disappear as living tongues. Currently, efforts are under way among American Indian organizations to safeguard Indian tribal lands and to strengthen tribal autonomy. These efforts do not include specific emphasis upon language maintenance.

2. Of the colonial languages spoken by 16th, 17th, and 18th century colonizers, English, Spanish, French, and German continued to be spoken in the 19th and 20th centuries, but Russian, Swedish, and Dutch did not survive. Their use in the U.S. today is a result of their re-introduction with immigrant status. Of these languages Spanish has the greatest number of speakers in this country. The ancestry of most Spanish speakers in the United States is not European but Mexican-Indian. To the large indigenous Spanish-speaking population, there have been added in recent years large contingents from Mexico, Puerto Rico, Cuba, and other quota-free Spanish American countries. Thus Spanish has dual colonial-immigrant status.

The situation of French as a colonial language is only superficially similar to that of Spanish. Most Franco-Americans are of post-colonial immigrant stock. German represents a mixture of colonial and immigrant statuses. Although a great variety of German dialects were spoken in colonial days, it is only in connection with several non-prestige variants—commonly called "Pennsylvania Dutch"—that linguistic continuity with colonial times has been maintained. The vast majority of German speakers in the U.S. today are of post-colonial origin.

From Theodore Andersson and Mildred Boyer, *Bilingual Schooling in the United States*, vol. 2 (1970), pp. 83–86.

3. Any consideration of language maintenance efforts in the U.S. must stress the immigrant languages, since these are the most numerous and their speakers have been exposed to the assimilative forces of American life for the shortest period of time. Mass immigration from Europe lasted from approximately 1880 to 1920. Subsequently, mass immigration has occurred only in the Latin American Spanish-speaking case. Millions of speakers of scores of languages arrived on our shores: peasants and townsmen, illiterates and literati, speakers of prestigious and speakers of officially unrecognized tongues, avowed language loyalists and others who had no particular awareness of their language. They, their children and grandchildren represent a great and largely untapped resource of language teachers and language learners. It is the purpose of this report to examine the nature and extent of these human resources and to suggest programs for activating and developing them.

The Question of Language Loyalty

The Americanization of immigrants has been explained on the basis of irresistible attractiveness of American mass-culture, the destruction of immigrant folkways under the impact of industrialization and urbanization, the openness and ampleness of the American reward system through public education to social mobility, the geographic mobility of our population, which favored adoption of a lingua franca and other equally recent and common cultural denominators, the emphases on childhood and youth and the outdating of adult values and patterns, and even an "Old World weariness" which immigrants purportedly carried with them at a subconscious level. Although the U.S. was born, grew up, and came of age during two centuries in which nationalism reached unsurpassed heights in western history, the vast majority of the millions of immigrants to the U.S. were innocent of nationalistic sentiments or ideologies in their daily lives. Ethnicity of a traditional, particularistic, and non-ideological character—rather than nationalism in its strident and symbolically elaborated manifestations—guided their behavior in most cases. The languages that they spoke were related to the countless acts of everyday life rather than to "causes" or ideologies. Indeed it was only *after* immigration that group and language maintenance sometimes became conscious goals. American "nationalism" has been non-ethnic from the very first. From the days of the Pilgrim fathers American leaders have ideologized morality, opportunity, progress, and freedom. Ethnicity has been considered irrelevant. There was no apparent logical opposition between the ethnicity of nationalism of incoming immigrants and the ideology of America. Individually and collectively immigrants could accept the latter without consciously denying the former. However, acceptance of the goals and values of America placed them on the road to accepting American life-styles, customs, and the English language. Just as there is hardly any ethnic foundation to American nationalism so there is no language awareness in conjunction with the use of English. The English language does not figure prominently in the scheme of values, loyalties, and traditions by which Americans define themselves as "American." Americans have no particular regard for English as an exquisite instrument, no particular concern for its purity, subtlety, or correctness. The fact that so few Americans command any other language than English is largely a result of educational failure, cultural provincialism, and the absence of pragmatic utility for bilingualism, rather than an outgrowth of any conscious attachment to English. Given the lack of ethnic and linguistic awareness roundabout them, the linguistic facility and interest of immigrants steadily diminished or atrophied once they had painlessly and unconsciously accepted the American dream.

Anti-foreigner movements (at times, more narrowly anti-Catholic ones) and the opposition to German language and culture during the two World Wars are clearly historical exceptions related to unusual circumstances on the national and international scenes. Most normal by far has been the unplanned attrition of minority cultures. More linguistic and cultural treasures were buried and eroded due to mutual permissiveness and apathy than would ever have been the case had repression and opposition been attempted. Immigrant minorities were virtually never forbidden to organize and maintain their own communities, organizations, schools, or publications.

Language loyalty in the U.S. could not but be related to the tenor of American-European relationships, and was at times fanned by the perpetuation on our shores of Old World rivalries and tensions. However, these animosities rarely had more than a brief or intermittent attraction for most immigrants. American social and economic realities were too novel and too inviting and the immigrant populations were too varied and scattered for this aspect of language loyalty to maintain firm footing.

There have always been some immigrants who viewed themselves explicitly as the preservers and saviors of their old country languages and heritages. These language loyalists founded political groups, schools, choral and dramatic societies, and literary and scholarly associations. They established publications at an intellectual level substantially higher than that of the mass-immigrant press or of the mass-English press. They organized societies, institutes, and congresses for the very purpose of linguistic and cultural self-maintenance. All in all, their long-term impact on most immigrant groups was probably negligible. The tradition of struggling for linguistic and cultural self-maintenance is an old one on American shores—even if not a particularly successful one.

To question the wisdom or the necessity or the naturalness of the de-ethnicization of immigrant populations strikes many as questioning the very legitimacy of America's national and cultural existence. Since "Americans" have no ethnic roots in past millennia, as do many other peoples of the world, the Americanizing process itself, i.e., the de-ethnicization of immigrants, takes on a central role in the formation of the national identity and national self-concept of most Americans. Nevertheless, ethnic groups and ethnicity, language loyalty and language maintenance still exist on the American scene. Even Americans of western European origin continue to recognize their ancestry and to partially define themselves in accord with it.

The future of ethnicity and of language maintenance in America is a function of the kind of America we would like to see. It is a problem for Americans of all backgrounds and on all economic levels. The fact that third and subsequent generations frequently continue to think of themselves in partially ethnic terms and frequently maintain positive attitudes and interests with respect to the heritages of their grandparents is a very significant fact about American life, a far more significant one than the fact that acculturation to general American patterns frequently begins in the very first generation. Theoretically, the American melting pot should have been even more successful than it has been. Perhaps the absence of well-defined or deeply-rooted American cultural patterns—which might have been substituted for immigrant cultures—is behind the ultimate failure of the melting pot as much as it is behind its success.

There has been a constant and growing interplay between public Americanization and private ethnicity throughout our brief national existence. The upshot of this process may be that ethnicity is one of the strongest unrecognized facets of American life—in politics, in religion, in consumer behavior, in life-styles, and in self-concepts.

A lack of attention—indeed a repression from awareness—has characterized our reaction to the efforts of minority cultural groups to maintain and develop their particular hertitages as vibrant (rather than as ossified or makeshift) lifeways. Only recently has a change of heart and a change of mind become noticeable. It is an open question whether this change represents an instance of "better late than never" or an instance of "too little and too late."

Francesco Cordasco

The Children of Immigrants in the Schools: Historical Analogues of Educational Deprivation

INTRODUCTION

American concern with immigration is nowhere better illustrated than by the Immigration Commission which the Congress convened on February 20, 1907. This Commission, chaired by Senator William P. Dillingham, published its massive *Reports* in 1911 and afforded a kaleidoscope of immigrant life in American society of such dimension that its deliberations became one of the great social documents of all time. If its conclusions (and the subsequent restrictive quotas derived from its judgments) are controversial, the data it assembled are nonetheless invaluable in piecing together the intricate mosaic of late 19th and 20th century American life and in furnishing a basis from which American national character and history are to be understood. The *Reports* furnished a statistical review of immigration (1819-1910); studied emigration conditions in Europe; compiled a *Dictionary of Races or Peoples*; studied immigrants in industry; studied the urban immigrant; surveyed the occupations of first and second generation immigrants, and the fecundity of immigrant women; studied the children of immigrants in the schools; studied immigrants as charity seekers; surveyed immigration and crime; studied steerage conditions, the importation and harboring of women for immoral purposes, and immigrant banks (all incongruously gathered in one volume); mapped changes in bodily form of the descendents of immigrants; surveyed Federal and state immigration legislation; reviewed the immigration situation in other countries; and collected statements and recommendations submitted by societies and organizations interested in the subject of immigration.[1] An impressive document, it influenced American policy for decades. Any one of its *Reports* supplies both a point of reference and a watershed of influence which can help explain subsequent American history. This is particularly apparent in its *Report on the Children of Immigrants in Schools* (vols. 29-33), which is a vast repository of data on the educational history of the children of the poor and the schools.

---

[1] United States Immigration Commission, *Report of the Immigration Commission*, 41 vols. (Washington: Government Printing Office, 1911), Vol. 42 (*Index of Reports of the Immigration Commission*, s. doc. no. 785, 61st Congress, 3rd Session) was never published.

From *The Journal of Negro Education*, vol. 42 (Winter 1973), pp. 44–53. Reprinted with permission.

THE MIGRATIONS

Since the keeping of records which were begun in 1819, it has been estimated that some 43 million human beings made their way into the United States of America, truly one of the greatest peaceful human migrations in the whole history of mankind. Of these, at least 40 million were of European origin and the remainder of widely scattered origins. The bulk of the migration in the period before 1819 (i.e., 1607-1819) came from Northern and Western Europe, and of this a preponderance came from the British Isles; the remainder was from other parts of Europe, and also included an estimated 300 thousand blacks, mostly brought in as slaves. The period between 1819-1882 is often referred to as the era of the "old migrations" in which some 10 million immigrants arrived, with the majority again originating in Northern and Western Europe. Between 1882-1921 ("the new migration"), the period of the greatest sustained migration, the migrants were largely of southern and eastern European origin (some 20 million) out of an estimated 23.5 million. Since 1921, with the imposition of quotas, immigration was drastically reduced, and an effort was made to maintain the basic population-composition as it existed in 1890 just prior to the great influx of southern and eastern Europeans. Since 1921, and especially after further reductions in 1929, average immigration annually has been about 200,000.[2]

The immigrants of the "new migrations" (1882-1921) differed not only in language and customs from earlier American residents, but arrived during those decades when the American "common school" had largely evolved into its framework of "a genuine part of that [American] life, standing as a principal positive commitment of the American people."[3] The children of the immigrants of this later period presented particular challenges to the American school. With reference to the period between 1880-1920 (particularly, the late 19th and early 20th centuries), this paper will present an overview of (1) the American school in form and function as it presented itself to the immigrant child, and (2) the response of the American school to the immigrant child.[4]

The American School in Form and Function

The immigrant child was the child of his own immigrant subcommunity within the American city in which his parents had settled. In this immigrant subcommunity (or "ghetto" which carries with it a pejorative connotation), the child was securely related to an organized social life which largely duplicated the customs and mores which his parents had transplanted to America. It was the school which introduced

---

[2] A vast literature exists on immigration. See Richard C. Haskett et al., "An Introductory Bibliography for the History of American Immigration," in *A Report on World Population Migrations* (Washington: The George Washington University Press, 1956), pp. 85-295. Particular reference should be made to Jeremiah W. Jenks and W. Jett Lauck, *The Immigration Problem* (New York: Funk and Wagnalls, 1917); and to the United States Immigration Commission, 41 vols. (Washington: Government Printing Office, 1911).

[3] Lawrence A. Cremin, *The American Common School: An Historic Conception* (New York: Bureau of Publications, Teachers College, Columbia University, 1951), p. 219.

[4] The paper limits itself to the experience in New York City, and largely to the period between 1890 and 1915. It is the writer's view that the experiences of the immigrant child in other American cities during this period would be essentially the same, and if different, the differences would be in terms of the size of the immigrant subcommunity, its spatial distribution within the greater urban context.

him to a different world, and it was the school which saw its role essentially as one of enforced assimilation. Cubberley, the educational historian, makes this vividly clear:

> Everywhere these people [immigrants] tend to settle in groups or settlements and to set up their own national manners, customs and observances. Our task is to *break up* their groups and settlements, to assimilate or amalgamate these people as a part of the American race, and to implant in their children, so far as can be done, the Anglo-Saxon conception of righteousness, law, order, and popular government, and to awaken in them reverence for our democratic institutions and for those things which we as people hold to be of abiding worth.[5]

By 1911, 57.5 per cent of the children in the public schools of 37 of the largest American cities were of foreign-born parentage; in the parochial schools of 24 of these 37 cities, the children of foreign-born parents constituted 63.5 per cent of the total registration.[6] "To the immigrant child the public elementary school was the first step away from his past, a means by which he could learn to assume the characteristics necessary for the long climb upward."[7] And by 1911 almost 50 per cent of the students in secondary schools were of foreign born parentage.[8] In American cities the major educational challenge and responsibility was the immigrant child.

The situation in New York City was not atypical. Serious deficiencies existed in the adequacy of available school facilities. In 1890, it was estimated that in New York City some 10,000 children, who were within the legal ages for school attendance, were without actual school accommodations, and this figure was undoubtedly conservative.[9] The passage of the Compulsory Education Act in 1895, stipulating that all children attend school between the ages of eight and sixteen years (with certain exceptions as to employment, etc.) exacerbated the situation in New York City, and because of the lack of accommodations, the Compulsory Education Act was to all intents inoperative.[10] The expansion of secondary education (three new high schools were opened in 1897) imposed the need for vast curriculum changes in the upper grades of the elementary school, with a concomitant awareness of the need for the expansion of manual training schools. When the Consolidation Act (January 1, 1898)

---

[5] Ellwood P. Cubberley, *Changing Conceptions of Education* (Boston: Houghton Mifflin, 1909), p. 16. See also Leonard P. Ayres, *Laggards in Our Schools* (New York: Russell Sage Foundation, 1909); and, as a point of dissent, Jane Addams, "The Public School and the Immigrant Child," *National Education Association Journal*, **46** (1908), pp. 99–102.

[6] United States Immigration Commission, op. cit., *Abstracts of the Immigration Commission Reports. The Children of Immigrants in Schools*, vol. 2, pp. 1–15.

[7] Alan M. Thomas, "American Education and the Immigrant," *Teachers College Record*, **55** (1953–54), pp. 253–267.

[8] See footnote #6, supra.

[9] New York City Department of Education, *Annual Reports of the City Superintendent of Schools to the Board of Education, 1898–1915.* See also New York City Commission on the Congestion of Population, *Report of the Committee, 1911.*

[10] The biennial school census in 1895 showed that there were 166,000 non-attendant children in the city who were entitled to enter school. See New York City Board of Education, *Report of Finance Committee on School Systems*, 1896, pp. 4–5.

created a greater New York bringing together the boroughs, the schools in the Manhattan and Bronx boroughs were divided into primary and grammar departments with separate classes for boys and girls, with the elementary schools consisting of seven grades. In the other boroughs the elementary school was organized into eight grades. The first New York City superintendent of schools, William H. Maxwell, addressed himself to the major problems of the expansion of facilities, the opening of more kindergartens, the uniformity of an eight-year elementary school, and the establishment of manual training schools; and to the problems of urbanization, mounting school enrollments (some 20,000 to 40,000 new students had to be accommodated each year) was added the increasing patterns of heavy immigration.[11]

It was against the background of these problems that the immigrant child presented himself to the New York City public schools. By 1900, approximately eighty per cent of the New York City population was either foreign-born or of foreign-parentage, and by 1910 a significant shift in the birthplace of the majority of the immigrants from the north to the south of Europe had occurred. For the schools, the non-English speaking child presented still another dimension to overwhelming problems.[12] *The Third Biennial School Census* in 1906 showed that 17 percent of the entire public school enrollment was foreign-born (113,740), and although there was some controversy about the accuracy of the figures (particularly, that the figures did not reflect cases of truancy and the number of children working illegally), the enormity of the problems presented to the schools was dramatically underscored.[13] The children of the more recent immigrants constituted the bulk of elementary and intermediate enrollments, while the children of earlier immigrants were generally in higher grades.[14] More symptomatic than any other factor of the general malaise of the schools was the pervasive phenomenon of the overage pupil who was classed under the

---

[11] For the population growth in New York City between 1890–1910, see U. S. Census Bureau, *Thirteenth Census of the United States, 1910, Supplement for New York City*, pp. 569–71; and for growth in school population, see New York City Department of Education, *Annual Reports of the City Superintendent of Schools*, 1899, *et seq.*

[12] See H. H. Wheaton, *Recent Progress in the Education of Immigrants*, U.S. Department of the Interior, Bureau of Education (Washington: Government Printing Office, 1915), in which it is noted that in 1910 there were in New York City 421,951 persons ten years of age or over who could not speak English, and over 245,000 in the same category who were illiterate.

[13] New York City Department of Education, *Annual Report of the City Superintendent of Schools, 1906–1907*. See also John D. Haney, *Registration of City School Children* (New York: Teachers College, Columbia University, 1910).

[14] See generally the United States Immigration Commission, op. cit., *The Children of Immigrants in Schools*, vols. 29–33; for New York City, see vol. 32, pp. 603–765. "On the other hand, there are several races which have an unusually high portion of their children in the schools. These are the Greeks, the North and South Italians, the Poles, the Roumanians, the Spaniards, and the Syrians. This may be due to the recent immigration of these races and the preponderance among their children of those of early ages, as well as to the fact that where the children are themselves born abroad and are ignorant of the English language they are frequently forced to begin their work in the public schools of the United States at a point considerably below that which corresponds to their age." (Ibid., p. 613). In its conclusions, the Immigration Commission noted: "Of the pupils who are children of foreign-born fathers, three races—the Portuguese, Slovak, and South Italian—show less than one percent in the high school." Abstracts of *Reports of the Immigration Commission*, vol. I, p. 43.

rubric "retardation" with all of its negative connotations. The Immigration Commission of 1911 found that the percentage of retardation for the New York City elementary school pupils was 36.4, with the maximum retardation (48.8%) in the fifth grade.[15] The Commission observed:

> .... thus in the third grade the pupils range in age from 5 to 18 years. In similar manner pupils of the age of 14 years are found in every grade from the first of the elementary schools to the last of the high schools. It will, however, be noted that in spite of this divergence the great body of the pupils of a given grade are of certain definite ages, the older and younger pupils being in each case much less numerically represented. It may, therefore, be assumed that there is an appropriate age for each grade. This assumption is the cardinal point in current educational discussion in regard to retardation. If it were assumed that there is a normal age for each grade, then the pupils can be divided into two classes— those who are of normal age or less and those who are above the normal age. The latter, or overage pupils, are designated as 'retarded.'[16]

Although the Immigration Commission concluded that the "races" which had most recently arrived in the United States (and in which a foreign language was used in the home) had a higher percentage of retardation, it cautioned against deriving from these data less mental ability, but rather ascribed the retardation to environmental and external circumstances that would be corrected within a generation.

That the educational system was inadequate to the problems presented is unquestioned. In the main, there was a slow shift from concern with the problems of physical facilities, of congestion, to the more important concern of the needs of immigrant children, with the problems of their maladjustment, "retardation," with the particular needs of ethnic groups, with the preservation of the multi-cultures which the children brought to the schools, and to the articulation of a learning situation which was fashioned out of new curricula and understandings.[17]

---

[15] United States Immigration Commission, op. cit., *The Children of Immigrants in Schools*, vol. 32, p. 609.

[16] Ibid., pp. 608–609. The Commission further noted: "Again certain races may be noted which have a less proportion of retarded children than has the group of native parentage. They are the Danish, the Finnish, the German Hebrew, the Roumanian Hebrew, the Magyar, the Norwegian, the Roumanian, the Russian, and the Swedish. It cannot fail to attract attention that many of these races are those of comparatively recent immigration. On the other hand, there are some races with a conspicuously high degree of retardation among the children. These are the French Canadian, the Greek, the Italian, the Spanish, the Spanish-American, and the Syrian." (Ibid., p. 614). General reference should be made to Leonard P. Ayres, *Laggards in our Schools* (New York: Russell Sage Foundation, 1909) which, in an effort to determine the causes of retardation, conducted studies in twenty-nine cities and which includes a detailed study of 20,000 children in fifteen Manhattan schools. Ayres concluded that slow progress (not late entrance) was the greatest factor in retardation.

[17] See generally Lawrence A. Cremin, *The Transformation of the School* (New York: Knopf, 1961), pp. 66–75; and particularly, Leonard Covello, "A High School and Its Immigrant Community: A Challenge and an Opportunity," *Journal of Educational Sociology,* 9:331–346, February 1936. For contemporary comparisons, see David Alloway and F. Cordasco, *Minorities and the American City: A Sociological Primer for Educators* (New York: David McKay, 1970).

THE RESPONSE OF THE AMERICAN SCHOOL
TO THE IMMIGRANT CHILD

In the effort to respond to the immigrant child, it is important to note at the out-set that no overall programs were developed to aid any particular immigrant group. Although there was little agreement as to what Americanization was, the schools were committed to Americanize (and to Anglicize) their charges. Ellwood P. Cubberley's *Changing Conceptions of Education* (1909), which Lawrence A. Cremin characterizes as "a typical progressive tract of the era,"[18] saw the new immigrants as "illiterate, docile, lacking in self-reliance and initiative, and not possessing the Angle-Teutonic conceptions of law, order, and government. . . ." and the school's role was (in Cub-berley's view) "to assimilate and amalgamate."

What efforts were made to respond to the needs of immigrant children were im-provised, most often directly in answer to specific problems; almost never was any at-tempt made to give the school and its program a community-orientation. The children literally left at the door of the school their language, their cultural identities, and their immigrant subcommunity origins.[19] The child's parents had virtually no role in the school;[20] and the New York City experience was not atypical in its leaving the im-migrant child to the discretion of the individual superintendent, a principal, or a teacher. In New York City no city-wide system or policy was developed to meet the special needs presented by the immigrant child. Instead, largely left to the management of district superintendents, constructs and programs evolved along the broad lines of individual promotion; English instruction for foreigners; the provision of special classes; and, in some instance, of special schools.

---

[18] Cremin, *The Transformation of the School,* op. cit., p. 68. "To Americanize, in this view, was to divest the immigrant of this ethnic character and to inculcate the dominant Anglo-Saxon morality." See also Frank V. Thompson, *Schooling of the Immigrant* (New York: Harper, 1920) for a more eclectic view; and for the more pragmatic efforts of the settlement houses and other non-school agencies, see Robert A. Woods et al., *The Poor in Great Cities; Their Problems and What Is Being Done To Solve Them* (New York: Scribner's, 1895); and Morris I. Berger, *The Settlement, the Immigrant and the Public School,* un-published Ph.D. dissertation, Columbia University, 1956.

[19] See the autobiography of Leonard Covello, *The Heart Is the Teacher* (New York: McGraw-Hill, 1958). It is significant to note that Covello, as an immigrant boy in East Harlem, was more influenced by the work of the evangelist Anna C. Ruddy, who had devoted years to social work in the East Harlem Italian community, than by the public schools. See Anna C. Ruddy [pseudonym, Christian McLeod], *The Heart of the Stranger* (New York: Fleming H. Revell, 1908); see also Selma Berrol, "Immigrants at School: New York City, 1900-1910," *Urban Education,* 4:220-230, October 1969.

[20] See Leonard Covello, *The Social Background of the Italo-American Child: A Study of the Southern Italian Family Mores and Their Effect on the School Situation in Italy and America,* edited and with an in-troduction by F. Cordasco (Leiden, The Netherlands: E. J. Brill, 1967). As late as 1938, Phyllis H. Williams in a study under the aegis of the Institute of Human Relations, Yale University, observed: "Current theories of child training in American schools stress the pupil's role as an individual rather than as a group member. Teachers frequently expect the American-born child of Italian stock to manifest purely American traits, to have sloughed off almost all of the culturally determined personality traits that characterize his parents. When they attribute any variation to ethnic differences, they usually do so in the case of a vice rather than a virtue—in a typically ethnocentric fashion." Phyllis H. Williams, *South Italian Folkways in Europe and America: A Handbook for Social Workers, Visiting Nurses, School Teachers, and Physicians* (New Haven: Yale University Press, 1938; reissued with an introductory note by F. Cordasco, New York: Russell & Russell, 1969), p. 132. The persistence of an ethnocentric rejection of the use of native languages in the instruction of non-English speaking children can be studied in the recent history (1966-67) of the

Julia Richman, district superintendent in New York City School Districts #2 and #3, was particularly responsive to the needs of immigrant children. She experimented with a new system of individual promotion (in essence, graded patterns of instruction geared to individual needs), and her writings show a growing awareness of the need for community liaison and support. [21] As early as 1903, other district superintendents (in Division I, embracing Manhattan south of 14th Street) were experimenting with a syllabus of instruction for teaching English to children who did not know the language. [22] Certain superintendents instituted special classes for immigrant children (extending from one month to a whole year) for basic instruction in English which would bring them to grade level. [23] And the most ambitious of the constructs devised was the large-scale introduction of special classes by Julia Richman throughout the school districts under her governance. These efforts by Julia Richman are worthy of special note.

In 1903, Julia Richman conducted an investigation in her school districts to determine why so many children who applied to leave school were not at the fifth grade level (legally, children could leave school by age 14); and she maintained that the clearest indication of the failure of the schools was in the fact that large numbers of children desiring to leave school for employment at age 14, were not at fifth grade level. Students who were 14 and had completed Grade 5A or its equivalent were eligible for work certification. Miss Richman found that pupils who were not progressing could be classified as follows: (1) foreign-born children longer than one year in the city were unwisely classified and too slowly promoted; (2) children who were turned away from school or kept for years on waiting lists in the days when principals had that privilege; (3) children "run out of school" for misconduct when records were kept less carefully than at present; (4) children excluded because of contagion in the days when medical personnel and nurses were not able to control this situation; (5) children who had been neglected in classes where substitutes were placed in charge of afternoon part-time classes; (6) disorderly children; (7) truants;

enactment of Title VII (Bilingual Education Act) of the Elementary and Secondary Education Act. See F. Cordasco, "The Bilingual Education Act," *Phi Delta Kappan,* 51:75, October 1969; and F. Cordasco, "The Challenge of the Non-English Speaking Child in American Schools," *School & Society,* 96:198–201, March 30, 1968, which is an adaptation of testimony before the Committee on Education and Labour of the U.S. House of Representatives in support of the proposed Title VII (June 29, 1967). See further Mario Fantini and Gerald Weinstein, *The Disadvantaged: Challenge to Education* (New York: Harper, 1968); and a critique-review by F. Cordasco, "Educational Pelagianism: The Schools and the Poor," *Teachers College Record,* 69:705–709, April 1968.

[21] All of Julia Richman's writings are important. See particularly the following: "A Successful Experiment in Promoting Pupils," *Educational Review,* 18 (June 1899), 23–29; "The Incorrigible Child," *Educational Review,* 31 (May 1906), 484–506; "The Social Needs of the Public School," *Forum,* 43 (February 1910), 161–169; "What Can Be Done in the Graded School for the Backward Child," *The Survey,* 13 (November 1904), 129–131.

[22] See Joseph S. Wade, "The Teaching of English to Foreigners in the First Two Years of Elementary School," *Social Work,* 2 (November 1903), 285–92.

[23] Basically, this technique was extensively used in meeting the English language needs of Puerto Rican children following the heavy migrations to American cities after World War II. See F. Cordasco and E. Bucchioni, *Puerto Rican Children in Mainland Schools: A Sourcebook for Teachers* (New York: Scarecrow Press, 1968).

(8) defectives (mental or physical); and (9) children whose individual needs were overlooked when promotions were made. [24]

On the basis of these findings, Julia Richman received permission from the Board of Superintendents to form special classes for these children in which a simplified and individualized course of study was to be used. Only the absolute essentials demanded by the compulsory attendance law were to be taught. [25]

By September 30, 1904, some 18 special classes had been instituted in School Districts 2 and 3; and a significant reversal was made in the earlier practice of placing the immigrant child, whatever his age, in the lowest or next lowest grade. And by the end of the 1904-05 school year, some 250 special classes (principally for non-English speaking children) were in operation. [26] As children acquired a competency in English, they were transferred to appropriate grades. Generally, an overall improvement was noted with continuing difficulties only with those students who were highly transient and for whom the continuity of instruction was interrupted. Yet, even these difficulties were minimized by special efforts and adaptations. [27] Further refinements of the special class concept led to the definition of three categories of placement: Grade C for foreign-born children who did not speak English; Grade D for those pupils who were approaching age 14, could not finish elementary school, and wished to obtain work certificates; and Grade E for those pupils who hoped to graduate but needed special help to enter the 7th grade. [28] There is little doubt that the special classes were an effective force in meeting the needs of the immigrant child; and a not inconsiderable number of native-born children received needed help as well. [29]

Although the special classes gave principals and teachers considerable latitude in dealing with the problems of immigrant children, no effort was made to change the basic course of study in the regular classes to which these children eventually moved. Out of mounting criticism that the New York City school curriculum was inflexible,

---

[24] Julia Richman, "What Can Be Done in the Graded School for the Backward Child," *The Survey*, **13** (November 1904), 129-130.

[25] Ibid., p. 130.

[26] New York City Department of Education, *Annual Report of the City Superintendent of Schools, 1904-1905*.

[27] Ibid., Appendix A, p. 137. Since the special classes were largely for non-English speaking immigrant children, lay observers of the public schools continued to call for restriction of immigration as a solution to school problems. Cf., Adele Marie Shaw, "The True Character of New York Public Schools," *World's Work*, **7** (December 1903), 4204-4221. More sympathetic to public school efforts (and often the catalyst which brought them into being) was The Public Education Association of New York City which had been formed in 1894. See the invaluable study by Sol Cohen, *Progressives and Urban School Reform: The Public Education Association of New York City, 1895-1954* (New York: Teachers College, Columbia University, Bureau of Publications, 1964).

[28] New York City Department of Education, *Annual Report of the City Superintendent of Schools, 1905-1906*.

[29] See the results of an investigation of special classes which was conducted in 1909-1910. New York City Department of Education, *Annual Report of the City Superintendent of Schools, 1911-1912*. See also, U.S. Bureau of Education Bulletin 51, *Education of the Immigrant* (Washington: Government Printing Office, 1913).

and not geared to the wide variety of needs exhibited by the children, came recommendations for industrial education, for vast curricular reforms (largely unmet) and the creation of schools for incorrigible boys[30] (the forerunner of the present day "600" schools). The emphasis on industrial education was a continuing reiteration of the need for manual education; a private manual training school had been established in New York City in 1887, and the city's Baron de Hirsch School (1891) trained boys for the mechanical and building trades.[31] And the emphasis on manual and trade education (no matter how inadequately met) may have been the surest symptom of a school system which found the children of immigrants uneducable along traditional lines.[32]

That the public schools in New York City were unable, or willing, to meet the challenge of immigrant children is readily apparent in the paucity of the concepts and programs which were fashioned; in the few educational reformers (e.g., Julia Richman) who responded constructively to the multitude of challenges; and particularly in the continuing criticism of the schools by a host of lay reformers; and in the variety of non-school agencies which were created to meet the very real problems which the schools ignored. Most of the social reformers directed their criticisms to the schools, and of these Jacob A. Riis, Robert Hunter, and John Spargo are but a few whose writings are valuable chronicles of the deficiencies of the schools; and despite its intricate involvements, The Public Education Association of New York City formulated a conception of the public school as "a legatee institution" whose responsibility (as the PEA saw it) was the entire problem of child life.[33] And central in the community mosaic of the urban Settlement House was provision for all those identities which poor youth sought and were denied in the schools.[34]

The schools reflected the attitudes prevalent at the time of the great immigrations which, in essence, held that the immigrant was a one-generation problem. Assimilation was an educational process, and if immigrant children got a "good"

---

[30] See Isaac Russell, "Is Our Public School behind the Times? James Creelman's Remedy for Existing Evils," *The Craftsman*. 20:141-143, May 1911; Paul Hanus, *School Efficiency: A Constructive Study Applied to New York City* (New York: World Book, 1913); for the "incorrigible" child, see Julia Richman, "The Incorrigible Child," *Educational Review*, 31:484-506, May 1906.

[31] See Lawrence A. Cremin, *The Transformation of the School*, op. cit. pp. 24-57.

[32] S. Cohen has cogently advanced the thesis that the industrial education movement was an attempt to block the social advance of immigrant children. See S. Cohen, "The Industrial Education Movement, 1906-1917," *American Quarterly*, 20:95-110, Spring 1968.

[33] Jacob A. Riis, *The Children of the Poor* (New York: Scribner's, 1892); Robert Hunter, *Poverty* [particularly the chapter entitled, "The Child"] (New York: Macmillan, 1904); John Spargo, *The Bitter Cry of the Children* (New York: Macmillan, 1907). See also F. Cordasco, ed., *Jacob Riis Revisited: Poverty and the Slum in Another Era* (New York: Doubleday, 1968); and F. Cordasco, ed., *The Social History of Poverty: The Urban Experience*, 15 vols. (New York: Garrett Press, 1969-1971) which reprints the works of many of the reformers, e.g., Robert Hunter, John Spargo, Jacob Riis, Charles Loring Brace, Hutchins Hapgood, and Robert A. Woods.

[34] On the Settlement House movement, see M. I. Berger, op cit.; and Robert A. Woods and Albert J. Kennedy, *The Settlement Horizon* (New York: Macmillan, 1922). On the educational and social aspirations of ethnic subcommunities, see Timothy L. Smith, "Immigrant Social Aspirations and American Education, 1880-1930," *American Quarterly*, 21:523-543, Fall 1969.

education, the parents would be assimilated with them. In the process, parents and community were neglected, if not ignored. There is some doubt that the school acted as the main device through which the child was assimilated, and if so, it did its job poorly. Certainly, the schools did not ameliorate the plight of the immigrant parent. If anything they provided little opportunity to the immigrant parent to obtain information as to what the aims and objectives of the schools were, and in this respect the schools and the parent were in continuing conflict. If New York City was typical, the urban schools provided no system-wide policy which dealt with the educational needs of immigrant children; and where programs were fashioned to meet these needs, there was no attempt made to differentiate between immigrant groups (e.g., the experience of Italian and Jewish children in New York City strongly documents this failure); instead children were lumped under the rubrics "native-born" or "foreign-born." If one discounts the multiplicity of disfunctional programs, rampant discrimination, authoritarian prejudice, it is still difficult to attribute the general patterns of failure to immigrant children or their parents. The blame for the failure lies almost wholly within the school and the dominant society which shaped its programs and articulated its cultural ideals.

Leonard Covello, who spent a half century in the New York City schools as a teacher and an administrator, himself an immigrant child in its schools, observed:

> Of no little importance was the fact that the Americanization programs were directed only toward people of foreign stock, without giving any consideration to the necessity of involving *all* Americans, regardless of the time of their arrival in the United States. But, above all, the earlier Americanization policies, by and large, denied or neglected the strength of, and the values in, the foreign culture of immigrant groups. The concept of Americanization was based upon the assumption that foreigners and foreign ideas and ways were a threat to American political, economic, social stability, and security. The infiltration of foreign culture, it was feared, would eventually bring about a deterioration of the American 'way of life.' Programs were designed, therefore, to suppress or eliminate all that was conceived of as 'foreign' and to impose upon the immigrant a cultural uniformity with an American pattern.[35]

---

[35] Leonard Covello, *The Social Background of the Italo-American Child*, op. cit. p. 411.

Francesco Cordasco

The Challenge of the Non-English-Speaking Child in American Schools

In an open-ended American society, education has afforded the essential entry point into the mainstream of American identity. Education has provided social mobility, and it has extended opportunity. In the peopling of the American continent and the creation of a democratic society, the schools have served as a basic vehicle of cohesion; in the transmission of a society's values, the American schools have ministered to children who brought with them myriad cultures and a multiplicity of tongues. More often than not (almost always in the urban immigrant citadels), the American school found its children in poverty and neglect; increasingly, the schools recognized that their success in the absorption of the child lay not only in meeting his cognitive needs, but equally in confronting the reality of the social context in which the child was found. A definite correlation existed between the cognitive achievement of the child vis-à-vis the socio-economic disadvantagement which he suffered.

The cornucopia of Federal legislation of the last few years did not discover poverty as a new or rare phenomenon in American society. What the Congress perceptively recognized was that many of our social institutions (particularly our schools) only partially were successful, and that many of our democratic ideals were mauled severely in the grim pathology of social disaffection, cultural assault, and enforced assimilation. It was not that our schools failed, but rather that their recorded failures were to be measured in the inadequacy of their response to the child who came to them formed in the context of another heritage, or in the articulation of a strange tongue. If there is a common denominator which must be sought in the millions of American children who presented themselves to a society's schools, it is poverty. And its ingredients (within the parameters of this poverty) were cultural differences, language handicaps, social alienation, and disaffection. In this sense, the Negro in-migrant rural poor huddled in the urban ghettos of the 1960's, the Puerto Rican migrant poor who seek economic opportunity on the mainland, and the Mexican-American poor, largely an urban minority, are not newcomers to the American schools, nor do they present American educators with new problems. The American poor, traditionally, are the ingredients out of which our social institutions have fashioned the sinews of greatness.

From *School & Society*, vol. 96 (March 30, 1968), pp. 198–201. Reprinted with permission.

A vast literature on the schools and poor children is being assembled.[1] The children of poverty have been described euphemistically as "culturally deprived," "disadvantaged," "disaffected," "alienated," "socially unready;" yet, what most educational historians have not seen and have not recorded is the continuing historical confrontation of American social institutions and the poor. The American "common" school evolved in a free society to train citizens "to live adequately in a republican society and to exercise effectively the prerogatives of citizenship . . ."[2] and in the process it encountered many difficulties. The greatest of these difficulties lay in its treatment of the "minority child" whose minority status was affirmed by his cultural, ethnic, religious, and linguistic differences, and all related to his presence in a social sector of severe socio-economic disadvantagement.

In its efforts to assimilate all of its charges, the American school assaulted (and, in consequence, very often destroyed) the cultural identity of the child; it forced him to leave his ancestral language at the schoolhouse door; it developed in the child a haunting ambivalence of language, of culture, of ethnicity, and of personal self-affirmation. It held up to its children mirrors in which they saw not themselves, but the stereotype middle-class, white, English-speaking child, who embodied the essences of what the American child was (or ought) to be. For the minority child, the images which the school fashioned were cruel deceptions. In the enforced acculturation, there was bitterness and confusion, but tragically, too, there was the rejection of the wellsprings of identity and, more often than not, the failure of achievement. The ghettoization of the European immigrant, in substance, is exactly analogous to the ghettoization of the Negro, Puerto Rican, and Mexican-American poor. A long time ago, Louis Wirth called attention to the vitality of the ghetto in its maintenance of the lifestyles, languages, and cultures of a minority people assaulted by the main institutions of a dominant society.

The schools, if only because of the sensitivity of their role, measured their successes sparingly; for it increasingly became apparent that, if the schools truly were to be successful, they would have to build on the strengths which the children brought with them—on ancestral pride, on native language, and on the multiplicity of needs and identities which the community of the children afforded.[3]

---

[1] See Yeshiva University, bulletins of the Informational Retrieval Center on the Disadvantaged; also, U.S. Department of Health, Education and Welfare, Office of Education, *The Education of Disadvantaged Children: A Bibliography* . . ., Aug. 15, 1966; and Helen Randolph, *Urban Education Bibliography* (New York: Center for Urban Education, 1967). We are witnessing a proliferation of books (mostly collections of articles) on the schools and the children of the poor, the best of which is the review of current issues and research edited by Harry L. Miller, *Education for the Disadvantaged* (New York: Free Press, 1967).

[2] Lawrence A. Cremin, *The American Common School: An Historic Conception* (New York: Bureau of Publications, Teachers College, Columbia University, 1951), pp. 213–214.

[3] It is instructive to note that the immigrant Catholic minority of the 19th century created its own schools as a direct response to the social disenfranchisement of its children by the dominant society. See J. A. Burns and Bernard Kohlbrenner, *A History of Catholic Education in the United States* (New York: Benziger, 1937). For an in-depth study of the acculturation of a minority's children, ethnicity and the American school, and the context of poverty and its challenge to the schools, see Leonard Covello, *The Social Background of the Italo-American School Child: A Study of the Southern Italian Mores and Their Effect on the School Situation in Italy and America*, edited and with an introduction by F. Cordasco (Leiden, The Netherlands: E. J. Brill, 1967). A graphic picture of the failings of the school in meeting the needs of children of the immigrant poor is in the address of Jane Addams before the National Education Association in 1897 (*Proceedings*, 1897, pp. 104–112).

The imposition of immigration quotas during 1920–24 largely ended the confrontation of the American school and the European immigrant bilingual child. In the course of the past quarter-century, the bilingual child in America, in the main, has been Spanish-speaking, encountered in growing numbers in the classrooms of American schools. In the major cities of the U.S. at the present time, it is the Spanish-speaking child (Mexican-American or Puerto Rican) who is the bilingual child, almost inevitably found in a context of poverty and reflecting a constellation of unmet myriad needs.

Faye L. Bumpass, Texas Technological University, recently testified before a Senate subcommittee on bilingual education. She observed: "In the five state area [Texas, New Mexico, Colorado, Arizona, and California], there exist today at least 1.75 million school children with Spanish surnames, whose linguistic, cultural and psychological handicaps cause them to experience, in general, academic failure in our schools or at best limit them to only mediocre success."[4] The average number of school years completed by the Anglo child in the Southwest is 12.1 years, for the Negro it is nine years, and for the Mexican-American it is 7.1 years. "The problems of the group [Mexican-Americans] include all of the inter-related complexities of low income, unemployment, migration, school retardation, low occupational aspirations, delinquency, discrimination and all of the problems that attend the intrusion of one culture upon another."[5] The Mexican-American child classically demonstrates that an almost inevitable concomitant of poverty is low educational achievement.[6]

The Commonwealth of Puerto Rico neither encourages nor discourages migration. As an American citizen, the Puerto Rican moves between the island and the mainland with complete freedom. If his movement is vulnerable to anything, it fluctuates only with reference to the economy on the mainland. Any economic recession or contraction graphically shows in the migration statistics.[7] How the Puerto Rican child has fared in the mainland schools is best illustrated in the experience in New York City, where Puerto Ricans have the lowest level of formal education of any identifiable ethnic or color group. Only 13% of Puerto Rican men and women 25 years of age and older in 1960 had completed either high school or more advanced study.

---

[4] *The New York Times*, June 18, 1967.

[5] From a development proposal submitted to the U.S. Commissioner of Education by the Department of Rural Education, National Education Association. Reported in *Congressional Record*, Jan. 17, 1967, p. S 357. See generally, Sen. Ralph Yarborough, "Two Proposals for a Better Way of Life for Mexican-Americans of the Southwest," *Congressional Record*, Jan. 17, 1967, pp. S 352–S 361.

[6] The best source on the educational problems of Mexican-American children is Herschel T. Manuel, *Spanish Speaking Children of the Southwest: Their Education and the Public Welfare* (Austin: University of Texas Press, 1965).

[7] The best source on Puerto Rican migration is the Migration Division of the Department of Labor, Commonwealth of Puerto Rico, which maintains a central mainland office in New York City and offices in other U.S. cities. It also maintains an office in Puerto Rico to carry out a program of orientation for persons who intend to migrate to the mainland. See Joseph Monserrat, *Puerto Ricans in New York City* (New York: Department of Labor, Migration Division, Commonwealth of Puerto Rico, 1967). See also *Bibliography on Puerto Ricans in the United States* (New York: Department of Labor, Migration Division, Commonwealth of Puerto Rico, April 1959). In 1964, the New York City Department of Health placed the Puerto Rican population in New York City at 701,500, representing 9.3% of the city's population. A projection of this study by the Migration Division of the Puerto Rico Department of Labor estimates the 1966 Puerto Rican population at 762,000.

Among New York's nonwhite (predominantly Negro) population, 31.2% had completed high school; and the other white population (excluding Puerto Ricans) did even better. Over 40% at least had completed high school.[8] In 1960, more than half (52.9%) of Puerto Ricans in New York City 25 years of age and older had less than an eighth-grade education. In contrast, 29.5% of the nonwhite population had not finished the eighth grade, and only 19.3% of the other whites had so little academic preparation.[9] Clearly, the critical issue for the Puerto Rican community is the education of its children, for the experience in New York City is a microcosm which illustrates all the facets of the mainland experience.

In the confrontation of the problems faced by Mexican-American and by Puerto Rican children, educators have not been without specific proposals. If one allows for those essential differences which relate to the history of both groups and their relationships vis-à-vis the dominant American society, the major problem presented to the American schools has been the legacy of poverty and the context of debilitating deprivation in which the children are found. In this sense, it can not be reiterated too strongly that the Spanish-speaking child is not unlike the child of poverty who presented himself to the American school in other eras. It is not that the school is inadequate to the needs of these children; the tragedy lies in the failure to use the experience gained by the schools, and the lessons learned, in the many decades past.

A persistent theme in all of the literature which deals with the minority child is the *absolute necessity* for the school to build on the cultural strengths which the child brings to the classroom: to cultivate in him ancestral pride; to reinforce (not destroy) the language he natively speaks; to capitalize on the bicultural situation; to plan bilingual instruction in Spanish and English for the Spanish-speaking child in the cultivation of his inherent strengths; to make use of a curriculum to reflect Spanish (and Puerto Rican) as well as American traditions; and to retain as teachers those trained and identified with both cultures. Only through such education can the Spanish-speaking child be given the sense of personal identification so essential to his educational maturation.[10] We only can lament the lost opportunities of other eras;[11] there is no excuse for failure at this historical and critical juncture in our society.

---

[8] The statistical indices of Puerto Rican poverty (and the related needs) are assembled best in *The Puerto Rican Community Development Project* (New York: Puerto Rican Forum, 1964), pp. 26–75. See also Monserrat, op cit.

[9] *The Puerto Rican Community Development Project*, op. cit., pp. 34–35, 39–41, and tables, pp. 43–44; see also F. Cordasco, "Puerto Rican Pupils and American Education," *School & Society*, Feb. 18, 1967, pp. 116–119; and F. Cordasco, "The Puerto Rican Child in the American School," *Journal of Negro Education*, **36**: 181–186, Spring 1967.

[10] See Herschel T. Manuel, op. cit.; also, "Bilingualism and the Bilingual Child: A Symposium," *Modern Language Journal*, **49**:143–239, March–April 1965; Yarborough, op. cit., particularly, pp. S 358–S 361. Eight colleges and universities in Texas are cooperating to develop a model for teaching Mexican-American children. Teachers from selected Texas public school systems attended a 1967 summer institute (NDEA, Title XI) at St. Mary's University, San Antonio, followed by in-service training during the school year, in the use of Spanish and English in first-grade teaching of children of Mexican ancestry. The institute is the first step toward the establishment of a number of demonstration centers featuring bilingual schooling. A New York City-sponsored Puerto Rican conference (April 15–16, 1967) called for bilingual education programs for Puerto Rican children, and the inclusion of Puerto Rican history and culture in the curriculum of the schools (*The New York Times*, April 17, 1967).

[11] See Covello, *The Social Background of the Italo-American School Child*, loc. cit. Looking back over a near half-century of service in the New York City public schools, Dr. Covello recently observed: "The

Congress has put forward a number of proposed bills to deal with the critical problem of the non-English-speaking child. In addition to H.R. 9840, introduced by Rep. James H. Scheuer (D.-N.Y.), bills have been introduced by Rep. Edward R. Roybal (D.-Calif.), Rep. Henry B. Gonzalez (D.-Tex.), and by others in the House, and by Sen. Ralph Yarborough (D.-Tex.). These bills seek to amend the Elementary and Secondary Education Act of 1965 to provide assistance to local educational agencies in establishing bilingual education programs.

In essence, the bills confront the basic problems of the non-English-speaking child in our schools. The bills seem to agree in the critical needs, not only in the categoric allocation of funds, but in the provision of programs which would promote closer home-school cooperation and provide high quality educational opportunities for children from non-English-speaking homes. If any basic difference exists in the bills, it remains primarily in the proposed Yarborough bill's limitation of its provisions to Spanish-speaking students, and its recommendation that Spanish be taught as the native language and English as a second language.

Neither of these differences is irresolvable. The limitation of the Yarborough bill to Spanish-speaking children quite obviously is a recognition that it is the Spanish-speaking child in our schools who, in the main, is non-English-speaking; and this is true not only in the Southwest, but in the major cities and many of the rural areas of America. However, nothing is lost by extending our definition to ". . . children from non-English-speaking, low income families" (H.R. 9840). On the matter of which primacy of language for instruction (Spanish or English?), attention must be paid to the needs of the children involved. It really is not a problem of which language is to be used, but rather of which language is most effective use to be made. It long has been an "ethnocentric illusion" in the U.S. that for a child born in this country English is not a foreign language, and virtually all instruction in schools must be through the medium of English. [12] All of the bills provide for planning and development of programs, including pilot projects to test the effectiveness of plans. Against this provision, the provisions of a final bill should allow for that flexibility out of which sound and effective programs will evolve. It really is not the primacy of language in the instructional process, but rather how a child is to be moved into an area of effective educational growth which will dictate practice.

The Scheuer Bill (H.R. 9840) provides a practicable vehicle to confront the critical needs of the non-English-speaking child. It provides for planning and development of programs, including pilot projects to test the effectiveness of plans, and the development and dissemination of special instructional materials; pre-service and in-service training programs for teachers and teacher aides involved in bilingual education programs; programs to upgrade the quality of the entire program of schools where large proportions of the children come from non-English-speaking, low-income families, including construction, remodelling, or renovation of facilities; intensive

---

Italian Department at the DeWitt Clinton High School began with one class in 1920 and by 1928 had a register of 1,000 students with a full four year course, and two 4th year classes. Cooperating with the Italian Teachers Association, parity for the Italian language was established in 1922 after a ten year campaign. *For during that period school authorities felt that having Italian students study the Italian language would segregate them from other students and retard their 'Americanization'—an old and often repeated story—an idea with which we very definitely took issue."* Congressional Record, May 16, 1967 [Italics added].

[12] See A. Bruce Gaarder, "Teaching the Bilingual Child: Research, Development, and Policy," in "Bilingualism and the Bilingual Child: A Symposium," op. cit., pp. 165–175.

early childhood programs; and bilingual and bicultural education programs for elementary and secondary school children to acquaint students from both English-speaking and non-English-speaking homes with the history and culture associated with each language. It also provides a whole range of supportive service for students, with participation by full-time nonpublic school students assured.

For millions of disadvantaged children, a Bilingual Education Act promises fuller participation in a free society.

Joshua A. Fishman

Language Maintenance in a Supra-Ethnic Age: Summary and Conclusions

THE CURRENT STATUS OF NON-ENGLISH LANGUAGE RESOURCES IN THE UNITED STATES

In 1960 the non-English language resources of the United States were undoubtedly smaller than they had been a decade or two previously. Nevertheless, they were still huge, both in absolute terms and relative to their 20th century high-water marks in the 1920's and 1930's.

Approximately 19 million individuals (11 per cent of the entire American population) possessed a non-English mother tongue in 1960. These mother tongues represent a very high proportion of those that have evolved to the point of becoming standard literary languages as well as many that have not yet reached this stage of development. Relative to 1940, the quantitative position of the colonial languages — Spanish, French, and German — has remained superior to that of all but the most recently reinforced immigrant languages. However, even in the case of most of the immigrant languages that did not benefit from post-war immigration and that suffered most from internal attrition and external apathy, some subgroups still retain sufficient cultural-linguistic intactness to maintain functional bilingualism and to provide good prospects of marked gain (in either functional or cultural bilingualism) with well designed and vigorous reinforcement efforts.

The non-English press boasted over 500 periodic publications in 1960 and continued to have a circulation of approximately five and one-half millions, as well as a "pass-along" readership estimated to be equally large. Although non-English dailies and weeklies have regularly lost circulation since 1930, monthlies have experienced circulation gains in recent decades. Non-English broadcasting also seemed to be in a far better state of health in 1960 than was usually expected to be the case — with over 1600 "stations" broadcasting more than 6,000 hours of non-English language programs every week in the continental United States. However, this picture largely reflects the continued strength of Spanish broadcasting, which alone accounts for two-thirds of all non-English broadcasting in the United States. Both the non-English press and non-English broadcasting (with the exception of Spanish broadcasting) are largely dependent upon and oriented toward a first-generation clientele. The latter, in turn, represent slightly less than half the claimants of almost all non-English mother

Joshua A. Fishman, *Language Loyalty in the United States* (1966), pp. 392–411. Reprinted with permission. **43** tongues in the United States. Thus, although immigrant status itself is not predictive of either language maintenance or language loyalty, both of these phenomena are heavily dependent upon immigrant status — with the colonial languages marking the only noteworthy exceptions to this generalization.

In 1960 there were at least 1800 (and probably a good many more) ethnic "cultural" organizations in the United States. Many, including the largest among them, serve first-, second-, and third-generation members. Nearly three-quarters of all ethnic cultural organizations favor maintenance of their non-English ethnic mother tongue. However, the very fact that ethnic organizations have been more successful than either the non-English press or non-English broadcasting in attracting second and third generation interest has also led most of them to exceedingly marginal and passive approaches to ethnicity and to language maintenance. The organizations represent bulwarks of structural more than of behavioral-functional pluralism.

The *most* active language maintenance institution in the majority of ethnic communities in the United States is the ethnic group school. Over 2,000 such schools currently function in the United States, of which more than half offer mother tongue instruction even when there are many "non-ethnics" and "other-ethnics" among their pupils. On the whole, they succeed in reinforcing or developing moderate comprehension, reading, and speaking facility in their pupils. They are far less successful in implanting retentivist language attitudes which might serve to maintain language facility after their students' programs of study have been completed, approximately at the age of fourteen. Although the languages learned by pupils in ethnic group schools are "ethnic mother tongues," rather than true mother tongues, the levels of facility attained usually are sufficient to provide a foundation for cultural bilingualism. This foundation, however, is rarely reinforced after the completion of study in the ethnic group school.

Mother tongue teachers in ethnic group schools rarely view themselves as powerful factors in determining language maintenance outcomes. They feel that their pupils do not accomplish much with respect to the more active domains of language maintenance. They typically report that their pupils become increasingly less interested in mother tongue instruction as they advance through the grades and attribute this (and other instructional difficulties) to parental apathy or opposition to the mother tongue. They tend to view the mother tongues they teach as not being among the most prestigeful in the United States (an honor reserved for French and Spanish almost exclusively). However, the determinants of language prestige (unlike the determinants of instructional difficulties) are attributed to "American" rather than to ethnic factors. When group maintenance is seen as being in conflict with language maintenance, the former is frequently preferred, except in the case of mother tongue teachers associated with very recent immigrant groups, most of whom reject the possibility of any such conflict.

The relationship between ethnicity, language, and religion remains strong, although the latter tends to withdraw from the tripartite association. Religion is organizationally "successful" in the United States, and therefore its less successful companions, ethnicity and language, lean upon it heavily for support. But the more "successful" religion becomes, the more de-ethnicized it becomes, the more amenable to mergers with other de-ethnicized churches, and the more disinterested in language maintenance. Language maintenance in historically ethnic churches is continued on a habitual (rather than an ideological-purposive) basis, on ethnic (rather than on religious) grounds, and in conjunction with adult (rather than youth) activities. The triple melting pot — leading toward de-ethnicized Catholicism, Protestantism, and Judaism — and the mere passage of time represent the two most prevalent religious solutions to the "embarrassment" of language maintenance. Traditional *ritual protection* of non-English vernaculars (such as exists in the Greek Catholic and Eastern Orthodox Churches) functions more as a significant delaying factor than as a crucial outcome factor in this connection.

Ethnic cultural-organizational leaders and rank-and-file ethnics display essentially similar patterns with respect to language maintenance efforts and processes. In both instances, immigrants are more retentive — within the family and outside it — than are second-generation individuals. Older children are more linguistically retentive than younger children, first children more so than last children, children more so than grandchildren, organizationally affiliated children more so than unaffiliated children. Whereas first-generation leaders consist of both cultural and organizational activists, second-generation leaders are almost exclusively organizational activists. Although they favor language maintenance, they do so with essentially non-ethnic rationales and their support for language maintenance is attitudinal rather than overt. Philosophies or rationales of bi-culturism and bi-lingualism are weak or non-existent.

There are two large worlds of non-English languages in the United States. One is the officially recognized and supported world of "foreign language" instruction in non-ethnic high schools and colleges. The other is the largely unrecognized and unsupported world of ethnic language maintenance efforts. These two worlds meet in the persons of foreign language teachers, over half of whom are of an immediate ethnic background appropriate to one of the languages they teach. Teachers of ethnically more infused, less prestigeful languages, (e.g., German and Italian, as contrasted with French and Spanish) — particularly those at the college and university level — are most likely to have been ethnically exposed and to be in favor of language maintenance efforts. However, these same teachers are also under the greatest strain toward professionalization and are, therefore, least inclined to utilize the resources of minority cultural-linguistic groups (native speakers, publications, broadcasts, choral-dramatic presentations) for instructional purposes (Fishman and Hayden 1964).

Detailed integrative case studies of six separate cultural-linguistic groups provide much independent support for the above generalizations. In general, language maintenance and language shift have proceeded along quite similar lines in the three high prestige colonial languages (French, Spanish, German) and the three low prestige immigrant languages (Yiddish, Hungarian, Ukrainian). Although differing widely with respect to period of settlement, numerical size, balance between low-culture and high-culture language retentivism, religious protection of the vernacular, and social mobility of their speakers, the drift has been consistently toward Anglification and has become accelerated in recent years. Differences between the six language groups seem to be great only in connection with the *rate of change* toward Anglification.

Among the Spanish and Ukrainian speakers sizable contingents of young and youthful bilinguals are still available. In the Ukrainian case this is primarily due to recent large immigration. In the Spanish case it is due to the absence of economic mobility. Symbolically elaborated ethnicity, language loyalty, and religious protection of the vernacular are absent in the Spanish case and present in the Ukrainian. All in all, certain pervasive characteristics of American nationalism (mobility on a non-ethnic, ideological, mass-culture base) and of most immigrant heritages (non-ideological ethnicity, cultural and economic "backwardness") seem to have been much more effective in jointly producing essentially similar outcomes than have the various uniquenesses of ethnic heritages or of immigrational-settlement patterns in safeguarding cultural and linguistic differences.

The modal characteristics of language maintenance efforts among southern and eastern European immigrants arriving during the period of mass immigration are roughly summarizable as follows:

a. Language is rarely a consciously identified or valued component of daily, traditional ethnicity. Ethnicity itself is minimally ideologized or organized in terms of conscious nationalistic or symbolic considerations.

b. Rapid immersion in the American metropolis and acceptance of American national values results in the fragmentation of traditional ways. Those fragments of ethnicity that are retained in a disjointed and altered fashion are usually insufficient for the maintenance of functional bilingualism beyond the first generation.

c. Ethnicity and language maintenance become increasingly and overly dependent on that major organizational institution previously available in the "old country" setting and most successfully transplanted to the United States: the Church. However, the Church has increasingly withdrawn from ethnicity and from language maintenance in order to pursue its own organizational goals.

d. Attempts to utilize the formal organizational mechanisms of high culture and of industrialized metropolitan and modern national life on behalf of language and culture maintenance proceed without benefit of a popular ideological base that might either compete with or be joined to American nationalism.

e. As a result, neither traditional intactness nor ideological mobilization is available to the second generation. "Revolts" are common when maximal claims are advanced by the first generation and become uncommon when such claims are no longer pressed.

f. Those of the second generation "outgrow" the fragmented ethnicity of the first but frequently retain an attachment to more marginal expressions of ethnicity via the Church, other organizations, and familial remnants of traditional ethnicity. While these have been insufficient for functional language maintenance, they have often preserved a positive attitude toward the ethnic language and culture. This positiveness becomes more evident as the second generation advances through adulthood.

g. The third generation approaches ethnicity with even greater selectivity, frequently viewing the ethnic mother tongue as a cultural or instrumental desideratum and viewing ethnicity as an area of appreciation or a field of study. De-ethnicized language maintenance elicits interest in the third generation although facility is rare.

Of all the foregoing, what can be considered new or striking in the light of previous studies or common knowledge? Certainly the availability of systematic empirical data — rather than anecdotal impressions — is new for many of the domains under discussion. The vastness of language maintenance efforts, even after generations of attrition, is certainly striking, but so is the fact that these efforts are so largely habitual and unfocused even within the very operation of organizations, schools, churches, and the mass media. The conscious, ideologically based and rationally directed efforts of language loyalists normally reach and influence only a small fraction of even the first generation of speakers of non-English languages. The uniformly changed role of religion with respect to language maintenance — from initially wholehearted support to implacable opposition or unmovable apathy — is also striking and hitherto largely unappreciated. Similarly notable is the fact that opposition to language maintenance in the second and third generations of immigrant stock is now most commonly on a low key and unideologized. The days of bitter language disputes seem to be over, even between the age groups formerly involved in such disputes. The continuation of favorable language maintenance sentiments much beyond the time of functional language maintenance is also striking, particularly in that it goes hand in hand with a continued acceptance of ethnicity and even a search for ethnicity of an appropriately selective and marginal nature. While language maintenance becomes a progressively weaker and smaller component of such ethnicity, organizational (including religious) involvement, cultural interests, and modified-disjointed festive acts become relatively more prominent and are maintained much longer. Thus it is that the most striking fact of all comes into focus — that a vast amount of marginal ethnicity can exist side by side with the gradual disappearance of language maintenance, with the two phenomena inter-acting and contributing to each other.

In summary, language maintenance in the United States is currently strongest among those immigrants who have maintained greatest psychological, social, and cultural distance from the institutions, processes, and values of American core society. Ideological protection of non-English mother tongues without concomitant withdrawal from interaction with American society (i.e., the pattern adopted by urban religionists and by secular-cultural nationalists in the United States) has been a somewhat less effective bulwark of language maintenance than has ethnic-religious separatism based upon intact rural "little traditions." Where neither ideological nor ethno-religious protection has obtained, language shift has proceeded in proportion to mobility within the larger sphere of American society, as reflected by indices of education, occupation, or income. Either type of protection has been exceedingly rare. As a result, between-group differences in language maintenance have come to reflect immigrational recency, settlement concentration, numerical size, and social mobility much more than differences in post-immigrational maintenance efforts. Within-group differences in language maintenance have also come to depend primarily on the same set of factors, together with rurality, and to a smaller but nevertheless noticeable degree upon conscious maintenance efforts.

Our current information concerning behaviors directed toward ethnic mother tongues on the part of their erstwhile and sometime speakers must be viewed in the perspective of the transitions that these tongues have most commonly experienced in the United States. From their original status as vernaculars of entire religio-ethnic communities they are now the vernaculars only of very recent or otherwise atypical sub-populations. Instead of their earlier use in all the domains of life related to the particular socio-cultural patterns of their speakers, they are now predominantly employed in fewer and particularly in symbolic or restricted domains. Nevertheless, concomitant with accelerated de-ethnization and social mobility, and concomitant with their relegation to fewer and narrower domains, non-English mother tongues have frequently experienced increases in general esteem during the past 15–20 years. They are more frequently viewed positively and nostalgically by older first- and second-generation individuals who had characterized them as ugly, corrupted, and grammarless in pre-World War II days. The third generations view them (almost always via translations) with less emotion but with even greater respect. Thus, instead of a "third generation return" (Hansen 1940) there has been an "attitudinal halo-ization" within large segments of all generations, albeit unaccompanied by increased use. Such a negative relationship between use rates and attitudinal positiveness over time was not foreseen by most earlier studies of language maintenance or language shift in immigrant contact settings. In the United States this development is an aspect of the continued and growing affective functioning of increasingly marginal ethnicity. In the absence of basic economic, geographic, cultural, or psychological separation between most ethnics and American core society, ethnic mother tongues survive longest at two extremes: the highly formal (the ritual-symbolic) and the highly intimate (the expressive-emotive). At these extremes they remain available to successive generations as reminders of ethnicity, and when needed, as reaffirmers of ethnicity.

At the level of overt behavioral implementation of maintenance or shift, most language reinforcement efforts — though much weakened by ideological and numerical attrition — continue along the traditional lines of information programs, religio-ethnic schools, periodic publications, broadcasts, cultural activities, etc. However, even in connection with language reinforcement efforts the transition to more marginal ethnicity and to more restricted language maintenance is evident. Thus, taking the field of ethnic periodic publications as an example, we note concomitant and continued shifts from more frequent to less frequent publications as well as shifts from all-mother-tongue, to mixed, to all-English publications. The process of de-ethnization has also brought with it a few novel avenues of reinforcement. As even the more "exotic" ethnic mother tongues (i.e., mother tongues not usually considered among the major carriers of European civilization and, therefore, most frequently associated with foreign ethnicity in the minds of average Americans) have ceased to be primarily associated with immigrant disadvantages or with full-blown religio-ethnic distinctiveness, these have been increasingly introduced as languages of study and research at the university, college, and public high school levels. Although bilingual public schools such as those that existed before the First World War have hardly ever been reintroduced, and although the bilingual college (or monolingual non-English college) which passed from the American scene at about the same time has also hardly ever been reintroduced, both are increasingly viewed as "experimental" possibilities on the part of non-ethnic (rather than ethnic) authorities. Seemingly, massive displacement has greater inhibitory impact on language planning efforts than it does on language reinforcement efforts. The latter are essentially conservative and seem to require less in the way of highly specialized leadership. The former are essentially modificatory and dependent upon expert linguistic advice in concert with compliance producing or persuasive authority. Thus archaic or rustic orthographic, lexical, and structural features continue to characterize most non-English mother tongues spoken in the United States and interference proceeds apace, both because planning and enforcing authorities are lacking and because the old find it more difficult to adopt conscious and systematic innovations.

Vocal advocates of language shift have practically disappeared, although institutional support for shift still exists along quiet but pervasive lines. Religious bodies have been particularly persistent in de-ethnicizing parishes and Anglifying church activities as they have gained in institutional autonomy and centralization. The Roman Catholic Church has been most active along these lines whereas Churches in which non-English languages are ritually protected (e.g., the Byzantine Rite Catholic and Eastern Orthodox Churches) have, by comparison, remained relatively conservative. In general, religion has more quickly and more successfully disassociated itself from ethnicity and arrived at independent legitimization in the United States than has the use of non-English mother tongues.

As for the cognitive aspects of language response, the marginalization of ethnicity has resulted in greater cognitive dissociation between ethnic identification and language maintenance. Far from being viewed as components of groupness (whether in the sense of resultant or contributing factors), non-English mother tongues are increasingly viewed in terms of non-ethnic cultural or non-ethnic practical considerations. At the same time, knowledge of language history, literature, and synchronic variants has remained rare.

The foregoing must not, however, be hastily accepted as constituting paradigms for the progress of language maintenance or language shift in all possible immigrant-based contact settings. It may be applicable only to those settings characterized by sharply unequal power configurations, by incorporation as the type of control, by marked plurality and recent immigration as the plurality pattern, by intermediate stratification and substantial mobility within the social structure, and by widespread mutual legitimization of acculturation and de-ethnization as accompaniments of urbanization, industrialization, mass culture, and ever-widening social participation (Schermerhorn 1963). In general, we know (or suspect) much more about the dynamics of language maintenance and language shift in the American immigrant contact situation than we do about these processes in settings involving indigenous populations utilizing more equally "official" languages (e.g., Riksmaal-Landsmaal, Spanish-Guaraní. Schwyzertütsch-Romansch, etc.). This imbalance has resulted in a skewing of conclusions and concepts among students of language maintenance and language shift.

If these findings have general significance it is primarily in their revealing that language shift may be accompanied by a heightening of certain attitudinal, cognitive, and overt implementational responses to languages that are being displaced. In general, ethnicity and culture maintenance appear to be much more stable phenomena than language maintenance. On the one hand, most immigrants become bilingual (i.e., English displaces the hitherto exclusive use of their mother tongue in certain kinds of interactions) much before they embark on de-ethnization or seriously contemplate the possibility of bi-culturism. On the other hand, marginal but yet functional ethnicity lingers on (and is transmitted via English) long after the ethnic mother tongue becomes substantially dormant or is completely lost. Curiously enough, the lingering of marginal ethnicity prompts and supports respect, interest, and nostalgia for the ethnic mother tongue, causing language loyalists to entertain renewed hopes for revitalization even though displacement is far advanced. Thus the very resultants of deep-reaching socio-cultural change carry with them seeds of further change and of reversal.

QUESTIONS AND INTERPRETATIONS

The foregoing findings invite comments and interpretations. Why has this state of affairs come into being? How is it to be understood, both in terms of American life and in terms of even wider relevance? Certainly it is not enough to say that too few have cared or that many have cared too little, since that too needs to be explained and since history records numerous instances of decisive impact of the few upon the many — in the domain of language, no less than in others.

In the planning stage of this study, the investigators were impressed with the tremendous spread of "input variance" relevant to the question uppermost in our minds. The socio-cultural worlds of carriers of non-English languages in the United

States reveal many and important differences: old immigrants and new immigrants, prestige languages and non-prestige languages, peasants and intellectuals, rurality and urbanness, religious reinforcement and nationalistic reinforcement, traditional ethnic roots and modern high culture roots, social mobility and its absence. It seemed only logical that the status of language maintenance efforts in the United States would vary significantly from one language to another, and that this variation, considered as a dependent or consequent variable, could be related to the tremendous variation in the cultural-linguistic carriers of language maintenance, considered as an independent or antecedent variable. Although this approach has revealed some moderately important and consistent relationships, these have been fewer than expected, and directionally uniform. Thus, upon concluding our study, we must be more impressed with the paucity of "output variance," particularly in long-range terms, and with the tremendous power of the intervening contextual variable to which all non-English speaking cultural-linguistic groups in the United States have been exposed: American nationalism.

The American Dream and the American Experience

The alchemists of old sought a universal solvent, an elixir, that could transmute all manner of baser metals into a single desired one. American nationalism may be viewed as such a solvent, although whether the cultural ingredients upon which it has acted were in any sense baser than the product that it has produced will always be open to question. Indeed, the solvent has not really been entirely effective as a solvent. Nevertheless, it *has* been a catalyst, and it *has* dissolved the basic ingredients of functional bilingualism: the desire and ability to maintain an intact and different way of life. It is this realization which has prompted us to suggest that the preservation and revitalization of America's non-English language resources (even for the purpose of cultural bilingualism) requires, first and foremost, several planned modifications in the goals and processes of American society.

American nationalism has been described as an extreme form of western European nationalism in that it is particularly non-ethnic and essentially ideological in nature (Kohn 1961[a]). Even the ethnicity of the early English-speaking settlers, who imparted to American nationalism ingredients of content and of direction that it has never lost, was strongly colored by the growing de-ethnization and ideologization of British life in the 17th and 18th centuries. There were, as there are today, Englishmen, Scotsmen, Welshmen, and Irishmen — and several regional varieties of each — but there was also (and, for many, primarily) Great Britain,[1] a supra-ethnic entity which increasingly involved all of the foregoing in supra-ethnic problems and processes (Kohn 1940). The supra-ethnic political struggles and the supra-ethnic religious struggles that had convulsed the British Isles for generations before the colonization of New England not only led to this colonization but also stamped it with a view of ethnicity as an aspect of social structure which was different from that of New France, New Spain, or New Amsterdam. The problems of religious diversity and of political participation were so much greater that the importance of purely ethnic manifestations in society paled by comparison. The ancient links between ethnicity and religion that existed in most other parts of Europe had already been weakened to the point that these were never fully re-established by British settlers in the New

---

[1] The terms "Britain" and "British" were originally derived from regionally delimited ethnic and linguistic entities in northern France and southern England. Their successive semantic metamorphoses, culminating in "Great Britain," are themselves products of centuries of de-ethnization and ideologization.

World. The relationships between man and God, between man and state, and between man and environment were formulated increasingly in non-ethnic terms. Even the term "Englishman" had political and ideological rather than ethnic connotations. Thus, a supra-ethnic outlook was transplanted, usually at a purely subconscious level. Later, as rivalries developed with colonists of non-British origin, with other colonial powers, with the mother country, and with the Old World itself, supra-ethnicity became a conscious value and a rally cry. By then it had already become a fact of life, even though not fully a way of life.

From the early supra-ethnic beginnings of American nationalism, the American Dream contained two recognizable components: those of process and those of promise. The components of process guaranteed personal freedom (and, therefore, political democracy and the separation of Church and State) as well as the determining use of reason (rather than ascribed status) in guiding public affairs. The components of promise held forth vistas of happiness in human affairs, limitless individual and collective advancement, and social inclusiveness in community affairs. In a very basic sense, each of these ingredients is supra-ethnic if not anti-ethnic. America offered initially and officially that which many today, all over the world, take to be the goals of all social evolution: freedom of physical, intellectual, and emotional movement in constantly expanding social, economic, and cultural spheres. American nationalism came to stand for all that was modern, good, reasonable, inclusive, and participationist in human relations. America has made good the promise of its nationalism for many millions and with dramatic rapidity.

The American Dream is crucial to language maintenance outcomes not only because of the importance of *primum mobile*. It is also crucial because, on the one hand, it has failed to answer certain questions of a substantive nature, and, on the other, most of our non-English speaking immigrants lacked any substantial counter-dream. In implying that freedom, equality, capacity, participation, and reason were sufficient guides to human behavior, it did not provide the substantive cultural ingredients of national life that both ethnicity and religion provide. In merely requiring an affirmation of its processes and promises it more quickly disarmed non-English speakers whose ethnicity had been transmuted and elaborated in consciously creative directions. In offering so much and seeming to ask so little in return, it overpowered the masses of immigrants whose primordial ethnicity was still largely intact and, therefore, still largely innocent of ideology. The overpowering nature of American nationalism is also an indication that it can be as uncompromising and as conformity-producing as the nationalisms known elsewhere throughout the world.

It is frequently claimed that Americanism processes and promises *require* cultural pluralism for their maturation and protection. Be this as it may, it is doubtless true that cultural pluralism was never explicitly "covered" by the formulators of the American Dream, nor has it been consciously and fully desired by the millions who subsequently subscribed to the Dream. Indeed, the prime factor leading most immigrants to our shores was the American Dream itself and its implicit contract and not any dream of cultural pluralism (Bruner 1956; Lerner 1958; Mead 1956). Not only was cultural pluralism a highly unlikely dream for most immigrants prior to their immigration, it was a rarely articulated or accepted dream after arrival. In most cases, ethnicity and language maintenance lived in America as they had in Europe: on a primarily traditional and non-ideological plane. Even when they crumbled or changed, they most commonly did so on a non-ideological basis. By and large, their carriers were conscious only of the American Dream, which is supra-ethnic in content. It is a Dream in which the Queen's English is no more than a "vehicle of communication" for the pursuit of perfection in human affairs, constant individual and collective advancement, and social inclusiveness in community processes. It is a vision which has spread round the world and excited envy, admiration, or both in distant places. Like most visions, it implies more than it specifies. The fact that it has emasculated both levels of functional ethnicity (upon one or another of which language maintenance has always relied), without at the same time providing for structural assimilation in more primary relationships (Gordon 1964), cannot clearly be used to its discredit — since it neither promised to maintain the former nor to attain the latter. That primordial ethnicity could not fully maintain itself under the impact of this Dream, and that ethnicity cannot fully and quickly disappear in a new world animated by this Dream alone, are as much due to the nature of ethnicity as to the Dream itself.

Ethnicity and Language Maintenance

Ethnicity designates a constellation of primordial awarenesses, sentiments, and attachments by means of which man has traditionally recognized the discriminanda that relate him to some other men while distinguishing him from others. Blood ties, geographic proximity, common customs and beliefs — these constitute primitive principles of human organization that are still very much in evidence throughout the world. So basic are they in socialization and in subsequent experience that they frequently appear as "givens" in nature. Even when man progresses to more complex and more abstract bases of social grouping (religion, ideology, the nation, the profession, even "mankind"), the earlier principles of interaction remain recognizable in his behavior and from time to time proclaim their dominance. Both levels of human organization seem to be required for meeting different personal and societal needs in the modern world. However, the kind and proportion of behavior actually guided by primordial considerations and the kind and proportion guided by considerations of a larger scale vary from country to country, from group to group, from person to person, and from occasion to occasion. Language may affect human behavior either through its more primitive, primordial or through its more modern, larger-scale involvements.

The folk-urban continuum (Redfield 1947, 1953) has been referred to in several of the foregoing chapters not because it is presumed that villages, cities and states are totally different environments, but because it casts light upon continuity and discontinuity in primordial behaviors when these are introduced into more modern political and social contexts (Geertz 1963). The fact that there are more nuances than clear-cut polarities in the rural-urban continuum (particularly when the continuum is viewed in historical and cross-cultural perspective [Benet 1963]) does not make the transition from predominantly rural to predominantly urban settings any smoother for those whose lot it is to quickly go from one to another. Under these circumstances, even without extirpation and transplantation, ethnicity and its various primordial components change in content, in saliency, and in relevance to daily life (Bruner 1961; Lewis 1952). There is no doubt that the mass of immigrants of the 1880–1920 period (upon whom language maintenance in the United States still largely depends in almost every case except Spanish and, perhaps, Ukrainian) hailed from far more rural, more homogeneous, more traditional, more ethnic contexts than those that they entered in the United States. There is no doubt that their language behavior was usually imbedded in ethnicity rather than in ideology. Finally, there is no doubt that language maintenance required (and usually did not find) a new foundation when its potential carriers came to feel at home in the American environment.

In its encounter with a non-traditional, secular world in which social interaction and social grouping are rationalized by forces emanating from progress and efficiency, justice and equality, nation and world, the ethnicity of underdeveloped and undermobilized populations has responded in two quite different ways. In many instances it has been symbolically elaborated and elevated to a higher order principle with claims for competitive legitimacy in the modern world of ideas and conscious loyalties. In other instances it has merely regrouped or restructured itself, changing in content, saliency, and part-whole articulation, but remaining far closer to the little tradition level from which it stems than to any modern Weltanschauung. While both of these transformations of old world ethnicity were attempted by immigrants to the United States, various circumstances conspired to make the latter approach much more common and much more acceptable than the former.

The relatively few intellectuals and political activists who sought to raise the ethnicity of rank-and-file immigrants to the level of religion, ideology, and nationalism by no means dismally failed. Indeed, given the difficulties they faced they were remarkably successful. They frequently united hitherto separated, particularistic ethnic populations into groups conscious of common nationality. They provided the energy and directing force that led many of the major formal organizations and undertakings of immigrants on American shores. They both pointed out and helped create Great Traditions in literature, history, and ideology which at least temporarily lifted their followers out of complete reliance on primordial ethnicity, provided them with pride in their heritage, and helped counteract feelings of insecurity vis-à-vis the accomplishments of American civilization. However, in the main and in the long run, they were unsuccessful and their fate may best be described as an alienation of the dedicated. They succeeded far better in foisting an identity between ethnicity and nationalism on the general, de-ethnicized American public (which reacted in typical early second-generation horror)[2] than they did in gaining acceptance of this same identity among their own co-ethnics. Their symbolic transmutations of everyday ethnic life probably led as many co-ethnics and their children to even more universalized, less ethnically delimited or rationalized interests in language, literature, and justice than to the kind of cultural-national self-definitions that these elites originally had in mind. In the last analysis they failed to permanently mobilize a sufficiently large proportion of their more primordially oriented co-ethnics, who were orientated in much more mundane directions. As a result, very little of language maintenance in the United States currently remains (or ever has been) under nationalistic ideological auspices.

Most immigrants to the United States, until comparatively recent times, may best be viewed as underdeveloped ethnic populations whose mobilization into modern life occurred under the aegis of the American Dream, the American city, and the American state (Steward 1951). They accepted the ideal norms of the new society round about them with relative and accelerating ease. In contrast to the relative disadvantage and lack of mobility that they had known in their own homelands they perceived and experienced rapid and marked improvements in their new homes

---

[2] Only rarely and comparatively lately have there been glimmers of recognition that behavioral ethnicity is essentially non-ideological and, therefore, that it poses no ideological threat to American nationalism. For this very reason ethnicity has always been far less of a danger to unity and loyalty in the United States (whether to American substantive ideology or to American procedural ideology) than the openly divisive and organizationally active ideologized forces that the United States has always recognized as legitimate: organized self-interest in economic, religious, and political pursuits.

(Shuval 1963). They eagerly accepted those values and norms that were required to maximize the benefits for which they had come. However, it is important for us to realize that their little traditions, though severely dislocated and weakened, showed an amazing capacity to regroup and even to innovate under these circumstances.

Although the ethnicity of immigrants to the United States did not become as ideologized or modernized as ethnic elites had hoped, it did move in that direction in the form of conscious organizational-associational activity. Indeed, as the ethnicity of daily life increasingly weakened, its organized associational transmutations appeared in bold and abnormal relief (Anderson and Anderson 1959/60). The churches, the organizations, the schools grew *pari passu* with the retreat of primordial ethnicity in the home and the neighborhood. The new expressions of ethnicity were well suited for urban, modern existence but they were also entities in themselves and had goals and needs of their own. They carried language maintenance as best they could and for as long as it served their own purposes. If the result has been markedly negative insofar as attaining or retaining functional bilingualism is concerned, it has been somewhat more positive with respect to other aspects of primordial ethnicity. Above all, the new instrumentalities preserve a new kind of ethnicity, simultaneously more conscious and more marginal than the old, but seemingly more capable of endurance in the American environment (or in other modern contexts). It is in this sense that ethnicity in the United States is not merely a vestigial remains but also a new creation on behalf of a kind of group solidarity and consciousness not provided for in the American Dream. In America, as elsewhere in today's world, circumstances bring about a modernization of ethnicity rather than its complete displacement. Whereas the majority of human interactions are governed by involvement, participation, and creativity on a larger scale of human organization, earlier, more primordial levels are still needed and still exist. It is not only non-Western intellectuals who currently vacillate between tradition and modernity (Shils 1961); it is not only non-Western peoples who currently alternate between emulation and solidarity in search of a more adequate great tradition (Orans 1959); most modern Americans and most modern Europeans do so as well. There are limits to the ability of larger-scale and more modern bonds and principles to solve the longings of mankind. The primordial and the modern show a capacity to co-exist side by side, to adjust to each other, and to stimulate each other.

The supra-ethnicity of the American Dream could not have found a better instrument for the enfeeblement of primordial ethnic particularities (including the displacement of ethnic languages) than the frenetic and polyglot American metropolis and the American "ways of life" which developed in it (Benet 1963; Bruner 1961). In these inauspicious surroundings the maintenance of ethnic languages became more conscious than it had ever been before, but without either a great tradition or a little tradition to maintain it. That it drew more strength from the latter than from the former seems quite natural under the circumstances of its carriers. Only in the case of two colonial languages — French and German — was a somewhat de-ethnicized and prestigeful great tradition available to buttress language maintenance among both intellectuals and common folk.[3] In connection with other languages, there was rarely any awareness or conviction that anything outstanding had been achieved nor the sophistication or experience needed to differentiate between assertive transmutations

---

[3] This is generally overlooked in discussions of the maintenance of major colonial languages in the United States. These have benefited not only from priority, numerical resources, concentration of settlement, prestige; and homeland reinforcements, but from the fact that Americans did not continually identify the great traditions of these languages with foreign nationalism.

of ethnicity and more purely creative transmutations on firmer ethnic foundations. The latter were rediscovered — selectively to be sure — by second and third generations. However, this came to pass only after the second generation had revolted against the irrationally all-encompassing claims of atomized ethnicity and after the remnants of primordial ethnicity were too feeble to seriously address similar claims to the third.[4]

Under the impact of American ideology and American mass culture, language maintenance turned for support first to the one and then to the other. The ideology closest to it was the religion with which it had been intimately associated on its home grounds. Indeed, as a result of centuries of co-existence, primordial ethnicity and religion had completely interpenetrated each other. At times each had come to the other's rescue (Jakobson 1945). Each had formed the other; each had changed the other. What better ally, then, for language maintenance in America than religion? Immigrant religions both courted and supported language maintenance, and religion was protected in American nationalism. Indeed, what other real ally was there?

Religion and Language Maintenance

Ethnic romanticists seem to view ethnicity in much the same way as religious mystics view religion: something pure, direct, unaltered, and unanalyzable. On the other hand, folk-immigrants, prior to arrival in the United States, may be said to have behaved as if their ethnicity were their religion. Each daily act, no matter how mundane, was within the pale of sanctity and colored by its hue. Subsequently, after varying exposure to modern American life, many immigrants came to behave as if their religion were their ethnicity. Religion came to be substituted for ethnicity and to preserve those remnants of primordial ethnicity that were amenable to it. Such preservation was rarely sufficient for the purposes of functional language maintenance.

As religiously-committed American historians look back upon the language issues that convulsed their Churches at one time or another, it strikes many of them that the linguistic particularism under which their predecessors labored were particularly misguided. How could anything as universal, as timeless, and as ultimate as religious truth ever have appeared to be inextricably dependent upon a particular vernacular (or even upon a particular sacred tongue)? The fact that religions have rendered various languages holy or have declared them to be particularly appropriate for the expression and preservation of religious attachments is conveniently overlooked when the advancement of religion—which may be distinguished from the advancement of religiosity—dictates that the bonds with particular languages need to be sundered. The Lord giveth and the Lord taketh away, in languages as in all else, and in sacred languages almost as much as in vernaculars.

---

[4] Generational designations are still employed too sweepingly and generational processes described too grossly in most discussions of American immigrant phenomena. Each generation passes through childhood, adolescence, maturity, and old age. It is unlikely that its ethnic attitudes and behaviors or its relationships with its "older generation" remain invariant during its life-span. Furthermore, the second generation whose adolescence occurred during the 1920's and 1930's was probably quite different from the second generation whose adolescence corresponded with the 1950's and 1960's, if only because their American environments, their ethnic communities, and their respective "older generations" were much different at these two points in time. Indeed, whereas native-born children of mixed parentage classically have been grouped together with the second generation in census studies (as well as in others), it may now be more appropriate to group them with the third, in view of the accelerated pace of acculturation. All of these matters remain to be studied.

Not only are the historical bonds between language and religions frequently overlooked in examining the particular bonds that existed during earlier stages of immigration to the United States, but the specific benefits to the Churches accruing from these bonds are generally ignored. Frequently, no effort is made to indicate the light in which the maintenance of particular vernaculars was viewed in former days, namely as a form of ethnic traditionalism firmly associated with religious traditionalism and, therefore, conducive to religious loyalty. Rather than a factor which strengthened immigrant Churches as organizations and institutions at a time when they were particularly weak, language maintenance is now preferably viewed as a temporary device of an established Church seeking to safeguard the faith of childish and unruly immigrants susceptible to the wickedness of the great city and to the blandishments of competing creeds. It is in this vein that a recent study recognizes "the immigrant phase" of the Catholic Church as one in "which the primary challenge was to guard the faith of Catholics and to defend the Church against calumnies" (Deedy 1963):

> Looking back now, one of the curiosities of those years is the absence from the Catholic press of any strong notion of solidarity in faith or in patriotism. Catholic readers were first Irish or German or Slovak, then Catholic. . . . Catholic publications played party to this folly by catering to the nostalgias, culture, and nationalism of the particular immigrant group served. . . . There was frequently cause to wonder whether a given publication was first Catholic or first Irish, German, French, and so on.

Obviously, language maintenance presented a very special problem to the Roman Catholic Church. In contrast to the national Protestant Churches which dealt with immigrants of a single ethnic origin, and unlike the Greek Catholic and Eastern Orthodox Churches that had long ago become decentralized along separate national lines, the Roman Catholic Church in America was simultaneously Irish, Anglified, "Americanist," and centralized. Whereas the other immigrant Churches lacked de-ethnicized, English-speaking American roots, the Roman Catholic Church as a result of over a century of effort had already developed such roots by the time masses of non-English speaking Catholics arrived. Horrified by the "regressive" centrifugal prospects of re-ethnization, the Catholic hierarchy in America may well have become (and remained) the second major organized de-ethnicizing and Anglifying force in the United States, next to the American public school system. What appeared to be at issue was not merely the hard-won beachhead of American respectability (for a Church that had been recurringly exposed to anti-papism and knownothingism), not only the loyalty of younger, English-speaking parishioners, but the very structural unity and authority of the Church itself, as various ethnic groups sought the kinds of parish government, the kinds of parish organizations, the kinds of religious services, the kinds of religiously sanctioned and sanctified ethnic practices that were in keeping with *their* particular Catholic traditions. No wonder, then, that a policy of strenuous resistance was developed in connection with language maintenance and other manifestations of ethnic particularism. Mass immigration was still in high gear when this policy of resistance culminated in Pope Leo XIII's encyclical of January 22, 1899, *Testem Benevolentiae,* "which praised the spirit and the progress of the Church in America, but which deplored the 'contentions which have arisen . . . to the no slight detriment of peace'" (Deedy 1963). The promulgation of this encyclical is correctly taken as ushering in the "post-immigration period" (even though mass immigration continued for another generation) in that ethnic parishes, like the ethnic press, "came tightly within the orbit of church authority." The apostolic letter "had the effect of dropping a blanket of silence" and of producing "a speedy metamorphosis," such that the 20th century was entered in a spirit "subdued and reserved, if not completely docile," a spirit conducive to a "truly American church, indeed" (Deedy 1963). Several of our studies reveal the lengths to which various Catholic and non-Catholic ethnic groups went in their lack of docility on behalf of ethnic and linguistic continuity. Nevertheless, from that day to our own, language maintenance in the United States has not been able to look upon organized religion as a dependable source of support.

Basically, the retreat of American religious bodies from the arena of language maintenance is due to much more pervasive factors than a papal encyclical which influenced only Roman rite Catholics at best. By the same token, recent actions of the Ecumenical Council permitting the use of vernaculars in the mass and in other Roman Catholic religious rituals can hardly be expected to materially strengthen language maintenance. The separation of religion from life as a result of secularization, ritualization, and organizational primacy is what is most fundamentally involved in this retreat. Indeed, the forces leading to the de-ethnization of formerly ethnic religions in the United States are quite similar to those that have affected ethnic organizations, ethnic schools, and "Ethnic ideologies." All continue to retain remnants of ethnicity, and these remnants function as bulwarks of ethnicity, and of language maintenance for the first generation which can fill them out and join them together via memories and sentiments, if not via overt behaviors. However, they cannot function as such for subsequent generations, in whose case they serve rather to smooth the path to further de-ethnization and to successively more selective, and more marginal, and reformed ethnicity.

Mass Culture and Language Maintenance

As ethnicity has become increasingly unable to support language maintenance, and as religion has grown increasingly unwilling to do so, the needs, values, and institutions of American society have been pointed out and appealed to on its behalf. Is it not good to know several languages? Is it not important? Does it not contribute to success in life? Does it not contribute to the national welfare? Should it not be publicly supported? These appeals all involve the utilitarianization of behavior and, as a result, they are, themselves, atraditional and supra-ethnic. That knowledge must be useful is an American bias of long standing. If bilingualism can be proved to be both good and useful, then we shall obviously "do something about it." If language maintenance can be made out to be concretely useful to the country and to the man in the street, it may yet be accorded a place of honor within American mass culture. However, there is a basic antithesis between ethnicity and mass culture.

Mass culture produces (or induces) both conformity and fluidity. On the one hand, it manufactures, popularizes, and distributes products—including cultural products—for a mass market. In this sense it is dependent upon standardization of products and homogenization of tastes and is, therefore, diametrically opposed to both particularism and traditionalism. However, once having replaced the old with the new, it establishes a cycle of replacement, both as a psychological principle and as a factor of the economy. Thus, tastes and behaviors are not merely widely homogenized. They are also rendered more fluid, more responsive to fashionability and obsolescence, and therefore more widely homogeneous even with a constantly changing repertoire or inventory. While social differentiations based on nativity, religion, age, sex, and class do not disappear—indeed, they become the best predictors of life style variables (Wilensky 1964)—behavior becomes more widely uniform and more widely changeable within and across these lines of differentiation, particularly as rich societies become richer and as the impact of abundance becomes more visible. Thus it is that the conformity-producing and the change-producing aspects of American mass culture are related to each other, and are in concerted opposition to the rooted particularism of primordial ethnicity. Mass culture has effectively reduced the hold of either behavioral or structural ethnicity, in the United States and elsewhere, as the two have come into greater contact. This has usually led to the further erosion of ethnically-based language maintenance among those for whom no other firm basis for language maintenance has existed. Incongruities between structure and culture in American life are undeniable. Nevertheless, they may well represent a transitional stage on the road to a more congruent alignment via mass culture and affluence. Both structural lag and growing accommodation are evident today.

The inroads of mass culture on ethnicity become clear to us, first of all, in connection with our consideration of the transmittal of language maintenance within the family. They become additionally apparent in connection with participationism in the American dream and in metropolitan life. The adolescent period appears to be the juncture at which the impact of mass culture on ethnically-based language maintenance is most clearly felt. In traditional society the problem of adolescent transition is significantly attenuated. There is far greater continuity and identity between the values, behaviors, and skills of the family and those of the larger society. Indeed, there is frequently no marked transition from the one to the other. Youth movements arose in modern Europe primarily as a result of the problems of middle-class youth faced by the barriers of social and economic dislocation in entering an increasingly non-familial type of society. In their case the values, behaviors, and skills required by society seemed particularly unclear or non-continuous with those of the family. This has been much less so for either lower-class or upper-class youth. Until comparatively recently there was little mass culture in Europe which could provide a transitional buffer between the experienced ethnic patterns of the family and the uncertain patterns of adult life outside the family. As a result, adolescent youth movements arose and middle-class adolescence was quite properly viewed as a sociological and political phenomenon rather than a psychological one, as it has long appeared to be in the United States. Here, an adolescent culture has developed, relying completely on mass culture as a non-institutional transition between family patterns of values, behaviors, and skills and those of middle-class society or the oncoming family of procreation. The adolescent of ethnic origin was particularly caught up by American mass culture, for in his case the discontinuity between family and society was most marked.

Indeed, the facts of life were such that in the United States ethnic society itself (to the extent that it existed) became decidedly and increasingly discontinuous with the ethnic family. To whatever extent it could, given the impact of metropolitan life, the family most frequently attempted to cling to ethnic traditions in a primordial, holistic manner. However, ethnic society (the ethnic Church, the ethnic organization, the ethnic school) tended increasingly toward organizational structure, toward ritualized ideology and pragmatic ethnicity, i.e., toward discrete, useful, and organizationally-dominated expressions of marginal ethnicity. The family's store of daily, holistic ethnicity actually became largely unnecessary for entry into ethnic society. At the same time, ethnicity traditionally made no provision for age homogeneous groups, whether adolescent or other. Thus the ethnic adolescent came to view his family's values, behaviors, and skills as doubly malfunctional: malfunctional for a role in ethnic society and malfunctional for a role in general society. Faced by conflicting total claims, the usual result was revolt on the one hand and a headlong pursuit of mass culture on the other.[5]

However, as was true with respect to American urbanization and American nationalism, mass culture need not be viewed entirely as a debilitating factor in language maintenance. It also contains shreds of reinforcement. Adolescents grow up and mass culture becomes less exclusively dominant the more they find a place for themselves in adult society. The ethnic ex-adolescent comes to derive certain stabilizing satisfactions from marginal ethnicity, particularly in a society built upon the shifting sands of mass culture. Just as over-acceptance of ethnicity in childhood led to its over-rejection in adolescence, so over-rejection, in turn, is frequently followed by re-evaluation and by ideological and behavioral selectivity. Thus de-ethnization and re-ethnization follow upon each other, perhaps in cycles of decreasing intensity, while the ubiquity of mass culture tends to render both processes meaningful. Of course, the re-ethnization of the adult second generation (which may actually be more responsible for that of the third than has usually been appreciated) is manifestly insufficient for language maintenance on an ethnic base. Indeed, de-ethnicized language maintenance must, of necessity, be far different from that which we have emphasized here. It must derive its impetus from the American Dream and from American mass culture, instead of directly or indirectly from ethnicity. If this were to be accomplished, language maintenance not only would be much changed (and therefore possibly much more attractive to ethnics), but it might contribute to the reformulation of its new-found protectors as well.

REFERENCES

Anderson, R. T., and Anderson, G., "Voluntary Associations and Urbanization: A Diachronic Analysis," *American Journal of Sociology,* **65** (1959/60), 265–273.

Banks, A. S., and Textor, R. B., *A Cross-Polity Survey* (Cambridge, Mass., M.I.T. Press, 1963).

Benet, F., "Sociology Uncertain: The Ideology of the Rural-Urban Continuum," *Comparative Studies in Society and History,* **6** (1963), 1–23.

Brault, G. J., "Some Misconceptions about Teaching American Ethnic Children Their Mother Tongue," *Modern Language Journal,* **48** (1964), 67–71 (in press).

Bruner, E. M., "Primary Group Experience and the Process of Acculturation," *American Anthropologist,* **58** (1956), 605–623.

———, "Urbanization and Ethnic Identity in North Sumatra," *American Anthropologist,* **63** (1961), 508–521.

Deedy, J. G., Jr., "The Catholic Press: The Why and Wherefore," in *The Religious Press in America,* Martin E. Marty et al. (New York, Holt, Rinehart and Winston, 1963).

Fishman, J. A., and Hayden, R. G., "The Impact of Exposure to Ethnic Mother Tongues on Foreign Language Teachers in American High Schools and Colleges," in *Language Loyalty in the United States,* J. A. Fishman et al. (New York, Yeshiva University, 1964), Chapter 13. (Mimeo.) Also *Modern Language Journal,* **48** (1964), 262–274.

Geertz, C., "The Integrative Revolution: Primordial and Civil Politics in the New States," in *Old Societies and New States* (New York, Free Press, 1963), pp. 106–157.

Gordon, M., *Assimilation in American Life* (New York, Oxford University Press, 1964).

---

[5] The less frequent revolt among recent second generation adolescents might, therefore, well be attributable to a three-way lessening of distance between the ethnic family and general society, between the ethnic family and ethnic society, and between ethnic society and general society.

Hansen, M., *The Immigrant in American History* (Cambridge, Mass., Harvard University Press, 1946).

Hughes, E. C., "Race Relations and the Sociological Imagination," *American Sociological Review*, **28** (1963), 879–890.

Jakobson, R., "The Beginnings of National Self-Determination in Europe," *Review of Politics*, **7** (1945), 29–42.

Kohn, H., "Genesis of English Nationalism," *Journal of the History of Ideas*, **1** (1940), 69–94.

———, *American Nationalism* (New York, Collier, 1961) (a).

———, *The Idea of Nationalism: A Study in Its Origin and Background* (New York, Macmillan, 1961) (b).

Lerner, D., *The Passing of Traditional Society* (Glencoe, Ill., Free Press, 1958).

Lewis, O., "Urbanization without Breakdown: A Case Study," *Scientific Monthly*, **75** (1952), 31–41.

Mead, Margaret, *New Lives for Old* (New York, Morrow, 1956).

Orans, M., "A Tribe in Search of a Great Tradition; The Emulation-Solidarity Conflict," *Man in India*, **39** (1959), 108–114.

Redfield, R., "The Folk Society," *American Journal of Sociology*, **42** (1947), 293–308.

———, "The Natural History of the Folk Society," *Social Forces*, **31** (1953), 224–228.

Schermerhorn, R. A., "Toward a General Theory of Minority Groups," paper presented at the 58th Annual Meeting of the American Sociological Association, Los Angeles, August 28, 1963.

Shils, E., *The Intellectual between Tradition and Modernity: The Indian Situation* (= *Comparative Studies in Society and History*, 1961, Supplement I).

Shuval, Judith T., *Immigrants on the Threshold* (New York, Atherton, 1963).

Steward, J. H., "Levels of Socio-Cultural Integration: An Operational Concept," *Southwestern Journal of Anthropology*, **7** (1951), 374–390.

Usesm, J., "Notes on the Sociological Study of Language," *SSRC Items*, **17** (1963), 29–31.

Wilensky, H. L., "Mass Society and Mass Culture," *American Sociological Review*, **29** (1964), 173–197.

Francesco Cordasco

Educational Enlightenment Out of Texas: Towards Bilingualism

It has long been an ethnocentric illusion in the United States that, for a child born in this country, English is not a foreign language and virtually all instruction in the schools must be through the medium of English. Some of our states (New York included) have mandated this ethnocentrism in a plethora of statutes which expressly forbid instruction in any language but English. Of course this is not difficult to understand. Despite the ideals of a democratic society in which the schools were to serve as a basic vehicle of cohesion, the schools instead became the agencies of social disaffection, cultural assault, and enforced assimilation. How could it have been otherwise, since the schools had to minister to children who brought with them myriad cultures and a multiplicity of tongues? More often than not (almost always in the urban immigrant citadels) the American schools found their children in poverty and neglect. If there is a common denominator which must be sought in the millions of American children who presented themselves to a society's schools, it is poverty. And its ingredients (within the parameters of this poverty) were cultural differences, language handicaps, social alienation, and disaffection. In this sense, the Negro huddled in the urban ghettos, the Puerto Rican poor in search of economic opportunity on the mainland, and the Mexican-American poor, largely an urban minority, are not newcomers to the American schools, nor do they present American educators with new problems. The American poor, traditionally, are the ingredients out of which our social institutions have fashioned the sinews of greatness.

In its efforts to "assimilate" all of its charges, the American school assimilated (and in consequence very often destroyed) the cultural identity of the child; it forced him to leave his ancestral language at the schoolhouse door; it developed in the child a haunting ambivalence of language, of culture, of ethnicity, and of self-affirmation. It held up to its children mirrors in which they saw not themselves, but the stereotyped middle-class, white, English-speaking child who embodied the essences of what the American child was (or ought) to be. For the minority child, the images which the school fashioned were cruel deceptions. In the enforced acculturation there were bitterness and confusion; but tragically, too, there was the rejection of the well-springs of identity, and more often than not, the failure of achievement. The ghettoization of the European immigrant is, in substance, exactly analogous to the ghettoization of the Negro, Puerto Rican, and Mexican-American poor. Louis Wirth, a long time ago, called attention to the vitality of the ghetto in its maintenance of the life-styles,

From *Teachers College Record*, vol. 71 (May 1970), pp. 608–612. Reprinted with permission.

languages, and cultures of a minority people assaulted by the main institutions of a dominant society.

When the Congress discovered poverty in the enactment of the Economic Opportunity Act of 1964, and fashioned the cornucopia out of which the schools have plucked endless "goodies," the schools largely fashioned programs born out of this new federal largesse which reflected their continuing pursuit of the stereotyped middle-class, white, English-speaking child in whose image all of our children were to be cast. And so Head Start taught its children middle-class table manners; the Neighborhood Youth Corps took its social adventurers to museums and opera houses whenever they could be found; Upward Bound, too, became preoccupied with the cultural refurbishing of its charges and took for granted miraculous cognitive blossoming; and Title I Programs of the Elementary and Secondary Education Act did a whole host of things which were designed to elevate "culturally deprived" children to levels of middle-class conformism, *de rigueur*.

THE NON-ENGLISH SPEAKING CHILD

Those of us who have been concerned with Puerto Rican children in our major cities have for some time struggled with what was actually a very old problem. If all children presented themselves to the American schools with many differences, how graphic was the immediate difference epitomized in the non-English speaking child. The history of the American school has not been the evangelical triumph which the New England sage and historian Ellwood Cubberley sketched in such bold relief; rather, the non-English speaking child (almost inevitably in a context of poverty) was the easy victim of cultural assault, and his ancestral language was at once a target against which the school mounted relentless resources.

Against this tragic background and quixotic effort, largely unnoticed, has been a "sleeper" amendment to the Elementary and Secondary Education Act which in essence would propose that we wash away the haunting ghosts of ethnocentrism and cultural affectation, and turn to the meaningful cultivation of individual differences which better reflect the pluralistic base out of which the children of an open society truly come.

THE SLEEPER AMENDMENT

The history of this "sleeper" amendment is a good illustration of what Kenneth Clark has characterized as "the dilemmas of power." Where would one have sought the power in the Congress to recognize the particular needs of Puerto Rican children, if previous Congresses had chosen largely to ignore those millions of children who were non-English speaking who had passed through the portals of the school? The tactic here was obviously to relate the Puerto Rican child to the needs of another group long indigenous in our society but equally long disenfranchised, and for whom English was not the native language. In the five state area of the Southwest (Texas, New Mexico, Colorado, Arizona, and California) there are at least 1.75 million school children with Spanish surnames, whose linguistic, cultural and psychological handicaps cause them to experience, in general, academic failure in our schools, or at best limit them to only mediocre success. The Mexican-American child classically demonstrated that an almost inevitable concomitant of poverty was low educational achievement. Thus, it was out of unlikely Texas that an extraordinary amendment to the ESEA was proposed: an unlikely provenance, since one would have expected that the provisions of this liberal and enlightened amendment would have been born in the great egalitarian citadels of the North.

On January 17, 1967 Ralph Yarborough (D.-Texas) introduced in the Senate of the United States S.428, which proposed "To amend the Elementary and Secondary Education Act of 1965 in order to provide assistance to local educational agencies in establishing bilingual American education programs and to provide certain other assistance to promote such programs." At long last the Congress had before it legislation which would legitimatize the cultivation of individual differences in our schools. Understandably, Senator Yarborough was concerned with the problems of his Mexican-American constituents, but his bill explicitly noted that: "For the purpose of this Title, Spanish-speaking elementary and secondary students means elementary and secondary school students born in, or one or both of whose parents were born in, Mexico or Puerto Rico, and, in states for which such information is available, other students with Spanish surnames." The very proposal of the bill was tantamount to the recognition that Mexican-American children had been neglected by American schools. But Senator Yarborough's legislation went far beyond this elemental recognition. It proposed (1) bilingual educational programs; (2) the teaching of Spanish as the native language; (3) the teaching of English as a second language; (4) programs designed to impart to Spanish-speaking students a knowledge of and pride in their ancestral culture and language; (5) efforts to attract and retain as teachers promising individuals of Mexican or Puerto Rican descent; and (6) efforts to establish closer cooperation between the school and the home. What extraordinary proposals! Those millions of children who had been denied what a mature society was now proposing might well have served as a Greek chorus intoning social amens.

As was to be expected, Senator Yarborough's bill (which had as co-sponsors both Mr. Javits and Mr. Kennedy of New York) created a flurry of activity in the House (though largely unnoticed outside the Congress) and a veritable spate of companion House bills were proposed, chief amongst which was H.R. 9840 mounted by James H. Scheuer (D.-New York). Congressman Scheuer would have everything that Senator Yarborough had proposed, but he chose not to accept the Yarborough bill's limitation of its provisions to Spanish-speaking students. For Congressman Scheuer the school would respond in much the fashion that Yarborough proposed, no matter what the student's native language might be, and Congressman Scheuer simply chose to increase five-fold the allocations which Senator Yarborough had proposed ($25,000,000 as against $5,000,000 for fiscal 1967–68), and further to allow participation by full-time nonpublic school students (children in parish schools).

TOWARDS BILINGUALISM

There are of course some objections which have been raised against the legislation. Some linguists have objected to the pegging of the bill to the poverty context, and have been adamant in proposing that the bill be unrestricted in its provisions and allow the cultivation of a vast bilingual resource. But this is truly another problem. What the legislation has really proposed (no matter how awkwardly, and with full cognizance of all the programming intricacies which will have to be worked out) is that the social institution which is the school and which serves the children of an open society must build on the cultural strengths which the child brings to the classroom: to cultivate in this child ancestral pride; to reinforce (not destroy) the language he natively speaks; to cultivate his inherent strengths; and to give this child the sense of personal identification so essential to his social maturation. We can only lament the lost opportunities of other eras. The legislation proposes that there is no excuse for failure at this juncture in our society. Senator Yarborough's "sleeper" legislation will have thrust greatness upon him, and Texas will have become in educational history as illustrious as Massachusetts. In August 1967 his Senate Bill 428 was unanimously reported out of the Senate Sub-Committee on Education, and in the closing sessions of the 90th Congress became law. In the long interim which followed, a reluctant Congress finally authorized $7.5 million for fiscal 1969.

Secretary of Health, Education, and Welfare Robert H. Finch said on February 12, 1969, that he considered prompt, massive upgrading of bilingual education one of the major imperatives confronting HEW. He announced at the same time that he was establishing a new post, Special Assistant to the Commissioner of Education for Bilingual Education, as a first step in meeting this challenge. Proposals requesting some $47 million were received prior to the December 20, 1968, deadline from local agencies in 40 states, the District of Columbia, and Puerto Rico. Following review of the proposals by a panel of outside experts, selected applicants were asked by the Office of Education to submit formal proposals by May 5, 1969, for final evaluation. From a $7.5 million budget for the program for fiscal 1969, direct grants are to be made to those agencies that propose programs and activities which present innovative solutions to bilingual education problems. Projects must focus on schools that have a high concentration of children of limited English-speaking ability and who come from families earning less than $3,000 per year. Emphasis may be on planning and developing research projects; conducting pilot projects to test the effectiveness of plans; developing special instructional materials; and providing training for teachers, teacher aides, and counselors. Bilingual educational activities may be designed to impart to students a knowledge of the history and culture related to their languages; establish closer cooperation between the school and the home; and provide preschool and adult educational programs related to bilingual education.

Seventy-seven public school agencies in 27 states have been invited by the U.S. Office of Education to prepare formal proposals for grants under the authority of the $7.5 million Bilingual Education Program, Title VII of the Elementary and Secondary Education Act, as amended. These education agencies were selected from 312 which submitted preliminary proposals to the U.S. Office of Education by the December 20, 1968 deadline. Approved projects will be operating during the 1969–70 school year.

2

Typology and Definitions

Since we are faced with various combinations of various factors, any single definition of bilingual schooling would be either too wide or too narrow to be of any use in planning and research, for what is true for one combination of factors may be untrue for another. And since the causes and effects of bilingual schooling are to be found outside the school, it is important to take these into consideration. What is needed, therefore, is not another definition of bilingual schooling or bilingual education but a classification of the field to account for all possible types—in other words, typology.

William F. Mackey

Definitions of
Bilingual Education

*Bilingualism for me the fundamental
problem of linguistics . . . .
—Roman Jakobson*

The terms "bilingual," "bilingualism," "bilingual schooling" seem to carry their meaning clearly within them. And yet a discussion involving any one of these words soon reveals the strikingly different concepts that people have of them.

Thinking primarily of the non-specialist reader, the distinguished scholar and authority on bilingualism, Einar Haugen, has prepared the following succinct definitions of "language," "dialect," "correctness," and "bilingualism."

Language. The word "language" is ambiguous and may easily be misunderstood. We exclude at once such meanings as "the language of flowers" or "the language of mathematics," where it refers to any code that is used for communication. As scientific linguists use the word, "language" is a specifically human form of communication in which sounds (or as a substitute for these, letters) are combined into words and sentences in order to convey meanings from one person to another. The capacity to perform this remarkable feat is inborn in every normal child, and within the first four years of his life he will quite inevitably acquire the sounds, the grammar, and the basic vocabulary of whatever language he hears around him. Being human, he will never acquire it in exactly the same form as it is used by those he hears it from, which is the reason that languages gradually change over time. In this scientific sense of language every human being has at least one language, his first language, sometimes called his mother tongue. He may go on to learn a second and a third later, or he may have two first languages, which he learns in his earliest childhood; in either case he is a "bilingual" by our definition, as will appear later. The main point is that no matter what the social status or the educational achievement of his environment, what he learns is a language in the strict scientific sense, just as an orchid and a dandelion and a tumbleweed are all plants, regardless of their social and economic value.

Dialect. It has long been recognized that there are many different languages in the world and that many of them (perhaps all) have branched off from each other by regular changes over long periods of time. Isolation has been the primary factor in this change, since people who communicate regularly tend to stay together in their

From Theodore Andersson and Mildred Boyer, *Bilingual Schooling in the United States*, vol. 1 (1970), pp. 7–13.

language in order to make sure that they are understood. It is also well known that every language is spoken in a variety of dialects and that such dialect differences have been the beginning of all the different languages of the world that have branched off from one another. So English and German are by origin dialects of Germanic that grew into separate languages, just as Spanish and French are dialects of Latin; and, farther back, just as Latin and Germanic are dialects of a long-lost Indo-European language. The differences that separate any two dialects of the same language may consist of differences in sounds, grammar, or vocabulary; as long as these are not great enough to make understanding impossible, we may still speak of them as dialects in the strictly linguistic sense. Each speaker has his own personal dialect, which is sometimes called an "idiolect," but in the main he shares with the fellow members of his community a dialect that is part of the cultural heritage of the community. To those whose first language it is, the dialect carries all the meanings and overtones of home, family, love, and friendship. It is the instrument of their thinking and feeling, their gateway to the world.

Correctness. Dialects differ not only in their linguistic structure but also in the attitudes which people hold towards them. Every dialect, no matter who speaks it, is objectively equally good for the expression of what its speakers have a need to express. Its sounds are equally easy to pronounce and its grammar equally easy to master for those who learn them as part of their first language. Its vocabulary reflects the cultural level of its speakers, and it can be expanded by training and education from the simple basic vocabulary of childhood to that of the most complex scientific and philosophical thought. Only a few dialects have been so expanded and made into standard languages for the use of whole nations, with standards of correctness which are imposed through the school systems. English and Spanish are among such standard languages. But in the general population common dialects of these languages continue to be spoken and serve as the daily medium of living communities. Any attitude that implies that these are "wrong" or "bad" is built on a standard of correctness which overlooks the validity of these dialects within their communities. A dialect that may be called "non-standard" or even "sub-standard" English or Spanish usually has long roots in history and is for those who use it a valid language, through which alone its users can express their full personalities. The importance of the mother tongue in instruction has only recently been recognized by many educators. They have overlooked that the mother tongue may for many children be the very "non-standard" dialect which the educators are trying to eliminate by teaching standard dialect. When the differences are not between one dialect and another, but between wholly distinct languages, the necessity of giving full consideration to this problem becomes even more pressing.

Bilingualism. There have been many attempts to produce an exact definition of bilingualism, but the only agreement among its various users is that it refers to the knowledge and use of two languages by the same persons. Some writers emphasize the *use* of the languages, e.g., Weinreich (1953), who defined bilingualism as "the practice of alternately using two languages" (similarly Mackey 1962, Brooks 1969). Since it is quite possible to be bilingual without using one of the two languages one knows, others have emphasized the *knowledge* or competence of the speakers, e.g., Haugen (1956), who defined a bilingual as "one who knows two languages" (so also Bloomfield, 1933, who spoke of "control of two languages"). Another difference in the use of the term is that some scholars extend it to include the mastery of more than two languages (in recognition of the fact that the phenomena involved are essentially similar), which is more precisely referred to as *multilingualism* or *polyglossy*. By contrast, one who knows only one language is called a *monolingual* or a *unilingual*.

Within this framework, however, the major problem is that bilinguals differ widely both in their knowledge and in their use of the two languages they master. Knowledge may extend from a few scraps of language to the mastery possessed by a highly educated native speaker and writer. The usual definition has been a rather narrow one, summed up in Bloomfield's use of the term "native-like control" (1933); a German writer, Maximilian Braun, demanded "active, completely equal mastery of two or more languages." Such bilinguals are rare, if they exist at all, and most students prefer a wider definition. In trying to set a lower limit, Haugen (1953) suggested that this be the ability of a speaker to "produce complete meaningful utterances in the other language." Diebold (1961) went a step further in including also a passive knowledge, which required the users only to *understand* speakers of another language, not to speak the language themselves.

Bilinguals may thus be classified according to their skill in their two languages along a more or less infinite scale. Broadly considered, there are bilinguals who have one dominant and one secondary language, while there are others who are reasonably balanced. There are bilinguals who switch easily from one language to the other, and some who find it extremely difficult and confusing to do so. It is very common to find bilinguals who have specialized their use of the languages, so that they can speak of some topics in one and of others in the other.

In considering bilingualism as a "problem" we must not forget that for millions of people throughout the world bilingualism is no problem at all. In many countries it is quite simply a way of life for all or some communities and occasions no particular comment; for educated persons in many countries it is a matter of course that one speaks and even writes more than one language. The problem arises only when a population through emigration or conquest becomes a part of a community where another language is spoken and this language is imposed on them through the school system or by other authorities. We may call this "asymmetrical bilingualism," an example of which is the topic of this book.

To Haugen's definitions, we add two other brief statements on the meaning of "dialect" and its relation to "standard."

All languages have dialects. The so-called "standard" is but itself a dialect, and in many language areas there are both regional standard dialects (e.g., London vs. San Francisco vs. Sydney, or Madrid vs. Mexico City vs. Buenos Aires), and non-standard dialects in the same areas, each with its regional hue. Furthermore, language is constantly changing, indeed nowhere faster than among speakers of "standard" dialects; and many of the features of present "non-standard" dialects simply represent survivals of elements which were once in "standard" use, rather than, as is so often erroneously assumed, "corruptions" of the standard. (Rudolph Troike)

It might be easier for non-linguists to understand the adequacy of non-standard dialects if they were thought of in terms of *different dialects for different purposes*. Every educated speaker of standard English uses the following varieties: formal written style for written reports, technical articles, and the like; formal spoken style for public speeches or lectures; informal written style for personal letters; informal colloquial spoken style for conversation with family and colleagues. For the speaker of non-standard English, the normal, adequate dialect for use in the beginning stages of education is his own non-standard dialect. He needs to learn standard colloquial for use with possible employers, etc.; he needs to learn standard colloquial written style for business letters; he may eventually also need to control the more formal spoken and written styles and certainly he will need to understand them. (Sarah Gudschinsky)

As Fishman puts it, individuals who have meaningful roles in a variety of milieus acquire competence in several varieties of language or dialect. It is a proper function of the school, not to destroy the learner's native dialect, but to assist him in acquiring such additional dialects or languages as may be of value to him.

The Description and Measurement of Bilingualism

For two decades or more linguists have become increasingly concerned with the description (definition) and measurement of bilingualism. In 1952 William F. Mackey, one of the leading students of bilingualism, wrote:[1] "The inadequacy of definition . . . . is not the only theoretical drawback to the study of bilinguals. There is also the lack of any adequate sytstem of classification and measurement. The problem of classification includes the following factors: levels of proficiency, similarity and differences between languages, the social function of each language, the effects, through bilingualism, of one language upon another." Writing on the same subject again in 1956, Mackey suggested that: "The solution to the problem of definition is to consider bilingualism (or multilingualism) not as an absolute but as a relative concept. The question should not be simply 'Is a person bilingual?' but rather 'How bilingual is he?' . . . Such a definition would put the subject on a more stable theoretical basis and would open the way to a systematic measurement of the *degree* of bilingualism. It would lead to classifications which would include the following divisions:

1. The number of languages involved . . . .
2. The type of languages used . . . .
3. Influence of one language upon another . . . .
4. Degree of proficiency . . . .
5. Vacillation . . . .
6. Social function"[2] . . . .

The Report on an *International Seminar on Bilingualism in Education* held in Aberystwyth, Wales, August 20–September 2, 1960,—and sponsored by the United Kingdom National Commission for UNESCO—contributed further to the description of bilingualism. The Report proposes the following key elements in the description of individual bilingualism, followed by charts for recording analytical observations under each heading:

I. Number — i.e. the number of languages used by the individual (e.g. language A and language B).

II. Type — i.e. the linguistic relationship between language A and language B.

III. Function — i.e. the conditions of learning and use of the two languages.

IV. Degree — i.e. proficiency in each language.

V. Alternation — i.e. "switching" from one language to another.

VI. Interaction — i.e. the way in which the languages affect each other linguistically, namely by importation and substitution.

---

[1] *Pédagogie-Orientation* (de l'Université Laval) vol. II, no. 6 (1952), p. 137.

[2] "Toward a Redefinition of Bilingualism," *Journal of the Canadian Linguistic Association,* vol. 6 (March 1956), p. 31.

Encouraged by his colleagues at Aberystwyth, William Mackey prepared in 1962, *The Description of Bilingualism.*[3] in which he elaborated his earlier thinking into a general framework around the concepts of *degree, function, alternation,* and *interference.*

In June 1967 the Canadian National Commission for UNESCO sponsored at the University of Moncton, New Brunswick, an International Seminar on the Description and Measurement of Bilingualism. Publication of the report is now being awaited.

It may inferred from the foregoing that the description of bilingualism is far from having found its definitive expression. It touches too many specialized disciplines. In the conclusion of *The Description of Bilingualism* Mackey provides an admirable persepective:

> Bilingualism cannot be described within the science of linguistics; we must go beyond. Linguistics has been interested in bilingualism only insofar as it could be used as an explanation for changes in a language, since language, not the individual, is the proper concern of this science. Psychology has regarded bilingualism as an influence on mental processes. Sociology has treated bilingualism as an element in culture conflict. Pedagogy has been concerned with bilingualism in connection with school organization and media of instruction. For each of these disciplines bilingualism is incidental; it is treated as a special case or as an exception to the norm. Each discipline, pursuing its own particular interests in its own special way, will add from time to time to the growing literature on bilingualism (see bibliographies in Haugen, 1956, Weinreich, 1953, and Jones, 1960). But it seems to add little to our understanding of bilingualism as such, with its complex psychological, linguistic, and social interrelationships.
>
> What is needed, to begin with, is a perspective in which these interrelationships may be considered. [4]

Bilingual Schooling or Bilingual Education

While such efforts at more nearly complete description move forward, what is bilingual schooling? We take as our working definition that of the Draft Guidelines to the Bilingual Education Program, which seems sufficiently broad: "Bilingual education is instruction in *two languages* and the use of those two languages as mediums of instruction for any part of or all of the school curriculum. Study of the history and culture associated with a student's mother tongue is considered an integral part of *bilingual education.*"

Some Misconceptions

Finally, having sampled authoritative definitions and settled on those that seem adequate to the purposes of the Bilingual Education Act, we come to what appears to us to be misconceptions that need to be rectified.

---

[3] *Canadian Journal of Linguistics,* vol. 7, no. 2 (Spring 1962), p. 71.

[4] Ibid., pp. 84–85.

Confusion of ESL (English as a Second Language) and Bilingual Education

One widely held misconception is that ESL is a form of bilingual education. As we shall see, ESL *is* an important component of bilingual education; but unless the home language is used as a medium for teaching a part or the whole of the curriculum, we believe education cannot properly be called bilingual. To call ESL programs bilingual only causes confusion. Thus, for example, in a U.S. Office of Education report of Projects to Advance Creativity in Education (PACE) entitled "Bilingual Education Projects—SR-68-25 Projects Funded in FY 1966, FY 1967, and FY 1968," there are reported descriptions of selected planning and operational programs funded under Title III of the Elementary and Secondary Education Act. The foreword, dated August 12, 1968, defines bilingual education as "the use of two different languages, such as English and German, in the regular classroom educational process." In spite of the title of the document and in spite of the definition of bilingual education given, the list includes projects which are definitely *not* covered by the definition. Thus, "bilingual education" is used as an official label to designate not only ESL projects, but also a project for the transfer of student records by data processing equipment and general cultural awareness programs. Such indiscriminate use of the term renders it meaningless.

What's in a Name?

Spanish-surname persons in the Southwest are frequently called bilinguals though they may have no knowledge of Spanish at all. Misclassification on the basis of name is likely to continue until we recognize that the term "bilingual" is inappropriate unless the person concerned does indeed have some knowledge of two languages. The "nationality" of his surname is an unreliable indicator of which language or languages an American speaks.

In California we were informed that the word "bilingual" has acquired a disparaging connotation ("uneducated"). We keep the term and use it in its technical sense, remembering, as Haugen has said above, that "in many countries (bilingualism) is quite simply a way of life. . . ."

On the subject of definitions there is no easy stopping-place. Specialists in linguistics—especially psycholinguistics and sociolinguistics—in psychology, in sociology, in anthropology, and in education are all busily studying various forms of bilingualism, diglossia, and bilingual education. Each passing year will see the progressive refinement of terms and concepts. For our present purposes we believe that the definitions here given will serve as an adequate basis for the following study.

William F. Mackey

A Typology of
Bilingual Education

There are few countries where one cannot find some instances of bilingual education. In the past decade the demand for bilingual education has been increasing in most parts of the world. In the developing or emerging nations the demand is caused by the rise in the status of one or more of the vernacular languages combined with the need to maintain an international language for purposes of secondary and higher education. In other nations, where the official language has already attained international status, a changing climate of tolerance toward minorities has often made it possible for ethnic groups speaking a language other than that of the national majority to organize with official approval their own schools in their own language.

Some of these changes have been the results of regional necessity; others are the fruits of local accommodations, based on purely political motives. It is important that the pressures of politics be distinguished from local linguistic needs. And linguistic needs must not be confused with linguistic desires. Language minorities have often been the victims of emotional exploitation from within by the few who can use it as a lever to personal political power.

One of the pawns in the politics of local minorities has been the question of bilingual schooling. This is a question which often arouses bitter conflicts which are rarely resolved by the sort of objective analysis and impartial study needed. The situation is aggravated by the lack of knowledge on the advantages and disadvantages of bilingual education and on the conditions under which it is useful or harmful.

What has made it difficult to obtain such knowledge is the lack of some stable references to the many sorts of bilingual education and also because of the lack of standard measures for the numerous variables.

Schools in the United Kingdom where half the subjects are taught in English are called bilingual schools. Schools in Canada in which all subjects are taught in English to French Canadian children are called bilingual schools. Schools in the Soviet Union in which all subjects except Russian are taught in English are bilingual schools, as are schools in which some of the subjects are taught in Georgian and the rest in Russian. Schools in the United States where English is taught as a second language are called bilingual schools, as are parochial schools and even weekend ethnic schools.

Bilingual situations of entirely different patterns have unwittingly been grouped together under "bilingual schools" and used as a basis for research on bilingual education. This is partly because the concept of "bilingual school" has been used

From Theodore Andersson and Mildred Boyer, *Bilingual Schooling in the United States*, vol. 2 (1970), pp. 64–82.

without qualification to cover such a wide range of uses of two languages in education. The term "bilingual school" means many things, even within the same country, and in any discussion is likely to mean different things to different persons. It cannot therefore, in its present denotation, be taken as an object for research.

Since we are faced with various combinations of various factors, any single definition of bilingual schooling would be either too wide or too narrow to be of any use in planning and research, for what is true for one combination of factors may be untrue for another. And since the causes and effects of bilingual schooling are to be found outside the school, it is important to take these into consideration. What is needed, therefore, is not another definition of bilingual schooling or bilingual education but a classification of the field to account for all possible types—in other words, typology.

Since bilingual education contains so many variables, a systematic classification of them in the form of a typology could be of help in designing experiments and in talking about bilingual education; it could contribute to the systematization of bilingual school programs and suggest ways of coordinating research and development in this expanding area of enquiry. As a preliminary to any typology, it is necessary to determine how much it will take into account.

Since the terms "bilingual education" and "bilingual school" are used to cover a wide range of different cases, it will be advantageous to have the widest possible inclusion. Otherwise we would have more use for definitions than for a typology. Instead of trying to change any current usage, we shall simply adopt the most inclusive. This will enable us to classify cases ranging from the unilingual education of bilingual children in unilingual communities to the bilingual education of unilingual children in bilingual communities. It will make it possible to include schools where some or all subjects are in the other language. It is necessary to isolate and classify all types of bilingual education before measuring their components. This is preliminary to any research.

In order to be of use to researchers, such a typology has to be entirely objective and based on criteria that are observable and quantifiable. Such criteria may be found in the pattern of distribution of languages in (1) the behavior of the bilingual at home, (2) the curriculum in the school, (3) the community of the immediate area within the nation, and (4) the status of the languages themselves. In other words, bilingual education is a phenomenon in four dimensions. Let us take a look at the first.

1. THE LEARNER IN THE HOME

If we study the language behavior of the learner at home in relation to the language requirements of his school, we find that, classified according to language usage, there are five types of bilingual learner.

A learner who speaks only one language at home and the same language in the school, even though it may not be the language of the community, is in quite a different position from that of the learner who uses two languages at home and the same two at school.

Without going into the degree of language proficiency, which will be accounted for below, we may divide our five types into two categories: those covering learners from unilingual homes (U) and those from bilingual homes (B). In each category, there are the cases where one home language is used as a school language (+S) and those where no home language is used as a school language (—S); in the bilingual category there are the cases where both home languages are used as school languages (+SS). This gives us our five types of learner:

1. Unilingual home: language is school language (U+S).
2. Unilingual home: language is not school language (U—S).
3. Bilingual home: languages include one school language (B+S).
4. Bilingual home: languages exclude school languages (B—S).
5. Bilingual home: languages include both school languages (B+SS).

Trilingual, quadrilingual, and other multilingual cases are simply numerical extensions of the above.

If we use a small square for the home, a larger one for school, and shading for the languages, we may visualize the types thus:

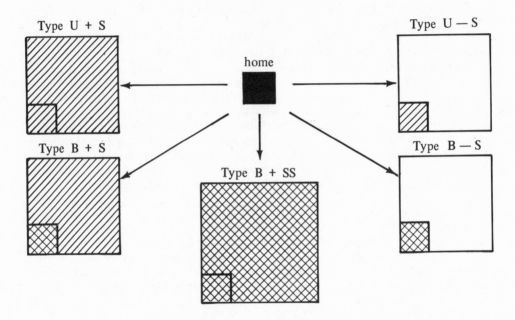

Type U + S

Type U — S

home

Type B + S

Type B — S

Type B + SS

2. THE CURRICULUM IN THE SCHOOL

Belonging to any one of these five types, each learner, with his acquired language habits ranging anywhere from complete unilingualism in one language to complete unilingualism in the other, enters a school where the importance and uses of the languages may not correspond to what they are at home. His place on the scale of bilingual usage—the ratio of his use of his two languages—is likely to be different from that of the school. Only at the extreme ends of the scale, the unilingual school for the corresponding unilingual learner (U+S), are the two points likely to correspond exactly. In all other cases, there is no guarantee that the ratio of bilingualism in the entering language behavior of the learner will correspond to the linguistic assumptions of a bilingual curriculum. For the curriculum patterns of bilingual schools vary as to (1) medium of instruction, (2) development, (3) distribution, (4) direction, and (5) change.

(1) The medium of instruction may be one language, two languages, or more; in other words, the school may have a single medium (S) or a dual medium (D) curriculum. (2) The development pattern may be one of maintenance (M) or two or more languages, or of transfer (T) from one medium of instruction to another. (3) The distribution of the languages may be different (D) or equal and the same (E). (4) The direction may be toward assimilation into a dominant culture, toward acculturation (A), or toward integration into a resurgent one, that is, toward irredentism (I). Or it may be neither one nor the other, but simply the maintenance of the languages at an equal level. In this case, the languages may be equal but different (D), or equal and equivalent (E). (5) Finally, the change from one medium to another may be complete (C) or gradual (G).

2.1 Medium: Single or Dual

Schools may be classified according to their languages used to convey knowledge, in contradistinction to the languages taught as subjects. Knowledge may be conveyed in one language, in two, or more.

2.1.1 Single-Medium Schools (S)

Single-medium schools are bilingual insofar as they serve children whose home language is different from the school language, the area language, or the national language. This may be the only language used for all subjects at all times.

2.1.2 Dual-Medium Schools (D)

In contradistinction to the type of school using a single medium of instruction are those which use two media—both the home and the second language, as the case may be, to convey knowledge. These are the dual-medium schools. Some subjects are taught in one language, some in the other language. In parts of Wales, history, geography, literature, and the fine arts are taught in Welsh; mathematics, social studies, biology, and other sciences are taught in English. Dual-medium schools vary not only in what is taught but also in how much. It is thus that they may be distinguished and classified. They can be compared quantitatively by measuring the amount of time devoted to the use of each language.

So far, we have made only a static or synchronic distinction between bilingual schools—single-medium and dual-medium schools. But since education is progressive by its nature, these distinctions must also be viewed developmentally, that is, on a time scale.

2.2 Development: Transfer or Maintenance

If we examine bilingual schools on the time scale, that is, from the point of view of the distribution of the languages from the first to the last year of the school's programme—or a section of it—we find two patterns: the transfer pattern and the maintenance pattern, both applying to single- and dual-medium schools.

M E D I U M	Development	Transfer	Maintenance
	Single		
	Dual		

2.2.1 Transfer (T)

The transfer pattern has been used to convert from one medium of instruction to another. For example, in some nationality schools in the Soviet Union a child may start all his instruction in his home language, perhaps that of an autonomous Soviet republic, and gradually end up taking all his instruction in the language of the Soviet Union. In schools of this type, the transfer may be gradual or abrupt, regular or irregular, the degree of regularity and gradualness being the variables available to distinguish one school from another.

2.2.2 Maintenance (M)

Contrariwise, the object of the bilingual school may be to maintain both languages at an equal level. This is often the pattern when both are languages of wider communication or are subject to legal provisions in the constitution which oblige schools to put both languages on an equal footing. The maintenance may be done by differentiation or by equalization.

2.3 Direction: Acculturation or Irredentism (A-I)

The direction taken by the curriculum may be toward the language of wider culture, toward acculturation; or toward that of the regional, national, or neo-national culture—the direction of irredentism.

2.4 Distribution: Different or Equal (D-E)

The subjects in the curriculum may be distributed differently, using different subjects for each; or equally, alternating or repeating the instruction from one language to the other.

2.5 Change: Complete or Gradual (C-G)

The change in direction or distribution may be complete and abrupt—using, for instance, one language one year and the other language the next—or gradual—adding more and more instruction in the other language.

2.6 Curriculum Patterns

The interplay of these basic distinctions generates a limited number of possible patterns, as illustrated in the following figure:

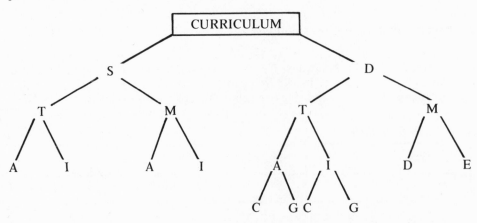

The distinctions between single (S) and dual (D) medium schools, accultural (A) and irredental (I), transfer (T) and maintenance (M), and complete (C) and gradual (G) change generate ten possible types of curriculum patterns. These are: SAT, SAM, SIT, SIM, DAT(C), DAT(G), DIT(C), DIT(G) DDM, and DEM. Let us see what each of these involves.

What is patterned in bilingual schooling is the use of two or more languages, one, all, or neither of which may be native to the learner and have a certain degree of dominance in his home environment. Any of the five types of home-school language relationships described above may enter the curriculum patterns described below. To represent these we shall take the unilingual home, where the language used may or may not be the school language or one of the school languages.

The curriculum, made up of subjects (vertical columns) and time units in which they are taught (horizontal columns) will be symbolized in a grid:

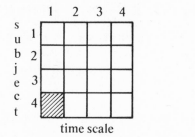

time scale

The home is placed beside the school, covering the lower left corner of the grid. It makes use of a language which may be different from that of the school, of the community, or of the nation. The extent to which the language is used is not a question of type but a matter of measurement—not of "what" is used, but of "how much." (See 4.1).

2.6.1 Type SAT (Single-Medium Accultural Transfer)

SAM

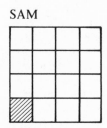

This type may transfer the language of learning from that of the home to that of the school. It may be completely accultural in that it takes no account of the language of the home. This type of single-medium acculturation is common among schools attended by the children of immigrants; for example, the English medium schools of Italian or French immigrants in the United States.

2.6.2 Type SAM (Single-Medium Accultural Maintenance)

SAT

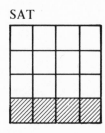

In some cases, as in the bilingual schools of certain parts of Canada, the home language or dominant home language is taught as a subject, without however being used as a medium of instruction. The maintenance of the home language as a subject may be the avowed purpose, as in the English-medium schools for French Canadians in Western Canada.

2.6.3 Type SIT (single-Medium Irredental Transfer)

SIT

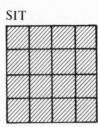

The converse also goes by the name of bilingual schooling. Here the home or dominant home language is used as a medium. Examples of this may be found in the multiple cases of language transfer, along the borderlands of Europe, resulting from the reconquest of territory. Witness, for example, the history of transfer of languages of instruction along the frontiers of the former Austro-Hungarian Empire.

2.6.4 Type SIM (Single-Medium Irredental Maintenance)

SIM

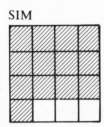

In some schools the dominant or formerly dominant national language is maintained as a school subject, as in the case of English in certain Gaelic schools of the West of Ireland.

The common characteristic of all these single-medium schools is that only one language is used to transmit knowledge—a single language is used as a medium of instruction in all school subjects (although another language may be taught as a school subject, as it is in unilingual schools). For this reason we call these bilingual schools single-medium schools.

2.6.5 Type DAT (dual-Medium Accultural Transfer)

DAT-C

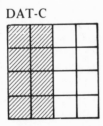

This type which, for obvious reasons of power and prestige is a common type, prepares children to take the rest of their education in a language or a dialect which is not dominant in the home—often a language of wider communication. Many of the schools in the emerging nations were, before they emerged, of this type. English in Africa was sometimes used after the third year. In other parts of Africa it was gradually introduced from the first year.

DAT-G

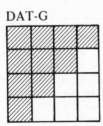

2.6.6 Type DIT (Dual-Medium Irredental Transfer)

DIT-C

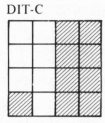

Conversely, in areas long dominated by a foreign language, the medium of instruction may revert to the language of the home, the foreign language being kept as a subject. Early Arabization of schooling in the Sudan illustrates this type.

DIT-G

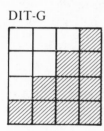

2.6.7 Type DDM (Dual-Medium Differential Maintenance)

DDM

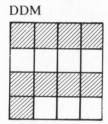

In maintaining two languages for different purposes, the difference may be established by subject matter, according to the likely contribution of each culture. Often the culture-based subjects like art, history, literature, and geography are in the dominant home language. Bilingual schools in certain parts of Wales are of this type.

2.6.8 Type DEM (Dual-Medium Equal Maintenance)

DEM

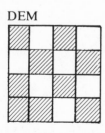

In some schools, as those found in certain parts of Belgium, South Africa, and Canada, it has been necessary—often for political reasons—not to distinguish between languages and to give an equal chance to both languages in all domains. This is done by alternating on the time scale—day, week, month, or year—from one language to the other.

We have seen that, from the point of view of patterning, the curriculum of bilingual schools can be distinguished between single- and dual-medium schools, each following transfer or maintenance patterns—transfer being accultural or irredental, maintenance based on differentiation or equalization.

These patterns may remain stable or evolve, slowly or rapidly, along with changes in pressures and policies. If, for example, one studies the changes in the laws of Louisiana during the past century, one notices several changes in approved patterns of bilingual schooling. The law of 1839 assumes the existence of both French and English single-medium schools. The constitution of 1879 authorizes that all subjects be given in both languages (Article 226). Whereas the 1898 constitution authorizes the teaching of French only as a subject (Article 251). In the constitution of 1921 all allusion to French disappears. Recent cultural accords between Louisiana and Quebec again encourage the use of French in instruction.

It is necessary, however, to distinguish between the patterns of language education used in a community and their avowed purposes. For example, a community may have language maintenance as its purpose, but be saddled with a transfer-type curriculum.

3. THE COMMUNITY IN THE NATION

Any one of these ten types of curriculum patterns (SAT, SAM, SIT, SIM, DAT-C, DAT-G, DIT-C, DIT-G, DDM, DEM) may function in a number of different types of language areas and national states.

It makes a great difference whether one of the languages used in school is that of the surrounding community, or that of the wider community. The home and community contexts in which the language is used must be taken into consideration if the language is to be used in school, since it is on the assumption of usage and consequent knowledge that the teaching is based. There is a difference, for example, in using English as a medium of instruction in one of the special language schools of Kiev and using it as a medium of instruction in the Ukrainian bilingual schools outside Edmonton.

The following are the possibilities of area and national contextual settings in which the above curriculum patterns may appear.

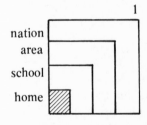

1. The school may be located in a place where the language of both the area and the nation is not that of the home.

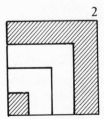

2. It may be in a country where the language of the home but not that of the area is the national tongue.

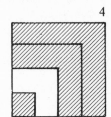

3. Conversely, the language of the area and not of the nation may be that of the home.

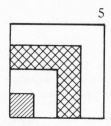

4. Both area and national language may be that of the home.

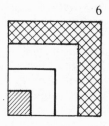

5. The national language may not be that of the home but the area may be bilingual with both the home and national languages being used.

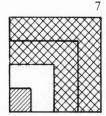

6. Conversely, the country may be bilingual and the area unilingual.

7. Both the area and the country may be bilingual.

8

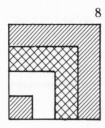

8. The area may be bilingual and the national language may be that of the home.

9

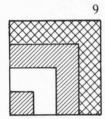

9. Finally, the country may be bilingual and the area language that of the home.

The typology so far elaborated has been based on variations in language patterning in the usage of the nation, the area, and the school; but much depends on which languages are used and what sort.

Certain languages may be worth maintaining regardless of the community. If Spanish and French, for example, are regarded as legitimate specialties for the unilingual, why should they not also be for the bilingual whose other language is one of these? On the other hand, the language may not lead far, even though the probability of community maintenance may be high.

If each of these nine contexts can absorb each of the ten types of curriculum patterns, then there are ninety basically different patterns of bilingual schooling, giving us the typology which appears in the appended figure. Each of these ninety patterns may absorb one or more of the five home-school categories. If we eliminate mutually exclusive combinations, this leaves some 250 integrated types, ranging from (U—S) SAT 1 to (B+SS) DEM 9.

This should permit us to plan for the elaboration of objective distinctions between bilingual education and bilingual schooling. For example, a bilingual classroom with a DAT curriculum pattern may contain learners with different patterns of bilingual education, depending on the category of relationship with the home language. All five types may find themselves in the same classroom, all doing the same thing. Whether it is wise to put them in the same class is another question; but it cannot be answered until something is known about the different home language behavior patterns of the learners. What type of curriculum pattern is suitable for which type of bilingual is a question yet to be resolved.

A number of these curriculum patterns may be in operation within the same school system, in the same area, or in the same country. Which type of curriculum is most appropriate for which type of area is another question.

Before any of these questions can be answered with any degree of certainty some means must be found of quantifying the variable within each type. All that the typology can do at present is to enable us to distinguish one bilingual educational situation from another in order to observe both of them systematically. But within each type there may be quantitative variations. The DAT type, for example, indicates that some school subjects are taught in one language and some in another; it does not tell us which ones or how many. It is only by using the typology to obtain a more detailed profile of each program of bilingual schooling that it will be possible to find out exactly what is going on in any area in the field of bilingual education, as compared with what is going on some place else. This is what has been attempted in the appended questionnaire, designed as it is to pattern descriptions of bilingual schooling into the typology for purposes of study and comparison.

The greatest problem of pattern quantification, however, remains in the fourth area—that of the contact between the languages themselves.

4. THE LANGUAGES IN THE PATTERN

The component common to all types at all levels is language. In fact, the entire typology may be viewed as a series of patterns of distribution of two or more languages in the area of the learner, within the home, the school, the area, and the nation.

This common component is itself a variable. So that each language appears in each pattern at a certain degree of intensity. Any planning or research design has to take this into account in trying to fit persons into the right patterns. For it makes a difference whether or not a child's proficiency in one or more languages is on a par with that of the rest of the class, and whether the level of proficiency is sufficient for the language to be used as a medium of instruction.

In order to understand the nature of the language variable in bilingual education it is important to make a distinction between the function of the languages, their status, and the linguistic and cultural differences between them.

4.1 The Functions of the Languages

The languages involved in bilingual education may have different functions in the home, in the school, and in the country.

4.1.1 Languages in the Home

The learner brings to the school a pattern of language behavior and a configuration of language dominance. It is not only a question of which language is involved, but to what extent.

There is a wide range of possible variation in the competence of the learner in each of his languages Each language may be of a standard acceptable for unilingual education, or only one may be acceptable to a unilingual teacher, or neither may be comparable in degree to the language proficiency of unilingual speakers.

To study what happens to this entering behavior under the influence of bilingual schooling, standardized screening instruments are needed—both wide-mesh and fine-mesh. We need easily used and validated wide-mesh screens for quantitative analysis of bilingual population samples. We need fine-mesh screens for small laboratory-type studies and depth analysis of individual cases. There is need for the application of language proficiency measures suitable for bilingual children.

But the child's proficiency may be limited in some domains and extensive in others, depending on his pattern of language behavior outside the school; he may, for instance, speak about certain things in one language to his father and about others in another language to his mother and her relatives. There is need therefore for simple scales to measure the degree of dominance in each of the child's domains.

If the child comes from a home where two or more languages are used, he may find it difficult to separate them. The extent and degree of language mixture may vary considerably from one bilingual child to the next, and from one domain to another. Tests will be needed to show how well a bilingual child keeps his languages apart.

4.1.2 Languages in the School

The language component also varies within the school—in the curriculum and in inter-pupil communication.

It is first important to determine the sort and amount of both languages used in the classroom. Two identical curriculum patterns may vary in the proportion of time devoted to each language. This is measurable by simple computation. But they may also vary in the domains in which each language is used. In one curriculum the second language may be used for history and geography; in the other it may be used for science and mathematics. In practice, each curriculum pattern would have to be quantified for each language in terms of proportion and domain of use. (See appended questionnaire.)

What is the language of the playground and of the street? In inter-pupil communication, it makes a difference how many of the other learners speak the language or languages of the child, and to what extent. It also makes a difference whether or not the child uses the same language at play as he does in school or at home. Some simple measure of the use of language or languages in the immediate context of the learner's activity would be a help in planning for bilingual education.

4.1.3 Languages in the Community

The extent to which the language or languages of the school may be used in the area in which it is located is an important variable in the language education of the child. Some measurement of this is prerequisite to any planning or research into bilingual education.

The role that each language plays in the nation is also of importance. It makes a difference whether both or only one of the languages is rated as official or national. The legal status of a language may be limited to a juridical subdivision of the nation. Both the proportion of the population using each language and its distribution throughout the nation may have some influence on the curriculum pattern selected. So will the international status of the languages and the distance between them.

4.2 The Status of the Languages

If the languages involved are languages of wider communication, like Spanish and French, the bilingual situation is bound to be different from those involving local languages like Navajo. It is also important to find out the extent to which each language is dynamic or recessive, concentrated or diffuse, both at the international and at the national or regional level.

4.2.1 International Status

In order to determine the international status of a modern language as one factor in planning the curriculum, languages in a bilingual school may be rated according to five indices:

1. Degree of standardization.
2. Demographic Index: Population figures.

3. Economic Index: Population/Gross national product.
4. Distributional Index: Number and spread of areas in which the language is spoken.
5. Cultural Index: Annual production of printed matter/Cumulative production.

4.2.2 National or Regional Status

The dialects of the languages used may differ in the extent to which each deviates from the norm or norms that may have been established for them. If two international languages are used as instructional media, the dialect version of one may differ little from the standard speech comprehensible anywhere the language is used. The other language, however, may be available in the area only in a local sub-standard variety. And this variety may not be the same, either as the one used in the home, the school, or the nation. The Alemanic home dialects of German Switzerland, for example, are far removed from the sort of Standard German taught in Swiss schools.

4.3 The Differences between the Languages

The rapidity with which a learner is likely to understand another language, used to teach him school subjects, depends on the degree of difference or distance between both languages. Because of the close relationship between Portuguese and Spanish, a learner whose mother tongue is Portuguese may take less time to learn to understand instruction given in Spanish than instruction given in more distant languages like English or Chinese.

This same similarity, which facilitates understanding (listening and reading) may be the cause of multiple mistakes in speaking and writing—due to the interference caused by the closeness of both languages. We need measures of the closeness and mutual intelligibility of the languages involved in bilingual instruction and means of predicting the effects of the languages on the comprehension and expression of the bilingual learner.

Regardless of similarities and differences in structure and vocabulary, the two languages may differ considerably in available cultural concepts. For example, Hungarian is genetically as distant from English as is Eskimo; but it is culturally closer, since both English and Hungarian embody many common European cultural concepts, which can be assumed as a basis for bilingual education. Before making use of this variable in research into bilingual education, however, it would be most useful to determine some way of quantifying it.

CONCLUSION

Once we have reduced our language variables to appropriate measures within the various types of bilingual education, it will be easier to analyze and classify specific cases.

It is only after we have taken all the variables into account and applied appropriate measures of them that we can achieve any degree of certainty in our planning in this important and complex field. Toward this end it is hoped that this preliminary typology may be of some help.

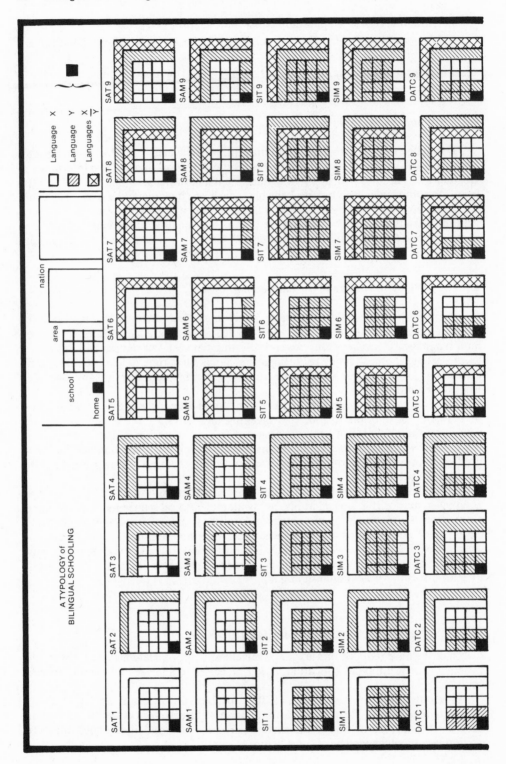

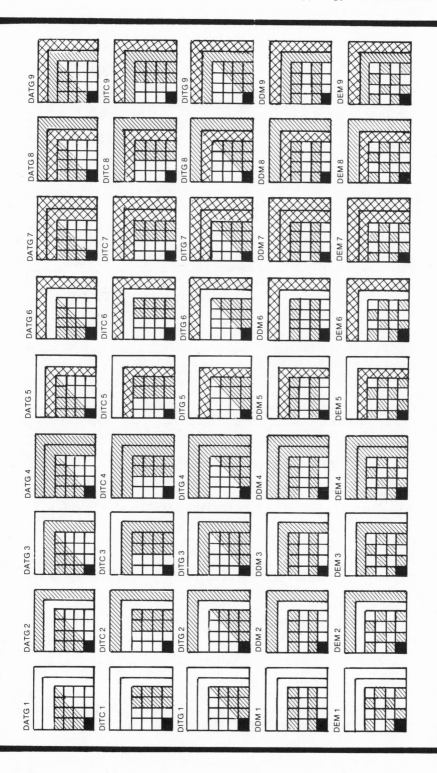

ATTACHMENT B

Name of institution or school system: _____	CURRICULUM
	PATTERNS
Address: _____	IN
Name of person responding to questionnaire:	BILINGUAL
_____	EDUCATION

1. Home language(s) of pupils: _____
2. Language(s) used in teaching: _____
3. Number of months of instruction a year: _____
4. For how many years has program presently described been operating? _____
     Is it experimental ☐   or operational ☐   ?

5. How many schools are included? _____
6. How many learners are involved? _____
7. How many teachers are involved? _____
8. Are there any teachers for special subjects? _____
     Which subjects? _____
9. How long is the subject or class period? (in minutes) _____
     If it varies, please explain. _____
10. Do you select pupils for the bilingual program? _____
     How do you select them? _____
11. Approximately what proportion of learners speak
     a) only English? _____
     b) no English? _____
12. Does the learner do his written work in a language other than English?
     English? _____   Which language? _____
     At what level? _____   What proportion? _____
13. At the end of the program here described, what type of school or program do the students enter?
     _____
14. Outside the class, how often do your pupils use English to communicate among themselves?
     _____

     NEVER   SELDOM   SOMETIMES   OFTEN   ALWAYS
      ☐   ☐   ☐   ☐   ☐

15. What are some of the main problems you have noticed in operating this program? Please feel free to comment at length. _____
     _____

SUBJECTS	2-year-olds	3-year-olds	4-year-olds	5-year-olds	6-year-olds	Grade 1	Grade 2	Grade 3	Grade 4	Grade 5	Grade 6	Grade 7	Grade 8	Grade 9	Grade 10	Grade 11	Grade 12	Other

Footnotes and comments: _____

Most usual language of inter-pupil communication outside class is: _____

ONE sheet per school

Name of school:_____
_____

INSTRUCTIONS

1. List in left-hand column under *subjects* names of subjects taught in the school. For example:

ENGLISH _____
HISTORY _____
GEOGRAPHY _____

2. Starting with the first year described in your program (horizontal list), indicate by grade the language in which the subject is being taught. Use first letter of language in appropriate square: French (F), Spanish (S), English (E), Navajo (N) etc.

ENGLISH	E	E	E	E
HISTORY	S	S	E	E
GEOGRAPHY	S	S	S	S

3. If both languages are systematically used in alternation (e.g. English + Spanish), indicate thus ⊏E/S⊐ and explain system in footnote. Do not include casual use of other language by the teacher.

4. If class teaching is in one language (e.g. Spanish) and pupils' schoolbooks in the other, indicate thus ⊏E/S⊐

Jeffrey W. Kobrick

The Compelling Case
for Bilingual Education

In 1968 a Spanish-speaking community worker named Sister Frances Georgia, observing certain children "visibly roaming the streets" of Boston, conducted a door-to-door survey in a Puerto Rican section of the city. Of the 350 Spanish-speaking school-aged children she found, 65 per cent had never registered in school; many others rarely attended or had dropped out. Armed with these facts, Sister went to the Boston School Department to seek help in locating and providing meaningful programs for Spanish-speaking children who were out of school. Skeptical, Boston school officials told her to produce the "warm bodies"; if she did, they said, "seats" would then be found.

At about the same time, leaders from Boston's poverty communities formed a "Task Force on Children out of School" to investigate the way the school system dealt with poor children generally. Among other things, the task force found that as many as half of Boston's estimated 10,000 Spanish-speaking school children were not in school. Between 1965 and 1969 only four Puerto Rican students graduated from Boston high schools.

Three years later, through the efforts of Sister Frances Georgia, community leader Alex Rodriguez, the Boston task force, and two key legislators, Education Committee Chairman Michael Daly and House Speaker David Bartley, Massachusetts passed the nation's first comprehensive state bilingual education law.

The law declares that classes conducted exclusively in English are "inadequate" for the education of children whose native tongue is another language and that bilingual education programs are necessary "to ensure equal educational opportunity to every child." Massachusetts thus became the first state to *require* school districts to provide bilingual programs for children whose first language is not English. (Other states including New York, California, Illinois, and Texas have laws *permitting* local school districts to provide bilingual programs.) The law calls for the use of both a child's native language and English as mediums of instruction and for the teaching of history and culture associated with a child's native language. It authorizes state expenditures of up to $4-million a year to help districts meet any extra costs of bilingual programs.

The Massachusetts law is a carefully constructed and innovative piece of legislation that hopefully will stimulate legislative efforts elsewhere. Indeed, because the federal Bilingual Education Act has been so underfunded—"Congress has been appropriating drops," notes Senator Walter Mondale, "when showers or even downpours are needed"—there is a critical need for state legislation and funding in areas

From *Saturday Review*, April 29, 1972. Reprinted with permission.

where there are substantial numbers of Puerto Rican, Chicano, Indian, and other non-English-speaking children. The U.S. Office of Education estimates that five million children attending public schools "speak a language other than English in their homes and neighborhoods." And increasing evidence reveals the almost total failure of our monolingual, monocultural school systems to provide for these children's educational needs.

In New York City alone, 250,000 Puerto Rican children attend the public schools. The estimated dropout (or "pushout") rate for these students has been put as high as 85 per cent. Of those who survive to the eighth grade, 60 per cent are three to five years below reading level. Nor is the plight of thousands of Puerto Rican children any better in the schools of Bridgeport, Chicago, Philadelphia, Newark, Hoboken, or Paterson. In "The Losers," a report on Puerto Rican education in those cities, Richard Margolis writes: "Relatively speaking, the longer a Puerto Rican child attends public school, the less he learns."

Between two and three million Spanish-speaking children attend school in five Southwestern states where, as Stan Steiner shows in *La Raza: The Mexican Americans,* the schools serve only to "de-educate" any child who happens not to be middle class. More than a third of the Spanish-speaking children in New Mexico's schools are in the first grade, and over half of those in grades above the first are two years or more overage for their grade level. One Texas school board required "Spanish-surname" children to spend three years in the first grade until a federal court stopped the practice. Chicanos are still put into classes for the mentally retarded on the basis of intelligence tests administered only in English; again, federal courts are in the process of abolishing this form of discrimination. The average number of school years completed by the Chicano in the Southwest is 7.1 years.

Statistics relating to the education of the more than 200,000 Indian children in public or Bureau of Indian Affairs schools are equally dismal. In 1960, 60 per cent of adult Indians had less than an eighth-grade education. Today the Indian dropout rate is more than twice the national average and in some school districts is 80 or 90 per cent. In an all-Indian public elementary school near Ponca City, Oklahoma, 87 per cent of the children have dropped out by the sixth grade. In Minneapolis, where some 10,000 Indians live, the Indian dropout rate is more than 60 per cent. In Washington, Muckleshoot children are automatically retained an extra year in first grade; and the Nook-Sack Indians automatically are placed in slow-learner classes.

One reason schools are failing in their responsibility to these children is that they offer only one curriculum, only one way of doing things, designed to meet the needs of only one group of children. If a child does not fit the mold, so much the worse for him. It is the child who is different, hence deficient; it is the child who must change to meet the needs of the school.

During the first four years of life, a child acquires the sounds, the grammar, and the basic vocabulary of whatever language he hears around him. For many children this language is Spanish or Cree or Chinese or Greek. Seventy-three per cent of all Navajo children entering the first grade speak Navajo but little or no English. Yet when they arrive at school, they find not only that English is the language in which all subjects are taught but that English dominates the entire school life. Children cannot understand or make themselves understood even in the most basic situations. There are schools where a child cannot go to the bathroom without asking in English. One little boy, after being rebuffed repeatedly for failure to speak in English, finally said in Spanish: "If you don't let me go to the bathroom, maybe I piss on your feet."

The effects of this treatment on a child are immediate and deep. Language, and the culture it carries, is at the core of a youngster's concept of himself. For a young child especially, as Theodore Andersson and Mildred Boyer point out, "Language carries all the meanings and overtones of home, family, and love; it is the instrument of his thinking and feeling, his gateway to the world." We all love to be addressed, as George Sánchez says, *en la lengua que mamamos* ("in the language we suckled"). And so when a child enters a school that appears to reject the only words he can use, "He is adversely affected in every aspect of his being."

With English the sole medium of instruction, the child is asked to carry an impossible burden at a time when he can barely understand or speak, let alone read or write, the language. Children are immediately retarded in their schoolwork. For many the situation becomes hopeless, and they drop out of school. In other cases, believing the school system offers no meaningful program, parents may fail to send their children to school at all.

Schools seem unmoved by these results. At any rate, the possibility of hiring some teachers who share a child's culture and could teach him in a language he can understand does not occur to them. Since the curriculum is in English, the child must sink or swim in English.

The injustice goes further: Having insisted that a child learn English, schools make little or no constructive effort to help the child do so. Instead schools assume, or expect, that any child in America will "pick it up" without any help from the school. Alma Bagu tells this story about a little Puerto Rican girl's day in school in New York:

> Sitting in a classroom and staring at words on a blackboard that were to me as foreign as Egyptian hieroglyphics is one of my early recollections of school. The teacher had come up to my desk and bent over, putting her face close to mine. "My name is Mrs. Newman," she said, as if the exaggerated mouthing of her words would make me understand their meaning. I nodded "yes" because I felt that was what she wanted me to do. But she just threw up her hands in despair and touched her fingers to her head to signify to the class I was dense. From that day on school became an ordeal I was forced to endure.

Like most of the people teaching Spanish-speaking or Indian children, Mrs. Newman presumably did not know the child's language. Yet she treated a five- or six-year-old as "dense" for the crime of not knowing hers.

The variety and perversity of the abuses committed against children are unending. In New York it is not unknown for teachers to lecture Puerto Rican students on how rude it is to speak a "strange" language in the presence of those who do not understand it. In the Southwest, where it is widely believed that a child's native language itself "holds him back," children are threatened, shamed, and punished for speaking the only language they know. Stan Steiner tells of children forced to kneel in the playground and beg forgiveness for speaking a Spanish word or having to write "I will not speak Spanish in school" 500 times on the blackboard. One teacher makes her children drop a penny in a bowl for every Spanish word they use. "It works!" she says. "They come from poor families, you know."

These are not the isolated acts of a few callous teachers. America's intolerance of diversity is reflected in an ethnocentric educational system designed to "Americanize" foreigners or those who are seen as culturally different. America is the great melting pot, and, as one writer recently stated it, "If you don't want to melt, you had better get out of the pot." The ill-disguised contempt for a child's language is part of a broader distaste for the child himself and the culture he represents. Children who are culturally different are said to be culturally "deprived." Their language and culture are seen as "disadvantages." The children must be "reoriented," "remodeled," "retooled" if they are to succeed in school.

Messages are sent home insisting that parents speak English in the home or warning of the perils of "all-starch diets" (which means rice and beans). Children are preached middle-class maxims about health and cleanliness. The master curriculum for California's migrant schools prescribes "English cultural games," "English culture, music, and song," "English concept of arithmetic"; nowhere is there mention of the Indo-Hispanic contributions to the history and culture of the Southwest. When Robert Kennedy visited an Indian school, the only book available on Indian history was about the rape of a white woman by Delawares. Even a child's *name* is not his own: Carlos becomes Charles; María, Mary.

Humiliated for their language and values, forced to endure the teaching of a culture that is unrelated to the realities of their lives, it is no wonder that children withdraw mentally, then physically, from school. "School is the enemy," said a Ponca Indian testifying before Congress. "It strikes at the roots of existence of an Indian student."

Far from accomplishing its professed aim of integrating minorities into the "mainstream," the monolingual, monocultural school system has succeeded only in denying whole generations of children an education and condemning them to lives of poverty and despair. There is no more tragic example of the fruits of such policies than that of the Cherokees.

In the nineteenth century, before they were "detribalized," the Cherokees had their own highly regarded bilingual school system and bilingual newspaper. Ninety per cent were literate in their own language, and Oklahoma Cherokees had a higher English literacy level than native English-speakers in either Texas or Arkansas. Today, after seventy years of white control, the Cherokee dropout rate in the public schools runs as high as 75 per cent. The median number of school years completed by the adult Cherokee is 5.5. Ninety per cent of the Cherokee families in Adair County, Oklahoma, are on welfare.

Obviously, no particular "program," not even a bilingual one, can be expected to cure all this. The remark of the 1928 Meriam Report on Indian education holds true today: "The most fundamental need in Indian education is a change in point of view."

Bilingual-bicultural education is perhaps the greatest educational priority today in bilingual communities. Its aim is to include children, not exclude them. It is neither a "remedial" program nor does it seek to "compensate" children for their supposed "deficiencies." It views such children as *advantaged,* not disadvantaged, and seeks to develop bilingualism as a precious asset rather than to stigmatize it as a defect. The very fact of the adoption of a program recognizing a child's language and culture may help to change the way the school views the child. It may help to teach us that diversity is to be enjoyed and valued rather than feared or suspected.

There are also strong arguments supporting the pedagogical soundness of bilingual education. Experts the world over stress the importance of allowing a child to begin his schooling in the language he understands best. Such a policy makes it more likely that a child's first experience with school will be a positive rather than a negative one. Moreover, as John Dewey and others have said, language is one of the principal tools through which children learn problem-solving skills in crucial early years. Policies that frustrate a child's native language development can cause permanent harm by literally jamming the only intellectual channel available to him when he arrives at school. Those who would concentrate on teaching a child English overlook the fact that it takes time for a child unfamiliar with the language to achieve a proficiency in it even approaching that of a child raised in an English-speaking home. In the meantime, struggling to understand other academic subjects, children fall hopelessly behind. In a bilingual program, by contrast, two languages are used as mediums of instruction; a child is thus enabled to study academic subjects in his own language at the same time he is learning English. Bilingual programs teach children to read their own language and to understand, speak, read, and write English (in that order). Language is oral. It is *"speech* before it is reading or writing." When a child enters school already speaking and understanding a language, he is ready to learn to read and write it. A program that prematurely forces English on a child can guarantee his eventual illiteracy in that language.

The "English-only" approach also misses the prime opportunity to teach a child to read his own language. Recent experience indicates that development of literacy in one's native language actually enhances the ability to learn English. When the Navajos evaluated their own bilingual school at Rough Rock, Arizona, they found that the children were more proficient in both languages than they would have been "if you tried to stuff English down the throat of a child who can't understand what you're talking about." Nancy Modiano reports similar results in a highly controlled experiment with Indian children in Chiapas, Mexico. The children who had read first in their native language showed greater proficiency in reading *Spanish* (the national language) than their control peers who had been instructed solely in Spanish. Modiano explains that the children were much more confident about learning to read in a language they already knew; having learned the mechanics of the reading act, they could apply their skill in learning to read another language.

In addition to facilitating the learning of English, bilingual education has other benefits. It helps to correct what Bruce Gaarder, former chief of the U.S. Office of Education's modern language section, has called "an absurdity which passeth understanding." More than $1-billion a year is spent on foreign language instruction. "Yet virtually no part of it, no cent, ever goes to maintain the native language competence which already exists in American children." Bilingual education also allows English-speakers to learn a second language far more effectively than they could in a foreign language program, because their classmates are native speakers. And it develops and enhances children's intellectual capabilities. Bertha Treviño found that in the Nye School, outside Laredo, Texas, both Spanish- and English-speaking children learned mathematics better bilingually than they did when taught in English alone. In Montreal, children who were educated bilingually scored higher on both verbal and nonverbal intelligence tests and "appeared to have a more diversified set of mental abilities" than their monolingual peers.

Despite the promise of bilingual education, however, only a handful of programs were in operation in the United States during the 1950s and 60s. In fact, prior to 1968, twenty-one states, including California, New York, Pennsylvania, and Texas, had laws requiring that all public school instruction be in English. In seven states, including Texas, a teacher risked criminal penalties or the revocation of his license if he taught bilingually.

In the late 1960s the Chicanos in the Southwest and other groups mounted a widespread campaign for bilingual, bicultural education. In 1967 Senator Ralph Yarborough of Texas introduced a bilingual education bill in Congress, which finally passed, in modified form, as an amendment to Title VII of the Elementary and Secondary Education Act of 1965.

The psychological impact of the federal Bilingual Education Act, a landmark in our history, cannot be overestimated. It reversed a fifty-year-old "one-language" policy and committed the moral force of the national government to meeting "the...educational needs of the large numbers of children of limited English-speaking ability in the United States." The act provided financial assistance to local educational agencies for, among other things: "(1) bilingual educational programs; (2) programs designed to impart to students a knowledge of the history and culture associated with their languages; (3) efforts to establish closer cooperation between the school and the home."

This commitment by the federal government has slowly influenced states and local communities. Since 1968 eleven states have passed laws permitting local school districts to provide bilingual instruction and, as stated earlier, one state, Massachusetts, has required school districts to provide bilingual education programs (although participation by the children is voluntary).

Nevertheless, even today very few children enjoy the "luxury" of bilingual education. Title VII has become a highly selective program presently serving only 88,000 of an estimated five million non-English-speaking children. The problem rests primarily with the funding structure of Title VII, which has proved singularly unable to stimulate comparable state and local efforts. The federal act, for example, pays the entire cost of the programs it supports. But since Title VII is grossly underfunded, the federal programs necessarily remain limited. If a local government wishes to institute additional bilingual programs, it must appropriate money from local funds. There is no provision for sharing costs across levels. Thus each level of government becomes reluctant to support a comprehensive bilingual program because it fears it alone will bear the possibly large costs of the program. If, however, costs were shared among the different levels of government—federal, state, and local—each agency might be willing to contribute more.

The Massachusetts legislation provides a needed innovation in this respect. The law requires school districts to offer bilingual programs but provides for state reimbursement of that portion of the cost that *exceeds* the district's average per pupil cost. For example, if a district's annual expenditure per child is $800 and the cost to offer bilingual education is $1,000, the district will be reimbursed $200. The philosophy of the Massachusetts law is that a local school district has an obligation to spend at least as much for the education of a bilingual child as it does for the education of any other child. The funding formula thus allows state money to go much further than if the state alone bore the cost. By redirecting money from the regular program to a program that better serves the needs of the non-English-speaking child, scarce resources are put to much more productive use.

The appeal here, however, is not to expediency. Many children in this affluent land are being denied their fundamental right to equal educational opportunity. To the needs of these children society must respond, and now.

Francesco Cordasco

Puerto Ricans on the Mainland: The Educational Experience

THE MIGRATION AND MAINLAND EXPERIENCE: AN OVERVIEW

In February 1971, the U.S. Census Bureau published its November 1969, sample-survey estimate that the fifty states and the District of Columbia had 1,454,000 Puerto Rican residents—811,000 born on the island, 636,000 born in the states and district, 1,000 in Cuba, and 6,000 elsewhere. In March 1972, the Census Bureau released preliminarily final state population totals from the 1970 census for three categories—persons of Spanish language, persons of Spanish family name, and Puerto Ricans. Puerto Rican counts were for three states only—New York (872,471; 5% of the state population); New Jersey (135,676; 2% of the state population); and Pennsylvania (44,535).

Puerto Ricans have been on the mainland for many years; in the 19th century, a small colony of Puerto Ricans, gathered largely in New York City, worked for the independence of the island. After the annexation of the island in 1898 by the United States, a continuing migration to the mainland began. In 1910 some 1,500 Puerto Ricans were living in the United States; by 1930, they numbered close to 53,000. The migration was reversed during the depression of the 1930s; and again was substantially impeded by World War II in the early 1940s. After the end of World War II (and concurrent with the advent of cheap air transport) it increased steadily until it reached its peak in the early 1950s (in 1953, *304,910* persons left the island and *203,307* returned, leaving a net balance of *74,603*). The state of the economy on the mainland has always been an indicator of the migration. The decline in Puerto Rican migration to the mainland in 1970 and continuing into 1971 was precisely due to economic hardship in the states. [1]

---

[1] For Puerto Rico passenger traffic for fiscal years 1940-1969, see the reports of the Puerto Rico Planning Board. The major source of information on Puerto Rican migration is the Department of Labor, Migration Division, Commonwealth of Puerto Rico. See further, H. C. Barton, Jr., "The Employment Situation in Puerto Rico and Migratory Movements between Puerto Rico and the United States," *Summary of Proceedings: Workshop on Employment Problems of Puerto Ricans* (New York: Graduate School of Social Work, New York University, 1968). See also, *The New York Puerto Rican: Patterns of Work Experience,* U.S. Department of Labor, Bureau of Labor Statistics (Middle Atlantic Region), New York, 1971.

In a prescient book on Puerto Rican Americans, the Jesuit sociologist Rev. Joseph P. Fitzpatrick observes that Puerto Ricans have found it difficult to achieve "community solidarity" and suggests that they may work out adjustment "in very new ways" differing from those of past immigrants (technically, as American citizens, Puerto Ricans are migrants to the mainland United States); and Father Fitzpatrick cogently observes:

A book about the Puerto Ricans in mainland United States, with a special focus on those in New York City, is very risky but also is very necessary. It is risky because the Puerto Rican community is in a state of turbulent change in a city and a nation which are also in a state of turbulent change. So many different currents of change affect Puerto Ricans at the present time that it is foolhardy to attempt to describe this group adequately or put them into focus. Nor is it possible to point out clearly any one direction in which the Puerto Rican community is moving in its adjustment to life on the mainland. Its directions are often in conflict, and no single leader or movement has given sharp definition to one direction as dominant over others. . . . What is most needed at this moment of the Puerto Rican experience, both for Puerto Ricans and other mainland Americans, is *perspective*: a sense of the meaning of the migration for everyone involved in that migration, for the new-comers as well as the residents of the cities and neighborhoods to which the Puerto Ricans come.[2]

How varied the Puerto Rican experience on the mainland has been can be best indicated by the sharp contrasts provided in four juxtaposed excerpts from Puerto Rican reactions registered over a period of time.

In 1948, J. J. Osuna, the distinguished Puerto Rican educator, on a visit to New York City schools, observed:

As far as possible something should be done in Puerto Rico to discourage migration of people who do not have occupations to go into upon their arrival in this country, or of children whose parents live in Puerto Rico and who have no home in New York. Too many people are coming, hoping that they may find work and thereby better themselves economically, and in the case of the children, educationally. It is laudable that they take the chance, but the experience of the past teaches us that as far as possible, people should not come to the continent until they have secured employment here.[3]

---

[2] Joseph P. Fitzpatrick, *Puerto Rican Americans: The Meaning of Migration to the Mainland* (Englewood Cliffs, N.J.: Prentice Hall, 1971), p. xi. The Puerto Rican migration is, in many ways, a unique phenomenon for the United States. "The Puerto Ricans have come for the most part in the first great airborne migration of people from abroad: they are decidedly newcomers of the aviation age. A Puerto Rican can travel from San Juan to New York in less time than a New Yorker could travel from Coney Island to Times Square a century ago. They are the first group to come in large numbers from a different cultural background but who are, nevertheless, citizens of the United States. They are the first group of newcomers who bring a cultural practice of widespread intermingling and intermarriage of people of many different colors. They are the first group of predominantly Catholic migrants not accompanied by a native clergy. Numerous characteristics of the Puerto Ricans make their migration unique." (Fitzpatrick, p. 2)

[3] J. J. Osuna, *Report on Visits to New York City Schools* (Government of Puerto Rico). Reprinted in F. Cordasco and E. Bucchioni, *Puerto Rican Children in Mainland Schools: A Sourcebook for Teachers* (Metuchen, N.J.: Scarecrow Press, 1968), pp. 227–239.

In 1961, Joseph Monserrat, at the time Director of the Migration Division, Commonwealth of Puerto Rico, in speaking on "Community Planning for Puerto Rican Integration in the United States," cautioned that:

> If all Puerto Ricans were to suddenly disappear from New York City, neither the housing problem nor other basic issues confronting the city would be solved. In fact, without the Puerto Ricans, New York would be faced with one of two alternatives: either "import" people to do the work done by Puerto Ricans (and whoever was imported from wherever they might come would have to live in the very same buildings Puerto Ricans now live in for the simple reason that there is nothing else); or industries would have to move to other areas where there are workers, causing a severe economic upheaval in the city. Obviously, neither one is a viable solution. Nor will the stagnation of the past resolve our dilemma.
> . . . The Puerto Rican, although he comes from a close knit neighborhood in the Commonwealth, has found the best possibility for social action and self-improvement on the city-wide level. The community of Puerto Ricans is not the East Side or the South Side. It is New York City, Lorain, Chicago, Los Angeles, Middletown. City living is learned living. The migrants must be helped to learn the facts of city life and how to function effectively as a pressure group in a pressure group society.[4]

Both of these statements are in stark contrast to the ideology of revolution and separatism evident in the animadversions which follow. First, from a spokesman for "La Generación Encojonada":

> Violence is the essence of a colonial society. It is established as a system in the interests of the ruling classes. Colonial society "is the meeting of two forces, opposed to each other by their very nature, which in fact owe their originality to that sort of substantification which results from and is nourished by the situation in the colonies. Their first encounter was marked by violence and their existence together . . . was carried on by dint of a great array of bayonets and cannon." Puerto Rican history has been witness to this violent confrontation between people and oppressor. We see it in daily events: in schools, churches, factories, the countryside, in strikes, demonstrations, and insurrections. As soon as an individual confronts the system, he feels its violence in the way of life colonialism imposes on him: the feudal-type exploitation in the countryside, the capitalist exploitation in the cities.
> The lifeblood of every colonial society is the profit it offers to its exploiters. Its basis is the authority of an exploiting system—not the authority that comes from a majority consensus, but the paternal authority with which a minority tries to justify a system beneficial to it. Around that system is built a morality, an ethic, rooted in the economic co-existence of colonizers and colonized. Thus the system envelops itself in forms that create the illusion of sharing, of a brotherhood and equality that don't exist. The Puerto Rican elections held every four years exemplify this. We must not confuse the ox with the fighting bull, the cause with the problem, the root with the branches.[5]

---

[4] Joseph Monserrat, "Community Planning for Puerto Rican Integration in the United States," [an address at the National Conference on Social Welfare, Minneapolis, Minnesota, May 1961]. Published in F. Cordasco and E. Bucchioni, op. cit., pp. 221–226.

[5] Juan A. Silén, *We, The Puerto Rican People: A Story of Oppression and Resistance* (New York: Monthly Review Press, 1971), pp. 118–119. Originally, *Hacia una Visión Positiva del Puertorriqueño* (Rio Piedras: Editorial Edil, 1970).

And from a theoretician for the Young Lords Party, spawned in the socio-pathology of the urban barrio:

To support its economic exploitation of Puerto Rico, the United States instituted a new educational system whose purpose was to Americanize us. Specifically, that means that the school's principal job is to exalt the cultural values of the United States. As soon as we begin using books that are printed in English, that are printed in the United States, that means that the American way of life is being pushed . . . with all its bad points, with its commercialism, its dehumanization of human beings.

At the same time that the cultural values of America are exalted, the cultural values of Puerto Rico are downgraded. People begin to feel ashamed of speaking Spanish. Language becomes a reward and punishment system. If you speak English and adapt to the cultural values of America, you're rewarded; if you speak Spanish and stick to the old traditional ways, you're punished. In the school system here, if you don't quickly begin to speak English and shed your Puerto Rican values, you're put back a grade—so you may be in the sixth grade in Puerto Rico but when you come here, you go back to the fourth or fifth. You're treated as if you're retarded, as if you're backward—and your own cultural values therefore are shown to be of less value than the cultural values of this country and the language of this country.[6]

It is no accident that this strident voice registers anger particularly with the schools; for, it is in the schools that Puerto Rican identity is subjected to the greatest pressures, and it is the educational experience on the mainland which, for Puerto Ricans, is generally bad and from which despair and alienation emerge. It is in mainland schools that the dynamics of conflict and acculturation for Puerto Ricans are best seen in clear perspective; and it is a grim irony that, generally, educational programs for Puerto Ricans have failed despite the multitudinous educational experiments encapsulated in those new attentions born in Johnsonian America to the culture of the poor and the massive programmatic onslaughts on poverty. In the Puerto Rican mainland communities, there has been a subtle shift (following Black models) from civil rights and integration to an emphasis on Puerto Rican power and community solidarity.

And the Puerto Rican poor in their urban barrios have encountered as their chief adversaries the Black poor in the grim struggle for anti-poverty monies and for the participative identities on Community Action Programs (funded by the Office of Economic Opportunity) which are often the vehicles and leverages of political power in the decaying American cities; additionally, a Puerto Rican professional presence in schools and a myriad of other institutional settings has been thwarted by exiled middle-class Cuban professionals. "Most of the Cubans are an exiled professional middle-class that came to the United States for political reasons. They are lauded and rewarded by the United States government for their rejection of Communism and

---

[6] David Perez, "The Chains That Have Been Taken off Slaves' Bodies Are Put Back on Their Minds," *Palante: Young Lords Party,* photographs by Michael Abramson; text by Young Lords Party and Michael Abramson (New York: McGraw-Hill, 1971), pp. 65–66. Palante is the Spanish equivalent of "Right On" or "Forward." The Young Lords Party is a revolutionary political organization formed in New York City in 1969. The concerns of the Young Lords Party range from prisons and health care to sexism; they have cleaned up the streets of *El Barrio,* organized free breakfast programs for school children, and conducted door-to-door testing for lead poisoning and tuberculosis. See Frank Browning, "From Rumble to Revolution: The Young Lords," *Ramparts Magazine,* vol. 9 (October 1970), pp. 19–25; and Richard C. Schroeder, *Spanish-Americans: The New Militants* (Washington: Editorial Research Reports, 1971).

Fidel Castro. The Cubans lean toward the political right, are fearful of the involvement of masses of poor people. Being middle-class they are familiar with 'the system' and operate successfully in this structure. They are competitive and upwardly mobile. 'They have little sympathy for the uneducated poor.' (Hilda Hidalgo, *The Puerto Ricans of Newark, New Jersey* [Newark: Aspira, 1971], p. 14)."

It is hardly strange that the Puerto Rican community has looked to the schools, traditionally the road out of poverty, as affording its best hope for successfully negotiating the challenges of a hostile mainland American milieu.

THE EDUCATIONAL EXPERIENCE OF PUERTO RICANS: THE BITTER LEGACY OF THE PAST

The Children of the Past

American schools have always had as students children from a wide variety of cultural backgrounds; and the non-English-speaking child has been no stranger in American urban classrooms. If we are to understand the problems which Puerto Rican children encounter in mainland schools, it is instructive to look at the experience of other children (non-English-speaking and culturally different) in American schools. A huge literature (largely ignored until recently) exists on the children of immigrants in the schools. No document on this earlier experience is more impressive than the *Report of the Immigration Commission* (1911) whose *Report on the Children of Immigrants in Schools* (vols. 29–33) is a vast repository of data on the educational history of the children of the poor and the schools.[7] By 1911, 57.5% of the children in public schools of 37 of the largest American cities were of foreign-born parentage; in the parochial schools of 24 of these 37 cities, the children of foreign-born parents constituted 63.5% of the total registration.[8] "To the immigrant child the public elementary school was the first step away from his past, a means by which he could learn to assume the characteristics necessary for the long climb upward."[9] And by 1911, almost 50% of the students in secondary schools were of foreign-born parentage.[10] In American cities, the major educational challenge and responsibility was the immigrant child.

In the effort to respond to the needs of the immigrant child, it is important to note that no overall programs were developed to aid any particular immigrant group. Although there was little agreement as to what Americanization was, the schools were committed to Americanize (and to Anglicize) their charges. Ellwood P. Cubberley's *Changing Conceptions of Education* (1909), which Lawrence A. Cremin characterizes

---

[7] United States Immigration Commission, *Report of the Immigration Commission,* 41 vols. (Washington: Government Printing Office, 1911). *The Report on the Children of Immigrants in Schools* (vols. 29–33) has been reprinted (5 vols.) with an introductory essay by F. Cordasco (Metuchen, N.J.: Scarecrow Reprint Corp., 1970).

[8] U.S. Immigration Commission, op. cit., *Abstracts: The Children of Immigrants in Schools,* vol. II, pp. 1–15.

[9] Alan M. Thomas, "American Education and the Immigrant," *Teachers College Record,* vol. 55 (April 1954), pp. 253–267.

[10] See footnote 8, supra.

as "a typical progressive tract of the era," [11] saw the immigrants as "illiterate, docile, lacking in self-reliance and initiative, and not possessing the Anglo-Teutonic conceptions of law, order, and government...," and the school's role was (in Cubberley's view) "to assimilate and amalgamate."

What efforts were made to respond to the needs of the immigrant children were improvised, most often directly in answer to specific problems; almost never was any attempt made to give the school and its program a community orientation. The children literally left at the door of the school their language, their cultural identities, and their immigrant subcommunity origins. [12] A child's parents had virtually no role in the schools; [13] and the New York City experience was not atypical in its leaving the immigrant child to the discretion of the individual superintendent, a principal, or a teacher.

Against such a lack of understanding and coordinated effort in behalf of the children of the poor it is hardly strange that the general malaise of the schools was nowhere more symptomatic than in the pervasive phenomenon of the overage pupil who was classed under the rubric "retardation" with all of its negative connotations. The Immigration Commission of 1911 found that the percentage of retardation for the New York City elementary school pupils was 36.4 with the maximum retardation (48.8%) in the fifth grade. [14] The Commission observed:

> ...thus in the third grade the pupils range in age from 5 to 18 years. In similar manner pupils of the age of 14 years are found in every grade from the first of the elementary schools to the last of the high schools. It will, however, be noted that in spite of this divergence the great body of the pupils of a given grade are of certain definite ages, the older and younger pupils being in each case much less numerically represented. It may, therefore, be assumed that there is an appropriate age for each grade. This assumption is the cardinal point in current educational discussion in regard to retardation. If it were assumed that there is

---

[11] Lawrence A. Cremin, *The Transformation of the School* (New York: Knopf, 1961). "To Americanize, in this view, was to divest the immigrant of his ethnic character and to inculcate the dominant Anglo-Saxon morality." (Ibid.)

[12] See the autobiography of Leonard Covello, *The Heart Is the Teacher* (New York: McGraw-Hill, 1958). It is significant to note that Covello, as an immigrant boy in East Harlem, was more influenced by the work of the evangelist, Anna C. Ruddy, who had devoted years to social work in the East Harlem Italian community, than by the public schools. See Anna C. Ruddy [pseudonym, Christian McLeod], *The Heart of the Stranger* (New York: Fleming H. Revel, 1908); see also Selma Berrol, "Immigrants at School: New York City, 1900–1910," *Urban Education*, vol. 4 (October 1969), pp. 220–230.

[13] See Leonard Covello, *The Social Background of the Italio-American Child: A Study of the Southern Italian Mores and Their Effect on the School Situation in Italy and America*, edited and with an introduction by F. Cordasco (Leiden, The Netherlands: E. J. Brill, 1967); and also, Leonard Covello, "A High School and Its Immigrant Community: A Challenge and an Opportunity," *Journal of Educational Sociology*, vol. 9 (February 1936), pp. 331–346. "Where the Italian community was studied, it was subjected to the ministrations of social workers (who concentrated on the sociopathology inevitable in a matrix of deprivation and cultural conflict) or to the probing of psychologists who sought to discern and understand the dynamics of adjustment." F. Cordasco, *Italians in the United States* (New York: Oriole Editions, 1972), p. xiii.

[14] United States Immigration Commission, *The Children of Immigrants in Schools*, op. cit., vol. 32, p. 609.

a normal age for each grade, then the pupils can be divided into two classes—those who are of normal age or less and those who are above the normal age. The overage pupils at the upper end of the scale are designated as "retarded." [15]

At best, it is a dismal picture whose poignant and evocative pathos is etched in the faces of the children imprisoned in the cheerless classrooms of the era. [16] It could have been otherwise: in the lower East Side of New York City the efforts of District School Superintendent Julia Richman, at the turn of the century, pointed in the more rewarding directions of community awareness, of building on the cultural strengths which the child brought to the school; and the near quarter-century tenure (1934-1957) of Leonard Covello of Benjamin Franklin High School in New York City's East Harlem, dramatically underscored the successes of the community centered school. But Julia Richman and Leonard Covello were the exceptions, not the rule; and it is hardly fortuitous that they came out of the emerging Jewish and Italian subcommunities, for these very identities help explain their responsiveness to the immigrant child. [17]

PUERTO RICAN CHILDREN IN THE SCHOOLS

The Early Years

It is in the perspectives of these earlier experiences that the educational failures of the Puerto Rican child are to be viewed and understood. Committed to policies of Americanization, the schools neglected the cultural heritage of the Puerto Rican child, rejected his ancestral language, and generally ignored his parents and community. And these policies were in keeping with the traditional practices of the schools.

The Puerto Rican community in New York City is the largest on the mainland, and its experience would be essentially typical of other mainland urban communities. As early as 1938, the difficulties of the Puerto Rican child in the New York City schools are graphically (if passingly) noted:

> Many Puerto Rican children who enter the public schools in New York speak or understand little English. The children who are transferred from schools in Puerto Rico to those in New York are usually put back in their classes so that they are with children who are two or three years younger than they are.

---

[15] Ibid., pp. 608-609.

[16] See many of the contemporary photographs taken by the social reformer Jacob Riis and reproduced in his books, particularly, *The Children of the Poor* (New York: Scribner, 1892); and generally, in F. Cordasco, ed., *Jacob Riis Revisited: Poverty and the Slum in Another Era* (New York: Doubleday, 1968). See also, Robert Hunter, *Poverty* [particularly the chapter entitled, "The Child"] (New York: Macmillan, 1904); and John Spargo, *The Bitter Cry of the Children* (New York: Macmillan, 1907).

[17] Julia Richman has, unfortunately, been neglected; she is one of the great urban school reformers in a period marked by hostility and contempt for the children of the poor. All of her writings are important. See particularly the following: "A Successful Experiment in Promoting Pupils," *Educational Review,* vol. 18 (June 1899), pp. 23-29; "The Incorrigible Child," *Educational Review,* vol. 31 (May 1906), pp. 484-506; "The Social Needs of the Public Schools," *Forum,* vol. 43 (February 1910), pp. 161-169, "What Can Be Done for the Backward Child," *The Survey,* vol. 13 (November 1904), pp. 129-131. For Covello, see footnote 13, supra; and his "A Community Centered School and the Problem of Housing," *Educational Forum,* vol. 7 (January 1943); and "A Principal Speaks to His Community," *American Unity,* vol. 2 (May 1944).

Americans who are teaching Puerto Rican children express the opinion that these children have had less training in discipline and in group cooperation than American children. Lacking the timidity of the children in this country, they sometimes act in an unrestrained and impulsive manner. One large agency in the settlement, which has dealt with Puerto Rican children for many years, reported that under proper conditions Puerto Rican children are responsive, easily managed, and affectionate. In contrast to this, another large institution said that for some reason which they could not explain the Puerto Rican children were more destructive than any group of children with whom they had had contact. All the evidence obtainable shows the relation of unsatisfactory home conditions to difficulties at school. During the past few years the desperate economic condition of these families has caused them to move so frequently that it has often been difficult to locate the children when they did not attend school. [18]

In December, 1946, Dr. Paul Kennedy, then President of the New York City Association of Assistant Superintendents, appointed a committee "to study and report on the educational adjustments made necessary by the addition of the 400,000 Puerto Ricans who have lately become residents of this city." The suprisingly comprehensive report prepared by this committee considered native backgrounds; migration to the mainland; problems of assimilation; the education of the Puerto Rican pupil; and made a number of recommendations. [19] That the report was anchored in the past is evident in its caution that "Although the Puerto Rican is an American citizen, the adjustment he must make in this city is like that of immigrants to this country from a foreign land." The report counted "13,914 pupils enrolled [June 1947; by October 1970, 260,040 were enrolled] in the public elementary and junior high schools of the city who originally came from Puerto Rico"; and further grimly observed: "there is no doubt but that many pupils coming from Puerto Rico suffer from the double handicap of unfamiliarity with the English language and lack of previous educational experience, sometimes approaching complete illiteracy. Malnutrition and other health deficiencies contribute to the educational problem of the schools. The overcrowding at home and the restlessness on the street carry over into the school in the form of nervousness, extreme shyness, near tantrums, and other behavior characteristics which are the more difficult for the teacher to understand because of the language barrier." (p. 38)

---

[18] Lawrence R. Chenault, *The Puerto Rican Migrant in New York City,* with a foreword by F. Cordasco (New York: Russell & Russell, 1970; originally, Columbia University Press, 1938), p. 146. See also, C. P. Armstrong, *Reactions of Puerto Rican Children in New York City to Psychological Tests, A Report of the Special Committee on Immigration and Naturalization* (State of New York: Chamber of Commerce, 1935) which Chenault used but (in keeping with the temperament of the time) noted "It is not the purpose of this study to raise the question of the innate ability of the migrant." Perhaps the earliest notice of Puerto Ricans in New York City is the unpublished typescript (14 pp.) on file in the office of the National Urban League, William E. Hill, *Porto Rican Colonies in New York* (1929).

[19] *A Program of Education for Puerto Ricans in New York City: A Report Prepared by a Committee of the Association of Assistant Superintendents* (New York: Board of Education, 1947). The report (106 pp.) was mimeographed with what appears to be a very limited circulation. "For years, boys and girls from Puerto Rico have entered the public schools of New York City. For the most part they came into Spanish Harlem, arriving in such small numbers that their admission to school was accepted routinely. Together with other non-English speaking children from European countries, they were placed in "C" classes, and gradually assimilated into the regular program of the school. There was no reference then to a 'Puerto Rican problem' in the schools." (p. 3).

The Committee also undertook the first study of "reading progress" among Puerto Rican pupils who were new admissions to the elementary and junior high schools; and it made a series of recommendations, chief among which was the establishment of special classes ("C" classes) for Puerto Rican children "for whom at least a year's time is needed for preliminary instruction and language work before they are ready for complete assimilation in the regular program." Although the report was generally neglected, it represented the first systematic study undertaken on the mainland to call attention to the needs of Puerto Rican children.

Attention has been called to J. J. Osuna's *Report on Visits to New York City Schools* in 1948 (see footnote #3). In 1951, a Mayor's Committee on Puerto Rican Affairs in New York City was convened and considered the needs of Puerto Rican pupils;[20] and in 1953, Dr. Leonard Covello, then Principal of Benjamin Franklin High School in East Harlem, consolidated and articulated into schematic form for consideration the various proposals which had been made up to that time to deal with the needs of Puerto Rican children in the schools.[21]

Finally, in 1953, the New York City Board of Education presented in booklet form the results of a study initiated by its Division of Curriculum Development.[22] This brief report indicated a new awareness of the importance of using Spanish in instructing Puerto Rican children, of the need for knowledge of Puerto Rican cultural backgrounds, and of the need for a fully developed educational program for Puerto Rican children; and it served as a prologue to *The Puerto Rican Study* which was initiated in 1953.

The Puerto Rican Study

The Puerto Rican Study was, for its time, one of the most generously funded educational studies ever undertaken.[23] The Fund for the Advancement of Education provided a grant-in-aid of a half million dollars and "contributions equivalent in amounts authorized by the Board of Education made the study a vital operation in the school system." (*Foreword*) It was not completed until 1957, and it was finally

---

[20] Mayor's Committee on Puerto Rican Affairs in New York City, "Puerto Rican Pupils in American Schools," *Report of the Subcommittee on Education, Recreation and Parks* (New York: 1951). Part of the report is reprinted in Cordasco and Bucchioni, op. cit., pp. 246–253.

[21] Leonard Covello, "Recommendations Concerning Puerto Rican Pupils in Our Public Schools" (Benjamin Franklin High School, May 1, 1953). This is an invaluable document, and is published in Cordasco and Bucchioni, op. cit., pp. 254–259. Attention should also be called to *Education of the Non-English Speaking and Bilingual (Spanish) Pupils in the Junior High Schools of Districts 10 and 11, Manhattan* (June 1952), prepared at the request of New York City Assistant Superintendent Clare C. Baldwin. The report noted that "every school in Districts 10 and 11 has some Puerto Rican children on its register."

[22] *Teaching Children of Puerto Rican Background in New York City Schools* (New York: Board of Education, 1953).

[23] *The Puerto Rican Study, 1953–1957, A Report on the Education and Adjustment of Puerto Rican Pupils in the Public Schools of the City of New York* (New York: Board of Education, 1958). For some of the backgrounds of the report, see J. Cayce Morrison, *A Letter to Friends of Puerto Rican Children* (1955); and his "The Puerto Rican Study—What It Is; Where It Is Going," *Journal of Educational Sociology,* vol. 28 (December 1954), pp. 167–173.

published in April 1959. It is, unquestionably, the fullest study ever made of the Puerto Rican educational experience on the mainland; and, in a broader sense, it remains one of the most comprehensive statements yet made, not only of the Puerto Rican school experience, but of the educational experience of the non-English-speaking minority child in the American school.[24] As such it is an invaluable document in American educational historiography, with all of the contemporary relevancies which the 1960s have defined (and continuing into the 1970s) with reference to ethnicity, the minority child, the contexts of poverty, and the educational needs of the "disadvantaged" child. It is strange that, in the proliferating literature on the minority child and the schools, *The Puerto Rican Study* should have been neglected; and its neglect may be due to its appearance before the advent of the Johnsonian anti-poverty programs of the 1960s with their educational components, and to the inevitable fate of sponsored reports whose implementation and evaluation are seldom realized or avoided for a variety of reasons.

The Puerto Rican Study's objectives are clearly stated:

> In a narrow sense, *The Puerto Rican Study* was a four-year inquiry into the education and adjustment of Puerto Rican pupils in the public schools of the City of New York. In a broader sense, it was a major effort of the school authorities to establish on a sound basis a city-wide program for the continuing improvement of the educational opportunities of all non-English-speaking pupils in the public schools.
>
> While the *Study* was focused on the public schools in New York City, it was planned and conducted in the belief that the findings might be useful to all schools, public and private, that are trying to serve children from a Spanish-language culture. As the *Study* developed, it seemed apparent that it might have values, direct or indirect, wherever children are being taught English as a second language. (p. 1)

It sought answers to the following specific problems: (1) What are the most effective methods and materials for teaching English as a second language to newly-arrived Puerto Rican pupils? (2) What are the most effective techniques whereby the school can promote a more rapid and more effective adjustment of Puerto Rican parents and children to the community and of the community to them?

As the *Study* progressed, its staff developed two series of related curriculum bulletins—*Resource Units* organized around themes and designed for all pupils, and a *Language Guide Series* which provided the content and methods for adapting the instruction to the needs of the pupils learning English (the *Study* lists the *Units* and

---

[24] The only comparable work is Leonard Covello's *The Social Background of the Italio-American School Child* (see footnote #13). For the contiguity and relationships of the Italian and Puerto Rican communities in East Harlem, see F. Cordasco and R. Galattioto, "Ethnic Displacement in the Interstitial Community: The East Harlem (New York City) Experience," *Phylon: The Atlanta University Review of Race & Culture,* vol. 31 (Fall 1970), pp. 302–312. *The Puerto Rican Study* was released officially by the New York City Board of Education on April 6, 1959. See *New York Times,* April 7, 1959: "Dr. John H. Theobold, the Superintendent of Schools, said that a 'substantial number' of recommendations and findings in the study had already been implemented. Teaching materials, courses of study and guides developed by the project, he said, are now being used. He said there were now 2,255 special classes for Puerto Rican children in the elementary and 346 such classes in the secondary schools."

Series). The *Study* also furnished a detailed description of the Puerto Rican children; devised a scale to rate English-speaking ability; and constructed a detailed program for the in-service education of teachers (Chapter 17). [25]

The Recommendations of *The Puerto Rican Study*

Its recommendations ("Where *The Puerto Rican Study* Leads") are both a blueprint and design for effectively meeting the needs of Puerto Rican children, and they impinge on all those facets of the experience of the minority child which are interrelated and which, if neglected, impede social growth and cognitive achievement. Simply listed (without the capsuled rationales which accompany them), they represent a skeletal construct as meaningful today as when they were formulated:

1. Accept *The Puerto Rican Study*, not as something finished, but as the first stage of a larger, city-wide, ever improving program for the education and assimilation of non-English-speaking children.
2. Take a new look at the philosophy governing the education of the non-English-speaking children in New York City schools.
3. Recognize that whatever is done for the non-English-speaking child is, in the long run, done for all the children.
4. Use the annual school census as a basic technic in planning the continuing adaptation of the schools to the needs of the non-English-speaking pupils.
5. Recognize the heterogeneity of the non-English-speaking pupils.
6. Formulate a uniform policy for the reception, screening, placement, and periodic assessment of non-English-speaking pupils.
7. Keep policies governing the grouping of non-English-speaking pupils flexible. Place the emphasis upon serving the needs of the individual pupil.
8. Place special emphasis on reducing the backlog of retarded language learners.
9. Recognize "English as a second language" or "the teaching of non-English-speaking children" as an area of specialization that cuts across many subject areas.
10. Use the curricular materials developed by *The Puerto Rican Study* to achieve unity of purpose and practice in teaching non-English-speaking pupils.

---

[25] *The Resource Units* and the *Language Guide Series* are invaluable aids for the teacher who is looking for materials for the instructional program for Puerto Rican children; equally valuable (and developed as part of *The Puerto Rican Study*) is Samuel M. Goodman, *Tests and Testing: Developing a Program for Testing Puerto Rican Pupils in Mainland Schools* (New York: Board of Education, 1958). Admittedly, *The Resource Units* and the *Language Guide Series* were intended (in their emphases) to facilitate a more rapid adjustment to the American way of life (in keeping with the ethos of *The Puerto Rican Study* and its period), but this does not detract from their value as cognitive aids. *The Puerto Rican Study* and its ancillary materials are a complete conspectus for the education of Puerto Rican children measured against the principles discussed in Theodore Andersson and Mildred Boyer, *Bilingual Schooling in the United States,* 2 vols. (Austin, Texas: Southwest Educational Development Laboratory, 1970); and Vera P. John and Vivian M. Horner, *Early Childhood Bilingual Education* (New York: Modern Language Association of America, 1971). Notice should also be made of the materials describing the programs at the Bilingual School (Public School #211, Bronx, N.Y.) which incorporate many of the recommendations of *The Puerto Rican Study*. The most completely developed Bilingual School in the United States is Public School #25 (Bronx, N.Y.) whose programs are essentially based on the recommendations of *The Puerto Rican Study*.

11. Capitalize on the creative talent of teachers in finding ways and means of supplementing and of improving the program for teaching non-English-speaking pupils.

12. Recognize and define the school's responsibility to assist, counsel, and cooperate with the parents of non-English-speaking pupils in all matters pertaining to the child's welfare.

13. Take a new look at the school's opportunity to accelerate the adjustment of Puerto Rican children and their parents through advice and counsel to parents on problems normally considered to be outside the conventional functions of the school.

14. Staff the schools to do the job: to help the new arrival to make good adjustment to school and community; to help the non-English-speaking child to learn English and to find his way successfully into the mainstream of the school's program.

15. Staff the proper agencies of the Board of Education to maintain a continuing program for the development and improvement of curricular materials and other aids to the teaching of non-English-speaking pupils.

16. Staff, also, the proper agencies of the Board of Education, and set in motion the processes to maintain a continuing assessment or evaluation of technics, practices and proposals.

17. Take a new hard look at the psychological services provided for non-English-speaking children, especially for Puerto Rican children.

18. Through every means available, make it clear that the education of the non-English-speaking children and their integration in an ever-changing school population is the responsibility of every member of the school staff.

19. Maintain, improve, and possibly expand the program of in-service preparation initiated through *The Puerto Rican Study* for training special staff to assist in accelerating the program for non-English-speaking children.

20. In cooperation with the colleges and universities of Metropolitan New York, create a dynamic program to achieve unity of purpose and more adequate coordination of effort in the education of teachers and of other workers for accelerating the program in the schools.

21. Use the varied opportunities available to develop an ever improving cooperation between the Department of Education in Puerto Rico and the Board of Education in New York City.

22. In cooperation with the responsible representatives of the government of the State of New York, continue to explore the mutual interests and responsibility of the city and the state for the education and adjustment of non-English-speaking children and youth.

23. Think of the City of New York and the Commonwealth of Puerto Rico as partners in a great enterprise.

No full scale implementation of *The Puerto Rican Study* was attempted. Much of what the *Study* recommended appears again in the New York City Board of Education *Educating Students for Whom English Is a Second Language: Programs, Activities, and Services* (1965), a pamphlet-review of subsequent programs which emphasized teacher training programs, particularly the exchange of teachers between New York and Puerto Rico. All kinds of reasons can be advanced for the failure to implement *The Puerto Rican Study,* and these might include teacher and Board of

Education resistance; the struggles which were to ensue over community participation, and decentralization; the rapidly politicizing community/school contexts with their attendant ideological quarrels; the absence of qualified personnel; and the accelerating growth of the Puerto Rican community which simply overwhelmed many of the schools. Whatever the reasons (and no reason or a combination of reasons provides an acceptable explanation), the *Study* was more than a million dollar white elephant. Its achievements (however incompletely implemented) included the following:

1. Developed two series of related curriculum bulletins—*Resource Units* and *Language Guides*—for use in teaching English to non-English-speaking pupils. These are keyed to New York City courses of study but may be easily adapted to courses of study in other school systems. They are adapted to the maturity level of children, grade by grade in the elementary school, and in terms of need for special instruction in English during the early secondary school years.

2. Developed a guide for teaching science—resource units and sample lessons—to Puerto Rican pupils who are still trying to learn English; and a guide for teaching occupations to teen-age Puerto Rican pupils in high school who wish to qualify for occupational employment.

3. Developed a battery of tests, measures, and data-gathering technics for use with Puerto Rican pupils in the mainland schools. Among these were a tape-recorded test for measuring the ability of non-English-speaking pupils to understand spoken English, a scale for rating ability to speak English, a bilingual test of arithmetic, and a process for screening new arrivals and for following their progress through periodic reviews.

4. Through an educational-ethnic-social survey of several thousand children in New York City elementary and junior high schools, obtained a profile of the characteristics of pupils of Puerto Rican background in relation to other pupils in the same grades and schools.

5. Through testing thousands of pupils, obtained estimates of the potential abilities as well as of the present performance of Puerto Rican pupils in relation to their peers, i.e., other pupils of the same age and grade in the same schools.

6. Through a variety of studies of individual children from kindergarten through the tenth grade or second year of high school, gained revealing information concerning the problems of Puerto Rican children in achieving cultural-educational-social adjustment in New York City schools.

7. Through a survey of the relations of schools to Puerto Rican parents, defined the problems confronting the schools, formulated criteria for determining the schools' role, and made some estimate of the cost in terms of personnel needed to help facilitate or accelerate the cultural adjustment of Puerto Rican parents.

8. Through analysis of previously established positions and of new positions established on an experimental basis, developed criteria for determining the necessity for special staff in schools to enable them to serve the needs of Puerto Rican and foreign-born or non-English-speaking children.

9. Through two years of experimentation with different procedures, developed proposals for an in-service program to reach all teachers required to teach non-English-speaking pupils.

10. Through participation in three summer workshops sponsored in part by the Board of Education of the City of New York at the University of Puerto Rico, formulated proposals for the development of the annual workshop as a continuing means of promoting better mutual understanding and cooperation between the school system of New York City and the school system of Puerto Rico.

11. Through the surveys and testing of thousands of children, devised a plan for obtaining a uniform census of all Puerto Rican and foreign-born children in the schools. Administration of census, through consecutive years, will give the Board of Education data for predicting with a high degree of accuracy pending changes in the ethnic composition of pupil population by school, school district, school level, borough and city.

12. The gradation of ability to speak English as defined by *The Puerto Rican Study* in its scale for rating ability to speak English was used by the Commissioner of Education of the State of New York in defining non-English-speaking pupils as a basis for the distribution of additional state aid appropriated by law. (pp. 9–10)

In themselves, these achievements (and the recommendations) were to become the measuring criteria against which continuing needs were to be delineated.[26]

BEYOND *THE PUERTO RICAN STUDY*

The Bilingual Education Act

Much of the effort in behalf of the educational needs of Puerto Rican children in the 1960s must be viewed and understood in the light of the massive federal interventions in education largely initiated by the enactment of the Elementary & Secondary Education Act of 1965, and its subsequent amendments.

The passage by the Congress in 1968 of the Bilingual Education Act (itself, Title VII of the ESEA) reaffirmed and strengthened many of the recommendations of *The Puerto Rican Study,* even though the *Study* had largely fallen into undeserved neglect. The struggle for a national bilingual education act represented a continuing fight against the ethnocentric rejection of the use of native languages in the instruction of

---

[26] The failure to implement *The Puerto Rican Study* led to great agitation and continuing demands from the Puerto Rican community. The first Citywide Conference of the Puerto Rican Community (April 1967) in its published proceedings (*Puerto Ricans Confront Problems of the Complex Urban Society* [New York City: Office of the Mayor, 1968]) presented recommendations for the education of Puerto Rican children, essentially a repetition of those made by *The Puerto Rican Study.* And in 1968, Aspira (an organization founded in 1961 by the Puerto Rican Forum to promote higher education for Puerto Ricans) convened a national conference of Puerto Ricans, Mexican-Americans, and educators on "The Special Educational Needs of Urban Puerto Rican Youth." The conference's published report (*Hemos Trabajado Bien* [New York: Aspira, 1968]), in its recommendations, reiterated most of those of *The Puerto Rican Study.* The Aspira conference also commissioned a report on Puerto Ricans and the public schools, Richard J. Margolis, *The Losers: A Report on Puerto Ricans and the Public Schools* (New York: Aspira, 1968). This brief report chronicles visits to sixteen schools in seven cities and "makes no explicit recommendations. Its purpose is to put the problem in sharper focus and on wider display, not to promote any single set of solutions." Margolis' report is a devastating indictment of those schools which neglected Puerto Rican children, and of programs which largely were encrusted with all the bitter abuses of the past: it appears inconceivable that the practices he describes could have been occurring a decade after the publication of *The Puerto Rican Study.*

non-English-speaking children; [27] and, in our view, the successful enactment of the Bilingual Education Act represented a movement away from the "ethnocentric illusion" in the United States that for a child born in this country English is not a foreign language, and virtually all instruction in schools must be through the medium of English; even more importantly, the Act was a national manifesto for cultural pluralism and bicultural education, and in this sense may prove the most socially significant educational legislation yet enacted.

The Act recognized "the special education needs of the large numbers of children of limited English speaking ability in the United States," and declared "it to be the policy of the United States to provide financial assistance to local educational agencies to develop and carry out new and imaginative elementary and secondary school programs designed to meet these special educational needs." The main priorities of the Act are the provision of equal educational opportunities for non-English-speaking children; the strengthening of educational programs for bilingual children; and the promotion of bilingualism among all students. A great number of programs have come into being as a result of the Act, and although the programs are of differing (and in some instances of dubious) quality, the programs affirm the practicability of meeting the needs of the non-English-speaking child. [28] Use of the principles and recommendations of *The Puerto Rican Study* would strengthen programs for Puerto Rican children, as even a casual examination would affirm.

The Realities of Program Implementation

In the last analysis, it is the *programs* which address themselves to the educational needs of the Puerto Rican child which must be evaluated with recommendations made for continuing improvement. The evaluation of the following particular program for Puerto Rican children in a large urban school district and the recommendations which were made for its improvement and expansion are, in themselves, instructive: they delineate the contemporary educational experience for the Puerto Rican child, and they point the way to further meeting the needs.

The recommendations which are subjoined derive from a study and evaluation of the educational programs for Puerto Rican students underway in the Jersey City (N.J.) school district in 1971-1972. [29] Over 5,000 Puerto Rican pupils (out of a total school register of some 38,000) were in the city's schools. The recommendations provide a profile of contemporary Puerto Rican educational experience (practice that leads itself to improvement), generally encountered on the mainland.

---

[27] See F. Cordasco, "The Challenge of the Non-English-Speaking Child in American Schools," *School & Society*, vol. 96 (March 30, 1968), pp. 198-201, which is an adaptation of testimony before the Committee on Education and Labor of the U.S. House of Representatives in support of the proposed Title VII (June 29, 1967); and for the history of the legislation, see F. Cordasco, "Educational Enlightenment Out of Texas: Toward Bilingualism," *Teachers College Record*, vol. 71 (May 1970), pp. 608-612; and F. Cordasco, "The Bilingual Education Act," *Phi Delta Kappan*, vol. 51 (October 1969), p. 75. The Bilingual Education Act, Title VII (P.L. 90-247; 20 U.S.C. 880b) authorized expenditure of $25 million in Fiscal 1971.

[28] For a list and description of some of the problems, see "Bilingualism," *The Center Forum*, vol. 4 September (1969), p. 20-26; and Vera P. John and Vivian M. Horner, op. cit., pp. 15-107.

[29] F. Cordasco and Eugene Bucchioni, *Education Programs for Puerto Rican Students: Evaluation and Recommendations* (Jersey City: Board of Education, 1971), pp. 27-37.

PROGRAM RECOMMENDATIONS

Elementary Level

1. The basic recommendation to be made for the elementary schools involves the establishment of functional bilingual programs wherever there are Puerto Rican students in attendance. The basic premise of bilingual education involves the use of Spanish to provide instruction in most curriculum areas when English is not the mother tongue of the children and when there is insufficient fluency in English to profit from school instruction in that language. Thus, for example, instruction in basic curriculum areas such as mathematics, social studies, etc., would be in Spanish. At the same time that instruction is given in the basic content areas in Spanish, an intensive program in the teaching of English as a second language must be conducted. As children develop greater fluency in English, additional instruction in the basic curriculum areas should be given in English. This approach would assist children in becoming equally fluent in both Spanish and English, and at the same time it would also assist children to develop the appropriate knowledges and skills in curriculum areas other than Spanish and English. Bilingual education should also provide for the teaching of Spanish as a second language for those children who are dominant in English. Such programs should begin in September 1972.

    At the present time in the bilingual classes in the Jersey City schools, this approach is not in widespread use. Teachers who speak Spanish are used for the most part to interpret what the English speaking teacher has said, and (as noted above) often at the same time, a practice resulting in considerable confusion. In addition, the practice of assigning two teachers to a room, one of whom functions as an interpreter, represents poor utilization of personnel, both educationally and financially.

2. The bilingual program recommended by the evaluators would also necessitate the regrouping of participating children more carefully. In addition to using the traditional criteria for grouping, in a bilingual education program it is necessary to develop parallel classes or sections of children who are dominant in either English or Spanish. In developing bilingual programs, however, it is essential that priority be given in class assignment to children who are dominant in Spanish, rather than to those dominant in English, because the greatest immediate need exists for children who are dominant in Spanish and who cannot derive as much educational value as possible from school programs conducted solely in English.

3. It is recommended that two schools [perhaps, Public School No. 16 in view of the very large number of Puerto Rican students in attendance] develop complete bilingual programs beginning with the kindergarten and including each grade in the school. In other schools, bilingual classes should be established as needed.

4. A committee on bilingual education at the elementary school level should be established immediately in order to plan for the development of bilingual programs in Public Schools Nos. 2 and 16, and in other schools of Jersey City where there are large Puerto Rican enrollments. The bilingual education committee will also give attention to the development of a bilingual curriculum encompassing the usual curriculum areas as well as the teaching

of English as a second language, and the history and culture of Puerto Rico as an integral part of the elementary school curriculum. The present Hispanic Culture Committee is a beginning; but it must deal with a Puerto Rican studies curriculum and only ancillarily with Hispanic cultures in general. Membership on the committee should include parents, teachers, principals and should also make provision for student input.

5. A city-wide Puerto Rican advisory council composed of parents, high school and college students and community leaders should be established. The advisory council can advise school officials on the needs, aspirations, sentiments and responses of the Puerto Rican community insofar as educational matters are concerned. The existence of a community advisory council will assist in making public schools with large numbers of Puerto Rican students "community schools," furnishing educational and other much needed services to the Puerto Rican community. Such an advisory council on a city-wide basis [and articulated with local advisory councils for specific schools] will provide much needed community participation in education in Jersey City for the Puerto Rican community.

6. Parochial schools with large numbers of Puerto Rican students should also participate in special programs funded with federal monies.

7. All communications from school officials to parents should be available in both English and Spanish.

8. Additional Puerto Rican personnel should be recruited for positions at all levels in the public schools including teachers, principals, school secretaries, a curriculum specialist, teacher aides, etc. Special attention should be turned immediately to the employment of a curriculum specialist in bilingual education.

9. At the present time, no city-wide coordinating effort involving existing bilingual programs is available in Jersey City. It is recommended, therefore, that a city-wide office at the level of coordinator for bilingual education be established. This office will have jurisdiction over planning, developing, implementing, supervising and evaluating all bilingual education programs, programs in the teaching of English as a second language, and other special service programs for Puerto Rican elementary school children and high school students. The office would also provide liaison with the Puerto Rican community.

10. Bilingual classes as envisaged in recommendation #1 should be made available in the Summer of 1972. [The period January 1972 to June 1972 should be used as a planning period for the bilingual programs to be established in the Summer and Fall of 1972].

11. It is recommended that provision be made for the establishment of a continuing consultancy in the implementation of the recommendations contained in this report. Consultants would work with school officials and members of the Puerto Rican community in the implementation of the recommendations and would assist in the development of other programs and special services that may be needed by the children of the Puerto Rican community.

12. Parent education programs conducted in both Spanish and English should be developed for the Puerto Rican community.

13. An in-service program for teachers and other school personnel should be developed as soon as possible. Current and past efforts in Jersey City in the areas of in-service courses include the offering of a course in "Teaching English as a Second Language" that was to be given in the 1970/71 school year, beginning in November, 1970 and a request to develop and finance an "In-Service Course Involving Philosophy, Approaches and Methodology of Bilingual Education," to be given during the 1971/72 school year. In-service efforts should be expanded, and should include both professionals participating directly in bilingual programs or English as a second language programs as well as other professionals in the Jersey City Public Schools who may not be participating in special programs for Puerto Rican children but who do work with Puerto Rican children in regular classes. Such an extensive in-service program might be developed and offered during the regular school year, or might be given as a special summer institute for participating personnel.

14. Greater numbers of Puerto Rican student teachers should be recruited from Jersey City State College. An expanded student-teaching "practicum" drawn from the cadres of Puerto Rican students at Jersey City State College represents an important source for recruiting larger numbers of Puerto Rican personnel for employment in the Jersey City Public Schools.

15. A continuing and expanded liaison between the Jersey City Public Schools and Jersey City State College is recommended. Here, an important beginning and model [Title VII, at School No. 16] has been provided by Professor Bloom and Jersey City State College personnel.

Secondary Level

1. The city-wide Community Advisory Council described in recommendations for elementary schools would also turn its attention to secondary education and make recommendations relevant to the educational needs of Puerto Rican high school students in Jersey City.

2. A testing and identification program should be developed at the secondary level. Such a program would attempt to identify Puerto Rican students in need of intensive instruction in English as a second language or in other important school subjects such as reading.

3. A special committee to deal with secondary education for Puerto Rican students should be established, with the membership drawn from teachers, principals, guidance personnel and other school professionals; and including parents and students from the Puerto Rican community. The committee should give special attention to the current basic offerings: industrial arts, college preparatory, business and general studies. It should consider ways of increasing the holding power of the secondary schools so that greater numbers of Puerto Rican students remain in high school and graduate.

4. Special work study programs for Puerto Rican students might be developed in connection with the basic offerings now available. Such work study programs could become a very significant phase of the industrial arts and business education programs, and should, consequently, carry high school credit.

5. An immediate attempt should be made to increase the number of Puerto Rican students in the college preparatory program. This can be done by teachers, guidance personnel and administrators. More information about current high school programs should be made available, and students should become familiar with the implications of selecting specific programs and the out-of-school consequences of enrollment in any given program. In addition, talent-search programs might be initiated to increase the number of Puerto Rican students entering college.

6. Secondary school teachers should participate in in-service programs dealing with the education of Puerto Rican students.

7. It is recommended that high school students having little fluency in English be given basic instruction in Spanish in the various classes required in the four curricula. Instruction in Spanish would be in addition to intensive instruction in reading, writing and speaking English as a second language. When high school students have achieved a sufficient degree of fluency in English, they may then receive all or most of their instruction in English. Bilingual education at the high school level at the present time is essential, and it is especially important when large numbers of students are dominant in Spanish rather than in English. It should be remembered that it was not possible to secure from school officials data concerning the number of Puerto Rican high school students dominant primarily in Spanish.

8. At present, a secondary school curriculum committee is working on a course of study in Puerto Rican history. The work of this committee should be accelerated and a course of study in Puerto Rican history and culture should be developed as rapidly as possible. The committee might then turn its attention to the development of a course of study dealing with the Puerto Rican experience on the mainland. At present, there are no student members of this committee. Students should be a significant and contributing part of this committee. Indeed, greater participation by high school students in the decisions affecting their school careers is vital, and it becomes especially crucial when there are large numbers of students dropping out of high school programs as is true for many Puerto Rican students.

9. The high schools should make available to all high school students without cost all special examinations such as the National Education Development Tests or the College Boards. Such examinations now require the payment of fees by candidates taking them. There may be many Puerto Rican and other students unable to take the examinations which require the payment of fees because of inability to afford the funds required.

10. The continuing consultancy referred to in recommendations for elementary schools should encompass secondary education as well as elementary education.

11. It is recommended that an experimental program involving independent study be instituted for those students who are considering leaving high school before graduation. This program would provide the opportunity for independent study under supervision, for which credit leading to a high school diploma would be given. Such a program would also provide for attendance in organized classes in the high schools, especially where remedial or advanced programs are required. Students would participate in developing their programs. Such supervised independent study programs could be

related to jobs which students leaving high school before graduation may have secured.

12. It is recommended that additional Puerto Rican personnel be recruited for employment in Jersey City secondary schools. The two Puerto Rican guidance counselors at Ferris High School are an important beginning.

These recommendations are, essentially, reaffirmations of the cogency of those made years earlier in *The Puerto Rican Study*. One cannot help but wonder how different meaningful educational opportunity for Puerto Rican children might have been had *The Puerto Rican Study* been implemented. In its cautions and admonitions, *The Puerto Rican Study* was prophetic: "A study, however good, never solves problems. At best it finds solutions that will work. To translate proposed measures into practice is the greater task. At the very best it will take three to five years to translate the proposals of *The Puerto Rican Study* into an effective program.... The real question is, how rapidly can the school system move?... There are thousands of Puerto Rican children in New York City schools who have been here two, three, four or more years and are still rated as language learners. The task is twofold—to salvage as many as possible of those currently retarded, and to reduce the numbers that thus far have been added annually to the list. The time to begin is now—a year gone from a child's life is gone forever." (p. 237)

BIBLIOGRAPHY OF SELECTED REFERENCES

I. *General Bibliographies*

[Cordasco, Francesco]. *The People of Puerto Rico: A Bibliography.* New York: New York Department of Labor, Migration Division, Commonwealth of Puerto Rico, 1968. Some 500 entries.

Cordasco, Francesco with Eugene Bucchioni and Diego Castellanos. *Puerto Ricans on the United States Mainland: A Bibliography of Reports, Texts, Critical Studies and Related Materials.* Totowa, New Jersey: Rowman & Littlefield, 1972. An annotated bibliography of 754 main entries dealing with bibliographical resources; the migration to the mainland; the island experience; conflict and acculturation on the mainland; education on the mainland; and social needs encompassing health, housing, employment, and other human needs.

Cordasco, Francesco and Leonard Covello. *Studies of Puerto Rican Children in American Schools: A Preliminary Bibliography.* New York: Department of Labor, Migration Division, Commonwealth of Puerto Rico, 1967. Some 450 entries. Also published in *Education Libraries Bulletin 31*, Institute of Education, University of London, Spring 1968, pp. 7-33; and in *Journal of Human Relations*, vol. 16 (1968), pp. 264-285.

Dossick, Jesse. *Doctoral Research on Puerto Rico and Puerto Ricans.* New York: New York University, School of Education, 1967. Dissertations completed at American mainland universities.

II. *General Studies*

Burma, John H. *Spanish-Speaking Groups in the United States.* Durham, N.C.: Duke University Press, 1954. Includes a sketch of "the Puerto Ricans in New York" (pp. 156-187). Burma assumes that there is a fundamental "unity of culture" among diverse groups put together because they speak the same language. In light of the widely differing historical backgrounds which have given rise to different cultures among Spanish-speaking groups the assumption does not seem valid.

Chenault, Lawrence. *The Puerto Rican Migrant in New York City.* New York: Columbia University Press, 1938. Reissued with a New Foreword by F. Cordasco. New York: Russell & Russell, 1970. The one book that puts together data available on the early movements to New York City of Puerto Rican migrants. Includes a discussion of the various ways these movements affect the established community and the migrants.

Cordasco, Francesco and David Alloway. "Spanish Speaking People in the United States: Some Research Constructs and Postulates," *International Migration Review,* vol. 4 (Spring 1970), pp. 76–79.

Fitzpatrick, Joseph P. *Puerto Rican Americans: The Meaning of Migration to the Mainland.* Englewood Cliffs, N.J.: Prentice Hall, 1971. An overview and trenchant study with materials on the dynamics of migration: the problem of identity; the family; problem of color; religion; education; welfare. See *New York Times,* September 12, 1971, p. 96.

Glazer, Nathan and Daniel P. Moynihan. "The Puerto Ricans." In *Beyond the Melting Pot: The Negroes, Puerto Ricans, Jews, Italians, and Irish of New York City,* 2nd ed., by Nathan Glazer and Daniel Moynihan. Cambridge: M.I.T. and Harvard University Press, 1970. Puerto Ricans in New York City are discussed in terms of who migrates to the United States; their relationship to the island of Puerto Rico; business, professional, labor opportunities, and average earnings in New York; and the effect of migration on the culture of the migrants. The Puerto Ricans are compared and contrasted with immigrant groups [1st ed., 1963]. The 2nd edition updates some of the material and includes a new introductory essay and analysis.

Lewis Oscar. *La Vida: A Puerto Rican Family in the Culture of Poverty—San Juan and New York.* New York: Random House, 1966. 669 pp. Begins with a long introduction which describes Lewis' methods, the setting, and the family involved in the study. A discussion of the theory of the "culture of poverty" is included. The rest of the book is the story of a Puerto Rican family, as told by the members of the nuclear family and some of their relatives and friends. See also Oscar Lewis, *A Study of Slum Culture: Backgrounds for La Vida.* New York: Random House, 1968. Provides the general background, data, and statistical frame of reference for *La Vida.*

Mills, C. Wright; Clarence Senior; and Rose Goldsen. *The Puerto Rican Journey: New York's Newest Migrant.* New York: Harper, 1950. Reissued, New York: Russell & Russell, 1969. A carefully researched field study of the Puerto Rican population in two core areas of New York City. The study was done in 1948 by a research team of the Bureau of Applied Social Research of Columbia University. Although many of its statistics are now out of date, the book deals with basic concepts, such as the factors in "adaptation," cultural and language differences, and their influence on the progress and problems of the migrants. Includes much data on the characteristics of the Puerto Ricans in the two core areas—family, age, sex, education, occupation, income, etc.

"[The] Puerto Rican Experience on the United States Mainland," *International Migration Review,* vol. II (Spring 1968). Entire issue devoted to a comprehensive account of the experience.

Puerto Rican Forum. *Puerto Rican Community Development Project.* New York: 1964. This report was developed as the basis for an antipoverty, economic opportunity project, and is subtitled "A Proposal for a Self-Help Project to Develop the Community by Strengthening the Family, Opening Opportunities for Youth and Making Full Use of Education." The forum is a private agency, with a professional and secretarial staff of New Yorkers of Puerto Rican background. It has received some financial support from foundations to develop its proposal. Thus the concern in this report is to highlight the problems—income, housing, education, family, etc.—that confront the Puerto Rican community in New York City, though not all of its population. Data are presented to support the thesis that Puerto Ricans generally are not well off and need to make much more rapid gains in a contemporary technical, urban society such as New York. As a Forum summary indicates, the report is advanced as a rationale for a project "which takes into consideration both the problems of poverty in New York City and the complex realities of the cultural community pattern of the Puerto Rican New Yorker." The report is not intended to be a rounded picture of the total Puerto Rican population in New York City. Read from the point of view of its purpose, it is an illuminating study.

Sexton, Patricia. *Spanish Harlem: Anatomy of Poverty.* New York: Harper & Row, 1965. Report by a sociologist who spent part of two years "getting acquainted" with East Harlem. Shows awareness that she is dealing with the pathologies of a minority of the area's population ("still, the majority of the people are self-supporting"). However, she does not gloss over the problems that confront many of the self-supporting, low-income urban dwellers. The book is informed by the important insight of the need for "the poor" to be involved in working out their destiny. See F. Cordasco. "Nights in the Gardens of East Harlem: Patricia Sexton's East Harlem," *Journal of Negro Education,* vol. 34 (Fall 1965), pp. 450–451; and F. Cordasco. "Spanish Harlem: The Anatomy of Poverty," *Phylon: The Atlanta Review of Race & Culture,* vol. 26 (Summer 1965), pp. 195–196.

III. *Education*

Anderson, Virginia. "Teaching English to Puerto Rican Pupils," *High Points* (March 1964), pp. 51–54.

"Bilingualism," *The Center Forum,* vol. 4 (September 1969). Entire issue is given to analysis of Title VII (Elementary and Secondary Education Act), programs and related matters. Includes an important annotated bibliography.

Bucchioni, Eugene. *A Sociological Analysis of the Functioning of Elementary Education for Puerto Rican Children in the New York City Public Schools.* Unpublished doctoral dissertation, New School for Social Research, 1965.

Cordasco, Francesco. "The Puerto Rican Child in the American School," American Sociological Association *Abstract of Papers,* 61st Annual Meeting (1966), pp. 23–24.

Cordasco, Francesco. "Puerto Rican Pupils and American Education," *School & Society,* vol. 95 (February 18, 1967), pp. 116–119. Also, with some change, in *Journal of Negro Education* (Spring 1967); and *Kansas Journal of Sociology,* vol. 2 (Spring 1966), pp. 59–65.

Cordasco, Francesco. "The Challenge of the Non-English Speaking Child in the American School," *School & Society,* vol. 96 (March 30, 1968), pp. 198–201. On the proposal for the enactment of the Bilingual Education Act (Title VII, Elementary and Secondary Education Act), with historical background.

Cordasco, Francesco. "Educational Pelagianism: The Schools and the Poor," *Teachers College Record,* vol. 69 (April 1968), pp. 705–709.

Cordasco, Francesco and Eugene Bucchioni. *The Puerto Rican Community of Newark, N.J.: An Educational Program for Its Children.* Newark: Board of Education, Summer 1970. A detailed report on the implementation of a program for Puerto Rican students.

Cordasco, Francesco and Eugene Bucchioni. *Education Programs for Puerto Rican Students.* [Jersey City Public Schools]. Jersey City: Board of Education, 1971. Evaluation and recommendations.

Cordasco, Francesco and Eugene Bucchioni. *Newark Bilingual Education Program, 1970–1971.* Newark: Board of Education, 1971. Evaluation report of a massive program for Puerto Rican students.

Cordasco, Francesco and Eugene Bucchioni. *The Puerto Rican Community and Its Children on the Mainland: A Sourcebook for Teachers, Social Workers and Other Professionals,* 2nd ed., Metuchen, N.J.: Scarecrow Press, 1972. "The original structuring of the text has been retained, and it is within this framework that new materials have been interpolated. New materials have been added to Part I (Aspects of Puerto Rican Culture) whose basic design is to afford a politico-cultural kaleidoscope of island life; to Part II (The Puerto Rican Family), bringing into clear focus the family's transition to mainland life; to Part III (The Puerto Rican Experience on the Mainland: Conflict and Acculturation), in bringing into sharp view the new politicization of the mainland experience; and to Part IV (The Puerto Rican Experience on the Mainland: Puerto Rican Children in North American Schools) in affording additional materials on bilingual education and in providing outlines for course content and staff-training. Appended to the bibliography are selected additional references." (Preface to the 2nd ed.)

Cordasco, Francesco and Eugene Bucchioni. "A Staff Institute for Teachers of Puerto Rican Students," *School & Society,* vol. 99 (May 1972).

Díaz, Manuel and Roland Cintrón. *School Integration and Quality Education.* New York: Puerto Rican Forum, 1964.

Hemos Trabajado Bien. A Report on the First National Conference of Puerto Ricans, Mexican-Americans and Educators on the Special Educational Needs of Puerto Rican Youth. New York: Aspira, 1968. Includes a series of recommendations.

John, Vera P. and Vivian M. Horner. *Early Childhood Bilingual Education.* New York: Modern Language Association, 1971. Invaluable. Includes a "Typology of Bilingual Education Models"; excellent documentation and bibliography.

Margolis, Richard J. *The Losers: A Report on Puerto Ricans and the Public Schools.* New York: Aspira, 1968. An important report on visits to a number of schools with description and evaluation of programs for Puerto Rican children.

Morrison, J. Cayce, Director. *The Puerto Rican Study: 1953–57.* New York: New York City Board of Education, 1958. Final report of the most complete study of the impact of Puerto Rican migration on the public schools of New York City, and how schools were affecting Puerto Rican children and their parents. Though sponsored by the New York City Board of Education, matching grant-in-aid of half a million dollars from the Fund for the Advancement of Eduation made the study possible. Specialized studies were done within the framework of the large-scale study. These smaller studies focused on the "socio-cultural adjustment" of the children and their parents, and digests are presented in final report. About a third of the book deals with the special non-English-speaking program developed by the city school system. Description of some of the methods and materials developed is included. Study discovered some unresolved problems in the areas of learning, effective grouping of pupils, staffing those schools with Puerto Rican children, and teacher education. Study led to many research and curriculum publications, and 23 major recommendations, all designed to achieve three purposes: ". . . [developing] better understanding of the children being taught, [relating] the teaching of English to the child's cultural-social adjustment, [improving] the integration of ethnic groups through the school's program" (p. 247). With respect to the children, the major conclusion is contained in the following statement: "The children of Puerto Rican background are exceedingly heterogeneous. This is true of their native intelligence, their prior schooling, their aptitude for learning English, and their scholastic ability . . ." (p. 239). Reprinted with an introductory essay by Francesco Cordasco. New York: Oriole Editions, 1972.

[Puerto Rican Children] "Education of Puerto Rican Children in New York City." *The Journal of Educational Sociology,* vol. 28 (December 1954), pp. 145–192. An important collection of articles.

U.S. Senate, Committee on Labor and Public Welfare, Special Sub-Committee on Bilingual Education. *Bilingual Eduation: Hearings.* 90th Congress, 1st session. Part 1, May 1967. Part 2, June 1967. On Title VII (Elementary and Secondary Education Act) which was enacted in 1968.

Francesco Cordasco

Spanish Speaking Children in American Schools

The agreement signed last year in Federal Court by the New York City Board of Education "to establish a major new program to improve the education of all Spanish-speaking pupils" explicitly acknowledges the unmet educational needs of Spanish-speaking children in American schools. Although the non-English speaking child comes to American classrooms with a multiplicity of tongues (e.g., French, Italian, Portuguese, Russian, and some 13 American Indian languages), the overwhelming number of N/E children are Spanish speaking.

Latest Census Bureau figures report about 10.8 million persons of Spanish origin in the United States, comprising nearly 5.2 percent of the nation's population. Persons of Mexican origin make up more than half of the Spanish group, with some 6.5 million persons; Puerto Ricans are next with more than 1.5 million, followed by Cubans with 689,000; and there are some 2 million other persons of Latin American origin.

The N/E child's educational problem begins with a rejection of his language, reaffirmed in the rejection of his culture and heritage of which his language is an extension. And it often results in his effective exclusion from the processes of education.

The U.S. Senate Select Committee on Equal Educational Opportunity (whose *Report* was published in 1972) concluded that "some of the most dramatic, wholesale failures of our public school systems occur among members of language minorities." Some examples of this failure were presented in testimony before the Committee:

In Boston, 62 percent of the Puerto Rican adults are illiterate in both English and Spanish.

In 87 New York City schools with Puerto Rican majorities, 85 percent are below grade level in reading and a third are 2 years below grade level.

In Chicago, Puerto Rican public school children are an average of 4 years behind in reading.

Spanish surnamed students in California leave the 12th grade 3-1/2 years behind, and in Illinois, 5 years behind.

Texas describes 40 percent of its Spanish-speaking citizens as functional illiterates.

Philadelphia's Puerto Rican dropout rate is 70 percent.

The average Chicano [Mexican] child in the Southwest drops out of school by the 7th year.

From *The International Migration Review*, vol. 9 (Fall 1975), pp. 379-382.

119

The Senate Select Committee was told that what was needed was to develop the N/E child's proficiency in communicative skills first through instruction in his native language, i.e., bilingual education, which, although its components are essentially undefined, is instruction in *two* languages, the use of both English and the child's mother tongue as media of instruction in the school's curriculum. Dr. Armando Martinez, Director of *Puente* [a Puerto Rican self-help group] in Boston, testified before the Senate Committee: "To think that a non-English speaking child can learn to read and write in a language that he cannot speak is totally unrealistic. To continue forcing on our children the triple disadvantage of having to learn to speak English—a period of 2 to 3 years—before learning to read or write . . . is unjust. The result of this practice kills whatever motivation the child brings to the classroom, and breeds in him a strong feeling of inadequacy."

With limited resources of their own, states and school districts have relied principally upon two Federal programs to try to meet the needs of the N/E child: Title VII of the Elementary and Secondary Education Act, known as the Bilingual Education Act, and the "English as a Second Language" (ESL) program funded under Title I of ESEA. Neither of these programs has been funded at a level which is adequate to even begin to meet the needs of N/E children. In FY 1975, New York City expects to receive some 9 million dollars under Title VII, ESEA.

At least four states (Illinois, Massachusetts, California, and New Jersey) have laws providing for special instruction for children who do not speak English, and the 1974 U.S. Supreme Court ruling in *Lau v. Nichols,* which required San Francisco schools to provide bilingual education to non-English speaking pupils (largely Chinese), will undoubtedly accelerate this trend.

The New York City Board of Education's new program to improve the education of "all Spanish-speaking pupils whose difficulties with English impede their learning" was begun in October, 1974, and is to be fully implemented throughout 1975. Aspira of New York, Inc., and Aspira of America, Inc. [Puerto Rican educational counseling groups] had brought a class-action suit which charged that the city school system failed to meet the needs of Spanish-speaking children, causing high truancy and dropout rates among Puerto Rican students. New York City Schools Chancellor Irving Anker said that 25,000 to 65,000 of the city's 1.1 million students would be involved in the new bilingual program. Victor Marrero, Chairman of the Puerto Rican Legal Defense and Education Fund, Inc., estimated the number of pupils to participate in the program at 40,000 to 100,000. Chancellor Anker noted that the city school system had received (1974–75) a supplemental allocation from the city of $11 million for bilingual education and that "even without the new program the system would have had to provide for the education of these youngsters."

According to the consent decree signed in Federal Court, the New York City Board of Education agreed:

> To devise "an improved method for identifying and classifying children who are Spanish-speaking or Spanish-surnamed according to their ability to speak, read, write and comprehend English and Spanish."

> To draw up a list of pilot schools that will offer the new bilingual program by October 30th, 1974. The program should start in these schools in February, 1975.

> To have implemented the full program by September, 1975 in all schools where children need the special program.

The program is being administered by the Board's recently created Office of Bilingual Education headed by Hernan La Fontaine, who had been principal of the first completely bilingual school in the history of New York City. This school [P.S. #25; District #7] was opened in September, 1968, largely as a result of the passage of the Bilingual Education Act in 1967. The bilingual educational program developed over the years at P.S. #25, itself enthusiastically supported by the Puerto Rican community, should, according to La Fontaine, furnish a model for the proposed citywide program.

The presently proposed program for the N/E child in New York City is the latest of a number of proposals which extend back to 1947 when "A Program of Education for Puerto Ricans in New York City" was officially approved by the Board of Education. In 1951 the "Mayor's Committee on Puerto Rican Affairs in New York City" issued a conspectus for educational reform; and in 1958 *The Puerto Rican Study,* a four-year million-dollar "Report on the Education and Adjustment of Puerto Rican Pupils in the Public Schools of the City of New York" was adopted and promptly forgotten. The issues were raised again in 1968 when Mayor John V. Lindsay convened a "Citywide Conference of the Puerto Rican Community." And in 1972 (when the Puerto Rican school dropout rate was New York City's worst—57 percent, compared with 46 percent for blacks and 29 percent for others), a major expansion of bilingual education was urged in a Board of Education study presented to the then School Chancellor Harvey B. Scribner, "to change the present conditions which are contributing to the failure of Puerto Rican children in the classroom."

The Federal Court consent decree "to improve the education of all Spanish-speaking pupils" will be monitored with cautious optimism both in and outside New York City.

Rolf Kjolseth

Bilingual Education Programs in the United States: For Assimilation or Pluralism?

Recent legislation[1] and financial support[2] for bilingual education programs in the United States are held by many to indicate a basic liberal breakaway from an earlier "language policy" and social context which successfully assimilated several waves of the most diverse immigrant groups into mainstream monolingual American society.

One often hears, especially from those who in one capacity or another are promoting these new programs, that they will favor cultural bilingualism and pluralism, that is, the democratic coexistence of ethnic and nonethnic groups.

This paper seeks to critically examine this thesis within a sociolinguistic perspective which, necessarily, considers the relevance and effects of bilingual programs upon language use beyond the school within the wider community.

However, an analysis of specific programs must first be prefaced by a few introductory remarks. These will touch upon the role of the school in community social change, sketch the concepts and method by which the analysis will proceed, and very briefly describe the social context of the communities in which these bilingual programs are embedded.

It would be a mistake to overestimate what any school can accomplish or to overvalue the significance of a student's performance if it is restricted only to the domain of the school itself. The school is only one domain in the life space of individuals and communities. Language cannot "live" there, although it may receive important impulses. The life of a language depends first and foremost upon its use[3] in other

---

[1] Federal legislation was enacted January 2, 1968, as Title VII of the Elementary and Secondary Education Act of 1965. The text of this law is reproduced by Andersson (1970, vol. 2, 1-6).

[2] Although forty-five million dollars was authorized for the first three fiscal years, actual appropriations, which are granted on a one-year basis, have been only half of that authorized. Fishman (1970) discusses the politics involved.

[3] Sociolinguistic research has clearly shown that there is no necessary, invariable, or universal correlation between *attitudes* toward a language (ethnolinguistics) and actual patterns of language *use* (dominance configuration) within a speech community. For an early treatment of language use patterns see Schmidt-Rohr (1933, 178-92). Landmann (1968) offers a fascinating historical account of a case (Yiddish) where negative attitudes concurred with increasing use of the ethnic language and vice versa. Nevertheless, there is presently and inordinate research emphasis upon attitudes which tacitly assumes them to be adequate indicators of language behavior.

This article is a revised version of a paper originally presented in the section on "Sociological Perspectives on Bilingual Education" of the Sociolinguistics Program at the Seventh World Congress of Sociology held in Varna, Bulgaria, September 14–19, 1970. Reprinted with permission.

domains. When a person has skills in two languages, this individual bilingualism, if it is to be stable, must be sustained by diglossic[4] norms of community language use (Fishman, 1967). Hence a bilingual program which fosters bilingual use outside the school and norms of stable and balanced diglossia is one which can be said to promote linguistic pluralism, whereas a program which restricts or inhibits bilingual use in other than school domains and erodes diglossic community norms is one which must be characterized as promoting linguistic assimilation.

In other words, a bilingual program's social effectiveness is seen in the school domain's qualitative and quantitative effect upon the *use* of each language in other community domains.

Hard evidence on varying programs' differential effects upon community language-use patterns must come from comparative empirical community research of diachronic shifts in the dominance configurations of specific groups. However, prior to this, a provisional and substitute route via secondary research can be used to cast some light on the question of the likely effects of bilingual programs as currently structured.

We can consider any bilingual program as being composed of a set of structural options resulting from basic policy decisions. I have considered a large set and selected a nonexclusive subset of some fifteen which appear most relevant[5] in terms of having a potential effect upon language use outside the school. Thus each of these options is held to be potentially relevant in affecting language use within the community either in the direction of ethnic language maintenance or shift depending upon whether or not the option is taken and/or how it is filled or operationalized.

To simplify this presentation, all the options judged likely to produce ethnic language shift can be collected into an ideal-typical and extreme "assimilation model" and all those options which tend to foster ethnic language maintenance into a polar "pluralistic model." These two models therefore represent two extremes on a continuum of possible structures of bilingual education programs.

However, before presenting the two models, a number of contextual restrictions are in order because it must be clear that no feature of a bilingual education program can be considered shift- or maintenance-fostering in and of itself. It is only within specific sociocultural contexts of great complexity that any program feature takes on relevance in one direction or the other.

Although these contextual features themselves merit an entire essay, I can only index a few here in order to suggest the frame of reference to which this analysis is restricted.

To speak of bilingual programs in the United States, the site of one of the most massive language shifts in world history while half the world's population is characterized by stable intragroup bilingualism (Macnamara, 1967), is to speak of quite a special case. Furthermore, I will restrict the context of my remarks to bilingual programs for Spanish-speaking Americans—the nation's largest foreign language

---

[4] "Diglossia," coined by Ferguson (1959) and expanded by Gumperz (1964b) and Fishman (1965, 1967, 1971) describes or characterizes a society wherein two or more language varieties are normatively employed, each for separate, complementary functions or domains. Diglossia is therefore a multilingual "opportunity structure" which sustains bilingualism in individuals who, as they move from a social context dominated by one language to another dominated by norms of appropriateness for a second language, will be constrained to switch idioms and so in the normal round of everyday life will use both languages and thereby naturally maintain their bilingualism through the only means possible—use.

[5] Gaarder (1967) discusses some of these program options, as does Mackey (1970).

minority and second largest ethnic minority[6]—with particular reference to Mexican Americans, or, as many more recently prefer to designate themselves, Chicanos.

This group's ancestors came as colonial conquerors in the sixteenth century and were in turn conquered in the nineteenth century.[7] Since then Mexican Americans have continued to grow in numbers through natural increase[8] and continuing immigration.[9] They are concentrated primarily in urban centers in five Southwestern states[10] and possess a rich folk culture.[11] The overwhelming majority are poor[12] ("lower-class"), politically powerless,[13] sharply discriminated against, and residentially segregated whether in urban or rural settings. Furthermore, Spanish is only a prestige idiom in the United States where there are irrelevant numbers of Spanish

---

[6] Estimates vary because the government has not included language items in its census questionnaires and has grouped Mexican Americans together with "whites." The Mexican American Population Commission of California places the number of "Americans of Hispanic origin" at 9.2 million as of 1971. "Hispanic origin" includes, in order of relative magnitude, Mexicans, Puerto Ricans, Cubans, and other Latin Americans. By conservative estimate (John and Horner, 1971, 2) there were over 4 million Mexican Americans in the United States by 1971. Fishman (1966, 42) estimates 3.4 million claimants of Spanish as their mother tongue in 1960.

[7] Don Juan de Onate arrived on the banks of the Rio Grande River on Ascension Day, 1598, claiming all the eye beheld for Spain (Steiner, 1969, 331-32). Mexican hegemony was broken by the war between Mexico and the United States in 1846, which United States General Ulysses S. Grant characterized as the "most unjust [war] ever waged by a stronger against a weaker nation." (Steiner, 1969, 362). As a consequence Mexico lost what has since become Texas, New Mexico, Arizona, and much of California, Nevada, Utah, and Colorado—an area comprising one-third of the United States (Steiner, 1969, 57).

[8] According to the 1960 U.S. census, the median age of Mexican Americans was 17 years and their high birth rate is reflected in 709 children under 5 years of age per 1,000 women age 15 to 49 (compared to 613 for Blacks and 455 for Anglos).

[9] The periods of largest immigration were 1920-29 (487,775) and 1955-64 (432,573). A number of factors such as the elimination of the "bracero" program (post 1965) and the extremely rapid mechanization and automation of all industries, including agricultural, has severely reduced job opportunities for the unskilled and has considerably reduced more recent immigration.

[10] The 1960 census estimates that 87.2% of the Mexican origin population lives in the Southwest: California 40.1%, Arizona 6.0%, Colorado 1.2%, New Mexico 2.0%, and Texas 37.9% (Loyo, 1969, 35). They are primarily urban dwellers: 85.4% in California and New Mexico, 69.3% in Arizona, and 78.6% in Texas (Steiner, 1969, 42).

[11] This oral culture is now beginning to be collected and published in the Chicano press, especially such periodicals as *Con Safos, La Raza,* and *El Grito.* Steiner (1969, 405-06) lists the addresses of twenty-six newspapers. Romano (1969) has recently edited a collection of native Chicano literature.

[12] Only 4.6% of the Mexican Americans were professionals (vs 15.1% for Anglos) according to the 1960 census. Taking all white-collar jobs together (professional, managerial, proprietors, sales, and clerical) 19% of the Mexican-American population held such positions vs 46.8% of the Anglos. Of all Spanish-surnamed families in the Southwest in 1960, 34.8% were estimated as living at or below the "poverty level," meaning their annual family income was less than $3,000 in 1959 (Loyo, 1969, 78).

[13] For example, although one million Mexicans and Mexican Americans live in Los Angeles, making it the third largest "Mexican" city in the world (after Mexico City and Guadalajara), districts have been so completely gerrymandered that they do not have a single representative on the City Council (Steiner, 1969, 188-89).

speakers. Where Spanish speakers are a relatively large group, it is an idiom held in considerable contempt.[14]

These few indicators only suggest some of the principal dimensions of the social context which must be kept in mind as we now consider first the pluralistic and then the assimilation models of bilingual education programs.

THE PLURALISTIC MODEL

This program is one initiated by a group of ethnic and nonethnic community leaders in consultation with teachers and school administrators who form a continuing committee to both advise and control the program's operation. The bilingual program is a social issue around which the ethnic community becomes politically mobilized. The program's administration provides reciprocal control between the school and the community. Its reception and development are thereby tied into community decision making and public opinion formation.

Before the program is actually begun, empirical research is conducted locally to ascertain: (1) the dominance configuration of the ethnic and nonethnic languages for several social categories of speakers in the community, (2) the linguistic features of the specific varieties of ethnic language spoken locally, and (3) the attitudes of various social categories of community residents toward both the local and nonlocal ethnic language varieties. These investigations thus provide locally valid information which is utilized in the planning of the program components such as: the selection of linguistic varieties to be included in the classroom repertoire, the choice of instructional materials, and the determination of teacher in-service training components. These investigations additionally provide baseline data for later diachronic evaluations of the program's effects upon community language and language-related variables of both a behavioral and attitudinal nature.

The teacher(s) and aides in the bilingual program are of local, ethnic origin, newly appointed to the program, and receive special training to develop their communicative competence in using local and regional ethnic varieties of language and culture, their knowledge of ethnolinguistics (partly based on the preprogram community research), mother-tongue instruction methods, and techniques for teaching English to speakers of other languages (TESOL).[15] The teachers live and are active in the local ethnic community and are members of the program's coordinating com-

---

[14] This might be formulated as "the Law of Anglo love of ethnic irrelevance," or the "Disneyland preference for symbolic ethnicity," i.e., the more locally irrelevant an ethnic language and culture is, the higher its social status, and the more viable it is locally, the lower its social status. Fishman (1966) has noted this attitude in the United States with respect to the most diverse ethnic languages and concluded that "as long as these languages and cultures are truly 'foreign' our schools are comfortable with them. But as soon as they are found in our own back yards, the schools deny them." This amounts to honoring the dead while burying the living.

[15] Gaarder (1970) implies the desirability of separate teachers for each language. However, such a division would exemplify for the pupils a complete contradiction of the program's verbally stated goal of fostering true biculturals and bilinguals. In such a program pupils are enjoined to become what the actions of their teachers and aides manifest as impossible. Actions speak louder than words. Rosenthal and Jacobson (1968) have carefully demonstrated the impact of such nonverbal messages on pupils and their motivations. Naturally teacher and aide training is a serious problem. Equally important is the question, "What kind of training in which linguistic varieties of each language and with what level of literacy for specific grade level positions?"

mittee. Their cultural and linguistic ideologies favor, and their behavior manifests, stable biculturalism and bilingualism. In summary, the teachers are effective bilingual and bicultural role models for their students.

The bilingual program is "two-way" with members of both the ethnic and nonethnic groups learning in their and the other's language (Stern, 1963) and classes are ethnically mixed (nonethnic on a voluntary basis) from the beginning, or, if initially segregated, they become mixed by the third or fourth grade (Gaarder, 1967).

Initially the medium of instruction is dual, using the local ethnic and core group's dialects[16] and both are presented by the same teacher. Each dialect receives equal time and equal treatment, initially through the presentation of a lesson in the student's strongest, or principal language variety, followed by presentation of the same materials in the second language variety, i.e., in the principal language variety of the nonethnic children.[17] Later, when students have a better command of the second language variety, the class may alternate from one to the other without doubling or repeating the same materials in the other. Physical education and play periods permit the use of all language varieties. Some programs may later develop towards using the two linguistic varieties for separate but essential and socially significant subject areas without relegating either to unimportant purposes. Gradually the two standard varieties (ethnic and nonethnic) are introduced but never completely supplant some use of the dialects[18] and do not disturb the overall ethnic to nonethnic language balance. The development trend of the program, which lasts a minimum of nine years, is toward maintenance of both languages, i.e., all four varieties.[19]

---

[16] This option for beginning instruction in the medium of locally normative language varieties is predicated on the dictum that "language teaching should be based on the resources that the child brings to the classroom" (Labov, 1971, 55). The American Association of Teachers of Spanish and Portuguese has recently recommended that "Especially in the case of learners whose dialect differs markedly from world standard (Spanish), the first weeks, months—in some cases, the entire first year—should focus patiently on developing their self-confidence as speakers and writers and readers of their *own kind* of Spanish" (Gaarder, 1971, 5, emphasis in original). Note however that the everyday term "dialect"—as opposed to the sociolinguistic term "language variety"—always contains sociocultural and political judgments (Fishman, 1972). Hence social conflicts often become manifest in decisions about whether or not a particular language variety is to be considered a "dialect" or not. It is a curiosity that Gaarder (1971) includes Barker (1971) in his references as she opens her book with a scathing condemnation of Pachuco Spanish—a widespread ethnic language variety spoken in the Southwest. Careful empirical research on intralanguage varieties and their educational significance has been conducted by Labov (1966), Stewart (1965, 1969), Dillard (1969), and Baratz and Shuy (1966) among others. Much of this work has focused on the varieties of English spoken by Blacks. Gumperz (1970a and 1970b, 1969a) has pioneered work on Chicano speech involving rapid Spanish/English switching and Kjolseth et al. (in preparation) are presently analyzing the grammar and social functions of such speech. Rayfield (1970) has analyzed similar switching patterns involving Yiddish and English.

[17] This is intended to facilitate the ethnic child's acquisition of a variety of the nonethnic language which is *appropriate* (Hymes, 1966, 22-23) in local peer level communication. Thus both ethnic and nonethnic pupils initially add a language variety to their linguistic repertoires which is appropriate for local communication with their outgroup peers, thereby favoring second language *use* by members of both groups in intergroup conversation outside the classroom.

[18] One place where "dialects" have an unquestionably appropriate place in classroom activities at all grade levels is that of creative writing, especially about relevant sociocultural topics.

[19] Of course, as the pupil progresses, new stylistic levels in both languages (informal, careful, formal, ceremonial) are added to the classroom repertoire.

The content of the bilingual curriculum stimulates ethnic community language-planning efforts and includes considerable attention to the local and regional cultures of both the ethnic and core groups in such a way as to provide a natural context for alternate use of both dialect and standard varieties. The results of research on local attitudes toward language varieties, their speakers, and bilingualism,[20] as well as information on vocational opportunities in education, industry, commerce, and government requiring or facilitated by bilingualism are presented first indirectly, and later directly.[21]

Demonstration classes are held for parents from all groups to promote understanding of the bilingual program and its methods as well as to encourage interest in a parallel program of bilingual adult education. In general the adult program is organized in ways analogous to that of the students but with materials adjusted to the age group: ethnically mixed classes, dual medium with equal time and treatment of the language varieties, an early emphasis on dialects, preferably the same teacher and similar content areas as in the children's program, information on bilingual vocational counseling, and local attitudes toward language varieties and their speakers.

A number of extracurricular activities involve both parents and children from both groups; for example, a lending library might be established with a variety of materials such as comics, magazines, newspapers, and books for a spectrum of interests, social-class levels, and age groups.

A series of public lectures and articles in local newspapers give information on the range of school and school-related programs, their rationale, organization, evaluation, and progress. Emphasis is placed on the program's interest in cultivating local varieties of language and culture for all groups. The community board of the bilingual program acts as the central controlling and coordinating body for this set of bilingual-bicultural activities in, near, and outside the school.

Evaluative research on the program considers not only changes in individual language skills and attitudes (as well as the traditional measures of academic achievement) but also tests for (sub-) *group qualitative and quantitative measures of the frequency of use of different language varieties in domains outside the school.* The emphasis is sociolinguistic.

The most important dimensions of the pluralistic bilingual program can be briefly summarized:

1. This program acts as a continuing stimulus to civic development and organization within the ethnic community and encourages a democratic forum for the resolution of conflicts and differing interests within and between the ethnic and nonethnic communities.

2. The teaching personnel are, on ascriptive, achieved, and behavioral grounds, credible exemplifications for ethnic and nonethnic students and parents of successfully operative bilinguals and biculturals.

3. Paralleling the composition of administrative control with its egalitarian distribution of power among diverse community interest groups, the linguistic and cultural content of the pluralistic program might be metaphorically

---

[20] A clear understanding of the content and social basis for local prejudices against different language varieties and their speakers is essential for "nondefensive cultural self-defense."

[21] Much more attention needs to be paid to presently nonexistent occupational categories which are, however, necessary in meeting the needs of the local ethnic community's majority.

characterized as "horizontally" articulated, emphasizing the complementarity of different varieties of situationally appropriate culture and language. This along with an increased awareness of ethnolinguistics encourages the student to become active in a variety of settings, use a number of linguistic varieties, and become experienced in switching between them. Language skills and cultural perspectives are added without progressively destroying his home language and culture. Furthermore, these developments take place in *both* groups. The success or failure of this program is most penetratingly indicated by the degree to which it encourages, engenders, and insures norms of appropriateness for non-English language varieties in community domains other than the school.[22]

THE ASSIMILATION MODEL

This bilingual program is initiated by the school without any community-based advanced planning. If a school-community advisory group is formed, it is without real powers to control the program. Community "involvement"[23] is encouraged and community control is avoided.

The teacher is either a nonethnic or, if a member of the ethnic group, one who lives in a nonethnic residential area and is either generally inactive in ethnic community affairs or active only in conservative elitist ethnic organizations and causes whose concerns and interests are distant from those which represent and speak to the basic everyday problems of the local ethnic majority. Transferred from some other class already within the school, this teacher will nevertheless have received some special in-service linguistic and cultural training for the position. This will not have included any significant concern for local ethnic culture, local language varieties (especially his or her competence in its *use*), or ethnolinguistics, but will have centered almost exclusively upon teaching a standard variety[24] of the ethnic language as a

---

[22] Any program's goals are reflected in three principal places: (1) the program's *statement* of goals, (2) the program's *structure* or design options, and (3) the teleology, hypotheses, and *research emphasis* of the program's evaluative component. The first is the weakest of the three as an indicator of what the program is, in fact, striving for.

[23] "Community involvement" is presently a popular euphemism which veils nonreciprocal rights between professionals who "serve" and the laity who are "served." Lay members opine and recommend while professionals decide and execute. "Involvement" is a well-known management technique long used in industry and designed to give those most directly affected by policy the feeling of influence rather than real influence itself. The U.S. Office of Education's Title VII Manual (USOE, 1970, 31–34, and Andersson, 1970, vol. 2, 7–20) *requires* community "involvement" and fails to make any recommendation concerning community control. It is interesting to note that only two existing programs funded by the federal government have anything like clear community control features built into them: Coral Way and Rough Rock (John and Horner, 1971, 28–31 and 17–20 respectively). Each is also unique in another, perhaps very relevant way. Coral Way serves a community whose ethnic members are primarily "middle-class," i.e., close in social status to the educational professionals. Rough Rock on the other hand serves an exclusively Navajo community which is geographically very isolated from any nonethnic communities. For these reasons, neither provides a very relevant example because most programs are located in urban areas with a high concentration of "lower" class ethnics. Much more exemplary for having some community control features and a strong bilingual curriculum are Public Schools 25 and 155 in New York City (John and Horner, 1971, 52–56).

[24] This standard variety may be careful or formal "middle-class" Mexico City Spanish, "world Spanish" (Gaarder, 1971), or even academic Castilian Spanish. All are likely to be related to, but very

mother tongue (and as a medium of instruction) and the language's "high" culture. The teacher's attitudes with respect to language tend to be exclusive and purist, viewing "interference," whether from the ethnic dialect or English, as a major "problem" and local dialect as categorically improper and "incorrect." [25] Biculturalism of "high" culture and bilingualism of the "proper" variety are held to be worthy goals attainable only with great effort by his students, who are held to suffer from "cultural deprivation." [26]

---

distant from the locally appropriate and most frequently used ethnic language varieties of the Chicano community where a federally funded program is located, especially as the law requires demonstrating a concentration of ethnic families with annual family incomes below $3,000!

At a bilingual school in southern California in 1971 this writer was informed by a bilingual aide, who lived in the Mexican-American barrio, that she and the other first grade aides "envied" the "more correct" Spanish of the master teacher, who does not live in the barrio. One of the first grade readers being used (published in Madrid) was found to contain many vocabulary items (four on one particular page) which a "middle-class" Mexican college graduate would not understand. The master teacher admitted having had to look up these terms in her dictionary—also published in Madrid. The terms were nevertheless justified as "better Spanish" although they are obviously inappropriate in any natural speech setting locally.

It should be added that we are notoriously ignorant about what actually happens in classroom interaction and what language varieties are actually included in the classroom repertoire. Lewis (1970) offers a seminal exploratory study of problems of cross-cultural communication between teachers and students.

[25] The "high/low" metaphor in popular usage characterizing linguistic and cultural varieties as well as social classes is, unfortunately, often uncritically adopted into the working vocabulary of social science. As Goudsblom (1970) shows, "high" systematically implies "better," "freer," and "stronger." Descriptively it would be more responsible and useful to identify language *varieties* and conceive of them sequentially in the order learned.

The purist approach might be characterized as a kind of cultural and linguistic imperialism, for it posits a single variety (of language or culture) as "correct" for all domains. Other varieties are felt to be in *competition* with the one they seek to impart in the school. These other varieties are a "problem." Herndon (1969, 9) conveys the feeling of teachers toward such phenomena, noting that it is "something which happens all the time . . . but which isn't supposed to happen. A problem. You were supposed to believe in, and work toward, its nonexistence." Rather than *adding* a linguistic variety to the child's repertoire (Gumperz, 1964a and 1964b; 1965; and 1969b and 1969c), it is felt that the school-approved "high" variety should *replace* the child's "low" variety. Steiner (1969, 212–15) refers to this as "de-education," i.e., the belief that the "lower-class" Mexican-American child "has to be de-educated before he can be re-educated," and adds that currently in the United States, "the de-education of La Raza is indeed overachieved."

Sociolinguistic factors underlie these pervasive purist beliefs. Labov (1971, 52) points out that "in a number of sociolinguistic studies it has been found that women are more sensitive to prestige forms than men—in formal style [. . .] and teachers in the early grades are women, largely from the lower middle class. This is the group which shows the most extreme form of linguistic insecurity, with the sharpest slope of style shifting."

[26] Labov (1971, 65) has affirmed that, "linguists . . . without a single dissenting voice . . . concur that this [cultural or verbal deprivation] is a superficial and erroneous interpretation of the very data presented in support of it." Nevertheless, this brutal term of sociocultural coercion has become very popular among educators. "Middle-class" ignorance of "lower-class" culture and language is rarely recognized. This is hardly surprising in view of the nonreciprocal power relations (see footnote 23 above) between the groups involved. To this one can add the ethnolinguistic fact (Wolff, 1964) that many teachers *will not,* and so *cannot,* comprehend a linguistic or cultural variety which they hold to be "inferior" and "reprehensible." Hymes (1966, 34) has suggested the need for a conference on the "cultural deprivation" of "middle-class" teachers while noting its unlikelihood. Finally, economic deprivation is frequently (and conveniently) equated with "cultural deprivation."

The end result of these factors is a kind of "educational colonialism" with the "priests of education" busily "civilizing the savages."

The program is one-way with classes only for ethnic students. It is held that there is no reason for nonethnics to participate, or, if they do, that one must bend to the insufficient interest or ingrained prejudices of nonethnics and their parents.

The program, which lasts a maximum of three years, may begin with either the ethnic standard as a single medium, or with the ethnic and nonethnic standards as dual mediums of instruction. However, as rapidly as is pragmatically deemed possible, the time and treatment of the nonethnic standard is increased so that within a relatively short period of time the ethnic standard is used only for limited, nonessential subjects. Insofar as reading or writing skills in the ethnic standard are taught, it is the minimum considered necessary for establishing the base skills for their transfer to the nonethnic standard. Basically the developmental trend in all the program's features is towards rapid and near complete transfer to the nonethnic standard. The school's policy is essentially a "burnt bridges" approach: the ethnic language is seen only as a bridge to the nonethnic language—one to be crossed as rapidly as possible and then destroyed, at least as a legitimate medium of general instruction, although some voluntary classes in it as a foreign language may be maintained.

Apart from some early consideration of distant, ethnic-related culture,[27] the content of the curriculum emphasizes nonethnic, non-"lower class" interests and values. Ethnolinguistic matters are conspicuous by their absence and bilingual vocational counseling, if included, focuses upon traditionally stylized nonethnic characterizations of vocations, the exercise of which have been either antithetical or irrelevant to the existent culture of the ethnic majority, e.g., teaching, academic research, diplomacy, and positions with large supranational corporations.

Demonstration classes and public lectures may be held for ethnic parents in order to convince them of the value of the program and to interest them in an adult education program.

If an adult bilingual education program is offered, its structure is in most ways similar to the children's program. Its goal is functional literacy in the nonethnic standard via the ethnic standard if necessary. Almost all effort is focused upon English as a second language (ESL) component.

Extracurricular activities, whether recreational or more serious, for young or old or both, tend to radiate a "high" and distant, ethnic-related culture.

Evaluation of the assimilation program is primarily focused upon testing the *quality of individual performances within the school setting* on a host of skill, aptitude, and attitude measures. The bias is narrowly academic, linguistic, and psychological.[28]

Summarizing the essential dimensions of the assimilation program we see that:

1. Because originated from "above" by elites and administered in taken-for-granted, traditional ways by nonethnic and supraethnic interests and forces, this program is likely to discourage ethnic community organization among the

---

[27] Emphasis is thus on "symbolic ethnicity" rather than upon existentially persistent traditions. See also footnote 14 above.

[28] Some examples in each area are: *academic;* frequency of disciplinary problems, absenteeism, dropout rates, and academic achievement scores in all subject areas, *linguistic;* word recall, translation, and sentence-completion performance measures as well as tests for phonological, morphological, and syntactic "interference," *psychological;* attitudinal, interest, and "intelligence" test scores, etc. "Interference" and "intelligence" merit being enclosed in quotation marks in the opinion of this writer because, although originally developed in social science as neutral terms, they have both come to be frequently *used* by the educational establishment as symbolic justifications for crude and iniquitous methods of social control.

large majority and to stifle open appraisal of intragroup and intergroup conflicts.

2. The teacher exemplifies the ability of elite members of dominant cultures to
   master and propagate a "superior" brand of ethnic culture and language.[29]
3. The linguistic and cultural content of the assimilation program is
   metaphorically a "vertically" articulated one implying power and hegemony.
   It emphasizes the superiority or inferiority of different varieties of language
   and culture and encourages restricting use to correct forms of school-approved
   varieties in all domains of usage. This may be successful in alienating the
   student from the ethnic language and culture of his home and community if
   there are few or no extraschool domains where the careful "middle-class"
   standard ethnic variety is appropriate. Preexistent stereotypes on varieties of
   language and culture, their speakers and carriers, held by youth and adults in
   both groups are unaltered or reinforced by these and other measures such as
   newspaper articles which describe the bilingual program as bringing "cultural
   enrichment" and a literate standard language to the "culturally deprived" and
   illiterate.

ANALYSIS

Which of these models do current bilingual programs approximate? To answer
this question we now turn to the materials on bilingualism available through the
Educational Resources Information Center (ERIC, 1969) of the U.S. Office of
Education (USOE) in order to examine the available reports and weigh their relevant
structural features in terms of the two polar models.

This procedure presents two problems. First this file contains a collection of
reports on programs existing in 1969 but cannot be taken to constitute anything like a
representative sample of all bilingual educational efforts. A second drawback in using
these materials is that reports currently present great problems of comparability
because there is no adherence to even a minimal set of reporting categories such as
numbers of hours of instruction in each language, or materials taught in each
language. In order to make such reports more useful for secondary analyses, the
USOE should develop and sanction adherence to minimal reporting criteria such as
the National Institute of Mental Health has encouraged with its program of model
reporting areas for mental health statistics. This is an urgent need.[30]

Nevertheless, in spite of these two methodological problems inherent in the data
used here, the results of this secondary analysis reveal such an overwhelmingly clear
and one-sided trend that we can assume it gives us a picture of what kinds of bilingual
education programs are currently multiplying in the United States.

---

[29] Because pupils may more easily identify with an ethnic teacher, they may be even more effective than
nonethnic teachers in implanting in the pupils a sense of shame and inferiority with respect to the local
varieties of ethnic language and culture. Steiner (1969, 176–77) quotes one barrio leader as observing, "no
one is more frightened, smug, and conservative, and harder on our people, than the typical schoolteacher
... who has escaped from the barrios in a two-car port and a king-sized bed." Thus, for many, social
mobility is up-and-*out* of the barrio. One's distance from the barrio is signaled geographically (suburbia),
culturally ("high" ethnic culture), and linguistically ("correct" Spanish). In view of this it should be clear
that local control and ethnic teachers are in themselves no panacea of guarantee of a pluralistic program.
See also footnote 25 above.

[30] Mackey (1970, 80–82) has proposed a useful questionnaire which is an important step in the needed
direction.

The finding is that *the great majority of bilingual programs (well over 80 percent) closely approximate the extreme of the assimilation model,* while the remaining few are only moderately pluralistic.

Thus, in direct contradiction to the usual program's statement of goals, the structure of "typical" programs can be expected to foster not the maintenance but rather the accelerated demise of the ethnic mother tongue.

This is to say that in most cases the ethnic language is being exploited rather than cultivated—weaning the pupil away from his mother tongue through the transitional use of a variety of his mother tongue in what amounts to a kind of cultural and linguistic "counterinsurgency" policy on the part of the schools. A variety of the ethnic language is being used as a new means to an old end. The traditional policy of "Speak Only English" is amended to "We *Will* Speak Only English—just as soon as possible and even sooner and more completely, if we begin with a variety of the ethnic language rather than only English!"

In light of this, the benefits to the ethnic language and culture optimistically supposed by many to be somehow inherent in any bilingual education program become suspect as one realizes that some (and today most) types of bilingual programs may achieve much more effectively what the earlier monolingual policy could not do.

The appearance of bilingual programs does indeed represent a new policy, but as currently structured, most seem designed as a change from an earlier policy of simple repression to a more "modern" and sophisticated policy of linguistic counterinsurgency.

I do not suggest however that those directly involved in bilingual programs consciously intend these consequences; most are undoubtedly dedicated and well-intentioned.

The relevant issue today is not simply monolingual vs bilingual education, but more essentially what *social* goals will serve the needs of the *majority* of ethnic group members and what *integrated set* of program design features will effectively realize them. Currently most programs are patchwork affairs, each searching for some distinctive gimmick and focusing its rhetoric and design toward the individual pupil in isolation from his family, peers, neighborhood, and community.

If this evaluation seems harsh, it may be important to the reader to know that since the above analysis of the ERIC data and its conclusion that most bilingual programs strongly foster assimilation and language shift, three important studies reviewing an even larger number of programs, many of which were more recently initiated, have all come to a similar conclusion.

For example, Gaarder (1970) has analyzed the official USOE program descriptions of all seventy-six bilingual education projects federally funded in the first year of Title VII operation and polled all project directors. He notes that "the disparity between aims and means is enormous," adds that "only six aim eventually to provide bilingual schooling at all grade levels, 1–12," and concludes, "'bilingual education'... can serve the ends of either [Anglo] ethnocentrism or cultural pluralism."

The same trend again becomes clearly evident as one reads the many program descriptions reproduced by John and Horner (1971, 15–100) and Andersson and Boyer (1970, vol. 2, 241–91). John and Horner (p. 187) conclude with a warning: "Educational innovations will remain of passing interest and little significance without the recognition that education is a social process. If the school remains alien to the values and needs of the community, if it is bureaucratically run, then the children will not receive the education they are entitled to, no matter what language they are taught in."

More recently Andersson (1971, 24–25), after noting a steady decline in the number of proposals for bilingual education programs received by the U.S. Office of Education (315 for 1970, 195 for 1971, and 150 for 1972), concludes that, "the obstacles to success are indeed formidable. Perhaps the greatest of these is the doubt in many communities that the maintenance of non-English languages is desirable."

Yet exactly this pervasive doubt that ethnic language maintenance is desirable might be an important reason for promoting more *assimilation* programs.

Again the more basic issue is, "*What type* of bilingual programs?"

All this is not even surprising when one considers that the assimilation program is essentially an expression of the present social structures of most United States communities with sizable ethnic populations. The school has always been an institution representative of the powerful community interest groups and their mainstream beliefs. The majority of Chicanos simply do not at present have either the sociopolitical power or the detailed and clear policy on language and culture necessary for their indigenous varieties of language and culture to be recognized in an institution for social *control* such as the school, which in all societies is one of the traditional sites where the results of overt and covert sociopolitical and cultural conflicts are operationalized in what, in English, we somewhat euphemistically call "school policies," rather than "cultural politics."

The difference between "policies" and "politics" is no idle matter of just words, but a consequential distinction implying two completely different modes of distributing power. "Policies" are generally understood to represent decisions appropriately made by professionals—in this case educators, administrators, and researchers. "Politics," however, directly implies the appropriateness of rights of influence and control (not just "involvement") in the decision-making process for lay or nonprofessional constituencies, especially those most directly affected—in this case the parents and children of the ethnic majority within the Chicano community.

To the typical Southwestern nonethnic American, the pluralistic program for Chicanos must sound radical, for it seems to him to assume a host of factors which his social upbringing has taught him are absent. Where is the ethnic community ideology, interest, and consensus necessary for promoting an ethnic-based bilingualism and biculturalism? Where are there ethnics with the prerequisite basic training needed for recruitment into such a program? How can an "illiterate dialect" be considered appropriate for use in the school? What culture does a "culturally deprived" group have worthy of inclusion in an academic program? And many ethnic members, especially those of the elite, have adopted these same views, which makes even more understandable the tendency to propose only "high" cultural and linguistic varieties as acceptable for a program proposal.

Indeed the pluralistic program *is* one which in many ways runs against the tide and almost appears to present a dilemma.

If the assimilation program is an expression of the status quo social structures, the pluralistic program is an expression of planned social change, and its introduction itself presupposes some basic social changes in intraethnic ideologies and power relations.

Fishman and Lovas (1970, 215) have suggested that "bilingual education in the United States currently suffers from three serious lacks: a lack of funds (Title VII is pitifully starved), a lack of personnel (there is almost no optimally trained personnel in this field), and a lack of evaluative programs (curricula, material, methods)."

Realizing that these are real problems, let us nevertheless assume that more money, trained personnel, and evaluative programs *are* forthcoming in the future. Will this assure any change away from the community demise of the ethnic language?

This question lends greater weight to the principal concern of Fishman and Lovas, who emphasize that most needed is greater sociological understanding of the social consequences of bilingual programs.

While one cannot predict the types of bilingual education programs which are likely to appear should more funds, personnel, and materials become available, there would appear to be a strong possibility that the result will not be pluralistic programs. One possibility is of course the proliferation of more numerous assimilation programs.

However, some changes may also be expected. Because the progressive phasing out of the ethnic language as a medium of instruction, or what Mackey (1970) calls a "transfer" curriculum, clearly achieves language shift *within* the school domain, and because a program in which the ethnic language continues to have a role as a medium of instruction throughout the progressive grades (a "maintenance" curriculum) obviously realizes ethnic-language maintenance *within* the school domain, many influential proponents of bilingual education are coming to recognize the exploitation of the ethnic language inherent in the transfer curriculum and are advocating the institution of more maintenance curricula.

No sociological acumen is required to see this much.

However, if planners of new programs focus almost exclusively upon the "time and treatment" curriculum issue, the following may easily happen: one begins with what is essentially a near ideal-typical assimilation program (which includes a school transfer curriculum) and inserts in its place a maintenance curriculum while retaining all the other features of the model. Such a change would be from a transfer-assimilation to a maintenance-assimilation program.

To call it a maintenance-assimilation program implies a contradiction, namely, that while realizing ethnic language maintenance within the school, it simultaneously promotes ethnic language shift within the community.

Is such a result possible? I would hypothesize not only that it is, but that there are sociological reasons for expecting that in certain social contexts, a maintenance-assimilation program may be an even *more* potent, albeit less visible, instrument of linguistic counterinsurgency than the transfer-assimilation method.

A few reasons for such a possibility can be most concisely suggested by a schematic outline of postulates, assumptions, and hypotheses which, it is recognized, can only be confirmed or refuted by future empirical research. (It should be clear that in my opinion most of the following hypothetical consequences are considered undesirable.)

The basic question is, "What are the diachronic effects of the maintenance-assimilation program on the local community dominance configuration?"

Postulate 1: Significant types of language shift may remain veiled unless in addition to the distinction between the ethnic and the nonethnic languages, intraethnic language varieties are differentiated. For purposes of this discussion only two varieties will be distinguished: the informal local ethnic language variety (ELV_L) vs. a supranational world (Gaarder, 1971) ethnic language variety (ELV_W).

Postulate 2: A speaker will view his stronger language in a more differentiated manner than he will his weaker language. That is, members of the ethnic speech community will be more aware of, and sensitive to, differential competence in their command of distinct *intra*ethnic language varieties than they will be to either their differential *inter*language (ethnic vs. nonethnic), or nonethnic *intra*language competence. For example, a member of the ethnic majority who is confident in his command of an informal ethnic language variety may, when faced with a situation requiring "correct" usage (ELV_W), become painfully aware of his felt inability and therefore opt to switch into the variety of the nonethnic language which he commands, although, for a native speaker of the nonethnic language this variety may be felt to be far from formal. However, if fellow ethnic community members constitute his audience (see assumption 2 below), such an interlanguage switch may be accepted as "more formal" than an intraethnic language variety switch because they hold similar norms highly differentiating varieties of their mother tongue and stereotyping the second language.

Assumptions:

1. The maintenance-assimilation program emphasizes ELV_W exclusively, i.e., either excludes ELV_L from the classroom repertoire completely or only tolerates it passively, e.g., the teacher does not overtly chastise a child for using ELV_L but will never use it herself.

2. The ethnic community is vertically stratified into a large "lower-class" majority and a small "middle-class" minority. Both tend to be residentially segregated from each other and from the nonethnic population—the majority more so than the minority.

3. The ethnic majority has broad competence in ELV_L and very limited competence in ELV_W, while the ethnic minority has more competence in ELV_W than in ELV_L.

4. Subjectively both the ethnic majority and minority sharply distinguish ELV_L from ELV_W.

5. Most members of the ethnic majority uncritically accept the ethnic minority's cultural and linguistic norms and their ethnolinguistic beliefs which characterize ELV_L as "low" "inexpressive," "incorrect," etc., and the ELV_W as "high," "eloquent," "correct," etc.[31]

Hypothesis 1: The maintenance-assimilation program will tend to *increase the use of ELVW* in those community domains which: (a) play a secondary role in the ethnic majority's everyday communication networks, (b) fulfill formal and ceremonial functions, or (c) tend to be governed by channel constraints or nonreciprocal rights firmly establishing one group as predominantly senders and another as predominantly receivers,[32] i.e., are domains which tend to be controlled by the minority elite and assign a passive-receptive role to the majority. Some examples of such domains would be the formal parts of festive, ceremonial, and political gatherings, and mass media such as radio, television, and newspapers.

Hypothesis 2: The maintenance-assimilation program will tend to *decrease the use of ELVL* in those community domains which: (a) play a primary role in the everyday communication networks of the ethnic majority, (b) fulfill intimate, casual, and informal functions, or (c) are governed by reciprocal rights of participants, so that all persons involved engage in the productive and receptive use of language which is mutually controlled by the partners to the speech event.

---

[31] There is an impressive array of supporting evidence for assumptions 4 and 5. Only a few examples can be given here. Alvarez (1967) calls Spanish "calo" a "snarl language." See also Barker (1971) and footnote 16 above. Even Haugen (1962) has characterized a number of normative dialect forms as "pathological."

[32] These terms are taken from Hymes (1964) paradigm of speech events.

Hypothesis 3: The maintenance-assimilation program will tend to *decrease the overall use of ethnic language vis-à-vis the nonethnic language* due to the greater prevalence and salience of informal over formal domains in the everyday life space of the ethnic majority. To use a quasi "evolutionary" metaphor, this result would amount to a sort of social "selection" of a "higher" species of the ethnic language—relegated however to a near vestigial or marginal role in community interaction. Ethnic language use in the community is thus "purified" and "elevated" while simultaneously isolated from the core functional concerns of the majority, where it is replaced by the nonethnic language, which is more categorically approved without such fine or detailed distinctions between its various varieties as are made between those of the ethnic language as briefly sketched in Postulate 2 above. It is as if the ethnic language were gaining legitimacy through death and supporters of such a trend felt "better a noble death than an ignominious life," that is, better the more restricted use of a "high" variety than a wider use of a "low" one.

The above hypotheses focus upon the ethnic majority. What might be the consequences for the ethnic minority?

Hypothesis 4: If the above postulates, assumptions, and hypotheses are valid, the maintenance-assimilation program might be expected to *increase* the use of ELVw within the communication networks of the ethnic minority elite and increase their control over the ethnic majority in local affairs while at the same time increasing the ethnic minority's opportunities for social mobility beyond either local or ethnic boundaries. The ethnic minority elite would thus become more dominant over, while simultaneously less dependent upon, and more divorced from, the local ethnic majority. This might place them in a particularly advantaged position for being easily co-opted by supraethnic interests dedicated to a colonial policy of indirect rule and make more difficult any attempts on the part of the ethnic majority to form independent sources of power and influence.[33]

Summarizing this series of hypotheses, one might say that if the transfer-assimilation program represents the ethnocentric triumph of nonethnic over ethnic values and interests, then in a sense the maintenance-assimilation program may bespeak a sociocentric victory of the ethnic minority elite over the ethnic majority's interests and values.

However, all these hypotheses, which suggest currently unanticipated consequences, must be put to empirical test.

As research can generally only discover what it sets out to find, adequate empirical tests can only be constructed by persistently holding on to the fundamental question: "What are the *social* consequences of particular bilingual education strategies upon the changing patterns of *community* language *use?*" And as the four hypotheses above seek to make clear, even such studies are likely to cast a net too coarse to catch the most significant changes unless a finer net is spun which recognizes the internal heterogeneity of the ethnic community and differentiates between intraethnic language varieties, and their communicative roles, status, and consequences for intraethnic community social and political organization.

From the contradiction between current statements of goals for bilingual programs and their likely outcomes—given their present (and likely future) structures—it would appear that many if not most bilingual programs are being unintentionally, yet falsely, represented to those most directly affected by them, that is, the pupils and parents of the ethnic majority.

---

[33] A recent example of such attempts at the development of independent sources of power is the formation of a third political party in 1970 and 1971 in several Southwestern states.

CONCLUSION

From this one can conclude that future sociolinguistic research in this field has not only a scholarly but also an urgent democratic need to fulfill. Only by developing our knowledge of the longer range social consequences which specific programs have in their particular, heterogeneous, and stratified community contexts, and by developing an awareness of the range of possible alternative bilingual education models, can the real conflicts always involved in such projects become more visible and the interest groupings affected have a basis for developing a more enlightened stand towards the introduction and development of desired programs.[34]

POSTSCRIPT

From the perspective of the above analysis it is particularly significant that at the time of the writing of this amended version (September 1971), after numerous communications with the U.S. Office of Education and correspondence with Project BEST (in New York City), which is engaged in a systematic review of the approaches used in every evaluative research component attached to each federally funded bilingual program in the United States, it has been possible to determine that *currently there is not a single study planned to determine program effects upon community diglossia.*

Such a glaring absence presents a phenomenon which itself deserves detailed investigation and should attract persons interested in the sociology of science and knowledge.

Why does this notorious research lacuna exist? Will it persist? Certain factors seem to maintain it. Psychologists, educators, and linguists far outnumber sociolinguists in the education research establishment. Also, the laymen, teachers, and administrators promoting bilingual education programs have primarily been members of the ethnic minority elite and nonethnics who are generally uninterested in, or directly opposed to, many of the characteristics of the pluralistic model presented here. Existing programs naturally have a built-in interest in testing themselves on measures where they are likely to show "success" and justify their expenditures in terms which will be persuasive and adequate for those who decide upon the continuation of programs and the allocation of funds. On the basis of current trends, one could conclude that for those who presently decide, community language maintenance in general and maintenance of the ethnic majority's cultural and linguistic varieties in particular is manifestly irrelevant or simply not considered desirable.

There are, nevertheless, some positive signs. Fishman (1966 and 1971) has developed, applied, and refined the diglossic approach in several studies of different ethnic groups in the United States. Several centers for the preparation of

---

[34] The emphasis of this essay has admittedly been critical. The reader should not lose sight of the fact that a few pluralistic programs do exist. Additionally, many powerfully assimilationistic programs are admittedly very effective in reducing disciplinary problems, dropout rates, and absenteeism as well as promoting higher levels of academic achievement. Also, a strictly Anglo-oriented "cost analysis" of assimilation programs should show them to be a "good investment" and even a "bargain": i.e., that they are effective in keeping youth off the streets, out of juvenile hall (courts), and will result in fewer of them in the future appearing on welfare and unemployment rolls.

The point, however, is that these traditional school- and budget-oriented goals can be achieved while simultaneously threatening or destroying community diglossia and hence the future of the ethnic community as such.

sociolinguists have been developed in recent years. Gaarder (1971) has drawn attention to the significance of the relations between intraethnic language varieties and recommended the importance of giving local varieties a place in the classroom repertoire. And finally, within the Mexican-American community itself new political movements, leaders, and ideas more concerned with the future of the ethnic majority are being developed which are beginning to critically reexamine those of the ethnic elite minority.

Only one thing is certain. Not only do we not know what the major *social* consequences of different types of bilingual education programs are, but unless current trends and research priorities are basically altered, we are not going to know either—until too late, when the consequences have already been wrought and become sufficiently massive so as to be evident to all. But the important questions will then be of only historical interest.

Would it not be shamefully irresponsible to wait for such a postmortem?

REFERENCES

Alatis, J. E. (ed.). *Bilingualism and Language Contact: Anthropological, Linguistic, Psychological, and Sociological Aspects.* Report of the Twenty-First Annual Round Table Meeting on Linguistics and Language Studies, *Georgetown Monograph Series on Languages and Linguistics,* No. 23. Washington, D.C.: Georgetown University Press, 1970.

Alvarez, G. R. "Calo: The 'Other' Spanish." *ETCC* (Journal of the International Society for General Semantics), **24**:1 (1967), 7-13.

Andersson, Theodore. "Bilingual Education: The American Experience." Paper presented at a conference sponsored by the Ontario Institute for Studies in Education. Toronto, Canada, March 1971.

—— and Mildred Boyer. *Bilingual Schooling in the United States,* 2 Vols. Washington, D.C.: USGPO, 1970.

Baratz, Joan, and Roger Shuy (eds.). *Teaching Black Children To Read.* Washington, D.C.: Center for Applied Linguistics, 1966.

Barker, Marie Esman. *Español para el bilingüe.* Skokie, Ill.: National Textbook Company, 1971.

Dillard, J. L. "How To Tell the Bandits from the Good Guys, or What Dialect to Teach?" *The Florida FL Reporter* (Spring/Summer 1969), 84-85 and 162.

ERIC File on Bilingualism. A list of the materials in this file and information on how they may be ordered appears in *The Linguistic Reporter* (Center for Applied Linguistics, Washington, D.C.), **11**:3 (June 1969), 6-7.

Ferguson, C. A. "Diglossia," *Word,* **15** (1959), 325-40.

Fishman, Joshua A. *The Sociology of Language: An Interdisciplinary Social Science Approach to Sociolinguistics.* Rowley, Mass.: Newbury House, 1972.

——, R. L. Cooper, and Roxana Ma et al. *Bilingualism in the Barrio.* (Language Sciences Series) Bloomington, Ind.: 1971.

——. "The Politics of Bilingual Education." In J. E. Alatis, op. cit., 1970, 47-58.

—— and John Lovas, "Bilingual Education in Sociolinguistic Perspective." *TESOL Quarterly,* **4**:3 (September 1970).

. "Bilingualism with and without Diglossia: Diglossia with and without Bilingualism." *Journal of Social Issues,* **23**:2 (1967), 29-38.

——. *Language Loyalty in the United States.* The Hague: Mouton, 1966.

——. "Who Speaks What Language to Whom and When?" *Linguistique,* **2** (1965), 67-88.

Gaarder, A. Bruce. "Teaching Spanish in School and College to Native Speakers of Spanish." A report commissioned by the Executive Council of the American Association of Teachers of Spanish and Portuguese. Mimeo., 1971.

————. "The First Seventy-Six Bilingual Education Projects." In J. E. Alatis, op. cit., 1970, 163-78.

————. "Organization of the Bilingual Schools." *Journal of Social Issues,* **23**:2 (1967), 110-20.

Goudsblom, Johan. "On High and Low in Society and in Sociology: A Semantic Approach to Social Stratification." A paper presented at the 7th World Congress of Sociology, Varna, Bulgaria, September 1970.

Grebler, Leo, Joan W. Moore, and Ralph C. Guzman et al. *The Mexican American People: The Nation's Second Largest Minority.* New York: Free Press, 1970.

Gumperz, J. J. "Verbal Strategies in Multilingual Communication." In J. E. Alatis, op. cit., 1970a, 129-47.

————. "Sociolinguistics and Communication in Small Groups." Working Paper No. 23. Berkeley, Calif.: Language Behavior Research Laboratory, April 1970b.

———— and E. Hernandez. "Cognitive Aspects of Bilingual Communication." Working Paper No. 28. Berkeley, Calif.: University of California Language Behavior Research Laboratory, December 1969a.

————. "Communication in Multilingual Societies." *Cognitive Anthropology.* Ed. S. A. Tyler. New York: Holt, 1969b, 435-49.

————. "Theme." *The Description and Measurement of Bilingualism.* Ed. Louis Kelley. Toronto: University of Toronto Press, 1969c, 242-53.

————. "Linguistic Repertoires, Grammars and Second Language Instruction." *Report of the Sixteenth Annual Round Table Meeting of Linguistics and Language Studies.* Ed. Charles W. Kriedler. Georgetown University Monograph Series on Languages and Linguistics, No. 18. Washington, D.C.: Georgetown University Press, 1965, 81-90.

————. "Linguistic and Social Interaction in Two Communities." *American Anthropologist,* **66**:2 (1964a), 37-53.

————. "Hindi-Punjabi Code Switching in Delhi." *Proceedings of the International Congress of Linguistics.* Ed. Morris Halle. The Hague: Mouton, 1964b.

Haugen, Einar. "Schizoglossia and the Linguistic Norm." *Georgetown Monograph Series on Languages and Linguistics,* No. 15. Washington, D.C.: Georgetown University Press, 1962, 63-73.

Herndon, James. *The Way It Spozed To Be.* New York: Bantam, 1969.

Hymes, Dell. "On Communicative Competence." Mimeo., 1966.

————. "Introduction: Toward Ethnographies of Communication." *American Anthropologist,* **66**:6, Part 2 (December 1964), 1-34.

John, Vera P., and Vivian M. Horner, *Early Childhood Bilingual Education.* New York: MLA, 1971.

Kjolseth, Rolf, Nora Margadant, David Lopez, and Enrique and Carmen Lopez. *Chicano Talk.* In preparation.

Labov, William. "The Place of Linguistic Research in American Society." *Linguistics in the 1970's.* Prepublication edition. Washington, D.C.: Center for Applied Linguistics, 1971, 41-70.

————. *The Social Stratification of English in New York City.* Washington, D.C.: Center for Applied Linguistics, 1966.

Landmann, Salcia. *Jiddisch: Abenteur einer Sprache.* 3. Auflage. Muenchen: Deutscher Taschenbuch Verlag, 1968.

Lewis, Louisa. "Culture and Social Interaction in the Classroom: An Ethnographic Report." Working Paper No. 38. Berkeley, Calif.: University of California Language Behavior Research Laboratory, November 1970.

Loyo, Gilberto. "Prologo." Manuel Gamio. *El Immigrante mexicano: La Historia de su vida.* Mexico: Universidad Nacional Autonoma de Mexico, 1969, 5–80.

Mackey, William F. "A Typology of Bilingual Education." In T. Andersson and M. Boyer, op. cit., 1970. II, 63–82.

Macnamara, John. "Bilingualism in the Modern World." *Journal of Social Issues,* **23**:2 (1967), 1–7.

Rayfield, Jr. R. *The Languages of a Bilingual Community.* The Hague: Mouton, 1970.

Romano-V., Octavio Ignacio (ed.). *El Espejo/The Mirror: Selected Mexican-American Literature.* Berkeley, Calif.: Quinto Sol Publications, 1969.

Rosenthal, Robert, and Lenore Jacobson. *Pygmalion in the Classroom: Teacher Expectation and Pupils' Intellectual Development.* New York: Holt, 1968.

Schmidt-Rohr, George. *Mutter Sprache.* 2. Auflage, Jena: Eugen Diederichs Verlag, 1933.

Steiner, Stan. *La Raza: The Mexican Americans.* New York: Harper & Row, 1969.

Stern, H. H. (ed.). *Foreign Languages in Primary Education.* Hamburg: UNESCO Institute of Education, 1963.

Stewart, William. "On the Use of Negro Dialect in the Teaching of Reading." In J. Baratz and R. Shuy, op. cit., 1969.

———. "Urban Negro Speech: Sociolinguistic Factors Affecting English Teaching." *Social Dialects and Language Learning.* Ed. Roger Shuy. Champaign, Ill.: National Council of Teachers of English, 1965, 10–18.

United States Office of Education. "Manual for Project Applicants and Grantees: Programs under Bilingual Education Act (Title VII, ESEA)." Draft, March 20, 1970.

Wolff, Hans. "Intelligibility and Inter-Ethnic Attitudes." *Language in Culture and Society.* Ed. Dell Hymes. New York: Harper & Row, 1964, 440–45.

Joshua A. Fishman

The Politics of
Bilingual Education

Unlikely Dreams Can Come True

As the "Language Resources Project" which I headed from 1960-1963 was drawing to a close, I began to put the finishing touches on a report which was ultimately to appear as the volume *Language Loyalty in the United States.* I wrote the report itself during a fellowship year at the Center for Advanced Study in the Behavioral Sciences, commonly known as the "Think Tank" or the "Leisure of the Theory Class." Those of you who know it—in the beauty of its location, overlooking the Stanford campus and the lower Bay—will understand what I mean when I suggest that it provides the scholar with opportunity for even more detachment from the trials and tribulations of society than does his ordinary academic existence. There it was that I first wrote my chapter on the "preservation" of our unrecognized non-English language resources. There it was that I first suggested that one of the necessary steps for the preservation of American bilingualism was an agency of government that would be responsible for safeguarding and augmenting the cultural and linguistic resources that our country has so often ignored and even snuffed out. I distinctly remember feeling triply removed from reality while writing that particular chapter, for few things seemed as unlikely then as the possibility that within five years there might be a Bilingual Education Act and at least some of the funds and staff needed to make it functional.

If such unlikely dreams can be realized in this age of miracles, then it may not be too unrealistic to hope that language scholars, language teachers, and other genuine friends of bilingual education will yet learn how to influence and strengthen the Bilingual Education Act and how to put its funds to better use. After all, we have arrived at a day and age when interest groups—even those on college campuses—engage in concerted action as never before in order to attain their goals. It is my hope that the friends of bilingual education too can rise to a more active position than that of going to conferences, writing and reading papers, and agreeing to spend the funds that come their way as a result of the efforts of those who refuse to be even once removed from the real world of affairs and of power.

Having devoted the past decade entirely to academic matters pertaining to bilingualism and to sociolinguistics more generally, it may also be that I now want to atone, in part, for my own sins by trying to "tell it as it is," rather than delivering yet another academic paper and leaving the responsibility for influencing the Act itself entirely to professional politicians.

In James E. Alatis (ed.), *Bilingualism and Language Contact* (Washington: Georgetown University Press, 1970, pp. 47–58. Reprinted with permission.

Some Lessons in Elementary Actmanship

Our childhood lessons in civics—particularly the chapters once studied in "how a bill becomes a law"—have not really prepared us to cope with the realities of influencing legislation. Were this not the case, we would realize that the latter is a never-ending process requiring continual attention and cultivation rather than self-satisfaction and mustering out of forces at the end of a session in which the votes and the authorizations have seemingly gone our way. However, in this respect we—language scholars and language teachers interested in bilingual education—have fully confirmed our amateur political standing—a standing shared with most citizen groups—by retiring from the field of battle once the authorization for funds has been approved. That is when the real action begins.

What we have not realized—and probably do not really comprehend to this very day—is that an authorization is just that and nothing more. However, once authorizations are signed and the jubilant citizen groups go home to celebrate their little victories, the legislative process gets down to the real business of appropriations. Authorizations are not appropriations! Hardly any educational appropriations are as much as 50% of what their respective authorizations mentioned. The final authorization for the Bilingual Education Act was 45 million dollars over a three-year period. We were sufficiently inexperienced to be elated by the immensity of that paltry sum. How naive we were! The appropriation was only 7.5 million dollars and it provided nothing beyond a one-year period! (See Table below.)

Funds for Bilingual Education Under Title VII: ESEA

Fiscal year	Authorization	Appropriation	Expenditure
1968	15 million	_____	_____
1969	30 million	7.5 million	7.5 million
1970	40 million	21,250,000	_____
1971	Senate Subcommittee on Educ. recom. 80 million		
1972	100 million		
1973	135 million		

This, too, we must learn. While authorizations may cover several years most appropriations are for one year only and, therefore, without constant attention on the part of those who are interested, appropriations may be conveniently allowed to lapse or may be cut drastically. No amount of talk about grandiose new authorizations will prevent this unless constituents and lobbyists are immediately at hand and vocally so. Thus, this fall the Senate Subcommittee on Education recommended an authorization for bilingual education (in conjunction with considering the extension of the ESEA) of more than three hundred million dollars over a five-year period. After this recommendation had gained the attention and praise it deserved (or, at least, the attention and praise it was intended to elicit), the Senate voted to appropriate a far smaller sum for fiscal year 1970 (some 25 million dollars). This sum the House-Senate Appropriations Conference finally adopted, not without serious attempts to reduce it further (to 15 million dollars). At this point the President's budgeteers, hacking away at the entire HEW appropriation, knocked bilingual education down to 10 million dollars for fiscal 1970 and its final funding is still in doubt.

Appropriations Committees

We were not—and are not today—prepared for the appropriations committees and their ability to emasculate programs or even to gut them entirely. Appropriations committees can and do write limitation riders into acts so that the funds they grant may not be utilized for certain purposes which may well be mentioned in the initial authorizing legislation. Unfortunately, bilingual education is particularly vulnerable to mistreatment at the appropriations stage. These committees—like many other crucial operative committees of Congress—are often controlled by chairmen for whom bilingual education is hardly a live issue. Indeed, one of the reasons that bilingual education has fared so poorly in appropriations committees thus far is that it is viewed as being primarily a regional problem (Southwest, Florida, and the New York Metropolitan area) rather than a matter that all Congressmen and Senators need to worry about. Another and more important reason why appropriations committees have not dealt kindly with bilingual education authorizations is that the entire matter of bilingual education is viewed as just one more anti-poverty measure, one more effort to help the disadvantaged. As such, there are many who take the position that Title I of ESEA and other appropriations are available to combat these two widespread ills and, therefore, why appropriate much more for "the same purpose again" via Title VII?

It is my considered opinion that the only way to convince appropriations committees to take bilingual education seriously is to convince them (a) that it is not merely a sectional matter, and (b) that is is not merely yet another part of the anti-poverty program. Thus, while it may well be true that whatever has been appropriated for bilingual education in the past few years is primarily due to the Mexican-American vote and the poverty issue, I am convinced that neither of these provide optimal pressure or optimal rationale for the future growth of bilingual education. More about this later.

Lobbying for Bilingual Education

Who can continually try to influence Senators and Congressmen via a flow of information concerning the need for bilingual education? Who can continue to exert pressure—which means personal visits as well as organized calls and telegrams—directed toward members of the appropriations committees? Who can maintain regular contact with thousands upon thousands of language teachers and language scholars so that they will know what pertinent legislation is being considered in Congress and who is for it or against it? Who can bring into action a "quick contact network" all over the country to elicit the protests and the plaudits that are needed in order to gain Congressional support for bilingual education? Who can watch closely how a new act is being staffed and implemented by the Washington bureaucracy and keep it from being interpreted into an early grave or into a far cry from what its original supporters had had in mind? Obviously, all of these things cannot be done—and done both well and repeatedly—by amorphous citizen groups. What is needed is obviously a lobby for bilingual education. It is equally obvious to me, however, that we cannot at this time hope for an organized lobby that spends all of its time fighting for bilingual education and for that alone. That takes time to establish, and funds, and consensus, and experience—none of which we now have. What then do we have that might pinch-hit for a bilingual education lobby? We have allies who lobby for bilingual education *too* because bilingual education presents them with another opportunity to obtain funds for the things they are independently interested in.

The organized voices that have been raised on behalf of bilingual education have been of two kinds: educational and ethnic. It is my contention that we who are interested in bilingual education per se (whether as a way to language maintenance, to cultural pluralism, to overcoming the educational retardation of many non-English-speaking learners, or as part of the educational right of every family to self-respect and to cultural integrity) must begin to cultivate friends and influence groups in each of these camps, many of which already maintain lobbies in Washington and throughout the country.

The power of lobbies is that—like mutual funds—they continue to work all of the time, not only when the heat's on. Most Congressmen and Senators are too busy ever to hear about bilingual education in the normal course of events. There is simply too much going on for them to be able to function at any but a highly selective level. At that level only that which is either very well recommended or very powerful gets through the filter imposed for purposes of sheer self-preservation. Lobbyists make it their business to know which of his colleagues any particular Congressman or Senator looks up to or looks upon as bellwethers to be followed in co-sponsoring or supporting bills that are being considered. Lobbyists know to whom in their home territories each Congressmen or Senator is indebted, whom he respects, whom he knows. Lobbyists find individuals favorable to their own positions from among such people and they arrange to take them along when they plan their campaign of visits to Congressman X or Senator Z. These visits go on all of the time, including those times when all concerned are relaxed, have time, and no vote is pending. Those are the times when many future votes are gained or lost.

The Education and the Ethnic Lobbies

Among the most effective friends that bilingual education has had thus far has been NEA in general and its West Coast office in particular. Indeed, when I was invited to testify on behalf of the Bilingual Education Bill in the spring of 1968, I found that another giving testimony at the same session was a representative of the Adult Education Section of the NEA. Quite naturally, he not only supported the bill but suggested that its wording be changed so as to clearly include adult education in its provisions. Clearly, bilingual education represented another arena in which adult education and its practitioners could grow and prosper. And why not? and what about rural education? and special education? and vocational education? and higher education? and day-care nurseries? and early childhood education? and reading instruction? and science education? etc., etc. All of these together (recently conjoined as the Emergency Committee for the Full Funding of Education Programs) and each of them separately could be interested in bilingual education—for their *own* sake as well as for *its* sake. One by-product of doing so would be to counter the currently widespread and erroneous impression that bilingual education is only for the poor; indeed, that it is primarily to eradicate a disease of the Puerto Rican and Mexican-American poor, namely, greater facility in Spanish than in English!

Which brings us to another lobby that I believe we must cultivate on behalf of bilingual education, namely the ethnic lobby. When I testified on behalf of bilingual education, there were several others testifying who represented various Mexican-American groups and associations. But where were the Franco-Americans, the Italo-Americans, the Polish-Americans, the German-Americans, the Ukrainian-Americans, the Chinese-Americans, the Jewish-Americans, etc., etc.? That they are potentially very interested in bilingual education may be seen from the fact that the American Council for Nationalities Services distributed news releases about the 1967 bill in some two dozen languages to hundreds and hundreds of ethnic publications and radio programs throughout the country. However, this potential lobby on behalf of bilingual education still remains essentially unorganized and unconvinced. This is a great pity, I believe, for not only must bilingual education serve all of them if it is to be a genuine expression of America's sociocultural and educational maturity (rather than merely a sop to the "poor Chicanos," so that they don't become too nasty), but by doing so it can attract a new force in support of education measures which the education lobby itself might welcome.

The ethnic lobby—and the Congressmen and Senators who respond to it—often speaks for somewhat insulated and conservative groups that are disposed to budget-cutting on matters not of explicit interest to them. Since the liberalization of the immigration laws a few years ago—and since the Soviet-American detente—this lobby has been looking around for a "good disease" to champion. Bilingual education with its implications for ethnic and linguistic maintenance could well entice this lobby and those responsive to it into the general education camp. If we want the education lobby to fight part of this good fight on behalf of bilingual education, we must be on the alert for new allies that we can contribute to the general struggle of the education lobby. The addition of the ethnic lobby to the push for more and for more genuine bilingual education would also help overcome the restricted regional image that bilingual education currently has, and would help give it a more diversified reality and a more varied substance. However, this lobby will remain lost to us, I believe, as long as the Act's poverty criterion excludes them. The poverty criterion must be eliminated from the act, both for sound philosophical as well as for sound tactical reasons!

Coming: Real Bilingual Education

Both the logic and the psychologic of bilingual education are leading in the same direction—in the direction of more genuine concern with bilingual curricula for various models and ideals of societal bilingualism. The day is coming when more and more genuine bilingual education, for all those who want it, regardless of income, mother tongue or language dominance, will be part of the variegated picture of American education. At that time it will not be a mere euphemism for programs in English as a Second Language which, though unquestionably essential, constitute only one part and one kind of dual language education. It will not be just a promissory note to the poor, nor a left-handed contribution to increasingly vocal and organized (though still exploited and dispossessed) Hispanos and Indians. It will be available to my children and grandchildren, and to yours, because it is too good to keep it from all the people. But if that time is to come as quickly as it should, as it could, as it must—without threats and animosities and confrontations—it requires that *we* become *more* than merely language scholars and language teachers. It requires that we become political activists, political realists, and political sophisticates, even more so than those who have pressured the Bilingual Education Act into its current stage. Bilingual education needs more than crumbs and deserves more than crumbs. The more rapidly we build it into the concerns of the education lobby and the more we strengthen that lobby with the new friends that bilingual education is in a good position to attract, the more rapidly it will get more than crumbs—which is all it is getting today.

A Practical Suggestion, in Parting

What I have suggested above is merely a "pitch" and, like any "pitch," it requires a "follow through" if it is to amount to anything. The alliance that I have called for (not to mention an even grander alliance incorporating Pan-American business and economic interests, United Nations supporters, and yet others) will not be fashioned spontaneously. It requires a few people, a little money, and a little help to get it rolling. Perhaps this is where we, language teachers and language scholars, could contribute most by taking the lead. Could not TESOL, ACTFL, NEA, and the AATs designate one dedicated and informed person each, to begin with, to form an ad hoc committee in Washington, D.C.? Could not these leading agencies of our profession pro-rate among themselves the initially modest expenses for the stationery, postage, reference materials, typing, and a bit of travel necessary in order for such an ad hoc group to begin the task? The task is a sizable one, but many others have done it before and some of them would be very willing to show us how and what. We need a clearing house and headquarters for information (e.g., current names and addresses of key Congressmen and their administrative assistants; reports on pertinent legislation pending and amendments needed; material on bilingual education for press, radio, TV, and school boards; reports on successful experiments and projects in bilingual education; analyses of the difficulties encountered, etc., etc.). It is high time for *us* to do "*our* thing."[1]

DISCUSSION

Robert J. Di Pietro, Georgetown University: I'd like to say, first of all, that I agree wholeheartedly with Professor Fishman. The problem to me, though, seems that we have to convince not so much the ethnic groups who face the issue of bilingualism, but the general American population, the so-called "silent majority," that there is a value in knowing and being educated in more than one language. This, I think, is a general problem in the English-speaking world.

Fishman: I'd like to suggest a possible modification of that. Most Americans would agree that it is fine to know other languages. There are just a couple of qualifications that come after that. It is very nice to know other languages (a) provided it is French, (b) provided it is the French of Paris, and (c) provided your parents don't speak French at home.

Robert Lado, Georgetown University: I would like to support the urgent plea of Professor Fishman and I hope that action will follow. I would also like to support the

---

[1] I am grateful to the following individuals for their comments on the first draft of this paper as a result of which I have made many changes and additions to it: Professor Theodore Andersson (Southwest Educational Development Laboratory), Joe Carter (Administrative Assistant to Senator George Murphy of California), Dr. Bruce Gaarder (Basic Studies Branch, Division of College Programs, Bureau of Educational Personnel Development, USOE), Larry Horwitz (Administrative Assistant to Congressman John Conyers, Jr. of Detroit), and Monroe Sweetland (West Coast Regional Office, NEA). Of course, I alone am responsible for the views (or errors) presented and do not mean to imply that the foregoing friends of bilingual education have any responsibility at all for either.

last comments. I fought a battle for ten years to permit the children of speakers of the languages in which we give a major, to major in those languages. I fought hard and I got it through, and then when I spent two years away in Spain on a Fulbright grant, I came back to find it had been pushed aside. There seems to be something that isn't liked in permitting a child of an Italian family to major in Italian or to permit a child of any other language that we teach to major in that language. I would like to support the idea that we should provide a lobby and should move toward really full-fledged bilingual education all the way from prekindergarten to college, and if we succeed in this, the United States will truly be one of the leading nations of the world in this area.

Joan Baratz, Education Study Center: I'd like to broaden the scope of the discussion a little. I think we are not simply talking about language programs and we are not simply trying to educate the country in general and Congressmen in particular about the fact that it would be nice to have multilingual speakers and bilingual programs in this country. We have to recognize that what Mr. Fishman suggests is really attacking a basic fabric of the American dream in terms of what a melting pot is and what America is like. When we are talking about not eradicating the second language through bilingual education, what we are really talking about is kind of revolutionary—we are talking about reconceptualizing what America is and what it should be. It is not a simple language problem.

Fishman: I think that is very true, very well put, but also very desirable; I'm sure it doesn't frighten you and it doesn't frighten me. The major blessing of the current turmoil in our lives is that it is exactly due to the fact that people are reconceptualizing America, are more demanding with respect to new dreams, are more eager to realize dreams that were always there. I'd like to tell you about that best kept secret in the world, a book called *Language Loyalty in the United States,* which most fully documents the existence of the dream of a bilingual America, a dream that people might be fully accepted in this country not merely by erasing themselves, but by being themselves. That dream has been dreamt ever since the days of the Pilgrims, because they came exactly in order to maintain themselves as they were rather than to change, and so did many groups since then. That has been an American dream for as long and longer than the country has existed, and it is high time that it came to be realized for blacks, for Hispanos, and for immigrants and their children and grandchildren. We are finally coming to realize that this is not the best of all possible countries, that it could be improved in many ways to make it so, and I believe this is one of the most vital avenues of improvement, precisely because it has so long been overlooked by some and denied by others.

P. B. Pandit, Cornell University: I'm really touched by this very eloquent plea to make America a multilingual country. I would like to ask Dr. Fishman, since he has coedited a book on linguistic problems of developing countries where most of the authors have considered the developing countries to be very unfortunate because of the great diversity and variety of languages. Having done so, and having considered countries with many languages as problem countries, I would like to ask Dr. Fishman what would be his interpretation of the American situation when it becomes multilingual. Multilingualism is also looked upon as symptomatic of barriers in communication by these writers; in what way would such multilingualism affect the development of mass media in particular and technology in general?

Fishman: It is quite true that the coincidence between underdevelopment and multilingualism is very high, but it is the same kind of coincidence that John Macnamara and Einar Haugen were speaking about last night: the coincidence between bilingualism and lower IQ scores in this country and elsewhere. There is no necessary connection between these factors. There are several highly stable and economically very advanced multilingual societies in the world today, and there are, as we know, a very large number of very unstable, very miserable, problem-plagued and problem-ridden monolingual countries in the world today. I don't think we have to worry that the Bilingual Education Act or the fostering of genuine bilingualism in the United States for those who want it will be the ruination of the country. The ruination of the country is more likely to come, as it always has in the past, by the insidious implication that by forgetting the problems, by forgetting oneself, by overlooking one's parents, by throwing away treasures that are rightfully one's heritage, one could help the country. I think that is far more of an insidious, unrecognized type of underdevelopment than the kind of multilingual and multicultural development that I have been advocating.

John Gumperz, University of California, Berkeley: I would like to ask Dr. Fishman two questions. Does he feel that too much money is being spent on poverty programs? In other words, he said that the Bilingual Education Act has been associated with poverty programs. We are living in a year that all funds for education are being cut. In my own university we are having something like a 50% cut in EOP programs. This is the first year that we have begun to admit minority group students in large numbers, and it is also the first year that we have no funds to support such students. Now, what would he like to do about this in real terms?

The second question is not related. In a paper which I believe was published in *Anthropological Linguistics,* Dr. Fishman discusses the language problems of what he calls underdeveloped nations, and specifically choice of national language. In talking about the choice of English—he uses the term "rationality"—he says rational choices are made when English is chosen. In countries who choose their own native language, the choice is said to be motivated by sentiment. In other words, he implies that people give in to their sentiments when they choose their own native language, but when they choose English this is called a rational decision. Now how does he reconcile this with his position about multilingualism in the United States; is he advocating that we too make "sentimental" rather than "rational" choices?

Fishman: We don't happen to have a state legislature backing Yeshiva University, but we have had many cuts too. I'm genuinely alarmed that all these cuts are taking place, and I oppose them as strenuously as I can. Nevertheless, one must take care not to be for bilingual education only if there is money for it, or only if there is enough money for everything else, or only in the end of all things when the state will wither away. Of course, I didn't begin to say that there is too much money for poverty programs in the United States today; I said there was a complete misunderstanding of bilingual education and the Bilingual Education Act; so much so that it was seen as just one more poverty program and therefore, since some Congressmen and Senators have thought that lots of money was being put into poverty programs, they felt there was no need to put any aside for bilingual education if it was just one more minor, funny kind of poverty program. There obviously is not enough money going into poverty programs. However, in pleading for more funds for bilingual education I am not really competing with the poverty programs. at all. A country that has been able to waste money the way we have wasted it for the worst causes ought to be able to amply support bilingual education and still have greatly increased funds for the poverty program as well. There is no necessary competition between them and it shouldn't be thought of in that way.

Secondly, it is not at all my conviction that where English or another language of wider communication is chosen, it is actually chosen in terms of more rational appeals, nor that where the national language is chosen for government, education, etc., by a developing country, it is actually chosen in terms of more sentimental appeals. My point is that the actors themselves in the new language drama going on through the Third World commonly approach the problem as if this were the case. That is, the announced appeals on behalf of English or other world languages are that the country will be helped to develop economically; that its ties with the English-speaking countries or other major centers of power will be strengthened; its scientists will be more closely in touch with scientists all over the world; all of these being advanced as very rational, instrumental, and modern reasons. However, when such advice is adopted, the resulting policies always have affective or sentimental consequences as well, since technical and operative integration always leads to sociocultural integration and vice versa. Similarly, those who plead on behalf of the national language often stress the national heritage, the national past, the national beauty, national ideals, national character, and talk about these things as if they were unrelated to or more important than practical, operative, instrumental concerns.

But actually the brunt of my paper was to show that both of these considerations (the instrumental and the sentimental) are always present together, that they always contribute to each other, and that all countries have always, in connection with language problems, given attention to both simultaneously or at different stages in their development. My advocacy of bilingual education in the United States is therefore based on both instrumental and sentimental grounds, precisely because these grounds always co-occur. Our problem is that we have a world which is highly uneven in terms of development and highly variegated in terms of the stages and types of social problems being experienced and, therefore, we do have a world today in which the haves are shouting to the have-nots: "Be rational, be reasonable, be successful, be like me, ... use English!"

A. Bruce Gaarder

Bilingual Education: Central Questions and Concerns

An examination of bilingual education that does not first take into account different kinds of bilingualism itself would be futile. Without such an accounting, there would be no point of reference, for bilingual education necessarily flows out of and into some kind of bilingualism, and there are many different kinds.

For our purpose here, the most fundamental distinction is between voluntary bilingualism, developed in individuals, and obligatory bilingualism, which is a collective or group phenomenon. In the former case, the individual becomes bilingual of his own free will or that of his parents. The new skill is acquired from members of the family, tutors, or servants, from sojourns abroad, in special schools, or from simple foreign language study. Obligatory, collective bilingualism takes two main forms, but the principal one is the result of contact and conflict between two peoples in a single state or under a single government: a dominant people and a dominated people. The latter group becomes bilingual by necessity, from their need to eat, to survive.

Thus, the bilingualism of Americans or Frenchmen or Argentinians who learn Russian or German is voluntary, elitist, academic. The bilingualism of Puerto Ricans or Mexican-Americans (Chicanos) who have to learn English, of Catalans in Spain who must learn Spanish too, of Indians in South or North America who must learn Portuguese or Spanish or English—this is obligatory and collective. The dynamics—social, political, pedagogical—of the two kinds of dual-language acquisition are different and incompatible.

FACTORS AFFECTING COLLECTIVE BILINGUALISM

In addition to the obligatory form of bilingualism that appears when one people is subordinated to another, it is not uncommon for a single people to use and prefer to use two languages. Examples of this are the Arabic nations, each of which has its own vernacular Arabic and also uses Koranic Arabic; Greece, where Katharevusa and *dimotiki* are common; the German cantons of Switzerland, where the population is generally bilingual in Schwyzertütsch and standard German. What differentiates this form of collective bilingualism from the other is the lack of inter-group conflict and the fact that there is no competition between the languages, since each is used by its speakers for a different set of purposes. Collective bilingualism in these cases—commonly known as diglossia—is a stable relationship.

Reprinted by permission from *New York University Education Quarterly*, vol. 6., no. 4, Summer 1975. ©
 New York University.

The political stance toward linguistic and cultural diversity is another factor in the dynamics of bilingualism. Some countries notable for a strongly assimilative stance toward their minority peoples are the United States (despite the bilingual education movement and wishful wisps of cultural pluralism), France, Spain, and South American nations except Paraguay. The objective in states favoring assimilation is to promote national unity even if minority-group cultures and languages must thereby be eliminated.

Among the nations which—for whatever reason—practice true cultural pluralism are Switzerland, the Soviet Union, Czechoslovakia, Yugoslavia, Belgium, Finland, and in a very special way, Paraguay. This is usually done by means of laws which recognize the right of minority people to cultural autonomy or a status closely approaching that autonomy and which safeguard each people's language from aggression by others.[1] Cultural autonomy commonly means the right and the means to establish schools and colleges, to publish and use the air waves, to conduct business and legal matters, to practice religion and everything else in one's own language. It commonly supports the ideal of unilingualism, although not to the exclusion of learning one or more additional languages. There is recognition of the important difference between foreign language instruction and the much more powerful—and dangerous—use of the second tongue as a medium of school instruction.

Cultural autonomy is usually based on separate territories, but in some cases when two peoples live dispersed among each other there is recourse to the personal principle, which gives to each person language rights wherever he finds himself. Paraguay is unique because the merging there of two peoples, the indigenous and the European, has been marked by a oneness that includes retention and cultivation of the Guaraní language by a majority of the people in a stable, diglossic, non-competitive relationship with Spanish.[2]

Two other important factors in the dynamics of bilingualism are power (political and economic) and prestige (the prestige of the languages concerned). Usually the power factor is overriding and is merely reinforced by the prestige of the more powerful people's language. In a few notable cases, however, the prestige of a language is great enough to override superior political and economic power. Examples of this latter anomaly are found in Belgium and the Republic of South Africa. In both these nations a Dutch-speaking people (Flemish and Afrikaaners) have achieved hegemony—over the French-speaking Walloons in Belgium and the English-speaking people in South Africa. The enormously greater prestige of French and English exercises such power of attraction over Flemish and Afrikaaner families that they begin by becoming bilingual and end by becoming French- or English-speaking, and in both countries it has been found necessary to restrict severely the likelihood of bilingualism.

A final major factor (there are many more, but they cannot be identified here) is the extent, in demographic terms, of the bilingualism. Collective, compulsory bilingualism (two languages and peoples, one dominated by the other within a single nation) is essentially a transitional means of communication between two

---

[1] Jean Falch, *Contribution à l'étude du statut des langues en Europe*, Québec: Presses de l'Université Laval, 1973; and Bernard Touret, *L'aménagement constitutionelle des Etats de peuplement composite*, Québec: Presses de l'Universite Laval, 1973.

[2] Joan Rubin, *National Bilingualism in Paraguay*, unpublished doctoral dissertation, Yale University, 1963. Chapter VII appears in *Readings in the Sociology of Language*, Joshua A. Fishman, ed., The Hague: Mouton, 1970.

monolingual peoples. Here it should be borne in mind that it is invariably a one-sided phenomenon: the subordinated people alone becomes bilingual, the dominant one does not; the subordinate people's tongue alone (except in the anomalous cases noted above) suffers linguistic interference, with distortion of its syntax and swamping of its lexicon. As soon as most of the dominated people become speakers of both languages there is no further need for both of them, and the weaker tongue disappears. We then say that a language shift has occurred.

It follows that collective, compulsory bilingualism is an unstable, self-destructive linguistic phenomenon, for no people needs two languages for the same set of purposes. Therefore it matters a great deal, in terms of the imminence and danger of language shift, whether only a few people have become bilingual or whether almost all have so become.

The five major dynamic factors of collective bilingualism—its inevitability, the political stance, power, language prestige, and demography—plus its instability, plus the factors of religion and race and the wide variation of people's attitudes toward their language or languages—all these elements and more combine variedly to show fifty-four essentially different, contrasting kinds of bilingualism. [3]

OBLIGATORY BILINGUALISM IN THE UNITED STATES

After the above brief overview of bilingualism, some points become apparent about the language situation in the United States. First, it should be plain that there are fundamental, irreconcilable differences between, on the one hand, the millions of students in schools and colleges who are studying foreign languages and, on the other hand, the many more millions—perhaps one-tenth of our population—who have no choice about speaking two languages. For the first group learning the new language is an elitist gesture of cultural enrichment; for the others it is a form of assimilation which they would find almost impossible to avoid.

Why, it will be asked, cannot the second kind of bilingualism be as enriching as the first? The answer, not at all clear and unequivocal, is that it can be, indeed often is, but somehow in the great majority of cases it is not. Consider for a moment that at least half of all of our teachers of foreign language—predominantly those who teach the uncommon tongues—are native speakers drawn from the ranks of obligatory bilinguals. Consider too some possible reasons for the persistence of bilingualism in Mexican-Americans, in the Puerto Ricans in continental United States, and in native American Indians. What weight should be given to the fact of their being in large part "visible" minorities in a racist society and to the consequent negative factors of isolation, poverty, illiteracy, and discrimination? There are of course more positive factors which must be weighed too: the proximity of Mexico and Puerto Rico, the ease of travel, the historical primacy of these peoples (they are either aboriginal or identify ethnically with the aboriginals), and their professed unwillingness to be assimilated—to become like everyone else and lose their distinctive language and culture.

What then of bilingual education (the use of two languages, one of them English, as mediums of school instruction, plus emphasis on the history and culture of the children's forebears)? Can it be seen as other than encouragement to bilingualism? Yet, in view of the self-destructive nature of compulsory bilingualism, can bilingual education be other than a way of hastening the disappearance of all folk languages except English?

---

[3] A. Bruce Gaarder, "Political Perspective on Bilingual Education," unpublished manuscript, 1974.

PEDAGOGICAL AND OTHER IMPLICATIONS

There were only a few examples of bilingual education in the United States in recent times—including what may still have been the best attempt, Coral Way Elementary School in Dade County, Florida—before the Bilingual Education Act was passed in 1968. That act may fairly be called a national response to the Spanish-speakers' struggle for social justice. It was intelligently and ambiguously worded to give equal comfort to those who wanted bilingual education to be a mere one-way bridge to English and to those who hoped it might be extended into the secondary schools to maintain and develop full competence and literacy in Spanish and the other non-English tongues. Also out of political expediency, and most unfortunately in the view of those who saw each of the languages as the chief manifestation and instrument of a culture and a people, the act included a poverty criterion for use in identifying its beneficiaries. This has had the effect of stigmatizing bilingual education as an educational medicine specific to the poor and disadvantaged. It might instead have been seen as a superior kind of education for possibly superior children.

There was nothing in the writings of those who provided the rationale for bilingual education to show that they were aware of the dilemma posed by the transitory, self-destructive nature of obligatory bisocietal bilingualism. "Research findings" were quickly produced to show that the child would less likely be retarded if allowed to learn in its mother tongue instead of being forced to delay a year or two or three until sufficient competence had been acquired in the use of English to permit its unrestricted use for instructional purposes. Other findings showed the greater ease with which a Spanish mother-tongue child becomes literate in comparison with one whose mother tongue is English, given the extraordinary incongruencies between the English pronunciation and writing systems. And so on. Not until 1973 did it occur to me that the only rationale either needed or worthy of being heeded for teaching a child through its mother tongue is the simple proposition that it is a fundamental human right for every people to rear—and educate—its children in its own image and language. [4]

Meanwhile, under the stress of creating proposals for the first Bilingual Education Act grants by 1969, patterns of federal and local administration of the program were quickly developed. It is my perception that the most significant of these was a tendency to minimize the importance of employing in bilingual education programs only well-prepared teachers and administrators, strongly literate in the non-English tongue and highly knowledgeable of the other culture. [5]

In retrospect it is not difficult to explain this attitude, even apart from the unavoidable haste in launching the national program. First, it would be unthinkable not to use—for example—the Spanish speakers themselves in the new effort to improve the education of their children. Yet, unavoidably, most of them are victims of educational policy which in the past denigrated their mother tongue, discouraged them from using it, and virtually assured their illiteracy in it. Second, due in part to the studied ambiguities of the Bilingual Education Act, there was from the beginning an inclination among school people to define bilingual education as any special educational treatment given to bilingual children, including the exclusive teaching of

---

[4] Theodore Andersson and Mildred Boyer, "A Rationale for Bilingual Schooling," in *Bilingual Schooling in the United States*, Vol. I, Washington, D.C.: U.S. Government Printing Office, 1970.

[5] A. Bruce Gaarder, "The First Seventy-Six Bilingual Education Projects," in *Monograph Series on Languages and Linguistics*, No. 23, James. E. Alatis, ed., Washington, D.C.: Georgetown University, 1970.

English "as a second language." Third, although it might have been possible to set standards of training and competence for the teachers, it would have been difficult (in personal and political terms) to rule out of a local program any teacher, already employed there, who was "bilingual" and then to bring in supposedly more competent outsiders, even members of the same ethnic group. Who would make the judgments? Fourth, there was no existing program of suitable training in the teacher training institutions, because no precedent existed for preparing teachers to work professionally through the medium of a non-English tongue. Fifth—and perhaps most weighty—it soon became politically inexpedient among important segments of the speakers themselves to suggest that teachers should use *el español común* (world standard Spanish) for school work,[6] rather than a vernacular somewhat analogous to "black English."

The result—one result—was that I had occasion in 1970 to identify one group of about thirty native Spanish speakers regularly employed and responsible for the Spanish side of bilingual education in Colorado and New Mexico, not one of whom had ever read a book in Spanish. Another such group in 1971 did not know the Spanish alphabet. Previous experience with similar groups of teachers in California attests to the same situation there. All of them were graduates of American schools and colleges, educated exclusively through English.

Another result of the negligible emphasis on strong literacy in the non-English tongue has been the preponderant use of English for professional purposes related to bilingual education: publications, meetings, record keeping, etc., and, most importantly, teacher training. With very few exceptions, I have found that the plans of studies in master's degree and doctoral programs offered in "bilingual education" consist essentially of a selection of standard education courses in English; a course or so in the history and culture of the minority people, also in English; something dealing with the "theory" or history of bilingual education, also in English, plus an invitation to enroll for courses in the institution's department of foreign languages.[7]

In contrast with this, it can be averred that in any other country where a minority people has won the right to educate its children through its own language, one of the first major concerns would be the establishment of a normal school to train the teachers. And the school would be staffed by educated, highly literate members of the minority language group and conducted exclusively in that language.

INCOMPATIBLE GOALS OF BILINGUAL EDUCATION

Enough has been written here to lead us to the centermost of all concerns: the goal or goals of bilingual education. Clearly there are three major ones, each in basic opposition to the others: (1) development of a more effective, more "humane" one-way bridge to English; (2) more effective education for children whose mother tongue is not English, plus the long-term development and maintenance of that mother tongue; (3) provision of a source of jobs in education and of preferential treatment for members of the ethnic groups involved.

---

[6] On this subject see Estelle Chacón, "Pochismos," *El Grito,* 3:1 (1969): 34–35; and Uvaldo Palomares, "Psychological Factors Teachers Must Recognize in the Bicultural Child," *Proceedings, National Conference on Bilingual Education,* Austin, Texas: Dissemination Center for Bilingual Bicultural Education, 1972, pp. 210–220.

[7] The Education Amendments of 1974 Act, which amended and expanded significantly the original Bilingual Education Act of 1968, mandates that "for the fiscal year ending June 30, 1975, not less than 100 fellowships leading to a graduate degree shall be awarded . . . for preparing individuals to train teachers for programs of bilingual education." Additional fellowships are to be awarded in subsequent years.

The U.S. Office of Education and Albert Shanker, president of the American Federation of Teachers, exemplify espousal of the first goal. Their view is very widely shared. In a letter to Senator Joseph Montoya of New Mexico dated November 15, 1974, the Commissioner of Education, Terrell H. Bell, discussing the question of ends and means, wrote:

> I maintain that the proper goal of federally-supported Bilingual/Bicultural Education Programs is precisely that stated in the OE [Office of Education] staff paper cited in your letter—namely, "to enable children whose dominant language is other than English to develop competitive proficiency in English so that they can function successfully in the educational and occupational institutions of the larger society. . . . What we know about the educational process tells us that the most effective and the most humane way to achieve this English language competency is through a Bilingual/Bicultural approach.

Mr. Shanker makes that position clear in an article related to the consent decree won by the plaintiffs in *ASPIRA v. New York City Board of Education,* which mandates substantive instruction in Spanish for children whose English-language deficiencies prevent them from participating in the learning process in the New York City schools. Speaking in *New York Teacher* for January 26, 1975, Shanker said, "It should be made clear that this kind of instruction is transitional, and that children should be moved into regular instruction in English on an on-going basis as their English language skills are strengthened." Reiterating the transitional nature of bilingual education, he said that the bilingual programs should "self-destruct." "That is, the ultimate goal is to integrate non-English speaking children into the regular school program as quickly as possible."

The second goal was expressed typically by Spanish-speaking Senator Montoya in a letter to the U.S. Commissioner of Education on October 11, 1974.

> It is my view . . . . that bilingual education must have as its goal the fulfillment of what is inherent in its title: two languages. Children learn to speak a language at home or in their community. The school is, ideally, the place where children learn to read and write in that language, thus becoming literate. . . . If a bilingual program is available in his school, he can learn to speak two languages instead of one, and because he is instructed in two languages (as the law directs for bilingual programs) he can soon become literate in two languages instead of one.

It is safe to say that a great many—perhaps most—of the speakers of non-English languages wish that their languages and cultures could be maintained and strengthened. Perusal of the consent decree referred to above—from the point of view of the Puerto Rican—substantiates this statement. It is also safe to aver that very few of them know what would be required in terms of political, economic, and educational change in order to make that wish come true.

The third goal, jobs and preferment, is uncomfortably evident in what was said above about the lack of academic soundness in much that is called bilingual education at both the school level and the university level.

There is increasingly convincing evidence that educational policy which requires non-English mother-tongue children to be educated exclusively through English is severely detrimental to them. There is little evidence that bilingual education, as it is now practiced, is offsetting that detriment. A situation that used to be seen, ethnocentrically, as "the handicap of bilingualism"—and still is, very widely and for the same reason—is coming to be viewed as a denial of equal educational opportunity. The evidence of detriment comes chiefly from studies related to the measurement of intelligence and, to a lesser extent, of achievement. Stated summarily, the case rests on three points: use of non-Spanish-speaking testers, use of English as the testing medium, and use of tests which are culture-bound to the English language milieu. These factors, separately and combined, have been found to depress severely the performance of Spanish mother-tongue children.[8] However much the I.Q. testing program alone might be improved, the failure to provide equal educational opportunity (insofar as formal schooling is concerned) for Spanish-speaking children would be as great as ever in any classroom where the medium is English and the teacher other than a Spanish speaker well-trained to teach through Spanish.

EVALUATION

All that has been said above suggests the difficulty of evaluating the effectiveness of a national program involving (in the 1972–73 school year) twenty-four languages and "dialects" in twenty-nine of the states, plus Guam, the Mariana Islands, Puerto Rico, and the Virgin Islands, and over 100,000 students in 652 schools.[9] Examination of the best attempt thus far to evaluate the bilingual education program suggests additional complications. In 1973, under contract with the U.S. Office of Education, an excellent "process evaluation" was made of a random sample of thirty-four projects supported under the Bilingual Education Act and serving Spanish-speaking children.[10] Emphasis on the Spanish speakers—even as in this essay—was justified on grounds of consistency plus the fact that about 80 percent of the Bilingual Education Act projects deal with the Spanish language. The following observations on some of the findings of the evaluation are to be read in the light of what was said above about the dynamics of bilingualism.

The 14,043 children in the thirty-four projects were classified solely on the basis of "language dominance": 8,765 Spanish-dominant, 4,008 English-dominant, and 1,270 undetermined. This must be considered together with the Office of Education's official *Manual for Project Applicants and Grantees* (1971) which says that "children whose dominant language is English and who attend schools in the project area should be encouraged to participate, and provisions should be made for their par-

---

[8] Forty-seven randomly selected Spanish-speaking "retarded" children, half from urban, half from rural backgrounds in California were reexamined in the Spanish language by Spanish-speaking psychologists, and it was found that 42 of the 47 scored above the I.Q. ceiling of the mental retardate classification; 37 scored 75 or higher; over half scored 80 or above; 16 percent scored 90 or more. This was part of the evidence presented in *Diana, et al. v. (California) Board of Education,* which led U.S. District Court Judge Robert E. Peckham to rule on February 5, 1970 that thenceforth school officials would be required a) to explain any disproportionate assignment of Spanish-speaking children to classes for mental retardates, and b) to have prepared an I.Q. test normed to the California Spanish-speaking child population; and that such children will be tested in both Spanish and English and be allowed to respond in either tongue. See also James Vásquez, "Measurement of Intelligence and Language Differences, *AZTLAN,* **3**:1 (1973): 155–163; and Jane R. Mercer, "Current Retardation Procedures and the Psychological and Social Implications on the Mexican-American," paper prepared for Southwestern Cooperative Education Laboratory, Albuquerque, April 1970.

[9] *Guide to Title VII ESEA Bilingual Bicultural Projects in the United States,* Austin, Texas: Dissemination Center for Bilingual Bicultural Education (6504 Tracor Lane, 78721), 1973.

[10] *A Process Evaluation of the Bilingual Education Program, Title VII, Elementary and Secondary Education Act,* Vol. I. Washington, D.C.: Development Associates, 1973.

ticipation in order to enhance the bilingual and bicultural aspects of the program." The same manual cities as a characteristic of approved bilingual education programs that "provision is made for increasing the instructional use of both languages for both groups in the same classroom."

What this means is that Anglo monolinguals and Spanish-speaking monolinguals (or bilinguals) are together in the same classroom, receiving instruction at the same time. Not only is there a basic incompatibility in such groupings in terms of the dynamics of bilingualism, as noted above, there is also a kind of pedagogical incompatibility. Teaching that uses Spanish as the medium of instruction for Spanish-speaking pupils permits vigorous, authentic, full use of that tongue. It is a much more powerful teaching mode than and basically incompatible with teaching Spanish as a foreign language, which is inescapably required if there are English monolinguals in the class.

A disastrous compromise is possible: rapid switching by the teacher from one language to the other. I have seen this done continuously in projects in South Texas. The conclusion there was that the miraculous language learning of which young children are capable was not taking place, for the pupils had but to wait a few seconds to receive the same message in their own tongue. Language switching is a manifestation of acculturation and of the difficulty of keeping the two languages entirely separate.

The official evaluation had much to say about the extent of the teachers' preparation. Of the 510 teachers, only 22 had "lived for an extended period" in a Spanish-speaking country. There were no data on the extent to which any of these had actually studied through Spanish. Of the 510, 393 were "bilingual," but the evaluators noted that "the extent of functional bilingualism of teachers and aides was not determined."

Two of the 34 projects had no bilingual teachers and instead used bilingual aides. The project directors voiced a common concern for the inadequacy of their teachers' preparation. Most directors provided "orientation" and some in-service training for their staffs. One project sent the entire staff to Mexico two successive summers for five weeks of intensive training.

Regarding teaching materials in Spanish, the evaluation noted that most teachers found those published elsewhere to be somehow inadequate and that in many projects the bilingual staffs were preparing their own. It also referred extensively to the more than 20,000 items of published Spanish-language materials collected throughout the Spanish-speaking nations specifically for use in bilingual education projects. Of these it was observed that "teacher evaluation sheets show that foreign materials tend to be too difficult for American children." Even more revealingly, the evaluators remarked of those imported publications, "The language is evidently too difficult for those who are not fluent speakers and readers of Spanish."

About pupil achievement the evaluators had little to say. The pupils' "language competence in both English and Spanish was not measured" by the projects' staffs. "Spanish language skills of English-dominant students were imparted only minimally by current attempts at teaching subjects in Spanish." During about two-thirds of the school day "content" was taught in English; in one-third it was taught in Spanish. Some projects professed to be devoted to the transitional language-bridge philosophy; others professed to be aiming at long-term maintenance and development of the non-English mother tongue. The evaluators found marked incongruity between those professions and what was actually happening in the projects.

The major concerns raised in this essay seem to be of little concern to those involved most closely in bilingual education. The questions raised and implied are not being answered. At the very least this suggests that before an evaluation of bilingual education in terms of pupil achievement is attempted, each project might well be scrutinized to see if what is happening there corresponds reasonably well to its stated aims. This would require careful consideration of the social, political and pedagogical dynamics of bilingualism. At the most it suggests that bilingual education could still be used to meet the noblest goals of the most generous of its supporters.

Linguistic Perspectives

A goal of education, bilingual or other, presumably is to enable children to develop their capacity for creative use of language as part of successful adaptation of themselves and their communities in the continuously changing circumstances characteristic of contemporary life. And linguistics indeed has already addressed itself to this goal, as witnessed by the concern within descriptive theory for the "creative aspect of language use" and the recognition of the role of the child's first language long advocated by many linguists and anthropologists. In both respects, however, linguistics falls short until it is able to deal with ways of speaking in relation to social meanings and situations, until, in short, the starting point of description is not a sentence or text, but a speech event; not a language, but a repertoire of ways of speaking; not a speech community defined in equivalence to a language, but a speech community defined through the concurrence of rules of grammar and rules of use.

Dell Hymes

Joshua A. Fishman

Bilingual Education and the Future of Language Teaching and Language Learning in the United States

Language teachers in general and modern language teachers in particular constitute one of the primary target audiences of the sociology of language. I have tried to recognize this audience in many of my writings—and not only to teach its members but also to learn from them. For both of these reasons I would have been delighted to address this distinguished gathering of chairmen of departments of foreign languages under ordinary circumstances, and I am therefore *doubly* delighted to do so having just completed the first draft of a "Sociology of Bilingual Education" and being invited to talk about it to you. Perhaps I should apologize for initially adapting the stance of "Let's not talk about *me* (a sociologist of language), let's talk about *you* (language teachers)" and then immediately following that up by "What do *you* think of *my* book?" We are all too human and just as "chickens must dream of chicken feed" (Yiddish proverb) so sociologists of language must "do their thing" and there is no getting away from it.

AN EXCITING FIELD

I have been a "language teaching watcher" for many years and my impression is that yours is an exciting field. During the past third of a century, there has been as much innovative theory, curricular and methodological rethinking, and sophisticated debunking in the language teaching field as in the much stressed mathematics-sciences field. This says a great deal about the intellectual vitality of the field of language teaching and it clearly distinguishes it (as well as math-sciences) from the social sciences and the humanities, which regrettably have remained comparatively quiescent in terms of revisions in instructional theory or methodology. Indeed, the *growing* relationship between the language field and the math-science field on the one hand (in terms of the forces that shape American life and American education) and the shrinking relationship between the language field and the humanities-social sciences field on the other hand, is related both to the *heights* and to the *depths* that American language teaching has experienced since the beginning of World War II.

From an Address to the Association of Departments of Foreign Languages, Modern Language Association (New York: December 27, 1974). Reprinted with permission.

EXTRA-SOCIETAL AND EXTERNAL SOCIETAL INFLUENCES

During and immediately after World War II—war needs themselves being among the most dramatic influences that American language teaching has *ever* experienced—the most influential ideas shaping American language teaching methods were derived from linguistics and from psychology. I refer to these as *extra-societal* influences since neither the view that gave primacy to syntax and phonology over lexicon and use, nor the view that gave primacy to listening comprehension and to speech over reading and writing, had any societal image, purpose or function explicitly in mind. They did not attempt to cope with the question: "What should be the role of subsequent languages in the life of the learner and in the life of society?" There was absolutely no conscious "language-in-society" model underlying either of these powerful methodological approaches, both of which are still very much with us today.

Although the same extra-societal designation is *not* true with respect to the *second most powerful force* influencing American language teaching during the past third of a century—here I refer to the post-sputnik panic and the realization that language expertise was vital for defense related purposes—that force was an *external* societal factor rather than an internal one. The threat of Soviet technological modernization imposed itself upon us from outside our own boundaries and even when language instruction responded to that threat with all the "non-deliberate" speed at its command, it never (well, "hardly ever") linked up its contribution to national defense with the indigenous language resources internal to American society. The "Language Resources Project" that I headed from 1960-1963, and that resulted in my *Language Loyalty in the United States,* tried to provide such an internal societal link, but it was an idea whose time had not yet quite come. The common American approach to language learning (and, indeed, the common approach of the language teacher per se to the commodity he was "pushing") was that additional languages are useful or crucial for our national well-being *particularly* if such languages are (a) learned in school rather than in the context of home and community, (b) learned as a mature adult (in college and graduate school), (c) learned as a target, in itself, rather than as a process for the mastery of other material, and (d) are exotic to the American content in terms of easy access to the learner.

THE ASCENDENCY OF SOCIETAL CONCERNS

Let us quickly skip over all that the concentration on external threat enabled foreign language teaching to accomplish. The rapid expansion (indeed duplication) of programs, increase in positions, and mushrooming of student incentive funds has been recounted many times. Let us turn immediately to the realization that during the past decade (1965-1975) most of the impetus for change in language teaching and language learning has had strong indigenous societal roots, although the former external exposure is also still present. In this past decade language teaching in the United States has had to respond, as never before, to internal social issues and social needs such as the urban disadvantaged, the alienation of youth, the ethnic minorities, the rebirth of ethnicity among some whose parents fancied that they had escaped from it, and, most recently, the fiscal crunch. Many of these societal needs and re-emerging lost-continents have hit language instruction *directly,* in that the high priorities given to them have left proportionately fewer taxpayer and foundation dollars for other needs. In addition the educational establishment's reaction to those needs and pressures has often hit language instruction *indirectly,* by permitting greater latitude to student choice of subjects to be studied, greater opportunity for "alternative" forms and contents of education, and, correspondingly, lesser insistence on language learning as new subjects and as new populations enter our high schools, colleges and universities.

For one reason or another, language enrollments have generally been dropping, language requirements have been fading, the attack on language learning has been mounting, and—as in all times of strife and disappointment—the time and mood are ripe for a new saviour. Language teaching in the United States needs a new panacea, a good bet, a stimulating idea, a rallying cause, or, at the very least, a straw to clutch at in the form of an unbeatable method. It is at this point that bilingual education enters the picture to save Little Red Riding Hood from the Big Bad Wolf.

BILINGUAL EDUCATION AND COMPENSATORY EDUCATION

There is growing recognition in language teaching circles—as in education circles more generally—that a sizable proportion of the disadvantaged lack facility in English—not to mention standard school English—and that if their educational progress is not to be appreciably delayed and diluted, they had best be taught most subjects in their non-English mother tongues, at least until ESL gets through to them. The recent *Lau* decision of the Supreme Court may soon foster a nation-wide approach along these lines, and yet, with all of its welcome relief for all children whose English is really insufficient for the burden of educational effort, I doubt that it will do much for language instruction. Bilingual education that is merely compensatory, merely transitional, is merely a desperate attempt to fight fire with fire. If a non-English mother-tongue is conceptualized as a disease of the poor, then in true vaccine style this disease is to be attacked by the disease bacillus itself. A little bit of deadened mother tongue, introduced in slow stages in the classroom environment, will ultimately enable the patient to throw off the mother tongue entirely and to embrace all-American vim, vigor and vitality.

My own evaluation is that compensatory bilingual education is not a good long term bet, neither for language teaching nor for bilingual education per se. The multi-problem populations on whose behalf it is espoused—underprivileged, unappreciated, alienated—cannot be aided in more than an initial palliative sense by so slender a reed as compensatory bilingual education. Populations that would present well nigh insuperable problems to our schools and to all of our establishment institutions, even if they were *monolingual* English speakers, will not cease being such problems merely because they are offered a year or two of introductory education primarily in their non-English mother tongues. Their problems and our hang-ups are not that simple to overcome.

Bilingual education "sold" as a compensatory promissory note will disappoint us all—teachers and citizens alike. It will not solve the basic societal problems of the non-English speaking poor and, therefore, will not solve their basic educational problems. It will soon be just another educational panacea gone sour and, language teaching as well as bilingual education as a whole will both suffer needlessly as a result of having made yet another bad bet.

BILINGUAL EDUCATION AND ETHNIC LEGITIMACY

There is another rationale for bilingual education and it might well be of somewhat greater interest to language teachers and to American society at large. Thanks to our recent ethnicity binge it recognizes the non-English mother tongues and cultures in our midst as things of beauty, to be maintained and treasured forever and ever. It recognizes these languages and cultures not for manipulative, compensatory and transitional purposes, but as basic ingredients of a healthy *individual* self-concept and of sound *group* functioning. Groups that are deprived of their languages and cultures are dislocated groups. Such groups have no alternative but to dump dislocated and alienated students on the doorstep of the school and of all other institutions of the larger society. Greater *self*-acceptance among non-English mother tongue children (including acceptance of their parents and their traditions and their immediate societies), and greater mutual acceptance between such children and the American mainstream, will also foster greater genuine school progress. Bilingual education under this rationale is *group maintenance* oriented, and, as a result, not merely a compensatory, transitional "quickie."

Note, however, that it too has an unstated assumption, namely that bilingual education is needed only for the "unmeltable ethnics." Such a view is still patronizing—although "patronizing once-removed"—in that it assumes that non-ethnics are beyond or above bilingual education and "all that." Language and ethnicity are still assigned to the "outer fringe," beyond the propriety of White Anglo-Saxon Protestantdom. Enlightened patronization would not be a propitious approach to strengthening the impact of mathematics or history in American education or in American life and I predict that, welcome though it may be among the Navajos, it will do little or nothing for the place of language learning in our schools and in our society more generally.

BILINGUAL EDUCATION FOR ENRICHMENT

In various parts of Canada (and not only in French Canada) economically comfortable English speaking parents are voluntarily sending their eager youngsters to primarily-but-not-entirely French schools. Such "immersion schools" for societally favored youngsters also exist in France, Germany, Latin America, the Soviet Union, the Arab world, Italy, Belgium, not to mention many, many parts of Africa and Asia. They bring together two languages of wider communication—rather than one pitifully small language and one gargantuanly large one. They involve the populations most able to pay for a good education and most likely to succeed educationally and societally—rather than those least favored in these respects. They require the most advantaged to *stretch further* educationally and, thus, are really an enrichment for the rich. They continue, albeit at a somewhat more accessible level, the bilingual education tradition practiced by most elites from the days of the ancient Egyptians, Greeks and Romans on. They are eminently successful and therefore attract the best students, teachers, administrators. Regrettably, such schools are almost unknown in the public sector of American education.

Of course, bilingual education for enrichment also involves some unspoken assumptions, just as does compensatory and group maintenance bilingual education. It assumes that it is particularly the well-off who not only stand to gain by an additional cultural exposure but that, indeed, they are the very ones for whom such an exposure is an acceptable and even a powerful motivating argument. My own view is that enrichment (or immersion) bilingual education is the best way of demonstrating the *academic* and *societal* advantages of bilingual education. I am sure that it is *this* kind of bilingual education that could become the most reliable prop for language teaching in the United States, just as it has become such in some of the countries I have mentioned. Such a prop would be more than a fad, more than a nostrum, if it were ever to catch on. It represents bilingual education not only at its best but at its broadest. However, I am not sure that "middle America," in whose image most of our secondary and higher educational institutions are shaped, is quite ready for it, or ever will be.

BILINGUAL EDUCATION IN SOCIOLINGUISTIC PERSPECTIVE

Let me close by viewing both bilingual education and language teaching in sociolinguistic perspective. If there is anything that bilingual education has to contribute to language teaching more generally it is its maximization of *language learning for the communication of messages that are highly significant* for senders and receivers alike, both in their individual as well as in their actual and potential societal capacities. There is simply no way in which language teaching which focuses on language as a *target of instruction* can fully capture the total impact upon the learner which is available to language teaching which also capitalizes upon language as the *process of instruction*. Because bilingual education does just that—particularly in its enrichment guise, but also in its compensatory and group maintenance guises which definitely have a validity of their own (although of a more temporally or demographically restricted nature)—it provides a powerful and world-wide boost to language teaching. However, like every potential solution it poses potential problems as well.

Is the American public mature enough for enrichment-oriented bilingual education? Are we and our colleagues in the language teaching profession mature enough to move toward it rather than to reject it because of our personal inadequacies and societal biases? My own tendency is to view the future in optimistic terms. I see the future of language teaching and language learning in the United States as including a greater variety of rationales, goals and methods than has hitherto been the case. I see bilingual education among them, and I see more language teachers able to engage in it than previously, whether for compensatory, group maintenance or enrichment purposes. Indeed, I see American bilingual educators being able to engage in *various kinds* of bilingual education, rather than merely in one kind or another, depending on the students and communities to which they are addressing themselves. Finally, I see more second language teachers also able to engage in bilingual education and more bilingual educators being able to engage in second language instruction, rather than two quite distinct groups of language practitioners, as is most often the case in the USA today.

As for bilingual education itself, it cannot be the panacea for all the ills that plague American language teaching today. It is *but one* opportunity to revitalize language teaching among many. It is itself *internally diversified* into compensatory, group maintenance and enrichment streams and must not be viewed as one undifferentiated blob. It has its own problems of training and funding. It can no more *remake society, education,* nor even *language teaching* than can any other partial solution to all-encompassing and multifaceted problems. It should not be underrated, but it should not be *oversold* on false premises. It has functions that go above and beyond language teaching. However, I know that it is *here to stay* as a *world-wide phenomenon* today, with outcroppings in well over 100 countries, and I trust that our beloved America too will profit from it and contribute to it in the days to come.

Muriel Saville-Troike

Bilingual Children:
A Resource Document

CHILD LANGUAGE ACQUISITION

1. How Language Is Learned

A normal child can learn any language to which he has adequate exposure. If he hears and responds to two languages in his environment, he will become a bilingual.

Much of a child's language development is completed before he ever comes to school. By the age of six months an infant has produced all of the vowel sounds and most of the consonant sounds of any language in the world—including some that do not occur in the language his parents speak. If the child hears English spoken around him, he will learn to discriminate among those that make a difference in the meaning of English words (the *phonemes*), and he will learn to disregard those that do not. If the child hears Spanish spoken around him, he will learn to discriminate among some sounds the English-speaker learns to ignore, as the *r*'s in *pero* "but" and *perro* "dog," and to disregard some differences that are not distinctive in Spanish, but vital to English word-meaning, as the initial sounds of *share* and *chair*.

The average child has mastered most of the distinctive sounds of his first language before he is three years old, and he controls most of its basic grammatical patterns before he is five or six. Complex grammatical patterns continue to develop through the school years, and he may add new vocabulary items even through adult life.

No child has to be trained to learn language. Given even minimally favorable environmental circumstances, he will gain substantial control of the language(s) regularly spoken in his vicinity within the first three or four years of his life.

This feat is little short of miraculous, and we are not at all sure how it is accomplished. The nature of our speculations has changed radically in the past decade, primarily due to recent developments in the field of psycholinguistics. These hypotheses have extensive implications for language development programs during early childhood.

It has been suggested by some that primary language acquisition is in large part the result of the child's natural desire to please his doting parents, who wait impatiently for him to utter a recognizable word. Yet even the offspring of relatively indifferent parents acquire language, as do children of parents who are completely deaf—if there is another at least minimal source of language in his environment.

It has been suggested by others that a child's language acquisition is purposive, that he develops language because of his urge to communicate his wants and needs to

Excerpts from *Bilingual Children: A Resource Document* (Arlington, Virginia: Center for Applied Linguistics 1973), pp. 14–42.

his caretakers. Research indicates, however, that talking develops as an activity that a child indulges in for its own sake. Up to the age of about 18 months, "talk" tends to accompany action or activity rather than being a substitute for it (Gesell 1940). Within his limited sphere of activity, communicative needs seem to be satisfied by gesture and such extra-lingual vocalization as squeals, whines, grunts, and cries.

Perhaps the most widely held view is that a child learns language by imitation. It is true that some of a child's initial language learning can be attributed to his imitation of the sounds around him, but many of his utterances are quite original and cannot be explained as imitations at all. Furthermore, according to this theory, an adult's role would be to correct the child when he is wrong in his language use and to reinforce him when he is correct. In fact, there seems to be no evidence that either correction or reinforcement of phonology and grammar occurs often enough to be an important factor. Parents do correct such "bad language" as "pee-pee" (Gesell 1940), and misstatements of fact, but not immature grammatical forms (Brown, Cazden and Bellugi 1969). The same lack of correction is found from India to Samoa as well (Slobin 1968).

Current research does support the following conclusions:

a. Language Is Uniquely Human

Animal noises relate to biological states and processes, such as hunger, courting, danger signals, and anger. Animals cannot be trained to use these noises inappropriately; that is, they cannot switch noises and use one in a situation which would normally call for another (Lenneberg 1970b).

Further, although the great apes evidently have the physiological capacity to produce speech sounds, none has developed anywhere near the skill of any young child. And all of us who talk regularly to cats or dogs know that no matter how rich a linguistic environment we provide, we never get even one word in return.

Animals certainly develop communication systems, and some (like the dolphin's) seem quite complex, but none even approach the abstractness and complexity of the grammar of a two year old child.

b. Children Have An Inherent Predisposition To Learn Language

This must be assumed in order to explain several facts:

1. Children around the world begin to learn their native language at the same age, in much the same way, and in essentially the same sequence.
2. Children have acquired most of the basic operations in language by the age of four, regardless of their language or social environment.
3. Children can understand and create novel utterances; they are by no means limited to repeating what they have heard, and many child speech patterns are systematically different from those of the adults around them.

In viewing the ability to acquire language in terms of genetic predisposition, we are saying that part of language structure is genetically "given" to every human child. We view English and every other language as an incredibly complex system which no child could possibly *learn* in his early years to the degree he exhibits mastery over it. As remarkable as his ability to create new sentences is, his ability to recognize when a string of common words does *not* constitute a grammatical sentence in the language, such as *Give please some me milk,* is even more so. He has never been told, surely, that that particular group of words is not an English sentence, but he knows. If a child had to consciously learn the set of abstract principles which indicate which groups of words are sentences in his language as opposed to those which are not, only the smartest would learn to talk, and it would take them many more years than it does.

A hypothesis for which there is a good deal of support is that a great many of these abstract principles are common to all languages, as opposed to the principles that are language specific, and that those that are universal are "programmed" into each human child just by virtue of his being human. These would be language-related genetic specifications, which would not be sufficient in themselves to account for language acquisition, but would account for a child's ability to process the smorgasbord of sounds and words that he hears and come up with essentially the same structures (in the same sequence) as every other child.

c. Children Learn To Talk

They will never acquire language unless they hear it. Lenneberg (1970a) draws a useful analogy between learning language and eating:

> Biology takes over [in learning to talk] in basically the same fashion as it does when the child metabolized protein after eating. He uses the proteins but not in ready-made form. They are broken down into polypeptides and amino acids and reassembled according to built-in purposes, purposes embodied in the genetic codes that determine the directions of protein synthesis and serve the needs of his maturing body.
>
> The child needs language for survival just as he needs food. The information he receives from us may be regarded as raw material of a sort. It passes via auditory channels into the central nervous system where it is "absorbed," broken down into its elements, and resynthesized in the achievement of varied and complex language skills (p. 12).

Even if the universal properties of language are preprogrammed in the child, he must learn all of those features which distinguish his native language from all other possible human languages. He will learn to speak only the language(s) he hears around him, no matter what his linguistic heritage. An American-born child of Japanese or Greek ancestry will never learn the language of his grandparents if only English surrounds him.

A child must learn those properties of his language that are not universal, that are not necessary in all human languages. For instance, in French we find the sounds (ö) and (ü). English does not contain these sounds, nor do many other languages. (ö) and (ü) are possible language sounds, but their occurrence in an individual language is accidental. A burp and a cough, on the other hand, are not sounds of English or French. They are not found in any language nor could they be; this is not accidental. The child does not have to learn that such noises are not possible language sounds; he "knows" this innately in much the same sense as he invariably "knows" he can manipulate his hands and sets about grasping things with them as soon as his motor development permits.

Consider how innate knowledge of possible language structure saves the child from countless useless hypotheses about how the language he is in the process of acquiring works. For example, in English we say *The baby is hungry* and *Is the baby hungry?*; *Your brother is here* and *Is your brother here?* Note that in each case the question may be formed from the statement by moving the third word, counting from the left, to the leftmost position in each string of words. However, this rule would also generate *In John is New York?* from *John is in New York,* and *Girl the little is here?* from *The little girl is here.*

The utterances of children in the process of acquiring language deviate in many ways from those of adults, but children never make the kind of mistakes just illustrated. There is no human language which signals meaning by moving every third or fifth or seventh word to the beginning of the sentence, nor could there be one. It appears that only certain kinds of hypotheses can occur to the child because the mind works in certain ways and not in others.

If this were not so, we would have difficulty accounting for the fact that the sentences one child produces at various levels of language development, although often not conforming to adult models, are very similar to those of other children at the same level of development in all other language communities. They make the same kinds of mistakes.

One universal process in language which children make extensive use of in their language development is analogy. An English-speaking child hears and uses forms like *cat:cats; dog:dogs;* and *book:books.* He unconsciously formulates a generalized rule for English plurals and correctly uses *rat:rats* without ever hearing that particular construction before. If his extension to *foot:foots* meets disapproval, he will revise his rule and learn the exception; if he escapes early correction, he will continue to use *foots* until some experience brings the "error" to his attention.

Language is learned in the sense that a child cannot acquire it unless he is in an appropriate environment, and in the sense that he will develop whatever specific variety of language (pronunciation, grammar, and vocabulary) is unique to his family's social group.

d. Children Learn Different Styles of Speech and Paralinguistic Behavior

Even young children are aware of the changing appropriateness of different styles of speech with different communicative contexts, and can interpret and use a variety of gestures, facial expressions, and other paralinguistic devices common to their own culture.

For example, a Spanish-speaking five year old in a California kindergarten started speaking English with a lisp, although he did not lisp in Spanish. The answer was his English-speaking friend, who had recently lost his front teeth. (The Spanish-speaker was obviously using a peer model for his English, and not his teacher.) As he made more English-speaking friends, he acquired a normal pronunciation, but he continued to lisp when the deviant pronunciation was appropriate—whenever he talked to his lisping friend.

Another example is provided by a linguistics professor in Texas who is from a dialect region where *creek* is pronounced (krɪk); his wife pronounces it (krik). His five year old son asked if he could go fishing in the (krik) one afternoon. The three year old daughter corrected him, saying, "Don't you know you're supposed to say (krik) to Mommy and (krɪk) to Daddy?"

Many more supporting examples are coming from experience in school integration. Young children add the appropriate dialect forms when they wish to identify with their new friends. Anglo children are adding the nonstandard English forms of their Black and Spanish-speaking classmates as well as the other way around.

Learning is also undoubtedly involved in this aspect of language acquisition and socialization, but there has evidently been no research at all in this area. We can safely assume that the process varies in different linguistic communities, however, and can speculate that it involves:

1. Some degree of imitation. There would be cultural differences in who provides the model, in what contexts, and to what extent.
2. Explicit correction by adults. This is likely to be minimal (again depending on the culture), but occurs whenever someone says to a child, "That's not a nice way to talk," or "Don't look at me like that," or imparts any other rule of sociolinguistic etiquette.
3. Feedback from social interaction. The reactions of others to any specific speech style or behavior, though often unconscious, probably constitute the most potent force in this process.

An analysis of the body movements of older bilingual children while they were using both languages suggests that a child will use only those characteristic of his native language if it is socially more prestigious, but will tend to modify his gestures and body position in the second language if it has higher status than his first (Brown and Bellugi 1964). When a child's parents each speak a different language natively, this study of French/English bilinguals shows the child (boy or girl) will adopt the paralinguistic system of the mother.

e. There Is a Cutoff Point for Language Development

Progress in language development usually stops at about the age of puberty—no matter what level has been reached. Mentally retarded children, who have had a slower rate of development (but in the same relative sequence), are likely never to develop a complete adult grammar for this reason.

Another consequence is seen in learning a second language:

The extent of a foreign accent is directly correlated with the age at which the second language is acquired. At the age of three or four practically every child entering a foreign community learns to speak the new language rapidly and without a trace of an accent. This facility declines with age. The proportion of children who speak the second language with an accent tends to increase, but very slowly, so that by the age of 12, perhaps 1% or 2% pronounce words differently from native speakers. A dramatic reversal of form occurs during the early teens, however, when practically every child loses the ability to learn a new language without an accent (Lenneberg 1970a:9-11).

This has important implications for education because it means that fluent bilinguals are not developed in high school and college foreign language programs. Our bilingual children are the "advantaged" in this physiological sense. They have the innate capacity and the potential linguistic environment to accomplish what many of us have failed to do well in all our years of schooling.

2. How Mothers Talk to Children

A mother's language generally seems to follow the model her child sets, and not vice versa. She simplifies both her word choice and grammar, adding more complex structures as her child does, although her notion of "simplicity" does not correspond to the actual sequence in language acquisition. She imitates the child much more frequently than he imitates her.

In this imitation, mothers often provide expansions of the child's utterances. This process is of disputed importance. Brown and Bellugi (1964), Cazden (1966), and Lenneberg (1960, 1967, 1970) would argue that such expansions are not necessary for language learning, and perhaps do not even facilitate it. Others, such as Slobin (1967), think expansions by adults are quite important to linguistic development.

The answer to this controversy would be extremely important to all personnel in early childhood education interested in facilitating language learning in their programs. Additional research in this area is clearly needed, particularly when we add the complexities of development in two languages. A few studies have been made of minority group mothers talking to their children, but they seem very unreliable. We can only be sure that these mothers do not talk to their children as much as middle class white mothers do in the presence of a linguist, psychologist, or tape recorder.

While we lack information on just what, how, and how much a mother's language use contributes to child language development, we know that early linguistic stimulation is essential. And we should remember that the child is an active participant in this process, interacting with his social environment.

3. Sequence of Language Development

We may view the child's developing in his first language as evolving into a more and more complex set of rules. This acquisition tends to correlate with increasing maturation. In the earlier stages, at least, increasing maturation seems to be more reliably definable in terms of motor development than chronological age.

Because the levels of language development can be delineated and studied, it is possible to talk about "child grammar," that is, to devise a set of rules to describe the kinds of sentences a child can produce or understand at a given maturational level (Menyuk 1969). The sentences which a child can process at a particular developmental stage are not viewed as failures on the part of the child to produce sentences of the same grammatical form as adults, but are considered the normal output of all children at that level of development. As the child matures, so do his language abilities. Since certain grammatical processes are more complex than others, they require a higher maturational level of the child than simpler ones. In order to master complexities in his first language which are beyond his present linguistic grasp, what the normal child needs is additional time, not additional stimuli (Piaget 1955).

Linguists probably know more about the child's acquisition of his phonological system than they do about other aspects. The first sounds an infant makes are reflexive (0–3 months) and associated with physiological states. During the next "babbling" period (3–12 months), he demonstrates almost unlimited phonetic capability, producing sounds that will have no later use in his language. When a child first begins to distinguish meaningful speech sounds, he has only one consonant and one vowel, and can produce words like [mama]. The next step is differentiating between a labial consonant (like [m]) and a non-labial (like [d]) allowing [dada] as well. The next distinction is between back and front vowels (as [a] and [i]).

The process of splitting of sounds continues until the child has mastered the whole inventory of phonemes in the language. Then the process stops. Some problem pairs are [t]:[k], [Θ]:[f], [w]:[r], and [l]:[y] because of their acoustic similarity. The most dissimilar sounds in his language are distinguished first, and the most similar last. Most sounds are controlled by a three year old, and all by the age of about seven.

Semantics, or meaning, is basic to all language learning. Brown (1973) suggests that the first meanings are an extension of Piaget's "sensorimotor intelligence." A child is innately capable of distinguishing objects, recognizing relationships, and learning that environmental experiences can be expressed with language. All children in the first stage of language acquisition (18 to 24 months) have the same repertoire of operations and relations to express this meaning, whatever their first language. These include naming, negation, action and object, location, possession, and attribute.

In the second stage, children learn noun and verb inflections, means for expressing spatial relations, and some auxiliary forms in grammar. Although most basic structures have been acquired by four or five, the acquisition of syntax continues at least through age ten and perhaps never terminates completely (C. Chomsky 1971).

The *rate* of a child's progression through these and subsequent stages will vary radically among children, but the *order* of development is invariant across both children and languages. The rate is influenced by both family interaction variables and intelligence, while the order has been "primarily determined by the relative semantic and grammatical complexity of constructions" (Brown 1973:59).

4. Language and Physical Maturity

The following correlations of motor and language development are taken from Lenneberg's "On Explaining Language" (1970c:4):

Age	Motor Milestones	Language Milestones
0,5	Sits using hands for support; unilateral reaching	Cooing sounds change to babbling by introduction of consonantal sounds
1	Stands; walks when held by one hand	Syllabic reduplication; signs of understanding some words; applies some sounds regularly to signify persons or objects, that is, the first words
1.5	Prehension and release fully developed; gait propulsive; creeps downstairs backward	Repertoire of 3 to 50 words not joined in phrases; trains of sounds and intonation patterns resembling discourse; good progress in understanding
2	Runs (with falls); walks stairs with one foot forward only	More than 50 words; two-word phrases most common; more interest in verbal communication; no more babbling
2.5	Tiptoes 3 yards (2.7 meters); walks stairs with alternating feet; jumps 0.9 meter	Vocabulary of some 1000 words; about 80 percent intelligibility; grammar of utterances close approximation to colloquial adult; syntactic mistakes fewer in variety, systematic, predictable
	Jumps over rope; hops on one foot; walks on line	Language well established; grammatical anomalies restricted either to unusual constructions or to the more literate aspects of discourse

5. Language and Concept Development

Given the complexity of language, it is no wonder that even adults with their mature intellects seldom attain native fluency in a new language. But children, with their limited memories, restricted reasoning powers, and as yet almost non-existent analytical abilities, acquire perfect fluency in any language to which they are consistently exposed. The ability to acquire language could not be dependent upon intellectual powers alone.

The argument has been presented that children universally accomplish this feat because the human infant is genetically endowed with the ability to do so. All available evidence indicates that this ability to acquire a native language is not a function of general intelligence. A 12-year-old child with an IQ of 50 is in control of a linguistic code. His IQ will degenerate to about 30 by the age of 20, yet he will not lose his linguistic ability (Lenneberg, Nichols, and Rosenberger 1964). At the same time, a child with a clearly superior IQ will not necessarily begin to speak earlier, or with better results than a child of ordinary intellect (Gesell 1940). These facts would be difficult to explain if the ability to acquire language were simply a facet of general intelligence.

Yet language and concept development are inexorably related. There are absolute correspondences between the level of cognitive development and the type of relationships that can be verbalized, and mental age correlates more closely than chronological age with many of the kinds of sentences children understand.

Those who work with linguistically diverse children should view with suspicion all claims that the developmental sequence of concepts is universally the same. There is good reason to believe that this sequence is influenced by the child's culture to some extent.

It may be influenced by his language, since language facilitates (and to some extent may determine) the categorization of experience (Segil 1964). Navajo children appear to categorize objects much more frequently along the dimensions of shape and use than do English-speakers of the same age, for instance, and relatively less frequently by color and size. This might be explained by their language, which requires categorization by shape as a basic grammatical process and the concept of use in nominalization, or naming.

These correlations do not mean that language is entirely *necessary* for cognition. Deaf children organize experience in much the same way as those who hear, and all children can solve many kinds of problems without being able to verbalize them. The reverse is very unlikely; expression in language cannot precede cognitive development.

When a second language is learned as an adult, the process is one of learning new labels for concepts that are already developed. In early childhood bilingual contexts, a child is learning to express many brand new concepts in one language or the other, and language and concept development cannot be separated. This suggests that careful attention should be paid to their developmental sequence in the child's particular culture—for the sake of the child's emotional well being as well as efficiency. It is also important to decide which language to use to express which concepts if linguistic interference is to be minimized.

6. Boys vs. Girls

Even young children can be reliably identified as to sex by judges who hear only their recorded voices. This is not a difference in pitch, but is identifiable in the formant patterns recorded by a sound spectograph (Sachs 1972). This suggests that part of language acquisition is developing cultural patterns for marking sex-identification in speech.

Psycholinguistic studies of language development are not finding girls to be superior, which is at variance with older tests. Berko (1958), for instance, measured children's ability to extend the rule for forming the past tense of *melted* to new forms. She found no significant difference between scores of boys and girls at seven age levels from 4 to 7 years.

A significant difference in second language learning was found to be in favor of *boys* in a Fresno, California, kindergarten program (Manning and Brengelman 1965). It is a probable example of how child-rearing practices are an important variable, at least in how the children respond to both tests and to second language instruction. The Mexican-American boys in the classes tended to be much more extrovertive, and much more actively involved in the second language drills and games. The Mexican-American girls talked less, participated less, and evidently learned less in the program.

The better grades and higher achievement scores which girls receive in school is undoubtedly a cultural factor in our society, and not due to any advantage they have been alleged to have in language development.

It is important to add that the results of the Fresno program which show more active boys to be better language learners is also an artifact of our culture. That program was based on "learning by doing." There is no reason why different methods would not be equally successful for children with different styles of learning.

7. The Effects of Socio-Economic Status

We often hear the claim that economic deprivation and the social conditions associated with it tend to interfere with language development in children. We need to view such claims very skeptically, since the poor performance of a linguistically and culturally different group of children on various tests is usually only reflective of the linguistic and cultural bias of the tests being used, or of the testing situation itself.

This deficit hypothesis is held by many who are in the field of bilingual education. In a handbook for educators published by the Office of Education, for instance, Ulibarri states, "The teacher must remember that the child coming from an impoverished environment has had little language development in either his native vernacular or in English" (1969:38). And Engelman (1969) has said that migrant Spanish-speaking children in the Midwest must begin learning English from scratch because they come to school with no concepts at all.

There are research reports which to some extent support this notion of linguistic retardation among children of low socio-economic status (SES): Jones and McMillan (1973) find their speech to be "less fluent and grammatically less complex," and Quisenberry (1971) finds significant lag in their syntactic maturity at age four. Although the lower SES children in these studies tend to be from minority groups in the United States, there is some data from other language communities as well. In a study of Italian children in Rome, Parisi (1971) finds that SES differences appear in language development at about 3 1/2 years and that the split gradually widens, especially between 5 1/2 and 6.

Not all researchers agree: Templin (1957) reports an SES difference in language production at age 3, but says there is no indication of cumulative deficit; Shriner and Miner (1968) find no SES differences in children's language structures; and Evans (1971) finds no SES (or Mexican-American/Anglo) differences in auditory discrimination or repetition tasks. In a fairly extensive study of the language maturity of children in Baltimore and the surrounding area, Entwisle (1967) found low SES first graders living in slums more advanced linguistically than higher SES children in the suburbs (although by the third grade the slum children lagged behind).

One safe conclusion is that we are not sure what children do *not* know about their language. Another is that both children and languages are exceedingly complex. Part of the disparity in the research results cited above is due to the selective view each takes of what aspect of language to measure: number of words used per sentence; ratio of modifiers to nouns and verbs; percentage of subordinate structures; patterns of word association responses. Tests of "language development" are not all testing the same thing. Part of the disparity is due to what complete language system is being selected from; in most cases it is the middle class adult speech community to which the testor belongs, and different groups of children will have different degrees of experience with it. Part of the disparity is due to diversity in child/testor rapport.

We should not deny the importance of language testing because of this complexity, although we should reject the stereotypes which some of them support. These are potentially very damaging to the self-fulfillment, social development, and educational achievement of many bilingual children. In a positive sense, finding out what children *do* know about their language is an important prerequisite to understanding and accepting them where they are, to using their diverse linguistic and cultural experiences as resources upon which to build.

8. Finding Out What Children Know

A principal in one Texas school was so upset with a language assessment program being used on his "disadvantaged" kindergarten students, he called one of the testors into his office, pointed to a picture on the wall, and said, "Tell me everything you can about *this*."

The woman stumbled over a few incoherent words (scoring "non-verbal," no doubt), but of course gave no true sample of her linguistic competence in response. Although such a demand is outside the bounds of normal communication, and often threatening to children as well as to the adult in this instance, this questioning method is currently in wide use to determine the language proficiency of young children.

If the Texas principal had not been trying to make a point about unfair testing techniques, this situation would never have arisen between two adults. We don't talk to "people" like that.

There are often appropriate differences in the linguistic code used between adults and between an adult and a child, including different word choice, grammatical complexity, intonation, and such paralinguistic factors as gesture, facial expression, and posture. It should always be remembered that these differences are largely culture specific, and a child from one culture can easily misinterpret the intent of an adult from another group.

The culture of the school is closest to middle-class white norms, but it utilizes some unique linguistic patterns. Some of these patterns have extended down into early childhood programs as well, and may be seen as inhibitors of spontaneous interaction.

Labov (1970) lists these potentially inhibiting practices as:

1. Aggravated commands. We say "Do as you're told" and "Talk to me" to children, but never to adults.
2. Repeating what the child has just said.

3. Obvious lying. This is usually done to force answers to questions the adults obviously already know the answer to.

4. Demanding "correct" answers to moral questions, rather than factual questions, even in tests supposedly designed to measure a child's control of his language.

When the verbal context is an artificial testing situation, or any context which is threatening, there is little reason to expect a natural response from a child.

There are no completely appropriate language evaluation measures for young children from linguistically and culturally diverse backgrounds. Natural speech can only be elicited in natural communicative contexts, and listening to children talk to each other in the course of work and play will provide more reliable information on their fluency and ability to express themselves than any formal techniques.

For an adult to find out what a child is thinking, what he knows, he should talk to the child very simply and directly. He should avoid the inhibiting aggravated commands, repetitions, lies, and moral injunctions. He should *listen*.

BECOMING BILINGUAL

1. Learning a Second Language

While it seems to be much easier for a young child to acquire a second language than it is for an adult to, even he cannot learn it as he did his first. For one thing, a child entering kindergarten at age five has spent his waking hours for four years mastering his native language, but the school has only a few hours a day to bring the child to the same level of competence in the second language if he is to achieve successfully in an English-speaking school. This is one reason why the presentation of sounds, structure, and vocabulary must be made in a way which efficiently shortcuts the time required for learning English if he has immediate need for it in first grade. Bilingual programs do not put the same time constraints on learning the second language.

Another major difference in first and second language acquisition is that a child's first language learning is closely related to his cognitive development. He acquires his language at about the same time as he expands his conceptual powers. Second language learning during the school years has an entirely different relationship to conceptual maturation. In general, a child learns his first language to express the new meanings he perceives in his environment; in a second language, he usually learns new forms to express concepts he has already assimilated.

First and second language acquisition share at least one important feature: the learning rate of both depends in part on the child's need and opportunity to use the language to communicate.

There appear to be extensive differences in the language learning faculties of children and adults which suggest that different methods and materials are appropriate for each age group. We are sure that abilities differ, but the bases for these differences are largely unknown at the present time. They may result from neurological changes, from loss of an ability (such as eidetic imagery), from a shift of set or attention, or because of the adult's greater richness in semantic associations. Major differences include (Ervin-Tripp 1968):

a. Children show a greater readiness to learn the language of their contemporaries in a new linguistic environment, to join the group.

  b. Children enjoy rote memorization, while adults prefer solving intellectual problems.
  c. Adults emphasize the content of language, often neglecting its formal system.
  d. Children are more perceptive to the sounds of a language, adults to its meaning.
  e. Children relate speech more to the immediate context, while adults may attach it to related thoughts not immediately relevant.
  f. Children usually learn new words through sensory activities, adults in a purely verbal context.
  g. Children can make linguistic abstractions—learn about structures never directly presented to them, but adults have a greater capacity to remember stated grammatical rules.
  h. Children are less subject to interference from their native language systems than are adults.

2. Interference Phenomena

As a child develops his control over his own native language, the linguistic habits involved in the perception and production of the language become increasingly fixed. Although all physiologically normal children are born with the capacity to produce any sound used in any language, as they get older, they lose the flexibility to produce other sounds. More importantly in some respects, they learn to hear all sounds in terms of the particular set of sound-categories used in their own language. "Foreign" sounds are not heard as such, but rather are unconsciously and automatically pigeonholed in one of the pre-existing categories of the native language. Spanish speakers, for example, commonly hear English *ship* and *sheep* as identical, because the differences in these vowel sounds are not distinctive in Spanish. English speakers, conversely, commonly have difficulty in recognizing the difference between the *r*-sounds in Spanish *pero* "but" and *perro* "dog." It is not that they are inherently incapable of hearing the particular differences, but rather that they have been conditioned *not* to, by their previous experience with their own language.

Comparable problems occur in grammar and vocabulary, all of which result from the natural tendency of a speaker to carry over the habits of his native language into the second, or to translate from one into the other. All of these problems of perception and use of a second language which are due to the native language habits of a child are termed linguistic *interference*.

Many interference problems can be predicted and explained through contrastive analysis (a procedure for comparing two languages: see Saville and Troike 1971). Such analysis is also useful in ordering the elements of the second language so that they may be presented in a graded sequence. Being aware of systematic differences between languages is a useful prerequisite for developing teaching methods and materials. Because languages are systematic, a child's speaking habits will not be effectively altered by piecemeal "correction" of his native habits as he learns English, and such an approach may inhibit fluency in any case. The new elements of English need to be taught as part of a new language *system* which will be added to the child's total linguistic competence.

Because language is essentially a social phenomenon, learned in a social context, and used to communicate with others in a society, it is not surprising that some social factors also interfere with second language learning. We need to perceive and understand cultural as well as linguistic differences in our students if we are to teach effectively.

The most important factor in the home affecting second language learning is the attitude of the parents toward their own speech community, toward the school, and toward the prospects of acculturation. Also important are the educational level of the parents, the degree to which the child interacts with the second language community, and the child's ordinal rank among the children in the family. The oldest child may have no reinforcement at home for his second language experiences, while a younger child will have brothers and sisters who may also be learning the second language at school.

It should not be surprising that we sometimes find factors in the schools themselves which interfere with a child's second language learning. Where these occur, they include:

a. Inappropriate teaching methods and materials.
b. Limited peer associations: little need or opportunity to communicate in the second language.
c. Negative attitudes toward the child's language and culture.
d. Low expectations of learning capacity.
e. Administrative segregation of linguistic minorities into "special" classes.

3. Optimum Age for Second Language Learning

A good motto might be "the sooner the better" for learning a foreign language—prior to age six, if at all possible.

Lenneberg's research (1970a) reports that any child of three or four can learn a foreign language without a non-native accent if the context is favorable, but that this ability diminishes with age. Further substantiation for this view comes from Penfield (1965) who argues that only a young child can establish a completely new center in the brain for the second language system. After about age twelve, a speaker passes out of this formative period and the initially uncommitted part of the brain he could have used has been taken over for other functions.

Some evidence to the contrary cannot be taken very seriously. Hakes (in Ulibarri 1969:116) says, for instance, "... interference and negative transfer are more common with the bilingual than with the monolingual student." Granted that a child will not experience interference from his second language if he doesn't have one, but this doesn't answer our question. At what age can a child most efficiently learn a second language?

Despite the neurological evidence favoring early childhood, there are other considerations. One is the child's first language development; there is some reason to believe that a child will experience more interference between language systems if the second is added before the first is completely developed (at about age ten). Another is the child's self-concept; some hypothesize that a child may not see himself as a stable whole if he has two cultural identities before one is accepted, that he will grow up between two languages and two cultures, a condition known as *anomie*. There are many instances of a bilingual child refusing to understand or use one of his languages for a period of time, essentially choosing one identity and rejecting the other.

If a child living in the United States does not speak English, he has no choice other than to become bilingual. The optimum age for introducing English to him as a second language depends on several social factors as well as on the neurological ones. If he lives in a monolingual non-English-speaking community and will have access to a bilingual program in first grade, the early childhood years can perhaps best be spent on first language development and enrichment. If this same child will not have access to a bilingual program, however, it is probable that he will experience frustration and failure in first grade unless he has prerequisite English language skills. A high priority should be placed in this case on teaching him English as a second language during early childhood. This is important, since a child whose initial experience with school is failure can seldom be reclaimed in remedial programs. He rarely catches up.

A child in a bilingual home and community with positive attitudes toward both of his languages and cultures can probably benefit from the neurological advantages of early second language development without running risks of a negative or amorphous self-identity.

4. Psychological Factors

It has long been recognized that attitudinal factors are very important in learning, and second language learning is no exception. If a child has a positive attitude toward the English-speaking community and wants to relate to it, he will learn English better. If an English-dominant social group puts a stigma of inferiority on a child's native language, it can easily create a barrier to learning.

Teachers need to be as sensitive to their own attitudes as to the child's. The way they feel about their cultural and linguistic identity is an important factor in the way they relate to children of the same or different cultural backgrounds. Most teachers are members of the middle class, accept its values, and feel justified in demanding middle-class standards from all children. Teachers who have recently migrated to the middle class from lower-class origins may reject children from the same background because they are a threat to their change of identity.

A teacher who recognizes these feelings in herself should be able to control this rejection and become a positive model for the children to identify with. Unrecognized, such feelings must create a source of negative identity and conflict.

Motivation is another key factor in second language learning. Every child learns a great deal of his language from his peer group, and one of his strongest motivations for learning language is his desire to communicate with them. We should therefore provide as much opportunity for inter-child communication as possible. Programs which assign English-speaking children to one area and non-English-speaking children to another are failing to recognize or utilize one of the most powerful psychological factors in language learning. Children from diverse language backgrounds will readily learn to communicate with one another when they have both need and opportunity to do so.

PROFILES OF BILINGUAL CHILDREN

1. Mexican-American Children

Everyone who lives in the Southwestern United States "understands" Mexican-Americans, their values, their problems, and their life-style. To prepare teachers of Mexican-American children (in case the teachers come from another part of the country or lack assurance in their classroom practices), the educational literature and local curriculum guides provide handy lists of these cultural traits. Mexican-Americans are reported as typically:

  a. Passive. They accept their poor lot in life, saying, "Que será, será."
  b. Non-competitive. They lead a peaceful rural existence and do not care to join the urban rat race. Nor is much attention paid to such competitive aspects of school as test scores and grades.

c. Present-oriented. They work to satisfy present needs, and not for future goals. (This explains the lack of importance the family places on their children's education.)

Many Mexican-American children are considered "alingual" as well—without language. They speak only a mixture of Spanish and English, really neither one, or they don't talk at all. This is blamed on their noisy, crowded home environment and the number of children in each family, which prevents the mother from talking much to any one of them.

In fact, almost no generalizations about Mexican-Americans can be substantiated by objective research if one does not begin with the invalid assumption that the "Mexican-American culture" is a monolithic whole. There are important regional, social class, and rural/urban differences in the population which are seldom taken into account when data are reported.

Little is really known about the values Mexican-American children learn by being members of that ethnic group. The passive stereotype is commonly applied by the dominant group in a society to minorities, and it may reflect a coping style developed by historically oppressed people in this country to avoid calling attention to themselves or "getting into trouble." It is interesting that the stereotype is being maintained even while such formerly "passive" minorities as Blacks, Chicanos, and Indians are rapidly changing to a much more active coping style.

This contradiction was dramatized several years ago when a well-known Mexican psychologist reported on his cross-cultural studies during a meeting at the National University in Mexico City. At the very time he was presenting his statistically-impressive evidence that Mexicans are passive, the University was just beginning to recover from a full-scale student riot. His conclusions were drawn from the responses to such multiple-choice questions as, "What would you do in case of an earthquake?" Texas-Anglo students included in the study were judged "active" for responding that they would run outside, while Mexicans were judged "passive" for responding that they would stay inside. These responses prove only that Mexicans know more about earthquakes than do Texans. Californians, too, stay inside in doorways during an earthquake if they are in an area of tall buildings, and it usually takes only one such experience for their children to learn such "passivity." (Such fallacious interpretations of data clearly show the general need in research to be sensitive to cultural bias.)

A study of the cooperative vs. competitive behavior of Anglo, Black, Mexican-American, and Mexican elementary school children (Madsen and Shapira 1970) shows the Anglos and Blacks most competitive, with Mexican-Americans somewhat less, but still much more so than the Mexicans. This may well be an urban/rural difference instead of an ethnic one, however, since the Mexican group was rural and only about 20% of the Mexican-Americans in the Southwest still live in rural areas. It may also be a social-class difference, since Wasserman (1971) reports more cooperative behavior among "blue-collar children"—whether Mexican-American, Black, or Anglo. Another study by Kagan and Madsen (1971) included four- and five-year-old children and showed no differences at all at that age. Only 3% of the moves of each group in the test rates "competitive," and no group behavioral differences appeared along this dimension until ages seven to nine. Yet another study (Del Campo 1970) finds that Mexican-American children score *higher* on competitive values than do Anglos.

Concern for present needs rather than future gratification is a well-documented characteristic of those who live in poverty. There is absolutely no basis for the stereotype which attributes this to Mexican-Americans as an ethnic group. As for parental interest in education, Mexican-American families place about the same emphasis on education as any other families (Anderson and Johnson 1971). Educators must look elsewhere to explain the high degree of academic failure these children experience.

Claims that Mexican-American children are "alingual" are based on inappropriate testing techniques and misunderstanding about the nature of language and linguistic diversity.

Most Mexican-American children already have two well-developed language systems before they enter school, although they may speak "nonstandard" dialects of one or both. It is quite natural for them to switch from one language to the other, as do adults in bilingual communities, although they should also learn to keep the two codes separate on more formal occasions as they mature linguistically. What is sometimes called "Tex-Mex" is a regional variant of Spanish with some English borrowings in the lexicon. Words like *troca* for "truck" also occur commonly in the Spanish of Northern Mexico.

Even older children's Spanish is often deprecated by educators who do not understand the nature of language. An educator in Texas writes:

> He speaks Spanish with his playmates. But it is an impoverished Spanish, a language which has been culturally "beheaded" by its forced separation from its own literary heritage.

Another, from Arizona, says:

> The fact that the pupil's home language is a colloquial Spanish may be only one additional handicap, no more important than other cultural handicaps.

Conclusions that Mexican-American children's English is stronger than their Spanish (e.g., Cornejo 1973 and Swanson and DeBlassie 1971) may also be based on linguistic naïveté. Those who always speak one language at home and always speak the other in a different domain (like school or work) learn the vocabulary for each domain only in the relevant language. A child may know only the Spanish terms for furniture or cooking utensils found at home, for instance, and only English for such uniquely scholastic objects as chalkboard and filmstrip projector, or terms in subjects like geography and science which he might never discuss at home. Even bilingual teachers who were educated themselves in monolingual English schools have experienced considerable initial difficulty teaching these subjects in Spanish.

Intelligence and achievement tests in Spanish (particularly when normed in Puerto Rico or Mexico) are often just as inappropriate for these children as those in English, and are just as unreliable. It is little wonder that so many studies find Mexican-American children have a lower IQ than Anglo children.

Although there are several reliable descriptions of the language of Mexican-American children (Lastra 1969, Carrow 1971, González 1970, 1973), there are serious needs for further research, including:

a. Studies of regional and social variation in adult Spanish-speaking communities in the United States. (Child language needs to be described in terms of the adult speech around him, and not a different norm.)
b. Studies of language development in the same region by children from different socio-economic levels.
c. Studies of code-switching phenomena, by adults and by children, and in different contexts.

    d. Studies of the acquisition of social rules governing language use.

    e. Studies of second language acquisition controlled for age, socio-economic level, and learning context.

Denying the stereotypes that appear in the educational literature does not mean denying all differences. The "average" Mexican-American family does differ from the "average" Anglo family in size, occupational level, and economic status; a larger percentage of the Mexican-American population belongs to the Catholic church; a larger percentage maintains bilingual competencies than any other ethnic group; and a disproportionate number of Mexican-American children do fail in school.

Those who fail are most likely to be different from the mainstream Anglo norms in most of these respects, by definition the "unacculturated." A primary goal of early childhood programs has often been to try to eliminate these differences, to change the children and/or their families to fit the educational system they will enter. An alternate possibility, at least theoretically proposed by advocates of bilingual/bicultural programs, is to accept and build upon individual and social differences, to change the educational system to fit linguistically and culturally diverse children.

2. Puerto Rican Children

The Puerto Rican population is geographically divided by the sizeable chunk of the Atlantic Ocean which lies between the Island of Puerto Rico and the U.S. mainland. Historically the population of Puerto Rico is a racial and cultural combination of Spanish, African, and Taino, and currently the mainland group is a heterogeneous mixture of temporary residents, recent migrants, older migrants, and native-born.

The Puerto Rican community in the United States is in a state of turbulent change, and the differences which have developed among the Islanders and the mainland groups have thus far prevented that change from taking a single, unifying direction. Migration has brought new problems to adults and their children; the older mainlanders still feel ties to the Island, but also feel their own situation is not always understood by those in Puerto Rico.

Much of the controversy focuses on education and language policy, on the desired amount of acculturation to the dominant U.S. language and culture.

The still-lingering resentment against U.S. imperialism in Puerto Rican education is understandable when we read of the language policy imposed in the Island in the first half of this century (Cremer 1932):

> The unifying effects of a language are strong. A double language practice is disintegrating in effect.
>
> One of the handicaps to uniformity of language usage is the unwillingness of the older generation to cooperate for the benefit of their children and the nation at large.
>
> Since the United States is a major nation of the world, Puerto Rico can well get the pace from a growing and ascending nation and learn the expression of the ways of a great people.

The Puerto Ricans constitute New York's newest and youngest minority group. They account for one fourth of the New York state school population and 70% of the non-English speakers in New York City. With a median income of only $3500, one third are on public welfare.

Poverty and the pressures of cultural displacement and change are sufficient to account for most of the other problems which beset Puerto Rican parents and children: breakdown of the traditional family structure, emotional disorientation, discrimination, and educational failure.

The family roles for the traditional Puertorriqueño were clearly defined, but both poverty and affluence are eroding this structure. In a large city like New York, there is often more opportunity for an unskilled or undereducated woman to find employment than her husband, removing her from the traditional family role and creating many conflicts for the male ego. On the other hand, a breakdown of these roles with more even distribution of labor and responsibility is also a result of higher socio-economic status and assimilation (McCauley 1972). More general evolutionary factors may also be at work, since there is a change in this direction throughout Latin America which cannot be considered assimilation to Anglo-American culture.

There are large numbers of "abandoned" children reported in both Puerto Rico and New York. The traditional extended Island family copes with this problem, but the different family patterns in New York have deprived children of this security.

> Traditional features of Puerto Rican culture (machismo, the practice of the mistress, consensual unions, the culture of poverty) have created a problem of abandonment in the past. In the process of migration, the cultural patterns whereby people sought to cope with the consequences of abandonment are easily lost (Fitzpatrick 1971:159).

A further breakdown in family structure occurs as children are exposed and educated to different values than their parents hold. The resulting changes in attitudes and behavior are often seen as disrespectful, and can be very threatening.

There has been a very high rate of mental illness in the Puerto Rican populations of both the Island and New York, especially in the form of schizophrenia (Malzberg 1956, Fitzpatrick 1971). The reasons usually given for this are only speculative, but it must be taken as an indication of the very strong cultural pressures being felt in the Puerto Rican community. Young children are not exempt from these emotional pressures, and often express feelings of inferiority.

Discrimination against Puerto Ricans in New York has been partially for racial reasons, by both Blacks and Anglos, and partially for economic reasons. Although certainly victims of complex circumstances beyond their control, the large percentage of Puerto Ricans on welfare rolls engenders resentment from many overburdened taxpayers.

A reflection of these attitudes may be found in the nature of references to Puerto Ricans in English vs. Spanish dailies in New York City (Fishman and Casiano 1969). Although the English language papers showed little interest in the Puerto Rican community at all, except when there were violent disturbances in Spanish Harlem, the reporting they did was much more of their needs and problems. Little note was taken during the months surveyed of Puerto Rican leaders, social functions, holidays, or creativity.

As measures of educational failure, Puerto Rican children have the highest dropout rate of any ethnic group in New York, and a great many adults are still functionally illiterate. The current problems of Puerto Rican students are attributed to such factors as the low education and socio-economic levels of their parents, English language deficiencies, and misunderstanding or insensitivity on the part of their teachers. Attitudinal factors within the Puerto Rican community also affect student achievement, however. Dulay and Pepe (1970) report that Puerto Rican children's

English proficiency correlates to a high degree with whether or not their parents wish to return to the Island.

Objective information on these children is meagre. We know that traditional child-rearing practices differentiate sexual roles from a very early age, and these make a significant difference in educational attitudes and performance. For one thing, Puerto Rican girls show a higher anxiety pattern than boys when in a situation where they are threatened with failure, as when taking a test. The boys' low anxiety is probably a function of the cultural attitude toward their admission of anxiety (Siu 1972).

Three- and four-year-old Anglo and Puerto Rican children have been observed and compared while responding to a "demanding cognitive task" (Hertzig, et al. 1968). The differences in this case were not believed to be due to differences in socio-economic level (although this was evidently not controlled), but in home experiences:

a. Focus on social interaction rather than tasks.
b. Age at which independence is expected.
c. Regarding toys as entertainment rather than education.

The behavioral responses of both groups to nonverbal tasks were essentially the same, but these differences were noted:

a. Puerto Rican children were less likely to attempt the task (introduced by a Spanish-speaking testor).
b. Puerto Rican children were less likely to verbalize their response.
c. Puerto Rican children were much more likely to "work" on nonverbal tasks rather than on verbal ones. (Anglo children responded about the same to both.)

There is solid evidence that the Puerto Rican children attending Spanish Harlem day care centers are just as intelligent as children of other ethnic groups (Hertzig, et al. 1968, using Draw-a-Man and Spanish directions), but they show high resistance to taking a test. When compared with Chinese children, Puerto Ricans react more strongly to test situations where threatened with possible failure, and they are less confident (Siu 1972).

It seems quite probable that even very young Puerto Rican children, for reasons of cultural conditioning and environmental experiences, bring different attitudes and reactions to educational contexts than children of other ethnic groups. If early childhood personnel are to meet their needs, relieve their anxieties, and develop their potentials, we need to know a great deal more about the positive experiences upon which to build.

There is little question that their Spanish language development is one of these strengths. Although most Puerto Rican parents want their children to learn English as a second language, Spanish is very solidly the language of the home. In Puerto Rico, Spanish is the dominant language in all domains, including the school. A large percentage of the population cannot be considered to know enough English to be classed as bilingual.

Although there are no published descriptions of language acquisition in Puerto Rico or Spanish Harlem, there has been extensive study of adult speech in the bilingual New York community (Fishman, et al. 1971). A fairly early study of five-year-old speech in Spanish Harlem day care centers (Anastasi and de Jésus 1948) indicates that these children are using longer and more complex sentences than their

Black and Anglo peers, but this needs replication and extension in a current psycholinguistic framework.

The English spoken by Puerto Rican children has been described by Williams (1972) and Wolfram (1972). The latter, studying the speech of second generation bilinguals in New York, reports there is significant interference from Black English. This is an interesting sociolinguistic phenomenon which indicates not only language contact, but probable attitudinal factors at work.

A strong language shift towards English has been observed among mainland Puerto Ricans, but this is a trend that may well be reversed. Given Puerto Rican attitudes, experiences, and child-rearing practices, and the positive U.S. position toward education in two languages, a stable bilingualism may be cultivated in Puerto Rican children for some time to come.

3. Indian Children

For more than a century one of the heaviest stones in the "white man's burden" has been the education of American Indian children. The main purpose of the school has been assimilation, whether the methods were coercive or persuasive. Indian education was effected to alienate children from their own people. The use of Indian languages was forbidden and English was imposed as the sole medium of instruction.

In the 1880's, the Commissioner of Indian Affairs reported:

> The first step to be taken toward civilization, toward teaching the Indian the mischief and folly of continuing in their barbarous practices, is to teach him the English language. . . . We must remove the stumbling-blocks of hereditary customs and manners, and of those language is one of the most important (Brewton 1968).

Assimilation to the American way of life is still considered by many to be the primary goal of Indian education, although the clause is now often added, "while retaining Indian identity." There is less intolerance of the use of Indian languages now than formerly, but we still find many signs that teachers and administrators are not completely sympathetic toward Indian languages, discouraging, if not actually forbidding them in the school.

This educational system has been grossly ineffective, as judged from the high degree of absenteeism, academic retardation, and dropouts. Many reasons for this failure have been offered. We are all familiar with these reasons which have been repeated in nearly every research report on American Indian children which has been published in recent years. However, a careful look at the statistics in some of these same reports shows that these reasons are far less well supported than has been supposed, and that indeed a very different situation is often the case.

We are told that Indian parents are apathetic toward formal education, and that the children's home environment is not supportive of the school, but 76% of the high school students in one study reported that members of their families are interested in college work, and 57% reported that their fathers like to read at home (Bass 1969).

We are told that Indian students are "shy" and "lazy." Such reports are based on the observations of experienced teachers working with diverse tribes. Apaches are also reported to be "hostile," "mean," and "dumb," Ute children are "undependable," "uncooperative," and "inattentive," Pomos "lack interest and incentive for education." There is no research to support the validity of such stereotypes, but their existence is well documented. The most common attitude is one of condescension—often well-meant, but always critical. According to the Coleman report, approximately one fourth of all elementary and secondary school teachers of Indian students indicate that they would prefer not to be teaching Indians.

We are told Indians are mentally deficient, despite psychological evidence to the contrary. Although scores on specific tests will vary, intelligence fits a normal distribution in all ethnic groups and is comparable from group to group. Differences in IQ, therefore, cannot explain the failure of the schools to teach Indian children, but the dominant culture's negative stereotype that the Indian really is mentally inferior may be a partial explanation since it affects teachers' expectations.

We are told that Indians have a low self-concept. The Coleman report indicates that the pupil attitude factor has a stronger relation to achievement than all the "school" factors together, and that Indian students in the 12th grade have the lowest self-concept of all minority groups tested. These data and similar interpretations of the Havighurst study (1955) have been widely accepted, but should be examined for ethnocentric bias. The low self-concept is deduced largely from students' feelings that they have little or no control over their environment. Many Indian cultures do not believe that actively controlling natural forces is desirable, or even reasonable. This research does not seem to take into account Indian perception of what constitutes a positive self-concept, but rather evaluates the Indian self-concept in terms of white, mainstream values.

We are also told that Indians are unable to adapt to the white man's culture. In fact, the history of most American Indians has been a continuing process of adaptation to new people and new environments. The vast majority have accepted our family structure, our form of government, and our religion. Many have adopted our language to the extent of losing the use of their own. Although almost 300 distinct American Indian languages and dialects are still spoken in the United States (including Alaska), approximately 60% of these now have fewer than 100 speakers and are in imminent danger of extinction.

Finally, we are told that the Indians' failure to acquire necessary competence in English is responsible for their academic failure. It is, of course, difficult for proponents of this argument to explain why even in Indian communities where only English is spoken there remains the pervasive problem of low achievement and high dropout rate.

Most research on Indian children has been carried out by anthropological observers who live in a community for often a year or more, describe the society's structure, values, and roles, record behavioral data which indicate child-rearing practices and other common phenomena, and collect information on ceremonial functions. (A professional joke in this field is that the typical Navajo family is composed of five people: a father, a mother, two children, and an anthropologist.) Although there is no foolproof safeguard against biased observers any more than there is against biased tests and questionnaires—and we should always look critically at generalizations based on either—anthropologists have provided considerable relevant information.

Few pronouncements can be made about "Indian children" as a group, since the many tribes maintaining their identity in the United States are very heterogeneous with regard to language, culture, and even physical (racial) traits. There are, however, a few social values and practices that are quite wide-spread among the various Indian communities.

The concept of autonomy, or individual right, has been traditionally valued by Native American tribes of the Southwest, Plains, and Eastern Woodlands (e.g., Navajo, Cheyenne, Sioux, and Iroquois). Their nineteenth century Anglo conquerors could never understand why one "chief" could not commit all of "his people" to a treaty or a single course of action, and educators in this century have despaired over parents who respected the right of children to decide whether or not they wanted to attend school. These same groups decided on joint action by consensus, with majority rule an alien concept imposed more or less successfully from the outside.

Child-rearing practices are often very lenient when compared to Anglo standards, with little or no physical punishment used. Children are commonly disciplined by teasing, ridicule, or fear (as with Hopi Kachinas). Their learning of physical tasks is more through observation than verbal instruction, but many social and religious lessons are taught through stories. (A number of studies suggest that the visual perception and visual memory of Indian children raised in these groups are much higher than that of their Anglo age-mates [Kleinfeld 1970, Lombardi 1970, Cazden and John, in CAL 1968].)

The verbal dimension causes much of the conflict Indian children experience with Anglo adults. Anglos, on the one hand, assault Indian language conventions through ignorance or negative attitudes. In return, part of the basis for conflict rests on the Indian children's misunderstanding of the sociolinguistic factors involved in speaking English, a completely neglected component in the teaching of English as a second language. These factors include purposes and means of learning, expectations regarding linguistic behavior in encounter situations, and attitudes toward language use.

Communicative conflict may begin on the first day of school for an Indian child. The school setting is strange, the buildings and furnishings often unlike any he has known. Perhaps he does not understand English, and even if he understands the surface structures of the language, he may not be familiar with the way it is used. In the first place, the strange teacher talks to him right away, and it may be his custom to keep silence initially with unfamiliar people and situations. He would then not respond verbally, following the social rules he has learned, and thus would fulfill the teacher's stereotype of "shy" and "unresponsive."

When the first question the teacher asks is, "What is your name?" she creates an additional dimension of cultural conflict if the child is from one of the many groups that do not believe in saying their own name. She is asking the child to violate a religious taboo. If the child is Navajo, for instance, she violates additional taboos if she talks about or depicts a bear in the classroom, or tells stories about some of the other hibernating animals before they are asleep. Her normal voice projection level may frighten the Navajo child, who often interprets this as anger. (Conversely, his low voice level contributes to the erroneous image of Navajo children as shy.) The eye contact expected or even demanded by white teachers is not considered polite or respectful by Navajos, who avoid looking directly at the person they are addressing.

This catalogue of differences can continue, with each new dimension explaining some of the conflicts between Indians and whites in the areas of education (and politics). Since the beginning, we have paid little attention to cultural differences among the Indian tribes, to differences in value systems, and in learning styles. We have never accepted, nor even understood, Indian children. It should surprise none of us that we have failed to educate the vast majority.

In the past, the Indians who did succeed had to learn in forms that we imposed. There is a strong counter-movement now to return control of Indian education to Indian communities (see recommendations in CAL 1973). This also seems to be an inevitable direction for early childhood programs to follow. It will require the training of many Indian men and women to work in child development centers, and the sensitizing of other personnel to the goals and values each community has for its children, to fulfill the expected need.

Because the extinction of many Indian languages is such a concern to Native Americans, where their children are still learning to speak the ancestral languages, early childhood personnel should be additionally required to understand and speak them, too.

REFERENCES

Anastasi, Anne, and Cruz de Jésus. "Language Development and Nonverbal IQ of Puerto Rican Children in New York City." *Journal of Abnormal and Social Psychology,* vol. 48 (1953), pp. 357–366.

Brown, Roger. *A First Language.* Cambridge: Harvard University Press, 1973.

———, and Ursula Bellugi. "Three Processes in the Child's Acquisition of Syntax." *Harvard Educational Review,* vol. 34 (1964), pp. 133–151.

Carrow, Elizabeth. "Comprehension of English and Spanish by Pre-School Mexican-American Children." *Modern Language Journal,* vol. 55 (1971), pp. 299–306.

Cazden, Courtney B. "Subcultural Differences in Child Language." *Merrill-Palmer Quarterly,* vol. 12 (1966), pp. 185–219.

———, and Vera John. "Learning in American Indian Children," in *Styles of Learning Among American Indians: An Outline for Research.* Washington: Center for Applied Linguistics, 1968.

[Center for Applied Linguistics.] *Recommendations for Language Policy in Indian Education.* Washington: Center for Applied Linguistics, 1973.

Chomsky, Carol. *The Acquisition of Syntax in Children.* Cambridge: M.I.T. Press, 1971.

Cornejo, Ricardo. "The Acquisition of Lexicon in the Speech of Bilingual Children," in Paul Turner, ed., *Bilingualism in the Southwest.* Tucson: University of Arizona Press, 1973, pp. 67–93.

Del Campo, Philip E. "An Analysis of Selected Features in the Acculturation Process of the Mexican-American Elementary School Child." Unpublished doctoral dissertation, International University, 1970.

Ervin-Tripp, Susan. *Becoming a Bilingual.* Washington: Center for Applied Linguistics, 1968.

Evans, J. S. "Word-Pair Discrimination and Imitation Abilities of Pre-School Economically Disadvantaged Native Spanish-Speaking Children." Unpublished doctoral dissertation, University of Texas, 1971.

Fishman, Joshua A., et al. *Bilingualism in the Barrio.* The Hague: Mouton, 1971.

———, and Heriberto Casiano. "Puerto Ricans in Our Press." *Modern Language Journal,* vol. 53 (1969), pp. 157–162.

Fitzpatrick, Joseph. *Puerto Rican Americans: The Meaning of Migration to the Mainland.* Englewood Cliffs, N.J.: Prentice-Hall, 1971.

Gesell, Arnold. *The First Five Years of Life.* New York: Harper, 1940.

González, Gustavo. *The Acquisition of Questions in Texas Spanish: Age Two–Age Five.* Washington: Center for Applied Linguistics, 1973.

———. "The Acquisition of Spanish Grammar by Native Spanish Speakers." Unpublished doctoral dissertation, University of Texas, 1970.

Hertzig, Margaret E., et al. *Class and Ethnic Differences in the Responsiveness of Pre-school Children to Cognitive Demands.* New York: Society for Research in Child Development, 1968. (Serial No. 117.)

Kagan, Spencer, and Millard C. Madsen. "Cooperation and Competition of Mexican-American and Anglo-American Children of Two Ages Under Four Instructional Sets." *Developmental Psychology,* vol. 5 (1971), pp. 32–39.

Kleinfeld, Judith S. *Cognitive Strength of Eskimos and Implications for Education.* [ERIC ED 45 281] 1970.

Labov, William. "Finding Out About Children's Language." Unpublished paper presented to the Hawaii Council of Teachers of English, April 1970.

Lastra, Yolanda. "El hablar y la educacíon de niños de origen mexicano en Los Angeles." Paper read at Fifth Symposium of the Interamerican Program on Linguistics and Language Teaching. São Paulo, Brazil, January 5, 1969.

Lenneberg, Eric H. *Biological Foundations of Language.* New York: John Wiley and Sons, 1967.

_____. "The Biological Foundations of Language," in Mark Lester, ed., *Readings in Applied Transformational Grammar.* New York: Holt, Rinehart and Winston, 1970, pp. 10–46.

_____. "On Explaining Language," in Doris V. Gunderson, ed., *Language and Reading.* Washington: Center for Applied Linguistics, 1970.

_____, et al., eds. *New Directions in the Study of Language.* Cambridge: M.I.T. Press, 1964.

Lombardi, Thomas D. "Psycholinguistic Abilities of Papago Indian School Children." *Exceptional Children,* vol. 36 (1970), pp. 485–493.

Madsen, Millard C., and A. Shapira. "Cooperative and Competitive Behavior of Urban Afro-American, Anglo-American, Mexican-American, and Mexican Village Children." *Developmental Psychology,* vol. 3 (1970), pp. 16–20.

Malzberg, Benjamin. "Mental Disease Among Puerto Ricans in New York City, 1949–51." *Journal of Nervous and Mental Disease,* vol. 123 (1956), pp. 457–465.

Manning, John C., and Frederick Brengelman. *Teaching English as a Second Language to Kindergarten Pupils Whose Native Language Is Spanish.* Fresno: Fresno State College, 1965.

McCauley, Margaret A. "A Study of Social Class and Assimilation in Relation to Puerto Rican Family Patterns." Unpublished doctoral dissertation, Fordham University, 1972.

Menyuk, Paula. *Sentences Children Use.* Cambridge: M.I.T. Press, 1969.

Parisi, Domenico. "Development of Syntactic Comprehension in Preschool Children as a Function of Socioeconomic Level." *Developmental Psychology,* vol. 5 (1971), pp. 186–189.

Penfield, Wilder. "Conditioning the Uncommitted Cortex for Language Acquisition." *Brain,* vol. 88 (1965), pp. 787–798.

Piaget, Jean. *The Language and Thought of the Child.* Cleveland: World Publishing Co., 1955.

Saville, Muriel R., and Rudolph D. Troike. *A Handbook of Bilingual Education.* Washington: Center for Applied Linguistics, 1971.

Segil, Irving E. "The Attainment of Concepts," in Martin L. Hoffman and Lois W. Hoffman, eds., *Review of Child Development Research.* New York: Russell Sage Foundation, 1964.

Shriner, T. H., and L. Miner. "Morphological Structures in the Language of Disadvantaged and Advantaged Children." *Journal of Speech and Hearing Research,* vol. 11 (1968), pp. 605–610.

Siu, Ping K. *The Relationship Between Motivational Patterns and Academic Achievement in Minority Group Children.* Final report. [ERIC ED 63–443] 1972.

Slobin, Dan I. "Imitation and Grammatical Development in Children," in N. S. Endler et al., eds., *Contemporary Issues in Developmental Psychology.* New York: Holt, Rinehart and Winston, 1967, pp. 437–443.

Swanson, E., and R. DeBlassie. "Interpreter Effects on the WISC Performance of First Grade Mexican-American Children." *Measurement and Evaluation in Guidance,* vol. 4 (1971), pp. 172–175.

Ulibarri, Horacio. *Interpretative Studies on Bilingual Education.* Washington: U.S. Office of Education, 1969.

Wasserman, S. A. "Values of Mexican-American, Negro, and Anglo Blue-Collar Children." *Child Development,* vol. 42 (1971), pp. 1624–1628.

Williams, George M. *Puerto Rican English: A Discussion of Eight Major Works Relevant to Its Linguistic Description.* New York: Columbia University Press, 1972.

Dell Hymes

Bilingual Education: Linguistic vs. Sociolinguistic Bases

Bilingual education is a sociolinguistic subject par excellence. The skills of linguists are both necessary and insufficient. The role of linguistics in research on bilingual education may seem to be a matter only of application of a linguistics already given. The contrary is the case. Research on bilingual education requires a kind of linguistics not yet fully constituted. The use of linguistics in such research challenges linguistics to develop conceptual and methodological tools able to deal adequately with the place of speech in human life—with the place of actual speech competencies in actual lives.

A goal of education, bilingual or other, presumably is to enable children to develop their capacity for creative use of language as part of successful adaptation of themselves and their communities in the continuously changing circumstances characteristic of contemporary life. And linguistics indeed has already addressed itself to this goal, as witnessed by the concern within descriptive theory for the "creative aspect of language use" (Chomsky 1965, 1966) and the recognition of the role of the child's first language long advocated by many linguists and anthropologists. In both respects, however, linguistics falls short until it is able to deal with ways of speaking in relation to social meanings and situations, until, in short, the starting point of description is not a sentence or text, but a speech event; not a language, but a repertoire of ways of speaking; not a speech community defined in equivalence to a language, but a speech community defined through the concurrence of rules of grammar and rules of use.

The leading view of the nature of linguistic competence and creativity has been dubbed "Cartesian linguistics" (Chomsky 1966), not as a historically exact label, but in recognition of a direction given to theory of language in the period following Descartes by an emphasis on the nature of mind as prior to experience, and an analytic, universalizing, reconstituting methodology (cf. Cassirer 1955, Ch. I, "The Philosophy of the Enlightenment"). In similar vein, one may dub a subsequent tradition of thought "Herderian linguistics" (Hymes 1970a), not as a historically exact label, but in recognition of a direction given to theory of language in the period following Herder (1744–1801) by an emphasis on language as constituting cultural identity (cf. Barnard 1965: 117, 118, 142), and on a methodology of sympathetic interpretation of cultural diversity sui generis—Herder coined the German verb *ein-*

From James E. Alatis (ed.), *Bilingualism and Language Contact* (Washington: Georgetown University Press, 1970), pp. 69–76. Reprinted with permission.

fühlen—if within a larger universal framework. (The two traditions might be labelled "Enlightenment" and "Romantic," but the individual names perhaps are better, in that they less imply two mutually exclusive periods, or simple uniformity within each.)

"Cartesian" and "Herderian" approaches have contributed much to our knowledge of language. In the past the differences between the two approaches have been salient, but here what matters most is what they have fundamentally in common: isolation of *a* language as the object of linguistic description; equation of a language with a speech community (or culture); taking of the social functions of language as external, given, and universally equivalent; restriction of study of the structure of language to units and relations based on reference.

The emergence of sociolinguistics is in important part a response to social needs; but as an intellectual stage in the history of linguistics, the recent history of sociolinguistics can be seen as a response to the hegemony of "Cartesian" and "Herderian" assumptions, first, by critical analysis of the assumptions themselves, and, secondly, by effort to replace them. Just as Boas, Sapir, Bloomfield, Pike, and others can be seen as concerned to develop concepts and methods adequate to the description of all languages, so the current work of Ervin-Tripp, Fishman, Gumperz, Labov, and others can be seen as concerned to develop concepts and methods adequate to the description of speech communities. And where Boas, Sapir, Bloomfield, Pike, and others had to empty some concepts of normative or ethnocentric content (e.g. "inflection," "incorporation" vis-à-vis compounding), extend some (e.g. *morphème*), and invent others (e.g. phoneme), with regard to grammars, so have contributors to sociolinguistics today the task of emptying, extending, and inventing with regard to the identification and organization of ways of speaking.

Mrs. Philips' work is a contribution to the empirical task. In the rest of my remarks I shall sketch some of the critical analysis associated with it, with regard to "Cartesian" concepts of competence and creativity, and "Herderian" concepts of language in the speech community.

The concern with competence and creativity in Chomsky's "Cartesian" linguistics is an advance toward sociolinguistics, but, on analysis, an advance more nominal than real. To make competence central, rather than *la langue*, to reconcile the sphere of creativity with that of structure, does focus discussion on actual human beings and their abilities, and regard them as acquirers and shapers of culture, rather than merely as "culture-bearers." Just such a transformation was projected for anthropology and linguistics by Sapir in his last writings (see discussion in Hymes 1970b). But whereas Sapir turned attention to "living speech," understood as requiring that received categories be reconsidered within the matrix of social interaction, Chomsky's "Cartesian" linguistics seems a cogent, thoroughly thought out perfection of the impulse to the autonomy of language that spurred so much of structural linguistics and in an earlier stage, Sapir himself. From origin as possibly a physico-chemical accident to the assumptions of wholly fluent use free of situation in a homogenous community, any dependence of language on social interaction and adaptation is excluded.

In brief, Chomskyan "competence" is restricted to knowledge and, within knowledge, to knowledge of grammar. Much of what would normally be considered part of a speaker's knowledge and ability is excluded. Much of what one would need to study to understand actual individual competence is not "competence" but "performance." In effect, two senses of "performance" are confounded: a negative sense, in which "mere" performance is that superficial behavior which linguistics must seek to go beneath, and an implicitly positive sense, in which "performance" is everything other than grammar that contributes to acceptable speech. The confusion tends to give the positive contents of "performance" the negative association, and in any case, the dichotomy is used to relegate all but grammar to a secondary status. The constitutive role of social factors is ignored, as is knowledge of them, yet identification and motivation are found to be key factors in sociolinguistic change (Labov 1966, Le Page 1969). Performances, as events, have no admitted structure of their own.

The "creative aspect of language use," like "competence," promises more than it contains. It is analyzed (Chomsky 1966) in terms of the possibility of producing an indefinitely large number of sentences, free of immediate stimulus control, that are yet appropriate. But a sentence might be new, free of stimulus control, and bizarre. Appropriateness entails a relation to situation. Competent speakers have knowledge of the structure and meaning of sentences and of the structure and meaning of situations and the relations between the two as well. Just as "Cartesian" linguistics reduces competence to knowledge of grammar, so it reduces "creativity" to novelty.

Those concerned with linguistic aspects of education and with sociolinguistic theory must thank Chomsky for making competence and creativity central to linguistic theory, but must reconstruct the concepts for themselves. [1]

"Cartesian" and "Herderian" linguistics differ most obviously with regard to the place of differences among languages. There is not, to be sure, a complete opposition. The most celebrated early figure in the "Herderian" tradition, W. von Humboldt, was concerned with universals as well as specific difference, as were Boas, Sapir, and Whorf later. Indeed, what Herder, von Humboldt, and Goethe are linked by is a conception of form that links the individual and universal. The notion of form is linked to that of creativity, and individuality, both, so that in contrast to the "Cartesian" sense of particularity and uniqueness of personality (language, culture) as negative limitation, such limitation is seen as positive. It is not the absence of universality, but realization of a universal power. The universal finds realization only in the actuality of the particular; form is truly acquired only through the power of self-formation (Cassirer 1961: 20–25.) (On this development, see Cassirer 1950: 224–5, 252; 1955: 32–36; 1961: 20–26. On von Humboldt as having found his way into the study of language through his concern with the characterization of individuals and individual peoples, see Lammers 1936 and Leroux 1958: 69, n. 2).

Chomsky treats von Humboldt in terms of his continuity with the general approach of the Enlightenment; he acknowledges but omits much of that aspect of von Humboldt which, according to Cassirer, is his distinctive achievement. He follows von

---

[1] A sociolinguistic critique of "Cartesian" linguistics is markedly parallel to the critique by Marx of Feuerbach. By substituting "Chomsky" (or "Cartesian linguistics") for "Feuerbach," and "linguistic" for "religious," one has a remarkably applicable statement:

> "Chomsky resolves the linguistic essence into the *human* essence. But the essence of man is no abstraction inhering in each single individual. In its actuality it is the ensemble of social relationships.
> "Chomsky, who does not go into the criticism of this actual essence, is hence compelled:
> (1) to abstract from the historical process and to establish linguistic intuition as something self-contained, and to presuppose an abstract—*isolated*—human individual;
> (2) to view the essence of man merely as 'species,' as the inner dumb generality which unites the many individuals *naturally*" (i.e. not socially).
> (Quoted from Easton and Guddat 1967: 402.)

I do not think one can abandon some conception of a generic human nature (human essence), as the thesis might be taken as saying; but the man for whom Chomsky's competence and theory is a model is indeed an isolated man in the abstract. There is nothing to be said about men (or women).

Humboldt in concern with the universal power, but neglects von Humboldt's understanding of form as something not given, but historically emergent and acquired.[2] The treatment of von Humboldt is in keeping with the treatment of competence and creativity.

The "Herderian" approach, as developed by von Humboldt is indeed the approach needed in sociolinguistics. The focus, however, must be changed from a language, as correlate of a people, to persons and their ways of speaking. The inadequacy of a monolingual approach has long been recognized and, indeed, no one has ever denied the obvious facts of multilingualism, the prevalence of linguistic diversity in the world. The difficulty remains that in informal thought one tends to fall back on the Herderian model of one language, one people, one culture, one community—the Hopi and their language, etc., (on the persistence of "savage anthropology" of this sort, see Fontana 1968), because we are only beginning to have sociolinguistic models and taxonomies adequate to thinking in terms of multilingual situations. But, as the work of Gumperz, Labov, and others has shown, more than plurality of languages is involved.

First of all, what counts as a language boundary cannot be defined by any purely linguistic measure. Attitudes and social meanings enter in as well. Any enduring social relationship or group may come to define itself by selection and/or creation of linguistic features, and a difference of accent may be as important at one boundary as a difference of grammar at another. Part of the creativity of users of languages lies in the freedom to determine what and how much linguistic difference matters. The alternative view, indeed a view often taken, conceals an unsuspected linguistic determinism. (For a recent issue of this sort, involving the notion of ethnic unit and mutual intelligibility, cf. Hymes 1968.)

Secondly, speech communities cannot be defined in terms of linguistic features alone in another respect. Their definition must comprise shared knowledge both of one or more primary varieties, and of rules for their use. Differential knowledge of a linguistic variety aside (and that is of course of importance), a person who is a member of a speech community knows not only a language but also what to say. A person who can produce all and any of the sentences of a language, and unpredictably does, is institutionalized. For some range of situations, itself to be empirically determined and perhaps varying significantly across communities, a competent member of the speech community knows what to say next. And just as there are *Sprachbunde*, defined by linguistic features shared across language boundaries, so there are *Sprechbunde*, defined by shared rules of speaking. (I owe this notion to J. Neustupný.) And such sharing of speech rules across languages may extend not only in space but also through time. The Ngoni of Africa, for example, mostly no longer speak Ngoni, but use the language of the people in Malawi whom they conquered. However, they use it in Ngoni ways, ways whose maintenance is considered essential to their identity. Analogous situations obtain in some American Indian communities.

In general, both theory and relevance to education require that one break with the equation between a named language and a functional role. Functional role is primary and problematic (cf. argument of Hymes 1966). The means that serve a given function

---

[2] One might argue that transformational generative grammar ought by rights to be especially concerned, as was von Humboldt, with individual form. By establishing that marked departures from universal, or natural, features and relations entail costs, it is able to recognize the great extent to which languages, or rather their speakers, pay such costs, and to appreciate the power of the sociohistorical forces that motivate such payment.

are to be empirically determined. Beyond cognitive differences possibly attributable to differences of language, there are cognitive differences due to differences in speaking. There is interference not only between phonologies and grammars, but also between norms of interaction and interpretation of speech. One must take the vantage point of the person acquiring competence in speech in a community, and discover the number and organization of ways of speaking that result.

The notions of rules of co-occurrence and rules of alternation recently developed by Ervin-Tripp are general and neutral concepts for discovering the organization of linguistic features in a community, comparable to concepts developed for discovering phonological and grammatical structure. They rely upon the fundamental notion of contrastive relevance, but generalize it to the contrastive relevance of "stylistic" features as well as features of reference. (Vowel length for emphasis is as much a contrastive feature of English or Wasco Chinook as /m/ : /n/ to distinguish morphemes.) And the step from the identification of features to organized sets of features is, to repeat, an empirical one, governed by analysis of other components of speech events as well. The step is not, repeat not, taken by automatically referring features to a "named" language known externally and prior to investigation. Rules of co-occurrence identify styles; rules of alternation identify their social meanings and contrastive relevance in use. (This last is the step that the approach to styles of Pike [1967] fails to take.) The notion "ways of speaking" calls particular attention to the fact that members of a speech community have a knowledge such that speech is interpretable as pertaining to one or another genre, and as instancing one or another speech act and event.

In sum, there is no quarrel with the "Cartesian" concern for universals and the human mind. There is much concern with the "Herderian" concern for individuation and emergent form. Only the focus of theory and description changes, from rules of language to rules of speaking. It is the latter that are fundamental, embracing the former as one constituent. And an understanding of rules of speaking is indispensable to understanding failures and to increasing success in bicultural education.

REFERENCES

Barnard, F. M. 1965. Herder's social and political thought, from enlightenment to nationalism. Oxford, Clarendon Press.

Cassirer, Ernst. 1950. The problem of knowledge. Philosophy, science, and history since Hegel. New Haven, Yale University Press.

———. 1955. The philosophy of the enlightenment. Boston, Beacon Press. (Princeton University Press, 1955; German original, Tübingen, 1932).

———. 1961. The logic of the humanities. New Haven, Yale University Press. (German original, Göteborg, 1942.)

Chomsky, Noam. 1965. Aspects of the theory of syntax. Cambridge, M.I.T. Press.

———. 1966. Cartesian linguistics. New York, Harper and Row.

Easton, Lloyd D. and Kurt H. Guddat, eds. 1967. Writings of the young Marx on philosophy and society. Garden City, New York, Doubleday.

Ervin-Tripp, Susan M. 1971. On sociolinguistic rules: alternation and co-occurrence. In John J. Gumperz and Dell Hymes, eds., Directions in sociolinguistics. New York, Holt, Rinehart, and Winston.

Fontana, Bernard L. 1968. Savage anthropologists and unvanishing Indians in the American Southwest. Paper read before the 67th Annual Meeting of the American Anthropological Association, Seattle, Washington, November 21.

Hymes, Dell. 1966. Two types of linguistic relativity: some examples from Amerindian ethnography. In William Bright, ed., Sociolinguistics, 114-158. The Hague, Mouton.

——. 1967. Why linguistics needs the sociologist. Social Research 34 (4): 632-647.

——. 1968. Linguistic problems in defining the concept of "tribe." In June Helm, ed., Essays on the problem of tribe, 23-48. Proceedings of the 1967 annual spring meeting of the American Ethnological Society. Seattle, University of Washington Press.

——. 1970a. Linguistic aspects of comparative political research. In Robert T. Holt and John E. Turner, eds., The methodology of comparative research, Ch. VII. New York, The Free Press.

——. 1970b. Linguistic method of ethnography. In Paul Garvin, ed., The problem of method in linguistics. The Hague, Mouton.

——. 1971. On communicative competence. Philadelphia, University of Pennsylvania Press.

Labov, William A. 1966. The social stratification of English in New York City. Washington, D.C., Center for Applied Linguistics.

Lammers, Wilhelm. 1936. Wilhelm von Humboldts Weg zur Sprachforschung 1785-1801. Berlin.

Le Page, R. C. 1969. Problems of description in multilingual communities. Transactions of the Philological Society, 1968, 189-212. London.

Leroux, Robert. 1958. L'anthropologie comparée de Guillaume de Humboldt. Publications de la Faculté des lettres de l'Université de Strasbourg, Fascicule 135. Paris, Société d'éditions.

Pike, K. L. 1967. Language in relation to a unified theory of the structure of human behavior. The Hague, Mouton.

Susan U. Philips

Acquisition of Rules for Appropriate Speech Usage

INTRODUCTION

Recent studies of North American Indian education problems have indicated that in many ways Indian children are not culturally oriented to the ways in which classroom learning is conducted. The Wax-Dumont study (Wax, Wax and Dumont 1964) of the Pine Ridge Sioux discusses the lack of interest children show in what goes on in school and Wolcott's (1967) description of a Kwakiutl school describes the Indian children's organized resistance to his ways of organizing classroom learning. Cazden and John (1968) suggest that the "styles of learning" through which Indian children are enculturated at home differ markedly from those to which they are introduced in the classroom. And Hymes has pointed out that this may lead to sociolinguistic interference when teacher and student do not recognize these differences in their efforts to communicate with one another (Hymes 1967).

On the Warm Springs Indian Reservation, in central Oregon, where I have been carrying out research in patterns of speech usage during this past year, teachers have pointed to similar phenomena, particularly in their repeated statements that Indian children show a great deal of reluctance to talk in class, and that they participate less and less in verbal interaction as they go through school. To help account for the reluctance of the Indian children of Warm Springs (and elsewhere as well) to participate in classroom verbal interactions, I am going to demonstrate how some of the social conditions governing or determining when it is appropriate for a student to speak in the classroom differ from those which govern verbal participation and other types of communicative performances in the Warm Springs Indian community's social interactions.

The data on which discussion of these differences will be based is drawn, first of all, from comparative observations in all-Indian classes in the reservation grammar school and non-Indian or white classes in another grammar school at the first and sixth grade levels. The purpose here is to define the communicative contexts in which Indian and non-Indian behavior and participation differ, and to describe the ways in which they differ.

After defining the situations or social contexts in which Indian students' verbal participation is minimal, discussion will shift to consideration of the social conditions in Indian cultural contexts which define when speaking is appropriate, attending to children's learning experiences both at home and in the community-wide social activities in which they participate.

From James E. Alatis (ed.), *Bilingualism and Language Contact* (Washington: Georgetown University Press, 1970), pp. 77–101.

The end goal of this discussion will be to demonstrate that the social conditions which define when a person uses speech in Indian social situations are present in classroom situations in which Indian students use speech a great deal, and absent in the more prevalent classroom situations in which they fail to participate verbally.

There are several aspects of verbal participation in classroom contexts which should be kept in mind during the discussion of why Indians are reluctant to talk. First of all, a student's use of speech in the classroom during structured lesson sessions is a communicative performance in more than one sense of "performance." It involves demonstration of sociolinguistic competency, itself a complex combination of linguistic competency and social competency involving knowledge of when and in what style one must present one's utterances, among other things. This type of competency, however, is involved in every speech act. But in classrooms there is a second sense in which speaking is a performance that is more special, although not unique, to classroom interactions. In class, speaking is the first and primary mode for communicating competency in all of the areas of skill and knowledge which schools purport to teach. Children communicate what they have learned to the teacher and their fellow students through speaking; only rarely do they demonstrate what they know through physical activity or creation of material objects. While writing eventually becomes a second important channel or mode for communicating knowledge or demonstrating skills, writing as a skill is to a great extent developed through verbal interaction between student and teacher, as is reading.

Consequently, if talk fails to occur, then the channel through which learning sessions are conducted is cut off, and the structure of classroom interaction which depends on dialogue between teacher and student breaks down and no longer functions as it is supposed to. Thus while the question "Why don't Indian kids talk more in class?" is in a sense a very simple one, it is also a very basic one, and the lack of talk a problem which needs to be dealt with if Indian children are to learn what is taught in American schools.

CULTURAL AND EDUCATIONAL BACKGROUND OF THE WARM SPRINGS INDIANS

Before embarking on the main task of the discussion outlined above, some background information on the setting of the research, the Warm Springs Indian Reservation, is necessary to provide some sense of the extent to which the cultural, linguistic, and educational situation there may be similar to or different from that of North American Indians in other parts of the country.

Today the reservation of 564,209 acres is populated by some 1500 descendants of the "bands" of Warm Springs Sahaptin, Wasco Chinook, and Paiute Indians who gradually settled there after the reservation was established in 1855. The Warm Springs Indians have always been the largest group numerically, followed by the Wasco, with the Paiutes so small in number that their influence in the culture of the reservation has been of relatively small significance. Although they spoke different languages, the Warm Springs and Wasco groups were geographically quite close to one another before the reservation was established, and were culturally similar in many respects. Thus after over a hundred years together on the reservation, they presently share approximately the same cultural background.

The "tribe," as the Indians of Warm Springs now refer to themselves collectively, today comprises a single closely integrated community with strong tribal leadership which receives the full backing of the people. Until after World War II the Indians here experienced considerable poverty and hardship. Then in the 1950s, they received two large sums of money, first in compensation for reservation land which had originally been purchased from the Indians for considerably less than it was worth, and then in compensation for the loss of fishing rights along the Columbia River when the construction of The Dalles Dam caused their fishing sites to be covered with water. Rather than distribute all these funds to individual members of the tribe, which was the practice on other reservations in the area at that time, tribal leaders invested some of the money in tribal economic enterprises, notably a saw mill where reservation timber is processed, and a small resort.

With the income from these enterprises, and drawing as well on various forms of federal aid available to them, the tribe has developed social programs to help members of the tribe in a number of ways. Chief among their concerns is the improvement of the education of their children, whom they recognize to be less successful in school than their fellow non-Indian students. Tribal leaders have taken numerous important steps to increase the educational opportunities of their young people, including the establishment of a scholarship program for college students, a tribal education office with half a dozen full-time employees supervising the tribally sponsored kindergarten, study halls, and community center courses, and the federally sponsored programs such as VISTA, Head Start, and Neighborhood Youth Corps. Their education office employees also act as liaisons between parents of children with problems in school, and the administrators and teachers of the public schools which the children attend. In sum, the tribe is doing everything within its means to provide the Warm Springs children with the best education possible.

Despite their efforts, and those of the public school officials who are under considerable pressure from tribal leaders to bring about changes in the schools which will result in the improvement of the academic performance of Indian students, the Indians continue to do poorly in school when compared to the non-Indian students in the same school system.

One of the most important things to know about the schools the Indian children attend is the ethnic composition of their classes. For the first six grades, Warm Springs children attend a public school which is located on the reservation. Here their classmates are all Indians and their teachers are all non-Indians or whites. After the first six grades, they are bussed into the town of Madras, a distance of fifteen to thirty miles, depending on where one lives on the reservation. Here, encountering their fellow white students for the first time, the Indian students are outnumbered by a ratio of five to one. From the point of view of tribal leaders, it is only when they reach the high school, or ninth grade, that the Indian students' "problems" really become serious, for it is at this point that hostility between Indian and non-Indian is expressed openly, and the Indian students' failure to participate in classroom discussions and school activities is recognized by everyone.

There is, however, abundant evidence that Indian students' learning difficulties begin long before they reach the high school. The statistics which are available on their educational achievements and problems are very similar to those which have been reported for Indians in other parts of the country (Berry 1969). On national achievement tests the Warm Springs Indian children consistently score lower than the national average in skills tested. Their lowest scores are in areas involving verbal competencies, and the gap between their level of performance on such tests and the national averages widens as they continue into the higher grade levels (Zentner 1960).

Although many people on the reservation still speak an Indian language, today all of the Warm Springs children in school are monolingual speakers of English. The dialect of English which they speak, however, is not the Standard English of their teachers, but one which is distinctive to the local Indian community, and which in some aspects of grammar and phonology shows influence from the Indian languages spoken on the reservation.

In addition, there is some evidence that many children are exposed to talk in the Indian languages which may affect their acquisition of English. Because older people on the reservation are very concerned about the Indian languages dying out, many of them make a concerted effort to teach young children an Indian language, particularly the Warm Springs Sahaptin. Thus some infants and young children are spoken to consistently in both Warm Springs Sahaptin and English. Every Indian child still knows some Indian words, and many informants report that while their children refuse to speak the Warm Springs Sahaptin—particularly after they start school—they understand much of what is said to them in it.

The effects of the acquisition of a very local dialect of English and the exposure to the Warm Springs language on classroom learning are difficult for local educators to assess because children say so little in the presence of the teachers. Observations of Indian children's verbal interactions outside the classroom indicate a control and productive use of linguistic rules that is manifested infrequently in classroom utterances, indicating that the appropriate social conditions for speech use, from the Indians' point of view, are lacking. It is this problem with appropriate social contexts for speaking that will now be considered in greater detail.

CONDITIONS FOR SPEECH USE IN THE SCHOOL CLASSROOMS

When the children first enter school, the most immediate concern of the teachers is to teach them the basic rules for classroom behavior upon which the maintenance of continuous and ordered activity depend. One of the most important of these is the distinction between the roles of teacher and student. In this there is the explicit and implicit assumption that the teacher controls all of the activity taking place in the classroom and the students accept and are obedient to her authority. She determines the sociospatial arrangements of all interactions; she decrees when and where movement takes place within the classroom. And most important for our present concern with communication, she determines who will talk and when they will talk.

While some class activities are designed to create the sense of a class of students as an organized group with class officers, or student monitors carrying out various responsibilities contributing to the group, actual spontaneous organization within the student group which has not been officially designated by the teacher is not encouraged. It interferes with the scheduling of activities as the teacher has organized them. The classroom situation is one in which the teacher relates to the students as an undifferentiated mass, much as a performer in front of an audience. Or she relates to each student on a one-to-one basis, often with the rest of the class as the still undifferentiated audience for the performance of the individual child.

In comparing the Indian and non-Indian learning of these basic classrooms distinctions which define the conditions in which communication will take place, differences are immediately apparent. Indian first graders are consistently slower to begin acting in accordance with these basic arrangements. They do not remember to raise their hands and wait to be called on before speaking, they wander to parts of the room other than the one in which the teacher is conducting a session, and talk to other students while the teacher is talking much further into the school year than do students in non-Indian classes. And the Indian children continue to fail to conform to classroom procedure much more frequently through the school year.

In contrast to the non-Indian students, the Indian students consistently show a great deal more interest in what their fellow students are doing than in what the teacher is doing. While non-Indian students constantly make bids for the attention of their teachers, through initiating dialogue with them as well as through other acts, Indian students do very little of this. Instead they make bids for the attention of their fellow students through talk. At the first grade level, and more noticeably at the sixth grade level, with new teachers, Indian students often act in deliberate organized opposition to the teacher's directions. Thus, at the first grade level, if one student is told not to put his feet on his chair, another will immediately put his feet on his chair, and he will be imitated by other students who see him do this. In non-Indian classrooms, such behavior was observed only at the sixth grade level in interaction with a substitute teacher.

In other words, there is, on the part of Indian students, relatively less interest, desire, and/or ability to internalize and act in accordance with some of the basic rules underlying classroom maintenance of orderly interaction. Most notably, Indian students are less willing than non-Indian students to accept the teacher as director and controller of all classroom activities. They are less interested in developing the one-to-one communicative relationship between teacher and student, and more interested in maintaining and developing relationships with their peers, regardless of what is going on in the classroom.

Within the basic framework of teacher-controlled interaction, there are several possible variations in structural arrangements of interaction, which will be referred to from here on as "participant structures." Teachers use different participant structures, or ways of arranging verbal interaction with students, for communicating different types of educational material, and for providing variation in the presentation of the same material to hold children's interest. Often the notion that different kinds of material are taught better and more efficiently through one sort of participant structuring rather than another is also involved.

In the first type of participant structure the teacher interacts with all of the students. She may address all of them, or a single student in the presence of the rest of the students. The students may respond as a group or chorus in unison, or individually in the presence of their peers. And finally, student verbal participation may be either voluntary, as when the teacher asks who knows the answer to her question, or compulsory, as when the teacher asks a particular student to answer, whether his hand is raised or not. And always it is the teacher who determines whether she talks to one or to all, receives responses individually or in chorus, and voluntarily or without choice.

In a second type of participant structure, the teacher interacts with only some of the students in the class at once, as in reading groups. In such contexts, participation is usually mandatory rather than voluntary, individual rather than chorus, and each student is expected to participate or perform verbally, for the main purpose of such smaller groups is to provide the teacher with the opportunity to assess the knowledge acquired by each individual student. During such sessions, the remaining students who are not interacting with the teacher are usually working alone or independently at their desks on reading or writing assignments.

A third participant structure consists of all students working independently at their desks, but with the teacher explicitly available for student-initiated verbal interaction, in which the child indicates he wants to communicate with the teacher by raising his hand, or by approaching the teacher at her desk. In either case, the interaction between student and teacher is not witnessed by the other students in that they do not hear what is said.

A fourth participant structure, and one which occurs infrequently in the upper primary grades and rarely, if ever, in the lower grades, consists of the students being divided into small groups which they run themselves, though always with the more distant supervision of the teacher, and usually for the purpose of so-called "group projects." As a rule such groups have official "chairmen," who assume what is in other contexts the teacher's authority, in regulating who will talk when.

In observing and comparing Indian and non-Indian participation or communicative performances in these four different structural variations of contexts in which communication takes place, differences between the two groups again emerge very clearly.

In the first two participant structures where students must speak out individually in front of the other students, Indian children show considerable reluctance to participate, particularly when compared to non-Indian students. When the teacher is in front of the whole class, they volunteer to speak relatively rarely, and teachers at the Warm Springs grammar school generally hold that this reluctance to volunteer to speak out in front of other students increases as the children get older.

When the teacher is with a small group, and each individual must give some kind of communicative verbal performance in turn, Indian children much more frequently refuse, or fail to utter a word when called upon, and much less frequently, if ever, urge the teacher to call on them than the non-Indians do. When the Indian children do speak, they speak very softly, often in tones inaudible to a person more than a few feet away, and in utterances which are typically shorter or more brief than those of their non-Indian counterparts.

In situations where the teacher makes herself available for student-initiated communication during sessions in which students are working independently on assignments which do not involve verbal communication, students at the first grade level in the Indian classes at first rarely initiate contact with the teachers. After a few weeks in a classroom, they do so as frequently as the non-Indian students. At the sixth grade level, Indian students initiate such relatively private encounters with teachers much more frequently than non-Indian students do.

When students control and direct the interaction in small group projects, as described for the fourth type of participant structure, there is again a marked contrast between the behavior of Indian and non-Indian students. It is in such contexts that Indian students become most fully involved in what they are doing, concentrating completely on their work until it is completed, talking a great deal to one another within the group, and competing, with explicit remarks to that effect, with the other groups. Non-Indian students take more time in "getting organized," disagree and argue more regarding how to go about a task, rely more heavily on appointed chairmen for arbitration and decision-making, and show less interest, at least explicitly, in competing with other groups from their class.

Observations of the behavior of both Indian and non-Indian children outside the classroom during recess periods and teacher-organized physical education periods provide further evidence that the differences in readiness to participate in interaction are related to the way in which the interaction is organized and controlled.

When such outside-class activity is organized by the teachers, it is for the purpose of teaching children games through which they develop certain physical and social skills. If the games involve a role distinction between leader and followers in which the leader must tell the others what to do—as in Simon Says, Follow the Leader, Green Light, Red Light, and even Farmer in the Dell, Indian children show a great deal of reluctance to assume the leadership role. This is particularly true when the child is appointed leader by the teacher and must be repeatedly urged to act in telling the others what to do before doing so. Non-Indian children, in contrast, vie eagerly for such positions, calling upon the teacher and/or other students to select them.

If such playground activity is unsupervised, and the children are left to their own devices, Indian children become involved in games of team competition much more frequently than non-Indian children. And they sustain such game activities for longer periods of time and at younger ages than non-Indian children. While non-Indian children tend more to play in groups of two and three, and in the upper primary grades to form "friendships" with one or two persons from their own class in school, Indian children interact with a greater number of children consistently, and maintain friendships and teams with children from classes in school other than their own.

In reviewing the comparison of Indian and non-Indian students' verbal participation under different social conditions, two features of the Warm Springs children's behavior stand out. First of all, they show relatively less willingness to perform or participate verbally when they must speak alone in front of other students. Second, they are relatively less eager to speak when the point at which speech occurs is dictated by the teacher, as it is during sessions when the teacher is working with the whole class or a small group. They also show considerable reluctance to be placed in the "leadership" play roles that require them to assume the same type of dictation of the acts of their peers.

Parallel to these negative responses are the positive ones of a relatively greater willingness to participate in group activities which do not create a distinction between individual performer and audience, and a relatively greater use of opportunities in which the point at which the student speaks or acts is determined by himself, rather than by the teacher or a "leader."

It is apparent that there are situations arising in the classroom which do allow for the Indian students to verbalize or communicate under or within the participant structures which their behavior indicates they prefer; otherwise it would not have been possible to make the distinctions between their behavior and that of non-Indians in the areas just discussed. However, the frequency of occurrence of such situations in the classroom is very low when compared to the frequency of occurrence of the type of participant structuring in which Indian students fail to participate verbally, particularly in the lower grades.

In other words, most verbal communication which is considered part of students' learning experience does take the structure of individual students speaking in front of other students. About half of this speaking is voluntary insofar as students are invited to volunteer to answer, and half is compulsory in that a specific student is called on and expected to answer. In either case, it is the teacher who establishes when talk will occur and within what kind of participant structure.

There are many reasons why most of the verbal communication takes place under such conditions. Within our particular education system, a teacher needs to know how much her students have learned or absorbed from the material she has presented. Students' verbal responses provide one means—and the primary means, particularly before students learn to write—of measuring their progress, and are thus the teacher's feedback. And, again within our particular educational system, it is not group, but individual progress with which our teachers are expected to be concerned.

In addition, it is assumed that students will learn from each other's performances both what is false or wrong, and what is true or correct. Another aspect of this type of public performance which may increase educators' belief in its efficacy is the students' awareness that these communicative acts *are* performances, in the sense of being demonstrations of competency. The concomitant awareness that success or failure in such acts is a measure of their worth in the eyes of those present increases their motivation to do well. Thus they will remember when they make a mistake and try harder to do well to avoid public failure, in a way which they would not, were their performances in front of a smaller number of people. As I will try to demonstrate further on, however, the educators' assumption of the validity or success of this type of enculturation process, which can briefly be referred to as "learning through public mistakes," is not one which the Indians share, and this has important implications for our understanding of Indian behavior in the classroom.

The consequences of the Indians' reluctance to participate in these speech situations are several. First of all, the teacher loses the primary means she has of receiving feedback on the children's acquisition of knowledge, and is thus less able to establish at what point she must begin again to instruct them, particularly in skills requiring a developmental sequencing, as in reading.

A second consequence of this reluctance to participate in speech situations requiring mandatory individual performances is that the teachers in the Warm Springs grammar school modify their teaching approach whenever possible to accommodate, in a somewhat ad hoc fashion, what they refer to as the Indian students' "shyness." In the first grade it is not easy to make very many modifications because of what teachers perceive as a close relationship between the material being taught and the methods used to teach it. There is some feeling, also, that the teaching methods which can be effective with children at age six are somewhat limited in range. However, as students go up through the grades, there is an increasing tendency for teachers to work with the notion, not always a correct one, that given the same body of material, there are a number of different ways of "presenting" it, or in the terms being used here, a range of different participant structures and modes of communication (e.g. talking versus reading and writing) which can be used.

Even so, at the first grade level there are already some changes made to accommodate the Indian children which are notable. When comparing the Indian first grade classes with the non-Indian first grade classes, one finds very few word games involving students giving directions to one another being used. And even more conspicuous in Indian classes is the absence of the ubiquitous Show and Tell or Sharing through which students learn to get up in front of the class, standing where the teacher stands, and presenting, as the teacher might, a monologue relating an experience or describing a treasured object which is supposed to be of interest to the rest of the class. When asked whether this activity was used in the classroom one teacher explained that she had previously used it, but so few children ever volunteered to "share" that she finally discontinued it.

By the time the students reach the sixth grade, the range of modes and settings for communication have increased a great deal, and the opportunity for elimination of some participant structures in preference to others is used by the teachers. As one sixth grade teacher put it, "I spend as little time in front of the class as possible." In comparison with non-Indian classes, Indian classes have a relatively greater number of group "projects." Thus, while non-Indian students are learning about South American history through reading texts and answering the teacher's questions, Indian students are doing group-planned and executed murals depicting a particular stage in Latin American history; while non-Indian students are reading science texts and answering questions about how electricity is generated, Indian students are doing group-run experiments with batteries and motors.

Similarly, in the Indian classes "reports" given by individual students are almost nonexistent, but are a typical means in non-Indian classes for demonstrating knowledge through verbal performance. And finally, while in non-Indian classes students are given opportunities to ask the teacher questions in front of the class, and do so, Indian students are given fewer opportunities for this because when they do have the opportunity they don't use it. Rather, the teacher of Indians allows more periods in which he is available for individual students to approach him alone and ask their questions quietly where no one else can hear them.

The teachers who make these adjustments, and not all do, are sensitive to the inclinations of their students and want to teach them through means to which they most readily adapt. However, by doing so, they are avoiding teaching the Indian children how to communicate in precisely the contexts in which they are least able, and most need to learn how to communicate if they are to do well in school. The teachers handicap themselves by setting up performance situations for the students in which they are least able to arrive at the evaluations of individual competence upon which they rely for feedback to establish at what level they must begin to teach. And it is not at all clear that students do acquire the same information through one form of communication as they do through another. Thus these manipulations of communication settings and participant structures, which are intended to creatively transmit knowledge to the students through the means to which they are most adjusted, may actually be causing the students to completely miss types of information which their later high school teachers will assume they picked up in grammar school.

The consequences of this partial adaption to Indian modes of communication become apparent when the Indian students join the non-Indian students at the junior and senior high school levels. Here, where the Indian students are outnumbered one to five, there is no manipulation and selection of communication settings to suit the inclinations of the Indians. Here the teachers complain that the Indian students never talk in class, and never ask questions, and everyone wonders why.

CONDITIONS FOR SPEECH USE IN THE WARM SPRINGS INDIAN COMMUNITY

To understand why the Warm Springs Indian children speak out readily under some social conditions, but fail to do so under others, it is necessary to examine the sociolinguistic assumptions determining the conditions for communicative performances, particularly those involving explicit demonstrations of knowledge or skill, in the Indian community. It will be possible here to deal with only some of the many aspects of communication which are involved. Attention will focus first on the social structuring of learning situations or contexts in which knowledge and skills are communicated to children in Indian homes. Then some consideration will be given to the underlying rules or conditions for participation in the community-wide social events that pre-school children, as well as older children, learn through attending such events with their families.

The Indian child's pre-school and outside-school enculturation at home differs from that of many non-Indian or white middle-class children's in that a good deal of the responsibility for the care and training of children is assumed by persons other than the parents of the children. In many homes the oldest children, particularly if they are girls, assume these responsibilities when the parents are at home, as well as when they are not. Frequently, also, grandparents, uncles and aunts assume the full-time responsibility for care and instruction of children. Children thus become accustomed to interacting with and following the instructions and orders of a greater number of people than is the case with non-Indian children. Equally important is the fact that all of the people with whom Indian children form such reciprocal nurturing and learning relationships are kinsmen. Indian children are rarely, if ever, taken care of by "baby-sitters" from outside the family. Most of their playmates before beginning school are their siblings and cousins, and these peer relationships typically continue to be the strongest bonds of friendship through school and adult life, later providing a basis for reciprocal aid in times of need, and companionship in many social activities.

Indian children are deliberately taught skills around the home (for girls) and in the outdoors (for boys) at an earlier age than many middle-class non-Indian children. Girls, for example, learn to cook some foods before they are eight, and by this age may be fully competent in cleaning a house without any aid or supervision from adults.

There are other areas of competence in which Indian children are expected to be proficient at earlier ages than non-Indian children, for which the means of enculturation or socialization are less visible and clear-cut. While still in grammar school, at the age of 10 or 11, some children are considered capable of spending afternoons and evenings in the company of only other children, without the necessity of accounting for their whereabouts or asking permission to do whatever specific activity is involved. At this same age, many are also considered capable of deciding where they want to live, and for what reasons one residence is preferable to another. They may spend weeks or months at a time living with one relative or another, until it is no longer possible to say that they live in any particular household.

In general, then, Warm Springs Indian children become accustomed to self-determination of action, accompanied by very little disciplinary control from older relatives, at much younger ages than middle-class white children.

In the context of the household, learning takes place through several sorts of somewhat different processes. First of all, children are present at many adult interactions as silent but attentive observers. While it is not yet clear how adult activities in which children are not full participants are distinguished from those in which children may participate fully, and from those for which they are not allowed to be present at all, there are clearly marked differences. What is most remarkable, however, is that there are many adult conversations to which children pay a great deal of silent, patient attention. This contrasts sharply with the behavior of non-Indian children, who show little patience in similar circumstances, desiring either to become a full participant through verbal interaction, or to become completely involved in some other activity.

There is some evidence that this silent listening and watching was, in the Warm Springs culture, traditionally the first step in learning skills of a fairly complex nature. For example, older women reminisce about being required to watch their elder relatives tan hides when they were very young, rather than being allowed to play. And certainly the winter evening events of myth-telling, which provided Indian children with their first explicitly taught moral lessons, involved them as listening participants rather than as speakers.

A second type of learning involves the segmentation of a task by an older relative, and the partial carrying out of the task or one of its segments by the child. In household tasks, for example, a child is given a very simple portion of a job (e.g. in cleaning a room, the child may begin by helping move the furniture) and works in cooperation with and under the supervision of an older relative. Such activities involve a small amount of verbal instruction or direction from the older relative, and allow for questions on the part of the child. Gradually the child comes to learn all of the skills involved in a particular process, consistently under the supervision of an older relative who works along with him.

This mode of instruction is not unique to the Warm Springs Indians, of course; many non-Indian parents use similar methods. However, there are aspects of this type of instruction which differ from its use among non-Indians. First of all, it is likely to be preceded by the long periods of observation just described when it occurs among the Indians. The absence of such observation among non-Indian children is perhaps replaced by elaborate verbal instructions outlining the full scope of a task before the child attempts any part of it.

A second way in which this type of instruction among the Warm Springs Indians differs from that of non-Indians is the absence of "testing" of the child's skill by the instructing kinsman before the child exercises the skill unsupervised. Although it is not yet clear how this works in a diversity of situations, it appears that in many areas of skill, the child takes it upon himself to test the skill unsupervised and alone, without other people around. In this way, if he is unsuccessful, his failure is not seen by others. If he is successful, he can show the results of his success to those by whom he has been taught, whether it be in the form of a deer that has been shot, a hide tanned, a piece of beadwork completed, or a dinner on the table when the adults come home from work.

Again there is some evidence that this type of private individual's testing of competency, followed by public demonstration only when competency is fully developed and certain, has been traditional in the Warm Springs Indian culture. The most dramatic examples of this come from the processes of acquisition of religious and ritual knowledge. In the vision quests through which adolescents, or children of even younger ages, acquired spirit power, individuals spent long periods in isolated mountain areas, from which they were expected to emerge with skills they had not previously demonstrated. While some of these abilities were not fully revealed until later in life, the child was expected to be able to relate some experience of a supernatural nature which would prove that he had, in fact, been visited by a spirit. Along the same lines, individuals until very recently received and learned ritual songs through dreams and visions, which they would sing for the first time in full and completed form in the presence of others.

The contexts described here in which learning takes place can be perceived as a sequence, idealized, of three steps: (1) observation, which of course includes listening; (2) supervised participation; and (3) private, self-initiated self-testing. It is not the case that all acquisitions of skills proceed through such phases, however, but rather only some of those skills which Indian adults consciously and deliberately teach their children, and which the children consciously try to learn. Those which are learned through less deliberate means must to some extent invoke similar structuring, but it is difficult to determine to what extent.

The use of speech in the process is notably minimal. Verbal directions or instructions are few, being confined to corrections and question-answering. Nor does the final demonstration of skill particularly involve verbal performance, since the validation of skill so often involves display of some material evidence or nonverbal physical expression.

This process of Indian acquisition of competence may help to explain, in part, Indian children's reluctance to speak in front of their classmates. In the classroom, the process of "acquisition" of knowledge and "demonstration" of knowledge are collapsed into the single act of answering questions or reciting when called upon to do so by the teacher, particularly in the lower grades. Here the assumption is that one will learn, and learn more effectively, through making mistakes in front of others. The Indian children have no opportunity to observe others performing successfully before they attempt it, except for their fellow classmates who precede them, and are themselves initiated. They have no opportunity to "practice," and decide for themselves when they know enough to demonstrate their knowledge; rather, their performances are determined by the teacher. And finally, their only channel for communicating competency is verbal, rather than nonverbal.

Turning now from learning processes in the home to learning experiences outside the home, in social and ritual activities involving community members other than kinsmen, there is again considerable evidence that Indian children's understanding of when and how one participates and performs individually and thus demonstrates or communicates competence, differs considerably from what is expected of them in the classroom.

Children of all ages are brought to every sort of community-wide social event sponsored by Indians (as distinct from those sponsored by non-Indians). There is rarely, if ever, such a thing as an Indian community event which is attended by adults only. At many events, children participate in only certain roles, but this is true of everyone. Sociospatially and behaviorally, children must always participate minimally as do all others in sitting quietly and attentively alongside their elders.

One of the social features which characterizes social events that are not explicitly kin group affairs, including activities like political General Councils, social dinners, and Worship Dances, is that they are open to participation by all members of the Warm Springs Indian community. While different types of activities are more heavily attended by certain Indians rather than others, and fairly consistently sponsored and arranged by certain individuals, it is always clear that everyone is invited, both by community knowledge of this fact, and by explicit announcements on posters placed in areas where most people pass through at one time or another in their day-to-day activities.

A second feature of such activities is that there is usually no one person directing the activity verbally, or signalling changes from one phase to another. Instead, the structure is determined either by a set procedure or ritual, or there is a group of people who in various complementary ways provide such cueing and direction. Nor are there any participant roles which can be filled or are filled by only one person. In dancing, singing, and drumming there are no soloists, and where there are performers who begin a sequence and are then joined by others, more than one performer takes a turn at such initiations. The speaking roles are handled similarly. In contexts where speeches are appropriate, it is made clear that anyone who wants to may "say a few words." The same holds true for political meetings, where the answerer to a question is not necessarily one who is on a panel or council, but rather the person who feels he is qualified, by his knowledge of a subject, to answer. In all situations thus allowing for anyone who wants to to speak, no time limit is set, so that the talking continues until everyone who wants to has had the opportunity to do so.

This does not mean that there are never any "leaders" in Indian social activities, but rather that leadership takes quite a different form than it does in many non-Indian cultural contexts. Among the people of Warm Springs, a person is not a leader by virtue of holding a particular position, even in the case of members of the tribal council and administration. Rather, he is a leader because he has demonstrated ability in some sphere and activity, and many individuals choose to follow his suggestions because they have independently each decided they are good ones. If, for example, an individual plans and announces an activity, but few people offer to help him carry it out or attend it, then that is an indication that the organizer is not a respected leader in the community at the present time. And the likelihood that he will repeat his efforts in the near future is reduced considerably.

This type of "leadership," present today among the people of Warm Springs, is reminiscent of that which was described by Hoebel (1954: 132) for the Comanche chiefs:

> In matters of daily routine, such as camp moving, he merely made the decisions himself, announcing them through a camp crier. Anyone who did not

like his decision simply ignored it. If in time a good many people ignored his announcements and preferred to stay behind with some other man of influence, or perhaps to move in another direction with that man, the chief had then lost his following. He was no longer chief, and another had quietly superseded him.

A final feature of Indian social activities, which should be recognized from what has already been said, is that all who do attend an activity may participate in at least some of the various forms participation takes for the given activity, rather than there being a distinction made between participants or performers and audience. At many Indian gatherings, particularly those attended by older people, this aspect of the situation is reflected in its sociospatial arrangement: people are seated in such a way that all present are facing one another, usually in an approximation of a square, and the focus of activity is either along one side of the square, or in its center, or a combination of the two.

And each individual chooses the degree of his participation. No one, other than perhaps those who set up the event, is committed to being present beforehand and all participating roles beyond those of sitting and observing are determined by the individual at the point at which he decides to participate, rather than being prescheduled.

In summary, the Indian social activities to which children are early exposed outside the home generally have the following properties: (1) they are community-wide, in the sense that they are open to all Warm Springs Indians; (2) there is no single individual directing and controlling all activity, and to the extent that there are "leaders," their leadership is based on the choice to follow which is made by each person; (3) participation in some form is accessible to everyone who attends. No one need be exclusively an observer or audience, and there is consequently no sharp distinction between audience and performer. And each individual chooses for himself the degree of his participation during the activity.

If one now compares the social conditions for verbal participation in the classroom with the conditions underlying many Indian events in which children participate, a number of differences emerge.

First of all, classroom activities are not community-wide, but, more importantly, the participants in the activity are not drawn just from the Indian community. The teacher, as a non-Indian, is an outsider and a stranger to these events. In addition, by virtue of her role as teacher, she structurally separates herself from the rest of the participants, her students. She places herself outside the interaction and activity of the students. This encourages their cultural perceptions of themselves as the relevant community in opposition to the teacher, perhaps much as they see themselves in opposition to other communities, and on a smaller scale as one team is in opposition to another. In other words, on the basis of the Indians' social experiences, one is either a part of a group or outside it. The notion of a single individual being structurally set apart from all others, in anything other than an observer role, and yet still a part of the group organization, is one which children probably encounter for the first time in school, and continue to experience only in non-Indian derived activities (e.g. in bureaucratic, hierarchically-structured occupations). This helps to explain why Indian students show so little interest in initiating interaction with the teacher in activities involving other students.

Second, in contrast to Indian activities where many people are involved in determining the development and structure of an event, there is only one single authority directing everything in the classroom, namely the teacher. And the teacher is not the controller or leader by virtue of the individual students' choices to follow her, as is the case in Indian social activities, but rather by virtue of her occupation of the role of teacher. This difference helps to account for the Indian children's frequent indifference to the directions, orders, and requests for compliance with classroom social rules which the teacher issues.

Third, it is not the case in the classroom that all students may participate in any given activity, as in Indian community activities. Nor are they given the opportunity to choose the degree of their participation which, on the basis of evidence discussed earlier, would in Indian contexts be based on the individual's having already ascertained in private that he was capable of successful verbal communication of competence. Again these choices belong to the teacher.

CONCLUSION

In summary, Indian children fail to participate verbally in classroom interaction because the social conditions for participation to which they have become accustomed in the Indian community are lacking. The absence of these appropriate social conditions for communicative performances affect the most common and everyday speech acts which occur in the classroom. If the Indian child fails to follow an order or answer a question, it may not be because he doesn't understand the linguistic structure of the imperative and the interrogative, but rather because he does not share the non-Indian's assumption in such contexts that use of these syntactic forms by definition implies an automatic and immediate response from the person to whom they were addressed. For these assumptions are sociolinguistic assumptions which are not shared by the Indians.

Educators cannot assume that because Indian children (or children from other cultural backgrounds than that which is implicit in American classrooms) speak English, or are taught it in school, they have also assimilated all of the sociolinguistic rules underlying interaction in classrooms and other non-Indian social situations where English is spoken. If the children are to participate in the classroom verbal interaction upon which the learning process depends, they must first be taught the rules for appropriate speech usage in contexts where talking is necessary.

REFERENCES

Berry, Brewton. 1969. The education of American Indians: A survey of the literature. Prepared for the Special Subcommittee on Indian Education of the Committee on Labor and Public Welfare, United States Senate. Washington, D.C., Government Printing Office.

Cazden, Courtney B., and Vera P. John. 1968. Learning in American Indian children. In: Styles of learning among American Indians: An outline for research, 1–19. Washington, D.C., Center for Applied Linguistics.

Hoebel, E. Adamson. 1954. The law of primitive man. Cambridge, Harvard University Press.

Hymes, Dell. 1967. On communicative competence. MS due to be published in a volume edited by Renira Huxley and Elizabeth Ingram, tentative title: Mechanisms of language development. To be published by Centre for Advanced Study in the Developmental Science and CIBA Foundation, London.

Wax, Murray, Rosalie Wax, and Robert Dumont, Jr. 1964. Formal education in an American Indian community. Social Problems Monograph no. 1. Society for the Study of Social Problems, Kalamazoo, Michigan.

Wolcott, Harry. 1976. A Kwakiutl village and school. New York City, Holt, Rinehart and Winston.

Zentner, Henry. 1960. Volume II: education. Oregon State College Warm Springs Research Project.

DISCUSSION

Shaligram Shukla, Georgetown University: In your brief paper, Mr. Hymes, you mention Chomsky and his creative aspect of language use, etc. I would like to know what is the noncreative aspect of language use.

Hymes: This, in fact, touches on something which is quite important in language use. Creative, of course, is something for which there is not a single definition, but in Chomsky's use of it and in many people's sense of it, it is very much the sense of novelty, of innovation, of some sort of production of something which is in itself an instance occurring for the first time. That is fundamental and important to language in its role in human life. From an anthropological point of view, of course, one misses in that emphasis an equally, perhaps, important aspect of the role of language in human life which is the saying again of things which are valued, the perpetuation of traditional forms of speech, the satisfactions often of saying something which one's father has said in the same situation, and so forth. This is not necessarily an answer directly to your question, because if one takes the view which I was sketching in the paper, to analyze creativity as such one really has to relate the novelty of the utterance to the situation. One may have the kind of creativity which involves saying something which has been said before. No creativity there, perhaps, from Chomsky's point of view, with regard to the sentences, but if it is new in that situation, the novelty and creativity may be in recognizing the possibility of using this familiar utterance in this new circumstance. If I repeat a list I memorized, that would probably not be very creative.

Shukla: If you remember, in 1958 Charles Hockett said exactly the same thing, that in language you could say something that has never been said before. So why shouldn't people quote Hockett instead of Chomsky?

Hymes: Well, you know, in 20 minutes I don't discuss everybody who may have had something interesting to say. The reason we are discussing Chomsky is because most linguists read Chomsky and, unfortunately, don't read what Hockett said in 1958. I did, in fact, read what Hockett said at a previous Georgetown Round Table on ethnolinguistic implications, and thought it was one of his best articles; but I do think he was a bit hung up on the matter of ritual use. There again one has the same problem of being so hung up on the notion of novelty as to find it a mystery that people will do the same thing again.

Robert J. Di Pietro, Georgetown University: I have a footnote to add to Mrs. Philips' talk. You don't have to go to the Indian schools to find nonvocal children. All you have to do is sit in a foreign language class where students are expected to say something which they haven't really been taught. Also, "nonvocalism" has been noticed among Welsh children, among black Americans, and among many different groups trying to climb up into another economic class. The anthropological study of such groups often is as revealing of the anthropologist as it is of the people being studied. If it is true that an effort is being made to get the Navajo Indian children to act more like Anglo-Americans, we must also notice among universities and schools in various parts of this country the exact opposite trend in trying to destroy the usual type of teacher-student interaction. There is an attempt to set up new forms of interaction and reduce the authoritarian figure of the teacher and work toward more of a social grouping of student and teacher. Perhaps in succeeding to change the Navajo we will find that we ourselves have been changed.

Hymes: I think that of course it is not alright to decide for peoples what their own goals should be. Generally speaking, the Indians of Warm Springs want to succeed in education. On their own initiative they have used their funds to make it possible for every child who can finish high school to go to college. They themselves are constantly concerned and distressed at the failures as they perceive them in the schools. It was only possible for Mrs. Philips to do this work at Warm Springs because the people at Warm Springs accepted her and in fact considered what she was doing as relevant and of interest to them.

Philips: With regard to what kinds of changes one would want to introduce into a classroom situation, I like to think that it would depend on what the people in the community actually want, and not on any decisions that those of us who are outside of the situation would make for them. And while this kind of thing is possible at Warm Springs because of the small size of the tribe and the strong leadership they have, I don't know that it is possible in some of the other Indian situations. However, I would like for it to be more so; I want to see that kind of thing happening instead of us making the decisions.

Vera John, Yeshiva University: I think the size of the tribe is not necessarily a limiting factor in planning on Indian reservations. I'm sure that Dr. Roessel is going to speak to us during our lunch in greater detail about many important adventures in self-determination and education on the Navajo reservation. Traditional education for Indians has been so bad that throughout Indian communities all over the country there are very, very strong movements, on the part of tribal people, defining the role and purpose of education for Indian children by Indians. The big problem is that educational techniques very often lag behind in helping to implement new objectives, and I think it is in this area that we can be of assistance. That is, I think more and more Indian groups are saying, "We don't want the secondhand Anglo education that we have been exposed to; we want another form of education." The question is: Can the consultants, collaborators, and those members of the white community who are accepted in these endeavors, come up with something new? This is our challenge.

Walter A. Wolfram, Center for Applied Linguistics: I'm deeply sympathetic with your concern for functional uses of language, the ethnography of speech. What I would like to have clarified is exactly what you mean by rules. Do you, when you talk about rules, interpret this to be some sort of taxonomic framework for setting up participants, topics, settings, and so forth, into which certain linguistic styles might fit? Or do you conceive eventually of formalizing such types of rules so that they may have some generative type of capacity? At what stage is your development of these so-called rules in terms of their formal representation?

Hymes: Two things to say to that. Usually I mentally use the word "rules" in quotes, because the conception of "rule" itself is one which can be debated. Lamb, for example, would argue that it is not proper to speak of rules in this connection. I use the word "rules" for the same reason that I spoke of Chomsky rather than Hockett: because I'm trying to address linguists and the generally common terminology for dealing with these things, to point out the importance of certain things which are neglected. With regard to what I think the nature of these rules might be, it seems to me that we know rather little about it, that the kinds of notions which I think are most important at this time are those which are developed by Dr. Tripp, for example. In a recent paper of hers she talks about rules of co-occurrence and alternation. That seems to be a very good basis for it because it is a completely general and neutral approach which cuts across many of the difficulties which we have in thinking in terms of whole languages and so forth. One can discover empirically whatever styles or organizations of speech features may be present; and not only co-occurrence which brings together ways of speaking, but also alternation which enables one to deal with their substitution, one for the other, and their contrastive social uses, which is a point which Pike, for example, fails to take in his book. He talks about styles, but it is always complementary in relation to the ordinary linguistic structure, never taking that step to contrast styles in social circumstances. What form these would take is very difficult to say. A lot of people are concerned about this. I don't think anybody has the whole answer. David DeCamp, as you know (he spoke here last year), talks about scaling, and that obviously gets at some things. Dr. Tripp has used flow charts for getting at some kinds of relationships, and that seems to be the most economical and effective way of showing those relationships. It is very much an open matter here, I think.

Esperanza Medina-Spyropoulos, Georgetown University: I would like to comment on one of Professor Hymes' assertions, and I hope that my comments will tie in with Professor Shukla's remarks on the creative aspect of language use. Professor Hymes asserts that there is no quarrel with the Cartesian linguistics. If you will permit me, I would like to change for a moment the title of "Bilingual Education: Linguistic vs. Sociolinguistic Bases" to read: "Bilingual Education: Cartesian Linguistic Bases vs. Sociolinguistic Bases" and maintain that there should be, if not a quarrel, a careful evaluation of the Cartesian linguistics if we are to apply its principles to sociolinguistic studies. I would like to echo Professor Andree F. Sjoberg's remarks that the descriptive techniques of transformational linguistics (to which many sociolinguists subscribe) have had the effect of drawing the attention of linguists away from the sociocultural dimension of language. Clearly, the descriptive techniques developed by the generative grammarians represent great improvements in the study of language structure and there is no doubt that their impact will endure the test of time. However, some of the basic assumptions of the followers of Cartesian linguistics must be questioned, mainly their line of reasoning in regard to their view of man in relation to language; it seems to me that we have failed to recognize that there is a fundamental incompatibility between the assumptions underlying Cartesian linguistics and those basic to sociolinguistics as far as the basic view of man, mind, and language. Descartes sought to separate man from society; on the other hand, leading sociolinguists see the study of language as inseparable from the study of society and maintain that linguistic interaction is social interaction. Such a notion appears to be in contrast to that of the Chomskians, who are at present primarily interested in language structure as directly embedded in the fundamental character of the human mind, and apparently seem to exclude interest in societal structures and interactions. In regard to creativity, Cartesian linguists and their followers seem to view creativity in rather mechanistic terms: creativity involves far more than the generation of new sentences; the generation of new strings is essentially an automatic process and it results from the operation of certain grammatical rules which act as calibres or filters, rejecting the structures that are not acceptable. The search is now on for language universals, but once they are discovered, it will also be a rather mechanistic process if all the mind has to do is to select the applicable universals. Professor George Herbert Meade emphasizes the reflective nature of the human mind and says that it is not so much man's ability to create new sentences which sets him apart from the animals, but it is his ability to reflect on what he has said and to reflect on his capacity to conceptualize. In addition, we must remember that the Port Royal method never produced as fine and eloquent linguistic descriptions as did its rival, the empirical method, so I believe that sociolinguists should take issue with Cartesian linguistics to the extent of clarifying with insight their main tenets and adding further refinement to their model; for Chomsky himself speaks of the "absurdity of regarding the system of generative rules as a point-by-point model for the actual construction of a sentence by a speaker." (I must give credit to Professor Andree F. Sjoberg, University of Texas at Austin, for his lucid exposition of "The Socio-Cultural Dimension in Transformational Theory" presented at the Annual Meeting of the Linguistic Society of America, New York City, December 28–30, 1968).

Hymes: I find myself sometimes in a situation having to defend Chomsky first so that after I can criticize him the way I would like to. But in my text, at least, and I hope certainly implicit in the presentation, there is no quarrel with the Cartesian concern for universals in the human mind, which is less than accepting everything that goes under that name. Just to make my position clear, let me read you a footnote which maybe is kind of cute and maybe not. It goes as follows: "A sociolinguistic critique of Cartesian linguistics is markedly parallel to the critique by Marx of Feuerbach. By substituting 'Chomsky' for 'Feuerbach' and 'linguistic' for 'religious' one has a remarkedly apposite statement." (I'm now quoting Karl Marx): "Chomsky resolves the linguistic essence into the human essence, but the essence of man is no abstraction inhering in each single individual. In its actuality it is the example of social relationships." Chomsky, who does not go into the criticism of this actual essence, is hence compelled to abstract from the historical process and to establish linguistic intuition as something self-contained, and to presuppose an abstract, isolated, human individual, and to view the essence of man merely as "species," (that is in a generic sense), as the inner dumb generality which unites the many individuals naturally (i.e., not socially).

William Stokoe, Jr., Gallaudet College: I'd like to ask Mrs. Philips if she has noted a distinction between the ways that the Indians of Warm Springs Reservation and non-Indians communicate nonverbally; whether the nonverbal communicative interchange suggested by the square formation of social groupings plays a different role in the Indian participant interaction than in non-Indian participant situations.

Philips: I'm not quite clear on whether you mean that the organization of activity is in itself communicating something, or that by virtue of that organization, other things get done. I would say that this face-to-face kind of organization in itself allows for people to be able to see constantly how everybody is reacting to everything. It implies in itself a type of silent participation that you can't possible have when all the people are in a room like this facing toward the front. You have little idea how each other among you have responded to the same things that you have responded to, whereas the Indians would. They would know. I think that is one kind of thing that makes a difference.

Stokoe: You mentioned the difference between the imperative and interrogative structures of English which call for specific responses in some cultures. Isn't it so that some kind of signal or a certain kind of response comes from nonverbal cues rather than from the structure of the verbal utterance?

Philips: Yes, in some respects, but that wasn't what I was thinking about in this particular case. I was actually referring to some sociolinguistic discussions of things like questioning and answering (I don't know if anything like this has been published, but papers circulate). There has been some notion that a question implies an automatic response. Thus somebody might point out that a child knows that if he asks a parent a question the parent will have to respond to him. It is a way of engaging somebody in interaction. On the Indian reservation one of the first things that I heard was that it was possible to have an encounter with somebody where you ask them a question and they simply don't answer you, but they might come back and visit you a couple of days later and answer the question that you had asked them! This indicates a difference in the cultural assumptions about what the temporal obligations of the answerer are. That was what I was talking about in this particular case.

Programs, Practices, and Staff Development

Whatever the strengths, whatever the weaknesses of ... bilingual schooling projects ... they need help. If bilingual schooling, the noblest innovation in American education, is to succeed, it must have close, objective, encouraging attention from all sides. The projects need, above all else, formative evaluation by knowledgeable outside observers who—with the gentle pressure of the Office of Education's authority and responsibility to continue each grant only so long as the work is performed satisfactorily—can help each project to become a model of its kind. Without radical strengthening some could probably never become models. They should either be strengthened or abandoned.

A. Bruce Gaarder

A. Bruce Gaarder

The First Seventy-Six
Bilingual Education Projects

This essay examines certain salient features of the plans of operation of the first seventy-six bilingual schooling projects supported by grants under the Bilingual Education Act. It reveals what appears to be, in a large majority of them, such inadequate attention—time, resources, and understanding—to the other tongue, as compared to the attention paid to English that, on the whole, the concept of bilingual education represented by these plans of operation seems to be something less than the legislation and its advocates intended. I say "appears" and "seems" because the analysis was made from close reading of the official plans of operation, plus addenda and other correspondence in the files of the U.S. Office of Education, plus returns from a questionnaire sent to the project directors, rather than from direct observation of the projects in action. The qualifiers are required too because the development of language competency in children takes several years, and at this writing only the first half-year of the five years of the supporting grants has elapsed. [1]

The Congress couched its extraordinarily generous and innovative legislation in support of dual-language public schooling in terms that permit both the ethnocentrists and the cultural pluralists to see what they want to see in the Act. It could mean the merest token obeisance to the non-English mother tongue (N-EMT) and the culture it represents, or it could—as a fictitious example—support production for one of the American Indian tribal groups of a full panoply of teaching materials in their language for all the school subjects, the complete training of a corps of native speakers of that language and full implementation of the resulting curriculum from kindergarten through the twelfth grade, plus schooling for the parents in their native tongue. English, of course, could never be excluded.

The Office of Education has interpreted bilingual education officially to mean the use of two languages, one of which is English, as mediums of instruction ... for the same student population, in a well-organized program which encompasses part or all of the curriculum, plus study of the history and culture associated with a student's mother tongue.

As one might expect, of the 76 projects some—quite within their rights—proposed the use of the child's mother tongue for purposes of instruction as a "bridge" to English, to be crossed as soon as possible and then eliminated entirely or

---

[1] The author gratefully acknowledges much help and cooperation from the Office of Education staff which administers the Bilingual Education Act. Since their inception the projects have undergone constant modification to improve their effectiveness.

From James E. Alatis (ed.), *Bilingualism and Language Contact* (Washington: Georgetown University Press, 1970), pp. 163–178.

virtually so in favor of English as the sole medium. With these our special quarrel is that the bridge seems usually to be a one-way affair with no encouragement to pass back and forth freely, and is sometimes so short as perhaps not to reach the other side of the abyss. Most of the projects have planned to give a much more substantial role to the mother tongue as a medium of instruction in the regular school subjects. Many profess to aim for equal emphasis on the two languages and seek to develop in their pupils equal competence in the two. Here it is evident in most cases that, whether consciously or unconsciously, the emphasis is very far from equal.

In the plans of operation of all of the projects, there is a profession of emphasis on the "history and culture" of the child who has a mother tongue other than English. They want to strengthen his "sense of identity," his "self-concept." Here—as will be seen later in this essay—the disparity between aims and means is enormous. Every project attempts to provide improved and intensified instruction in English. This component, in most cases the principal focus of the project plan, cannot be described in this limited essay. Finally, each plan provides in-service training for its project teachers and aides, and occasionally, for other personnel. Suffice it to say, for the purpose of this brief overview, that the in-service training included in most cases a short orientation session before the fall term began, and periodic sessions are held during the academic year focused on the other culture, the teaching of English as a second language, and the teaching of and through the N-EMT. The important point to note is that this work is conducted in the great majority of the cases by the local project director or the bilingual coordinator.

A brief overview of the entire program: 76 separate projects in 70 different cities, each project to be funded for 5 years if work is performed satisfactorily.

Language (in addition to English)		*Projects*
Spanish		68
Spanish and Sioux	1	
Spanish and Pomo	1	
Spanish and Keresan and Navajo	1	
Spanish and Chinese	1	
Mexican-Americans	58	
Puerto Ricans	7	
Puerto Ricans and one other language group	2	
Mixed Spanish-speaking	2	
Cherokee		2
Chinese (Cantonese) (plus the one noted above)		1
French		1
Japanese		1
Navajo (plus the one noted above)		1
Portuguese		2
		76
In elementary schools only		54
In secondary schools only		8
In both		14

Most projects have begun the first year very modestly, with only one or a few classes of pupils at one or two grade levels only. Some are more ambitious. All expect to expand year by year for five years.

Total first year cost of 76 projects $7,500,000
Average cost   98,684

Are the "other-medium" teachers (those expected to teach some or all of the regular school subject areas through the children's mother tongue) adequately prepared for bilingual schooling? There is evidence that most of them are not. In most of the plans of operation the qualifications of the staff are carefully set forth. Forty-nine call for mere "bilingualism," or "conversational ability" in the other tongue. Six want "fluent" bilinguals; at least one specifies the ability to read, write, and speak the two languages; some say the teachers will be "hopefully" or "preferably" bilinguals. On the other hand, eleven either identified or demanded well qualified people; and in fifteen there is at least one person educated abroad and some were seeking one or more such teachers. The ethnic groups differ markedly in respect to teacher qualification, with the highest requirements found among those with easiest access to literacy, notably the Portuguese, Chinese, French, and Puerto Ricans.

In about 20 cases the plans contain no requirement that the director and other key project leaders be more than "bilingual," and in at least 28 cases not even that limited knowledge of the non-English tongue is demanded. Again, in a score of cases the specific requirements for the director and other key persons in respect to competence in the other language and the culture it represents are high.

The above and following comments on teacher adequacy should be read with the knowledge that to a large extent the projects expect to depend on the teaching services of aides, sometimes called para-professionals, "bilingual" individuals usually drawn from the community, rarely required to be literate in the non-English tongue, and paid disproportionately low wages. Sometimes the aides work with bilingual teachers. In other projects only the aides are expected to be bilingual, and the regular teachers, the "master" teachers, are Anglos. Much can be said in favor of bringing into the schools persons who represent fully the usually under-represented ethnic minorities. But if those representatives obviously have less professional status, less training, less authority and receive less money than the teachers, the other-medium side of the project is getting less than a full, fair trial.

One plan calls for 40 bilingual aides at two dollars per hour to "encourage and energize the parents." In another plan of operation for grade one (and eventually grades 1–3) the aides alone are to be bilingual, their English must be "demonstrably competent," but they need only "conversational competency" in the other tongue. Yet the hope is that they somehow are to be given "the factual basis to permit a useful comparison and analysis of the differences between Spanish and English as spoken languages in the classroom" and are expected to prepare teaching materials. In still another case the merely bilingual kindergarten and preschool aides will be given in-service training in language development in both tongues in "contrasting usage, translation, relationships, vocabulary development, concept development, and pronunciation," and they are expected to "improve the oral language facility" of both pupils and parents.

What is mere, hopeful, even fluent bilingualism or "conversational ability" in two languages? Since most of the projects plan to use their own local teachers, and since the American school system has provided virtually no opportunity for child speakers of non-English languages to maintain and develop those languages—indeed, it has commonly discouraged and denigrated such speaking—the merely bilingual person is a product of the very kind of schooling which bilingual education aims to correct. Members in most cases of social groups with strong oral traditions rather than literary ones, given a first chance at literacy at age 15 in the ninth grade under Anglo foreign language teachers who seldom speak the child's tongue and invariably use books designed for Anglo beginners, how many such bilinguals will have read as many as five books or written 50 pages in their mother tongue? There is indeed the possibility of college study of the tongue, and in some few cases the *vita* notes such college work. The most favored case recorded notes that each teacher has at least 21 college semester hours of Spanish. An elementary school teacher with a college major in a foreign language is a rarity indeed, and none turned up in the data. Nor is the weakness lessened by the assurance of two directors (who had set no special requirements for their bilingual aides) that the secretary is expected "to read and write" and "translate the materials." A third plan of operations sets no requirements beyond "bilingualism" for the teachers, but specifies that the project secretary must be proficient in writing both languages: "Accurate spelling and punctuation is a priority need for the secretary."

A quick look at what the other-medium teachers and aides are usually expected to do affirms the weakness of their training. "They are expected to teach through the non-English tongue such subject fields as mathematics, science, the social studies, and language arts." There is a common belief that the person who speaks two languages can say anything in one that he can say in the other. That is simply not true. The most common situation finds such a speaker facile in one or more "domains" of usage in one language, and in other domains in the other. Perhaps small talk and intimacy in one, business and formality in the other. Facility in the terminology of a game or a sport or a technology in one language, expression of religious feeling in the other. Arithmetic in only one. Professional matters in only one. Everyday affairs can probably be conducted in either, but no one can stand up and invent authentic translations of mathematics teaching terminology or the terminology of any other school subject.

"They are expected in most of the projects to create or assist in the creation of teaching materials in the non-English tongue." Little need be said here to make the point. It is currently lauded pedagogy to encourage teachers to choose freely among teaching materials and adapt them as needed in order to adjust to the pupils' individual differences, but how many teachers can be expected to write their own books? A few project plans of operation gave examples of locally produced writing in the other tongue. Some were well done. Most are exemplified by the following:

A formal letter:
Hemos estado trabajando bajo considerable obstáculos con respeto a la escritura de la proposición . . . La fecha . . . adelantada dos días para darles el beneficio de discusiones . . .

A printed announcement:
Si Ud. desea conversar con el professor, por favor márquelo en el espacio destinado a ello. . . . Su firma justificará que Ud. revisó la libreta de notas . . . Poner una nota es algo muy importante en la Escuela, además de ser el deseo de las Escuelas Públicas de _____, a fin de interpretar mejor a los alumnos y ayudar así a los padres. . . . Para un avance satisfactorio, es indispensable una asistencia regular y a tiempo. . . . *Hábitos De trabajo* Significa que siempre debe estar preparado con sus materiales y tareas, siga y escuche las direcciones que se le dan.

A formal letter to the parents:
. . . Uds. puede ayudar a su niño tener éxito en el colegio.

A formal printed announcement:
Hablando diariamente, escuchando, leyendo y escribiendo, son las pericias del idioma inglés. . . Substantivos vívidos y verbos como *canyon y amontonar* se acentúan.

Educational theory about success in school:
El suceso de un niño . . .

Teaching materials:
Si alguien en un carro quiere que vaya con el, tenga cortes, pero marchase y no entre su carro.

Maria, agarra tres pelotas. Ensename dos modos para decirme que tienes tres pelotas.

Formal publication:
Advancemos: Mano en Mano

Must one be a pedant to be disturbed by these examples of inordinate influence from English and violation of the structure of Spanish? I think not, for the implication in all but possibly one of the Title VII project plans is that the other-language medium, whether Spanish, Cantonese, French, or whatever, will be its "standard" form. No one has yet claimed that San Francisco Cantonese, the Portuguese of Providence, and the Spanish of San Antonio are separate linguistic systems whose exquisite aberrations should be polished and respected and set apart from the vulgar standard by their own contrastive analyses. One plan states that its bilingual teacher aides will be trained in "standard South American Spanish." The exception noted calls for someone to prepare "material in barrio Spanish," but not to the exclusion of standard writings.

In one plan the measurement of behavioral objectives includes listening to tapes of three sentences each in Castilian Spanish and British English and repeating them in "Mexican Spanish" and "United States English." This particular plan of operation emphasizes speech and drama at the junior high school level.

Since almost all of the project plans require the same bilingual teachers to be responsible for both the non-English and the English side of the program, these teachers are expected to represent and present authentically, fully, fairly, two cultures: that of the United States and that of the non-English mother tongue child's forebears. In most cases they must somehow interpret a third culture, the amalgam, because the Puerto Ricans in continental United States, and Mexican-Americans and Franco-Americans find that their cultural patterns are in essential ways different from either of the two parent cultures.

It is at the bastion of biculturalism rather than at the bastion of language alone that bilingual education will succeed or fail, and it is here that the doubts gnaw most painfully.

First of all, is it fair to expect a product of the amalgam, a product of the educational system and policy which bilingual education seeks to correct, to represent fairly and powerfully both of the parent cultures? Does not biculturalism—a word which appears repeatedly in the projects' aims—imply double perspective, not the perspective of two eyes, but of two pairs of eyes? The use of the same persons to explicate both cultures—rather than two sets of persons, one for the English medium and United States culture, one for the non-English medium and the culture it carries—is matched in a number of project plans by the decision to have the teachers and aides themselves produce the classroom materials dealing with the other history and culture. In some projects the history books and others in this area will be translations of United States, English language texts.

The following examples illustrate some of the ambivalence and uncertainty regarding the other-tongue history and culture:

One project means to establish in the children "a detachment towards the Spanish and English languages to enable the student to function in either his native or Anglo-Culture [sic] whenever he so chooses." Can language be thus successfully detached from culture?

One program "encompasses bilingualism with diglossia," by which is meant ". . . the socio-cultural context in which language learning takes place." But "many children's books have been translated into Spanish" (not, it should be understood, by the project's personnel) and "children's songs, singing games, and rhythmic activities will be translated into Spanish . . ."

In one plan the Mexican-American child is expected, on completion of the "Texas Government and History" course through Spanish, to demonstrate "respect for himself as an individual by over [sic] acceptance of various levels of ability and differing physical characteristics in others." Could this be the same as acceptance of one's lot?

"Cultural readings for literature, interdisciplinary materials from the social sciences and science materials will be translated (to Spanish) and modified for language instruction." Yet the purpose of these culturally oriented materials is supposedly to develop pride in the child's own heritage, to give him a new point of view, not merely the same one presented through another language.

In still another project, the teacher responsible for bicultural activities must have a high degree of competency in both tongues "because of requirements of both accurate and idiomatic translations."

As noted, the applicant for a Title VII bilingual education project has the right to propose the degree of emphasis on the non-English language and culture that his wisdom dictates. This is not the same, however, as declaring intention to do one thing and then, unwittingly, describing conditions which can be expected to frustrate that intention.

One project expects to develop the ability of all children, both N-EMT and EMT (English mother tongue), to pursue ordinary school subjects in either language, but it will teach the language arts and mathematics to N-EMT children in that tongue only enough to avoid retardation.

One project seeks "to develop his (the child's) ability to function in and through two languages" and develop his "competence needed to employ two linguistic systems separately and consciously as mediums for speaking (reading and writing) and thinking in the total curriculum . . ." But in the third year of the project, reading in Spanish will be included only if sufficient funding is available and community approval can be determined, and such subjects as mathematics will be taught in English only. Two other projects are virtually identical in this respect.

A hint of some notion of the concept of diglossia comes in one plan of operation which seeks to develop "coordinate bilingualism." The plan states that ". . . those areas in which the student must succeed in high school and college—for example, mathematics—will be taught in English . . ." and "those areas which the student associates with his own background, for example, native literature . . ." will be taught in Spanish.

One project means to "develop curriculum authentic in respect to Mexican-American culture," but for the program development specialists there is a formal requirement of expertise in setting "behavioral objectives" and no such requirement as a knowledge of Spanish.

One project aims at a "true, balanced bilingual program," but "English will become the major medium of instruction during the second grade."

In one of the plans, which provides work through the N-EMT in language, mathematics, and the social studies, only the aides are bilingual. The children show that they are learning "by responding in classes where the real teacher is Anglo to or through translators [sic] if necessary."

The plans of operation of the 76 projects are not entirely clear about the amount of time that will be devoted each day to instruction using the N-EMT as the medium. There is uncertainty on this point because the expression "bilingual program" sometimes means both tongues, sometimes only the N-EMT. Thus, in one, the "bilingual" part is four hours daily, but the breakdown, during the first quarter year, is three hours of ESL, and one of history taught through English and the N-EMT; and during the second quarter there are two hours of ESL, and two hours of history divided between the two languages. At least four programs favor the N-EMT. Thirty-four are either bridges or favor English markedly. Only six aim eventually to provide bilingual schooling at all grade levels, 1–12.

One project seems to have scheduled only 10–15 minutes' work daily in the other language. Another aims "to provide an opportunity for any student to become truly bilingual," yet it schedules only 25 minutes daily for the mother tongue as a medium.

The adverse criticism explicit and implied in much of the foregoing is not the whole story. Many strong, promising features are to be found among the 76 projects.

Both Albuquerque and Grants, New Mexico, see clearly that mere bilingualism does not prepare a teacher for this work.

Brentwood, California makes a point of the need for full literacy in both languages for teachers and aides.

Chicago makes two important points: (1) that the "bilingual" is not necessarily "bicultural" and may not be able to interpret fairly the other culture; for this purpose they want foreign exchange teachers, and (2) they clearly separate the languages, one in the morning, the other in the afternoon. New Haven also stresses the importance of not mixing the languages during a single class period.

One of the Del Rio, Texas projects has called on experienced teachers from Mexico for help with Spanish-medium tests, and has planned one three-day in-service training session in Acuña, Mexico. Edinburg, Texas arranged for its teacher trainers and the teacher in charge of Spanish language literacy to come from Mexico.

Gonzalez, California sees the importance of employing teachers who are "conversant with Spanish language approaches to the subjects taught," and declares that its staff "will make an effort to avoid producing materials in areas where specialized professional competence is of prime importance." The Naples, Florida project also stresses the employment of teachers able to give training through Spanish in all subject areas.

The Lansing project expects its other-medium teachers to have the baccalaureate and both bilingual and bicultural skills: "... ability to discuss in Spanish some of the major language learning problems of the bilingual child and the history and culture of the Spanish-speaking American."

Laredo, Texas (Laredo Independent School District), seemingly alone among the projects, recognizes the extra burdens of dual-medium teachers and has budgeted an annual bonus of 300 dollars for each one. Its plan also calls for bringing from Mexico a special teacher to be in charge of staff and materials development. The Laredo project's bilingual teachers are required to take the Modern Language Association Proficiency Test (in Spanish) for teachers and advanced students.

The Laredo, Texas (United Consolidated Independent School District) bilingual teachers all have earned at least 21 college semester hours in Spanish.

The New York Bronx project includes a six-weeks summer extension, three hours daily, alternating the languages, in language, reading, and mathematics. The New York Two Bridges project plan offers half of each day for native tongue subject matter classes, and views itself as building a bridge not to English, but on which the children can move easily back and forth.

The Providence, Rhode Island plan, seeking to assure that the N-EMT children develop full capacity for conceptualization through the mother tongue, gives less than equal time to English until the participants are in their fourth year of school. English as a second language study begins, nevertheless, in grade one, and they expect to achieve beginning literacy in English in grade two. They employ different teachers for each medium and secure educated, experienced trainers from abroad for the N-EMT work.

Milwaukee sees the importance of uniting its bilingual schooling project with the efforts of its regular foreign language teachers at the high school level, and will offer a history and culture course for both groups of students together.

The Rochester project provides different teachers for each of the mediums, insists on high literacy of all teachers and aides, plus demonstrated ability to teach school subjects through Spanish, and keeps the languages separated in time and place.

Whatever the strengths, whatever the weaknesses of the 76 bilingual schooling projects (and this essay gleaned from written accounts rather than direct observation cannot describe them with complete certainty), they need help. If bilingual schooling, the noblest innovation in American education, is to succeed, it must have close, objective, encouraging attention from all sides. The projects need, above all else, formative evaluation by knowledgeable outside observers who—with the gentle pressure of the Office of Education's authority and responsibility to continue each grant only so long as the work is performed satisfactorily—can help each project to become a model of its kind. Without radical strengthening some could probably never become models. They should either be strengthened or abandoned.

Bilingual schooling needs assistance from research-oriented scholars and other investigators who will answer some of the questions which project directors and teachers are asking:

1. How can project directors ascertain quickly and fairly the degree of scholarly competence of persons who might be employed as teachers or aides in the non-English medium?
2. How can the difference between requiring teachers to work through two languages and having separate teachers for each of the languages be made plain? (The cost is not a serious factor, for the length of the school day is fixed and each teacher usually works alone with a class at any given time.)

3. Bearing in mind the plague of constant borrowing and interference between the tongues in bilinguals who do not maintain separate domains in their lives for each tongue, how can the relative merit of keeping them separate (or mixing them) in respect to time, place, and teacher in the school be determined?

4. What are the administrative and legal impediments to bringing able, experienced teachers and other personnel from abroad, and how can they be overcome?

5. How can school materials of all kinds be produced for teaching American Indian children their own languages and through those languages as mediums of instruction?

6. There is need for a means of measuring the extent to which N-EMT children—even very young children—possess and control that tongue.

7. There is a great need for a search abroad for teaching materials written originally in the other language, both corresponding to the regular school curriculum in the project schools, and dealing with the "history and culture" of the N-EMT child's people and their forbears as viewed by themselves through their own language.

There are questions of methodology. Millions of young children three to eight or thereabouts have learned a second language in a complete, effortless, largely mysterious way, but the literature contains no record of anyone's having "taught" one to a child.

8. The main problem is to maintain at maximum effectiveness the circumstances which are known to facilitate natural learning by children when the new language is the necessary, unavoidable means to their involvement in pleasant, significant situations far beyond language itself, and still permit experimentation with highly structured lessons (drill, etc.) designed to increase the speed of learning.

9. Should parents whose English (or any other language) is heavily flawed be asked to speak English to their small children as a means of helping them learn that language? Their efforts will tend to offset those of the child's English teacher, and their failure to stress the mother tongue will offset the efforts of the mother tongue teacher.

10. What is the minimum amount of language contact time short of which children's ability to learn naturally a second language becomes ineffective? (One of the 76 bilingual schooling projects schedules only a 10–15 minute period daily for the second language.)

Beyond the concern for developing and refining the 76 projects and others like them and realizing, *in school,* the full potential of bilingual education, there are broader concerns yet unvoiced for the role of the non-English tongues—certainly this is applicable to Spanish—in the streets, the shops, the offices, the homes. Put otherwise, is it really possible to make a child vigorously literate in his mother tongue if that vigor and literacy are not somehow matched in public places and in the homes? Do children really read eagerly and widely if their parents read reluctantly and seldom? If there are very few books, few newspapers and almost no magazines? Can two languages co-exist stably in the same speakers and be expected to serve exactly the same purposes? Will not bilingual schooling, if it succeeds in raising the educational level of the bilinguals, thereby increase their control of English, their social and geographical mobility and so hasten the disappearance of the other tongue?

These are concerns for the adults, the parents, the intellectuals and, yes, for teachers of these tongues as "foreign" languages. "Bilingual education," we saw earlier, can serve the ends of either ethnocentrism or cultural pluralism.

DISCUSSION

Gerard Hoffman, Yeshiva University: I was particularly gratified to hear Dr. Gaarder's remarks, especially in light of his initial comment that the programs are supposed to focus on those whose mother tongue is not English. In observing our own project and in planning for the future—we are located in first grade at the moment and we expect to expand down and upward from kindergarten through grade 5 eventually—and in talking to people involved in other Title VII programs besides ours, I find that there is some sort of contradiction in the use of the term "bilingual education," especially in the minds of the people on the Board of Education with whom we have to deal, and the people in the local schools, namely the warning that Dr. Fishman made this morning that through Title VII Bilingual Education we are creating a monolingual people in English. I see that by use of the term "bilingual education" instead of "mother tongue instruction" there has been some confusion on the part of some people, and I wonder if Dr. Gaarder or somebody else in the Office of Education would comment on that.

Gaarder: I would like to have Miss Moore, who really knows more about this than I do, comment. Let me say this before she does begin, that I feel ashamed because it seems that I have, and I have indeed, emphasized some negative aspects. I simply ran out of time; the full paper will be published.

Margaret Moore, U.S. Office of Education: Would you repeat, please?

Hoffman: It seems to me that there is some confusion in the case of people we should be trying to reach—the nonlanguage teachers, the educators who are not versed in the field of bilingualism. There is some confusion in their minds as to the purpose of the bilingual act. I believe many of them feel that it is to create, not a bilingual community among the various groups that we are dealing with, but to give them a basic education in their native language with the eventuality of making them English speakers, or finishing their education in English rather than fostering bilingualism throughout the grades. There seems to be a tendency on the part of local educators to see bilingual education phasing out as you go up the grades.

Moore: There are various patterns of bilingual education throughout the Title VII projects. Some projects are following the approach that he has described. There are others that are not, but which are following a full bilingual program. Some projects have chosen not to develop an ideal, all-grades bilingual program. Perhaps for some the reason for choosing another pattern is related to the matter of educating school people in terms of attitudes and awareness of what bilingual education is. Perhaps for some the reason is related to their own analysis of local needs. I admit there are a variety of patterns depending on local needs, etc. Yet there are still those who are following the full bilingual concept.

The law stresses the use of at least two languages, and one of those languages must be English since that is one tool that the students will need in order to function in our society. But the law doesn't spell out specifically which patterns should be followed. Projects discovered early in the first year of operation that there is a problem choosing the pattern best suited to their needs. However, a pattern that is only an English as a Second Language program is not recognized by us as being the same as a bilingual education program.

Robert Lado, Georgetown University: This is Lado from Georgetown, a bilingual. I visited four or five or six—I don't know how many—of these 76 projects with Dr. Andersson and a number of others about a year ago, and I think that I share with Dr. Gaarder the high ideals that he has. I would like to see this America of ours really get there quickly, but I think that if he expects these first projects to achieve these ideals from the start, he is going to impose some impossible demands on this bilingual program, and I would like to give a little testimony, a couple of minutes.

I will mention two things I discovered when we visited these projects in San Antonio that may give us the magnitude of these problems, and then some very optimistic impressions. First, the taxi driver who took me to the hotel was a bilingual Mexican speaker, and I made him talk. I wanted to know how he felt about bilingualism, and he had very strong ideas. He said he did not want his daughter to study Spanish (he told me this in Spanish) because he wanted his daughter to marry a big shot from Washington. And I told him that I was from Washington, but that I was married and had many children, and besides that I liked studying Spanish and English. The problem, then, is that this negativism toward bilingual education is all over, and I do not think we can expect these 76 projects to change the United States from top to bottom overnight. This is asking too much, and if Dr. Gaarder is asking that much, then we are all going to fail and we might as well forget it. But we can expect other things.

I saw some schools where the bilingual programs were going on, and in one school I saw children watching four tubes with a transparent, colorless liquid in them, and they were being asked to reason, to see if they could discover if these four tubes had the same kind of liquid in them—they all looked like water. A child would make a statement, and he or she would be asked to come up to the front of the class and do something to the tubes—smell them, shake them, or pour them into something else—and the material inside the tubes would do different things. Then they would proceed to another step of reasoning in Spanish concerning some introduction to science. Then English-speaking children would do this in Spanish also, and Spanish-speaking children would do this in English in another class. To me this was so exciting that I said (and this is what Dr. Fishman says), "I wish that my children could have the advantage of this kind of bilingual growth in intellectual as well as linguistic material." Of course the answer was, "Your children cannot have this because they are not in the poverty category." And this is Dr. Fishman's recommendation, that we should strive to expand the bilingual education to those who are not in this $3,000 a year family income bracket. This is the optimistic impression which I got.

Then, on the negative side: In that same school I went to the library; I wanted to see how many books they had in Spanish, and the librarian didn't know. So I located *Ferdinand the Bull* in Spanish, and a couple of others like that. In my report to the office staff, I asked if something could be done about getting more Spanish books, or French books, or whatever, and I was encouraged by the tremendous effort that is being made to do this. This year, for example, a major program is going on to get Spanish books from all over the world into these schools.

Another impression on the negative side: In one school into which I walked, all the heroes on the walls were those heroes who became famous by fighting and beating the grandparents of the bilinguals in school. I assure you that my heart beat more slowly. The atmosphere according to the pictures was not bilingual or bicultural. On the other hand, in another school in the same district the pictures were bicultural, so much so that one of the members of the visiting team begged to see if he could get some of these pictures, and I think they are now hanging in Hawaii.

I think the situation is very promising. We cannot expect these 76 projects to turn America around overnight, but there is enough of a dawn here that we should support it at this time.

Eleanor Sandstrom, Title VII Project Director in Philadelphia: May I just try to get a statement across, because I am concerned about what Dr. Lado has just said, and I am very concerned that this fear of turning America around too soon is going to help the baby die instead of helping the baby grow. And one of my tremendous concerns is for some more directional effort from U.S.O.E. to support those areas where we are committed to bilingual education and "real bilingual education for both Anglo and Latino children in our particular city," and where we are trying to teach children in both languages, and we continually have to answer to the climate of school administrators who are concerned about whether these things are good or bad for their children. I would hope that groups such as TESOL and the Linguistic Society will support the things that both Dr. Fishman and Dr. Gaarder had to say here today.

Curtis Harvey

General Descriptions of Bilingual Programs That Meet Students' Needs

A look at bilingual education programs in operation across the nation presents the reviewer with a tremendous variety of program organization and implementation. At first glance, there would appear to be very little or nothing at all which would identify them as members of a basic instructional curriculum with common strategies. Several educators have made attempts to single out the common elements which are characteristic of bilingual programs in general. For example, Dr. Theodore Andersson, in his publication, "Bilingual Schooling in the United States,"[1] presents the following schematic developed by William F. Mackey.[2]

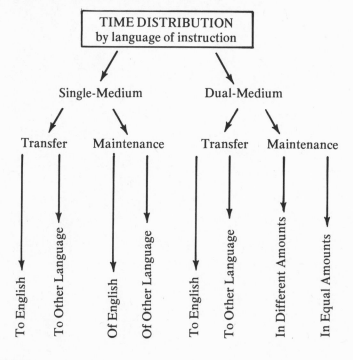

---

[1] Andersson, Dr. Theodore, and Mildred Boyer, "Bilingual Schooling in the United States," 1970.

[2] Mackey, William F., "A Typology of Bilingual Education," 1970.

From *Proceedings of the National Conference on Bilingual Education* [April 14–15, 1972] (Austin, Tex.: Dissemination Center for Bilingual Bicultural Education, 1973), pp. 252–264.

Dr. A. Bruce Gaarder, in an article entitled "Organization of the Bilingual School," [3] used the following chart developed by H. H. Stern. [4]

One-Way School:	Mother tongue added	{ Equal time and treatment
one group learning languages		Unequal time and treatment
	Second tongue added	{ Equal time and treatment
		Unequal time and treatment
	Segregated classes	{ Equal time and treatment
Two-Way School: two groups, each learning in its own and the other's language		Unequal time and treatment
	Mixed classes	{ Equal time and treatment
		Unequal time and treatment

As you can readily see from these two examples, efforts of this nature have a tendency to become rather confusing and are relatively meaningless to the average teacher or administrator who is not trained in the area of bilingual education and who is interested in trying to organize and implement a local program. Therefore, for the purposes of this discussion, let us attempt a different approach.

Basic to every educational program are the needs of the students for which it is developed. One of the major criticisms of today's "standardized curriculum" is the fact that it does not provide for individual variations among students. This has been substantiated time and time again as schools have failed to provide so many of our young people with the skills and knowledge needed to become positive contributors in today's society. The recognition of this failure has been accepted to some degree over the past years and many attempts have been made to develop programs which would alleviate the "problems." However, a close observation of many of these programs leaves a person with the feeling that they are beautifully developed on paper, but initiated with little or no foreknowledge of the children they serve, their characteristics and their specific needs as individuals. Here again, we have preconceived programs trying to mold the children into their structure and limitations, rather than making an attempt to change the curriculum of the program to provide for the needs of the children.

---

[3] Gaarder, Dr. A. Bruce, "Organization of the Bilingual School," 1967.

[4] Stern, H. H., *Foreign Languages in Primary Education: The Teaching of Foreign or Second Language to Younger Children*, 1962.

Saville and Troike[5] suggest a number of factors outside the direct control of the school which influence first and second language development. These factors may well be expanded to not only be concerned with children's language but also to relate to their total intellectual development as individuals in preparation for entrance into the school environment.

The nature of the child's preschool environment.

The personality traits of parents and their attitudes (attitudes towards the community, their work, the school, etc.).

Degree of association with adults.

Child-rearing practices in the home.

Number of siblings, and ordinal rank among them.

The attitude of the parents toward their own speech community and toward the second language group.

At this point, however, it might be well to mention the danger of identifying bilingual education as a remedial program. By thinking of bilingual education as a remediation for children who have not been able to function successfully in school and are, for one reason or another, not achieving at grade level according to our standards, we have allowed ourselves to be led into a trap by two common misconceptions: (1) The present curriculum is appropriate for every child and does not need changing, and (2) all children should be expected to progress at the same rate, regardless of individual differences, background, environment, culture, etc. In fact, we are associating bilingual education with failure from the very beginning which immediately creates a negative atmosphere.

Another erroneous concept that many people have been led to believe is the idea that bilingual education places an additional burden on an already crowded curriculum by increasing the number of subjects to be taught or by duplicating instruction, i.e. teaching a concept or lesson in one language and then repeating it in the second language. Obviously, neither of these approaches is practical or desirable; nor are they necessary. Bilingual education simply takes the already existing curriculum of a program and, through the use of the language the children speak and manipulate with facility, initiates instruction. This allows the children to focus their entire attention on the task of learning, continuing to expand their conceptual development without distraction and limitations caused by an unfamiliar language.

In 1967, Dr. A. Bruce Gaarder[6] listed four major reasons for providing instruction in the first language. Still quite appropriate today, they are:

1. to avoid or lessen scholastic retardation in children whose mother tongue is not the principal school language;
2. to strengthen the bonds between home and school;
3. to avoid the alienation from family and linguistic community that is commonly the price of rejection of one's mother tongue and of complete assimilation into the dominant linguistic group, and
4. to develop a strong literacy in the mother tongue in order to make it a strong asset in the adult's life.

---

[5] Saville, Muriel R., and Rudolph C. Troike, *A Handbook of Bilingual Education*, 1971.

[6] Gaarder, Dr. A. Bruce, "Organization of the Bilingual School," 1967.

Dr. Gaarder[7] also states the rationale for providing instruction in a second language which is not only applicable to non-English-speaking children, but also very appropriate for English dominant children. They are:

1. to engage the child's capacity for natural, unconscious language learning;
2. to avoid the problems of method aptitude, etc., which beset the usual teaching of second languages;
3. to make the second language as means to an end rather than an end in itself;
4. to increase second language experience without crowding the curriculum;
5. plus other well-known reasons such as to teach the national (dominant group) language, to provide a lingua franca or a world status language, for cultural enrichment, and economic gain.

Although the fifth point appears rather general it has taken on new and greater importance with today's focus on cultural awareness and identity in our society.

There are a number of factors which must be taken into consideration which play an important part in the structure and the effectiveness of a bilingual program. They will be determined by the characteristics of the children and the community to be served by the program and the availability of personnel for staffing. Considerable consideration must be given to the time allotment and distribution for each of the two languages. How each language will be used and the treatment that each will be given must be determined early in the planning process. It is important to know whether the language which is to be added to the previously existing system is the first or will be the second language for the children to participate in the program. The linguistic capabilities of the teachers must be known. Are they all bilingual or will there be monolingual teachers involved also?

The organizational pattern of a bilingual education program may vary, depending on the factors identified above and others. But a series of structures or "models"[8] have been developed which represent the basic generalizations that can be made about these patterns.

MODEL I

CONTENT

T I M E	First Language
	Second Language

In a program of this type instruction is equally divided between the children's first language and their second language. Typically, a school operating under this program will have instruction in the first language in the morning and instruction in the second language in the afternoon. Sometimes, specific content areas are selected for instruction in the first language and other areas are selected for instruction in the second language. In other instances the instruction in the second language is simply an extension of the content areas presented in the first language.

---

[7] Ibid.

[8] Southeastern Educational Laboratory, *Razón de Ser of the Bilingual School,* no date.

MODEL II

CONTENT

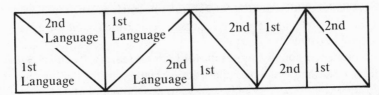

Again, the instruction is offered in both languages in a program of this nature. Approximately the same amount of time is given to each language, but any time-block may contain the two languages used in an integrated or blended manner or they may be maintained separately as depicted. Team teaching is a technique which adapts itself easily to this type of program. In both Model I and Model II, the children must have an equal command of both languages.

MODEL III

TIME

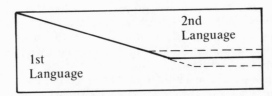

In a program of this design, instruction is initiated totally in the children's first language and the second language is introduced gradually. As mastery is obtained in the second language, less and less time is devoted to instruction in the first language until it is reduced to a "maintenance" level. In this case the first language may be presented as a subject itself in the curriculum, or any other content area could be selected to continue instruction in the first language. Basically, this type of program is known as transitional, providing instruction in the first language until the children are sufficiently fluent to operate successfully in the second language.

MODEL IV

TIME

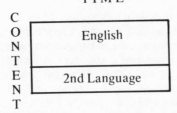

For the last model the program is predominantly in English. The second language is either taught as a subject itself or it is used for instruction in another selected content area. This is the basic design for most foreign language programs and does not actually qualify as bilingual instruction in the full meaning of the concept.

As was indicated earlier in this discussion, the major focal point of any school program, bilingual or otherwise, centers around the specific needs of the children who are to be involved. If it does not meet these needs, or if the needs themselves have not been identified, there is no way for us as educators to expect or even hope for positive results. It is stated in the Statewide Design for Bilingual Education[9] in Texas that: "The primary goal of Bilingual Education is successful achievement by the student of the goals of the educational process, using two languages, developing proficiency in both. . ." To achieve this broad goal, the Statewide Design further states that the local school districts will: "(1) Provide an environment conducive to learning, (2) Develop an effective program that will give each student an opportunity to make progress toward these goals, (3) Appraise the student's level of development of language, concepts, and experience (exercising care to avoid testing the student in his second language until he has sufficient control of the language so that his true verbal abilities can be measured), and (4) Have available sufficient numbers of personnel qualified to conduct the program."

More specifically, the Statewide Design identifies the following components as characteristic of a bilingual program that is developed to meet the individual needs of each child:

I. The basic concepts initiating the child into the school environment are taught in the language he brings from home.

Orientation to the classroom code of behavior and patterns of social interaction with his peers are developed by drawing from the child's resource of experiences and concepts and language which he has already learned in his home environment.

II. Language development is provided in the child's dominant language.

The sequential development of the four language skills, i.e., listening, speaking, reading, and writing, is continued in the language for which the child has already learned the sound system, structure, and vocabulary. This is exactly the same approach which has been used in the past. The only difference is the use of the dominant language of the child whose first language is not English. With this one change the child begins developing the skills with the use of his first language without having to wait until he learns his second language.

III. Language development is provided in the child's second language.

By utilizing second language teaching methodology, i.e., teaching the listening and speaking skills by use of audiolingual instructional techniques prior to teaching the reading and writing skills, the child immediately begins to learn a second language. For the English-speaking child this instruction is in the language of the other linguistic group involved in the program and, of course, English is taught to the child who comes from a non-English-speaking environment. Unique about this component of the program is the fact that the child does not have to relearn language skills. He has only to transfer these skills learned in his first language to the second language.

IV. Subject matter and concepts are taught in the child's dominant language.

Content areas which are considered to be critical to the intellectual and emotional development of the child and to his success in the school environment are initially taught through the use of the child's first language,

---

[9] *A Statewide Design for Bilingual Education,* Texas Education Agency, no date.

thereby permitting and encouraging the child to enter immediately into the classroom activities, drawing from all his previous experiences as a basis for developing new ideas and concepts.

V. Subject matter and concepts are taught in the second language of the child.

Since no language can be taught in a vacuum, content areas are also taught in the second language, providing the vocabulary and concepts which are needed for communication while the second language is being learned. Initially the number of ideas and concepts are necessarily few due to the limitations imposed by the amount of language the child controls. The teaching techniques are audiolingual in order to insure the development of listening and speaking skills. As the child's second language ability develops, more and more content is included and the other skills, reading and writing, are incorporated.

VI. Specific attention is given to develop in the child a positive identity with his cultural heritage, self-assurance, and confidence.

The historical contributions and cultural characteristics identified with the people of both languages involved are an integral part of the program. Both the conflict and the confluence of the two cultures are presented in the social development of the State and nation in order to create an understanding and appreciation of each in a positive rather than negative sense.

By providing the opportunities for successful participation and achievement, the child is encouraged to develop acceptance of himself and of others through social interaction. [10]

Briefly, the following Guidelines[11] compiled from research and reports from bilingual preschool programs, offer some practical suggestions and direction for establishing needs when a bilingual education program is under consideration.

1. The Community:
    Is it linguistically stable?
    If not, what nature of change is taking place and in what direction?
    What are the social relationships between the two languages?

2. The Composition of the Class (or School):
    Are all children non-English-speaking?
    Do some speak English fluently?
    Are there children who are deficient of appropriate experiences and background for the traditional school curriculum?

3. The Desires of the Parents:
    Do they want their children to become a part of the dominant Anglo culture quickly? (Do they send their children to Head Start to learn English?)
    Would they prefer that their children maintain a bilingual/bicultural outlook?

---

[10] *A Statewide Design for Bilingual Education,* Texas Education Agency, no date.

[11] Bernbaum, Marcia, *Early Childhood Programs for Non-English-Speaking Children,* PREP Report No. 31, 1972.

4. The Teachers:
   Are they bilingual?
   If not, is there a bilingual aide in the classroom?
   Are they knowledgeable of both cultures?
5. The Educational Future of the Children:
   Will they be going to an elementary school where only English is spoken and most of their classmates are Anglo?
   Will they remain in a bilingual/bicultural atmosphere?

BIBLIOGRAPHY

Andersson, Theodore and Mildred Boyer, *Bilingual Schooling in the United States,* Vol. I, Southwest Educational Development Laboratory, Austin, Texas, 1970.

Bernbaum, Marcia, "Practical Guidelines for the Teacher and Administrators," *Early Childhood Programs for Non-English-Speaking Children,* PREP Report No. 31, ERIC Clearinghouse on Early Childhood Education, University of Illinois, Champaign, Illinois, 1972.

Gaarder, A. Bruce, "Organization of the Bilingual School," *Journal of Social Issues,* Vol. XXIII, Number 2, 1967.

Mackey, William F., "A Typology of Bilingual Education," *Bilingual Schooling in the United States,* Vol. II, Southwest Educational Development Laboratory, Austin, Texas, 1970.

Razón de Ser of the Bilingual School, Southeastern Education Laboratory, Atlanta, Georgia, n.d.

Saville, Muriel R. and Rudolph C. Troike, *A Handbook of Bilingual Education,* Center for Applied Linguistics, Washington, D.C., 1970.

A Statewide Design for Bilingual Education, Texas Education Agency, Austin, Texas, n.d.

Stern, H. H. (Ed.), *Foreign Languages in Primary Education: The Teaching of Foreign or Second Languages to Younger Children* (Report on an International Meeting of Experts, April 9-14, 1962, International Studies in Education), UNESCO Institute of Education, Hamburg, 1963.

Carmen Elena Rivera

Administration, Supervision, and Implementation of a Bilingual Bicultural Curriculum

Frustrated, and at times disillusioned and embittered about the failure of their children to achieve, communities who have been speaking out for decades are now beginning to be heard in increasing numbers.

Educators are concurring with their critics. They are beginning to understand why the curriculum, which presently encompasses the educational offerings for the more privileged middle class child, is unacceptable. They are beginning to accept the fact that critical statements about the curriculum are no longer to be considered undemocratic or outrageous. For it is true that it is neither meaningful nor relevant. Language and cultural differences have not been recognized and when recognized, not respected. This explains its lack of success in lifting the educational sights of the much misunderstood and neglected Hispanic child.

Questions such as the following are now being directed to our educators for accountable responses:

Is it defensible to expect children to struggle to learn in a language they find unfamiliar or inadequate? Not when chapters of failures which are daily being added to our histories of education report fewer successes for the Hispanic than for other minority groups.

Is it conscionable to permit children to grow into adulthood with inferior and inadequate feelings about themselves? Not when we know that the majority culture in many instances feeds on the minority's inadequacies and failures to insure its own survival. That nebulous "self-concept" is no longer an abstraction for us. We can see it, hear it, talk about it and feel it. We can even measure it. The low scores frighten us.

In the light of what we have learned from the above, schools must therefore provide for the Hispanic child a curriculum that will insure his acquiring:

1. the necessary command of skills so that he can use language effectively for communication at all levels;
2. the assistance and encouragement essential to "find himself" within the cultural milieu of his own choice.

Our public schools will thus be honoring their commitment to the public they were historically designed to serve. This public consists of significantly larger numbers of Hispanics, who have heretofore been overlooked. This forgotten minority

From *Proceedings of the National Conference on Bilingual Education* [April 14–15, 1972] (Austin, Tex.: Dissemination Center for Bilingual Bicultural Education, 1973), pp. 105–120.

which began to make its mark in the sixties will continue to make an impact in the seventies. The introduction of bilingual, bicultural approaches to teaching the non-English-speaking in particular, and the urban poor Hispanic and non-Hispanic child in general, is facilitating this process.

It is disappointing that the paucity of funds is frustrating the efforts of many interested and concerned community leaders and committed educators to embark on needed bilingual programs. This will unfortunately continue to be the case until our own local city authorities begin to accept their responsibility to appropriate the monies necessary to run an efficient and effective school system.

Since the millenium is not yet near, and until such time as it is, the state and/or federal government, or both, should perhaps become more judicious in the allocation of its monies. By shifting their priorities, monies may begin to flow into programs designed to "save" our youth for meaningful participation and gainful employment, in a society, where, prognosticators tell us, only the best equipped intellectually and emotionally are slated for survival. The Title VII monies allocation has never been generous. The potential of Title I for financing bilingual programs is an unknown, largely because its role has not been recognized in this area.

The bilingual school curriculum that is the subject of this paper is that of an existing bilingual school which is in its third year of operation in New York City. As is certain to have occurred in other sectors of the country, much rhetoric preceded the reality of bilingual education in New York City. Our educational leaders had to readjust their thinking, and begin to dispel their unfounded fears, about the most pedagogically sound approach to teaching—the use of the vernacular. Laws directing and compelling schools to use English only as a medium of instruction had to be repealed, which historic event occurred in New York in 1967.

It was a year later, in 1968, that several of the more courageous members of the bilingual and educational community of District 12, where 211 is situated, forged ahead with plans to implement this novel, innovative approach. P.S. 25, a totally bilingual school located in another but neighboring school district, had already opened its doors. This fact was no doubt instrumental in pressing the leaders of District 12 to reach this major decision.

The acquisition of the C.S. 211 school building preceded the planning and organization of its bilingual, bicultural curriculum to be implemented that coming September of 1969. This was an abandoned building which had long outlived its usefulness as an industrial site. Within the space of close to eight months, this loft was converted into a beautiful and functional school, introducing the most modern features in school construction and design, such as open-wall classrooms, carpeted floors and acoustic ceilings. The term "open-wall classrooms" is self-explanatory. An entire area capable of containing four classrooms was kept "open" with only movable pieces of furniture serving as room dividers. The carpeted floors and acoustic ceilings were introduced to reduce the noise level that was certain to rise in decibels as the population of the "learning areas" was increased in numbers. This type of physical structure has facilitated the introduction of the non-graded type of organization and the utilization of team teaching—two other unique aspects of this very special school—aspects which have played a major role in the evolving of our bilingual bicultural curriculum.

This site selection, incidentally, reflects another changing concept. The overcrowding and overutilization of school buildings shortchanges the education of the minority-group child, for it often leads to part-time instruction. It definitely makes more sense to use abandoned commercial buildings—bowling alleys, catering centers, warehouses—which can be converted and refurbished for transformation into schools, particularly when the skyrocketing cost of new construction is making new structures exorbitant and unavailable.

In addition to obtaining a building so that a two-track bilingual school organization could be structured from the start, those administrative areas of immediate concern to its director had to be identified: the student body which had to come voluntarily; the staff which had to be competent, bilingual if possible, and necessarily committed to this type of organization and program; the location and acquisition of materials which had to complement a curriculum relevant to the needs of the child in terms of language, culture and content.

The initial planning and organization was conducted during a six-month period preceding the formal opening of the school. With the approval of a state urban aid proposal, monies for a much needed staff to work with, and an office to work in, became available. It was in addition possible to gain additional insights on bilingualism by visiting bilingual schools and programs outside of the New York City metropolitan area, such as Chicago, Miami and San Antonio. A teacher-training institute was organized and conducted during the Summer of 1969 for the essential orientation and training of the school's prospective teachers and paraprofessionals. Teachers who were unfamiliar with the styles of minority group children needed the opportunity of working with these children, if only in the familiarity and confines of the traditional box-like classrooms in already scheduled District summer school programs. Courses for accreditation by Lehman College, a neighboring city college, were among the offerings. These specific courses were designed to develop among the prospective teachers competencies in the teaching of Reading and the Second Language, two of the most important subjects of its curriculum. In addition, workshops were conducted during which time the rationale for bilingual education was proposed, and the philosophy, history and research of bilingual education discussed. The second language was also taught — Spanish and English — so that the monolingual English-speaking teachers particularly would gain or regain confidence to teach children with very specific second language problems.

The elements that were to differentiate the curriculum of this bilingual school—211—from that of neighboring non-bilingual schools, as well as other existing bilingual schools, began to emerge with the consideration of the following questions: What was our ultimate goal as a bilingual school? Was our school designed to specifically meet the unique language, cultural, and learning needs of its entire student body? Was its ethnic distribution to be given strong consideration in the structuring of its curricular design? The answers to these questions contributed to the unfolding of our curriculum. For example, at the time that we were recruiting and registering our children it appeared that more than 40 percent of our applicants would be non-Hispanic, largely Black American. It had been previously and mutually agreed that no child whose parents expressed an interest in the program would be denied admission to a school that was advertised as a two-track bilingual school. I did not find this to be at all untenable.

As a foreign language teacher of Spanish, I had always wanted to see the wider expansion of the Spanish language program in the elementary schools. Traditionally, as I am certain is true of other school systems throughout the nation, the learning of a foreign language in the early grades is the prerogative of the rich or the intellectually gifted. The schools that offer these enriched offerings have heretofore been located in the more affluent neighborhoods. The recipients are children whose reading scores are considerably above the national norms and whose own background of experiences has offered challenge and stimulation. But, is it not possible for the poor and the non-intellectually gifted to learn a foreign language at an early age? Cannot the study of the foreign language and its culture both stimulate and challenge a child and consequently enhance his learning capabilities? There is confirming evidence of this every day at 211.

The remaining 60% of the children whose parents expressed an interest in the program were Hispanic—largely of Puerto Rican origin or background. These were the children who would be significantly retarded in the mastery of the basic skills in Spanish, and in addition, as it soon became dramatically evident to all of us, in English as well. Can it not be possible to develop, strengthen and maintain the language arts skills of these children's vernacular so that they gain control and confidence in their home language? Is it not possible for these children to acquire skills, learn concepts and add to their fund of knowledge via their home language, their mother tongue, their vernacular? Can they not learn their second language—English—faster than other urban poor children who attend non-bilingual schools? They do, and we likewise see increasing evidences of this phenomenon.

A viable, functional, meaningful bilingual program therefore evolved as we were able to define what bilingualism meant to us, who our bilingual child was, what were to be the components of our bilingual program of instruction. The fact that the study of the literature, coupled with the examinations of bilingual programs in different sectors of the country, revealed that no standard definitions of bilingualism, the bilingual child and bilingual programs of instruction existed gave us the fortitude to think in terms of developing our own.

By "bilingualism" in our program we meant competency in the use of two languages as vehicles of communication, verbal communication as well as written communication, in consonance with the age, grade and achievement level of the child. The bilingual child in our program was one whose command of Spanish represented the whole continuum of language, that is, ranging from limited to a fluency unusual for his age and grade. Because for some of these children the stronger language appeared to be English they were classified as English Dominant. The Hispanic child who could not function effectively in English for learning purposes, that is, who had not developed decoding skills in English, was classified as Spanish Dominant. He was by and large the new arrival to this country. In some instances, he was the offspring of parents whose command of English was poor for a number of reasons: they may have been living in this country for just a few years; they may not have been exposed to the language because of the linguistic islands where they live and work, or they may have resisted adopting completely the new language because of plans to return to their homeland, Puerto Rico.

The bilingual bicultural person our comprehensive bilingual program is designed to produce is one who can use both languages effectively for communication at a level commensurate with his age, ability and interest, and, in addition, can transfer from one language to the other without losing what we characteristically refer to as *el hilo del pensamiento*—the thread of thought.

These introductory remarks lead us logically into a description of our comprehensive bilingual program of instruction, which is specifically designed to meet the cultural, language and learning needs of our three major language categories of children: Spanish Dominant, English Dominant and bilingual, distributed throughout the six grades with achievement levels running from readiness to seventh and eighth grades in reading and mathematics, ethnically distributed in the following manner: about 30% Black American, 70% Bilingual and/or monolingual Hispanic (mostly Puerto Rican). For the latter their knowledge and/or command of Spanish is ideally suited to the introduction and/or continuance of the bilingual curriculum for the major portion of the school day. For the former, the early introduction of a second language, Spanish, should contribute to the growth of bilinguals from the monolingual (English) component of our population, a desideratum when we reflect on the monolingual structure of our society — a reality that does not appear to perturb our educators.

In essence, our bilingual program at 211 is above all, and significantly so, a maintenance program:

1. The vernacular, be it English or Spanish, is respected, maintained, developed and strengthened. It is used to facilitate teaching of all content areas of the curriculum. To put it more explicitly, it is used as a tool for learning.

2. English is introduced and taught as a second language to the Spanish Dominant child. Spanish is likewise introduced and taught as a second language to the English (monolingual) speaking child. Spanish is taught as an enrichment subject to the bilingual child classified as English Dominant. If a child neither reads nor writes Spanish, the focus will be on developing those skills that will give him practice and eventual command of the necessary reading and writing skills.

3. In addition to teaching the language, we also program children for instruction in the second language. The subject area of the curriculum specifically selected for this purpose was Mathematics, which in 1970 was taught for 15 minutes a day in the second language. The following year it was taught in the second language during two 45-minute periods a week. This year it is taught for approximately five 45-minute periods a week. Concepts are introduced in the child's vernacular with provisions made to conduct the required practice and drill part of the lesson in the second language. This coming school year Science, in addition to Mathematics, will be taught in the second language.

4. The development of knowledge, consequent understanding and respect for the cultural heritage of our two main language and ethnic groups is an additional facet of the program which differentiates our curriculum from that of the average school.

What I have described thus far has been the use of Spanish in the instructional process, as a first and/or second language and as a vehicle for the teaching of content. We have dealt more with the product than with the process. And I realize that in this particular instance we are all interested in how we reach our ultimate objective of developing and adding to the projected bilingual bicultural society we all envision for the future.

There is a term usually appended to that of curriculum — materials — that needs to be discussed at this time. Teachers are interested in knowing what they have to teach. They express interest and concern with the how (methodology). But we know that they are even more concerned with the what — which is materials — at times not realizing that weakness in approach can vitiate the quality of the materials.

This is the greatest weakness of a bilingual program. The dearth of materials reported a few years ago still exists. The location of materials in Spanish for our three groups of language learners — Spanish as Second Language (S.S.L.), Spanish for Spanish Speakers (Bilingual Children) (S.E.) and Spanish for non-English Speakers (Spanish Dominant), became for us a long and arduous task. When, in addition, these materials had to meet the additional requirements of legibility, attractiveness, price, reading level, language, and, above all, relevancy, the task became almost monumental.

Via local distributors (The Materials Acquisition Project in San Diego, California, has a nationwide list of them), we have acquired many of our materials in Spanish. One of them is an entire series (in Mathematics); others are selected titles for expanding and enriching the skills, knowledges and conceptual framework of the other subject areas such as Science and Social Studies. Our own American publishers have in the past few years begun to recognize the emerging needs among educators for these materials and are responding to these needs, as evidenced by the following titles.

These are materials that have served to meet the immediate needs of teachers. They should be closely examined because selection for local needs often varies.

For SSL—Spanish as a Second Language—we have made available for teacher selection and use the following titles:

The Langford and Parnel Series of Allyn and Bacon *(Yo Sé Leer, Venga a Ver)*

The Saavedra Tirsa Series of Ginn & Co. *(Como Se Dice, Somos Amigos)*

The Bishop Series of the National Textbook Co. *(Hablan Los Niños).*

As with other subject areas, titles are not prescribed for particular levels. Teachers have guides available. Our own school S.S.L. Committee makes suggestions regarding procedures, practices and curricular content in terms of the structure and vocabulary that should be mastered by a child at his own particular level.

For SE—Spanish Enrichment—materials must be available to encompass the language and interest levels of children who range in grades from one to six, some of whom are already independent readers in the two languages, and many who command one skill but who may be seriously lacking in the others. The curricular offerings for these children must of necessity vary. Many of the materials are teacher prepared, distributed and shared. A committee of S.E. teachers is charged with the responsibility of coordinating this instructional component in the school.

Several commercially prepared materials have nevertheless been acquired for use in this area:

The *Me Gusta Leer* series of Allyn and Bacon is recommended for use with children who are independent readers in English but who have no reading skills in Spanish.

The Laidlaw Spanish Basal Readers, which provide a *cartilla (Aprendemos a Leer)* and proceed to a grade level 6—*Páginas de Ayer Y Hoy*—is again recommended for children in the English Dominant (bilingual children) classes who are independent readers in English.

There are books printed in Latin America that are widely used: The Añorga Series on *Elementos gramaticales* and on *Lectura.* Añorga also has an *Ortografía funcional.*

For those children who are already in the upper grades, and whose verbal facility in Spanish has been rated as poor, books on suggested conversational dialogues are available. One of these is the Dixon books on *Conversación en Español.*

There are several library titles, either translations of American classics or adaptations of Spanish classics, whose potential for use with these children was early recognized. Segmar of Buenos Aires has an animal series that is attractive, legible and popular. The Western Press has the *Libros de Oro del Saber* which are also extensively used.

The focus on E.S.L.—English as a Second Language—is on developing and/or strengthening aural-oral skills. After the child is familiar with reading skills in his own language he is introduced to reading in English.

Many of the publishing companies have produced instructional materials in the form of texts, readers, tapes and records:

McGraw-Hill (Let's Speak English)

Houghton-Mifflin (Introducing English of Lancaster)

American Book Co. (We Learn English)

Ginn & Co. (Core English I and II)

The Michigan Oral Lessons Series (with structured oral language lessons for the teaching of English and Spanish to the young child)

Teachers are free, in addition, to use other titles and aids as resources in their daily preparation.

For the teaching of Reading to Spanish speakers who are classified E.S.L., we use the *Serie Básica* of Laidlaw Brothers which is the reading series used in Puerto Rico. Our problem in this area arises in effecting the extension of individualized reading. What we have done thus far is to prepare our own Reading units with the limited titles we have available to us. To these units we must append exercises that have to be individually prepared, since instructions must be clear and the exercises such that they test particular comprehension skills. It should again be stressed that not until a child can decode in his own language is he introduced to reading in the second language.

In the fields of Mathematics, Social Studies and Science, teachers follow the courses of study and/or curriculum guides issued by our Central Board of Education. Commercial textbook companies study these guides and follow them closely in evolving the kind of printed material teachers look for in developing suggested units with their children.

Books in Mathematics which incorporate all the modern mathematics language and concepts have been published in English with parallel editions in Spanish. One such publisher is Laidlaw Brothers. There is the *Fondo Educacional Interamericano, S.A. Math* series which is the Spanish parallel of Addison Wesley's series. All these series follow the Modern Mathematics philosophy and likewise have excellent teacher guides.

To teach Science, we likewise have a parallel series in Schneider Science Books of D. C. Heath & Co. This translation was produced and pilot tested in Puerto Rico by Puerto Rican teachers with Puerto Rican children.

The area of Social Studies presents by far the greatest problem. Parallel translations are not commercially available for the lower grades. Teachers must therefore translate these materials and prepare their own worksheets. Many are quite adept. They have the necessary resourcefulness, ingenuity and imagination to introduce concepts and develop the activities necessary and important for developing understanding and appreciation among children. Others are not so endowed and bemoan the dearth of materials in these areas. There is no doubt that teacher requests should whenever possible be honored. However, the paucity of printed materials can at times provide teachers with an excellent opportunity to develop their own resources. They can encourage children to play a major role in their own intellectual development. Sometimes we forget that despite the lack of ability to express themselves in fluent, fluid Spanish, and/or English, children have acquired knowledge, skills and ideas as a result of having explored their own immediate work about them. This is an opportune area, therefore, for teachers to use multi-faceted approaches, such as research and investigation through use of library materials, cooking ethnic foods, making dioramas and exhibits, where an informal approach in second language communication can be effectively expected. The skillful, inspiring teachers will elicit from children what they know and will in turn, as the facilitators in the learning process, help them build a system of order out of what may be a disarray of facts and a confusion of ideas.

Reading and research material should be on hand and immediately available on many topics and all levels to meet our children's varying needs. Where the printed material is missing in Spanish, the aid of the staff should be enlisted in developing novel approaches to obtaining this material. The SCDC (Spanish Curricular Development Center), located in Miami Beach, for example, is producing, among other strands, a Social Science strand. Although the kits available are for the first grade, basic concepts are presented in a spiral basis, much as it is in Modern Mathematics, with particular emphasis in learning strategies for independent growth and discovery. The activities presented furnish teachers with ideas for the conduct of their own lessons on a level beyond the first grade. (For beginning learners the activities should be followed as suggested, with provision made for the utilization of the great variety of audio-visual and manipulative materials that accompany all their kits.)

We hope that as the program continues teachers will acquire the skills necessary to translate, adapt and/or develop their own materials. They are already involved in this aspect. With the possible availability of Title VII monies we expect that this will be an area that will receive our largest share of attention. A great need which likewise exists is material written in the sociocultural context of the child, which should encompass the Puerto Rican and the Black experience, reflect a poor urban environment and be permeated by an ambient where different styles of communication coexist—two languages in both their standard and non-standard forms.

It is difficult to expound on curriculum and materials, to describe process fully, if all aspects of the school design are not fully recognized and understood. A bilingual bicultural program must respect and reflect the language and learning needs of the children in terms of skills development and conceptual growth, as well as their physical, emotional and social needs: Spanish Dominant, English Dominant, Bilingual, Hispanic, Puerto Rican, Black, Independent, Non-Independent readers, all grades, with achievement on a continuum from readiness to grade six and above at the elementary level.

In view of this diversity and in order to organize for effectiveness and efficiency we began to group children for the purpose of reducing, wherever possible, the existing wide ranges of achievement. Grouping is now a school-wide practice in the areas of Reading, Language, (Spanish as a Second Language, English as a Second Language, Spanish Enrichment) and Mathematics in the Second Language (Spanish and English).

In addition, all our teachers have become teachers of language. Very few, however, came to our program trained to teach the second language. In order to help teachers develop and strengthen their skills in this area, workshops on a regular basis on school time have been organized. Demonstrations, observations and conferences are scheduled with individual teachers and groups of teachers. We now anticipate using Title VII monies to likewise assist our teachers in strengthening this aspect of their teaching.

The role of the administrator in planning and organizing a bilingual curriculum has been delineated above in terms of his concern for the availability of courses of study, curriculum guides and materials. He plays a major role in developing the skills, competence and confidence of that person who will play a key role in reaching the major objectives of the program—the teacher. He likewise should play an important, if not a major, role in those organizational aspects described at the outset, since a building is important, teachers must be recruited, selected and licensed, children enrolled and parental involvement enlisted.

There is an additional area of interest and concern not mentioned above. This has to do with how the public views bilingual education and the questions they are likely to ask, to wit: Is this program a procedure for further alienating the ethnic groups of a community? Will the learning of a Second Language (Spanish) retard even more the child's progress in Reading in English? If so, since many of the children of the urban poor are already severe retardates in reading, should they not read more in their vernacular instead of less? If you teach a non-English-speaking child in his own language, when is he going to learn English? When is he going to be Americanized, to enter the "mainstream of American Society," to be "melted" in the proverbial pot that never existed? Can the poor urban child (English monolingual) really learn Spanish?

Anyone involved in bilingual education must have the answers to the above questions at his fingertips. Although parents have exercised their option in enrolling their children in this particular bilingual school, my experience has been that in several cases the last consideration in their minds was bilingual education and its assets or debits. This was and is true of the Hispanic as well as the non-Hispanic parent. They must be assured and convinced that they have made a wise educational choice.

For every child positive results are already noticeable at P.S. 211, which attests to the validity of this approach.

The morale of the teachers is higher than that at other schools with which I have been associated.

The upgrading in the total reading performance is highly indicative of the fact that the children are learning.

While most of our children are bussed, there is a minimum of irregular attendance. Our rate of mobility is likewise lower.

School-community ties have been strengthened. Attendance at meetings is excellent and parental visits to the school are quite frequent.

It is not a segregated school in terms of its being a Puerto Rican School. The percentage of Puerto Rican children and Black is about 65/35. They are both benefiting greatly.

The Puerto Rican child is learning content and developing skills while at the same time he is learning English. No one is hopelessly attempting to teach him skills and concepts in a language he doesn't understand.

The Black Child profits from group work, team teaching and a second language, the learning of which has always been one of the rewards of being intellectually gifted and, if not "rich," in this school he has the opportunity of increasing his future options in the labor market.

The promise that our program holds for bridging cultural barriers and lifting achievement levels is being realized. The Black child and the Puerto Rican together are learning to recognize and value each other's cultural values since the Puerto Rican heritage and culture and the Afro-American heritage and culture are daily interwoven into the school curriculum.

They will be at the vanguard of the cultural pluralism movement when they reach maturity. This is the hope all of us see as a possibility of fulfillment in a school where its educators are dedicated to fulfilling the goals established for a bilingual bicultural curriculum.

Gloria Zamora

Staff Development for Bilingual/Bicultural Programs— A Philosophical Base

Bilingual/Bicultural Education serves as a positive response to the need for equal educational opportunity for the thousands of children in the United States whose first language is other than English.

In the 60's when the first national efforts to initiate bilingual education programs in the United States were made, our children were called "culturally disadvantaged" and their home language was called a "problem" or a "handicap."

In 1972, many people still consider Spanish, or French, or Chinese, or any language other than English a "handicap." Culture and language are problems or handicaps only when the school fails to see them as assets and fails to capitalize upon them as sources for learning and intellectual development.

Before the staff development component of any bilingual program can be determined it will be necessary to examine the philosophical base of the program, for from the philosophy flows the design or model for all the components.

Investigation of bilingual/bicultural programs throughout the United States reveals a wide philosophical difference.

1. There are those programs that use the dominant language only as a "bridge" to help the child move into English as quickly as possible.

2. There are programs that look upon bilingual education strictly as an oral language development program, with heavy emphasis on ESL.

3. There are programs that translate the existing English curriculum into the home language and call it bilingual education. Perhaps it is bilingual, but it is no better than what we had before and it definitely is not bicultural.

4. There are programs that utilize the dominant language to stimulate cognitive development, extend the knowledge and use of the mother tongue and develop the knowledge and use of the second language, English—all of this enhancing the self-concept because the program treats the culture and home language of the students as positives.

The philosophy of the Edgewood Independent School District, in all of its programs, is the latter. We are not working with "handicapped" or "disadvantaged" children, but with "atypical" children. The district's "Theory of Incompatibilities"[1]

---

[1] The "Theory of Incompatibilities" was developed by Dr. José Cárdenas and Miss Bambi Cárdenas.

From *Proceedings of the National Conference on Bilingual Education* [April 14–15, 1972] (Austin, Tex.: Dissemination Center for Bilingual Bicultural Education, 1973), pp. 299–303.

serves as the rationale from which the staff development component flows. Briefly, when one examines the typical school structure, it is quite evident that there are incompatibilities between it and the atypical children we serve.

These incompatibilities have been identified and grouped into five major categories: poverty, culture, language, mobility and societal perceptions. It is our responsibility as educators, then, to reduce the incompatibilities not by changing the child (as has been so unsuccessfully done) but by changing the institution. We will examine each of the incompatibilities and responses to the incompatibilities in detail in order to formulate the staff development component. Let us also bear in mind that staff development must include administrators, supervisors, teachers, teacher-aides and parents—everyone who works with the child.

POVERTY

The typical instructional program fails to take into account the effects of poverty: a large child-to-adult ratio in the home, the absence of typical adults in a family, the dissipation of adult energies in meeting the basic necessities of life, the relative absence of communication media in the home, the absence of toys and activities that stimulate intellectual development and the deprivational effects of inadequate housing, malnutrition and poor health.

What implications does this have for staff development?

CULTURE

What is culture? It is much more than the art and music of a people. It is their value system, their life style and their language. Traditional curriculum is oriented to an ethnic group and a culture incompatible with the culture of minority groups. Our children have been called "culturally disadvantaged" when in reality they are culturally different children who become culturally deprived only after culturally-biased institutions succeed in damaging the fabric of culture through consistent and heavily armed attack.

Does this have implications for staff development?

LANGUAGE

This third incompatibility between the instructional program and the characteristics of the learner is an element of culture so significant in its role as an impediment to learning that it must be listed separately. It is readily apparent that an incompatibility exists when a Spanish-speaking child is placed in an English-language instructional program. It is at this point that we must reexamine our philosophy. Shall we eradicate this language "problem," this "handicap," and move him into English as rapidly as possible? Or shall we recognize his home language as a marvelous asset which should be recognized, nurtured and developed?

What implications does this have for staff development?

MOBILITY

To a large extent, the instructional program for typical children is one designed for stable populations. The sequence and continuity in the instructional activities assumes that the child participating in them also acquired previous and often prerequisite learnings and that the same child will be present to participate in subsequent and often dependent learning activities. This is a dangerous and false assumption to make wherever there is a high mobility factor. The problems of poverty often necessitate migrant labor, or relocation within the school attendance zones. The education of these children suffers from a lack of sequence and continuity.

How can staff development help reduce this incompatibility?

SOCIETAL PERCEPTIONS

The perceptions that people in a child's educational environment have of that child, as well as the child's own perceptions of himself, maximally affect the level of success or failure enjoyed by the child in an educational program. Teachers' expectations for atypical minority-group children tend to become self-fulfilling prophecies. Teacher attitudes and resultant teacher behavior may substantially alienate the child from the instructional program. Consistently poor performance in an instructional program which is incompatible with his cultural and learning characteristics further enhances the negative perceptions the child has of himself. Thus, we find the child in a vicious cycle involving negative feelings which lead to failure, further reinforcing negative feeling and perpetuating poor performance.

What can we do in staff development to help counteract negative perceptions?

INTERRELATEDNESS AND INTERDEPENDENCE

The five categories of incompatibilities do not operate independently of each other. Mobility alone is not necessarily disabling. It is mobility coupled with poverty, with language, with culture, with negative perceptions which produces disastrous educational problems.

Dealing with these incompatibilities in our educational system is analogous to the medical treatment of a sick person. If he has a brain tumor, a ruptured appendix, and a cerebral hemmorhage, the finest surgery for removal of the brain tumor will not be sufficient to save his life.

Bilingual education, too, is doomed to failure if we respond only to language. Let us develop programs that respond to all of the incompatibilities. For the teacher and the staffs of bilingual programs, let me say that love is not enough—we must develop some new methodologies, curricula and staffing patterns in order to respond to all of the incompatibilities.

Francesco Cordasco
and Eugene Bucchioni

An Institute for Preparing Teachers of Puerto Rican Students

Elementary and secondary school Puerto Rican students are confronted by the usual array of educational difficulties and emotional and social problems related to poverty or low-income status. In addition, Puerto Rican students demonstrate the life styles, values, and normative understandings and responses characteristic of Puerto Rican culture. The lack of specially trained teachers prepared to work specifically with Puerto Rican students is a major factor affecting the quality of the educational program offered to Puerto Rican students. Furthermore, teachers who are not specially trained contribute significantly to conflict in schools with large Puerto Rican enrollments. The lack of professional skills in areas such as remedial reading for Puerto Rican students, conversational Spanish, the teaching of English as a foreign language, and guidance of Puerto Rican students, as well as the general lack of knowledge of Puerto Rican culture and of the Puerto Rican experience on the mainland, are additional factors contributing to unsuccessful school achievement and widespread academic retardation common among Puerto Rican students.[1]

The writers propose a Staff Development Institute for Elementary and Secondary School Teachers of Puerto Rican Students, which will be concerned, consequently, with the development of knowledge of, and insight into, Puerto Rican culture and the Puerto Rican experience in the U.S.; specific professional skills, such as remedial reading for Puerto Rican students, methods and materials for the teaching of English as a second language, and specific guidance procedures to be used with Puerto Rican students; conversational Spanish as spoken within the Puerto Rican community to enable teachers to relate to, and communicate more effectively with, both parents and children whose knowledge of English is very limited; and bilingual education—its philosophy, structure, objectives, curriculum, and methods and materials of instruction. Teachers, together with other school personnel, will participate in the program, forming teams of about four teachers from schools with high percentages of Puerto Rican students in attendance. The function of the team structure will be to provide a nucleus of individuals in selected schools so that a variety and diversification of professional skills will be available.

Each participant in the institute will take seminars entitled, "Puerto Rican Students in American Schools" and "Aspects of Puerto Rican Culture and History."

---

[1] See, generally, Francesco Cordasco and Eugene Bucchioni, *Puerto Rican Children in Mainland Schools: A Source Book for Teachers,* revised edition (New York: Scarecrow/Grolier, 1972).

Each member of a school team will choose from the following offerings: philosophy, structure and curriculum, and methods and materials of instruction in bilingual education; remedial reading for Puerto Rican students; teaching of English as a second language; conversational Spanish; and guidance of Puerto Rican students. Finally, a synthesizing seminar will be offered to each participant on the basis of level of teaching: elementary teachers will take "Elementary Education for Puerto Rican Children," and high school teachers will be expected to complete "Secondary Education for Puerto Rican Students."

The institute should be implemented through lectures, discussions, films, readings, field trips, and with extensive contact with members of the Puerto Rican community. An important feature of the institute should be the inclusion of many Puerto Rican professionals and other members of the Puerto Rican community in the various offerings and activities of the program.

Some attention should be given to the selection of participants in terms of the following criteria: reasonable competency and satisfactory service in a school; general social and emotional maturity; and commitment to the education of Puerto Rican students and to teaching in the Puerto Rican community.

Through interviews, letters of recommendation and the examination of the professional history of the applicants, an attempt should be made to select only those teachers who have a firm commitment to the education of Puerto Rican students, and who demonstrate the characteristics required for success in the institute and for implementation of learnings, skills, and knowledge derived from the institute in their respective schools. In addition, each participant selected should possess the leadership potential necessary for developing required changes as part of the team returning to each school. In this way, the impact of the institute will go beyond that of the participants alone, and will be extended to other members of the school staff, who will be encouraged to use the members of the team completing the institute as leaders or resource people in the education of Puerto Rican students.

Costs for the institute may be defrayed in part by Federal or by local funds, depending upon budgetary exigencies. Title I (Elementary and Secondary Education Act) funds may be budgeted appropriately within existing guidelines, and, where districts have applied for Title VII (ESEA) funds, the institute may be part of the program (within Title VII guidelines) for the education of non-English-speaking children.

Robert Miller and Francesco Cordasco

Conspectus for M.A. in Bilingual Education and M.A. in Teaching English as a Second Language: A Program Proposal

I. RATIONALE FOR SUBMITTING THIS COMBINED PROPOSAL

There are at least four cogent reasons for submitting a proposal for a degree in bilingual education at the same time as one in the teaching of English as a second language:

1. Bilingual education programs in the United States are at present intended *primarily* for children who do not speak English natively.
2. The teaching of English as a second language (TESL) has itself become a highly specialized discipline and is recognized as an integral and necessary component in any bilingual education program.
3. The State Board of Education of New Jersey has itself recognized the close association between the two disciplines by recently approving at the same time the certification proposals[1] in Bilingual Education and TESL that were submitted to them by the Bureau of Teacher Education and Academic Credentials.
4. Furthermore, since, as the State's own proposals show, there is a good deal of overlap among the courses required for certification in the two fields, it is possible to offer most of the total number of courses to teacher-trainees interested in either field. An important by-product of this arrangement is that such courses will reduce the number of staff members required to teach them and will increase the enrollment in each course offered.

II. INTRODUCTION AND RATIONALE FOR PROPOSING AN M.A. IN BILINGUAL EDUCATION

That bilingual-bicultural education[2] is a desirable educational goal is scarcely debatable any longer among our most thoughtful educators—nor is its inevitability.

---

[1] The M.A. proposals presented here include, of course, all of the courses that are required for certification alone.

[2] The shorter term "bilingual education" has been and will continue to be used throughout the remainder of this proposal to stand for the longer and somewhat more awkward expression "bilingual-bicultural education." This abbreviation is in line with general usage. "Bilingual (-bicultural) education" is usually defined as an educational program in which two languages are employed as mediums of instruction within the same school population.

The full significance of this movement has been aptly summarized in the following passage:[3]

> Bilingual-bicultural education has become one of the most significant and widespread movements in American education in the twentieth century. Not since the Renaissance has there been such a general acceptance of the idea that the goals of education might best be served by offering instruction in the native language of the learner. The passage of the Bilingual Education Act in 1968 helped bring about a major change in our educational philosophy, from a rejection or disparagement of other languages to a respect for their validity and their value as mediums for learning. The cultures of their speakers have come to be recognized as forming a valuable part of our national heritage, and as occupying an important place in our pluralistic society.
>
> Today, state after state is adopting legislation supporting or mandating bilingual-bicultural education. Recent court decisions, including one by the Supreme Court, are giving added impetus to this movement. In order to meet the urgent need for competent teachers trained to teach in bilingual-bicultural programs, colleges and universities are rapidly instituting teacher training programs, and state departments of education are moving to prepare or approve credentials in this field.

The following is a specific list of the major reasons given by respected educators, linguists, psychologists, sociologists, and administrators why bilingual education is a valuable enterprise:

1. It avoids scholastic retardation when the child's English is not adequate, thus providing equal educational opportunities for non-English-speaking children.
2. It strengthens the bonds between home and school.
3. It develops an understanding and respect for the child's mother tongue and the culture associated with it. This understanding and respect lead to a more positive self-image and better social and personal adjustment.
4. It puts to advantage the career potential of the non-English language.
5. It recognizes the basic right of every people to rear and educate its children in its own image.
6. It acknowledges the fact that a second language is learned better, for example, English by native Spanish speakers, and Spanish by Anglos, if some subject matter is taught through that medium rather than when the language is taught as an end in itself.
7. It grants recognition at last to the richness and diversity of our collective national linguistic and cultural heritage. It thus makes available a wider cultural experience to *all* members of our society.
8. It supports the contention that when children from diverse linguistic and cultural backgrounds learn each other's language and culture at an early age and in the same school, they are more likely to share greater mutual respect for each other as adults.

---

[3] From the Linguistic Reporter: A Newsletter in Applied Linguistics (October 1974).

Why a Master's Degree?

We feel that a Master's degree program in bilingual education is more urgent at this time than a Bachelor's degree for the following reasons:

1. There is an immediate need for teachers trained in bilingual education in the State of New Jersey. The recent (January, 1975) signing of S-811 bill, requiring bilingual education programs in districts which have twenty or more pupils of limited English-speaking ability, took effect July 1. If such districts are to be served, it seems obvious that the state must begin to rely, at least at first, on a reservoir of in-service teachers—especially foreign language teachers, English as a Second Language (ESL) teachers, teachers working in learning centers, and teachers who are bilingual but who may never have taught in their first language. We believe that these and other teachers will be seeking to enroll themselves in graduate programs in bilingual education (Montclair State has received many such requests in recent months), both in order to cope with the many unfamiliar problems posed by this new enterprise and to better secure their present teaching positions by attaining a graduate degree in this field.

2. As the demand for teachers of foreign languages diminishes and the demand for bilingual education teachers increases, Montclair State, along with the other State colleges, can expect many of its graduates, especially those in Spanish-Italian, education, linguistics, and TESOL, to pursue a graduate degree in bilingual education. That is to say, we have a ready-made reservoir of prospective graduate students in bilingual education already on campus.

Why Montclair State?

Judged by the combined criteria of geographical position and resources, both human and material, we feel Montclair State is uniquely endowed to offer a graduate program in bilingual education:

1. Of the fourteen school districts in New Jersey comprising 15% or more of Spanish-speaking and/or Spanish-surnamed students, eleven of them lie within reasonable commuting distance of Montclair State. They are:[4]

School District	*Percentage of Spanish-Speaking and/or Spanish-Surnamed*
West New York	63%
Union City	61%
Hoboken	56%
Perth Amboy	45%
Passaic	31%
Weehawken	23%
Paterson	22%
Elizabeth	19%
Dover	18%
Jersey City	17%
Newark	15%

[4] The chart is taken from Diego Castellanos, "The Hispanic Experience in New Jersey Schools" (Trenton: New Jersey State Department of Education, June 1973), pp. 17-18.

We expect a large number of teachers teaching in these districts to be seeking admission to the proposed graduate program in bilingual education at Montclair State.

2. Most of the courses that the state has tentatively proposed to be included in a Bilingual Education Certification Endorsement are either already being taught by the Linguistics Department of Montclair State (the only such department among the State Colleges offering a B.A. in Linguistics), or are about to be proposed by the Linguistics Department (those about to be proposed are Social Dialectology, Testing and Materials Preparation, Applied Linguistics, and Linguistics and Reading). Moreover, all of the required courses in the recently passed program leading to certification in the Teaching of English to Speakers of Other Languages (TESOL), which constitutes a major component in a bilingual education program, are offered by the Linguistics Department.

3. Because a program in bilingual education should rely upon the advice and expertise of persons who have taught and done research in the field, we consider Montclair State to be particularly fortunate in having Professor Francesco Cordasco on its campus. Professor Cordasco is a nationally-known authority and the author of many books and articles on the Puerto Rican child and his adjustment to the American educational system. We hope to be able to depend on Professor Cordasco's counsel throughout the development of the program.

4. Among the State Colleges of New Jersey, the Harry A. Sprague Library of Montclair State has the best collection by far of books and periodicals dealing with all aspects of bilingual education. Indeed, the collection compares favorably with those of the entire New York Metropolitan Area.

III. RATIONALE FOR PROPOSING AN M.A. IN TEACHING ENGLISH AS A SECOND LANGUAGE

As we stated in Section I above, besides being an important component of bilingual education the teaching of English as a second language is itself a highly specialized field. Being a native speaker of English does not automatically qualify a person to teach other people to speak English any more than the ability to speak any language natively so qualifies anyone. Furthermore, the teaching of English as a second language entails much more than teaching children the phonology, grammar, and vocabulary of English, although the knowledge and skills demanded of a teacher to accomplish even these tasks are considerable and are the subject of some controversy. The teacher must also be aware of the linguistic, cultural, and psychological factors that are critical in the development of the whole person and be aware of how these differ from one society to another. For example, the teacher of English as a second language must possess considerable knowledge of general learning theory, the differences between first and second language learning, the developmental stages of language learning, the various functions of language in different societies and the different cultural systems associated with those societies. The teacher of English as a second language must also be aware of the social, regional, and functional varieties of English, including their structure, development, and relations to the culture of English-speaking peoples. In many respects the teacher of English as a second language has a more difficult task than that of his colleagues in the modern foreign languages, for he is responsible for ensuring his pupils' success in their use of English at least throughout the remainder of their school career—and in various school subjects.

We feel that when the extent and degree of knowledge required to master the accomplishments described above are carefully considered, particularly in the context of a bilingual education program, the necessity and desirability for offering an M.A. in Teaching English as a Second Language becomes obvious.

IV. MATRICULATION REQUIREMENTS FOR AN M.A. IN BILINGUAL EDUCATION

1. A bachelor's degree based upon a four-year program in an accredited college.
2. At least six semester hours in linguistics, including general linguistics and the phonological and grammatical structure of American English.
3. A regular New Jersey teaching certificate in another field.
4. Demonstration of verbal and written proficiency in English and in one other language used also as a medium of instruction.

V. MATRICULATION REQUIREMENTS FOR AN M.A. IN TEACHING ENGLISH AS A SECOND LANGUAGE

1. A bachelor's degree based upon a four-year curriculum in an accredited college and whose field of concentration was the Teaching of English as a Second Language.

Or

2. A bachelor's degree based upon a four-year curriculum in an accredited college.
3. At least twelve semester hours in linguistics, including general linguistics and the phonological and grammatical structure of American English.
4. Evidence of native or near-native competency in English as determined by guidelines to be established by the State Department of Education.

VI. PROGRAM STRUCTURE

A total of eleven courses, i.e., 33 credits, will be required in addition to one elective course (3 credits) for either M.A.

VII. COURSES

		Credits
A. An elective for those candidates who lack sufficient matriculation requirements in linguistics.		
1. 1505/XXXX	Intensive Linguistics for Teachers	3
B. Courses required for either an M.A. in Bilingual Education or in TESL:		
1. 1505/XXXX	Applied Linguistics This course is a prerequisite for all other linguistics courses	3
2. 0821/XXXX	Interpersonal Relations of Children of Hispanic-American Bilingual and Bicultural Heritage	3
3. 1505/XXXX	Language and Culture	3

4.	1505/XXXX	Social Dialectology	3
5.	1505/XXXX	Linguistics and Reading	3
6.	1505/XXXX	Theory and Practice of Teaching English as a Second Language	3
7.	1505/XXXX	Materials Preparation and Resources in TESL and Bilingual Education	3
8.	1505/XXXX	Testing and Evaluation in TESL and Bilingual Education	3
9.	1505/XXXX or	Bilingual-Bicultural Field Experience 0829/XXXX	3

Total   27

C. Additional required courses for an M.A. in Bilingual Education: Credits

1.	1505/XXXX	Foundations of Bilingual-Bicultural Education	3
2.	0821/XXXX	Teaching Social Studies in Spanish in Bilingual and Bicultural Learning Environments	3
	or		
2'.	0821/XXXX	Teaching Mathematics and Science in Spanish in Bilingual and Bicultural Environments	3

Total   6

D. Additional required courses for an M.A. in TESL: Credits

1.	1505/XXXX	Problems in TESL	3
2.	1505/XXXX	TESL Field Experience	3

Total   6

E. Electives for candidates in both programs: Credits

1.	1505/XXXX	Intensive Linguistics for Teachers	3
2.	0821/XXXX	Cultural Pluralism in the United States	3
3.	0821/XXXX	The Hispanic-American Experience on the Mainland	3
4.	0821/560	Comparative Studies of Educational Systems	3

Additional electives, for example in the Reading Program and in the Anthropology Department, may be chosen in consultation with a faculty adviser.

F. 1505/XXXX   Foundations of Bilingual-Bicultural Education may be taken as an elective for M.A. candidates in TESL   3

VIII. COURSE DESCRIPTIONS

1. *Intensive Linguistics for Teachers*—This course will be an accelerated introduction to those areas of linguistics that are especially important for students in TESL and bilingual education.
2. *Applied Linguistics*—Examination of the applications that the disciplines of linguistics, psycholinguistics, and sociolinguistics have for the teaching of

second languages, English as a second language or as a Standard dialect, and for bilingual education. The course will also include study of the contributions these fields have made to our understanding of the reading process, of how language functions in the classroom, and of how language develops in children.

3. *Interpersonal Relations of Children of Hispanic-American Bilingual and Bicultural Heritage*—Survey and analysis of interpersonal relations of Hispanic-American children, including examination of cultural life style, psychosocial development, family socialization process and self-identity, and economic situation, which will enable the teacher of Hispanic-American students to deal effectively, constructively and empathetically in his relationships with these students.

4. *Language and Culture*—Survey of the relationship between linguistic and other socio-cultural variables (status, role, setting, topic, etc.) within a wide variety of the world's speech communities. The general survey will be followed by a close examination of the relationship as it applies to the chief minority groups of the United States, especially the Hispanic.

5. *Social Dialectology*—Study of the structure and functions of the major social dialects within the United States, including Black English and Puerto Rican English, and the relationships between non-standard varieties of English and Spanish to their standard varieties. The relevance of the study of social dialects for many kinds of pedagogical problems, including teacher attitudes and student motivation.

6. *Linguistics and Reading*—Survey and evaluation of the various insights which linguistics has contributed to our understanding of the reading process. Study of the differences between teaching reading to native speakers of a language, to non-native speakers, and to the teaching of reading to speakers of non-Standard English.

7. *Theory and Practice of Teaching English as a Second Language*—Study of the theory and methods of teaching English to non-English speakers in the U.S. Phonology, vocabulary, grammar, reading, composition, geographic and stylistic variation. Techniques in predicting and correcting errors made by non-English speakers.

8. *Materials Preparation and Resources in TESL and Bilingual Education*—Curriculum design, audio-visual materials, bibliographic resources, service organizations, professional associations and journals, use of language laboratories.

9. *Testing and Evaluation in TESL and Bilingual Education*—Construction and evaluation of diagnostic, achievement, and proficiency tests in TESL and bilingual education.

10. *Bilingual-Bicultural Field Experience*—Opportunity for teaching in bilingual school classrooms will be arranged for each student in the program.

11. *Foundations of Bilingual-Bicultural Education*—The rationale, history, and survey of existing models of bilingual education throughout the United States and the world. Study of program designs, the selection and training of teachers, and the role of community participation.

12. *Teaching of Social Studies in Spanish in Bilingual and Bicultural Learning Environments*—Seminar 30 hours, plus 15 hours conferences and practicum hours to be arranged in a bilingual learning environment.

The primary focus of this seminar is that participants are competent in terms of theoretics, methodology and content to teach Social Studies and Language Arts to bilingual students of Hispanic-American cultural heritage. Emphasis on the evaluation of methodology, and curriculum materials available in Social Studies and Language Arts for bilingual students.

13. *Teaching of Mathematics and Science in Spanish in Bilingual and Bicultural Programs*—Seminar 30 hours, plus 15 hours conferences and practicum hours to be arranged in a bilingual learning environment.

    The primary requirement of this seminar is that participants are competent, in terms of theoretics, methodology and content, to teach mathematics and/or science to Hispanic-American children. Special emphasis on evaluation of methodology and instructional materials available for bilingual instruction.

14. *Problems in TESL*—Intensive study and discussion of the major difficulties in the teaching of English as a second language or as a second dialect.

15. *TESL Field Experience*—Opportunity for teaching English as a second language will be arranged for each student in the program.

16. *Cultural Pluralism in the United States*—Seminar 30 hours, plus conferences.

    Central consideration will be given to an analysis of the significance of cultural pluralism as a positive factor in American education. Special emphasis will be given to the dynamics of cultural pluralism as they affect the educational experience of students of Hispanic-American cultural background as well as that of other minority groups of New Jersey.

17. *The Hispanic-American Experience on the Mainland*—Seminar 30 hours, plus conferences and field experience in a Hispanic-American community agency.

    A comparative analysis and examination of the dynamics of the Hispanic-American cultural and historical experience—Mexican Americans, Puerto Ricans, Cubans, Dominicans, and other Central and South American peoples—both in terms of its roots, as well as its manifestations on mainland United States. Particular emphasis will be placed on these factors: cross cultural conflicts, acculturation, enculturation, accommodations, attitudes, values and stereotypes present in society—and their effects upon the education experiences, identity, self-image and intellectual development of bilingual and bicultural children of Hispanic-American heritage.

18. *Comparative Studies of Educational Systems*—Relationship between social structure and the types of educational institutions; the struggle for change in industrialized societies; efforts for educational change in developing areas. Latin America, Germany, England, France, Soviet Union, Israel, India, China, Japan and selected areas of tropical Africa.

Francesco Cordasco

The New Bedford Project for Non-English Speaking Children

This evaluative memorandum derives from a visit (January 26–27, 1971) with the New Bedford Project for Non-English Speaking Children and from discussions with its Director, Mr. Joaquim Baptista. Since the elemental dynamics of the New Bedford social context in which non-English speaking children are found remain esentially those generally encountered, and the cognitive needs/acculturative processes remain those which American schoolmen have traditionally faced,[1] the visit affords adequate evidential data for a summary overview of the sociological backgrounds; for an exposition of the New Bedford Project For Non-English Speaking Children; with a notice of related components; and for recommendations for the Project's strengthening and evolving development.

BACKGROUND

New Bedford has the largest cohesive Portuguese community in America; in 1965, 50% of the city's population was of Portuguese origin, largely first and second generation Americans who still had known relatives in Portugal. The enactment of the Immigration and Nationality Act of 1965 has resulted in the immigration of some 20,000 persons annually from Portugal to the United States, 80% of whom settle in southeastern New England, principally in the cities of Providence, Fall River, and New Bedford.[2]

---

[1] See F. Cordasco, "The Challenge of the Non-English-Speaking Child in American Schools," *School & Society* (March 30, 1968), pp. 198–201; and for a massive repository of data on the educational history of the immigrant child and the American schools, see U.S. Immigration Commission: *Report of the Immigration Commission,* 41 vols. (Washington: Government Printing Office, 1911), vols. 29–33, *Report on the Children of Immigrants in Schools* [re-issued with an Introductory Essay by F. Cordasco, New York: Grolier-Scarecrow, 1970].

[2] There is virtually no contemporary information available on the Portuguese subcommunity of New Bedford. Informational memoranda (particularly, "Assessment of Needs"; and varia, dated January and May 1970) compiled by J. Baptista and his staff are invaluable in casting the New Bedford experience into meaningful current perspectives. The *Report on the Children of Immigrants in Schools,* in op. cit., does include data on New Bedford (and on Providence and Fall River) which provide information on 8,067 (for whom returns were secured) elementary school children, 68.2% of whose fathers were born abroad; 15.2% of whom were born abroad; and notes that of 1,358 Portuguese children, 45.9% were retarded (2 or more years older than the normal age for the child's grade). These data largely attest the neglect of the N/E speaking child in a prior era.

Thus, in New Bedford there is encountered a firmly established, cohesive ethnic subcommunity whose continuation and replenishment since the mid-1960s, and the revisions of the immigration statutes, have necessitated a continuing programmatic effort by the schools to meet the needs of the non-English speaking child. Although it would be difficult to determine what specific efforts (other than enforced assimilation) had been made in New Bedford to meet the needs of the non-English speaking child prior to the enactment of the Elementary and Secondary Education Act (1965), and the proliferation of Title I programs, it would be safe to assume that the non-English speaking child in New Bedford, as elsewhere, was forced into the traditional molds of the American school.[3] Joaquim Baptista reports that in 1965 there were 29 children enrolled in special non-English speaking classes which the New Bedford schools had maintained for years; although no mention is made of what was done in these N/E speaking classes, it may be assumed that they served as a transition and staging area for children who had no proficiency in English, and that cognitive retardation was endemic (for the N/E speaking child in and out of these special classes), with all of the patterns of enforced assimilation. By June of 1966, Baptista reports the articulation of a special non-graded program (headed by a director) for the N/E speaking New Bedford child with 303 children enrolled.[4] It is out of this non-graded program that the present program has evolved.

THE NEW BEDFORD PROJECT FOR THE N/E SPEAKING CHILD

The New Bedford Project for the N/E speaking child must be viewed in terms which attest both the needs and the effort. On May 1, 1970 out of a total New Bedford school registry of 16,288 children, 12.7% of the children were born in Portugal, 1.8% were of other foreign birth, and 4.3% (693 pupils) were enrolled in ESL ungraded classes. Obviously, the N/E speaking child existed in greater numbers (second generation, etc.), and the very flexibility of the registry in and out of N/E ungraded classes would be significantly higher than the figure reported.[5] Under the resourceful leadership of Director Joaquim Baptista, the New Bedford N/E Project has expanded its scope dramatically. In a variety of settings (units at individual schools; the Thompson Street School; and a rented school facility [a recently closed parish elementary school]), Baptista and his staff have created a highly functional, pragmatically oriented N/E program which includes some 13 ungraded classes, 10 ungraded transitional classes, and 9 graded classes. Seen in the light of the recent New Bedford experience, this is a remarkable achievement if only measured in quantitative terms. But its significance has important qualitative aspects: by using

---

[3] Generally, no philosophical or methodological *rationale* for the acculturation of the non-English speaking child existed before the enactment of the Bilingual Education Act in 1967 (Title VII, ESEA). Traditionally the N/E speaking child was "assimilated" with the consequent destruction of his native language, and a concomitant demeaning of his life-style, etc. See F. Cordasco, "Educational Englightenment Out of Texas: Towards Bilingualism," *Teachers College Record*, vol. 71 (May 1970), pp. 608–612. See also F. Cordasco, "The Bilingual Education Act," *Phi Delta Kappan* (October 1969), p. 75.

[4] See Baptista, varia, footnote no. 2. The sudden emergence of a formally structured N/E program in New Bedford was undoubtedly due to the fortuitously coincidental patterns of a rising immigration and the federal stimulus of the ESEA, and the New Bedford experience would not be atypical.

[5] See Baptista, "Assessment of Needs," footnote no. 2, supra.

ungraded classes (with close attention to chronological age and a learning continuum), and by providing a tripartite staged vestibule of transitional entry to regular classes, Baptista and his staff have articulated a highly flexible instrumentality which supports the N/E speaking child at the learning juncture at which he is found.

The ungraded school-related N/E speaking classes allow initial encounters: diagnostic, remedial, and cognitive; ungraded transitional classes (Thompson Street School) upgrade efforts and assure readiness for traditional placement; and the graded classes (within the rented school) create an N/E speaking learning center where a coordination of effort and an evolving curriculum for the N/E speaking child is taking shape. Within this highly functional organizational paradigm, the techniques employed are largely fashioned out of existing ESL methodologies with both their strengths and weaknesses.[6] It is not unanticipated that Baptista and his staff will move toward providing, within this pragmatic design, bilingual components which are a logical development in dealing with the learning needs of the N/E speaking child; and clear indications of the need for Bilingual orientations are cogently provided by Director Baptista in several memoranda.[7]

Related Components

Before making recommendations which will, hopefully, strengthen the New Bedford N/E speaking project, it is important to mention two related programs: A separate program, funded with Title VII (Bilingual Education Act, ESEA) monies, appears to be operating (although minimally deployed) outside the New Bedford N/E speaking project: allowing the patent incongruity of this effort outside the functional N/E speaking effort, it would appear that the Bilingual program is so integral a part of the effort in behalf of the N/E speaking child that its basic design and aim must be incorporated into the greater and more functionally operative N/E speaking effort.[8] Additionally, (in keeping with Congressional intents and sentiments recently expressed by U.S. Commissioner of Education Sidney Marland)[9] the proposal for "A Vocational Education Project for N/E Speaking Children and Adults"[10] should be implemented. The vocational education program would precisely allow a completely dimensional and fully articulated effort in behalf of the total N/E speaking New Bedford community; and this vocational orientation is exactly within the functional paradigm which Baptista and his staff have created.

---

[6] ESL techniques are best described in Mary Finocchiaro, *Teaching English as a Second Language*, rev. ed., (New York: Harper & Row, 1970).

[7] See "Bilingual Education Program", and "An Appraisal of the Need for Bilingual Education in New Bedford" (1970).

[8] The Bilingual Program in New Bedford is difficult to justify (despite its very modest size) outside the major N/E speaking effort. To the best of my knowledge, New Bedford is the only school system in which a bilingual project (even pilot-project in design) remains outside a major N/E speaking effort. See, in this connection, "A Selected List of Bilingual Programs at the Elementary School Level," *The Center Forum*, vol. 4 (September 1969), pp. 25–26.

[9] See *Education Daily*, January 25, 1971.

[10] *Proposal for a Vocational Education Project for Non-English Speaking Children And Adults* (New Bedford, 1970).

RECOMMENDATIONS

At the outset, it is imperative that the Bilingual Program (noted in *Related Components, supra*) should be absorbed into the N/E speaking project; and equally that the proposed vocational education program should be implemented. The total effort for the N/E speaking child and the community of which he is an integral part should operate under a single aegis. There is no doubt in my mind that Baptista and his staff are moving in the right directions. The fragmentation of the N/E speaking effort can only result in a diminution of both the quality and the evolving strength of the N/E speaking project. The logical development must be toward the incorporation of bilingual orientations and models into the N/E speaking project; and the awareness of this need has been cogently stated by the N/E speaking project staff.[11]

Bilingual orientations and models could, without difficulty, be incorporated into the tripartite model which the N/E speaking project has structured. The Project's operative model is, as has been noted, highly functional, and within this functionality bilingual orientations could only strengthen the N/E speaking child's growth along cognitive, acculturative, and socialization lines.

Since the N/E staff has created a flexible non-graded and graded structure (see "The New Bedford Project for the Non-English Speaking Child," supra), I will propose several models (elementary and secondary) which can be adapted within the existing structure. The strength of the existing structure lies in its allowance for ongoing transition, since the basic aim must be to move the N/E speaking child toward English proficiency and planned placement into the mainstream of the district's schools.[12]

First, as to some basic principles: (1) a Community Advisory Council should be created to assure that the N/E speaking project is responsive to community needs;[13] (2) children whose first language is Portuguese and who are dominant in that language should receive much of their instruction in Portuguese, with intensive work in English as a second language; and as children develop increasing fluency in English, they should receive greater amounts of instruction in English in the various curriculum areas; and (3) an additional major component of the curriculum should be the inclusion of the history and culture of Portugal: for the child whose first language is Portuguese and whose community is Portuguese, ethnic identity and self-esteem are essential parts of social maturation. The goals of the New Bedford N/E project should include the development of bilingualism; the greater levels of school achievement in the basic curriculum areas resulting from general instruction in the first language (i.e., Portuguese); and simultaneously, an increased proficiency in English which is essential for economic, occupational and academic reasons.

A typical daily schedule for the elementary bilingual class (allowing a graded or non-graded structure [combining, if necessary, grades 1, 2, 3, and 4; or combining grades 5 and 6, or grades 7 and 8]) would be as the following.

---

[11] See footnote no. 7, supra.

[12] Although the principal concern is with the Portuguese-speaking child, the need of the Spanish-speaking child (Puerto Rican) should not be ignored. The flexibility of the structure of the N/E speaking program does not preclude provision for the Spanish-speaking child.

[13] Cf., Henry M. Levin, *Community Control of Schools* (Washington: Brookings Institution, 1970) as basically illustrative of the social dynamics involved. Levin's title (the word "control") is misleading; the volume is an excellent commentary on a community's role in the schools. See also F. Cordasco, "Leonard Covello and the Community School," *School & Society*, vol. 98 (summer 1970), pp. 298–299.

Typical Schedule For A Portugese Dominant Class:

9:00- 9:45	Mathematics (in Portuguese)
9:45-10:30	English as a Second Language
10:30-11:15	Recreation
11:15-12:00	History and Culture of Portugal (in Portugese)
12:00- 1:00	Lunch
1:00- 1:45	Reading (in Portuguese)
1:45- 2:30	English as a Second Language

At the secondary level, much more adaptation is called for; but for a youngster whose first language is Portuguese, a typical weekly schedule follows:

1st Period	Mathematics in Portuguese
2nd Period	English as a Second Language
3rd Period	History and Culture of Portugal (in Portuguese) (Monday and Wednesday)
4th Period	Guidance Seminars in Portuguese (Monday and Wednesday)
5th Period	English as a Second Language (Tuesday and Thursday)

Coordinated with this core curriculum would be a gamut of secondary experiences intended to promote cognitive growth, social maturation, and guidance orientations. Vocational guidance sessions, whenever practicable, should be conducted by people in the community, from colleges, industry and government. These sessions should motivate students to aspire to, and to sustain, a seriousness of purpose.[14]

Of course, thought must be given to an in-service program for project teachers, to the recruitment of teacher-aides (from the community) and to a clearly delineated role for coordinators at the levels which have been structured. Two basic seminars should be offered (as soon as practicable) to teachers in the program: (1) History and Culture of Portugal; (2) The Educational Experience of the N/E Speaking Child in American Schools; and, on a continuing basis, seminars in Bilingual Education and in the formulation of a curriculum for the N/E speaking child.

The New Bedford Project for N/E Speaking Children has both strength and functionality. A bilingual orientation will enhance the strength and promote a more rapid assumption by the N/E speaking child of his place in the mainstream of the American school. In essence, efforts in behalf of the N/E speaking child should have a twofold

---

[14] These models, obviously, present both problems and challenges. In mathematics, personnel who are bilingual are difficult to find; and children might be grouped by level of proficiency in mathematics, as well as in the common dominant language. English as a second language need not be taught by a bilingual teacher; the children should be grouped according to their level of proficiency in English. In this important and vital effort, the course will teach the four language skills: comprehension, speaking, reading, writing. At the secondary level, children must learn English as soon as possible if they are to succeed in the high school disciplines which prepare them for higher education and other roles.

objective: (1) to assure cognitive growth; and (2) to build on the cultural strengths (language, life-styles) which the N/E speaking child brings to the portal of the school. The logical outcome should be an acculturative process which brings the N/E speaking child into the totality of the American experience; and it was this meaningful acculturation which the Congress proposed in its Title VII amendment to and extension of The Elementary and Secondary Education Act of 1965. [15]

---

15 "Basically, the Puerto Rican child is not a newcomer to the American school. In many ways he presents himself to a school and a society whose very nature is heterogeneous and variegated and to which the non-English speaking child is no stranger.... What is...important to the Puerto Rican child (and to American society) is the process of acculturation. How does the Puerto Rican child retain his identity, his language, his culture? In substance this remains the *crucial* problem, and in this crucial context, the role of the school in American society needs to be carefully assessed. If the Puerto Rican child is sinned against today, the tragedy lies in the continued assault against his identity, his language, and his cultural well-springs." F. Cordasco, "The Puerto Rican Child in the American School," *Journal of Negro Education* (Spring 1967), p. 185. These sentiments apply no less to the Portuguese speaking child in New Bedford.

Appendixes

Appendix A

AN OVERVIEW OF COURT DECISIONS AND
LEGISLATION AFFECTING BILINGUAL EDUCATION

The Context of Legislation—Major Federal
Court Decisions Relevant to Bilingual Education

Early Supreme Court decisions relevant to bilingual education concerned the constitutional rights of private schools to offer foreign languages as courses of instruction and the rights of students to attend such private schools in lieu of public schools.

In *Meyer v. Nebraska,* 262 U.S. 390 (1923), and *Farrington v. Tokushige,* 273 U.S. 284 (1927), the Supreme Court invalidated prohibitions against foreign language instruction in private schools. The statute in *Meyer* had prohibited all pre-eighth grade foreign language instruction and was found to violate the equal protection clause of the Fourteenth Amendment. The Hawaii territorial law in *Farrington* had included—in addition to regulations concerning subjects taught, textbooks used, and the political beliefs of instructors—a provision restricting foreign language instruction to one hour per day, six days per week, 38 weeks per year. The Court invoked the due process clause of the Fifth Amendment to invalidate the statute. (The Fourteenth Amendment equal protection clause applies only to the states. However, the Supreme Court has consistently held that the due process clause of the Fifth Amendment, which applies to the federal government and non-state American-flag jurisdictions, incorporates equal protection notions. See *Bolling v. Sharpe,* 347 U.S. 497 [1954].)

In *Pierce v. Society of Sisters,* 268 U.S. 510 (1925), the Court invalidated an Oregon law which had compelled attendance at public schools. The Court held that there is a constitutional right to attend a private school, though a state might prescribe a minimum curriculum or require that a private school meet reasonable safety or quality standards.

Recently, federal courts have directly addressed issues concerning the rights of limited English-speaking students in federally-assisted schools. In *Lau v. Nichols,* 414 U.S. 563 (1974), the Supreme Court relied on Title VI of the Civil Rights Act of 1964—a generally worded anti-discrimination statute—to invalidate the de facto exclusion of non-English-speaking students from federally assisted education programs. The Court held that a California public school district receiving federal funds must provide either bilingual or English-as-a-second-language programs whenever student members of a non-English-speaking minority are enrolled in large numbers in the district's schools.

Excerpts from *The Current Status of U.S. Bilingual Education Legislation* (Arlington, Va.: Center for Applied Linguistics, 1975), pp. 2–35.

In *Serna v. Portales,* 499 F. 2d 1149 (10th Cir. 1974), the court relied on *Lau* and affirmed a trial judge's discretionary power to order bilingual programs as a remedy in a Title VI case—at least where the only alternative remedial plan presented the trial court was a "token plan that would not benefit" the plaintiff students. *Serna,* supra, at 1154.

Federal Statutes

In addition to the general anti-discrimination provision of Title VI of the Civil Rights Act of 1964, several other federal statutes encourage bilingual education programs. Some grants for bilingual education have been made under Title I and Title III of the Elementary and Secondary Education Act of 1965. The Bilingual Education Act (Title VII of the Elementary and Secondary Education Amendment of 1967, amended in 1974), of course, has been a major source of federal money for bilingual education. Some bilingual teachers have benefited from grants under the National Defense Education Act. [Heinz Kloss, *Laws and Legal Documents Relating to Problems of Bilingual Education in the United States* (Washington: Center for Applied Linguistics, 1971), p. 6.]

Basic Trends in State Statutes

In 1971 Heinz Kloss was able to place each state in one or two of nine categories, according to whether their laws prohibited, permitted, or said nothing about non-English instruction in public, private or both public and private schools. At that time, 13 states—Alabama, Arkansas, Connecticut, Iowa, Kansas, Michigan, Minnesota, Montana, Nebraska, North Carolina, Oregon, South Dakota, and West Virginia—had statutes which required that English be the exclusive language of both public and non-public school instruction (other than foreign language instruction where the foreign language itself was the subject taught). Seven states—Delaware, Idaho, Indiana, Louisiana, North Dakota, Oklahoma, and Wisconsin—had such statutes applicable only to public schools. Two states—Massachusetts and Nevada—had similar statutes applicable only to non-public schools.

Sixteen states—Alaska, Florida, Georgia, Hawaii, Kentucky, Maryland, Mississippi, Missouri, New Jersey, Ohio, South Carolina, Tennessee, Utah, Vermont, Virginia, and Wyoming—had no statutes on the subject. Three states—Massachusetts, Nevada, and Rhode Island—had statutes applicable to non-public schools, but none applicable to public schools. Ten states—Arizona, Colorado, Delaware, Idaho, Indiana, Louisiana, New Mexico, North Dakota, Oklahoma, and Wisconsin—had statutes applicable to public schools, but none applicable to non-public schools.

Eight states—California, Illinois, Maine, New Hampshire, New York, Pennsylvania, Texas, and Washington—had statutes applicable to both public and non-public schools which expressly permitted non-English instruction in school subjects. Three states—Arizona, Colorado, and New Mexico—had such statutes for public schools. Rhode Island had a statute which expressly permitted non-public school instruction in a language other than English.

Since 1971, nine states have either repealed or amended their English-only statutes and now expressly or tacitly permit, or expressly require, local school districts to offer subject instruction in languages other than English. These states are Connecticut, Indiana, Kansas, Massachusetts, Michigan, Nevada, North Dakota, Oregon, and South Dakota.

Five states—Alaska, Florida, Maryland, New Jersey, and Utah—have taken action for the first time and now either permit or require local districts to provide non-English course instruction. Massachusetts and Rhode Island have enacted their first statutes applicable to public schools. Both describe circumstances under which a district must offer subjects taught in languages other than English.

Three states that formerly had only permissive legislation applicable to public and non-public schools now specify circumstances under which non-English instruction must be offered in public schools. These states are Illinois, Pennsylvania, and Texas.

One English-only state—Montana—and five states that expressly permitted non-English instruction in public schools—Arizona, California, Maine, New Mexico, and New York—have amended their statutes without changing their respective categories.

Twenty-two states have not altered their laws since 1971: Alabama, Arkansas, Colorado, Georgia, Hawaii, Idaho, Iowa, Kentucky, Mississippi, Missouri, Nebraska, North Carolina, Ohio, Oklahoma, South Carolina, Tennessee, Vermont, Virginia, Washington, West Virginia, Wisconsin, and Wyoming.

As of April, 1975, state laws fall into five categories. Seven states—Alabama, Arkansas, Iowa, Montana, Nebraska, North Carolina, and West Virginia—have English-only statutes applicable to both public and non-public schools.

Five states—Delaware, Idaho, Louisiana, Oklahoma, and Wisconsin—have English-only provisions applicable to the public schools.

Fourteen states—Georgia, Hawaii, Indiana, Kentucky, Mississippi, Missouri, Nevada, North Dakota, Ohio, South Carolina, Tennessee, Vermont, Virginia, and Wyoming—now have no provisions. Three of these states—Indiana, Nevada, and North Dakota—have entered this category since 1971 by simply repealing their English-only statutes.

Twenty-two states—Arizona, California, Colorado, Connecticut, Florida, Illinois, Kansas, Maine, Maryland, Massachusetts, Michigan, Minnesota, New Hampshire, New Jersey, New Mexico, New York, Oregon, Rhode Island, South Dakota, Texas, Utah, and Washington—have statutes which expressly or implicitly permit school districts to offer courses in a language other than English. Of these, six describe circumstances under which a school district must offer such courses.

Two states—Alaska and Pennsylvania—describe only circumstances under which non-English instruction in substantive courses is required.

Other American-Flag Jurisdictions

Before 1971, the Virgin Islands, Guam, the District of Columbia, Trust Territories of the Pacific, and the Panama Canal Zone had no statutory provisions specifying the language of instruction to be used in the classroom. Puerto Rico required the use of Spanish as the language of instruction.

Since 1971, only the Virgin Islands and Guam have undergone any legislative change. The Virgin Islands now require the Board of Education to provide courses in English and Spanish if special circumstances arise. Guam permits public schools to develop non-English programs for the Chamorro people.

American Samoa, though listed by Kloss as having no statutory provisions dealing with the language of instruction to be used in the classroom, has permitted non-English instruction in the public schools since 1962.

EXCERPTS FROM COURT DECISIONS, CONSTITUTIONS, AND STATUTES AFFECTING BILINGUAL EDUCATION

Federal Court Decisions*

Meyer v. Nebraska, 262 U.S. 390 (1923)

Forbidding the teaching in school of any other than the English language until the pupil has passed the eighth grade violates the guarantee of liberty in the Fourteenth Amendment of the Federal Constitution, in the absence of sudden emergency rendering the knowledge of the foreign language clearly harmful.

Ibid; from the Opinion of the Court

The Supreme Court of the State has held that the so-called ancient or dead languages "are not within the spirit or the purpose of the act." ...Latin, Greek, Hebrew are not proscribed; but German, French, Spanish, Italian and every other alien speech are within the ban. Evidently the legislature has attempted materially to interfere with the calling of modern language teachers, with the opportunities of pupils to acquire knowledge, and with the power of parents to control the education of their children.

It is said, that the purpose of the legislation was to promote civic development by inhibiting training and education of the immature in foreign tongues and ideals before they could learn English and acquire American ideals; and "that the English language should be and become the mother tongue of all children reared in this State." It is also affirmed that the foreign born population is very large, that certain communities commonly use foreign words, follow foreign leaders, move in a foreign atmosphere and that the children are thereby hindered from becoming citizens of the most useful type, and the public safety is imperiled.

That the State may do much, go very far indeed in order to improve the quality of its citizens, physically, and mentally, and morally, is clear; but the individual has certain fundamental rights which must be respected. The protection of the Constitution extends to all those who speak other languages as well as to those born with English on the tongue. Perhaps it would be highly advantageous if all had a ready understanding of our ordinary speech, but this cannot be coerced by methods which conflict with the Constitution—a desirable end cannot be prompted by prohibited means.

The power of the State to compel attendance at some schools and to make reasonable regulations for all schools, including a requirement that they shall give instructions in English, is not questioned; nor has challenge been made of the State's power to prescribe a curriculum for institutions which it supports.

Pierce v. Society of Sisters, 268 U.S. 571 (1925)

The fundamental theory of liberty upon which all government of this country rests, excludes any general power of the state, to standardize its children by forcing them to accept instruction from public teachers only.

---

* *Lau v. Nichols* and *Serna v. Portales Municipal Schools* new since Kloss's study.

The Oregon Compulsory Education Act...is an unreasonable interference with the liberty of the parents and guardians to direct the upbringing of the children, and in that respect violates the 14th Amendment.

Farrington v. Tokushige, 273 U.S. 284 (1927)

Acts of the Legislature of Hawaii relating to foreign language schools or the teachers thereof and regulations adopted thereunder by the Department of Public Instruction, taken as a whole, appear to infringe rights, under the Fifth Amendment, of owners of private Japanese schools, and the parents attending them. . . .

The due process clause of the Fifth Amendment affords the same protection to fundamental rights of private school owners, parents and children against invasion by the Federal Government and its Agencies (such as a territorial legislature) as it has been held the Fourteenth Amendment affords against action by a State.

Mo Hock Ke Lok Po v. Stainback, District Court Hawaii, 74 F. Supp. 852 (1944)

(854) The parents' right to have their offspring taught a foreign language is one of the fundamental rights guaranteed by the due process clause of the Fifth and Fourteenth Amendments. (856) ...It should be noted however, that to the fundamental parental right to secure for a child a foreign language so recognized in the Berea College and the Society of Sisters cases—that is, in the American isolationist period between 1909 and 1926—in today's world of the United Nations there has been added an equally profound international need for understanding between the peoples of a world of different tongues....(857) The Act...shows on its face a denial of the rights to acquire a foreign language to that half, or nearly half, of Hawaiian children of more than "average intelligence." ...In Hawaii there were 22,357 children in the first four grades. Of these at least 10,000 above average intelligence, the brighter ones, are denied the right then to begin to acquire a foreign language even with a tutor at home. We do not agree that such a denial...is warranted to seek the elimination of the harm it seeks to avoid for those of lesser ability.

Lau v. Nichols, 414 U.S. 563, 39 L. Ed 2d 1, 94 S. Ct 786 (1974)

Mr. Justice Douglas delivered the opinion of the Court: The District Court found that there are 2,856 students of Chinese ancestry in the school system who do not speak English. Of those who have that language deficiency, about 1,000 are given supplemental courses in the English language. About 1,800, however, do not receive that instruction. This class suit brought by non-English-speaking Chinese students against officials responsible for the operation of the San Francisco Unified School District seeks relief against the unequal education opportunities, which are alleged to violate, inter alia, the Fourteenth Amendment. No specific remedy is urged upon us.

Teaching English to the students of Chinese ancestry who do not speak the language is one choice. Giving instructions to this group in Chinese is another. There may be others. Petitioners ask only that the Board of Education be directed to apply its experience to the problem and rectify the situation. . . .

[T]here is no equality of treatment merely by providing students with the same facilities, textbooks, teachers, and curriculum; for students who do not understand English are effectively foreclosed from any meaningful education.

Basic English skills are at the very core of what these public schools teach. Imposition of a requirement that, before a child can effectively participate in the education program, he must already have acquired those basic skills is to make a mockery of public education. We know that those who do not understand English are certain to find their classroom experiences wholly incomprehensible and in no way meaningful.

We do not reach Equal Protection Clause argument which has been advanced but rely solely on Section 601 of the Civil Rights Act of 1964, 42 USC Section 2000d....

By Section 602 of the Act HEW is authorized to issue rules, regulations, and orders to make sure that recipients of federal aid under its jurisdiction conduct any federally financed projects consistent with Section 601. HEW's regulations 45 CFR Section 80.3 (b) (1), specify that the recipients may not:

(ii) Provide any service, financial aid, or other benefit to an individual which is different, or is in a different manner, from that provided to others under the program;....

(iv) Restrict an individual in any way in the enjoyment of any advantage or privilege enjoyed by others receiving any service, financial aid, or other benefit under the program.

Discrimination among students on account of race or national origin that is prohibited includes "discrimination...in the availability or use of any academic...or other facilities of the grantee or other recipient." Id., Section 80.5 (b).

Discrimination is barred which has that effect even though no purposeful design is presented: a recipient "may not...utilize criteria or methods of administration which have the effect of subjecting individuals to discrimination" or has "the effect of defeating or substantially impairing accomplishment of the objectives of the program as respects individuals of a particular race, color, or national origin." Id., Section 80.3 (b) (2).

It seems obvious that the Chinese-speaking minority receives fewer benefits than the English-speaking majority from respondents' school system which denies them a meaningful opportunity to participate in the educational program—all earmarks of the discrimination banned by the regulations. In 1970 HEW issued clarifying guidelines, 35 Fed Reg 11595, which include the following:

Where inability to speak and understand the English language excludes national origin–minority group children from effective participation in the education program offered by a school district, the district must take affirmative steps to rectify the language deficiency in order to open its instructional program to these students.

Any ability grouping or tracking system employed by the school system to deal with the special language skill needs of national origin–minority group children must be designed to meet such language skill needs as soon as possible and must not operate as an educational dead end or permanent track.

Concurring Opinion by Mr. Justice Stewart

[I]t is not entirely clear that Section 601 of the Civil Rights Act of 1964, 42 USC Section 2000d [42 USCS Section 2000d], standing alone would render illegal the expenditure of federal funds on these schools....

On the other hand, the interpretative guidelines published by the Office of Civil Rights...clearly indicate that affirmative efforts to give special training for non-English-speaking pupils are required by Title VI as a condition to receipt of federal aid to public schools. . . .

The critical question is, therefore, whether the regulations and guidelines promulgated by HEW go beyond the authority of Section 601. Last term, in *Mourning v. Family Publication Service, Inc.,* 411 US 356, 369, 36 L ED 2d 318, 93 S Ct 1652, we held that the validity of a regulation promulgated under a general authorization provision such as Section 602 of Title VI "will be sustained so long as it is 'reasonably related to the purposes of the enabling legislation.' *Thorpe v. Housing Authority of the City of Durham,* 393 US 268, 280–281 [21 L Ed 2d 474, 89 S Ct 518] (1969)." I think the guidelines here fairly meet that test. Moreover, in assessing the purposes of remedial legislation we have found that departmental regulations and "consistent administrative construction" are "entitled to great weight."

Concurring Opinion by Mr. Justice Blackmun

Against the possibility that the Court's judgment may be interpreted too broadly, I stress the fact that the children with whom we are concerned here number about 1,800. . . .

I merely wish to make plain that when, in another case, we are concerned with a very few youngsters, or with just a single child who speaks only German or Polish or Spanish or any other language other than English, I would not regard today's decision, or the separate concurrence, as conclusion upon the issue whether the statute and the guideline require the funded school district to provide special instruction. For me, numbers are at the heart of this case, and my concurrence is to be understood accordingly.

Serna V. Portales Municipal Schools, 499 F. 2d 1149 (10th Cir. 1974)

[T]he factual situation in the instance case is strikingly similar to that found in *Lau.* Appellees are Spanish-surnamed students who prior to this lawsuit were placed in totally English-speaking schools. There is substantial evidence that most of these Spanish-surnamed students are deficient in the English language; nevertheless no affirmative steps were taken by the Portales school district to rectify these language deficiencies...

While Spanish-surnamed children are required to attend school, and if they attend public schools the courses must be taught in English, Portales school district has failed to institute a program which will rectify language deficiencies so that these children will receive a meaningful education. The Portales school curriculum, which has the effect of discrimination even though probably no purposeful design is present, therefore violates the requisites of Title VI and the requirement imposed by or pursuant to HEW regulations. . . .

Appellants argue that even if the school district were unintentionally discriminating against Spanish-surnamed students prior to institution of this lawsuit, the program they presented to the trial court in compliance with the court's memorandum opinion sufficiently meets the needs of appellees. . . .

After reviewing the entire record we are in agreement with the trial court's decision. The record reflects a long-standing educational policy by the Portales schools that failed to take into consideration the specific needs of Spanish-surnamed children. After appellants submitted a proposed bilingual-bicultural program to the trial court a hearing was held on the adequacies of this plan. At this hearing expert witnesses pointed out the fallacies of appellants' plan and in turn offered a more expansive bilingual-bicultural plan. The trial court thereafter fashioned a program which it felt would meet the needs of Spanish-surnamed students in the Portales school system. We do not believe that under the unique circumstances of this case the trial court's plan is unwarranted. The evidence shows unequivocally that appellants had failed to provide appellees with a meaningful education There was adequate evidence that appellants' proposed program was only a token plan that would not benefit appellees. Under these circumstances the trial court had a duty to fashion a program which would provide adequate relief for Spanish-surnamed children. As the Court noted in *Swann v. Charlotte-Mecklenburg Board of Education,* 402 U.S. 1, 15, 91 S. Ct. 1267, 1276, 28 L. Ed. 2d 554 (1971), "[o]nce a right and a violation have been shown, the scope of a district court's equitable powers to remedy past wrongs is broad, for breadth and flexibility are inherent in equitable remedies." Under Title VI of the Civil Rights Act of 1964 appellees have a right to bilingual education. And in following the spirit of *Swann,* supra, we believe the trial court, under its inherent equitable power, can properly fashion a bilingual-bicultural program which will assure that Spanish-surnamed children receive a meaningful education.

The New Mexico State Board of Education stresses the effect the decision will have on the structure of public education in New Mexico. It is suggested that bilingual programs will now be necessitated throughout the state wherever a student is found who does not have adequate facility in the English language. We do not share SBE's fears. As Mr. Justice Blackmun pointed out in his concurring opinion in *Lau,* numbers are at the heart of this case and only when a substantial group is being deprived of a meaningful education will a Title VI violation exist.

Federal Constitution and Statutory Provision

Note:
1. Bilingual Education Act (880b) amended.
2. Adult Education Act 20 S1205 amended to include S1205 (a) (11)
3. Vocational Training Act 20 S1393 amended to include subchapter X
4. Emergency Aid Act 20 S1607 amended to include S1607 (c) (1)
5. Public Library Services and Construction 20 S351 (b) amended to include S351d (b) (4)
6. State Vocational Education Programs 20 S1262 amended to include S1262 (a) (4) (c)
7. Kloss omitted Section 601-Civil Rights Act of 1964. This was the statute construed in *Lau v. Nichols.*

U.S. Constitution, Fifth Amendment (1791)

No person shall . . . be deprived of life, liberty, or property, without due process of law; nor shall private property be taken for public use without just compensation.

U.S. Constitution, Fourteenth Amendment (1868)

No State shall . . . deprive any person of life, liberty, or property without due process of law, nor deny to any person within its jurisdiction the equal protection of the laws.

Bilingual Education Act (880b)

S880b Congressional declaration of policy; authorization of appropriations

(a) Recognizing—

(1) that there are large numbers of children of limited English-speaking ability;

(2) that many of such children have a cultural heritage which differs from that of English-speaking persons;

(3) that a primary means by which a child learns is through the use of such child's language and cultural heritage;

(4) that, therefore, large numbers of children of limited English-speaking ability have educational needs which can be met by the use of bilingual educational methods and techniques; and

(5) that, in addition, children of limited English-speaking ability benefit through the fullest utilization of multiple language and cultural resources,

the Congress declares it to be the policy of the United States, in order to establish equal educational opportunity for all children (A) to encourage the establishment and operation, where appropriate, of educational programs using bilingual educational practices, techniques, and methods, and (B) for that purpose, to provide financial assistance to local educational agencies, and to State educational agencies for certain purposes, in order to enable such local educational agencies to develop and carry out such programs in elementary and secondary schools, including activities at the preschool level, which are designed to meet the educational needs of such children; and to demonstrate effective ways of providing, for children of limited English-speaking ability, instruction designed to enable them, while using their native language, to achieve competence in the English language.

(b) (1) Except as is otherwise provided in this subchapter, for the purpose of carrying out the provisions of this subchapter, there are authorized to be appropriated $135,000,000 for the fiscal year ending June 30, 1974; $135,000,000 for the fiscal year ending June 30, 1975; $140,000,000 for the fiscal year ending June 30, 1976; $150,000,000 for the fiscal year ending June 30, 1977; and $160,000,000 for the fiscal year ending June 30, 1978.

(2) There are further authorized to be appropriated to carry out the provisions of section 380b-7 (b) (3) of this title $6,750,000 for the fiscal year ending June 30, 1974; $7,250,000 for the fiscal year ending June 30, 1975; $7,750,000 for the fiscal year ending June 30, 1976; $8,750,000 for the fiscal year ending June 30, 1977; and $9,750,000 for the fiscal year ending June 30, 1978.

(3) From the sums appropriated under paragraph (1) for any fiscal year—

(A) the Commissioner shall reserve $16,000,000 of that part thereof which does not exceed $70,000,000 for training activities carried out under clause (3) of subsection (a) of section 880b-7 of this title, and shall reserve for such activities 33 1/3 per centum of that part thereof which is in excess of $70,000,000; and

(B) the Commissioner shall reserve from the amount not reserved pursuant to clause (A) of this paragraph such amounts as may be necessary, but not in excess of 1 per centum thereof, for the purposes of section 880b-11 of this title.

S880b-1. General provisions—Definitions; English-speaking children, enrollment; application

(a) The following definitions shall apply to the terms used in this subchapter:

(1) The term "limited English-speaking ability," when used with reference to an individual, means—

(A) individuals who were not born in the United States or whose native language is a language other than English, and

(B) individuals who come from environments where a language other than English is dominant, as further defined by the Commissioner by regulations;

and, by reason thereof, have difficulty speaking and understanding instruction in the English language.

(2) The term "native language," when used with reference to an individual of limited English-speaking ability, means the language normally used by such individuals, or in the case of a child, the language normally used by the parents of the child.

(3) The term "low-income" when used with respect to a family means an annual income for such a family which does not exceed the low annual income determined pursuant to section 241c of this title.

(4) (A) The term "program of bilingual education" means a program of instruction, designed for children of limited English-speaking ability in elementary or secondary schools, in which, with respect to the years of study to which such program is applicable—

(i) there is instruction given in, and study of, English and, to the extent necessary to allow a child to progress effectively through the educational system, the native language of the children of limited English-speaking ability, and such instruction is given with appreciation for the cultural heritage of such children, and, with respect to elementary school instruction, such instruction shall, to the extent necessary, be in all courses or subjects of study which will allow a child to progress effectively through the educational system; and

(ii) the requirements in subparagraphs (B) through (E) of this paragraph and established pursuant to subsection (b) of this section are met.

(B) A program of bilingual education may make provision for the voluntary enrollment to a limited degree therein, on a regular basis, of children whose language is English, in order that they may acquire an understanding of the cultural heritage of the children of limited English-speaking ability for whom the particular program of bilingual education is designed. In determining eligibility to participate in such programs, priority shall be given to the children whose language is other than English. In no event shall the program be designed for the purpose of teaching a foreign language to English-speaking children.

(C) In such courses or subjects of study as art, music, and physical education, a program of bilingual education shall make provision for the participation of children of limited English-speaking ability in regular classes.

(D) Children enrolled in a program of bilingual education shall, if graded classes are used, be placed, to the extent practicable, in classes with children of approximately the same age and level of educational attainment. If children of significantly varying ages or levels of educational attainment are placed in the same class, the program of bilingual education shall seek to insure that each child is provided with instruction which is appropriate for his or her level of educational attainment.

(E) An application for a program of bilingual education shall be developed in consultation with parents of children of limited English-speaking ability, teachers, and, where applicable, secondary school students, in the areas to be served, and assurances shall be given in the application that, after the application has been approved under this subchapter, the applicant will provide for participation by a committee composed of, and selected by, such parents, and, in the case of secondary schools, representatives of secondary school students to be served.

(5) The term "Office" means the Office of Bilingual Education.

(6) The term "Director" means the Director of the Office of Bilingual Education.

(7) The term "Council" means the National Advisory Council on Bilingual Education.

(8) The term "other programs for persons of limited English-speaking ability" when used in sections 880b-10 and 880b-11 of this title means the program authorized by section 1607(c) of this title and the programs carried out in coordination with the provisions of this subchapter pursuant to section 1262(a) (4) (C) of this title and sections 1393 to 1393f of this title and section 1205(a) (11) of this title, and programs and projects serving areas with high concentrations of persons of limited English-speaking ability pursuant to section 315(b) (4) of this title.

Model programs

(b) The Commissioner, after receiving recommendations from State and local educational agencies and groups and organizations involved in bilingual education, shall establish, publish, and distribute, with respect to programs of bilingual education, suggested models with respect to pupil-teacher ratios, teacher qualifications, and other factors affecting the quality of instruction offered in such programs.

Regulations

(c) In prescribing regulations under this section, the Commissioner shall consult with State and local educational agencies, appropriate organizations representing parents and children of limited English-speaking ability, and appropriate groups and organizations representing teachers and educators involved in bilingual education.

S880b-7. Bilingual education programs—grants for certain programs and activities

(a) Funds available for grants under this part shall be used for—

(1) the establishment, operation, and improvement of programs of bilingual education;

(2) auxiliary and supplementary community and educational activities designed to facilitate and expand the implementation of programs described in clause (1), including such activities as

   (A) adult education programs related to the purposes of this subchapter particularly for parents of children participating in programs of bilingual education, and carried out, where appropriate, in coordination with programs assisted under the Adult Education Act, and

   (B) preschool programs preparatory and supplementary to bilingual education programs;

(3) (A) the establishment, operation, and improvement of training programs for personnel preparing to participate in, or personnel participating in, the conduct of programs of bilingual education and

   (B) auxiliary and supplementary training programs, which shall be included in each program of bilingual education, for personnel preparing to participate in, or personnel participating in, the conduct of such programs; and

(4) planning, and providing technical assistance for, and taking other steps leading to the development of, such programs.

(b) (1) A grant may be made under this section only upon application therefor by one or more local educational agencies or by an institution of higher education, including a junior or community college, applying jointly with one or more local educational agencies (or, in the case of a training activity described in clause (3) (A) of subsection (a) of this section, by eligible applicants as defined in section 880b-9 of this title). Each such application shall be made to the Commissioner at such time, in such manner, and containing such information as the Commissioner deems necessary, and

   (A) include a description of the activities set forth in one or more of the clauses of subsection (a) of this section which the applicant desires to carry out; and

   (B) provide evidence that the activities so described will make substantial progress toward making programs of bilingual education available to the children having need thereof in the area served by the applicant.

(2) An application for a grant under this part may be approved only if—

   (A) the provision of assistance proposed in the application is consistent with criteria established by the Commissioner, after consultation with the State educational agency, for the purpose of achieving an equitable distribution of assistance under this part within the State in which the applicant is located, which criteria shall be developed by his taking into consideration

      (i) the geographic distribution of children of limited English-speaking ability,

      (ii) the relative need of persons in different geographic areas within the State for the kinds of services and activities described in subsection (a) of this section,

      (iii) with respect to grants to carry out programs described in clauses (1) and (2) of subsection (a) of this section, the relative ability of particular local educational agencies within the State to provide such services and activities, and

(iv) with respect to such grants, the relative numbers of persons from low-income families sought to be benefited by such programs;

(B) in the case of applications from local educational agencies to carry out programs of bilingual education under clause (1) of subsection (a) of this section, the Commissioner determines that not less than 15 per centum of the amounts paid to the applicant for the purposes of such programs shall be expended for auxiliary and supplementary training programs in accordance with the provisions of clause (3) (B) of such subsection and section 880b-9 of this title;

(C) the Commissioner determines

(i)   that the program will use the most qualified available personnel and the best resources and will substantially increase the educational opportunities for children of limited English-speaking ability in the area to be served by the applicant, and

(ii) that, to the extent consistent with the number of children enrolled in nonprofit, nonpublic schools in the area to be served whose educational needs are of the type which the program is intended to meet, provision has been made for participation of such children; and

(D) the State educational agency has been notified of the application and has been given the opportunity to offer recommendations thereon to the applicant and to the Commissioner.

(3) (A) Upon an application from a State educational agency, the Commissioner shall make provision for the submission and approval of a State program for the coordination by such State agency of technical assistance to programs of bilingual education in such State assisted under this subchapter. Such State program shall contain such provisions, agreements, and assurances as the Commissioner shall, by regulation, determine necessary and proper to achieve the purposes of this subchapter, including assurances that funds made available under this section for any fiscal year will be so used as to supplement, and to the extent practical, increase the level of funds that would, in the absence of such funds be made available by the State for the purposes described in this section, and in no case to supplant such funds.

(B) Except as is provided in the second sentence of this subparagraph, the Commissioner shall pay from the amounts authorized for these purposes pursuant to section 880b of this title for each fiscal year to each State educational agency which has a State program submitted and approved under subparagraph (A) such sums as may be necessary for the proper and efficient conduct of such State programs. The amount paid by the Commissioner to any State educational agency under the preceding sentence for any fiscal year shall not exceed 5 per centum of the aggregate of the amounts paid under this part to local educational agencies in the State of such State educational agency in the fiscal year preceding the fiscal year in which this limitation applies.

Distribution of funds; priority to needy areas

(c) In determining the distribution of funds under this subchapter, the Commissioner shall give priority to areas having the greatest need for programs assisted under this subchapter.

S880b-8. Indian children in schools—Tribal institution or organization considered to be local educational agency

(a) For the purpose of carrying out programs under this part for individuals served by elementary and secondary schools operated predominantly for Indian children, a nonprofit institution or organization of the Indian tribe concerned which operates any such school and which is approved by the Commissioner for the purposes of this section may be considered to be a local educational agency as such term is used in this subchapter.

Payments to Secretary of Interior for bilingual
education of children on reservations
by schools operated or funded by
Department of Interior; criteria

(b) From the sums appropriated pursuant to section 880b(b) of this title, the Commissioner is authorized to make payments to the Secretary of the Interior to carry out programs of bilingual education for children on reservations served by elementary and secondary schools for Indian children operated or funded by the Department of the Interior. The terms upon which payments for such purpose may be made to the Secretary of the Interior shall be determined pursuant to such criteria as the Commissioner determines will best carry out the policy of section 880b (a) of this title.

Annual report to Congress and President;
authority or obligation of Director unaffected

(c) The Secretary of the Interior shall prepare and, not later than November 1 of each year, shall submit to the Congress and the President an annual report detailing a review and evaluation of the use, during the preceding fiscal year, of all funds paid to him by the Commissioner under subsection (b) of this section, including complete fiscal reports, a description of the personnel and information paid for in whole or in part with such funds, the allocation of such funds, and the status of all programs funded from such payments. Nothing in this subsection shall be construed to relieve the Director of any authority or obligation under this part.

Assessment of needs of Indian children; submitted to
Congress and President

(d) The Secretary of the Interior shall, together with the Information required in the preceding subsection, submit to the Congress and the President, an assessment of the needs of Indian children with respect to the purposes of this subchapter in schools operated or funded by the Department of the Interior, including those State educational agencies and local agencies receiving assistance under the Johnson-O'Malley Act (section 452 et seq. of

Title 25) and an assessment of the extent to which such needs are being met by funds provided to such schools for educational purposes through the Secretary of the Interior.

S880b-9. Training activities—Grants and contracts for personnel training, special training programs, and training institutes; fellowships: number, report to congressional committees; stipends; funds limitation; application for purposes of section 880b-1 (a) (4) (E) of this title

(a) (1) In carrying out provisions of clauses (1) and (3) of the subsection (a) of section 880b-7 of this title, with respect to training, the Commissioner shall, through grants to, and contracts with, eligible applicants, as defined in subsection (b) of this section, provide for—

(A) (i) training, carried out in coordination with any other programs training auxiliary educational personnel, designed (I) to prepare personnel to participate in, or for personnel participating in, the conduct of programs of bilingual education, including programs emphasizing opportunities for career development, advancement, and lateral mobility, (II) to train teachers, administrators, paraprofessionals, teacher aides, and parents, and (III) to train persons to teach and counsel such persons, and

(ii) special training programs designed (I) to meet individual needs, and (II) to encourage reform, innovation, and improvement in applicable education curricula in graduate education, in the structure of the academic profession, and in recruitment and retention of higher education and graduate school facilities, as related to bilingual education; and

(B) the operation of short-term training institutes designed to improve the skills of participants in the programs of bilingual education in order to facilitate their effectiveness in carrying out responsibilities in connection with such programs.

(2) In addition the Commissioner is authorized to award fellowships for study in the field of training teachers for bilingual education. For the fiscal year ending June 30, 1975, not less than 100 fellowships leading to a graduate degree shall be awarded under the preceding sentence for preparing individuals to train teachers for programs to the need for teachers of various groups of individuals with limited English-speaking ability. For each fiscal year after June 30, 1975, and prior to July 1, 1978, the Commissioner shall report to the Committee on Education and Labor of the House of Representatives and the Committee on Labor and Public Welfare of the Senate on the number of fellowships in the field of training teachers for bilingual education which he recommends will be necessary for that fiscal year.

(3) The Commissioner shall include in the terms of any arrangement described in paragraph (1) and (2) of subsection (a) of this section provisions for the payment, to persons participating in training programs so described, of such stipends (including allowances for subsistence and other expenses for such persons and their dependents) as he may determine to be consistent with prevailing practices under comparable federally supported programs.

(4) In making grants or contracts under this section, the Commissioner shall give priority to eligible applicants with demonstrated competence and

experience in the field of bilingual education. Funds provided under grants or contracts for training activities described in this section to or with a State educational agency, separately or jointly, shall in no event exceed in the aggregate in any fiscal year 15 per centum of the total amount of funds obligated for training activities pursuant to clauses (1) and (3) of subsection (a) of section 880b-7 of this title in such year.

(5) An application for a grant or contract for preservice or inservice training activities described in clause (A) (i) (I) and clause (A) (ii) (I) and in subsection (a) (1) (B) of this section shall be considered an application for a program of bilingual education for the purposes of subsection (a) (4) (E) of section 880b-1 of this title.

"Eligible applicants" defined

(b) For purposes of this section, the term "eligible applicants" means—
(1) institutions of higher education (including junior colleges and community colleges) which apply, after consultation with, or jointly with, one or more local educational agencies;
(2) local educational agencies; and
(3) state educational agencies.

PART B—ADMINISTRATION

S880b-10. Office of Bilingual Education—Execution of functions of Commissioner

(a) There shall be, in the Office of Education, an Office of Bilingual Education (hereafter in this section referred to as the "Office") through which the Commissioner shall carry out his functions relating to bilingual education.

Director of Bilingual Education; appointment; delegation of functions

(b) (1) The Office shall be headed by a Director of Bilingual Education, appointed by the Commissioner, to whom the Commissioner shall delegate all of his delegable functions relating to bilingual education.
(2) The Office shall be organized as the Director determines to be appropriate in order to enable him to carry out his functions and responsibilities effectively.

Report to Congress and President; contents

(c) The Commissioner, in consultation with the Council, shall prepare and, not later than November 1 of 1975, and of 1977, shall submit to the Congress and the President a report on the condition of bilingual education in the Naiton and the administration and operation of this subchapter and of other programs for persons of limited English-speaking ability. Such report shall include—
(1) a national assessment of the educational needs of children and other persons with limited English-speaking ability and of the extent to which such needs are being met from Federal, State, and local efforts, including
(A) not later than July 1, 1977, the results of a survey of the number of such children and persons in the States, and

(B) a plan, including cost estimates, to be carried out during the five-year period beginning on such date, for extending programs of bilingual education and bilingual vocational and adult education programs to all such preschool and elementary school children and other persons of limited English-speaking ability, including a phased plan for training of the necessary teachers and other educational personnel necessary for such purpose;

(2) a report on and an evaluation of the activities carried out under this subchapter during the preceding fiscal year and the extent to which each of such activities achieves the policy set forth in section 880b (a) of this title;

(3) a statement of the activities intended to be carried out during the succeeding period, including an estimate of the cost of such activities;

(4) an assessment of the number of teachers and other educational personnel needed to carry out programs of bilingual education under this subchapter and those carried out under other programs for persons of limited English-speaking ability and a statement describing the activities carried out thereunder designed to prepare teachers and other educational personnel for such programs, and the number of other educational personnel needed to carry out programs of bilingual education in the States and a statement describing the activities carried out under this subchapter designed to prepare teachers and other educational personnel for such programs; and

(5) a description of the personnel, the functions of such personnel, and information available at the regional offices of the Department of Health, Education, and Welfare dealing with bilingual programs within that region.

S880b-11. National Advisory Council on Bilingual Education Establishment; membership; Chairman; qualifications; representation of interested persons and geographic areas

(a) Subject to part D of the General Education Provisions Act, there shall be a National Advisory Council on Bilingual Education composed of fifteen members appointed by the Secretary, one of whom he shall designate as Chairman. At least eight of the members of the Council shall be persons experienced in dealing with the educational problems of children and other persons who are of limited English-speaking ability, at least one of whom shall be representative of persons serving on boards of education operating programs of bilingual education. At least three members shall be experienced in the training of teachers in programs of bilingual education. At least two members shall be persons with general experience in the field of elementary and secondary education. At least two members shall be classroom teachers of demonstrated teaching abilities using bilingual methods and techniques. The members of the Council shall be appointed in such a way as to be generally representative of the significant segments of the population of persons of limited English-speaking ability and the geographic areas in which they reside.

Meetings

(b) The Council shall meet at the call of the Chairman, but, notwithstanding the provisions of section 1233e(a) of this title, not less often than four times in each year.

Duties; report to Congress and President

(c) The Council shall advise the Commissioner in the preparation of general regulations and with respect to policy matters arising in the administration and operation of this subchapter, including the development of criteria for approval of applications, and plans under this subchapter, and the administration and operation of other programs for persons of limited English-speaking ability. The Council shall prepare and, not later than November 1 of each year, submit a report to the Congress and the President on the condition of bilingual education in the Nation and on the administration and operation of this subchapter, including those items specified in section 880b-10 (c) of this title, and the administration and operation of other programs for persons of limited English-speaking ability.

Personnel procurement; staff; information, and other assistance

(d) The Commissioner shall procure temporary and intermittent services of such personnel as are necessary for the conduct of the functions of the Council, in accordance with section 1233d of this title, and shall make available to the Council such staff, information, and other assistance as it may require to carry out its activities effectively.

PART C—SUPPORTIVE SERVICES AND ACTIVITIES

S880b-12. Administration; regulations; delegation of functions
(a) The provisions of this part shall be administered by the Assistant Secretary, in consultation with—
  (1) the Commissioner, through the Office of Bilingual Education; and
  (2) the Director of the National Institute of Education, notwithstanding the second sentence of section 1221e (b) (1) of this title; in accordance with regulations.
(b) The Assistant Secretary shall, in accordance with clauses (1) and (2) of subsection (a) of this section, develop and promulgate regulations for this part and then delegate his functions under this part, as may be appropriate under the terms of section 880b-13 of this title.

S880b-13. Research and demonstration projects—Bilingual education research; statement of purpose
(a) The National Institute of Education shall, in accordance with the provisions of section 1221e of this title, carry out a program of research in the field of bilingual education in order to enhance the effectiveness of bilingual education programs carried out under this subchapter and other programs for persons of limited English-speaking ability.

Competitive contracts

(b) In order to test the effectiveness of research findings by the National Institute of Education and to demonstrate new or innovative practices, techniques, and methods for use in such bilingual education programs, the Director and the Commissioner are authorized to make competitive contracts with public and private educational agencies, institutions, and organizations for such purpose.

Studies; instructional materials; national
clearinghouse of information

(c) In carrying out their responsibilities under this section, the Commissioner and the Director shall, through competitive contracts with appropriate public and private agencies, institutions, and organizations—

(1) undertake studies to determine the basic educational needs and language acquisition characteristics of, and the most effective conditions for, educating children of limited English-speaking ability;

(2) develop and disseminate instructional materials and equipment suitable for use in bilingual education programs; and

(3) establish and operate a national clearinghouse of information for bilingual education, which shall collect, analyze, and disseminate information about bilingual education and such bilingual education and related programs.

Periodic consultation with State and local educational
agencies and appropriate groups and organizations

(d) In carrying out their responsibilities under this section, the Commissioner and the Director shall provide for periodic consultation with representatives of State and local educational agencies and appropriate groups and organizations involved in bilingual education.

Authorization of appropriations

(e) There is authorized to be appropriated for each fiscal year prior to July 1, 1978, $5,000,000 to carry out the provisions of this section.

Section 601 of the Civil Rights Act of 1964 (42 U.S.C. 2000d)

No person in the United States shall on grounds of race, color, or national origin, be excluded from participation in, be denied the benefits of, or be subjected to discrimination under any program or activity receiving Federal financial assistance.

Adult Education (20 S1205)

S1205. State plans; submission to Commissioner; required provisions; hearing

(a) Any State desiring to receive its allotment of Federal funds for any grant under this chapter shall submit through its State educational agency a State plan. Such State plan shall be in such detail as the Commissioner deems necessary, and shall—

(b) provide that special assistance be given to the needs of persons of limited English-speaking ability (as defined in section 880b-1(a) of this title), by providing bilingual adult education programs in which instruction is given in English and, to the extent necessary to allow such persons to progress effectively through the adult education program, in the native language of such persons, carried out in coordination with programs of bilingual education assisted under title VII of the Elementary and Secondary Education Act of 1965 and bilingual vocational education programs under the Vocational Education Act of 1963;

Bilingual Vocational Training (20 S1393)

S1393. Congressional findings

The Congress hereby finds that one of the most acute problems in the United States is that which involves millions of citizens, both children and adults, whose efforts to profit from vocational training is severely restricted by their limited English-speaking ability because they come from environments where the dominant language is other than English; that such persons are therefore unable to help to fill the critical need for more and better trained personnel in vital occupational categories; and that such persons are unable to make their maximum contribution to the Nation's economy and must, in fact, suffer the hardships of unemployment or underemployment. The Congress further finds that there is a critical shortage of instructors possessing both the job knowledge and skills and the dual language capabilities required for adequate vocational instruction of such language-handicapped persons, and a corresponding shortage of instructional materials and of instructional methods and techniques suitable for such instruction.

S1393a. General responsibilities of Commissioner and Secretary of Labor; consultations; regulations and guidelines; approval and consistency with other promulgations

(a) The Commissioner and the Secretary of Labor together shall—
  (1) develop and disseminate accurate information on the status of bilingual vocational training in all parts of the United States;
  (2) evaluate the impact of such bilingual vocational training on the shortage of well-trained personnel, the unemployment or underemployment of persons with limited English-speaking ability, and the ability of such persons to contribute fully to the economy of the United States; and
  (3) report their findings annually to the President and Congress.
(b) The Commissioner shall consult with the Secretary of Labor with respect to the administration of this subchapter. Regulations and guidelines promulgated by the Commissioner to carry out this subchapter shall be consistent with those promulgated by the Secretary of Labor pursuant to section 871 of Title 29 and shall be approved by the Secretary of Labor before issuance.

S1393b. Authorization of appropriations

There are authorized to be appropriated $17,500,000 for the fiscal year ending June 30, 1975, to carry out the provisions of this subchapter.

S1393c. Authorization of grants and contracts; payments

(a) From the sums made available for grants under this subchapter pursuant to section 1393b of this title, the Commissioner is authorized to make grants to and enter into contracts with appropriate State agencies, local educational agencies, postsecondary educational institutions, private nonprofit vocational training institutions, and to other nonprofit organizations especially created to serve a group whose languages as normally used is other than English in supplying training in recognized occupations and new and emerging occupations, and to enter into contracts with private for-profit agencies and organizations, to assist them in conducting bilingual vocational training programs for persons of all ages in all communities of the United States which are designed to insure that vocational training programs are available to all individuals who desire and need such bilingual vocational training.

(b) The Secretary shall pay to each applicant which has an application approved under this subchapter an amount equal to the total sums expended by the applicant for the purposes set forth in that application.

S1393d. Uses of Federal funds

Grants and contracts under this subchapter may be used, in accordance with applications approved under section 1393f of this title, for—

(1) bilingual vocational training programs for persons who have completed or left elementary or secondary school and who are available for training by a postsecondary educational institution;

(2) bilingual vocational training programs for persons who have already entered the labor market and who desire or need training or retraining to achieve year-round employment, adjust to changing manpower needs, expand their range of skills, or advance in employment; and

(3) training allowances for participants in bilingual vocational training programs subject to the same conditions and limitations as are set forth in section 821 of Title 29.

S1393e. Applications—time and manner of submission; contents

(a) A grant or contract for assistance under this subchapter may be made only upon application to the Commissioner at such time, in such manner, and containing or accompanied by such information as the Commissioner deems necessary. Each such application shall—

(1) provide that the activities and services for which assistance under this subchapter is sought will be administered by or under the supervision of the applicant;

(2) set forth a program for carrying out the purposes described in section 1393d of this title; and

(3) set forth a program of such size, scope, and design as will make a substantial contribution toward carrying out the purposes of this subchapter.

Submission to State board or agency for comment; inclusion of comment

(b) No grant or contract may be made under this subchapter directly to a local educational agency or a postsecondary educational institution or a private vocational training institution or any other eligible agency or organization unless that agency, institution, or organization has submitted the application to the State board established under subchapter II of this chapter, or in the case of a State that does not have such a board, the similar State agency, for comment and includes the comment of that board or agency with the application.

S1393f. Application approval by Commissioner—Original applications; conditions

(a) The Commissioner may approve an application for assistance under this subchapter only if—

(1) the application meets the requirements set forth in subsection (a) of section 1393e of this title;

(2) in the case of an application submitted for assistance under this subchapter to an agency, institution, or organization other than the State board established under subchapter II of this chapter, the requirement of subsection (b) of section 1393e of this title is met; and

(3) in the case of an application submitted for assistance under this sub-chapter, the Commissioner determines that the program is consistent with criteria established by him, where feasible, after consultation with the State board established under subchapter II of this chapter, for achieving equitable distribution of assistance under this subchapter within that State.

(b) An amendment to an application shall, except as the Secretary may otherwise provide, be subject to approval in the same manner as the original application.

Emergency Aid (20 S1607)

S1607. Special programs and projects; grant and contract authority; bilingual education; eligibility, program committee

(a) (1) Amounts reserved by the Assistant Secretary pursuant to section 1603 (b) (2) of this title, which are not designated for the purposes of clause (A) or (B) thereof, or for section 1612 of this title shall be available to him for grants and contracts under this subsection.

(2) The Assistant Secretary is authorized to make grants to, and contracts with, State and local educational agencies, and other public agencies and organizations (or a combination of such agencies and organizations) for the purpose of conducting special programs and projects carrying out activities otherwise authorized by this chapter, which the Assistant Secretary determines will make substantial progress toward achieving the purposes of this chapter.

(3) The Assistant Secretary is authorized to make grants to, and contracts with, one or more private, nonprofit agencies, institutions, or organizations, for the conduct, in cooperation with one or more local educational agencies, of special programs for the teaching of standard mathematics to children eligible for services under this chapter through instruction in advanced mathematics by qualified instructors with bachelor degrees in mathematics, or the mathematical sciences from colleges or other institutions of higher education, or equivalent experience.

(b) (1) From not more than one-half of the sums reserved pursuant to section 1604(a) (3) of this title, the Assistant Secretary, in cases in which he finds that it would effectively carry out the purpose of this chapter stated in section 1601(b) of this title, may assist by grant or contract any public or private nonprofit agency, institution, or organization (other than a local educational agency) to carry out programs or projects designed to support the development or implementation of a plan, program, or activity described in section 1605 of this title.

(2) From the remainder of the sums reserved pursuant to section 1604(a) (3) of this title, the Assistant Secretary is authorized to make grants to, and contracts with, public and private nonprofit agencies, institutions, and organizations (other than local educational agencies and nonpublic elementary and secondary schools) to carry out programs or projects designed to support the development or implementation of a plan, program, or activity described in section 1605 of this title.

(c) (1) The Assistant Secretary shall carry out a program to meet the needs of minority group children who are from an environment in which a dominant language is other than English and who, because of language barriers and cultural differences, do not have equality of educational opportunity. From the amount reserved pursuant to section 1603(b) (2) (A) of this title, the Assistant Secretary is authorized to make grants to, and contracts with—

  (A) private nonprofit agencies, institutions, and organizations to develop curricula, at the request of one or more educational agencies which are eligible for assistance under section 1605 of this title, designed to meet the special educational needs of minority group children who are from environments in which a dominant language is other than English, for the development of reading, writing, and speaking skills, in the English language and in the language of their parents or grandparents, and to meet the educational needs of such children and their classmates to understand the history and cultural background of the minority groups of which such children are members;

  (B) local educational agencies eligible for assistance under section 1605 of this title for the purpose of engaging in such activities; or

  (C) local educational agencies which are eligible to receive assistance under section 1605 of this title for the purpose of carrying out activities authorized under section 1606(a) of this title to implement curricula developed under clauses (A) and (B) or curricula otherwise developed which the Assistant Secretary determines meets the purposes stated in clause (A).

In making grants and contracts under this paragraph, the Assistant Secretary shall assure that sufficient funds from the amount reserved pursuant to section 1603(b) (2) (A) of this title remain available to provide for grants and contracts under clause (C) of this paragraph for implementation of such curricula as the Assistant Secretary determines meet the purposes stated in clause (A) of this paragraph. In making a grant or contract under clause (C) of this paragraph, the Assistant Secretary shall take whatever action is necessary to assure that the implementation plan includes provisions adequate to insure training of teachers and other ancillary educational personnel.

(2) (A) In order to be eligible for a grant or contract under this subsection—

  (i) a local educational agency must establish a program or project committee meeting the requirements of subparagraph (B), which will fully participate in the preparation of the application under this subsection and in the implementation of the program or project and join in submitting such application; and

  (ii) a private nonprofit agency, institution, or organization must (I) establish a program or project board of not less than ten members which meets the requirements of subparagraph (B) and which shall exercise policy-making authority with respect to the program or project and (II) have demonstrated to the Assistant Secretary that it has the capacity to obtain the services of adequately trained and qualified staff.

(B) A program or project committee or board, established pursuant to subparagraph (A) must be broadly representative of parents, school officials, teachers, and interested members of the community or communities to be served, not less than half of the members of which shall be parents and not less than half of the members of which shall be members of the minority group the educational needs of which the program or project is intended to meet.

(3) All programs or projects assisted under this subsection shall be specifically designed to complement any programs or projects carried out by the local educational agency under section 1605 of this title. The Assistant Secretary shall insure that programs of Federal financial assistance related to the purposes of this subsection are coordinated and carried out in a manner consistent with the provisions of this subsection, to the extent consistent with other law.

Public Library Services and Construction (20 S351(d))

S351d. State plans and programs

Provisions of plan

(b) A basic State plan under this chapter shall—
(4) set forth the criteria to be used in determining the adequacy of public library services in geographical areas and for groups of persons in the State, including criteria designed to assure that priority will be given to programs or projects which serve urban and rural areas with high concentrations of low-income families, and to programs and projects which serve areas with high concentrations of persons of limited English speaking ability (as defined in section 880b-1(a) of this title).

State Vocational Education Programs

S1262. Uses of federal funds—Authorized purposes for grants
(a) Grants to States under this subchapter may be used, in accordance with State plans approved pursuant to section 1263 of this title, for the following purposes:
(4) (A) vocational education for persons (other than handicapped persons defined in section 1248(6) of this title) who have academic, socioeconomic, or other handicaps that prevent them from succeeding in the regular vocational education program;
(B) vocational education for handicapped persons who because of their handicapping condition cannot succeed in the regular vocational education program without special educational assistance or who require a modified vocational education program;
(C) vocational education for students of limited English-speaking ability (as defined in section 880b-1 (a) of this title) carried out in coordination with bilingual education programs under title VII of the Elementary and Secondary Education Act of 1965 and bilingual adult education programs under section 1205(a) (11) of this title.

National Defense Education Act (P.L. 85-864, Amended)

SEC. 303. (a) Any State which desires to receive payments under this part shall submit to the Commissioner, through its State educational agency, a State plan which meets the requirements of section 1004(a) and—

(1) sets forth a program under which funds paid to the State from its allotment under section 302(a) will be expended solely for projects approved by the State educational agency for

   (A) acquisition of laboratory and other special equipment (other than supplies consumed in use), including audiovisual materials and equipment, and printed and published materials (other than textbooks), suitable for use in providing education in science, mathematics, history, civics, geography, economics, industrial arts, *modern foreign languages,* English, or reading in public *elementary or secondary schools, or both,* [emphasis added] and of test-grading equipment for such schools and specialized equipment for audiovisual libraries serving such schools authorities, be used when available and suitable in providing education in other subject matter, and

   (B) minor remodeling of laboratory or other space used for such materials or equipment;

(2) sets forth principles for determining the priority of such projects in the State for assistance under this part and provides for undertaking such projects, insofar as financial resources available therefor make possible, in the order determined by the application of such principles;

(3) provides an opportunity for a hearing before the State educational agency to any applicant for a project under this part;

(4) provides for the establishment of standards on a State level for laboratory and other special equipment acquired with assistance furnished under this part;

(5) sets forth a program under which funds paid to the State from its allotment under section 302(b) will be expended solely for (A) expansion or improvement of supervisory or related services in public elementary and secondary schools in the fields of science, mathematics, history, civics, geography, economics, industrial arts, *modern foreign languages,* [emphasis added] English, and reading, and (B) administration of the State plan; and

(6) sets forth any requirements imposed upon applicants for financial participation in projects assisted under this part, including any provision for taking into account, in such requirements, the resources available to any applicant for such participation relative to the resources for participation available to the resources for participation available to all other applicants.

(b) The Commissioner shall approve any State plan and any modification thereof which complies with the provisions of subsection (a).

SEC. 305. From the sum reserved for each fiscal year for the purposes of this section under the provisions of section 302(a), the Commissioner is authorized to make loans to *private nonprofit elementary and secondary schools* [emphasis added] in any State. Any such loan shall be made only for the purposes for which payments to State educational agencies are authorized under the first sentence of section 301, and—

(1) shall be made upon application containing such information as may be deemed necessary by the Commissioner;

(2) shall be subject to such conditions as may be necessary to protect the financial interest of the United States;

(3) shall bear interest at the rate arrived at by adding one-quarter of 1 per centum per annum to the rate which the Secretary of the Treasury determines to be equal to the current average market yield on outstanding marketable obligations of the United States with redemption periods to maturity comparable to the average maturities of such loans as computed at the end of the fiscal year next preceding the date the application for the loan is approved and by adjusting the result so obtained to the nearest one-eighth of 1 per centum; and

(4) shall mature and be repayable on such date as may be agreed to by the Commissioner and the borrower, but such date shall not be more than ten years after the date on which such loan was made.

Appendix B

PROGRAM AND PROJECT DESCRIPTIONS (A SELECTION)

California

Upper Valley Intercultural Program
Placer County Office of Education
  AUBURN, CALIFORNIA 95603

Spanish (Mexican American)   Third funding year
Grades: PreK–3; 11 classes, 360 students (180 Anglo American, 180 Mexican American). Students not participating total 290 (145 Anglo American, 145 Mexican American).
Staff of 2 resource teachers, 5 directors, 5 evaluators and 6 aides paid from Title VII ESEA funds, 11 professionals and 5 paraprofessionals paid from state funds. Funds other than Title VII constitute 40 percent of the 1973–74 project budget.
Three schools: Silveyville, Carlin Coppin, Laugenour.

Staff development activities anticipated for 1973–74 included a two-week workshop, a one-week seminar and seven one-day workshops.
Activities in which the *project director* anticipated participating during 1973–74 included staff development, community dissemination of information, negotiations for funding, and proposal writing.
Instructional materials for the project are project-developed and produced and commercially produced. The project has developed a social studies guide for Kindergarten and grade 1, and materials on the history and culture of Mexico for grade 2. Anticipated materials development includes areas of SSL, a K–3 curriculum guide, ESL components, SSL, and a K–3 activities guide.
Content areas taught in the non-English (first) language of the student include reading, oral language development and social studies. The Spanish-speaking student is taught all areas in English, after a preview in Spanish. English-speaking students are taught social studies, oral language development and reading in Spanish. The classroom is organized so that instruction is in the student's dominant language, then reinforced by the model of the second language.

Adapted from *Guide to Title VII ESEA Bilingual Bicultural Projects* (Austin, Tex.: Dissemination Center for Bilingual Bicultural Education, 1974).

Title VII Bilingual Schools Program
Los Angeles City Unified School District
  LOS ANGELES, CALIFORNIA 90033

Spanish (Mexican American)   Fourth funding year
Grades: K-4; 80 classes, 2,000 students (70 Anglo American, 1,810 Mexican
American, 28 Chinese, 12 American Indian, 72 Black, 8 Filipino). Students not par-
ticipating in the project total 581 (33 Anglo American, 489 Mexican American, 14
Chinese, 6 American Indian, 35 Black, 4 Filipino).
Staff of 88 bilingual professionals and 44 bilingual paraprofessionals paid from Title
VII ESEA funds; 30 paraprofessionals paid from Los Angeles Unified School District
funds. Funds other than Title VII constitute 25 percent of the 1973-74 project
budget.
Five schools: Bridge Street, City Terrace, Huntington Drive, Second Street, San
Antonio de Padua.

Staff development activities anticipated for 1973-74 included a summer preservice
session for new teachers and inservice for all teachers.
Activities in which the *project director* anticipated participating were the summer
preservice, community involvement, staff recruitment and in-project evaluation. The
local education agency funds grades K-1 and participates in staff development.
Instructional materials for the project are primarily commercially produced. The
project has developed materials in English as a second language, reading in Spanish,
and Hispanic culture (music, games and riddles). Materials development anticipated
for 1973-74 included areas of previous development as well as mathematics.
Content areas taught in Spanish and English to students of all cultures include math,
science, health, safety, social studies and language arts.
Curriculum areas stressed at each level are: grades K-2—language arts, grades
3-4—language arts, social studies, health, safety and science. The classroom is
organized primarily into a learning center for individualized instruction by bilingual
teacher and aide.
Student achievement by students in second language learning is measured by written
tests and observations of verbal ability. Improvement in the pupils' self-concept is indicated by the results of the Self-Concepts Inventory.
The *Parent Advisory Group* met 9 times during 1972-73; activities included parent
workshops, classroom visitations, holiday celebration programs and work on the
Senate Bilingual Hearings. Community members assisted in the classroom and with
cultural activities.
Evaluation of students' progress is according to the project's Title VII evaluation
design schedule; an external audit is performed biannually.

Castelar Bilingual Education Program
Los Angeles Unified School District
  LOS ANGELES, CALIFORNIA 90012

Chinese, Spanish (Mexican American)   Third funding year
Grades: K-2; 12 classes, 330 students (248 Chinese, 82 Mexican American).
Staff of 13 bilingual professionals, 1 monolingual professional, 14 bilingual
paraprofessionals paid from Title VII ESEA funds; 3 professionals, 4 paraprofessionals and 5 volunteers, salaries paid from Los Angeles Unified School District

funds. Funds other than Title VII constitute 33 percent of the 1973-74 project budget.

One school: Castelar Elementary.

Staff development activities anticipated for 1973-74 included a preservice workshop.

Activities in which the *project director* anticipated participating during 1973-74 included staff development, budgeting of funds, materials development and social gatherings.

Instructional materials developed for use at the project include bilingual, bicultural filmstrips and tapes, and bicultural games. Anticipated materials development for 1973-74 included areas of Chinese, Spanish, and English curricula. Procedures used to disseminate materials to persons outside the Title VII program included mailing to other projects and distribution to programs in the school district.

Content areas taught in the first and second languages simultaneously include reading, handwriting, language arts, math, physical education and music. The classroom is organized in kindergarten for team teaching with a Chinese-speaking and a Spanish-speaking teacher (a Spanish aide and a Chinese aide make small group teaching possible); the first grade classroom is organized with alternating Chinese and Spanish classes for math, music and physical education.

Student achievement by pupils in language acquisition and academic progress is measured by standardized tests, taping, and criterion testing by teachers.

The *Parent Advisory Group* met 5 times during 1972-73; activities included holiday celebration programs and a review of the project and instructional materials.

Evaluation of students' progress is made by pre- and post-testing by teachers, evaluator and coordinator; a continuing process of evaluation is maintained throughout the year.

Project Esperanza
Salinas City School District
  SALINAS, CALIFORNIA 93901

Spanish (Mexican American)   Second funding year

Grades: K-2; 12 classes, 350 students (127 Anglo American, 219 Mexican American, 1 Chinese, 2 Indian, 1 Black). Students not participating in the project total 911 (306 Anglo American, 546 Mexican American, 22 Chinese, 37 Black).

Staff of 3 bilingual professionals, 1 monolingual professional, 14 bilingual paraprofessionals paid from Title VII ESEA funds; 9 professionals, 3 paraprofessionals, 25 volunteers, salaries paid from Salinas City School District funds. Funds other than Title VII constitute 50 percent of 1973-74 project budget.

Two schools: Sherwood, Roosevelt.

Staff development activities anticipated for 1973-74 included intergroup activities and inservice sessions.

Activities in which the *project director* anticipated participating during 1974 were planning, developing and implementing the program.

Instructional materials are primarily project-developed and produced; the project has developed materials in math. Anticipated materials development for 1973-74 was in areas of math and reading. The project produces periodicals and a brochure to disseminate information to persons outside the Title VII program.

Content areas for the non-English (first) language of the student are reading and math. Instruction in the second language—ESL and SSL—is in the area of language development; reading and mathematics are taught in both languages simultaneously. *Curriculum areas* stressed at each level are reading, math, and social studies. The classroom is organized primarily for small group instruction and for team teaching. Improvement in the pupils' self-concept and peer-group interaction has been evidenced by a decrease in absenteeism, celebration of holidays, and group interaction.

The *Parent Advisory Group* met 10 times during 1972-73; activities included participation in project planning, implementation, and evaluation. Screening and evaluative committees included parents, members of the business sector, public agencies, the clergy and service agencies. The program is evaluated internally.

Bilingual-Cultural Exchange Project (BICEP)
San Bernardino County Schools
    SAN BERNARDINO, CALIFORNIA 92401

Spanish (Mexican American)   Fourth funding year
Grades: K-7; 23 classes, 690 students (272 Anglo American, 404 Mexican American, 10 Portuguese, 4 Black).
Staff of 4 bilingual professionals, 1 monolingual professional, 7 bilingual paraprofessionals paid from Title VII ESEA funds; 23 professionals and 100 volunteers, salaries paid from district funds. Funds other than Title VII constitute 65 percent of the 1973-74 project budget.
Four schools: El Rancho (Chino), Paul Rogers (Colton), Lytle Creek and Richardson Junior High School (San Bernardino).

Staff development activities anticipated for 1973-74 included curriculum development, working with community volunteers and materials adaptation.

Activities in which the *project director* anticipated participating in 1973-74 included curriculum and program development, consultation to project sites and evaluation.

Instructional materials for the project are primarily adapted from commercial material by project personnel. The project has developed materials in areas of language arts, math, science, fine arts and history. Anticipated materials development for 1973-74 included the same areas; information and materials are distributed at regional workshops.

Content areas in Spanish and English are taught in an open classroom setting; curriculum comes from student interest and natural curiosity.

Student achievement by ethnic minority students in second language learning has been indicated by standardized tests; random interviews by an audit team indicate that third year students are reading and speaking Spanish with good facility. Academic progress by project participants has been shown by standardized tests to be greater than that of nonparticipants.

The *Parent Advisory Group* from Chino met 16 times in 1972-73; the Colton group met 32 times and the San Bernardino group met 51 times. Activities included parent volunteer planning, program development and implementation, and development of a procedure for evaluation.

Evaluation of students' progress is measured in proportion with goals set by parent, teacher, and child. The project evaluator meets monthly with each funded teacher to monitor teacher-pupil-parent developed objectives.

Materials Acquisition Project
San Diego Unified School District
  SAN DIEGO, CALIFORNIA 92113

Spanish, Portuguese   Fourth funding year
Staff of 6 professionals, 20.5 (manhour equivalence) supportive personnel.
This is a *special project* providing support to other Title VII ESEA programs with the purpose of making instructional materials published in Spanish- and Portuguese-speaking countries increasingly available to bilingual education classes in the United States.
The project's *goals* have been implemented through field testing, parallel curricula, publications and publicity, and acquisitions.
Field testing of materials during 1972–73 was carried out by 77 teachers from 19 sites who attended workshops at MAP, in addition to other teachers from 18 additional sites who had already received materials.
The *parallel curricula* program was responsible for the scheduling of workshops for 401 teachers representing 85 projects throughout the nation. Teachers selected materials at MAP for comparison with materials already in use; comparable skills and concepts being taught will be recorded, and the information collated and organized.
Publications and publicity involves publishing a monthly magazine, entitled Materiales en Marcha para el Esfuerzo Bilingüe Bicultural, averaging 20 pages per issue and including articles featuring outstanding materials in the MAP collection. Other activities include the preparation of pamphlets, displays, and traveling book kits and presentations and exhibits at conferences and conventions.
The *acquisitions* staff has been responsible for totally processing 3,659 items (as of May of 1973) encompassing the fields of elementary and secondary education and including tapes, records, charts, games, and slides. Items of the collection which are outstanding with regard to their potential value to bilingual programs in the United States are featured in articles in the magazine Materiales en Marcha.

Chinese Bilingual Pilot Project
San Francisco Unified School District
  SAN FRANCISCO, CALIFORNIA 94108

Cantonese (Chinese)   Fifth funding year
Grades 1–5; 11 classes, 300 students (120 Anglo American, 150 Chinese, 30 Black).
Staff of 11 bilingual professionals, 6 monolingual professionals and 7 bilingual paraprofessionals paid from Title VII ESEA funds; 5 paraprofessionals paid from school district funds. Funds other than Title VII constitute 33 percent of the 1973–74 project budget.
Three schools: Commodore Stockton, Patrick Henry, St. Mary's.
Staff development activities anticipated for 1973–74 included inservice training of bilingual teachers.
Activities in which the *project director* anticipated participating during 1973–74 included inservice teacher training, program evaluation, and community relations.
Instructional materials are both commercially produced and project-developed and produced. The project has developed materials in areas of Chinese festivals, songs, stories, games and art activities, as well as Chinese reading and writing materials.

Procedures used to disseminate materials and information to persons outside the Title VII program are the making available of brochures by mail and the display of booklets at conferences.

Content areas taught in Cantonese are Chinese reading and writing; reading and writing are taught in English as a second language. English-speaking students are taught Chinese as a second language; both languages are used simultaneously in teaching social studies, math and physical education. The classroom is organized in a variety of situations from large group instruction to individualized instruction.

Student achievement in second language learning by students of minority and majority cultures is indicated by the many students reading at grade level, and by the non-Chinese children being able to follow directions and enjoy a simple story in Chinese.

The *Parent Advisory Group* met 8 times during 1972–73; activities included an open house, a review of project aims and objectives and a Chinese music composition contest.

Evaluation of students' progress is made by means of pre- and post-testing in English as a second language, Chinese as a second language, and Chinese reading and writing.

Project to Advance Cultural Opportunities (PACO)
San Francisco Unified School District
   SAN FRANCISCO, CALIFORNIA 94131

Spanish (Mexican American)   Fourth funding year
Grades: K–5; 10 classes, 236 students (140 Spanish language dominant, 96 English language dominant).

Staff of 25 bilingual professionals, 5 monolingual professionals and 11 bilingual paraprofessionals paid from Title VII ESEA funds; 3 professionals and 2 paraprofessionals paid from other funds; 5 volunteers. Funding other than Title VII is provided by the San Francisco Unified School District and constitutes 70 percent of the 1973–74 project budget.

Three schools: Buena Vista Elementary, Marshall Elementary, Washington Irving Intermediate.

Staff development activities anticipated for 1973–74 included a week-long preservice workshop and regularly scheduled inservice workshop and regularly scheduled inservice sessions for staff, teachers and aides.

Activities in which the *project director* anticipated participating during 1973–74 included planning and implementation of the bilingual instructional program, assignments of regular and supportive staff, resource teachers and language specialists; coordination with project principals and other state and federal projects having input in bilingual education; and formulation of inservice training plans.

Instructional materials for the project are project-developed and produced, commercially produced, and adapted from commercial materials by project personnel. The project has developed materials in areas of reading readiness for kindergarten, social studies units, and elementary science materials for grades K–6.

Content areas taught in the non-English (first) language of the student are language arts, reading, social studies, science, culture and crafts. Areas taught in English (the second language) are language arts, math, science and reading. English-speaking students are taught Spanish as a second language, social studies, arts and crafts in

Spanish. The classroom is organized for teaming of teachers and paraprofessionals for dual-language, individualized instruction.

The *Parent Advisory Group* met 10 times during 1973–73. Activities included policy making, discussion of program progress, evaluation reports, creation of parent resource centers, parent-teacher workshops, a Community Open House, and Parent Unity Day.

Evaluation of students' progress is by means of an internal evaluator from the district's Department of Research and Evaluation. Interim and final evaluation reports are prepared.

Proyecto Anglo Latino
Alum Rock Union Elementary School District
  SAN JOSE, CALIFORNIA 95127

Spanish (Mexican American)   Fourth funding year
Grades: K–5; 10 classes, 324 students (59 Anglo American, 259 Mexican American, 3 Portuguese, 3 Black). Students not participating are 49 percent Anglo American, 50 percent Mexican American and 1 percent Black.

Staff of 2 bilingual professionals, 10 bilingual paraprofessionals and 1 clerk typist paid from Title VII ESEA funds; 10 professionals and 5 paraprofessionals paid from other funds. Funds other than Title VII are provided by district and voucher funds and constitute 70 percent of the 1973–74 project budget.

One school: Richard E. Conniff.

Staff development activities anticipated for 1973–74 included preservice and inservice sessions and bilingual conferences.

Activities in which the *project director* anticipated participating during 1973–74 included staff development, conferences, teaching Spanish and serving as assistant administrator for the school.

Instructional materials for the project are primarily those adapted from commercial material by project personnel. The project has developed materials for all subjects, a curriculum for grades K–3, and Spanish stories for use in grades 3 and 4. Anticipated materials development for 1973–74 included more Spanish stories and a curriculum for grades 4 and 5 in all areas.

All *content areas* are taught in Spanish and English to students of both cultures.

All *curriculum areas* are stressed at each level, especially reading and writing. The classroom is organized for small group instruction (10 children per adult), individual teaching, team teaching, listening centers and large group instruction with individual help.

Student achievement in second language learning and academic progress is measured by Peabody Picture Vocabulary Tests and the Conniff School Test of Basic Concepts; specific program objectives met with a high level of success.

The *Parent Advisory Group* met 10 times during 1972–73; activities included classroom visitations and participation, a monthly newsletter, cultural celebrations, a potluck dinner and writing Spanish stories for the program.

Evaluation of students' progress is by means of pre- and post-testing with project-developed and commercial instruments. Program evaluation for 1973–74 is performed by the district evaluation department and the Rand Corporation.

Bilingual Bicultural Education Program
Santa Ana Unified School District
SANTA ANA, CALIFORNIA 92701

Spanish (Mexican American)   Fifth funding year
Grades: PreK–3; 42 classes, 1,240 students (246 Anglo American, 994 Mexican American).
Staff of 24 bilingual professionals, 18 monolingual professionals, and 25 bilingual paraprofessionals paid from Title VII ESEA funds. Local funds constitute 65 percent of the 1973–74 project budget.
Five schools: Diamond Diagnostic, Fremont, Hoover, Monroe, Sierra.

Staff development activities anticipated for 1973–74 included conferences and workshops.
Activities in which the *project director* anticipated participating during 1973–74 included parent involvement and staff development.
Instructional materials for the project are project-developed and produced, commercially produced, and adapted from commercial material by project personnel. The project has developed measurement devices; curriculum development during 1973–74 included areas of testing and language arts.
Content areas taught in Spanish and English are language arts, mathematics and oral language.
Curriculum areas stressed at each level are language arts, math, language, and cultural studies. The classroom is organized for individualized instruction with some schools utilizing open space methods and others using self-contained classrooms.
Student achievement in second language learning is measured with criterion-referenced tests; a project-developed device is used to measure pupils' self-concept.
The *Parent Advisory Group* met 10 times during 1972–73; activities included in-service training, conferences, parent workshops and active contribution to the continuation proposal.
Evaluation of students' progress is on an ongoing basis and is accomplished by use of criterion-referenced measurement devices; an internal evaluator conducts ongoing visitations and observations.

Santa Paula Bilingual-Bicultural Project
Santa Paula School District
SANTA PAULA, CALIFORNIA 93060

Spanish (Mexican American)   Fifth funding year
Grades: K–8; 80 classes, 3,297 students (1,509 Anglo American, 1,775 Mexican American, 5 Chinese, 8 Black).
Staff of 2 bilingual professionals, 1 professional monolingual and 3 bilingual paraprofessionals paid from Title VII ESEA funds; 63 professionals, 27 paraprofessionals and 20 volunteers funded from other sources. Title VII funds constitute virtually all of the 1973–74 project budget.
Four schools: Grace Thille, Bedell, McKevett, Isbell JHS.

Staff development activities anticipated for 1973–74 included continued development of the bilingual reading program, inservice sessions, conferences and seminars.

Activities in which the *project director* anticipated participating during 1973–74 included staff and materials development and writing of proposals.

Instructional materials for the project are primarily project-developed and produced. The project has developed materials for a bilingual reading program, and in areas of bilingual oral language and bicultural studies. Anticipated materials development during 1973–74 included the same areas.

Content areas taught in the non-English (first) language of the student and in English as a second language include reading and bicultural oral language.

Curriculum areas stressed at each level are reading, oral language, foods, literature, and dances at the primary levels; anthropological studies at the intermediate levels; and history, politics and foods in the upper grades. The classroom is organized for small group, self-contained, team teaching, and individualized instruction.

Student achievement in second language learning and academic progress is measured with project-developed criterion-referenced tests as well as standardized tests; results have shown an average of 0.4 progress above grade level.

The *Parent Advisory Group* met monthly during 1973–74; activities included review and critique of the project, school visitations and planning sessions.

Evaluation of students' progress is by means of monthly criterion-referenced tests in reading and achievement tests. The evaluator makes on-site visits, holds teacher conferences, and prepares interim and final reports.

Media Research and Evaluation Center
San Ysidro School District
    SAN YSIDRO, CALIFORNIA 92073

Spanish (Mexican American)   Second funding year
Grades: PreK–6; 95 classes, 2,303 students (461 English language dominant, 1,842 non-English language dominant).
Staff of 6 administrators, 93 teachers, 10 specialists, 4 pupil personnel workers, 2 evaluators, 76 teacher aides, 5 community liaison workers, 4 clerks.
Four schools: Beyer, Sunset/La Mirada, Smythe, Willow.

Staff development activities anticipated for 1973–74 included a ten-day preservice workshop, a three-day and a two-day inservice workshop, and regularly scheduled inservice sessions for teachers, paraprofessionals and staff on selection and use of materials, and teaching methods.

Activities in which the *assistant superintendent* anticipated participating were administration of the project and coordination of instruction and evaluation.

Instructional materials for the project are primarily project-developed and produced. Anticipated materials development for 1973–74 included continued work by the Media Research and Evaluation Center in developing a long range research and evaluation design for bilingual education, and the monitoring of teacher, aide and parent and community performance in relation to curriculum redesign.

Content areas taught in a bilingual setting are Spanish, English, math, physical education, social studies, science, music, phonics, writing and art.

The *Parent Advisory Group* met monthly during 1972–73. Activities included general meetings, review of the program and participation in research surveys.

Evaluation of students' progress is by means of pre- and post-testing with the Otis-Lennon test, the Metropolitan Achievement Test, the state-mandated Cooperative Primary Test, and the Inter-American Series in Spanish and English. An external auditor prepared the audit report by means of on-site visitations and testing.

A Demonstration Bilingual-Bicultural Education Project
Stockton Unified School District
STOCKTON, CALIFORNIA 95202

Spanish (Mexican American)   Fifth funding year
Grades: K-6; 40 classes, 1,074 students (109 Anglo American, 453 Mexican
American, 4 Chinese, 2 American Indian, 371 Black, 135 of other ethnic groups).
Staff of 3 bilingual professionals, 8 bilingual paraprofessionals and 40 professionals
paid from Title VII ESEA funds. Title VII funds constitute 100 percent of 1973-74
budget.
Two schools: George Washington, Zachary Taylor.

Staff development activities anticipated for 1973-74 included a summer inservice
workshop and inservice training throughout the year.
Anticipated activities of the *project director* included staff development and program
implementation.
Instructional materials used in the project are both project-developed and produced
and commercially produced. The project has developed materials in areas of California history (4th grade), U. S. history (5th grade), Latin American history (6th grade)
and science (6th grade). Anticipated materials development for 1973-74 included expansion of bilingual social studies units, updating of parent handbooks and production of bilingual science units.
Content areas taught in Spanish and English to all students are social studies, science
and reading in Spanish.
Curriculum areas stressed at each level are: grades K-3—self concept, grade
4—California history, grade 5—U. S. history, grade 6—Latin American history
(science and reading in Spanish are stressed at each level). The classroom is organized
for small group instruction in a team teaching situation, learning centers, and individualized instruction.
Student achievement in second language learning and academic progress is indicated
by Cooperative Reading Tests, a parent survey, and teacher responses on IBM
"sense" cards.
The *Parent Advisory Group* met 5 times during 1972-73; activities included a summer camp, field trips, classroom materials preparation, ethnic foods preparation and
involvement in program planning and implementation.
Evaluation of students' progress is by means of pre- and post-testing in fall and
spring, teachers' objectives checklists, videotape critiques three times annually, and
periodic conferences. An internal evaluator prepares preliminary and final annual
evaluation reports with analysis of data gathered.

Project Hacer Vida
Coachella Valley Unified School District
THERMAL, CALIFORNIA 92274

Spanish (Mexican American)   Fourth funding year
Grades: 1-4; 639 students.
Staff of 10 professional bilinguals and 3 professional monolinguals. Title VII ESEA
provides funds for grades 3, 4 and the high school bilingual classes; the local school
district provides funds for grades 1 and 2.
Six schools: John Kelley, Oasis, Mecca, Peter Pendleton, Palm View, Westside.

Staff development activities anticipated for 1973-74 included an inservice workshop.
Instructional materials used in the project are commercially produced, project-developed and produced, and adapted from commercial material by project personnel. The project has developed criterion-referenced tests. Materials and material-related information is available by mail or visitations.
Content areas taught in English and Spanish are reading, language arts, math, social studies and cultural heritage.
Curriculum areas stressed at each level are: Grade 1—Conversational English and Spanish as second languages, grades 2-4—second language, according to students' needs, due to a mobile population. Classroom organization varies with the individual students' needs.
Student achievement by students of the majority and minority ethnic groups is measured by pre- and post-testing using project-developed criterion-referenced instruments.
The *Parent Advisory Group* met monthly in 1972-73; activities included production of a newspaper, participation in school celebrations of Mexican American holidays and attendance at bilingual conferences. Classroom presentations of vocations were made by members of the community.
Evaluation of students' progress is made by the project director who correlates results on pre- and post-testing with classroom organization.

Florida

Bilingual Education in the Miccosukee Day School
Miccosukee Day School (Miccosukee Corporation)
    MIAMI, FLORIDA 33144

Eelaponke (Miccosukee)   Second funding year
Grades: K-6; ungraded classes, 50 students (Miccosukee Indian).
Staff of 2 bilingual professionals, 1 monolingual professional and 2 bilingual paraprofessionals paid from Title VII ESEA funds; 4 professionals, 2 paraprofessionals and 10 volunteers, salaries paid from BIA contract funds. Funds other than Title VII constitute 40 percent of 1973-74 project budget.
One school: Miccosukee Day School.

Staff development activities anticipated for 1973-74 included work on curriculum, materials and learning the Indian language.
Activities in which the *project director* anticipated participating included materials development, administration, staff development and community involvement. The local education agency provides fiscal control.
Instructional materials used in the project are primarily project-developed and produced. The project has developed Eelaponke reading materials for the upper elementary grades and readiness materials featuring local environments. Anticipated materials development for 1973-74 included a complete K-1 program with materials for both English and Eelaponke instruction, as well as unsequenced upper elementary reading and social studies materials.
Content areas taught in Eelaponke are language, thinking, readiness and reading. English is used in teaching language comprehension. The classroom is organized in small homogeneous groupings in an ungraded situation (of 25 children K-3; some 4 to 6 groups may be formed).

Student achievement in second language learning and academic growth is indicated by accomplishment of the majority on criterion-referenced items on locally devised instruments.

The *Parent Advisory Group* met 10 times during 1972–73. Activities included a review of materials and the program, and the choosing of representatives to serve on a curriculum group, to decide an integrated curriculum from Head Start through the Upward Bound program.

Evaluation of students' progress is by pre- and post-testing with commercial and locally devised criterion-referenced tests. A contracted evaluator works with the director in the design phase and makes an interim and a final report.

Spanish Curricula Development Center
Dade County Public Schools
  MIAMI BEACH, FLORIDA 33139

Spanish (Cuban, Mexican American, Puerto Rican)   Fourth funding year
Grades: K–3; 10,080 students within the local education agency, 25,434 students in cooperating field trial centers in other bilingual projects around the nation.
Staff of 22 professionals, 29 support personnel, plus personnel detached for field service.

This is a *special project* with the current goal of creating Spanish language curricula in support of bilingual education programs in grades one through three. Materials are field tested in Dade County Public Schools and in 42 field testing centers nationwide; personnel in key projects serve as field trial coordinators for the Spanish Curricula Development Center and its companion project, the Curriculum Adaptation Network for Bilingual Bicultural Education.

Curriculum kits are available which contain instructional guides in five areas: Spanish language arts, social science, science and mathematics, fine arts, and Spanish as a second language. Support materials include books for pupils, visual supplements, packets of ditto masters, tape cassettes, and assessment activities for evaluation of pupil progress. Criterion-referenced achievement tests are also to be provided by the Center. Materials have regional editions for Mexican American, Cuban, and Puerto Rican pupils; the final revised editions are disseminated by the Dissemination Center for Bilingual Bicultural Education in Austin, Texas. Anticipated materials development during 1973–74 included review kits to supplement previously developed materials and teacher training kits to facilitate preservice and inservice training.

Collier County Bilingual Project
Collier County Public Schools
  NAPLES, FLORIDA 33940

Spanish (Mexican American)   Fifth funding year
Grades: 1–6; 21 classes, 672 students (298 Anglo American, 299 Mexican American, 75 Black). Students not participating in the project total 773 (269 Anglo American, 307 Mexican American, 197 Black).
Staff of 4 bilingual professionals and 6 bilingual paraprofessionals paid from Title VII ESEA funds, 16 professionals paid from local education agency funds. Funds other than Title VII constitute 73 percent of the 1973–74 project budget.

Four schools: Bethune, Highlands, Lake Trafford, Immokalee Middle School.

Staff development activities anticipated for 1973-74 included inservice sessions.

Activities in which the *project director* anticipated participating included evaluation, diagnosing, planning, inservice and budgetary control. The local education agency anticipated participating in purchasing and budgetary control.

Instructional materials for the project are primarily commercially produced.

Content areas taught in the non-English (first) language of the student and in English are math, science, health and language skills. English-speaking students are taught reading, math, and social studies in Spanish. In all areas, Spanish and English are used simultaneously.

Curriculum areas stressed at each level are: Grade 1—English as a second language, grade 2—reading and math, grade 3-6—Spanish as a second language, reading, math and social studies (culture). The classroom is organized primarily for small group and team teaching.

Student achievement in second language learning is measured by standardized tests, and indicated by teacher reports and parental comments.

The *Parent Advisory Council* met twice during 1972-73; activities included program planning and volunteer program coordination.

Evaluation of students' progress is made each nine weeks by teachers, and semiannually by standardized tests; the program is evaluated internally.

Illinois

Juan Morel Campos Bilingual Center
Chicago Board of Education District 6
   CHICAGO, ILLINOIS 60601

Spanish (Puerto Rican)   Fifth funding year
Grades: 6-8; 6 classes, 110 students (15 Anglo American, 15 Mexican American, 80 Puerto Rican).

Staff of 1 bilingual professional and 1 bilingual paraprofessional paid from Title VII ESEA funds; 8 professionals and 1 paraprofessional paid from Chicago Board of Education funds. Funds other than Title VII constitute 85 percent of the 1973-74 project budget.

Six schools: Von Humboldt, Lafayette, Schley, Sabin, Wicker Park, Chopin.

Staff development activities anticipated for 1973-74 included inservice periods and visitations to other centers.

Activities in which the *project director* anticipated participating included providing inservice training and administering and supervising the center.

Instructional materials used by the project are primarily those adapted from commercial materials by project personnel. The project has developed materials in science and English dialogues. Anticipated materials development for 1973-74 included units in multiethnic studies. A grant from the Right to Read Department of H.E.W. provided funds for dissemination of materials and production of an information capsule.

All *content areas* are taught in English and Spanish. English-speaking students are taught language skills, science and math in Spanish.

All *curriculum areas* are stressed at each level. The classroom is organized primarily for team teaching, with one teacher for the English component and the other for the Spanish component.

Student achievement in second language learning is measured with standardized and teacher-made tests; results show an increase in attainment of behavioral objectives.

The *Parent Advisory Group* met 7 times during 1972–73; activities included assistance in planning and production of assembly programs.

Evaluation of students' progress is made with teacher testing in terms of behavioral objectives.

Goudy Bilingual Center
Chicago Board of Education District 24
  CHICAGO, ILLINOIS 60601

Spanish (Cuban, Mexican American, Puerto Rican)   Fifth funding year
Grades: 4–6; 2 classes, 60 students (9 Anglo American, 12 Mexican American, 13 Puerto Rican, 2 Chinese, 2 American Indian, 3 Black, 26 Cuban, 3 Japanese). Goudy School students not participating in the project total 865 (390 Anglo American, 41 Mexican American, 43 Puerto Rican, 15 Chinese, 98 American Indian, 101 Black, 147 Cuban, 30 Japanese).

Students—totalling 205—will participate in other bicultural bilingual programs using local, state, and private funding.

Staff of 1 bilingual professional paid from Chicago Board of Education funds. Funds other than Title VII constitute 70 percent of the 1973–74 project budget.

One school: Goudy Elementary.

Staff development activities anticipated for 1973–74 included workshops, inservice and monthly meetings.

Activities in which the *project director* anticipated participating in 1973–74 included staff development and program implementation.

Instructional materials used by the project are project-developed and produced, commercially produced, and adapted from commercial material by project personnel. The project has developed materials for Bilingual workshops and in areas of social studies and Spanish language arts. Anticipated materials development for 1973–74 included areas of the arts, Spanish and language arts.

Content areas taught in Spanish are language arts, social studies and math. Areas taught in English include language arts, science, math and art. Social studies, math and science are taught in both languages simultaneously.

Curriculum areas stressed at each level are: primary—Spanish and English language arts; intermediate—language arts, social studies and math; upper—language arts, social studies (culture: arts and crafts). The classroom is organized for team teaching and individualized instruction situations.

Student achievement in second language learning is indicated by scores on pre- and post-tests, teacher-made tests, and classroom performance.

The *Parent Advisory Group* involved itself in proposal writing and contributing to program implementation.

Evaluation of students' progress is by means of pre- and post-testing with teacher-made and standardized tests.

Jackson, McLaren Bilingual Bicultural Center
Chicago Board of Education
  CHICAGO, ILLINOIS 60601

Spanish (Mexican American)   Second funding year
Grades: K-4; 10 classes, 180 students.
Staff of 4 bilingual professionals, 2 aides and a clerk paid from Title VII ESEA funds;
11 professionals and 4 paraprofessionals paid from Chicago Board of Education
funds. Funds other than Title VII constitute 80 percent of the 1973-74 project
budget.
Two schools: Jackson, McLaren.

Staff development activities anticipated for 1973-74 included area and city wide
workshops and federally funded inservice staff development programs.
Activities in which the *project director* anticipated participating included im-
plementation of program goals and staff development.
Instructional materials for the project are primarily project-developed and produced.
The project has developed materials in language instruction and social studies. An-
ticipated materials development for 1973-74 included areas of mixed culture and
bilingual teaching and techniques.
All *content areas* are taught in the non-English (first) language of the student and in
English (the second language). Spanish is used in teaching Spanish language, music,
and literature. Social studies, math and fine arts are taught in English and Spanish
simultaneously.
Curriculum areas stressed at each level are those prescribed by the Chicago Board of
Education. The classroom is organized as a cooperative unit as modified by the
Morrison plan.
Student Achievement in second language learning is indicated by improvement in
language arts and ability to communicate in basic Spanish.
The *Parent Advisory Group* met several times in 1972-73; activities included program
planning and implementation assistance in assembly programs and cultural
celebrations.
Evaluation of students' progress is accomplished by regular teacher evaluation and
pre- and post-testing with commercial instruments.

Kosciuszko Bilingual Center
Chicago Board of Education District 6
  CHICAGO, ILLINOIS 60601

Spanish (Mexican American and Puerto Rican)   Second funding year
Grades: K-4; 9 classes, 270 students (135 Mexican American, 135 Puerto Rican).
Staff of 6 bilingual professionals, 4 bilingual paraprofessionals and one clerk paid
from Title VII ESEA funds; 1 bilingual professional and 7 monolingual professionals
paid from Chicago Board of Education funds.
One school: Kosciuszko Elementary.

Staff development activities anticipated for 1973-74 included weekly on-site inservice
training.
Activities in which the *project director* anticipated participating during 1973-74 included project planning and implementation, staff development and community
relations.

Instructional materials used by the project are project-developed and produced, commercially produced, and adapted from commercial material by project personnel. The project has developed materials in the areas of language arts and science. Anticipated materials development for 1973–74 included areas of language arts, science, and Spanish as a second language.

All *content areas* are taught in the non-English (first) language of the student and in English, the second language. English-speaking students are instructed in all areas in Spanish as their understanding of the language increases. Math, language arts, and social studies are taught in both languages simultaneously.

Curriculum areas stressed at each level are language arts. The classroom is organized primarily for team teaching, with small groups and individualized type instruction.

Student achievement in second language learning is measured by city-wide and Title VII tests, as well as teacher observation.

The *Parent Advisory Group* met 8 times during 1972–73; activities included review, planning and evaluation of the program and classroom participation.

Evaluation of students' progress is by teacher-structured tests, teacher observation; city-wide tests and parents' evaluation.

William H. Seward Bilingual Bicultural Parent-Child Preschool Program
Chicago Board of Education Area B, District 26
 CHICAGO, ILLINOIS 60601

Spanish (Mexican American)   Second funding year
Grades: PreK–K; 8 half-day classes, 240 students (80 Anglo American, 160 Mexican American). Students not participating in the project total 831 (269 Anglo American, 562 Mexican American).

Staff of 5 bilingual professionals and 4 bilingual paraprofessionals paid from Title VII ESEA funds; the director, 2 professionals, nurse, counselor and school community representative paid from Chicago Board of Education funds. Funds other than Title VII constitute 10 percent of the 1973–74 project budget.

One school: William H. Seward Elementary.

Staff development activities anticipated for 1973–74 included a school inservice program, visitations, consultation service and university participation.

Activities in which the *project director* anticipated participating included coordinating the program, ordering and processing materials, community involvement and teacher inservice.

Instructional materials used by the project are primarily adapted from commercial material by project personnel. Anticipated materials development for 1973–74 included areas of language, math, and culture. Newsletters, visitations and the public media are used to disseminate information to persons outside the Title VII program.

Content areas taught in Spanish and English are language arts, math, social studies, science, art and music.

Curriculum areas stressed at each level are social studies, neighborhood resources, development of self-concept and proficiency in English and Spanish language, and culture. The classroom is organized primarily for small group and individualized instruction, utilizing the team teaching approach.

Student achievement in second language learning and improvement in self-concept and intercultural interaction is measured by teacher observation and standardized tests.

The *Parent Advisory Council* met 20 times during 1972–73; activities included planning and implementation of program goals and cultural exchange activities.

Evaluation of students' progress is by teacher observation and teacher administered tests, and by the Minnesota Child Development Inventory Test, administered by evaluators from the Department of Government Funded Programs of the Chicago Board of Education.

Montana

Chippewa-Cree Bilingual Education Project
School District No. 87
  BOX ELDER, MONTANA 59521

Cree (Chippewa)   Fourth funding year
Grades: K–3; 2 classes, 172 students (114 Cree Indian, 58 English language dominant).
Staff of 1 administrator, 8 teachers, 7 specialists, 1 evaluator, 7 teacher aides, 1 clerical person. Funding is provided virtually 100 percent by Title VII ESEA.
One school: Rocky Boy Elementary.

Staff development activities anticipated for 1973–74 included preservice for all personnel relative to program objectives, materials and teaching strategies; weekly inservice sessions in conjunction with Northern Montana College in Havre relative to Cree language, culture, teaching techniques, and curriculum development; and inservice sessions in objectives refinement and evaluative design.

Activities in which the *project director* anticipated participating during 1973–74 included supervision and coordination of instructional materials development and evaluation.

Instructional materials used by the project are primarily project-developed and produced. The project has developed a total of 7 Cree readers, written stories, legends, cultural and historical stories, sound filmstrips, bilingual tapes, animal posters, student worksheets and slides. Anticipated materials development during 1973–74 included continued collection on cassette tapes and in written Cree the accounts of legends, lullabies, songs, religious stories and many cultural anecdotes, as well as a Cree-English dictionary and a Cree-English phrase book.

Content areas taught in Cree are language, culture, history and math. English is used in teaching language arts, ESL and science. In an attempt to preserve the Indian culture, other areas are also taught: dancing—for music, motor skills and culture; beading—for color recognition, eye-hand coordination, counting and reading readiness; and dry meat making in the classroom situation. The classes are divided into English language dominant and Cree classes for language instruction.

The *Parent Advisory Group* met monthly during 1972–73; activities included classroom visitations, establishing community goals, and three commemorative dinners—the Little Bear Memorial Feast, which was attended by 300, The Rocky Boy Memorial Feast in April, and a feast commemorating the founding of the settlement.

Evaluation of students' progress is by project-developed instruments and English achievement tests. The interim report was prepared by the Division of Educational Research and Services at the University of Montana at Missoula; program evaluation was performed by an evaluator from Montana State University at Bozeman.

Crow Bilingual Education Project
Hardin School District 17-H
  CROW AGENCY, MONTANA 59022

Crow   Fourth funding year
Grades: K–4; 10 classes, 175 students (57 Anglo American, 118 Crow).
Staff of 2 bilingual professionals, 3 monolingual professionals and 11 bilingual
paraprofessionals paid from Title VII ESEA funds; 12 professionals and 2
paraprofessionals paid from other funds.
One school: Crow Agency Public School.

Staff development activities anticipated for 1973–74 included teacher training—in-
service and courses offered through the Career Opportunity Program and Montana
State University.
Activities in which the *project director* anticipated participating during 1973–74 included development of a Crow Math Curriculum and directing the project.
Instructional materials for the project are primarily project-developed and produced.
The project has developed Crow reading materials and Crow culture and history
lessons. Anticipated materials development for 1973–74 included a Crow reading
program and Crow grammar lessons.
Content areas taught in the non-English (first) language of the student include
spoken Crow and Crow reading. English (the second language) is used in teaching
spoken English and English reading. English-speaking students are taught spoken
Crow history and culture, social studies, math, science and history.
Curriculum areas stressed at the lower levels are oral language activities. Initial
reading material is in the child's dominant language. Culture, language, environment
and math-logic are the four areas of the curriculum being developed. The classroom is
organized primarily for large group instruction in a team teaching situation.
Student achievement in second language learning and academic growth is indicated
by higher gains on oral English tests than those at a similar, non-bilingual, reservation project, and students' scoring an average of the national mean on most sub-
tests of national achievement tests administered. The Crow Historical and Cultural
Commission met regularly during 1972–73 to provide instructional materials and participate in classroom activities. An extensive home visitation program provides interaction and informational feedback for the program.
Evaluation of students' progress is measured by published and project-developed tests
measuring change in language abilities, general reasoning and the affective domain.
An internal evaluator monitors teacher training, curriculum development, parent-
community relations, instruction, management and evaluation.

Northern Cheyenne Bilingual Education Program
Lame Deer Public School District No. 6
  LAME DEER, MONTANA 59043

Cheyenne   Second funding year
Grades: K–1; 8 classes, 120 students (23 Cheyenne Indian, 97 English language
dominant).
Staff of 1 director, 1 linguist, 1 curriculum coordinator, 1 evaluator, 6 teacher aides, 1
community liaison, 1.3 (manhour equivalence) clerical personnel, 1.5 artist and an
audiovisual specialist.

Two schools: Lame Deer Public, St.Labré's Mission School.

Staff development activities anticipated for 1973–74 included inservice lessons on Cheyenne orthography, two curriculum and lesson planning workshops and courses at Concordia College at Busby in teaching methods at the kindergarten level.

Activities in which the *project director* anticipated participating during 1973–74 included program planning and coordination of staff selection, staff evaluation, materials development and program evaluation.

Instructional materials used by the project are project-developed and produced and adapted from commercial materials by project personnel. The project has developed 20 hours of recorded songs and legends, 100 hours of indirect language material, a Cheyenne alphabet, stories for kindergarten and grade 1, an adult workbook for learning the new orthography, and cards and charts for classroom use. Anticipated materials development includes areas of written and oral Cheyenne in science, social studies, math and fine arts.

Curriculum areas are oral and written Cheyenne, and oral English. Content areas are science, language arts, culture and social studies. The classroom is organized primarily by grouping by ability in subject areas.

The *Culture Advisory Board* held monthly meetings during 1972–73; activities included planning and implementing the collection of legends, sayings, and songs. The Policy Advisory Board and the Educational Planning Committee held meetings twice monthly.

Evaluation of students' progress is by means of a locally developed language test and the Peabody Picture Vocabulary Test, with standardized tests administered but used in a minor role. The internal evaluator and a contracted external auditor prepare evaluation reports.

New Jersey

Bilingual Education in a Consortium
Lakewood Board of Education
  LAKEWOOD, NEW JERSEY 08701

Spanish (Puerto Rican, Cuban)   Fourth funding year
Grades: K–4 and 7–10; 23 classes, 685 students (242 Anglo American, 301 Puerto Rican, 4 Portuguese, 43 Black, 95 Cuban). Students in participating schools not participating in the project total 2,999 (1,397 Anglo American, 472 Puerto Rican, 10 Portuguese, 970 Black, 150 Cuban).

Staff of 15 bilingual professionals and 5 bilingual paraprofessionals paid from Title VII ESEA funds; 20 professionals and 4 paraprofessionals paid from Lakewood Board of Education, Title I, and Follow Through funds.

Six schools: Ella G. Clarke (Lakewood), Clifton Avenue (Lakewood), School Number 3 (Paterson), Grover Cleveland J.H.S. (Elizabeth), Jefferson H. S. (Elizabeth), Battin H. S. (Elizabeth).

Staff development activities anticipated for 1973–74 included preservice and inservice sessions and curriculum development.

Activities in which the *project director* anticipated participating in 1973–74 included continued staff development, community participation, field testing of materials and promotion of the bilingual program.

Instructional materials for the project are primarily those adapted from commercial material by project personnel. The project has developed materials in areas of Spanish reading, Spanish and English language arts, social studies (grades 7 and 10), math (7-10), and science (7-10). Anticipated materials development for 1973-74 included Spanish as a second language and continued work in similar areas.

Content areas taught in the non-English (first) language of the student include reading, math, science, social studies and Spanish. Areas taught in English (the second language) are social studies, math, science, reading and typing. English-speaking students are taught language skills and math in Spanish. Social studies, math and science are taught using Spanish and English simultaneously.

Curriculum areas stressed at each level are: K—reading readiness and language; grade 1—reading and language; grades 2-4—reading, language and science; grades 7-10—Spanish, English, and science. The classroom is organized primarily in learning centers (Lakewood), for small group instruction (Paterson), and for large group instruction by subject areas (Elizabeth).

The *Parent Advisory Group* met six times during 1972-73; activities included an open house, cultural celebrations, proposal preparation and implementation, and classroom visitation, observation and participation.

Evaluation of students' progress is by means of a variety of commerical and teacher-made tests; Bernard Cohen Research and Development provides program evaluation.

New Brunswick Bilingual Education—Better Communication
New Brunswick Board of Education
  NEW BRUNSWICK, NEW JERSEY 08901

Spanish (Puerto Rican)   Second funding year
Grades: K-2; 16 classes, 400 students (203 Spanish language dominant, 197 English language dominant).
Staff of 1 administrator, 16 teachers, 3 specialists, 2 pupil personnel workers, 8 teacher aides, 1 community liaison and 1 clerk. Funding other than Title VII ESEA is provided by other federal funds and state funds, and constitutes 60 percent of the 1973-74 project budget.
Four schools: Bayard, Nathan Hale, Washington, Livingston.

Staff development activities anticipated for 1973-74 included a six-week preservice institute to train teachers and paraprofessionals, courses in second language teaching and biculturation instruction, and a series of inservice workshops for the maintenance of skills, development of materials and the carrying out of self evaluation.

Activities in which the *project director* anticipated participating included project planning and coordination of all aspects of the program.

Instructional materials are primarily those adapted from commercial material by project personnel. Monthly materials development workshops were planned for 1973-74. The project has developed units in SSL, bilingual lessons, and ESL—including audiovisual aids, songs, poems and tests.

Content areas taught in combinations of mixed language, foreign language, vernacular and bilingual instruction are reading, language arts, music, art, physical education, social studies, science, arithmetic and cultural instruction.

The *Parent Advisory Group* met monthly during 1972-73; activities included planning, implementation and evaluation of project activities, providing transportation and baby care services to facilitate additional participation, and ESL and SSL four-week courses.

Evaluation of students' progress is by systematic collection and analysis of reliable and valid information on instructional achievement, derived from standardized tests, and based on instructional objectives stated in performance terms; also, on a narrative based on observations. An external evaluator and external auditor provide program evaluation and audit reports.

Project SELL (Spanish English Language Learning)
Union City Board of Education
   UNION CITY, NEW JERSEY 07087

Spanish (Cuban, Puerto Rican)   Fourth funding year
Grades: 1–5; 14 classes, 315 students (35 Anglo American, 245 Cuban, 20 Puerto Rican, 4 Chinese, 11 South American). Students not participating in the project total 767 (167 Anglo American, 483 Cuban, 61 Puerto Rican, 3 Chinese, 2 Black, 51 South American).

Staff of 6 bilingual professionals and 3 bilingual paraprofessionals paid from Title VII ESEA funds; 10 professionals paid from local education agency funds. Funds other than Title VII constitute 50 percent of the 1973–74 project budget.

One school: Roosevelt Elementary.

Staff development activities anticipated for 1973–74 included a five-week summer training institute, seminars, and weekly workshops.

Activities in which the *project coordinators* anticipated participating in 1973–74 included staff development, materials development, community involvement, teacher training and student instruction.

Instructional materials used by the project are primarily commercially produced. The project has developed materials in areas of Spanish and English as second languages, math, social studies and science in Spanish. Anticipated materials development for 1973–74 included areas of previous development as well as Spanish as a second language.

Content areas taught in the non-English (first) language of the student included language arts, math, social studies, science, and health. Areas taught in English included math, music, art, gym, shop and home economics. Spanish as a second language is taught to all English-speaking students. Language arts and math are taught in Spanish and English simultaneously.

Curriculum areas stressed at all levels are fifty percent ESL daily and fifty percent SLA daily. The classroom is organized so that students change rooms at midday for alternate native language and second language instruction.

Student achievement in second language learning is indicated by improved oral and writing ability.

The *Parent Advisory Council* met six times during 1972–73; activities included classroom visitations, adult language classes, Thanksgiving and patriotic celebrations, and program preparation.

Evaluation of students' progress is by means of quarterly project-developed progress tests and pre- and post-testing with the Inter-American Series (CIA) (reading), the Stanford Achievement Test (math), the Boehm Concept Test and the Scamin Self-Concept Test. An external evaluator makes regular visits to all components, reviews test results, materials developed and teacher evaluations, and makes statistical analyses of children's progress.

New Jersey Bilingual Education Program
Vineland Board of Education
VINELAND, NEW JERSEY 08360

Spanish (multiethnic)   Fifth funding year
Grades: K–5; 46 classes, 1,260 students (830 Spanish language dominant, 430 English language dominant).
Staff of 5 administrators, 54 teachers, 14 specialists, 1 evaluator, 9 teacher aides, 4 community liaison workers and 3 clerical personnel. Funds other than Title VII are provided by other federal funds and local funds, and constitute 50 percent of the 1973–74 project budget.
Four schools: P.S. 16 (Jersey City), McKinley (Newark), P.S. 10 (Perth Amboy), Dr. Mennies (Vineland).

Staff development activities anticipated for 1973–74 included a preservice orientation workshop, and inservice one-day workshops each two weeks consisting of lectures by consultants, intervisitations and demonstration classes; including topics of reading, team teaching, languague arts development, arithmetic, social studies and science.
Activities in which the *project director* anticipated participating during 1973–74 included coordination of project administration with the four site principals and liaison with local and federal agencies.
Instructional materials for the project are primarily commercially produced.
Content areas taught in Spanish and English are language arts in the dominant language, and language and reading in the second language, arithmetic, music, physical education, social studies and art. The classroom is organized for instruction in a team teaching situation; with Spanish and English used in the introduction, followed by simultaneous reinforcement.
The *Parent Advisory Group* met monthly during 1972–73. The anticipated parental development program, to include parents and interested persons district-wide, will include areas of The Bilingual Philosophy, The Bilingual Program, Involvement in Local School Issues, Helping My Child in a Bilingual Program, and What Toys Should I Buy My Child?
Evaluation of students' progress during 1973–74 is according to an experimental research design: the New Jersey Bilingual Education Program test instrument will be given to the students in the program and to a control group, in order to provide control group scores. Pre- and post-testing with standardized evaluation measures, a self-concept evaluative measure and observation checklists are used in evaluation. An internal evaluator performs program evaluation, and an external auditor prepares audit reports.

New Mexico

Albuquerque Public Schools Bilingual Bicultural Program
Albuquerque Public Schools
ALBUQUERQUE, NEW MEXICO 87102

Spanish (Mexican American)   Fifth funding year
Grades: K–6; 179 classes, 4,875 students.
Staff of 8 bilingual professionals and 10 bilingual paraprofessionals paid from state funds. Funds other than Title VII constitute 40 percent of the 1973–74 project budget. 179 professionals and 35 paraprofessionals paid from other funds.

Eighteen schools: Coronado, Riverview, Old Town, A. Montoya, Lamesa, Larrazola, East San José, Las Padillas, Five Points, Valle Vista, Mission, Longfellow, San Felipe, Carlos Rey, Lew Wallace, Duranes, Inez, Apache.

Staff development activities anticipated for 1973–74 included a three-week summer training session and a three-hour weekly inservice session.

Activities in which the *project director* anticipated participating included continued teacher training and curriculum development.

Instructional materials for the project are both project-developed and produced and adapted from commercial materials by project personnel. The project has developed materials in areas of social studies, math, science and language arts. Anticipated materials development for 1973–74 was in the areas of previous development. The project regularly produces a newsletter.

Content areas taught in the non-English (first) language of the student include science, math, social studies, language arts and literature. Enrichment activities are taught in English (the second language) and in the non-English second language. All content areas are taught in both languages simultaneously. The open classroom is the primary manner of classroom organization.

Student achievement in ethnic minority and ethnic majority pupils in second language learning is indicated by an average gain of 7 months in a 5-month period.

The *Parent Advisory Group* met 9 times during 1972–73; activities included recommending needed changes in the program and relaying information of the needs of the community.

Evaluation of students' progress is by means of criterion-referenced and pre- and post-testing. The Office of Evaluation of the Albuquerque Public Schools evaluates the program.

Southeastern New Mexico Bilingual Program
Artesia Public Schools
   ARTESIA, NEW MEXICO 88210

Spanish (Mexican American)   Fifth funding year
Grades: K–5; 22 classes, 750 students (226 Anglo American, 496 Mexican American and 28 Black). Students not participating total 2,163 (1,238 Anglo American, 869 Mexican American, 56 Black).

Staff of 6 bilingual professionals and 22 bilingual paraprofessionals paid from Title VII ESEA funds; 16 professionals and 30 volunteers, salaries paid from operational budget funds. Funds other than Title VII constitute 70 pecent of the 1973–74 project budget.

Seven schools: Roselawn, Yucca, Pate R and D, Eddy, Hillcrest, Sunset, Lake Arthur.

Staff development activities anticipated for 1973–74 included individualized instruction and revision of the Criterion-Referenced Skill Charts.

Activities in which the *project director* anticipated participating in 1973–74 included inservice and workshop training and expansion of the project to include all elementary children in the school district.

Instructional materials for the project are primarily those adapted from commercial materials by project personnel. The project has developed materials in areas of self-image, Spanish language arts, science, social studies, multiculturalism, evaluation, all areas of curriculum guidelines, paraprofessional training and criterion-referenced skill charts. Anticipated materials development included expansion of Spanish language arts program and resource materials for all areas of grade 5. Procedures used to disseminate materials to persons outside the Title VII program are displays, the State Department of Education requests, publications and periodic conventional media usage.

Content areas taught in the non-English (first) language of the student and in English (second language) included Spanish and English language arts, science, math, social studies, multiculturalism and Spanish and English as second languages. English-speaking students are taught all areas in Spanish in gradually increased proportion as proficiency develops. Art, music and physical education are taught in Spanish and English simultaneously.

Curriculum areas stressed at each level are K—readiness, grades 1 and 2—reading in dominant language, grade 3—reading in the second language, grades 4 and 5—reading in first and second languages (self-image stressed at levels 1 through 5). The classroom is organized primarily for small groups with individual skill instruction.

Student achievement in reading, language, and arithmetic is measured by a variety of instruments which indicate at least 5 per cent increase annually in most areas.

The *Parent Advisory Group* functions in an advisory capacity; activities include classroom presentations, cultural celebrations, and advisory and volunteer work.

Evaluation of students' progress is by means of pre- and post-testing on standard state-mandated instruments and criterion-referenced tests, and by skill charts according to the project's evaluation design.

New York State

Non-Graded Early Childhood, Bilingual/Bicultural Education Program
Beacon City School District
　BEACON, NEW YORK 12508

Spanish (Puerto Rican)　　　　　　　　　　　　　　　Second funding year
Grades: K–3; 12 classes, 300 students (Puerto Rican).
Staff of 16 professionals, 10 paraprofessionals. (Statistics for 1972–73.)
Three schools: South Avenue, Sargent, J. V. Forrestal.

Staff development activities anticipated for 1973–74 included inservice training sessions for teachers and aides.

Activities in which the *project director* anticipated participating included project administration and coordination of instruction, staff development and evaluation.

Instructional materials used by the project are primarily commercially produced.

Content areas taught in Spanish and English conform to New York State guidelines. The child's dominant language is used for instruction. The classroom is organized for small group instruction, and team teachers are assisted by teacher aides and parent volunteers.

The *Parent Advisory Group* held regularly scheduled meetings during 1972–73; activities included review of the continuation proposal and classroom visitation and volunteer services.

Evaluation of students' progress is by means of standardized tests. The program evaluator and external auditor prepare final evaluation reports.

Bilingual Education Program
Buffalo Board of Education
  BUFFALO, NEW YORK 14201

Spanish (Puerto Rican)   Third funding year
Grades: PreK–4; 12 grades, 193 students (26 Anglo American, 2 Mexican American,
144 Puerto Rican, 6 American Indian, 13 Black, 2 of other ethnic groups).
Staff of 5 bilingual professionals and 7 bilingual paraprofessionals paid from Title
VII ESEA funds; 9 professionals and 6 paraprofessionals paid from Title I and Buf-
falo Board of Education funds. Funds other than Title VII ESEA constitute 60.5 per-
cent of the 1973–74 project budget.
One school: Public School No. 76.

Staff development activities anticipated for 1973–74 included preservice and inservice
sessions, curriculum committees, graduate courses in elementary education and
parent-teacher conferences.
Activities in which the *project director* anticipated participating in 1973–74 included
proposal writing, staff development, parental involvement and project administration.
Instructional materials for the project are primarily commercially produced. The
project has developed materials in areas of Puerto Rican history and culture, math in
Spanish, and a science test. Anticipated materials development for 1973–74 included
areas of Puerto Rican culture and history, with a test, social studies, and a Puerto
Rican culture and history test.
Content areas taught in the non-English (first) language of the student and in English
(the second language) include science, math, language arts and social studies. Spanish
as a second language is used to teach concepts in science, social studies and math.
Curriculum areas stressed at each level are: PreK—motor coordination and self-
concept development; K—motor coordination, auditory and visual perception, math
concepts, language arts concepts and vocabulary; grades 1–4—language arts, math,
social studies, science and Puerto Rican culture. The classroom is organized primarily
for small group instruction (moving towards individualized instruction).
Student achievement in second language learning is measured by the Metropolitan
Achievement Test (Informal Reading Inventory) and the Inter-American Series.
The *Parent Advisory Group* met 20 times in 1972–73; activities included selection of
personnel, proposal recommendations, policy making and student field trips.
Evaluation of students' progress is by means of pre- and post-testing with the
Metropolitan Achievement Tests in Reading and Mathematics, the Inter-American
Spanish Reading Test and teacher-made tests. The program's evaluation design calls
for quarterly instructional evaluation and semi-annual auditor's reports.

Project Advance
North Rockland Central School District
  HAVERSTRAW, NEW YORK 10927

Spanish (Puerto Rican, Dominican)   Third funding year
Grades: K–4; 14 classes, 392 students (112 Anglo American, 1 Mexican American,
198 Puerto Rican, 1 Portuguese, 6 Black, 68 Dominican, 6 South American). Non-
participating students total 1,110 (985 Anglo American, 2 Mexican American, 48
Puerto Rican, 5 Chinese, 34 Black, 32 Dominican, 4 South American).

Staff of 5 bilingual professionals and 5 bilingual paraprofessionals paid from Title VII ESEA funds; 6 bilingual professionals and 6 monolinguals paid from local levy funds. Funds other than Title VII constitute 60 percent of the 1973-74 project budget.

Two schools: Haverstraw (grades K-3), West Haverstraw-Blauvelt (grade 4).

Staff development activities anticipated for 1973-74 included inservice continuation of training in the development and use of materials.

Activities in which the *project director* anticipated participating during 1973-74 included parental involvement in observation and evaluation teams, curriculum development and review of all materials and methods. The local education agency anticipated absorption of bilingual staff, materials and fiscal accounting.

Instructional materials for the project are primarily commercially produced. The project has produced a primary language (Spanish) adaptation to local needs, social studies and cultural materials, and SSL and ESL adaptations. Anticipated materials development for 1973-74 included syllabus materials in Spanish language arts, SSL and ESL, and audio cassettes of language through literature.

Content areas taught in the language of the student are math, science, social studies and health. Areas taught in English and Spanish (second languages) are math, science and social studies.

Curriculum areas stressed at each level are K—culture and readiness, grades 1-2—social studies and science, grade 3—math, social studies and science, grade 4—math, social studies and plants. The classroom is organized primarily in homogeneous groups by language dominance for modified team teaching with bilingual aides.

Student achievement in second language learning is indicated by 50 percent of the students' scoring at average chronological level in language, reading and math.

The *Parent Advisory Group* met 6 times during 1972-73; activities included a foreign language fair, international night, a salute to Santo Domingo, an adult education program and the evaluation team.

Evaluation of students' progress is by pre-, interim and post-testing by the evaluation consultant and teacher-devised progress assessment; Bernard Cohen Research and Development Associates served as program evaluators, making use of results of commercial tests, district guidelines, and a project adaptation of Spanish Curriculum Development Center strand tests in making the final report.

New York City

Public School 25—The Bilingual School
New York City Community School District No. 7
   BRONX, NEW YORK 10455

Spanish (Puerto Rican)   Fifth funding year
Grades: K-6; 30 classes, 763 students (467 Spanish language dominant, 296 English language dominant).

Staff of 31 professionals and 14 paraprofessionals. Funding other than Title VII ESEA is provided by Title I and local funds, and constitutes 15 percent of the 1973-74 project budget.

One school: P.S. 25.

Staff development activities anticipated for 1973-74 included postgraduate courses for teachers at New York University in the areas of language arts, math, applied linguistics, construction, use and interpretation of tests, and oral Spanish.

Activities in which the *project director* anticipated participating during 1973-74 included serving as school principal, administration of the program and coordination of the work of the separate components.

Instructional materials for the project are project-developed and produced and adapted from commercial material by project personnel. The project has developed a curriculum for levels K-2 for social studies in Spanish relevant to the Puerto Rican urban elementary school pupil, and a curriculum for Spanish as a second language for grades 3-6. Anticipated materials development during 1973-74 included a social studies curriculum in Spanish in three levels, and proficiency placement tests in Spanish and English.

Content areas taught in Spanish and English are language arts and the basic skills.

Student achievement in second language learning is measured by standardized tests, interviews and tape recording. The adult education component consists of beginning, intermediate and advanced courses in English as a second language and in Spanish as a second language.

Evaluation of students' progress is by means of monitoring by the project director and teachers, and by the General Ability and Reading Tests of the Inter-American Series. The program is evaluated by the Institute of Research and evaluation of Fordham University's School of Education; Mobicentrics, Inc. prepared the pre-audit report.

Project BEST (Bilingual Education Skills Training)
New York City Board of Education
    BROOKLYN, NEW YORK 11201

Spanish (Puerto Rican)   Fourth funding year
Grades: K-5; 55 classes, 1,680 students (1,300 Puerto Rican, 300 Black, 80 Hispanic).
Staff of 7 bilingual professionals, 1 monolingual professional, 11 bilingual paraprofessionals and 4 secretaries paid from Title VII ESEA funds; 1 professional and 1 secretary-clerk paid from New York State grant funds. Funds other than Title VII provided by tax levy funds, and constitute 75 percent of the 1973-74 project budget.
Ten schools: Community Schools 1, 40 and 116 (Community School District 7); Community Schools 47, 50, 61, 66 and 67 (Community School District 12).

Staff development activities anticipated for 1973-74 included on-site training workshops, classroom visits by the curriculum specialists and a symposium on teaching reading in a bilingual program.

Activities in which the *project director* anticipated participating during 1973-74 included visits to bilingual classes, district meetings, parental activities, membership in the Executive Planning Committee of the Annual Bilingual Conference; and responsibility for the administrative component and fiscal matters.

Instructional materials for the project are primarily commercially produced. The project has developed materials in teacher training, Spanish as a second language, a curriculum implementation model and evaluative instruments. Anticipated materials development for 1973-74 include revision of the instructional objectives for grades

1-5 and preparation of a recipe book through parent workshops. Areyto, the project newspaper, and a brochure are produced by the project.

Content areas taught in Spanish and English are science, math, social studies and experimental reading, with music, arts and crafts, and physical activities taught in the first language of the student. The percentage of instruction in the second language of the student increases to 50 percent by grade 5. Language arts, math and social studies are stressed at each level. The classroom is organized primarily for small group instruction in a team teaching situation.

Student achievement in second language learning and academic progress are measured by standardized tests and objectives lists; results indicate similar gains between project and control group students.

The *Parent Advisory Group* met 4 times during 1972-73; functions included parental input into the coordination of the program throughout the districts involved; regularly scheduled parent workshops are held in each of the participating schools.

Evaluation of students' progress is measured by means of pre- and post-testing with the Inter-American Prueba de Lectura and Test of Reading; student learning objectives are assessed by the teachers. The Bilingual Education Applied Result Unit (BEARU) administers tests and makes program evaluation reports.

Integrated Bilingual Demonstration Project for High Schools
N.Y.C. Board of Education, Office of High Schools
    BROOKLYN, NEW YORK 11201

Spanish (Puerto Rican)   Second funding year
Grades: 9-10; 30 classes, 360 students (250 native speakers of Spanish, 110 native speakers of English). Students not participating total 2,890 (1,866 native speakers of Spanish, 1,024 native speakers of English).
Staff of 6 teachers, 2 administrators, an evaluator, 6 educational assistants, guidance counselor and secretary.
One school: Eastern District High.

Staff development activities anticipated for 1973-74 included inservice sessions for the entire staff, and specialized preservice training from Long Island University.

Activities in which the *project director* anticipated participating included staff development, materials development and adaptation, and coordinating evaluative efforts.

Instructional materials for the project are project-developed and produced and adapted from commercial materials by project personnel. The project has developed teacher-made tests in social studies, math, English, Spanish, and science. A student bilingual publication, El Lorito, is produced at the project.

All *content areas* are taught bilingually. Math, language and social studies are emphasized at each level. Classrooms are organized for individualized instruction with the use of educational assistants.

Student achievement is measured by means of teacher-devised tests and standardized tests such as the Metropolitan Reading Test and Puerto Rican Scale A. Students are programmed individually, and after careful testing they are placed in the class level best suited to their needs.

The *Parent Advisory Group* met monthly during 1972-73; activities included review and informational feedback for the program, field trips, a Puerto Rican Day and holiday celebrations.

Evaluation of students' progress is by means of internal evaluation as well as observations by the Bureau of Educational Research.

Louis D. Brandeis High School Bilingual Program
N.Y.C. Board of Education, Office of High Schools
    BROOKLYN, NEW YORK 11201

Spanish (Puerto Rican), French (Haitian)   Second funding year
Grades: 9–10; 12 classes, 350 students (250 Spanish language dominant, 50 French language dominant, 50 English language dominant).
Staff of 1 administrator, 20 teachers, 2 specialists, 2.2 (manhour equivalence) pupil personnel workers and 1 clerk. Funding other than Title VII, provided by local and state funds, constitutes 60 percent of the 1973–74 project budget.
One school: Louis D. Brandeis High School.

Staff development activities anticipated for 1973–74 included a week-long preservice workshop, project-based monthly inservice training sessions, interproject visitations and graduate level courses for 10 teachers at New York University in teaching bilingual education and language courses.
Activities in which the *project director* anticipated participating during 1973–74 were project administration, coordination of efforts with the principal and assistant principals, and coordination of staff development and evaluation.
Instructional materials for the project are commercially produced and adapted from commercial material by project personnel. Anticipated materials development includes completion of outlines and courses of study in French and Spanish for high school science; history; and English, French and Spanish as second languages. A trilingual newsletter is produced at the project.
Content areas taught in French and Spanish and English are math, science, history, social studies and a second language. Other courses offered at the project are Haitian history, Latin American studies, biology, physical education, Afro-American history, typing and industrial arts.
The *Parent Advisory Group* held general meetings during 1972–73; activities included fund raising for charities, a volunteer tutorial service program, field trips, parent-teacher nights and classroom visitations.
Evaluation of students' progress is by standardized instruments; an external evaluator from the Bureau of Educational Research of the New York City Board of Education performs the program evaluation.

District One Bilingual Program
New York City School District No. 1
    NEW YORK, NEW YORK 10009

Spanish (Puerto Rican)   Third funding year
Grades: K–4; 15 classes, 375 students (300 Puerto Rican, 50 Black, 25 of other ethnic groups). Students not participating total 14,240 (10,500 Puerto Rican, 1,120 Chinese, 2,200 Black, 420 of other ethnic groups).
Staff of 5 bilingual professionals, 2 monolingual professionals and 8 bilingual professionals paid from Title VII ESEA funds; 15 professionals and 2

paraprofessionals paid from Title I and tax levy funds. Funds other than Title VII constitute 60 percent of the 1973–74 project budget.
Three schools: P.S. 20, 63, 134.

Staff development activities anticipated for 1973–74 included college courses toward the M.A. degree in bilingual education and 40 hours of inservice training.
The *project director* anticipated participating in project administrative duties.
Instructional materials used in the project are primarily commercially produced. Anticipated materials and development in 1973–74 included areas of Puerto Rican culture and Spanish enrichment.
Content areas taught in English and Spanish are different for each grade.
All *curriculum areas* are stressed at each level. The classroom is organized primarily for small groups within a classroom according to language for basic skills.
Student achievement in second language learning is measured by project-developed tests. Academic progress during 1972–73 was measured by the Metropolitan Achievement Test in reading in English, and a project-developed instrument for recording Spanish reading level.
The *Parent Advisory Group* met 20 times in 1972–73; activities included organizing subcommittees within each school, preparation for district bilingual conference and screening of teachers for the new year.
Evaluation of students' progress is by means of standardized achievement tests administered by project personnel.

Building Bilingual Bridges
New York City School District No. 2, Manhattan
   NEW YORK, NEW YORK 10002

Chinese, Spanish (multiethnic)   Fifth funding year
Grades: PreK–3; 8 classes, 225 students participating; students in the school total 1,020 (55 Anglo American, 347 Puerto Rican, 514 Chinese, 88 Black, 16 Spanish surnamed).
Staff of 7 bilingual professionals paid from Title VII ESEA funds; 3 paraprofessionals paid from local education agency funds. Funds other than Title VII constitute 50 percent of the 1973–74 project budget.
One school: P.S. 2, Manhattan.

The *project director* anticipated participating in curriculum preparation and staff training during 1973–74. The local education agency anticipated support of PreK, K and first grades.
Instructional materials for the project are primarily project-developed and produced. The project has developed materials in areas of social studies, science, math, language arts and English as a second language. Anticiapted materials development in 1973–74 included areas of previous development.
Content areas taught in the non-English (first) language of the student include social studies, math, science and language arts. Areas taught in English (second language) include those of the first language, reading and English as a second language. English speakers are taught language arts (stories and songs) in a second language. Areas taught in both languages simultaneously are social studies, math, language arts and science.

Student achievement by ethnic minority pupils in second language learning is indicated by results of post-testing with a project-devised ESL test. Academic progress is indicated by post-testing results in areas of storytelling ability in both languages, math and science. Parents of students assisted the project staff in curriculum preparation and testing.

Evaluation of students' progress is by means of objective measurements such as the M.A.T., L.T.L. tests, math, science, ESL and native language tests (criterion reference measures based on the project curriculum). An internal evaluator performs process or formative evaluation (on-going process) and product or summative evaluation (pre- and post-testing procedure).

District 3 Bilingual Program
New York City School District No. 3
  NEW YORK, NEW YORK 10025

Spanish (Puerto Rican), French   Third funding year
Grades: K–4; 12 classes; 360 students.
Staff of 12 professionals. (Statistics from 1972–73).
Ten schools: P.S. 9, 75, 84, 87, 145, 163, 165, 166, 179, and 191.

Staff development activities anticipated for 1973–74 included college courses for teachers and aides.

Activities in which the *project director* anticipated participating during 1973–74 included project administration and coordination of staff development and evaluation.

Instructional materials used by the project are primarily commercially produced.

Content areas taught in Spanish and English conform to New York State guidelines. Classrooms are organized with an open corridor design to encourage maximum pupil interaction, and the opportunity for individualized instruction.

The *Parent Advisory Group* held regularly scheduled meetings during 1972–73. Activities included review of the continuation proposal and classroom visitations.

Evaluation of students' progress is by means of standardized tests. A contracted external auditor performs the independent educational audit.

The Bilingual Mini-School
New York Community School District No. 4
  NEW YORK, NEW YORK 10035

Spanish (Puerto Rican)   Fourth funding year
Grades: 7–8; 6 classes, 160 students (105 Puerto Rican, 1 Portuguese, 32 Black, 1 Italian, 21 Dominican and other Latin American).
Staff of 5 bilingual professionals paid from Title VII ESEA funds; 3 professionals and 5 paraprofessionals paid from learning cooperative and tax levy funds. Funds other than Title VII constitute 12 percent of the 1973–74 project budget.
One school: The Bilingual Mini-School at J.H.S. 45 (Manhattan).

Staff development activities anticipated for 1973–74 included teacher training and curriculum development.

Activities in which the *project director* anticipated participating included staff involvement in administrative functions of the program, curriculum development and higher community participation.

Instructional materials for the project are primarily commercially produced. The project staff has developed a social studies curriculum and a guidance program. Anticipated materials development for 1973–74 included areas of social studies and English as a second language.

Content areas for the non-English (first) language of the student include math, science, Spanish language arts, music, science, shop, typing, social studies and English as a second language. Areas taught in English (second language) include language, social studies, shop, industrial arts, art and music. Spanish as a second language is taught to English speakers.

Curriculum areas vary according to language dominance of the individual group members and their general learning abilities. The classroom is organized for team teaching, small group and individualized instruction.

Student achievement in second language learning is indicated by increase in the number of students receiving high school diplomas instead of certificates, and advanced placement in high school Spanish courses.

The *Parent Advisory Group* met 3 times during 1972–73; activities included project orientation, class trips, participation in guidance and academic activities and advising in the development of the Title VII continuation proposal.

Evaluation of students' progress is by means of initial testing, quarterly report cards, teacher-made and standardized tests. Program evaluation was performed by P.R.C. Metranamics, Inc., by means of analysis of pre- and post-testing devices and quarterly visits.

The Dual-Bilingual Program—District No. 5, Manhattan
New York City Community School District No. 5
  NEW YORK, NEW YORK 10027

Spanish (Puerto Rican), French (Haitian)   Second funding year
Grades: K–3; 21 classes, 615 students (405 Spanish and French language dominant, 210 English language dominant). Students not participating total 10,600 (2,840 Spanish and French language dominant, 7,760 English language dominant).
Staff of 25 professionals and 37 paraprofessionals. Funding other than from Title VII ESEA is provided by Title I state and district funds, and constitutes 78 percent of the 1973–74 project budget.
Eight schools: P.S. 30, 36, 43, 46, 125, 156, 161, Annunciation.

Staff development activities anticipated for 1973–74 included weekly teacher training workshops and involvement of 14 teachers in the bilingual education graduate program of study at New York University.

Activities in which the *project director* anticipated participating during 1973–74 included project administration, materials acquisition, staff recruitment and development, and coordination of evaluation.

Instructional materials for the project are primarily commercially produced. The project produces a bilingual newspaper.

Content areas taught in the non-English (first) language of the student are reading and writing. Spanish, French and English as second languages, history, culture, social studies, reading, health, science and math are taught in a bilingual setting with teacher aides.

The *Parent Advisory Group* met monthly during 1972–73. Activities included open houses, a cultural program, bimonthly classroom visitations, and classroom presentations about the culture of Puerto Rico, Haiti and Africa.

Evaluation of students' progress is by means of the Inter-American Test of General Ability, Sanford Cohen's adaptation of the J. T. Dailey Test, daily logs, and project-developed criterion-referenced tests. Each program component was evaluated by Arawak Consulting Corporation; Alfred J. Morin and Associates prepared the final audit report.

Bilingual Focus for the 70's
New York City Community School District No. 6
 NEW YORK, NEW YORK 10033

Spanish (Puerto Rican)   Third funding year
Grades: K–4; 28 classes, 1,003 students.
Staff of 15 bilingual professionals and 2 non-professionals.
Five schools: St. Elizabeth, P.S. 115, 128, 132, 192 M.

Staff development activities anticipated for 1972–74 included ESL courses at a local university, and the training of a district community resource team by Intelicor to assist in testing and to learn about measurement.
Activities in which the *project director* anticipated participating during 1973–74 included coordinating the activities of project administration, budget, contracts, evaluation, community involvement, conferences, teacher training and instruction.
Instructional materials used by the project are primarily commercially produced.
Content areas taught in Spanish are language arts and social studies (Hispanic culture and history). Areas taught in Spanish and English are language arts, science, math, music, art and health. The classes are organized in conventional classrooms with use of bilingual professional assistance for individualized instruction.
Student achievement in second language learning is measured by interviews, observation and project-developed checklists.
The *Parent Advisory Group* met on a regular basis during 1972–73. Activities included development and implementation of parents and members of the community.
Evaluation of students' progress is by means of pre- and post-testing with the Cooperative Inter-American Test of General Ability and the Boehm Test of Basic Concepts (Spanish or English version). Intelicor performs program evaluation, and Alfred J. Morin and Associates prepare interim and final audit reports.

Oklahoma

Seminole Bilingual Education Program
Strother School District No. 14
 ADA, OKLAHOMA 74820

Seminole   Second funding year
Grades: K–3; 18 classes, 315 students (175 Anglo American, 129 Seminole, 11 Black).
Students not participating total 1,462 (839 Anglo American, 540 Seminole, 83 Black).
Staff of 2 bilingual professionals, 1 monolingual professional, 18 other professional staff, and 20 bilingual paraprofessionals paid from Title VII ESEA funds.
Six schools: Strother, Bowlegs, Justice, Sasakwa, Wolf, Pleasant Grove.

Staff development activities included a workshop in July for teacher and bilingual assistant and monthly workshops.

Activities in which the *project director* anticipated participating during 1973-74 included project and national workshops, tribal meetings and evaluation conferences, and project administration.

Instructional materials for the project are primarily project-developed and produced. The project has developed materials in areas of language, legends, stories, math, social studies, music, coloring books with legends, phonics books, lesson plans and calendars. Anticipated materials development in 1973-74 included all areas of previous development and workbooks in math and language.

Content areas taught in Seminole and in English to all students are math, language, social studies, science, health, and arts and crafts.

Curriculum areas stressed at each level are: K—oral language, math, music and culture; grades 1-3—language, math, social studies, music and culture. The classroom organization varies, but primarily used is the open classroom concept with small groups.

Student achievement in second language learning and academic progress is measured by a wide range of achievement tests and teacher and staff observations.

The *Parent Advisory Group* met 3 times during 1972-73; activities included review of programs, materials, academic progress and plans of the project. Parents contributed efforts and articles for state, local and national bilingual workshops.

Evaluation of students' progress is by means of standardized testing and classroom visitation. Program evaluation is by an external evaluator who develops and implements the project design in cooperation with the staff and project director.

Choctaw Bilingual Education Program
Broken Bow Public Schools
   BROKEN BOW, OKLAHOMA 74728

Choctaw   Fourth funding year
Grades: K-4; 20 classes, 901 students (564 Anglo American, 285 Choctaw, 52 Black). Students not participating total 479 (Anglo American).

Staff of 4 bilingual professionals, 11 professional monolinguals and 28 bilingual paraprofessionals paid from Title VII funds; 27 professionals, 18 paraprofessionals and 1 volunteer, salaries paid from local school district funds. Funds other than Title VII constitute 20 percent of the 1973-74 project budget.

Four schools: Battiest, Broken Bow, Smithville, Wright City.

Staff development activities anticipated for 1973-74 included continuation of a system of monthly workshops.

Activities in which the *project director* anticipated participating included materials development, fiscal duties and evaluation. The local education agency provided facilities for inservice workshops.

Instructional materials for the project are primarily project-developed and produced. The project has developed materials in areas of social studies and English as a second language. Anticipated materials development during 1973-74 included areas of social studies, listening and reading. Public media and a newsletter are used to disseminate project-related materials and information.

Content areas taught in the first and second language simultaneously are math, social studies and language arts.

Curriculum areas stressed at each level are language arts (K–4), social studies (grades 3–4), and math (grades 1–4). The classroom is organized primarily for large group instruction.

Student achievement in second language learning is measured by teacher reports and Michigan Oral Language Tests. Stanford Achievement Tests are used in measuring academic growth.

The *Parent Advisory Group* met 8 times during 1972–73; activities included participation in workshops and review of the program, including consultations and recommendations for change.

Evaluation of students' progress is a continuing process by means of Michigan Oral Language Tests and pre- and post-testing with standardized and locally developed instruments. An auditor serves as program evaluator, making on-site visits in September and June.

Cherokee Bilingual Education Program
Greasy Board of Education
  TAHLEQUAH, OKLAHOMA 74464

Cherokee   Fifth funding year
Grades: K–5; 25 classes, 582 students (374 Cherokee, 208 English language dominant).

Staff of 2 administrators, 25 teachers, 1 language instructor, 4 specialists, 25 teacher aides, 1 community liaison, 2.5 (manhour equivalence) clerical personnel, 1 Cherokee translator. Funding by Title VII ESEA provides virtually 100 percent of the 1973–74 project budget.

Four schools: Greasy School, Lost City School, Tenkiller School, Marble City School.

Staff development activities anticipated for 1973–74 included courses in the Cherokee language in cooperation with Northeastern State College, and a four-week workshop in bilingual education conducted by the project linguist.

Activities in which the *project director* anticipated participating included developing and implementing program goals, staff recruitment, program administration and evaluation.

Instructional materials used by the project include those adapted from commercial material by project personnel, and some which are project-developed and produced. Anticipated materials development includes a measurement device that will be able to determine ability to speak the Cherokee language. A monthly newsletter is produced by the project.

Content areas taught in English are reading, language arts, arithmetic, phonics, music and art. At least one area at each grade level is taught in Cherokee. The classroom is organized for a modified open classroom approach with individualized instruction.

The *Parent Advisory Group* met regularly during 1972–73. Activities included cultural enrichment tours, school visitations, adult education classes, attendance at the drama "Trail of Tears," and contribution of skills and knowledge in construction of cultural materials and development of language materials.

Evaluation of students' progress is by means of pre- and post-testing with standardized achievement tests, and teacher observations. The external auditor prepares interim and final reports; the program evaluation is by the internal evaluator.

Texas

HABLA—Helping Advance Bilingual Learning in Abernathy
Abernathy Independent School District
    ABERNATHY, TEXAS 79311

Spanish (Mexican American)   Fifth funding year
Grades: K-4; 15 classes, 401 students (190 Anglo American, 186 Mexican American, 25 Black). Students not participating total 118 (54 Anglo American, 50 Mexican American, 14 Black).
Staff of 2 bilingual professionals, 13 monolingual professionals and 6 bilingual paraprofessionals paid from Title VII ESEA funds. Funds other than Title VII constitute 56 percent of the 1973–74 project budget.
One school: Abernathy Elementary.

Staff development activities anticipated for 1973–74 included a Spanish extension course for teachers and aides, and inservice meetings.
Activities in which the *project director* anticipated participating in 1973–74 include parental involvement, staff development and the volunteer high school student program for the bilingual elementary program.
Instructional materials for the project are primarily those adapted from commercial material by project personnel. The project has developed bilingual videotapes and guides in the area of language development, math, storytelling and reading readiness. Anticipated materials development in 1973–74 included more videotapes and reading readiness materials.
Content areas taught in English and Spanish to all students are language development, math and reading; social studies is taught in English.
Curriculum areas stressed at each level are language arts and math. The classroom is organized primarily for small group instruction through teacher and aide efforts.
Student achievement in second language learning and academic progress is measured by standard evaluative instruments and teacher observations.
The *Parent Advisory Group* met 8 times in 1972–73; activities included plans for parental involvement and discussion of bilingual methods and evaluative measures.
Evaluation of students' progress is by means of teacher-devised tests and standard evaluative instruments, and performed by a bilingual evaluation team.

Project ABLE
Abilene Independent School District
    ABILENE, TEXAS 79603

Spanish (Mexican American)   Third funding year
Grades: K-4; 25 classes, 639 students (162 Anglo American, 76 Black, 401 Mexican American).

Staff of 1 administrator, 26 teachers, 1 specialist, 1 evaluator, 18 teacher aides, 3 community liaisons, 3 clerical personnel.
Three schools: Woodson Kindergarten, College Heights, Fannin.

Staff development activities anticipated for 1973-74 included a summer preservice workshop in conjunction with Hardin-Simmons University, inservice planning and training sessions.
Activities in which the *project director* anticipated participating included coordination of evaluation, instruction and materials development, and the production of a bilingual newsletter.
Instructional materials for the project are primarily those adapted from commercial material by project personnel. Criterion-referenced tests have been developed and continued work on them is anticipated.
Content areas taught bilingually in English and Spanish are reading readiness, language arts, math concepts and arithmetic, science, social studies, writing and physical education. The Distar reading program is used with reported success by the project.
The *Parent Advisory Group* met monthly during 1972-73; activities included recruitment of additional parents to visit the schools and to help with tutoring and special projects, classroom visitations, setting up and revising project objectives and assisting with student field trips.
Evaluation of students' progress is by means of project-developed criterion-referenced tests and standardized achievement tests. The program is evaluated internally, and audited by a consultant from the University of Texas at Austin.

Bilingual Early Childhood Education Program
Alice Independent School District
  ALICE, TEXAS 78332

Spanish (Mexican American)   Fourth funding year
Grades: K-4; 19 classes, 525 students (523 Mexican American, 2 Black). Students not participating total 1,004 (991 Mexican American, 13 Black).
Staff of 5 bilingual professionals and 13 bilingual paraprofessionals and 2 paraprofessionals paid from local education agency funds; 6 volunteers. Funds other than Title VII constitute 50 percent of the 1973-74 project budget.
Four schools: Mary R. García, Nayer, Sáenz, Salazar.

Staff development activities anticipated for 1973-74 included initiating a new advisory committee, inservice and preservice sessions, and a new Spanish science program for grade 4.
Activities in which the *project director* anticipated participating included personnel recruitment, inservice training, staff evaluation, videotaping, materials acquisition, and public relations presentations on television and radio.
Instructional materials for the project are both project-developed and produced, and adapted from commercial material by project personnel. The project has developed materials in areas of language arts, science and cultural heritage. Anticipated materials developed during 1973-74 included areas of language arts, social studies and science.
Content areas taught in Spanish and English are reading, language, math and science; social studies is taught in English.

Curriculum areas stressed at each level are: K—oral language; grade 1—language and reading; grades 2 and 3—language, reading and math; grade 4—language, reading, math and science. The classroom is organized for both large and small group instruction.

Student achievement in second language learning and academic progress is indicated by grade level achievement derived from test scores.

The *Parent Advisory Group* met 6 times during 1972-73; activities included staging nine bilingual children's programs, appearance on television on a panel discussion, meeting with Title I committee members and volunteer work in the classrooms.

Evaluation of students' progress is by means of a performance objectives checklist and pre- and post-test scores. An internal evaluator and external auditor evaluate the program.

Dissemination Center for Bilingual Bicultural Education
Education Service Center, Region XIII
AUSTIN, TEXAS 78721

This is a special service project serving all Title VII projects.　　　Second funding year
Staff of 6 professionals, 3 paraprofessionals. The Center is one hundred percent federally funded under Title VII of the Elementary and Secondary Education Act of 1965, as amended.

One of the *primary functions* of the Dissemination Center for Bilingual Bicultural Education is the acquisition, editing and publishing of instructional materials relevant to bilingual, bicultural education.

Cartel: Annotated Bibliography of Bilingual Bicultural Materials, published monthly, is designed to serve as an informative listing for educators, librarians and others interested in materials for use in bilingual, bicultural education. A subscription is sent to each program funded under Title VII ESEA. Subscriptions are available to all interested persons and organizations.

Among the *goals of the project* are: determining which project-developed (Title VII ESEA) and other relevant public domain materials are suitable for distribution; reproducing and distributing these materials on the basis of established needs of the projects; surveying instructional materials available commercially in the United States for the purpose of publishing annotated listings of suitable project-developed and commercial materials in all project languages (Cartel). Further goals are the implementation of a feedback system to determine effectiveness with specific target populations of selected materials; collecting, analyzing, and disseminating data on Title VII ESEA projects in progress; and effecting a positive increase in interproject communication throughout the country in order to decrease duplication of effort. The Dissemination Center publishes an annual Guide to Title VII ESEA Bilingual Bicultural Projects in the United States, and listings of bilingual teacher training programs in the states, as well as other informational items where demand is greatest.

A library of relevant materials and information serves as a base for *informational services*. The Center participates actively in pertinent conferences by exhibiting published materials and making frequent presentations regarding its functions and services.

The project is evaluated internally on a monthly basis by an internal evaluator, and reviewed by auditors contracted for by the Office of Education's Division of Bilingual Education.

Region XIII Bilingual Education Program
Education Service Center, Region XIII
 AUSTIN, TEXAS 78721

Spanish (Mexican American)   Fifth funding year
Grades: 1–5; 24 classes, 640 students (39 Anglo American, 589 Mexican American, 12 Black).

Staff of 3 bilingual professionals (administrative) are paid from Title VII ESEA funds; 17 bilingual professionals, 7 monolingual professionals, 9 bilingual paraprofessionals and 3.5 (manhour equivalence) additional staff are paid by the school districts in which the programs operate (not the LEA). The project budget is 100 percent ESEA Title VII.
Four schools: Lockhart Primary and Lockhart Intermediate (Lockhart I.S.D.), Zavala Elementary (Austin I.S.D.), Montopolis Community School (Private).

Staff development activities anticipated for 1973–74 included training in diagnostic and prescriptive techniques for the Spanish and English reading program.
Activities in which the *project director* anticipated participating during 1973–74 include staff development and supervision. The local education agency provides administrative, fiscal and consultative services.
Instructional materials for the project are primarily commercially produced. The project has developed materials in areas of culture, scope and sequence for the Spanish reading program, a parental involvement handbook and annotated bibliographies of materials used in the Region XIII program. Anticipated materials development for 1973–74 include a handbook for administrators, a curriculum guide and bilingual teacher training kit.
Content areas taught in Spanish and English are language arts, reading, math, social studies, science and health.
Curriculum areas stressed at each level are reading, math, social studies and science, with spelling and mechanics of language included at grade 2 and above. Subjects increase in complexity according to grade level. Team teaching, small group instruction, individual instruction, and the Montessori approach are used within the project.
Project participants scored significantly higher on Spanish reading tests at grades 2 through 5 than control group students. Tests of other areas indicated equal scores between the two groups. Both groups held positive attitudes toward both cultures.
The *Parent Advisory Group* met 10 times in 1972–73; activities included a review of and suggestions for the project, a parent education program, classroom assistance, field trips, parties and a newsletter.
Evaluation of students' progress is by pre- and post-testing with published instruments. Evaluation of the instructional program and management is continual; materials evaluation and parental evaluation are semiannual.

To Be Bilingual Is To Be Bicultural
Brownsville Consolidated Independent School District
 BROWNSVILLE, TEXAS 78520

Spanish (Mexican American)   Third funding year
Grades: K–2; 78 classes, 2,272 students (21 Anglo American, 2,251 Mexican American). Students not participating total 1,789 (36 Anglo American, 1,753 Mexican American).

Staff of 4 bilingual professionals and 30 bilingual paraprofessionals paid from Title VII ESEA funds; 26 paraprofessionals paid from Title I funds. Funds other than Title VII constitute 1 percent of the 1973–74 project budget.

Twelve schools: Cromack, Canales, Castañeda, Victoria Heights, Webb, Resaca, Clearwater, Skinner, Longoria, Putegnat, El Jardín, Villanueva.

Staff development activities anticipated for 1973–74 included area meetings and 20 inservice meetings.

Activities in which the *project director* anticipated participating included inservice meetings, project management, evaluation and material development.

Instructional materials for the project are primarily commercially produced. The project has developed materials in areas of social studies, bicultural studies, evaluation and science. Anticipated materials development for 1973–74 included areas of Spanish as a second language, Spanish reading and science. A newsletter is published by the project.

Content areas taught in Spanish and English simultaneously are social studies, science and math.

Curriculum areas stressed at each level are: K—oral ESL and SSL conceptual skills in the first language; grade 1—ESL, Spanish reading, instruction in two languages; grade 2—Spanish reading, English reading, instruction in both languages; bicultural activities are conducted at all levels. The classroom is organized for group teaching and team teaching with monolingual and bilingual teachers.

Student achievement in second language learning and academic progress is measured by locally devised and Spanish/English achievement tests.

The *Parent Advisory Group* met 6 times in 1972–73; activities included classroom observation and review of the proposal, budget, evaluation procedures and materials.

Evaluation of students' progress is by means of pretest in September, monitoring checklist in January and posttest in May. The program evaluator makes use of the process checklist, timeline and classroom observations.

Aprendemos En Dos Idiomas
Corpus Christi Independent School District
   CORPUS CHRISTI, TEXAS 78403

Spanish (Mexican American)   Fourth funding year
Grades: K–3; 22 classes, 560 students (511 Mexican American, 42 Black, 7 Anglo American). Students not participating total 575 (450 Mexican American, 120 Black, 5 Anglo American).

Staff of 25 bilingual professionals and 14 bilingual paraprofessionals paid from Title VII ESEA funds; 1 professional salary paid from Title I, state and local funds; 412 parent volunteers. Funds other than Title VII constitute 72.23 percent of the 1973–74 project budget.

Three schools: Crockett, Evans, Travis.

Staff development activities anticipated for 1973–74 included regional staff development and an inservice meeting with Gulf Coast Title VII projects.

Activities in which the *project director* anticipated participating during 1973–74 included budget negotiations, staff development, inservice, planning sessions, workshops and program administration.

Instructional materials for the project are primarily those adapted from commercial materials by project personnel. The project has developed materials in areas of reading and social studies. Further development is anticipated in the area of reading.

Content areas taught in the non-English (first) language of the student include reading, math, and social studies. Areas taught in English (the second language) include reading, science and health.

Curriculum areas stressed at each level include language arts, reading and math. The classroom is organized for instruction with self-contained classes, individualized and small group instruction, and cooperative and some team teaching.

Student achievement in second language learning is indicated by most students' scoring at grade level on standardized test. Improved self-concept and intercultural interaction is evidenced by the Self Social Constructs Test.

The *Parent Advisory Group* met 6 times in 1972–73. Activities included promoting the project in the community, assisting in mobilizing the community for resources, and meeting with staff to assist in writing the continuation application proposal.

Evaluation of students' progress is by means of pre- and post-testing with teacher-made, standardized and nonstandardized instruments. Evaluation of the program is performed by a Title VII evaluator.

Bilingual Bicultural Education Program
Crystal City Independent School District
  CRYSTAL CITY, TEXAS 78839

Spanish (Mexican American) Third funding year
Grades: K–4; 43 classes, 1,168 students (975 Mexican American, 3 Black, 2 Anglo American, 188 of other ethnic groups).

Staff of 5 bilingual professionals, 1 monolingual professional and 27 bilingual paraprofessionals paid from Title VII funds; 71 professionals, 43 paraprofessionals and 15 volunteers, salaries paid from local, state and other federal funds. Funds other than Title VII constitute 74 percent of the 1973–74 project budget.

Three schools: Zavala (K–2), Airport (grade 3), Grammar (grade 4).

Staff development activities included preservice and inservice training and videotaping of classrooms, with Community Teachers Program members participating.

Activities in which the *project director* anticipated participating during 1973–74 included coordination of meetings and activities with the three principals, preparation of a project brochure, continuation of the monthly newsletter, and coordination and planning of a radio program.

Instructional materials for the project are primarily project-developed and produced. The project has developed guides with sequential units in areas of math, social studies, grammar, writing skills, and vocabulary development in Spanish and English. Anticipated materials development in 1973–74 included word lists, reading materials, resource books for English and science, and a manual with different reading approaches in Spanish.

Content areas taught in the non-English (first) language of the student and in English (the second language) include social studies, math, and language arts, with oral language development stressed in English. English speakers are taught music and SSL in Spanish. Physical education, art and music are taught in both languages simultaneously.

Curriculum areas stressed at each level are Spanish and English language arts, math and social studies. The classroom is organized both for small group instruction with teachers, aides and interns having groups, and for nongraded departmental instruction.

Student achievement in second language learning and academic progress is indicated by improvement on project-developed and achievement tests in math, language and reading.

The *Parent Advisory Group* met 18 times during 1972–73; activities included suggestions concerning the program and the continuation proposal, selection of community teachers program participants, and assistance in classroom and at student programs.

Evaluation of students' progress is by means of pre-, mid- and post-testing with standardized instruments in Spanish and English, and teacher reports each six weeks. The program evaluator collects data and conducts individual and group meetings with teachers.

Bilingual Multicultural Education Program
Dallas Independent School District
    DALLAS, TEXAS 75204

Spanish (Mexican American)   Third funding year
Grades: K–4; 86 classes, 2,162 students (1,645 Mexican American, 240 Anglo American, 2 Oriental, 8 American Indian, 255 Black, 12 of other ethnic groups). Students not participating total 783 (461 Mexican American, 169 Anglo American, 1 Oriental, 8 American Indian, 134 Black, 10 of other ethnic groups).

Staff of 12 non-teaching and 70 teaching, bilingual professionals, 16 monolingual professionals and 2 bilingual paraprofessionals paid from Title VII funds; 6 professionals and 46 paraprofessionals paid from Title I and ESEA Bilingual funds. Funds other than Title VII constitute 50 percent of the 1973–74 project budget.

Ten schools: Gabe P. Allen, Sidney Lanier, Ben Milam, St. Ann, Benito Juárez, Sam Houston, William B. Travis, Fred Douglass, Maple Fawn, St. Mary of Carmel.

Staff development activities anticipated for 1973–74 included preservice sessions, inservice sessions and workshops, and university courses.

Activities in which the *project director* anticipated participating during 1973–74 included coordination of staff development and curriculum development, as well as participation in the evaluation of the four components. The project has developed materials in areas of social studies, Spanish reading, Spanish language arts, music, art, literature and science.

Anticipated *materials development* during 1973–74 included areas of communication skills (Spanish), science, social studies, and aesthetics. A newsletter, ¿Qué Tal? and a program brochure are published by the project.

Content areas taught in the non-English (first language) of the student include reading, social studies, science, aesthetics and math. Core English (ESL) is taught to Spanish speakers. English-speaking students are taught all areas, including SSL.

Curriculum areas stressed at each level are Spanish reading, science, social studies and aesthetics (art, music, literature). The classroom is organized in large groups by language dominance, small groups for reading, and a multi-age group.

Student achievement in second language learning and academic progress is measured by pre- and post-testing with criterion-referenced tests and achievement tests. Pupils' self concepts and peer-group interaction were measured by the "happy-sad" and "academic self" subscales and by the "peer-acceptance/ostracism" sub-scale of the Primary Self Concept Inventory.

The *Parent Advisory Group* met 11 times during 1972–73; activities included recommendations through Meriendas (parent education meetings) and participation in Quiosco (parent center).

Evaluation of students' progress is by means of unit tests at the end of each work unit and pre- and post-testing with language and curriculum-referenced tests. The program analyst and two assistant evaluators develop the evaluative design, administer tests, and interpret data in conjunction with the Department of Research and Evaluation.

Bilingual Education Program
San Felipe—Del Rio Consolidated Independent School District
  DEL RIO, TEXAS 78840

Spanish (Mexican American)   Fifth funding year
Grades: PreK–5; 67 classes, 1,294 students (1,251 Mexican American, 43 Black). Students not participating total 711 (701 Mexican American, 10 Black).

Staff of 14 bilingual paraprofessionals paid from Title VII ESEA funds; 72 professionals, 8 paraprofessionals and 2 volunteers, salaries paid from ESEA and local funds. Funds other than Title VII constitute 60 percent of 1973–74 project budget.

Eight schools: St. Joseph, Sam Houston (Kindergarten); Austin, Lamar, Travis, East Side, North Heights, Memorial (Elementary).

Staff development activities include four all-day workshops and periodic campus meetings.

Activities in which the *project director* anticipated participating during 1973–74 include state meetings and project administration.

Instructional materials for the project are primarily those adapted from commercial material by project personnel.

Content areas taught in the non-English (first) language of the student include reading, math, social studies and fine arts. All content areas are taught in English. English-speaking students are taught reading, fine arts and social studies in Spanish.

Curriculum areas stressed at each level are reading, math, social studies and fine arts. The classroom is organized for instruction primarily in module and self-contained classrooms.

Student achievement in second language learning is indicated by 70 percent of ethnic minority students' scoring 41 percent or better in English and Spanish, and 80 percent of ethnic majority students' scoring 51 percent or better in English on achievement tests.

The *Parent Advisory Group* met 9 times during 1972–73; activities included special instruction to parents, making teaching aids for classroom use, demonstrations on aspects of culture and a volunteer aide program.

Evaluation of students' progress is by means of Pruebas de Fin de Año, Stanford Achievement tests, the Peabody Picture Vocabulary Test, teacher evaluations and questionnaires. An internal evaluator performs project evaluation.

Edinburg Bilingual Program
Edinburg Consolidated Independent School District
EDINBURG, TEXAS 78539

Spanish (Mexican American)   Fourth funding year
Grades: K–5; 49 classes, 1,620 students (1,460 Mexican American, 160 of other
ethnic groups). Students not participating total 2,114 (1,875 Mexican American, 239
of other ethnic groups).
Staff of 5 bilingual professionals, 1 monolingual professional and 15 bilingual paraprofessionals paid from Title VII funds; 49 professionals and 34 paraprofessionals
paid from Title I—Migrant, C.O.P., and Title I—Regular funds. Funds other than
Title VII constitute 80 pecent of the 1973–74 project budget.
Six schools: Austin, Travis, Jefferson, Lee, Lamar, Hargill.

Staff development activities anticipated for 1973–74 included monthly inservice
training and videotaping of selected Title VII classes.
Activities in which the *project director* anticipated participating during 1973–74 included implementation of program, staff development, tests and instructional
materials development, and writing of the proposal. The local education agency expects to participate through materials development, field trips and evaluation instruments.
Instructional materials for the project are primarily project-developed and produced.
The project has developed materials in areas of language arts, science and social
studies. Anticipated materials development in 1973–74 included curriculum guides
for SSL and areas of cultural awareness and math.
Content areas taught in Spanish and English are math, science, social studies and
language arts, with SSL taught to English speakers. All *content areas* are stressed at
each level. The classroom is organized primarily for small group instruction.
Student achievement in second language learning and academic progress is indicated
by fewer retainees, an increased number of parents who desire for their children to
participate in the project, and of principals asking for expansion of the program on
their campus.
The *Parent Advisory Group* met 4 times during 1972–73; activities included explanation of program and implementation, discussion of the proposal and liaison aide
visitations.
Evaluation of students' progress is by means of locally devised language and unit tests
and commercial tests in English and Spanish. An internal evaluator performs ongoing
and final evaluations.

Project Alma
El Paso Independent School District
EL PASO, TEXAS 79925

Spanish (Mexican American)   Fourth funding year
Grades: K–4; 47 classes, 1,414 students (Mexican American). Non-participating
students total 287 (Mexican American).
Staff of 43 bilingual professionals, 4 monolingual professionals and 18 bilingual paraprofessionals paid from Title VII funds; 3 paraprofessionals and 5 volunteers, salaries
paid from local education agency funds. Funds other than Title VII constitute 80 percent of the 1973–74 project budget.

Three schools: Aoy, Hart, Roosevelt.

Staff development activities anticipated for 1973–74 included a preservice workshop and continuous inservice training.

Activities in which the *project director* anticipated participating during 1973–74 included staff development, testing and evaluation, and coordination of parental involvement and materials development.

Instructional materials for the project are primarily those adapted from commercial materials by project personnel. The project has developed materials in areas of music, art and math. Anticipated materials development during 1973–74 included areas of social studies, science and health. A newsletter is published by the project.

Content areas taught in Spanish are reading, social studies, music, art, health and science. Content areas taught in English are language, reading, arithmetic and spelling.

All *curriculum areas* are stressed at each level. The classroom is organized primarily for small group instruction.

The *Parent Advisory Group* met 11 times in 1972–73; activities included discussion of the program and recommendations, a classroom volunteer program and student field trips.

Evaluation of students' progress is by means of TOBE and CAT tests administered in September and May. An internal evaluator performs program evaluation.

Programa En Dos Lenguas
Fort Worth Independent School District
    FORT WORTH, TEXAS 76133

Spanish (Mexican American)   Fifth funding year
Grades: PreK–5; 99 classes, 2,906 students (775 Anglo American, 2,131 Mexican American).
Staff of 15 bilingual professionals, 1 administrator.
Eight schools: Charles Nash, M. G. Ellis, H. V. Helbing, Washington Heights, Circle Park, Denver Avenue, Brooklyn Heights, Worth Heights.

Staff development activities anticipated for 1973–74 included teacher workshops.

Activities in which the *project director* anticipated participating during 1973–74 included the teacher workshops, visiting and evaluating classrooms, and evaluating the implementation of the bilingual program.

Instructional materials for the project are project-developed and produced, and adapted from commercial materials by project personnel. The project has developed curriculum units for levels PreK and K, social studies units for grades 2 and 3, and reading tests and a reading continuum in Spanish. Anticipated materials development in 1973–74 included units for Kindergarten, and in social studies for grades 1–3; social studies guides for PreK, and a Spanish reading continuum.

Content areas taught in Spanish are SSL, language arts, math, social studies, reading and writing. Areas taught in English are ESL, basal reading, English readiness, math, writing and spelling.

All *curriculum areas* are stressed at each level, including music and art. The classroom is organized for large group instruction in a team teaching situation and for small group reading classes.

Student achievement in second language learning and academic progress is indicated by a mean of better than .05 on Stanford Achievement, Iowa Test of Basic Skills, TOBE and Peabody tests.

The *Parent Advisory Group* met 11 times during 1972–73; activities included a cinco de mayo program, classroom visitations and suggestions to the program's director.

Evaluation of students' progress is by means of pre-testing—in September with the Peabody, Stanford Binet, and Iowa tests, and post-testing in May with the Inter-American Series and TOBE tests. An internal evaluator provides program evaluation.

Early Childhood Learning Center Bilingual Program
Galveston Independent School District
GALVESTON, TEXAS 77550

Spanish (Mexican American)   Fourth funding year
Grades: PreK (3 and 4 years old); 4 classes, 97 students (6 Anglo American, 73 Mexican American, 15 Black, 3 of other ethnic groups).

Staff of 4 bilingual professionals and 6 bilingual paraprofessionals paid from Title VII ESEA funds; 4 professionals and 5 paraprofessionals paid from M.F.P. and Moody Foundation funds. Funds other than Title VII constitute 60 percent of the 1973–74 project budget.

One school: Early Childhood Learning Center.

Staff development activities anticipated for 1973–74 included inservice workshops, attendance at conferences, and visitation at bilingual schools.

Activities in which the *project director* anticipated participating during 1973–74 included staff and program development, state and international meetings, observation of classrooms and parental involvement.

Instructional materials used by the project are primarily commercially produced. The project is in the process of developing a supplementary curriculum.

Content areas taught in Spanish and English are visual, auditory, motor, language, ideas and concepts.

Curriculum areas stressed at each level are visual, auditory, motor, ideas and concepts, language, directed learning centers: science, dramatic play, art and reading fun. The classroom is organized for team teaching instruction with directed learning centers utilized by both Level I and Level II classrooms.

Student achievement in second language learning is measured by the Tests of Basic Experience (English and Spanish editions). Academic progress is measured by the TOBE, the Pre-School Attainment Record, the Minnesota Intelligence Test, the Oseretsky Tests of Motor Proficiency and Mastery Tests of the S.E.D.L. Curriculum.

The *Parent Advisory Group* met monthly during the school year; activities included a videotape program and the bilingual parent committee project.

Evaluation of students' progress is by means of unit and mastery tests administered at frequent intervals, and group process is measured by testing four random groups in four testing periods during the year. An external auditor provided interim and final educational audit reports, conducting on-site visits and analysis of testing results.

Bilingual Education Program
Houston Independent School District
HOUSTON, TEXAS 77027

Spanish (Mexican American)   Fifth funding year
Grades: K–12; 49 classes, 1,300 students (21 Anglo American, 1,175 Mexican American, 102 Black, 2 of other ethnic groups). Students not participating total 6,911 (387 Anglo American, 3,097 Mexican American, 22 Chinese, 3,405 Black).

Staff of 12 bilingual professionals, 2 monolingual professionals and 11.5 bilingual paraprofessionals paid from Title VII ESEA funds; 42 professionals and 11.5 paraprofessionals paid from local and state funds. Funds other than Title VII constitute 65 percent of the 1973-74 project budget.
Ten schools: Anson Jones, Bruce, Crawford, Lamar, Looscan, Ross, Ryan and Sherman Elementary Schools, Marshall Junior High School, Jefferson Davis High School.

Staff development activities anticipated for 1973-74 included preservice and inservice training for teachers and teacher aides.
Activities in which the *project director* anticipated participating during 1973-74 included staff development and administrative management. The local education agency purchases materials and provides salaries and stipends for teachers and teacher aides of the program.
Instructional materials are project-developed and produced, commercially produced and adapted from commercial material by project personnel. The project has developed materials in content areas for Kindergarten, a Spanish reading program for all levels, math, a supplement to Mis Primeras Letras, an Affective Domain Rating Scale, a Cognitive Domain Rating Scale, and a Spanish reading test. Anticipated materials development for 1973-74 included a Spanish resource book and a bilingual book about Texas history.
All *content areas* are taught in Spanish and English; the English dominant student is brought in from other classrooms to participate in Spanish language instruction in reading, writing and spelling.
All *curriculum areas* are stressed at each level. The classroom is organized primarily for small group and individualized teaching; the bilingual teacher and teacher aide use a variety of approaches.
The *Parent Advisory Group* met twice during 1972-73; the individual schools met at least once a month. The bilingual staff participates by informing the parents of the status of the program. The board is given an opportunity to meet to discuss instruction, inservice, curriculum development, dissemination and evaluation.
Evaluation of students' progress is by means of the Cognitive Rating Scale (project-developed), administered on a quarterly basis; the program is evaluated by pre- and post-testing in addition to the ongoing process evaluation.

Hacia Nuevos Horizontes
La Joya Independent School District
LA JOYA, TEXAS 78560

Spanish (Mexican American)   Fifth funding year
Grades: K-7; 55 classes, 1,553 students (15 Anglo American, 1,538 Mexican American).
Staff of 3 bilingual professionals and 19 bilingual paraprofessionals paid from Title VII ESEA funds; 55 professionals and 10 volunteers, salaries paid from other funds.
Three schools: Memorial Elementary, John F. Kennedy Elementary, Nellie Schooner Junior High School.

Staff development activities anticipated for 1973-74 included a workshop for volunteering mothers of students and inservice training sessions.
Activities in which the *project director* anticipated participating during 1973-74 included supervision of classrooms, testing and evaluation, parental involvement and staff meetings.

Instructional materials are project-developed and produced, commercially produced, and adapted from commercial materials by project personnel. The project has developed materials in areas of American and Mexican holidays, music, folk tales and curriculum guides. Anticipated materials development for 1973-74 included resource books on Mexican and American holidays, short stories and a book about Mexican American culture.

Content areas taught in Spanish and English are math, history, science, language, art and music.

Curriculum areas stressed at each level are: K-2—English and Spanish oral language, vowels, consonants, math, health, social studies and reading; grades 3-7—reading, math, science, history, social habits, language and physical education. The classroom is organized for large group instruction (part of the time in a team teaching situation) and for small group instruction.

Student achievement in second language learning and academic progress is indicated by results of pre- and post-testing with English and Spanish achievement tests.

The *Parent Advisory Group* met 4 times in 1972-73; activities included dissemination of program information to the community, a work session on budget and proposal for continuation, and volunteer classroom assistance.

Evaluation of students' progress is by means of published and project-devised instruments; an educational evaluator prepares a pre- and post-test report and provides the program evaluation.

United Bilingual Education Project
United Independent School District
   LAREDO, TEXAS 78040

Spanish (Mexican American)   Fifth funding year
Grades: 3-6; 35 classes, 1,403 students (512 Anglo American, 891 Mexican American).

Staff of 6 bilingual professionals and 3 bilingual paraprofessionals paid from Title VII ESEA funds; 29 professionals and 7 paraprofessionals paid from other funds; 5 volunteers. Title VII funds constitute virtually all of the 1973-74 project budget.

Four schools: Nye, Clark, United Intermediate, Mary Help of Christians Catholic.

Staff development activities anticipated for 1973-74 included inservice training and development of materials.

Activities in which the *project director* anticipated participating during 1973-74 included inservice training, community involvement, materials development and serving as consultant to other districts.

Instructional materials for the project are primarily project-developed and produced. The project has developed materials in areas of Spanish reading and Spanish language arts, materials for teacher inservice training, and Spanish testing materials. Materials development anticipated for 1973-74 included areas of oral language development, reading, and Spanish language usage.

All *content areas* are taught in Spanish and English concurrently. The sixth grade program is departmentalized.

Curriculum areas stressed at each level are language arts, social studies, science and math in K-5, and bilingual language in grade 6. The classroom is organized primarily in a team teaching situation; students are taught bilingually through structured lessons, and learning is enriched through the learning center approach.

Student achievement in second language learning is indicated by minority students showing a +8 and a +1.1 achievement growth in reading and language; majority culture students improved from 40 to 47 percent correct answers. Results on achievement tests indicate 7 months or more growth in 3 skill areas.

The *Parent Advisory Group* met 4 times during 1972-73; activities included promoting the program throughout the community, serving as volunteers in the classrooms, and assisting in materials development.

Evaluation of students' progress is by means of project-developed Spanish achievement tests and the C.T.B.S. achievement test administered in September and April, and informal audiotaping of students in October and May. The bilingual staff performs program evaluation.

McAllen Bilingual Education Program
McAllen Independent School District
  McALLEN, TEXAS 78501

Spanish (Mexican American)   Fifth funding year
Grades: 1-5; 40 classes, 1,066 students (1,016 Mexican American, 50 Anglo American). Students not participating total 1,072 (952 Mexican American, 4 Black, 116 Anglo American).

Staff of 5 bilingual professionals, 3 secretaries and 7 bilingual aides paid from Title VII ESEA funds; 40 teachers and 6 aides paid from local education agency, state and Title I funds. Funds other than Title VII constitute 29 percent of the 1973-74 project budget.

Six schools: Alvarez, Bonham, Sam Houston, Thigpen, Wilson, Zavala.

Staff development activities anticipated for 1973-74 included a preservice workshop, monthly inservice sessions, a Saturday workshop each month and visitations to other schools.

Activities in which the *project director* anticipated participating during 1973-74 included staff development, attending meetings, writing a curriculum and visiting classrooms.

Instructional materials for the project are primarily those adapted from commercial materials by project personnel. The project has developed materials in areas of culture, literature and SSL. Anticipated materials development for 1973-74 include the areas of culture and literature of the Rio Grande Valley, Mexico and Spain, and ESL for grades 1-3. A semiannual newsletter is published by the project.

Content areas taught in the non-English (first) language of the student include self concept, math, science, reading, social studies, fine arts, literature, culture and grammar. Areas taught in English are reading, language arts, science, math and social studies. Conversational Spanish is taught to English speakers.

Curriculum areas stressed at each level are: grade 1—self concept, math, reading and social studies; grades 2 and 3—social studies and reading; grades 4 and 5—reading, literature, culture and grammar. The classroom is organized primarily for small group instruction.

Student achievement in second language learning and academic progress is measured by the California Achievement Test, Inter-American Series tests, language samples and social studies and geography tests.

The *Parent Advisory Group* met monthly during 1972–73; activities included discussion of the program and making suggestions, visiting the classrooms, assisting in the classrooms, and serving as chaperones on field trips.

Evaluation of students' progress is by means of pre- and post-testing with locally developed tests of oral English and Spanish, self concept and social studies; the California Achievement Test for English reading, math and language arts; and the Prueba de Lectura of the Inter-American Series for Spanish reading.

Better Education through Bilingualism
Edgewood Independent School District
SAN ANTONIO, TEXAS 78237

Spanish (Mexican American) Fifth funding year
Grades: 1–5; 98 classes, 2,355 students (5 Anglo American, 2,335 Mexican American, 15 Black). Students not participating total 3,415 (388 Anglo American, 2,328 Mexican American, 699 Black).

Staff of 8 bilingual professionals and 40 bilingual paraprofessionals paid from Title VII ESEA funds; 189 professionals, 74 paraprofessionals and 100 volunteers, salaries paid from other federal funds, local funds, and state funds. Funds other than Title VII constitute 73 percent of the 1973–74 project budget.

Fourteen schools: Burleson, Cenizo Park, Coronado, Edgewood, Emma Frey, Gardendale, Guerra, H. B. González, H. K. Williams, Las Palmas, L. B. Johnson, Loma Park, Roosevelt, Stafford.

Staff development activities anticipated for 1973–74 included videotaping for self evaluation, demonstrations on implementing the project-developed curriculum, classroom management, needs assessment for inservice, new teachers' orientation and competencies development.

Activities in which the *project director* anticipated participating during 1973–74 include coordination of exchange teaching between bilingual and monolingual teachers, coordination of Title VII activities with the regular program, expansion of the program into grade 5, and teacher and parent training sessions.

Instructional materials for the project are primarily project-developed and produced. The project has developed materials in areas of language arts, social studies and math in Spanish. Anticipated materials development during 1973–74 included Spanish language arts for grades 4 and 5, math for grades 1–3 in conjunction with the Experimental Schools Project (E.S.P.), and social studies for grades 1–5 with the E.S.P.

Content areas taught in Spanish and English are language arts, math, social studies and science.

Curriculum areas stressed at each level are: grades 1 and 2—second language oral and written development; grades 1–5—content areas including language arts, math, social studies and science. The classroom is organized primarily for small group instruction and a one-to-one teaching basis using paraprofessionals and teacher aides.

Student achievement in second language learning is measured with the Linguistic Capacity Index for grade one (pre- and post-tests), and the Stanford Achievement Test for grades 2–4 (post-test).

Parent and community involvement activities include community-wide meetings throughout the year. Senators Joe Bernal and Henry B. González, the Title VII director, the special education director, the curriculum specialist, a board member, and the evaluator gave presentations. Other activities included nutrition and crochet classes, newsletters, classroom participation and cultural events.

Evaluation of students' progress is by means of standardized tests in a pre- and post-testing schedule. The program evaluator prepares the interim report in January and the final report in July.

Proyecto Bilingüe Intercultural
San Antonio Independent School District
  SAN ANTONIO, TEXAS 78207

Spanish (Mexican American)   Fifth funding year
Grades: K-1 and 6-7; 35 classes, 974 students (6 Anglo American, 966 Mexican American, 1 Chinese, 1 Black).

Staff of 3 bilingual professionals and 2 bilingual paraprofessionals paid from Title VII ESEA funds; 5 professionals and 3 paraprofessionals paid from local funds. Funds other than Title VII constitute 10 percent of the 1973-74 project budget.

Twenty-two schools within the San Antonio Independent School District participate in the project.

Staff development activities anticipated for 1973-74 included a series of one-day teacher workshops.

Activities in which the *project director* anticipated participating during 1973-74 included development and field-testing of materials, and implementation of a summative evaluation design for the multimedia project.

Instructional materials for the project are primarily project-developed and produced. The project has developed a Multimedia Learning System for levels K-1 which includes social studies and English and Spanish language arts, as well as J.S.C.D.P. instructional units for grades 6 and 7 in Texas history, math, science, social studies, and Spanish and English language arts. Anticipated materials development for 1973-74 included development and production of 30 J.S.C.D.P. units in all content areas for grades 6 and 7.

Content areas taught in the non-English (first) language of the student are social studies and reading; ESL, social studies, math and science are taught in English (the second language).

Curriculum areas stressed at each level are social studies and reading in K-3, and all content areas in grades 6 and 7. The classroom is organized for use of the interest centers concept by bilingual teachers for large and small group instruction, and small group instruction and individualized instruction with monolingual teachers, bilingual aides and interns.

The *Parent Advisory Group* participated through classroom visitations, reading and reviewing the Title VII proposal, and making recommendations to the director in the areas of planning, implementation, and evaluation of the program.

Evaluation of students' progress is by means of pre- and post-testing, with individual testing conducted with commercial and locally prepared instruments. The evaluation division of the San Antonio Independent School District administers an ongoing evaluation design of the management process.

Bibliography of
Selected References

General
Bibliographical Resources

A basic bibliographical resource is William F. Mackey, *International Bibliography on Bilingualism* (Quebec: Les Presses de l'Université Laval, 1972), which is a computer printout of an alphabetized and indexed checklist of 11,006 titles. Reference also should be made to Einar Haugen, *Bilingualism in the Americas: A Bibliography and Reference Guide* (Tuscaloosa, Ala: University of Alabama Press, 1965), and the valuable bibliographies in Theodore Andersson and Mildred Boyer, *Bilingual Schooling in the United States,* 2 vols. (Austin, Tex.: Southwest Educational Development Laboratory, 1970).

Major sources of continuing information are the CAL/ERIC Clearinghouse on Languages and Linguistics which is operated by the Center for Applied Linguistics (1611 North Kent Street, Arlington, Va., 22209); and the Dissemination and Assessment Center for Bilingual Education (6504 Tracor Lane, Austin, Tex., 78721) whose *Cartel: Annotated Bibliography of Bilingual Bicultural Materials* is a monthly listing providing project personnel with information about relevant materials in bilingual/bicultural education for their programs. Reference should be made to the publications catalog of the Georgetown University School of Languages and Linguistics (Washington, D.C., 20057), *e.g.,* sociolinguistics, general linguistics, and the school's "Working Papers on Languages and Linguistics" and "Round Table on Languages and Linguistics."

A variety of publications is available from the TESOL (Teachers of English to Speakers of Other Languages) Central Office (455 Nevils Building, Georgetown University, Washington, D.C. 20057). A valuable retrospective resource is Virginia F. Allen and Sidney Forman, *English as a Second Language: A Comprehensive Bibliography* (New York: Columbia University, Teachers College Press, 1966) which is a listing by subject categories of the special collection (English As a Foreign or Second Language) in the Teachers College Library. Newbury House Publishers (68 Middle Road, Rowley, Mass. 01969) is a specialized resource of materials in applied linguistics, sociolinguistics, and bilingual education texts.

A number of journals should be consulted; particularly useful are *Florida FL Reporter; Human Organization; Journal of Verbal Learning and Verbal Behavior; Language Learning; Linguistic Reporter; The Modern Language Journal;* and *TESOL Quarterly.*

In the areas of poverty, socioeconomic disadvantagement, the equality of educational opportunity and related concerns, reference may be made to Francesco Cordasco et al., *The Equality of Educational Opportunity: A Bibliography of Selected References* (Totowa, N.J.: Rowman and Littlefield, 1973); Francesco Cordasco (ed.), *Toward Equal Educational Opportunity: The Report of the Select Committee on*

Equal Educational Opportunity, U.S. Senate (New York: AMS Press, 1974), particularly Part V (Education of Language Minorities); and to Francesco Cordasco and David Alloway (eds.), "Poverty in America: Economic Inequality, New Ideologies, and the Search for Educational Opportunity," *Journal of Human Relations* vol. 20 pp. 234–396 3rd Quarter, 1972 [special issue] which includes articles on poverty contexts, minority responses to oppression, racial caste systems, the assimilation of Mexicans, and the educational neglect of black, Puerto Rican, and Portuguese children.

Special note should be made of Harold B. Allen's *A Survey of the Teaching of English to Non-English Speakers in the United States* (Champaign, Ill.: National Council of Teachers of English, 1966). Known generally as the TENES report, Dr. Allen's data are still very useful. In a class by themselves are the valuable explorations of Basil Bernstein of the effect of class relationships upon the institutionalizing of elaborated codes in the school, e.g., Basil Bernstein, *Class, Codes and Control* [vol. I: *Theoretical Studies Towards a Sociology of Language;* vol. II: *Applied Studies Towards a Sociology of Language;* vol. III: *Towards a Theory of Educational Transmissions*] (London: Routledge & Kegan Paul, 1973–75). Important bibliographical studies of the Center for Applied Linguistics should be noted: *A Bibliography of American Doctoral Dissertations in Linguistics, 1900–1964* (1968); *Reference List of Materials for English as a Second Language* (three parts, 1964, 1966, 1969); *Spanish and English of United States Hispanos: A Critical, Annotated, Linguistic Bibliography* (1975); and for native American Indian languages, the Center's *A Survey of the Current Teaching of North American Indian Languages in the United States and Canada* (1975). The Center has also published a *Vietnamese Refugee Education Series* (1975) which includes phrasebooks, cross-cultural materials, an annotated bibliography, a personnel-resources directory, and a colloquium on the Vietnamese language.

In a class by itself is the invaluable repository of documents which form the congressional bilingual education hearings out of which derived the enactment of the federal Bilingual Education Act as Title VII of the Elementary and Secondary Education Act (see Appendix A: An Overview of Court Decisions and Legislation Affecting Bilingual Education): *Hearings before the Special Subcommittee on Bilingual Education of the Committee on Labor and Public Welfare on S. 428, Parts 1–2,* 2 vols., 90th Cong., 1st Sess., 1967, and *Hearings before the General Subcommittee on Education of the Committee on Education and Labor on H.R. 9840 and H.R. 10224,* 90th Cong., 1st Sess., 1967.

A guide to much of the literature of social reform in American education which directly relates to the non-English-speaking child and his social milieu is conveniently available in Francesco Cordasco, "Social Reform in American Education: A Bibliography of Selected References," *Bulletin of Bibliography,* vol. 33, pp. 105–110, April/June 1976. This should be supplemented by reference to Dorothy Christiansen, *Bilingualism: Teaching Spanish Speaking Students* (New York: Center for Urban Education, 1969), a valuable bibliographical handlist.

A miscellanea of other titles are of value. A profile of doctoral dissertations on a large American minority community is available in Remigio U. Pane, "Doctoral Dissertations on the Italian American Experience Completed in the United States and Canadian Universities, 1908–1974," *International Migration Review,* vol. 9, pp. 545–556, Winter 1975. Many of the dissertations deal directly with bilingual/bicultural education, e.g., Walburga Von Raffler, *Studies in Italian-English Bilingualism* (Indiana University, 1953); and Herman C. Axelrod, *Bilingual Background and Its Relation to Certain Aspects of Character and Personality of*

Elementary School Children (Yeshiva University, 1952), a study of more than 1,200 children of Italian, Jewish, and Polish origin in public schools in the New York City area. Two state documents of special value are Diego Castellanos, *Perspective: The Hispanic Experience in New Jersey Schools* (Trenton: New Jersey State Department of Education, 1972); and *Bilingual/Bicultural Education—A Privilege or a Right?* (Chicago: Illinois State Advisory Committee to the U. S. Commission on Civil Rights, 1974). Of the multitude of materials issued by the New York City Board of Education addressed to the needs of the non-English-speaking child, *The Puerto Rican Study, 1953–1957* (see the 1972 reissue of the study in the entry for J. Cayce Morrison) has continuing value. A million dollars was expended on the study and its ancillary guides, but it has largely been neglected.

Bibliography

Aarons, Alfred C., Barbara Y. Gordon, and William A. Stewart (eds.): "Linguistic-Cultural Differences and American Education," *Florida FL Reporter,* vol. 7, 1969 [special anthology issue].

Abrahams, Roger D. and Rudolph C. Troike (eds.): *Language and Cultural Diversity in American Education* (Englewood Cliffs, N.J.: Prentice-Hall, 1972).

Adkins, Dorothy C.: *Cross-Cultural Comparisons of the Motivation of Young Children To Achieve in School* (1971). [ERIC ED 60 053]

———, F. D. Payne, and B. L. Ballif: "Motivation Factor Scores and Response Set Scores for 10 Ethnic Cultural Groups of Preschool Children," *American Educational Research Journal,* vol. 9, pp. 557-572, 1972.

Agheyisi, Rebecca and Joshua A. Fishman: "Language Attitude Studies: A Brief Survey of Methodological Approaches," *Anthropological Linguistics,* vol. 12, pp. 137-157, 1970.

Ainsworth, Len and Gay Alford: *Responsive Environment Program for Spanish-American Children* [Evaluation Report, 1971–72] (Lubbock, Tex.: Adobe Educational Services, 1972). [ERIC ED 068 219]

Alatis, James E. (ed.): *Bilingualism and Language Contact: Anthropological, Linguistic, Psychological, and Sociological Aspects,* Monograph Series on Languages and Linguistics no. 23 (Washington: Georgetown University Press, 1970).

Alexander, David J. and Alfonso Nava: *A Public Policy Analysis of Bilingual Education in California* (San Francisco: R & E Research Associates, 1976).

Alfaro, Manuel R., Jr., and Homer C. Hawkins: *The Chicano Migrant Child,* (1972). [ERIC ED 072 900]

Allen, Harold B. and Russel N. Campbell: *Teaching English as a Second Language: A Book of Readings,* 2d ed. (New York: McGraw-Hill, 1972).

Alloway, David N. and Francesco Cordasco: *Minorities and the American City: A Sociological Primer for Educators* (New York: McKay, 1970).

Altus, David M.: *American Indian Education: A Selected Bibliography,* supplement no. 2 (Washington: Superintendent of Documents, U.S. Government Printing Office, 1971). [ERIC ED 58 980]

Anastasi, Anne and Cruz de Jesus: "Language Development and Nonverbal IQ of Puerto Rican Children in New York City," *Journal of Abnormal and Social Psychology,* vol. 48, pp. 357-366, 1953.

Anderson, Nels (ed.): *Studies in Multilingualism* (Leiden, The Netherlands: Brill, 1969).

Andersson, Theodore: "Bilingual Education: The American Experience," *The Modern Language Journal,* vol. 55, pp. 427-440, November 1971.

——— and Mildred Boyer: *Bilingual Schooling in the United States,* 2 vols. (Austin, Tex.: Southwest Educational Development Laboratory, 1970).

345

Anisfeld, Moshe: *Language and Cognition in the Young Child* (1965). [ERIC ED 019 636]

Aquino, Federico: "La Identidad Puertorriqueña y la Educación," *Quimbamba* [Bilingual Education Quarterly], June 1972.

Arciniega, T. A.: *The Urban Mexican-American: A Socio-Cultural Profile* (Austin, Tex.: Southwest Educational Development Center, 1971).

Arndt, Richard: *La Fortalecita: A Study of Low-Income [Urban] Mexican-Americans and Implications for Education,* unpublished dissertation, University of New Mexico, 1970.

Arnold, Richard D. and Thommasine H. Taylor: "Mexican-Americans and Language Learning," *Childhood Education,* vol. 46, pp. 149–154, 1969.

[Aspira]: *Hemos Trabajado Bien: A Report on the First National Conference of Puerto Ricans, Mexican-Americans and Educators on the Special Educational Needs of Puerto Rican Youth* (New York: Aspira, 1968).

Barclay, Lisa F. K.: *The Comparative Efficacies of Spanish, English, and Bilingual Cognitive Verbal Instruction with Mexican-American Head Start Children* [Final Report] (1969). [ERIC ED 030 473]

Barik, H. C. and M. Swain: *Bilingual Education Project: Interim Report on the Spring 1972 Testing Programme* (Toronto: Ontario Institute for Studies in Education, 1972).

Barker, George C.: "Social Functions of Language in a Mexican-American Community," *Acta Americana,* vol. 5, pp. 185–202, 1947.

Barnes, F.: *A Comparative Study of the Mental Ability of Indian Children,* M.A. thesis, Stanford University, 1955.

Bebeau, D. E.: "Administration of a TOEFL Test to Sioux Indian High School Students," *Journal of American Indian Education,* vol. 9, pp. 7–16, 1969.

Bernal, Ernest M.: *Concept-Learning Among Anglo, Black and Mexican-American Children Using Facilitation Strategies and Bilingual Techniques,* unpublished dissertation, University of Texas at Austin, 1971.

Bernbaum, Marcia: *Early Childhood Programs for Non-English Speaking Children* (Albany: The State Education Department, SUNY, 1972).

Biglin, J. E. et al.: *A Study of Parental Attitudes and Values Towards Education on the Navajo and Hopi Reservations. Part I: A Summary of the Literature* (1971). [ERIC ED 62 070 77]

"Bilingualism," *The Center Forum,* vol. 4, 1969. [Entire issue devoted to programs and related matters.]

"Bilingualism and the Bilingual Child—A Symposium," *Modern Language Journal,* vol. 49, March–April 1965.

Bongers, Lael Shannon: *A Developmental Study of Time Perception and Time Perspective in Three Cultural Groups: Anglo-American, Indian-American and Mexican-American,* unpublished dissertation, UCLA, 1971.

Bortin, Barbara H.: *Bilingual Education Program Evaluation Report, Milwaukee Public Schools, 1969–70* (1970). [ERIC ED 708]

Brannon, J. B.: "A Comparison of Syntactic Structures in the Speech of Three and Four Year Old Children," *Language and Speech,* vol. 11, pp. 171–181, 1968.

Bright, William (ed.): *Sociolinguistics: Proceedings of the UCLA Sociolinguistics Conference, 1964* (The Hague: Mouton, 1966).

Brisk, M. E.: *The Spanish Syntax of the Pre-School Spanish American: The Case of New Mexican Five-Year-Old Children,* unpublished dissertation, University of New Mexico, 1972.

Broman, Betty: "The Spanish-Speaking Five Year Old," *Childhood Education,* vol. 41, pp. 362–364, 1972.

Brooks, R., L. Brandt and M. Wiener: "Differential Response to Two Communication Channels: Socioeconomic Class Differences in Response to Verbal Reinforcers Communicated with and without Tonal Inflection," *Child Development,* vol. 40, pp. 453–470, 1969.

Brophy, J. E.: "Mothers as Teachers of Their Own Preschool Children: The Influence of Socioeconomic Status and Task Structure on Teaching Specificity," *Child Development,* vol. 41, pp. 79–94, 1970.

Brown, Marie L. S.: *The Effect of Ethnicity on Visual-Perceptual Skills Related to Reading Readiness,* unpublished dissertation, University of Colorado, 1971.

Brown, Roger: *A First Language: The Early Stages* (Cambridge, Mass.: Harvard, 1973).

———— and Ursula Bellugi: "Three Processes in the Child's Acquisition of Syntax," *Language and Learning,* special issue of *Harvard Educational Review,* vol. 34, pp. 133–151, 1964.

Brussel, Charles B.: *Disadvantaged Mexican-American Children and Early Educational Experience* (1968). [ERIC ED 30 517]

Bryson, Juanita: *Comparison of Bilingual vs. Single Language Instruction in Concept Learning in Mexican-American Four Year Olds* (1970). [ERIC ED 062 043]

Bucklin, L. Brice: *Anglo and Latin: The Cultural Difference* (1970). [ERIC ED 44 977]

Bureau of Indian Affairs: *Bilingual Education for American Indians* (Washington: Bureau of Indian Affairs, 1971).

————: *A Kindergarten Curriculum Guide for Indian Children: A Bilingual-Bicultural Approach* (1970). [ERIC ED 65 236]

Burger, Henry C.: *Ethno-Pedagogy: A Manual in Cultural Sensitivity with Techniques for Improving Cross-Cultural Teaching by Fitting Ethnic Patterns* (Albuquerque, N.M.: SWCEL, 1968).

Burma, John H.: "A Comparison of the Mexican-American Subculture with the Oscar Lewis Poverty Model," in J. H. Burma (ed.), *Mexican-Americans in the United States* (Cambridge, Mass.: Schenkman, 1970), pp. 17–28.

————: *Spanish-Speaking Groups in the United States* (Detroit: Blaine Ethridge, 1974; originally Duke, 1954).

———— (ed.): *Mexican-Americans in the United States* (Cambridge, Mass.: Schenkman, 1970).

Burt, Marina K. and Heidi C. Dulay (eds.): *New Directions in Second Language Learning, Teaching, and Bilingual Education* (Washington: Georgetown University Press, 1975). [TESOL]

Canedo, Oscar Octavio: *Performance of Mexican-American Students on a Test of Verbal Intelligence,* unpublished dissertation, International University, 1972.

Cannon, Garland: "Bilingual Problems and Developments in the United States," *PMLA,* vol. 86, pp. 452–458, 1971.

Cárdenas, Blandina and José A. Cárdenas: "Chicano—Bright Eyes, Bilingual, Brown, and Beautiful," *Today's Education* [NEA Journal], pp. 49–51, February 1973.

Cárdenas, René: *Three Critical Factors That Inhibit Acculturation of Mexican-Americans,* unpublished dissertation, University of California, Berkeley, 1970.

Carrow, Elizabeth: "Auditory Comprehension of English by Monolingual and Bilingual Preschool Children," *Journal of Speech and Hearing Research,* vol. 15, pp. 407–412, 1972.

————: "Comprehension of English and Spanish by Preschool Mexican-American Children, *Modern Language Journal,* vol. 55, pp. 299–306, 1971.

Carrow, Sister Mary Arthur: "The Development of Auditory Comprehension of Language Structure in Children," *Journal of Speech and Hearing Disorders,* vol. 33, pp. 105–108, 1968.

Castañeda, Alfredo et al.: *New Approaches to Bilingual, Bicultural Education* (Austin, Tex.: Dissemination and Assessment Center for Bilingual Education, 1975).

Caudill, William and Lois Frost: *A Comparison of Maternal Care and Infant Behavior in Japanese-American, American, and Japanese Families* (1971). [ERIC ED 57 153]

Cazden, Courtney B.: "The Hunt for the Independent Variables," in Renira Huxley and Elizabeth Ingram (eds.), *Language Acquisition Models and Methods* (New York: Academic, 1971), pp. 41–49.

———· "The Situation: A Neglected Source of Social Class Differences in Language Use," *Journal of Social Issues,* vol. 26, pp. 35–59, 1970.

———: "Subcultural Differences in Child Language," *Merrill-Palmer Quarterly*, vol. 12, pp. 185–219, 1966.

——— (ed.): *Language in Early Childhood Education* (Washington: National Association for the Education of Young Children, 1972).

——— and Vera John: "Learning in American Indian Children," in *Styles of Learning among American Indians: An Outline for Research* (Washington: Center for Applied Linguistics, 1968).

———, ———, and Dell Hymes (eds.): *Functions of Language in the Classroom* (New York: Teachers College, 1972).

[Center for Applied Linguistics]: *Recommendations for Language Policy in Indian Education* (Arlington, Va.: Center for Applied Linguistics, 1973).

[———]: *Styles of Learning among American Indians: An Outline for Research* (Washington: Center for Applied Linguistics, 1968).

Chafe, Wallace L.: "Estimates Regarding the Present Speakers of North American Indian Languages," *International Journal of American Linguistics*, vol. 28, pp. 162–171, 1962.

Chilcott, John H. et al.: *Handbook for Pima and Maricopa Indian Teacher Aides,* (1970). [ERIC ED 44 221]

Ching, D. C.: "Reading, Language Development, and the Bilingual Child: An Annotated Bibliography," *Elementary English*, vol. 46, pp. 622–628, 1969.

Chomsky, Carol: *The Acquisition of Syntax in Children from Five to Ten* (Cambridge, Mass.: M.I.T., 1969).

Christian, Chester C. and John M. Sharp: "Bilingualism in a Pluralistic Society," in Dale Lange and Charles James (eds.), *The ACTFL Review of Foreign Language Education*, vol. 4 (Skokie, Ill.: National Textbook, 1972), pp. 341–375.

Christiansen, T. and G. Livermore: "A Comparison of Anglo-American and Spanish-American Children on the WISC," *Journal of Social Psychology*, vol. 81. pp. 1–14, 1970.

Christopherson, Paul: *Second-Language Learning: Myth and Reality* (London: Penguin, 1973).

Cintrón de Crespo, Patria: *Puerto Rican Women Teachers in New York, Self-Perception and Work Adjustment as Perceived in Themselves and by Others* [unpublished doctoral dissertation](New York: Teachers College, 1965).

Cohen, Andrew D.: *A Sociolinguistic Approach to Bilingual Education* (Rowley, Mass.: Newbury House, 1975).

Cohen, R., G. Fraenkel, and J. Brewer: "Implications for 'Culture Conflict' from a Semantic Feature Analysis of the Lexicon of the Hard Core Poor," *Linguistics*, vol. 44, pp. 11–21, 1968.

Cole, H. J. : *A Comparison of Associative Learning Rates of Indian and White Adolescents*, unpublished dissertation, University of Oklahoma, 1971.

Cole, Michael and Jerome S. Bruner: "Cultural Differences and Inferences about Psychological Processes," *American Psychologist*, October 1971.

Coleman, James: *Equality of Educational Opportunity* (Washington: U. S. Government Printing Office, 1966).

Coombs, L. Madison: *The Indian Student Is Not Low Man on the Totem Pole* (Lawrence, Kans.: Haskell Institute Press, 1972).

Cooper, James G.: *Perception of Self and Others as a Function of Ethnic Group Membership* (1971). [ERIC ED 57 965]

Cooper, R. L.: "Two Contextualized Measures of Degree of Bilingualism," *Modern Language Journal*, vol. 53, pp. 172–178, 1969.

Cordasco, Francesco: "Another View of Poverty: Oscar Lewis' *La Vida,*" *Phylon: The Atlanta Review of Race & Culture*, vol. 29, pp. 88–92, Spring 1968.

————: "The Challenge of the Non-English Speaking Child in the American School," *School & Society*, vol. 96, pp. 198–201, March 30, 1968.

————: "The Children of Columbus: Recent Works on the Italian-American Experience," *Phylon*, vol. 4, pp. 295–298, September 1973.

————: "The Children of Immigrants in Schools: Historical Analogues of Educational Deprivation," *Journal of Negro Education*, vol. 42, pp. 45–53, Winter 1973.

————: "Educational Enlightenment out of Texas: Toward Bilingualism," *Teachers College Record*, vol. 72. pp. 608–612, May 1970. see also, F. Cordasco: "The Bilingual Education Act," *Phi Delta Kappan*, October 1969.

————: *Immigrant Children in American Schools: A Classified and Annotated Bibliography. With Selected Source Documents* (New York: A. M. Kelley, Publishers, 1976).

————: *The Italian American Experience: An Annotated and classified Bibliographical Guide, With Selected Publications of the Casa Italiana Educational Bureau* (New York: Burt Franklin, 1974).

————: *Italians in the United States: A Bibliography of Reports, Texts, Critical Studies and Related Materials* (New York: Oriole Editions, 1972).

————: *Jacob Riis Revisited: Poverty and the Slum in Another Era,* (New York: Doubleday, 1968). [Immigrant children and the schools]

————: "Leonard Covello and the Community School," *School & Society*, vol. 98, pp. 290–299, Summer 1970.

————: "The New Bedford Project for Non-English Speaking Children," *Journal of Human Relations*, vol. 20, pp. 326–334, 3rd Quarter, 1972. [New Bedford, Mass., Portuguese community.]

————: "Nights in the Gardens of East Harlem: Patricia Sexton's East Harlem," *Journal of Negro Education*, vol. 34, pp. 450–451, Fall 1965.

————: "Puerto Rican Pupils and American Education," *School & Society*, vol. 95, pp. 116–119, February 18, 1967.

————: *Puerto Ricans on the Mainland,* The Balch Institute Historical Reading Lists, no. 24 (Philadelphia: The Balch Institute, 1976).

————: "Puerto Ricans on the Mainland: The Educational Experience, *Journal of Human Relations*, vol. 20, pp. 344–378, 3rd Quarter, 1972.

————: "Social Reform in American Education: A Bibliography of Selected References," *Bulletin of Bibliography*, vol. 33 pp. 105–110 (April-June 1976). (Immigrant children and contemporary context)

————: "Spanish-Speaking Children in American Schools," *International Migration Review*, vol. 9, pp. 379–382, Fall 1975. Also, with some change, *Intellect*, vol. 104, pp. 242–243, December 1975.

————: "Teaching the Puerto Rican Experience," in James A. Banks (ed.), *Teaching Ethnic Studies: Concepts and Strategies* (Washington: Council for the Social Studies, 1973), pp. 226–253.

————: (advis. ed.): *The Italian American Experience*, 39 vols. (New York: Arno/New York Times, 1975).

———— (ed.): *The Italian Community and Its Language in the United States. The Annual Reports of the Italian Teachers Association* (Totowa, N.J.: Rowman and Littlefield, 1975). [Reports of the New York City Italian Teachers Association, 1921-1938.] See review essay by Joseph G. Fucilla: *Italian Americana*, vol. 2, pp. 101–107, Autumn 1975.

———— (advis. ed.): *The Puerto Rican Experience,* 33 vols. (New York: Arno/New York Times, 1975).

—— (ed.): *Studies in Italian American Social History. Essays in Honor of Leonard Covello* (Totowa, N.J.: Rowman and Littlefield, 1975).

—— et al.: *Puerto Ricans on the United States Mainland: A Bibliography of Reports, Texts, Critical Studies and Related Materials* (Totowa, N.J.: Rowman and Littlefield, 1972).

—— and Eugene Bucchioni: *The Italians: Social Backgrounds of an American Group* (New York: A. M. Kelley, Publishers, 1974).

—— and ——: *The Puerto Rican Community and Its Children on the Mainland: A Sourcebook for Teachers, Social Workers and Other Professionals* (Metuchen, N.J.: Scarecrow Press, 1972).

—— and ——: *The Puerto Rican Experience: A Sociological Sourcebook* (Totowa, N.J.: Littlefield, Adams, 1973).

—— and ——: "A Staff Institute for Teachers of Puerto Rican Students," *School & Society*, vol. 99, Summer 1972.

—— and Leonard Covello: *Studies of Puerto Rican Children in American Schools: A Preliminary Bibliography* (New York: Department of Labor, Migration Division, Commonwealth of Puerto Rico, 1967). Also in *Education Libraries Bulletin*, Institute of Education, University of London, no. 31, pp. 7–33, Spring 1968. And in *Journal of Human Relations*, vol. 16, pp. 264–285, 1968.

—— and Rocco Galattioto: "Ethnic Displacement in the Interstitial Community: The East Harlem (New York City) Experience," *Phylon*, vol. 31, pp. 302–312, Fall. 1970. [Italians, Jews, and Puerto Ricans]

——, Maurie Hillson, and Henry A. Bullock (eds.): *The School in the Social Order: A Sociological Introduction to Educational Understanding* (Scranton, Pa.: International Textbook, 1970).

Cornejo, Ricardo: "The Acquisition of Lexicon in the Speech of Bilingual Children," in Paul Turner (ed.), *Bilingualism in the South West* (Tucson: University of Arizona Press, 1973), pp. 67–93.

——: *Bilingualism: Study of the Lexicon of the Five-Year-Old Spanish-Speaking Children of Texas*, unpublished dissertation, University of Texas at Austin, 1969.

Cortés, Carlos E. (advis. ed.): *The Mexican American*, 21 vols. (New York: Arno/New York Times, 1974).

Covello, Leonard: "Bilingualism: Our Untapped National Resource," *American Unity Magazine*, September–October 1960. Also in *La Prensa* [Spanish text], January 20, 1960.

——: "A High School and Its Immigrant Community," *Journal of Educational Sociology*, vol. 9, pp. 333–346, February 1936. [Benjamin Franklin High School, East Harlem, New York City.]

——: "Language as a Factor in Integration and Assimilation," *Modern Language Journal*, February 1939.

——: "Language Usage in Italian Families," *Atlantica*, October–November 1934; part II, December 1934.

—— : *The Social Background of the Italo-American School Child: A Study of the Southern Italian Family Mores and Their Effect on the School Situation in Italy and America*, edited and with an introduction by F. Cordasco (Leiden, The Netherlands: Brill, 1967; Totowa, N.J.: Rowman and Littlefield, 1972).

Crossland, F.: *Minority Access to College* [Ford Foundation report] (New York: Schocken Books, 1971).

Darcy, N. T.: "Bilingualism and the Measurement of Intelligence: Review of a Decade of Research," *Journal of Genetic Psychology*, vol. 103, pp. 259–282, 1963

Davidson, M. Ruth: *A Comparative Pilot Study of Two First-Grade Programs for Culturally-Deprived Mexican-American Children*, unpublished dissertation, University of Texas at Austin, 1967.

Del Campo, Philip E.: *An Analysis of Selected Features in the Acculturation Process of the Mexican-American School Child*, unpublished dissertation, International University, 1970.

Denzin, G. K.: "Genesis of Self in Early Childhood," *Social Quarterly*, vol. 13, pp. 291-314, 1972.

Department of Education and Science: *Bilingualism in Education* (London: H. M. Stationery Office, 1965).

Dickeman, Mildren: "The Integrity of the Cherokee Student," in Eleanor Leacock (ed.), *The Culture of Poverty: A Critique* (New York: Simon & Schuster, 1971), pp. 140-179.

Diebold, A. Richard, Jr.: *The Consequences of Early Bilingualism in Cognitive Development and Personality Formation* (1966). [ERIC ED 020 491]

Dielman, T. E.: "Childrearing Antecedents of Early School Child Personality Factors," *Journal of Marriage and the Family*, vol. 34, pp. 431-436, 1972.

Di Lorenzo, L. G. and R. Salter: "Evaluative Study of Prekindergarten Programs for Educationally Disadvantaged Children: Followup and Replication," *Exceptional Children*, vol. 34, pp. 111-119, 1968.

Donofrio, R. M.: *Situations and Language: A Socio-Linguistic Investigation* [Final report] (Washington: National Center for Research and Development, 1972). [ERIC ED 168 236]

Doob, C. F.: "Family Background and Peer Group Development in a Puerto Rican District," *Sociological Quarterly*, vol. 11, pp. 523-532, 1970.

Drach, Kerry, Ben Kobashigawa, Carol Pfuderer, and Dan Slobin: *The Structure of Linguistic Input to Children*, Working Paper no. 14, Language Behavior Research Lab. (Berkeley: University of California Press, 1969).

Drake, Diana: "Empowering Children through Bilingual/Bicultural Education," *Educational Forum*, vol. 40, pp. 199-204, January 1976.

Dulay, Heidi C.: "Goofing: An Indicator of Children's Second Language Learning Strategies," *Language Learning*, vol. 22, pp. 235-252, 1972.

Dumont, Robert V., Jr.: "Learning English and How To Be Silent: Studies in Sioux and Cherokee Classrooms," in C. B. Cazden et al. (eds), *Functions of Language in the Classroom* (New York: Teachers College, 1972), pp. 344-369.

———— and Murry L. Wax: "Cherokee School Society and the Intercultural Classroom," *Human Organization*, vol. 28, pp. 217-226, 1969.

Duphiney, Lorna: *Oriental-Americans: An Annotated Bibliography* (1972). [ERIC ED 60 136]

Dwyer, R. C. et al.: "Evaluation of Effectiveness of a Problem-Based Preschool Compensatory Program," *Journal of Educational Research*, vol. 66, pp. 153-156, 1972.

Dyke, R. B. and H. A. Witkin: "Family Experiences Related to the Development of Differentiation in Children," *Child Development*, vol. 36, pp. 21-55, 1965.

Early Childhood and School-Age Intensive Education Program: Evaluation of the ESEA Compensatory Education Program of the San Francisco Unified School District, 1968-69 Evaluation Report, San Francisco Unified School District (1970). [ERIC ED 041 066]

Eastman, Clyde: *Assessing Cultural Change in North-Central New Mexico* (1972). [ERIC ED 63 070]

Edelman, Martin: "The Contextualization of School Children's Bilingualism," *Modern Language Journal*, vol. 53, pp. 179-182, 1969.

Edwards, J. and C. Stern: "Comparison of Three Intervention Programs with Disadvantaged Preschool Children," *Journal of Special Education*, vol. 4, pp. 205-214, 1970.

Eggan, Dorothy: "Instruction and Affect in Hopi Cultural Continuity," *Southwestern Journal of Anthropology*, vol. 12, pp. 347-370, 1956.

Engle, Patricia L.: *The Use of Vernacular Languages in Education. Language Medium in Early School Years for Minority Language Groups*, Bilingual Education Series no. 3 (Washington: Center for Applied Linguistics, 1975).

————: *The Use of the Vernacular Languages in Education: Revisited*, a literature review prepared for the Ford Foundation Office of Mexico, Central America and the Caribbean, 1973. (Mimeo)

Epstein, Erwin (ed.): *Politics and Education in Puerto Rico* (Metuchen, N.J.: Scarecrow Press, 1970).

Ervin-Tripp, Susan: *Becoming a Bilingual* (1968). [ERIC ED 018 786]

———— : *Language Acquisition and Communicative Choice* (Stanford: Stanford, 1973).

Evans, J. S.: *Word-Pair Discrimination and Imitation Abilities of Preschool Economically-Disadvantaged Native-Spanish-Speaking Children*, unpublished dissertation, University of Texas at Austin, 1971.

———— and T. E. Bangs: "Effects of Preschool Language Training on Later Academic Achievement," *Journal of Learning Disabilities*, vol. 5, pp. 585–592, 1972.

Farmer, G. L.: *Education: The Dilemma of the Spanish-Surname American* (Los Angeles: University of Southern California Press, 1968).

Fedder, Ruth and Jacqueline Gabaldon: *No Longer Deprived: The Use of Minority Cultures and Languages in the Education of Disadvantaged Children and Their Teachers* (New York: Teachers College, 1970).

Feldman, Carol F.: *Concept Formation in Children: A Study Using Nonsense Stimuli and Free-Sort Task* (1969). [ERIC ED 031 306]

———— and M. Shen: "Some Language-Related Cognitive Advantages of Bilingual Five-Year-Olds," *Journal of Genetic Psychology*, vol. 118, pp. 235–244, 1971.

Feldman, David H.: *The Fixed-Sequence Hypothesis: Ethnic Differences in the Development of Spatial Reasoning* (1969). [ERIC ED 33 476]

Finnocchiaro, Mary: *Teaching English as a Second Language*, rev. ed. (New York: Harper & Row, 1969).

Fisher, John C.: "Bilingualism in Puerto Rico: A History of Frustration," *The English Record*, vol. 21, pp. 19–24, April 1971.

Fishman, Joshua A.: *Bilingual Education: An International Sociological Perspective* (Rowley, Mass.: Newbury House, 1976).

————: "The Implications of Bilingualism for Language Teaching and Language Learning," in Albert Valdman (ed.), *Trends in Language Teaching* (New York: McGraw-Hill, 1966), pp. 121–132.

————: *Language and Nationalism* (Rowley, Mass.: Newbury House, 1973).

————: *Language Loyalty in the United States* (The Hague: Mouton, 1966).

————: "The Measurement and Description of Widespread and Relatively Stable Bilingualism," *Modern Language Journal*, vol. 53, pp. 153–156, 1969.

————: "The Politics of Bilingual Education," in James E. Alatis (ed.), *Bilingualism and Language Contact* [Georgetown University Round Table on Languages and Linguistics, 1970] (Washington: Georgetown University Press, 1970), pp. 47–58.

————: "A Sociolinguistic Census of a Bilingual Neighborhood," *American Journal of Sociology*, vol. 75, pp. 323–339, 1969.

————: *Sociolinguistics: A Brief Introduction* (Rowley, Mass.: Newbury House, 1971).

———— (ed.): *Readings in the Sociology of Language* (The Hague: Mouton, 1968).

———— et al.: "Bilingualism in the Barrio," *Modern Language Journal*, vol. 53, March–April 1969.

———— et al. (eds.): *Language Problems of Developing Nations* (New York: Wiley, 1968).

———— et al. (eds.): "Problems of Bilingualism," *The Journal of Social Issues*, vol. 23, April 1967.

————and Heriberto Casiano: "Puerto Ricans in Our Press," *Modern Language Journal*, vol. 53, pp. 157–162, 1969.

————, Robert L. Cooper, and Roxana Ma (eds.): *Bilingualism in the Barrio*, Language Science Monographs no. 7, Indiana University (The Hague: Mouton, 1971).

———— and John Lovas: "Bilingual Education in a Sociolinguistic Perspective," *TESOL Quarterly*, vol. 4, September 1970.

Fitzpatrick, Joseph: *Puerto Rican Americans: The Meaning of Migration to the Mainland* (Englewood Cliffs, N.J.: Prentice-Hall, 1971).

Francescato, G.: "Theoretical and Practical Aspects of Child Bilingualism," *Lingua Stile*, vol. 4, 1969.

Freed, S. A. and R. S. Freed: "Technique for Studying Role Behavior," *Ethnology*, vol. 10, pp. 107–121, 1971.

Gaarder, A. Bruce: "Bilingual Education: Central Questions and Concerns," *New York University Quarterly*, vol. 6, pp. 2–6, Summer 1975.

————: *Essays on Bilingual Schooling in the United States* (Rowley, Mass.: Newbury House, 1976).

————: "The First Seventy-Six Bilingual Education Projects," in James E. Alatis (ed.), *Bilingualism and Language Contact* [Georgetown University Round Table on Languages and Linguistics, 1970] (Washington: Georgetown University Press, 1970), pp. 163–178.

————: "Organization of the Bilingual School," *Journal of Social Issues*, vol. 23, pp. 110–120, 1967.

[————, Chairman]: "The Challenge of Bilingualism," in *Reports of the Northeast Conference on the Teaching of Foreign Languages* (New York: Modern Language Association, 1965), pp. 57–101.

Gabet, Yvonne Helen Y.: *Birth-Order and Achievement in Anglo, Mexican-American and Black Americans*, unpublished dissertation, University of Texas at Austin, 1971.

Garbarino, M. S.: "Seminole Girl: The Autobiography of a Young Woman between Two Worlds," *Transaction*, vol. 7, pp. 40–46, 1970.

Garcia, A. B. and B. J. Zimmerna: "The Effect of Examiner Ethnicity and Language on the Performance of Bilingual Mexican-American First Graders," *Journal of Social Psychology*, vol. 87, pp. 3–11, 1972.

Gardner, R. C.: "Attitudes and Motivation: Their Role in Second Language Acquisition," *TESOL Quarterly*, vol. 2, pp. 141–150, 1968. [ERIC ED 024 035]

Geffert, Hannah N. et al.: *The Current Status of U. S. Bilingual Education Legislation*, Bilingual Education Series no. 4 (Washington: Center for Applied Linguistics, 1975).

Gerber, Malcolm: *Ethnicity and Measures of Educability: Differences among Rural Navajo, Pueblo, and Rural-Spanish-American First Graders on Measures of Learning Style, Hearing Vocabulary, Entry Skills, Motivation, and Home Environment Processes*, unpublished dissertation, University of Southern California, 1968.

Gievins, J. W., A. R. Neville, and R. E. Davidson: "Acquisition of Morphological Rules and Usage as a Function of Social Experience," *Psychology of the School*, vol. 7, pp. 217–221, 1970.

Gill, Joseph: *A Handbook for Teachers of Sioux Indian Students*, unpublished dissertation, University of South Dakota, 1971.

Goldman, R. and J. W. Sanders: "Cultural Factors and Hearing," *Exceptional Children*, vol. 35, pp. 489–490, 1969.

Gonzáles, James Lee: *The Effects of Maternal Stimulation on Early Language Development of Mexican-American Children*, unpublished dissertation, University of New Mexico, 1972.

González, Gustavo: "The Acquisition of Questions in Texas Spanish: Age 2–Age 5" (Arlington, Va.: Center for Applied Linguistics, 1973). (Mimeo)

————: *The Acquisition of Spanish Grammar by Native Spanish Speakers*, unpublished dissertation, University of Texas at Austin, 1970.

————: *The English of Spanish-Speaking Migrant Children: Preliminary Report* (Austin, Tex.: SEDL, 1969).

————: *A Linguistic Profile of the Spanish-Speaking First-Grader in Corpus Christi*, M.A. thesis, University of Texas at Austin, 1968.

Gordon, Susan B.: *Ethnic and Socioeconomic Influences on the Home Language Experiences of Children* (Albuquerque, N.M.: SWCEL, 1970).

————: *The Relationship between the English Language Abilities and Home Language Experiences of First Grade Children, from Three Ethnic Groups, of Varying Socioeconomic Status and Varying Degrees of Bilingualism*, unpublished dissertation, University of New Mexico, 1969.

Graves, Nancy B.: *City, Country and Child Rearing: A Tricultural Study of Mother-Child Relationships in Varying Environments*, unpublished dissertation, University of Colorado, 1971.

Grebler, Lee, J. W. More, R. C. Guzman et al.: *The Mexican-American People* (New York: Free Press, 1970).

Greenfield, L.: "Situational Measures of Normative Language Views in Relations to Person, Place and Topic among Puerto Ricans," *Anthropos*, vol. 65, pp. 602–618, 1970.

Gumperz, John J.: *Language in Social Groups* (Stanford: Stanford, 1972).

———— and Eduardo Hernández-Chavez: "Bilingualism, Bidialectalism and Classroom Interaction," in C. B. Cazden et al. (eds.), *Functions of Language in the Classroom* (New York: Teachers College, 1972), pp. 84–108.

———— and Dell Hymes (eds.): *Directions in Sociolinguistics: The Ethnography of Communication* (New York: Holt, 1972).

———— and ———— (eds.): "The Ethnography of Communication," *American Anthropologist*, vol. 66, 1964.

Gustafson, R. A.: *The Self-concept of Mexican-American Youngsters and Related Environmental Characteristics* (1971). [ERIC ED 053 195]

Gutiérrez, Arturo Luis: "The Implications of Early Childhood Education," in *Proceedings of the National Conference on Bilingual Education, April 14–15, 1972* (Austin, Tex.: Dissemination Center for Bilingual Bicultural Education, 1972), pp. 282–287.

Harkins, Arthur M. et al.: *Indian Americans in Omaha and Lincoln* (1970). [ERIC ED 47 860]

Harris, M. B. and W. C. Hassemer: "Some Factors Affecting the Complexity of Children's Sentences, the Effects of Modeling, Age, Sex and Bilingualism," *Journal of Experimental Child Psychology*, vol. 13, pp. 447–455, 1972.

Harvey, Curtis: "General Descriptions of Bilingual Programs That Meet Students' Needs," *Proceedings of the National Conference on Bilingual Education, April 14–15, 1972.* (Austin, Tex.: Dissemination Center for Bilingual Bicultural Education, 1972), pp. 252–264.

Has, Peter Yuan: *An Analysis of Certain Learning Difficulties of Chinese Students in New York City*, unpublished dissertation, New York University, 1955.

Haugen, Einar: "Bilingualism, Language Contact, and Immigrant Languages in the United States: A Research Report, 1956–1970," in Thomas Sebeok (ed.), *Current Trends in Linguistics*, vol. 10 (The Hague: Mouton, 1973), pp. 505–591.

————: *The Ecology of Language* (Stanford: Stanford, 1972).

Havighurst, Robert J.: *The National Study of American Indian Education* (Chicago: The University of Chicago Press, 1970).

Hayes, John R. (ed.): *Cognition and the Development of Language* (New York: Wiley, 1970).

Henderson, R. W.: *Environmental Stimulation and Intellectual Development of Mexican-American Children*, unpublished dissertation, University of Arizona, 1966.

—— and G. C. Merritt: "Environmental Backgrounds of Mexican-American Children with Different Potentials for School Success," *Journal of Social Psychology*, vol. 75, pp. 101–106, 1969.

Hepner, E. M.: *Self-Concepts, Values, and Needs of Mexican-American Underachievers (or Must the Mexican-American Child Adopt a Self-Concept That Fits the American School?)* (1970). [ERIC ED 048 954]

Hernández-Chavez, Eduardo et al. (eds.): *El Lenguaje de los Chicanos: Regional and Social Characteristics Used by Mexican Americans* (Arlington, Va.: Center for Applied Linguistics, 1975).

Hertzig, Margaret E.: "Aspects of Cognitive Style in Young Children of Differing Social and Ethnic Backgrounds," in J. Hellmuth (ed.), *Cognitive Studies II: Deficits in Cognition* (New York: Brunner/Mazel, 1971).

—— and Herbert G. Birch: "Longitudinal Course of Measured Intelligence in Preschool Children of Different Social and Ethnic Backgrounds," *American Journal of Orthopsychiatry*, vol. 41, pp. 416–426, 1971.

——, ——, Alexander Thomas, and O. A. Mendez: *Class and Ethnic Differences in the Responsiveness of Preschool Children to Cognitive Demands*, Monograph of the Society for Research in Child Development no. 117 (1968).

Hickey, T.: "Bilingualism and the Measurement of Intelligence and Verbal Learning Abilities," *Exceptional Children*, vol. 39, pp. 24–28, 1972.

Hilger, Sister Inez: *Arapaho Child Life and Its Cultural Background*, Smithsonian Institution, Bureau of American Ethnology bulletin 148 (Washington: U. S. Government Printing Office, 1952).

Hilton, Darla C.: *Investigation of Internalization and Phonological Rules in Monolingual and Bilingual Children*, M.A. thesis, University of Texas at Austin, 1969.

Hurt, M., Jr., and S. P. Mishra: "Reliability and Validity of the Metropolitan Achievement Tests for Mexican-American Children," *Educational and Psychological Measurement*, vol. 30, pp. 989–992, 1970.

Huxley, Renira: "Development of the Correct Use of Subject Personal Pronouns in Two Children," in Giovanni B. Flores d'Arcais and William J. M. Lavelt (eds.), *Advances in Psycholinguistics* (Amsterdam: North-Holland Publishing, 1970).

Hymes, Dell: "Bilingual Education: Linguistic vs. Sociolinguistic Bases," in James E. Alatis (ed.), *Bilingualism and Language Contact* [Georgetown University Round Table on Language and Linguistics, 1970] (Washington: Georgetown University Press, 1970), pp. 69–76.

——: *Foundations in Sociolinguistics: An Ethnographic Approach* (Philadelphia: University of Pennsylvania Press, 1974).

—— (ed.): *Language in Culture and Society: A Reader in Linguistics and Anthropology* (New York: Harper & Row, 1964).

—— (ed.): *Studies in the History of Linguistics: Traditions and Paradigms* (Bloomington: Indiana University Press, 1974).

Ianni, Francis A. J. and Edward Storey (eds.): *Cultural Relevance, Educational Issues: A Reader in Anthropology and Education* (Boston: Little, Brown, 1971).

Ingram, D.: "Transitivity in Child Language," *Language*, vol. 47, pp. 888–910, 1971.

Jakobovits, Leon A. and M. S. Miron: *Readings in the Psychology of Language* (Englewood Cliffs, N. J.: Prentice-Hall, 1967).

Jampolsky, L.: "Advancement in Indian Education," in *The Education of Indian Children in Canada*, symposium by members of Indian Affairs Education (Toronto: Ryerson Press, 1965).

Jayagopal, R.: *Problem Solving Abilities and Psychomotor Skills of Navajo Indians, Spanish Americans and Anglos in Junior High School*, unpublished dissertation, University of New Mexico, 1970.

Jensen, Arthur R.: "Learning Abilities in Mexican-American and Anglo-American Children," *California Journal of Educational Research*, vol. 12, pp. 147–159, 1961.

—— and William D. Rohwer, Jr.: *An Experimental Analysis of Learning Abilities in Culturally Disadvantaged Children* (1970). [ERIC ED 43 690]

Jensen, J. Vernon: "Effects of Childhood Bilingualism, I," *Elementary English*, vol. 39, pp. 132–143, 1962, also, "Effects of Childhood Bilingualism, II," *Elementary English*, vol. 39, pp. 358–366, 1962.

John, Vera P. and Vivian M. Horner: *Early Childhood Bilingual Education* (New York: Modern Language Association, 1971).

Johnson, Colleen L.: *The Japanese-American Family and Community in Honolulu: Generational Continuities in Ethnic Affiliation*, unpublished dissertation, Syracuse University, 1972.

Johnson, D. L. and C. A. Johnson: "Comparison of Four Intelligence Tests Used with Culturally Disadvantaged Children," *Psychological Reports*, vol. 28, pp. 209–210, 1971.

Jorstad, D.: "Psycholinguistic Learning Disabilities in Twenty Mexican-American Students," *Journal of Learning Disabilities*, vol. 4, pp. 143–149, 1971.

Justin, Neal: "Experiments in Bilingual Education," *School & Society*, January 1970.

——: "Mexican-American Achievement Hindered by Culture Conflict," *Sociology and Social Research*, vol. 56, pp. 271–279, 1972.

Kagan, Spencer and Millard C. Madsen: "Cooperation and Competition of Mexican-American and Anglo-American Children of Two Ages under Four Instructional Sets," *Developmental Psychology*, vol. 5, pp. 32–39, 1971.

—— and ——: "Rivalry in Anglo-American and Mexican Children of Two Ages," *Journal of Personality and Social Psychology*, vol. 24, pp. 214–220, 1972.

Karabinus, R. A. et al.: "Van Alstyne Picture Vocabulary Test Used with Six-Year-Old Mexican-American Children," *Educational and Psychological Measurement*, vol. 29, pp. 935–939, 1969.

Karadenes, Mark: *A Comparison of Differences in Achievement and Learning Abilities between Anglo and Mexican-American Children When the Two Groups Are Equated by Intelligence*, unpublished dissertation, University of Virginia, 1971.

Karnes, M. B., J. A. Teska, and A. S. Hodgins: "The Effects of Four Programs of Classroom Intervention on the Intellectual and Language Development of Four-Year-Old Disadvantaged Children," *American Journal of Orthopsychiatry*, vol. 40, pp. 58–76, 1970.

Kashinsky, M. and M. Wiener: "Tone in Communication and the Performance of Children from Two Socioeconomic Groups," *Child Development*, vol. 40, pp. 1193–1202, 1969.

Kee, Daniel W. and William D. Rohwer, Jr.: "Elaboration and Learning Efficiency in Four Ethnic Groups," paper presented at the American Educational Research Association Conference, Chicago, 1972. [ERIC ED 63 084]

Kelly, L. G. (ed.): *Description et mesure du bilinguisme/Description and Measurement of Bilingualism* (Toronto: University of Toronto Press, 1969).

Kennedy, Edward, Sen.: *Indian Education; Hearings before the Subcommittee on Indian Education of the Committee on Labor and Public Welfare, U.S. Senate* (Washington: U.S. Government Printing Office, 1969).

Kernan, Keith T.: "Semantic Relationships and the Child's Acquisition of Language," *Anthropological Linguistics*, vol. 12, pp. 171–187, 1970.

Kershner, J. K.: "Ethnic Group Differences in Children's Ability To Reproduce Direction and Orientation," *Journal of Social Psychology*, vol. 88, pp. 3-13, 1972.

Kessler, Carolyn: *The Acquisition of Syntax in Bilingual Children* (Washington: Georgetown University Press, 1971).

Keston, J. J. and C. A. Jiminez: "A Study of the Performance on English and Spanish Editions of the Stanford-Binet Intelligence Test by Spanish-American Children," *Journal of Genetic Psychology*, vol. 85, pp. 262-269, 1954.

Kiefer, W. Christie et al.: *Biculturalism: Psychological Costs and Profits* (1970). [ERIC ED 47 054]

Killian, J. R.: "WISC, Illinois Test of Psycholinguistic Abilities, and Bender Visual-Motor Gestalt Test Performance on Spanish-American Kindergarten and First Grade School Children," *Journal of Consulting and Clinical Psychology*, vol. 37, pp. 38-43, 1971.

Kimball, Solon T.: "Cultural Influences Shaping the Role of the Child," in George D. Spindler (ed.), *Education and Culture: Anthropological Approaches* (New York: Holt, 1963), pp. 268-283.

Kirk, S. A.: "Ethnic Differences in Psycholinguistic Abilities," *Exceptional Children*, vol. 39, pp. 112-118, 1972.

Kitano, Harry H. L.: *Japanese Americans: The Evolution of a Subculture* (Englewood Cliffs, N.J.: Prentice-Hall, 1969).

Kjolseth, Rolf: "Bilingual Education Programs in the United States: For Assimilation or Pluralism?" in Bernard Spolsky (ed.), *The Language Education of Minority Children* (Rowley, Mass.: Newbury House, 1972), pp. 94-121.

Kleinfeld, Judith S.: *Cognitive Strengths of Eskimos and Implications for Education* (1970). [ERIC ED 45 281]

————: *Instructional Style and the Intellectual Performance of Indian and Eskimo Students. Final Report* (1972). [ERIC ED 59 831]

————: *Some Instructional Strategies for the Cross-Cultural Classroom* (Juneau: Alaska State Department of Education, 1971). [ERIC ED 059 001]

Kloss, Heinz: *The American Bilingual Tradition in Education and Administration* (Rowley, Mass.: Newbury House, 1976).

Kobrick, J. W.: "The Compelling Case for Bilingual Education," *Saturday Review*, April 29, 1972.

Krear, Serafina: *Development of Pre-Reading Skills in a Second Language or Dialect* (1971). [ERIC ED 60 754]

————: "The Role of the Mother Tongue at Home and at School in the Development of Bilingualism," *English Language Teaching*, vol. 24, pp. 2-4, 1969.

Kuo, Eddie Chen-Yu: *Bilingual Socialization of Preschool Chinese Children in the Twin-Cities Area*, unpublished dissertation, University of Minnesota, 1972.

Kuttner, R. E.: "Comparative Performance of Disadvantaged Ethnic and Racial Groups," *Psychological Reports*, vol. 27, p. 372, 1970.

Kuzma, K. J. and C. Stern: "Effects of Three Preschool Intervention Programs on the Development of Autonomy in Mexican-American and Negro Children," *Journal of Special Education*, vol. 6, pp. 197-205, 1972.

Labov, William: "Finding Out about Children's Language," paper presented to the Hawaii Council of Teachers of English, 1970.

————: "The Logic of Nonstandard English," in Alfred Aarons et al. (eds.), "Linguistic-Cultural Differences and American Education," *Florida FL Reporter*, vol. 7, 1969 [special anthology edition].

————— and Clarence Robins: "A Note on the Relation of Reading Failure to Peer-Group Status in Urban Ghettos," *TC Record*, vol. 70, February 1969.

Lamarche, Maurice M.: *The Topic-Comment Pattern in the Development of English among Some Chinese Children Living in the United States*, unpublished dissertation, Georgetown University, 1972.

Lambert, Wallace E.: *Language, Psychology, and Culture* (Stanford: Stanford, 1972).

—————, R. R. Gardner, R. Olton, and K. Tunstall: "A Study of the Role of Attitudes and Motivation in Second-Language Learning," in Joshua A. Fishman (ed.), *Readings in the Sociology of Language* (The Hague: Mouton, 1968), pp. 473–491.

—————, J. Havelka, and C. Crosby: "The Influence of Language Acquisition Contexts on Bilingualism," *Journal of Abnormal and Social Psychology*, vol. 56, pp. 239–244, 1958.

————— and Chris Rawlings: "Bilingual Processing of Mixed-Language Associative Networks," *Journal of Verbal Learning and Verbal Behavior*, vol. 8, pp. 604–609, 1969.

————— and Y. Taguchi: "Ethnic Cleavage among Young Children," *Journal of Abnormal and Social Psychology*, vol. 53, pp. 380–382, 1956.

————— and Richard C. Tucker: *Bilingual Education of Children: The St. Lambert Experiment* (Rowley, Mass.: Newbury House, 1972).

Lampe, P. E.: "The Acculturation of Mexican-Americans in Public and Parochial Schools," *Sociological Analysis*, vol. 36, Spring 1975.

Landy, David: *Tropical Childhood: Cultural Transmission and Learning in a Puerto Rican Village* (New York: Harper & Row, 1965).

Lassey, William R. and Gerald Navratil: *The Agricultural Workforce and Rural Development: The Plight of the Migrant Worker* (1971). [ERIC ED 59 797]

Lastra, Yolanda: "El Hablar y la Educación de Niños de Origen Mexicano en Los Angeles," paper read at fifth symposium of the Inter-American Program of Linguistics and Language Teaching, São Paulo, Brazil, January 5–14, 1965.

Lemus-Serrano, Francisco: *Mother-Tongue Acquisition and Its Implications for the Learning of a Second Language*, unpublished dissertation, Claremont Graduate School, 1972.

Lenneberg, Eric H.: *Biological Foundations of Language* (New York: Wiley, 1967).

—————: "The Biological Foundations of Language," in Mark Lester (ed.), *Readings in Applied Transformational Grammar* (New York: Holt, 1970a).

—————: "The Capacity for Language Acquisition," in Mark Lester (ed.), *Readings in Applied Transformational Grammar* (New York: Holt, 1970b).

—————: "On Explaining Language," in Doris V. Gunderson (ed.), *Language and Reading* (Washington: Center for Applied Linguistics, 1970).

————— (ed.): *New Directions in the Study of Language* (Cambridge, Mass.: M.I.T., 1964).

Lesser, G. S., G. Fifer, and D. H. Clark: *Mental Abilities of Children in Different Social and Cultural Groups*, Monograph of the Society for Research in Child Development no. 102 (1965).

Levine, H.: "Bilingualism, Its Effect on Emotional and Social Development," *Journal of Secondary Education*, vol. 44, pp. 69–73, 1969.

Le Vine, R. A. "Cross-Cultural Study in Child Psychology," in P. H. Mussen (ed.), *Carmichael's Manual of Child Psychology*, vol. 2 (New York: Wiley, 1970), pp. 559–614.

Lewis, Gordon K.: *Puerto Rico: Freedom and Power in the Caribbean* (New York: Monthly Review Press, 1964).

Linton, Marigold: *Problems of Indian Children*: (1970). [ERIC ED 44 727]

Lombardi, Thomas D.: "Psycholinguistic Abilities of Papago Indian School Children," *Exceptional Children*, vol. 36, pp. 485–493, 1970.

Long, Barbara H. and Edmund H. Henderson: "Self-Social Concepts of Disadvantaged School Beginners," *Journal of Genetic Psychology*, vol. 113, pp. 41–51, 1968.

Mace, Betty Jane: *A Linguistic Profile of Children Entering Seattle Public Schools Kindergartens in September, 1971, and Implications for Their Instruction*, unpublished dissertation, University of Texas at Austin, 1972.

Mackey, William F.: *Bilingual Education in a Binational School: A Study of Equal Language Maintenance through Free Alternation*, (Rowley, Mass.: Newbury House, 1972).

———: *Bilingualism as a World Problem* (Montreal: Harvest House, 1967).

———: *Theory and Method in the Study of Bilingualism* (New York: Oxford University Press, 1976).

Macnamara, John: *Bilingualism and Primary Education* (Edinburgh: Edinburgh University Press, 1966).

———: "The Cognitive Strategies of Language Learning," in *Conference on Child Language, Preprints of Papers Presented at Conference, Chicago, Illinois, November 22–24* (Quebec: Laval University, International Center on Bilingualism, 1971), pp. 471–484.

———: "The Effects of the Instruction in a Weaker Language," *Journal of Social Issues*, vol. 23, 1967.

Madsen, Millard C.: *Developmental and Cross-Cultural Differences in the Cooperative and Competitive Behavior of Young Children* (1970). [ERIC ED 62 040]

——— and A. Shapira: "Cooperative and Competitive Behavior of Urban Afro-American, Anglo-American, Mexican-American and Mexican Village Children," *Developmental Psychology*, vol. 3, pp. 16–20, 1970.

Madsen, William: *Mexican-Americans of South Texas* (New York: Holt, 1964).

Maldonado Denis, Manual: *Puerto Rico: A Socio-Historic Interpretation* (New York: Random House, 1972).

Malkoc, Anna M. and A. H. Roberts: "Bilingual Education: A Special Report from CAL-ERIC," *Elementary English*, pp. 713–725, May 1970.

Manning, John C. and Frederick Brengelman: *Teaching English as a Second Language to Kindergarten Pupils Whose Native Language Is Spanish* (Fresno, Calif.: Fresno State College, 1965).

Manuel, Herschel T.: "Recruiting and Training Teachers for Spanish-Speaking Children in the South West," *School and Society*, vol. 96, March 30, 1968.

Margolis, Richard J.: *The Losers: A Report on Puerto Ricans and the Public Schools* (New York: Aspira, 1968).

Marjoribanks, K.: "Ethnic and Environmental Influences on Mental Abilities," *American Journal of Sociology*, vol. 78, pp. 323–337, 1972.

Martinez-Bernal, J. A.: *Children's Acquisition of Spanish and English Morphology Systems and Noun Phrases*, unpublished dissertation, Georgetown University, 1972.

Mazeika, E. J.: *A Descriptive Analysis of the Language of a Bilingual Child*, unpublished dissertation, University of Rochester, 1971.

McCarthy, Jacqueline: *A Study of the Leisure Activities of Taos Pueblo Indian Children*, unpublished dissertation, North Texas State University, 1970.

McCauley, Margaret A.: *A Study of Social Class and Assimilation in Relation to Puerto Rican Family Patterns*, unpublished dissertation, Fordham University, 1972.

McConnell, F.: "Language Development and Cultural Disadvantagement," *Exceptional Children*, vol. 35, pp. 597–606, 1969.

McNeill, David: *The Acquisition of Language: The Study of Developmental Psycholinguistics* (New York: Harper & Row, 1970).

———: *The Development of Language* (1967). [ERIC ED 017 921]

Melaragno, R. J. and G. Newark: "A Pilot Study to Supply Evaluation-Revision Procedures in First-Grade Mexican-American Classrooms," technical memorandum TM 3950/000/00 (Santa Monica, Calif.: Systems Development Corporation, May 17, 1968).

Mencher, Joan: *Child Rearing and Family Organization among Puerto Ricans in Eastville: El Barrio de Nueva York,* unpublished dissertation, Columbia University, 1958.

Menyuk, Paula: "Alternation of Rules in Children's Grammar," *Journal of Verbal Learning and Verbal Behavior,* vol. 3, pp. 480–488, 1964a.

———: *Sentences Children Use* (Cambridge, Mass.: M.I.T., 1969).

———: "Syntactic Rules Used by Children from Preschool through First Grade," *Child Development,* vol. 35, pp. 533–546, 1964b.

Mexican-American Cultural Differences: A Brief Survey to Enhance Teacher-Pupil Understanding (1969). [ERIC ED 41 665]

Mickelson, N. I. and C. G. Galloway: "Cumulative Language Deficit among Indian Children," *Exceptional Children,* vol. 36, pp. 187–190, 1969.

Mickey, Barbara H.: *A Bibliography of Studies Concerning the Spanish-Speaking Population of the American Southwest* (1969). [ERIC ED 42 548]

Middleton, John (ed.): *From Child to Adult: Studies in the Anthropology of Education* (Garden City, N.Y.: Natural History Press, 1970).

Miller, Louise B. and Jean L. Dyer: *Four Preschool Programs: Their Dimensions and Effects* (1972). [ERIC ED 69 411]

Miller, Max D.: *Patterns of Relationships of Fluid and Crystallized Mental Abilities to Achievement in Different Ethnic Groups,* unpublished dissertation, University of Houston, 1972.

Miller, M. R.: "The Language and Language Beliefs of Indian Children," *Anthropological Linguistics,* vol. 12, pp. 51–61, 1970.

Mishra, S. P. and M. Hurt, Jr.: "Use of Metropolitan Readiness Tests with Mexican-American Children," *California Journal of Educational Research,* vol. 21, pp. 182–187, 1970.

Moore, Joan W.: *Mexican Americans* (Englewood Cliffs, N.J.: Prentice-Hall, 1970).

[Morrison, J. Cayce (dir.)]: *The Puerto Rican Study, 1953–1957* (New York: Board of Education, 1958); reissued with an introductory essay by F. Cordasco (New York: Oriole Editions, 1972).

Mycue, E.: *Testing in Spanish and the Subsequent Measurement of English Fluency* (Denton, Tex.: Texas Women's University, 1968). [ERIC ED 026 193]

Nagy, Lois B.: *Effectiveness of Speech and Language Therapy as an Integral Part of the Educational Program for Bilingual Children,* unpublished dissertation, International University, 1972.

Natalicio, Diana: *Formation of the Plural in English: A Study of Native Speakers of English and Native Speakers of Spanish,* unpublished dissertation, University of Texas at Austin, 1969.

——— and Frederick Williams: *Repetition as an Oral Language Assessment Technique* (Austin, Tex.: Center for Communication Research, 1971).

Nava, Julian: "Cultural Barriers and Factors That Affect Learning by Spanish-Speaking Children," in John H. Burma (ed.), *Mexican-Americans in the United States* (Cambridge, Mass.: Schenkman, 1970), pp. 125–134.

Naylor, Gordon Hardy: *Learning Styles at Six Years in Two Ethnic Groups in a Disadvantaged Area,* unpublished dissertation, University of Southern California, 1971.

Ney, James W. and Donella K. Eberle (comps.): "Bilingual/Bicultural Education," *Linguistic Reports,* [CAL/ERIC Clearinghouse on Languages, Selected Bibliographies 2] vol. 17, no. 1, January 1975.

Nichols, C. A.: *Moral Education among the North American Indians* (New York: Teachers College, 1930).

Nuñez, Louis: *Puerto Ricans and Education,* Puerto Rican Heritage Lecture Series for

Bilingual Professionals, May 17, 1971 (New York: Board of Education of the City of New York).

O'Donnell, R. C., Wm. Griffin, and R. C. Norris: *Syntax of Kindergarten and Elementary School Children: A Transformational Analysis* (Champaign, Ill.: NCTE, 1967).

Ogletree, Earl J. and David Garcia: *Education of the Spanish Speaking Urban Child: A Book of Readings* (Springfield, Ill.: Charles C Thomas, 1975).

Ohannessian, Sirarpi: *The Study of the Problems of Teaching English to American Indians* (Washington: Center for Applied Linguistics, 1967).

Oksaar, Els: "Bilingualism," in Thomas Sebeok (ed.), *Current Trends in Linguistics,* vol. 9 (The Hague: Mouton, 1972), pp. 476–511.

Olim, E. G.: "Maternal Language Styles and Cognitive Behavior," *Journal of Special Education,* vol. 4, pp. 53–68, 1970.

Ortega, Luis (ed.): *Introduction to Bilingual Education* (New York: Las Americas, 1975).

Osborn, L. R.: "Rhetoric, Repetition, Silence: Traditional Requisites of Indian Communication," *Journal of American Indian Education,* vol. 12, pp. 15–21, 1973.

Ott, Elizabeth H.: *A Study of Levels of Fluency and Proficiency in Oral English of Spanish-Speaking School Beginners,* unpublished dissertation, University of Texas at Austin, 1967.

Owen, George M. et al.: *Nutrition Survey of White Mountain Apache Preschool Children* (1970). [ERIC ED 46 508]

Padilla, Elena: *Up from Puerto Rico* (New York: Columbia, 1958).

Paquita, Vivó (ed.): *The Puerto Ricans: An Annotated Bibliography* (New York: Bowker, 1973).

Parisi, Domenico: "Development of Syntactic Comprehension in Preschool Children as a Function of Socioeconomic Level," *Developmental Psychology,* vol. 5, pp. 186–189, 1971.

———: "Differences of Socio-Cultural Origin in the Linguistic Production of Pre-School Subjects," *Rassegna Italiana di Linguista Applicata,* vol. 2, pp. 95–101, 1970.

——— and Francesco Antinucci: "Lexical Competence," in d'Arcais and Levelt (eds.), *Advances in Psycholinguistics* (Amsterdam: North-Holland Publishing, 1970), pp. 197–210.

Parker, Ronald K. et al.: *An Overview of Cognitive and Language Programs for 3, 4, and 5 Year Old Children* (1970). [ERIC ED 70 534]

Paulston, Christina B.: *Implications of Language Learning Theory for Language Planning: Concerns in Bilingual Education,* Bilingual Education Series no. 1 (Washington: Center for Applied Linguistics, 1974).

Peak, E. and Wallace Lambert: "The Relation of Bilingualism to Intelligence," *Psychological Monographs: General and Applied,* vol. 126, pp. 1–23, 1962.

Pedreira, Antonio S.: *Bibliografia Puertorriqueña, 1493–1930.* (Madrid: Imprenta de Hernando, 1932); reissued with a foreword by F. Cordasco (New York: Burt Franklin, 1974).

Pelletier, Wilfred: "Childhood in an Indian Village," *Northian,* vol. 7, pp. 20–23, 1970.

Peñalosa, Fernando: "The Changing Mexican-American in Southern California," *Sociological and Social Research,* vol. 51, pp. 405–417, 1967.

———: *Chicano Multilingualism and Multiglossia* (1972). [ERIC ED 56 590]

Penfield, Wilder: "Conditioning the Uncommitted Cortex for Language Learning," *Brain,* vol. 88, pp. 787–798, 1965.

Pettit, George A.: *Primitive Education in North America,* University of California, Publications in American Archaeology and Ethnology no. 43, 1946.

Philips, Susan U.: "Acquisition of Rules for Appropriate Speech Usage," in James E. Alatis (ed.), *Bilingualism and Language Contact* [Georgetown University Round Table on Languages and Linguistics, 1970] (Washington: Georgetown University Press, 1970), pp. 77–101.

———: "Participant Structures and Communicative Competence: Warm Springs Children in

Community and Classroom," in C. B. Cazden et al. (eds.), *Functions of Language in the Classroom* (New York: Teachers College, 1972), pp. 370-394.

Piaget, Jean: *The Language and Thought of the Child* (Cleveland: World Publishing, 1955).

Pialorsi, Frank (ed.): *Teaching the Bilingual: New Methods and Old Traditions* (Tucson: University of Arizona Press, 1974).

Pineiro, Carlos Juan: "Estudios Puertorriqueños II," *Quimbamba* [Bilingual Education Quarterly], June 1973.

Platoff, Joan C.: *The Effect of Education and Race on the Language and Attitude Verbally Expressed by Mothers of Pre-School Children,* unpublished dissertation, New York University, 1972.

Poulsen, M. K.: *Automatic Patterning of Grammatical Structures and Auditory and Visual Stimuli as Related to Reading in Disadvantaged Mexican-American Children,* unpublished dissertation, University of Southern California, 1971.

Proceedings of the First Annual International Multilingual Multicultural Conference, San Diego, April 1-5, 1973. (Austin, Tex.: Dissemination Center for Bilingual Bicultural Education, 1973).

Proceedings of the National Conference on Bilingual Education, April 14-15, 1972 (Austin, Tex.: Dissemination Center for Bilingual Bicultural Education, 1972).

"Proposed Guidelines for the Preparation and Certification of Teachers of Bilingual-Bicultural Education in the United States," *Linguistic Reporter,* October 1974.

Proshansky, Harold M.: "The Development of Intergroup Attitudes," in L. Hoffman and M. Hoffman (eds.), *Review of Child Development Research,* vol. 2 (New York: Russell Sage, 1966), pp. 311-371.

Puidollars, Carmen: "Nuestra Lengua Vernácula: Base para un Currículo al Enseñar Niños Puertorriqueños," *Quimbamba* [Bilingual Education Quarterly], June 1973.

Purdy, J. D.: *Associative Learning Rates of Second, Fourth and Sixth Grade Indian and White Children Using a Paired-Associate Learning Task,* unpublished dissertation, University of Oklahoma, 1968.

Quijano, Teresa: *A Cross-Cultural Study of Six Differences among First-Graders on a Verbal Test,* M.A. thesis, Texas Women's University, 1968. [ERIC ED 026 191]

Raffler Engel, W. von: "Suprasentential and Substitution Tests in First Language Acquisition," *Bollettino di Psicologia Applicata,* 1968.

———: "Videotape in Dialectology," paper presented to the International Conference on Methods in Dialectology, Charlottetown, P.E.I., July 1972.

Ramírez, Manuel and Alfredo Castañeda: *Cultural Democracy, Bicognitive Development, and Education* (New York: Academic, 1974).

Ramírez de Arellano, Diana: *El Español: La Lengua de Puerto Rico—Aprecio y Defensa de Nuestra Lengua Materna en la Ciudad de Nueva York,* Puerto Rican Heritage Series for Bilingual Professionals (New York: Board of Education, 1971).

Rapier, J. L.: "Effects of Verbal Mediation upon the Learning of Mexican-American Children," *California Journal of Educational Research,* vol. 18, pp. 40-48, 1967.

Reboussin, R. and J. W. Goldstein: "Achievement Motivation in Navajo and White Students," *American Anthropologist,* vol. 68, pp. 740-744, 1966.

Reinstein, Steven and Judy Hoffman: "Dialect Interaction between Black and Puerto Rican Children in New York City: Implications for the Language Arts," *Elementary English,* vol. 49, pp. 190-196, 1972.

Rivera, Carmen E.: "Administration, Supervision, and Implementation of a Bilingual Bicultural Curriculum" *Proceedings of the National Conference on Bilingual Education, April 14-15, 1972* (Austin, Tex.: Dissemination Center for Bilingual Bicultural Education, 1972), pp. 105-120.

Robbins, Lynn: "Economics, Household Composition and the Family Cycle: The Blackfeet

Case," in June Helm (ed.), *Spanish-Speaking People in the United States* [proceedings of the American Ethnological Society Meeting] (Miami Beach, Fla.: 1968), pp. 196–215.

Rodriguez, Armando: "The Mexican-American Disadvantaged? Ya Basta!" in Alfred Aarons et al. (eds.), "Linguistic-Cultural Differences and American Education," *Florida FL Reporter,* vol. 7, 1969 [special anthology issue].

Rohner, Ronald P.: "Factors Influencing the Academic Performance of Kwakiutl Children in Canada," *Comparative Educational Review,* vol. 9, pp. 331–340, 1965.

Rosen, Carl L. and Phillip D. Ortego: "Resources: Teaching Spanish-Speaking Children," *The Reading Teacher,* vol. 25, pp. 11–13, 1971.

Rosenblatt, J.: *Cognitive Impulsivity in Mexican-American and Anglo-American Children,* unpublished dissertation, University of Arizona, 1968.

Rosenthal, Alan G.: *Pre-School Experience and Adjustment of Puerto Rican Children,* unpublished dissertation, New York University, 1955.

Samuels, S. Jay: "Psychological and Educational Considerations in Early Language Learning," in F. André Paquette (ed.), *New Dimensions in the Teaching of FLES* (New York: American Council on the Teaching of Foreign Languages, 1969).

Sanches, Mary: *Features in the Acquisition of Japanese Grammar,* unpublished dissertation, Stanford University, 1968.

———— and Ben Blount (eds.): *Sociocultural Dimensions of Language Use* (New York: Academic, 1975).

Sandler, L. et al.: "Developmental Test Performance of Disadvantaged Children," *Exceptional Children,* vol. 39, pp. 201–208, 1972.

Sapir, Edward: "Language and Thinking," in Charlton Laird and Robert M. Gorrell (eds.), *Reading about Language* (New York: Harcourt, Brace, 1971).

———— and Morris Swadesh: "American Indian Grammatical Categories," *Word,* vol. 2, pp. 103–112, 1946.

Sasser, C.: *Motor Development of the Kindergarten Spanish-Speaking Disadvantaged Child,* M.A. thesis, Texas Women's University, 1970. [ERIC ED 167 186]

Saville, Muriel R.: "Interference Phenomena in Language Teaching: Their Nature, Extent, and Significance in the Acquisition of Standard English," *Elementary English,* pp. 396–405, March 1971.

————: "Linguistic and Attitudinal Correlates in Indian Education," paper presented at the American Educational Research Association Convention, Chicago, 1972.

———— and Rudolph C. Troike: *A Handbook of Bilingual Education* (Washington: Center for Applied Linguistics, 1971).

Saville-Troike, Muriel: "Basing Practice on What We Know about Children's Language," in *Classroom Practices in ESL and Bilingual Education,* vol. 1 (Washington: Teachers of English to Speakers of Other Languages, 1973).

————: *Bilingual Children: A Resource Document,* (Bilingual Education Series no. 2) (Washington: Center for Applied Linguistics, 1973).

Say, Margaret Z. and William J. Meyer: *Effects of Early Day Care Experience on Subsequent Observed Program Behaviors* (1970). [ERIC ED 68 149]

Schmidt, L. and J. Gallessich: "Adjustment of Anglo-American and Mexican-American Pupils in Self-Contained and Team-Teaching Classrooms," *Journal of Educational Psychology,* vol. 62, pp. 328–332, 1971.

Selected Characteristics of Persons and Families of Mexican, Puerto Rican, and Other Spanish Origin (1972). [ERIC ED 70 546]

Serrano, Rodolfa G.: "The Language of the Four Year Old Chicano," paper presented at the Rocky Mountain Educational Research Association meeting, Boulder, Col., 1971. [ERIC ED 071 791]

Sharp, Derrick: *Language in Bilingual Communities* (London: E. Arnold, 1973).

Shaw, Jean W. and Maxine Schoggen: *Children Learning: Samples of Everyday Life of Children at Home* (1969). [ERIC ED 33 763]

Sherk, John K.: *A Word-Count of Spoken English of Culturally Disadvantaged Preschool and Elementary Pupils* (Kansas City, Mo.: University of Missouri Press, 1973).

Shriner, T. H. and L. Miner: "Morphological Structures in the Language of Disadvantaged and Advantaged Children," *Journal of Speech and Hearing Research,* vol. 11, pp. 605–610, 1968.

Shuy, Roger W. and Ralph W. Fasold (eds.): *Language Attitudes: Current Trends and Prospects* (Washington: Georgetown University Press, 1973). [Georgetown University School of Languages and Linguistics.]

Siegel, Irving E. et al.: *Psycho-Educational Intervention Beginning at Age Two: Reflections and Outcomes* (1972). [ERIC ED 68 161]

Silberstein, R.: *Risk-Taking Behavior in Pre-School Children from Three Ethnic Backgrounds* (Los Angeles: UCLA, Center for Head Start Evaluation and Research, 1969). [ERIC ED 042 486]

Silén, Juan A.: *We the Puerto Rican People* (New York: Monthly Review Press, 1971).

Simirenko, A.: *Socio-Economic Variables in the Acculturation Process: A Pilot Study of Two Washoe Indian Communities* [final report] (Reno: University of Nevada Press, 1966).

Siu, Ping Kee: *The Relationship between Motivational Patterns and Academic Achievement in Minority Group Children* [final report] (1972). [ERIC ED 63 443]

Skoczylas, Rudolph V.: *An Evaluation of Some Cognitive and Affective Aspects of a Spanish-English Bilingual Education Program*, dissertation, University of New Mexico, 1972. [ERIC ED 066 990]

Skrabanek, R. L.: "Language Maintenance among Mexican-Americans," *International Journal of Comparative Sociology*, vol. 11, pp. 272–282, 1970.

Slears, Brian: *Aptitude, Content and Method of Teaching Word Recognition with Young American Indian Children,* unpublished dissertation, University of Minnesota, 1970.

Slobin, Dan I.: "Children and Language: They Learn the Same Way All Around the World," *Psychology Today,* vol. 6, pp. 74–77, 82, 1972.

———: "Imitation and Grammatical Development in Children," in N. S. Endler, L. R. Boulter, and H. Osser (eds.), *Contemporary Issues in Developmental Psychology* (New York: Holt, 1967), pp. 437–443.

Smith, Frank and G. A. Miller: *The Genesis of Language: A Psycholinguistic Approach* (Cambridge, Mass.: M.I.T., 1966).

Smothergill, N. L., F. Olson, and S. G. Moore: "The Effects of Manipulation of Teacher Communication Style in the Preschool," *Child Development,* vol. 42, pp. 1229–1239, 1971.

Soares, Anthony T. and Louise M. Soares: "Self-Perceptions of Culturally Disadvantaged Children," *American Educational Research Journal,* vol. 6, pp. 31–45, 1969.

Solís, Juan D. (ed.): *Teacher Training Bibliography: An Annotated Listing of Materials for Bilingual-Bicultural Teacher Education* (Austin, Tex.: Dissemination and Assessment Center for Bilingual Education, 1975).

Southern, Mara and Walter T. Plant: "Differential Cognitive Development within and between Racial and Ethnic Groups of Disadvantaged Preschool and Kindergarten Children," *Journal of Genetic Psychology,* vol. 119, pp. 259–266, 1971.

Southwest Council for Bilingual Education: *Bilingual Education in Three Cultures,* annual conference report, Las Cruces, N.M., 1968. [ERIC ED 027 515]

Southwest Council of Foreign Language Teachers: *Our Bilinguals—Social and Psychological Barriers, Linguistic and Pedagogical Barriers* (El Paso: 1965). [ERIC ED 019 899]

Spector, S.: *Patterns of Difficulty in English in Bilingual Mexican-American Children* (1972). [ERIC ED 066 083]

Spellman, C. M.: *The Shift from Color to Form Preference in Young Children of Different Ethnic Background*, unpublished dissertation, University of Texas at Austin, 1968.

Spence, A. G., S. P. Mishra, and S. Ghozeil: "Home Language and Performance in Standardized Tests," *Elementary School Journal*, pp. 309–413, March 1971.

Spolsky, Bernard (ed.): *The Language Education of Minority Children: Selected Readings* (Rowley, Mass.: Newbury House, 1973).

Staples, R.: "Mexican-American Family: Its Modification over Time and Space," *Phylon*, vol. 32, pp. 179–192, 1971.

Stedman, James M. and Russell L. Adams: "Achievement as a Function of Language Competence, Behavior Adjustment and Sex in Young, Disadvantaged Mexican-American Children," *Journal of Educational Psychology*, vol. 63, pp. 411–417, 1972.

—— and Richard E. McKenzie: "Family Factors Related to Competence in Young Disadvantaged Mexican-American Children," *Child Development*, vol. 42, pp. 1602–1607, 1972.

Stern, Carolyn and Diane Ruble: *Teaching New Concepts to Non-English Speaking Preschool Children* (UCLA: 1970). [ERIC ED 054 903]

Steward, Margaret S.: *The Observation of Parents as Teachers of Preschool Children as a Function of Social Class, Ethnicity, and Cultural Distance between Parent and Child* (1971). [ERIC ED 57 925]

—— and David Steward: "The Observation of Anglo-, Mexican-, and Chinese-American Mothers Teaching Their Young Sons," *Child Development*, vol. 44, pp. 329–337, 1973.

Stodolsky, Susan S. and Gerald Lesser: "Learning Patterns in the Disadvantaged," *Harvard Educational Review*, vol. 37, pp. 546–593, 1967.

Sugarman, Susan: *A Description of Communicative Development in the Pre-Language Child*, unpublished honors thesis, Hampshire College, Amherst, Mass., 1973.

Suter, Larry E.: *Selected Characteristics of Persona and Families of Mexican, Puerto Rican, and Other Spanish Origin: March 1971. Population Characteristics: Current Population Reports.* [ERIC ED 65 224]

Swain, Merrill: "Bilingualism, Monolingualism, and Code Acquisition," in *Conference on Child Language, Preprints of Papers Presented at Conference, Chicago, Illinois, November 22–24 (1971).* [ERIC ED 060 748]

Swanson, E. and R. DeBlassie: "Interpreter Effects on the WISC Performance of First Grade Mexican-American Children," *Measurement and Evaluation in Guidance*, vol. 4, pp. 172–175, 1971.

Swanson, Maria M.: "Bilingual Education: The National Perspective," in Gilbert A. Jarvis (ed.), *The ACTFL Review of Foreign Language Education*, vol. 5 (Skokie, Ill.: National Textbook, 1974), pp. 75–127.

Swinney, J. S.: *The Development of Education among the Choctaw Indians*, M.A. thesis, Oklahoma A&M College, 1935.

Tagatz, G. E. et al.: "Effects of Ethnic Background, Response Option, Task Complexity and Sex on Information Processing in Concept Attainment," *Journal of Experimental Education*, vol. 39, pp. 69–72, 1971.

Taylor, M. E.: *Investigation of Parent Factors Affecting Achievement of Mexican-American Children*, unpublished dissertation, University of Southern California, 1969.

Tharp, R. and A. Meadow: "Changes in Marriage Roles Accompanying the Acculturation of the Mexican-American Wife," *Journal of Marriage and the Family*, vol. 30, pp. 404–412, 1968.

Thomas, Elizabeth: *The Conceptualization Process in Advantaged and Disadvantaged Kindergarten Children,* unpublished dissertation, University of Illinois, 1968.

Thomas, R. M.: *Social Differences in the Classroom: Social-Class, Ethnic and Religious Problems* (New York: McKay, 1965).

Thonis, Eleanor: *The Dual Language Process in Young Children* (1971). [ERIC ED 061 812]

Topper, Martin D.: *The Daily Life of a Traditional Navajo Household: An Ethnographic Study in Human Daily Activities,* unpublished dissertation, Northwestern University, 1972.

Tremaine, Ruth V.: *Syntax and Piagetian Operational Thought* (Washington: Georgetown University Press, 1975). [Georgetown University School of Language and Linguistics.]

Troike, Rudolph C. and Nancy Modiano (eds.): *Proceedings of the First Inter-American Conference on Bilingual Education* (Arlington, Va.: Center for Applied Linguistics, 1975).

Tucker, C. A.: "The Chinese Immigrant's Language Handicap: Its Extent and Its Effects," *Florida FL Reporter,* vol. 7, 1969.

Turner, Paul R. (ed.): *Bilingualism in the Southwest* (Tucson: University of Arizona Press, 1973).

Ulibarri, Horacio: *Interpretive Studies on Bilingual Education* (Washington: U.S. Office of Education, 1969).

[———— et al.]: *Bilingual Research Project: Final Report* (Albuquerque: University of New Mexico, College of Education, 1959).

United States Bureau of the Census: *American Indians: 1970 Census of Population* (Washington: U.S. Department of Commerce, 1973).

————: *U.S. Census of Population and Housing: Puerto Rican Population Survey Areas, Employment Profiles of Selected Low Income Areas,* Final Report PHC (3) (Washington: U.S. Government Printing Office, 1972).

United States Cabinet Committee on Opportunity for the Spanish Speaking: *The Spanish Speaking in the United States: A Guide to Materials* [with a Foreword by F. Cordasco] (Detroit: Blaine Ethridge, 1975; originally G.P.O., 1971).

United States Commission on Civil Rights: *Report 1: Ethnic Isolation of Mexican Americans in the Public Schools of the Southwest* (Washington: U.S. Government Printing Office, 1971).

————: *Report 2: The Unfinished Education* (Washington: U.S. Government Printing Office, 1971).

————: *Report 3: The Excluded Student: Educational Practices Affecting Mexican Americans in the Southwest* (Washington: U.S. Government Printing Office, 1972).

————: *Report 4: Mexican American Education in Texas: A Function of Wealth* (Washington: U.S. Government Printing Office, 1972).

————: *Report 5: Teachers and Students: Differences in Teacher Interaction with Mexican American and Anglo Students* (Washington: U.S. Government Printing Office, 1972).

Valencia, Atilano A.: *The Effects of Bilingual/Bicultural Education among Spanish-Speaking, English-Speaking and Sioux-Speaking Kindergarten Children,* a report of statistical findings and recommendations for Educational Unit No. 18, Scotts Bluff, Nebraska (Albuquerque, N.M.: SWCEL, 1970).

Van Duyne, H. J. and G. Gutierrez: "The Regulatory Function of Language in Bilingual Children," *Journal of Educational Research,* vol. 66, pp. 122–124, 1972.

Vane, J. R. and W. M. Davis: "Factors Related to the Effectiveness of Preschool Programs with Disadvantaged Children," *Journal of Educational Research,* vol. 64, pp. 297–299, 1971.

Varo, Carlos: *Consideraciones Antropológicas y Políticas en Torno a la Enseñunza del*

"Spanglish" en Nueva York (Rio Piedras: Ediciones Librería Internacional, 1971).

Vásquez, Hector I.: "Puerto Rican Americans," *National Elementary Principal,* volume 50, 1970.

Vildomec, V.: *Multilingualism* (Leiden, The Netherlands: Sythoff, 1963).

Von Maltitz, Frances Willard: *Living and Learning in Two Languages: Bilingual-Bicultural Education in the United States* (New York: McGraw-Hill, 1975).

Voyat, Gilbert and Stephen Silk: *Cross-Cultural Study of Cognitive Development on the Pine Ridge Indian Reservation,* The Pine Ridge Research Bulletin no. 11, 1970. [ERIC ED 070 541]

Wagenheim, Karl with Olga Wagenheim: *The Puerto Ricans: A Documentary History* (New York: Praeger, 1973). See also the author's *Puerto Rico: A Profile* (Praeger, 1970) and *A Survey of Puerto Ricans on the U.S. Mainland in the 1970s* (Praeger, 1975).

Walker, Willard: "An Experiment in Programmed Cross-Cultural Education: The Import of the Cherokee Primer for the Cherokee Community and for the Behavioral Sciences," unpublished manuscript, background paper for 1967 CAL Survey, 1965.

Walsh, Marie A.: *The Development of a Rationale for a Program To Prepare Teachers for Spanish-Speaking Children in the Bilingual-Bicultural Elementary School* (San Francisco: R & E Research Associates, 1976).

Wampler, H.: *A Case Study of 12 Spanish-Speaking Primary Children Concerning School Achievement and Socialization,* unpublished dissertation, Pennsylvania State University, 1972.

Wasserman, S. A.: "Values of Mexican-American, Negro, and Anglo Blue-Collar and White-Collar Children," *Child Development,* vol. 42, pp. 1624–1628, 1971.

Wax, Murray L. et al.: *Indian Education in Eastern Oklahoma: A Report of Fieldwork among the Cherokee* [final report] (1969). [ERIC ED 029 741]

——, Stanley Diamond, and Fred O. Georing, (eds.): *Anthropological Perspectives on Education* (New York: Basic Books, 1971).

——, Rosalie Wax, and R. V. Dumont, Jr.: *Formal Education in an American Indian Community,* supplement to *Social Problems* 11, no. 4, Society for the Study of Social Problems, monograph no. 1. 1964.

Wight, B. W., M. F. Sloniger, and J. P. Keeve: "Cultural Deprivation: Operational Definition in Terms of Language Development," *American Journal of Orthopsychiatry,* vol. 40, pp. 77–86, 1970.

Wilkinson, Andrew: *The Foundations of Language: Talking and Reading in Young Children* (New York: Oxford University Press, 1971).

Williams, Frederick: *Psychological Correlates of Speech Characteristics: On Sounding "Disadvantaged"* (Madison, Wis.: The University of Wisconsin Press, 1969).

—— (ed.): *Language and Poverty: Perspectives on a Theme.* (Chicago: Markham, 1970).

Williams, George M.: *Puerto Rican English: A Discussion of Eight Major Works Relevant to Its Linguistic Description* (New York: Columbia, c. 1971). [ERIC ED 051 709]

Witkin, H. A.: "A Cognitive-Style Approach to Cross-Cultural Research," *International Journal of Psychology,* vol. 2, pp. 233–250, 1967.

Wolcott, Harry F.: *A Kwakiutl Village and Its School* (New York: Holt, 1967).

Woodford, Protase: "Bilingual-Bicultural Education: A Need for Understanding," in Gilbert A. Jarvis (ed.), *The ACTFL Review of Foreign Language Education,* vol. 6 (Skokie, Ill.: National Textbook, 1974), pp. 397–433.

Worrall, Anita Denise: *Bilingualism and Cognitive Development,* unpublished dissertation, University of Washington, 1970.

Young, Rodney W.: "Development of Semantic Categories in Spanish-English and Navajo-English Bilingual Children," in *Conference on Child Language, Preprints of Papers Presented at Conference, Chicago, Illinois, November 22–24 (1971),* pp. 193–208. [ERIC ED 060 749]

Zamora, Gloria: "Staff Development for Bilingual/Bicultural Programs—A Philosophical Base" in *Proceedings of the National Conference in Bilingual Education, April 14–15, 1972* (Austin, Tex.: Dissemination Center for Bilingual Bicultural Education, 1972), pp. 299–303.

INDEX